MIDNIGHT MARQUEE #79

50th ANNIVERSARY
1963-2013

Midnight Marquee #79
50th Anniversary Issue
[1963-2013]

Editors
Gary J. Svehla
Aurelia Susan Svehla

Graphic Design Interior
Gary J. Svehla

Front Cover
Bill Nelson
The sad Monster from
Bride of Frankenstein

Back Cover
Dave Ludwig
Valdemar (Vincent Price) takes revenge on Carmichael (Basil Rathbone) from *Tales of Terror*

Copy Editor
Linda J. Walter

Writers
Anthony Ambrogio
Barry Atkinson
Edmund G. Bansak
Mark Clark
Jim Clatterbaugh
Bruce Dettman
Richard Klemensen
Jonathan Malcolm Lampley
Arthur Joseph Lundquist
Greg Mank
Don Mankowski
David Metzler
Stephen Mosley
Neil Pettigrew
Bryan Senn
Brian Smith
Gary J. Svehla
Steven Thornton
Neil Vokes

Artists
Allen K.
Robert Knox
David Ludwig
David Robinson

Special Thanks
Warner Home Video; Fox Home Video; Universal Home Video; Scream Factory; Kino Home Video; Matt Berry; Scott Essman; Richard Klemensen; David Colton and the CHFB; Bill Littman; Greg Mank; John Antosiewicz; Susan Svehla; George Stover; Mark Robinson; Dave "Charlie" Ellis

4	Mutterings at Midnight by Gary J. Svehla
6	Art Portfolio: The Monstrous Cinematic Artwork of Allen K.
13	**Part One: The Enduring Monster Culture and Its Fandom**
14	Monster-Mania Walks Among Us: Celebrating The 1950s, The 1960s and 50 Years of *Gore Creatures/Midnight Marquee* by Edmund G. Bansak
30	It All Started in 1963—Two Amazing Life-Long Journeys Through Monsterland byRichard Klemensen
40	The Monster Magazine Family Tree—50 Years of *Gore Creatures/Midnight Marquee* by Jim Clatterbaugh
44	How the Cult Culture of Horror Film Fandom Changed Over Five Decades by Gary J. Svehla
56	Art Portfolio: Monsters on the Loose from The 1950s, Captured by Robert Knox
61	**Part Two: The Midnight Marquee Legacy**
62	Early Tales of *Gore Creatures* by David Metzler
64	*Midnight Marquee* Memories by Gary J. Svehla
74	A Technological Fanzine Odyssey: 1963-2013 by Gary J. Svehla
97	Art Portfolio: The Evolution of Horror Film Fanzine Art: The Dave Robinson Portfolio
104	**Part Three: It's the Movies that Matter**

Playing at the Midnight Marquee

105 *Tower of London*—Pomp, Pageantry and The Macabre
   by Greg Mank

123 Diamond of Frankenstein—Field of Fear ... and Fun
   by Don Mankowski

127 The *Other* Lionel Atwill—Sinister, Vengeful and Perverse
   by Neil Pettigrew

141 The 13 Most Influential Horror Movies:
   The Grand Finale!
      Compiled by Anthony Ambrogio; Edited by
      Anthony Ambrogio and Gary J. Svehla

162 Favorite Top-50 Horror Movies of The Sound Era [1931-1999]
   by Gary J. Svehla

174 An Iconic Doomsday Moment: "Is Anyone There?"
   by Arthur Joseph Lundquist

176 *Thriller*'s Classic Horror Episodes—Season One
   by Gary J. Svehla

191 Lost Innocence, *Blood Demon* and Christopher Lee
   by Stephen Mosley

200 Seduced by Small-Town America,1950s-Styleby
   Gary J. Svehla

210 Déjà vu Boo!
   by Steven Thornton

224 Subterranean Chills—The Cave in Fantasy Cinema
   by Barry Atkinson

239 Shape of Fear to Come!
   by Steven Thornton

247 *Midnight Marquee*—Book Review
   by Gary J. Svehla

255 *Midnight Marquee*—DVD/Blu-Ray Review
   by Gary J. Svehla

Publisher
Midnight Marquee Press, Inc.
Gary J. Svehla
Aurelia Susan Svehla

Midnight Marquee #79, December 2013, is copyright © 2013 by Gary J. Svehla; *Midnight Marquee* is published annually at 9721 Britinay Lane, Parkville, MD 21234; e-mail Gary Svehla at midmargary@aol.com; websites: http://www.midmar.com; phone: 410-665-1198

Regular issues of the magazine are available for $10 (plus $2 shipping Media Mail; $7 Priority Mail) and may be ordered only one issue in advance. We ship internationally, but please request current international shipping rates before placing your order. The 50th Anniversary issue #79 is available for $20 (Media Mail shipping) in the U.S.A. or $27 (Priority Mail shipping) in the U.S.A.

Articles and art should be transmitted electronically (or via snail mail) and will remain the property of the writer/artist or copyright holder, who will retain all rights. If material intended for publication is sent to us via regular mail, it is the sender's responsibility to include return postage. No responsibility is taken for unsolicited material.

Editorial views expressed by writers are not necessarily those of the publisher, Midnight Marquee Press. Nothing may be reproduced or shared in any media without the expressed written permission of the publisher. Letters of comment addressed to *Midnight Marquee* or Gary Svehla and/or Susan Svehla will be considered for publication, unless the writer requests otherwise.

We enthusiastically solicit articles and artwork from professionals and novices alike, but it is best to discuss potential submissions in advance. Remember, *Midnight Marquee* emphasizes the classics of the Golden Age and those modern movies that appeal to that "golden age" philosophy and style (or movies that simply refuse to be ignored because of their audacity).

Mutterings at Midnight

It seems 1963 was a watershed year for half-century anniversaries. Even though The Rolling Stones were founded officially in 1962, they consider 1963 to be their actual year of origin since essential drummer Charlie Watts joined the band at the beginning of 1963. President John F. Kennedy was assassinated 50 years ago this year. Betty Friedan's *The Feminine Mystique*, one of the books responsible for the feminist revolution, appeared. The USPS inaugurated their nationwide Zip Code to move the mail faster. Marvel Comics' *X-Men* debuted in September of 1963. The push button telephone first appeared. Bob Dylan's second album, *The Freewheelin' Bob Dylan*, his breakout album, was released. The Beatles debuted their first album, *Please Please Me*, in England in 1963, the same album that was released in America one year later. *Dr. No*, the first James Bond movie starring Sean Connery, was released in the States in 1963 (after having been released in England a year earlier). Rev. Martin Luther King, Jr. delivered his "I Have a Dream" speech from the steps of the Lincoln Memorial. And on a considerably more minor level, I published (if you could call it that) my first issue of *Gore Creatures* during the summer of 1963, 50 years ago. Happy anniversary to one and all!

So many people assisted me in those early years, both in dreaming up the concept of my personal vision of a classic horror movie fanzine and maintaining it after its childish debut, that I would need a minimum of 10 pages of only names and a big thank-you at the top to credit all those responsible for this 50-year experiment. So many important contributors have come and gone. Some of these people were close Baltimore friends, even relatives, while others were long-distance colleagues who assisted in the magazine's development. While far too many of these people died, others simply vanished as their interests changed and life took them into myriad directions.

When FantaCon sponsored the publication of our book-a-zine 25th anniversary issue back in 1988, I conceived the vision of how to tell the tale. When I examined each new issue of the magazine, I was looking at a new chapter of my life, perhaps several months or half a year further down the road. Reading each issue, I was examining my life, as a pre-teen, a teenager, a finding-my-identity 20-something and as a fully adult 30-something. So besides presenting the best articles I could assemble, I told the story of our fanzine history (and the history of Gary J. Svehla) by giving a detailed look at each issue and examining those factors that shaped each issue. But in 1984 my focus changed as I embarked upon my journey through life with my lovely wife Aurelia Susan. The magazine was still pivotal in my life, but no longer would each issue tell the personal history in the same way it did before. Now my life was not centered upon the magazine's publication. I now had a life away from my fanzine that focused upon career, marriage/family and two emerging enterprises that also shaped my life—the debut of Midnight Marquee Press, Inc. in 1995 (our small press book publishing company) and the FANEX conventions in 1987. Simply stated, life was becoming more complex, splintering into many different directions. My artistic inclinations were not totally devoted any longer to *only* the magazine. And since the book publishing company was a serious business, with the purpose of growing and making profits and establishing itself as a financial livelihood, *Midnight Marquee* magazine became the more hobby-oriented labor of love that inspired all the rest. Don't get me wrong, *Midnight Marquee* was just as important and remained my personal passion, but that passion was now being

The 1930s through the 1960s remain the definitive years of horror cinema. Here we have Claude Rains as The Invisible One from *The Invisible Man* (1933).

pulled in several different directions and had to share time with other endeavors.

So for my 50th anniversary issue, I had to re-invent the method by which I would tell the history of my 50 years as editor and publisher of a labor-of-love horror film magazine. What had worked and been so successful for telling the history of the first 25 years would not be as successful for evoking the second half of the story. Of course I would have to touch upon some anecdotes and history already covered in the original 25th anniversary issue, since this latest anniversary issue would cover all 50 years and not only years 26 through 50. Yet, I did not want to merely repeat too many often told tales. So the challenge was a difficult one to navigate. I hope I have given enough fresh insight to those humble beginnings and tied the pre-Sue, pre-FANEX and pre-Midnight Marquee Press years to the decades that followed. First of all, Susan and I are planning an entire book devoted to FANEX, so I did not wish to cover that enterprise in any type of depth. That story will be shared, but later. But I wanted to create a fitting tribute to a magazine that was (hopefully) always larger than my own identity. I wanted to pay tribute to a cultural time period in the middle 20th century through the newly awakening 21st century that grew up on monster movies and related pop culture. I wanted to tie in to the horror film fandom sub-culture started by Forrest J Ackerman and Calvin Beck, supported by professional monster magazines, the *Shock Theater* TV packages, horror hosts, monster toys, model kits, bubble-gum cards and comic books. Even though most of us aging baby boomers do not wish to acknowledge the reality that such Monster Kid fandom is on the downslide and that the younger generation of fans, while they may continue to enjoy horror movies, they may enjoy them in different ways than our generation has. Nothing lasts forever. Not even *Midnight Marquee*.

This 50th anniversary issue is one of pride and prejudice. Looking back to 1958, when the first issue of *Famous Monsters of Filmland* emerged on magazine stands, and following through to 2013, where more horror movie magazines exist than ever before and large-scale horror film conventions pepper the United States and beyond, the fact resonates deep in my gut that the golden years of horror film fandom are behind us. As one generation extends the torch to another, I hope enough younger horror film fans exist (ones who consider the classics of old to be movies made well before *Halloween* and *Alien*) who still care about early cinema to keep the spirit of Universal, Hammer, Paramount, MGM, 20th Century Fox, Val Lewton, American International and even PRC and Monogram alive. Young people will always look to thrilling exploitative cinema for weekend kicks, but that mentality is a far different one than that of the cult culture that studies and reveres the past and still strongly maintains that the 1930s through the 1960s remain the definitive years of horror cinema. Such prejudiced eyes see the technological past (1931's *Frankenstein* was a mere few years removed from the silent cinema era) as being innovative and creatively explosive, an era where glistening black-and-white photography stands toe-to-toe with the iconic Hammer Technicolor photography of Jack Asher. And those of us who worship the past, we must remember to still keep our eyes open to the current horror film cinema, as difficult as it might be to find a few gems among all the debris and garbage (movies such as *The Conjuring* give hope to aging classic horror movie lovers).

I end by singing the mantra that classic horror cinema is not a chronological period of time, it is more an attitude and a philosophy. It emphasizes, remembers and looks forward to the following tenants of filmmaking—a good plot comes first and foremost; characterization (even among monsters and villains) matters most; make-up and special effects are subservient to everything else and should never stand alone front and center; a memorable musical soundtrack and sound editing coupled with lingering atmosphere created by the craft of cinematography (employing the artistry of lenses and light) is essential (the cheap shock of a musical stinger, a crescendoing musical score or staccato editing should be called out as the gimmick it is); the finest horror film craftsmanship creates a marriage of sound and vision where the plot is forwarded by both dialogue and cinematography, the artifice becoming mostly invisible to its transfixed audience. While the horror film genre shines brighter during some decades than others, over all, our favorite film genre is thriving and continues to produce examples of all extremes—dreck and drivel, mediocre endeavors, as well as failed or flawed classics, amid a few certified classics that will stand the test of time. And with horror movie fans, sometimes the most flawed examples become the interesting ones. So the most discriminating buffs

My bedroom during the early *Gore Creature* days. Notice the Aurora Monster Models, fan club celebrity photos, a poster, a shrunken head and a comic book cover.

can still enjoy the full spectrum of horror cinema—classics, innovative failures, grade Z junk, low-budget genius and mainstream blockbusters.

And we are proud to have been along for the ride, documenting the past, the current trends and looking optimistically to the future of horror cinema. Hopefully, over the past five decades we have served the genre faithfully, with passion and expertise.

Gary J. Svehla
July 2013

P.S.—So, what's in the future? We hope *Midnight Marquee* will return to a once yearly publication schedule and continue to do for the upcoming years what we have done for the past 50. Also, Sue and I hope to republish our run of issues as print copies (not PDF digital ones) that reproduce the original layouts. I see the project as a compilation one, with perhaps issues 1 through 30 compiled in one trade paperback edition. Thus for an affordable price collectors and fans will get their money's worth with *The Gore Creatures/Midnight Marquee Archives, Volume One*. What we need is continued support, both with sales and written contributions to keep the magazine vital. And what has happened to the lost art of letter writing? Reader response has always been important to us. So as we move beyond our 50 years of publication, we hope to respectfully revisit our past, yet look to the future. As the Rolling Stones labeled their 50th anniversary tour, let us all rally around that war cry, "Fifty Years and Counting."

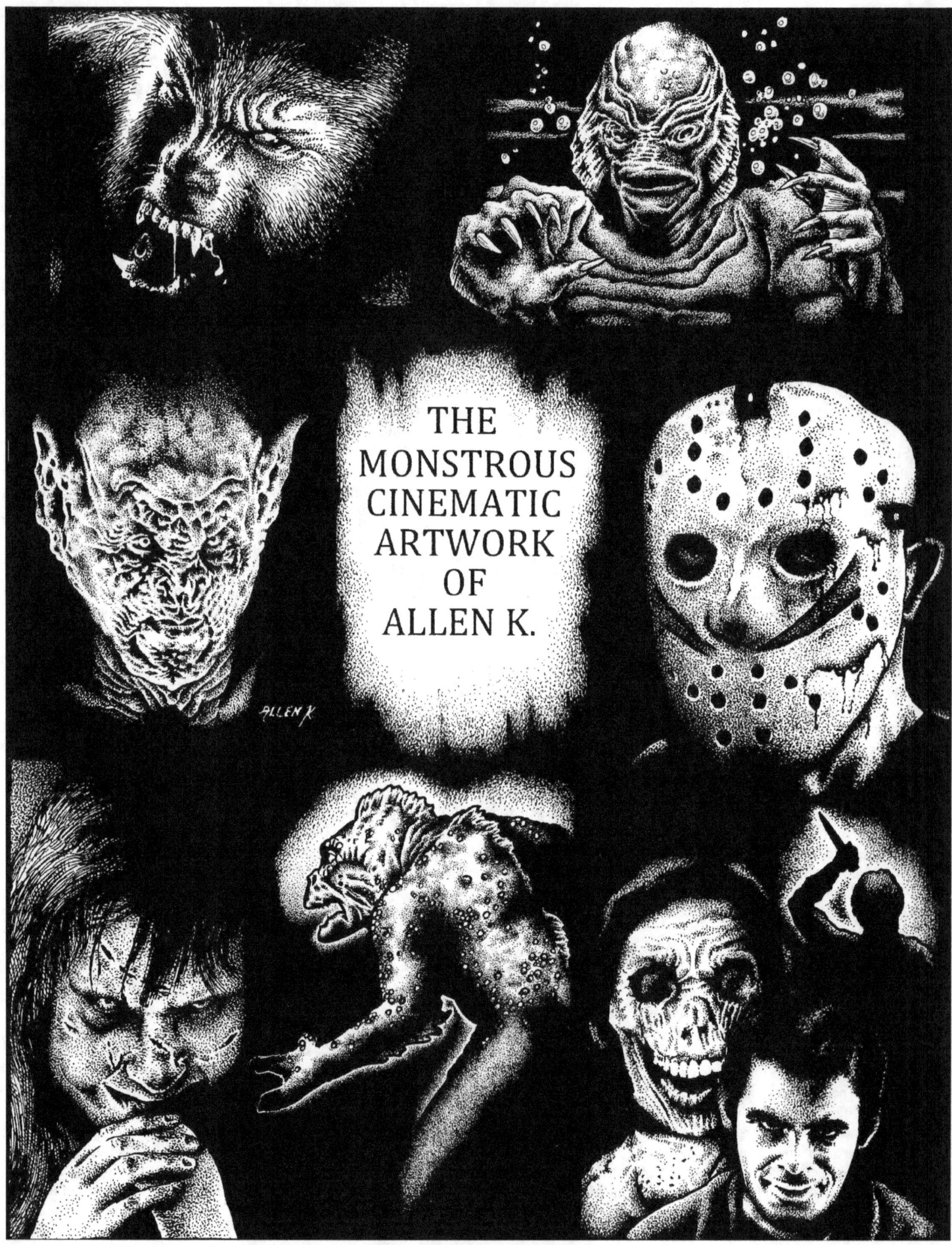

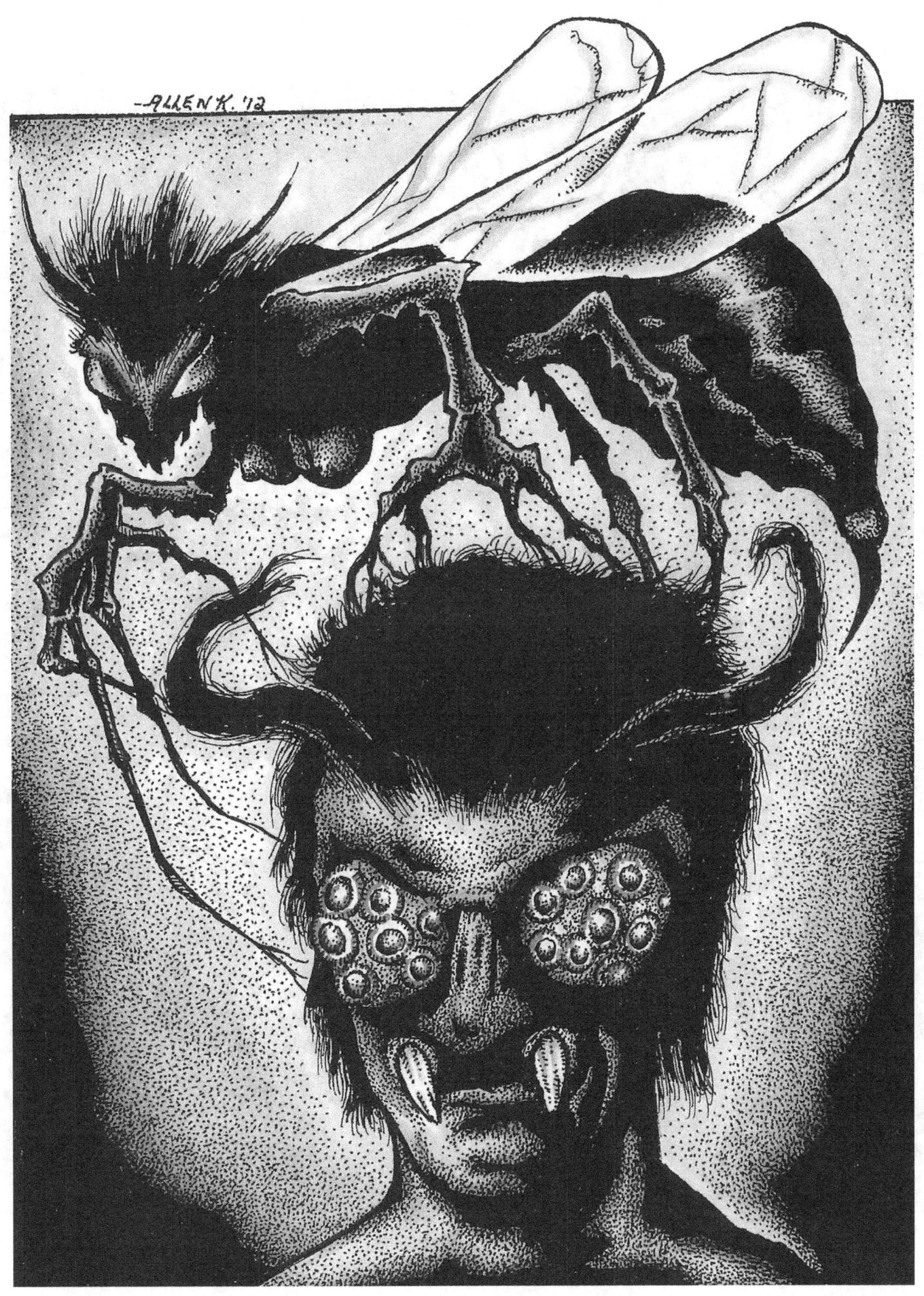

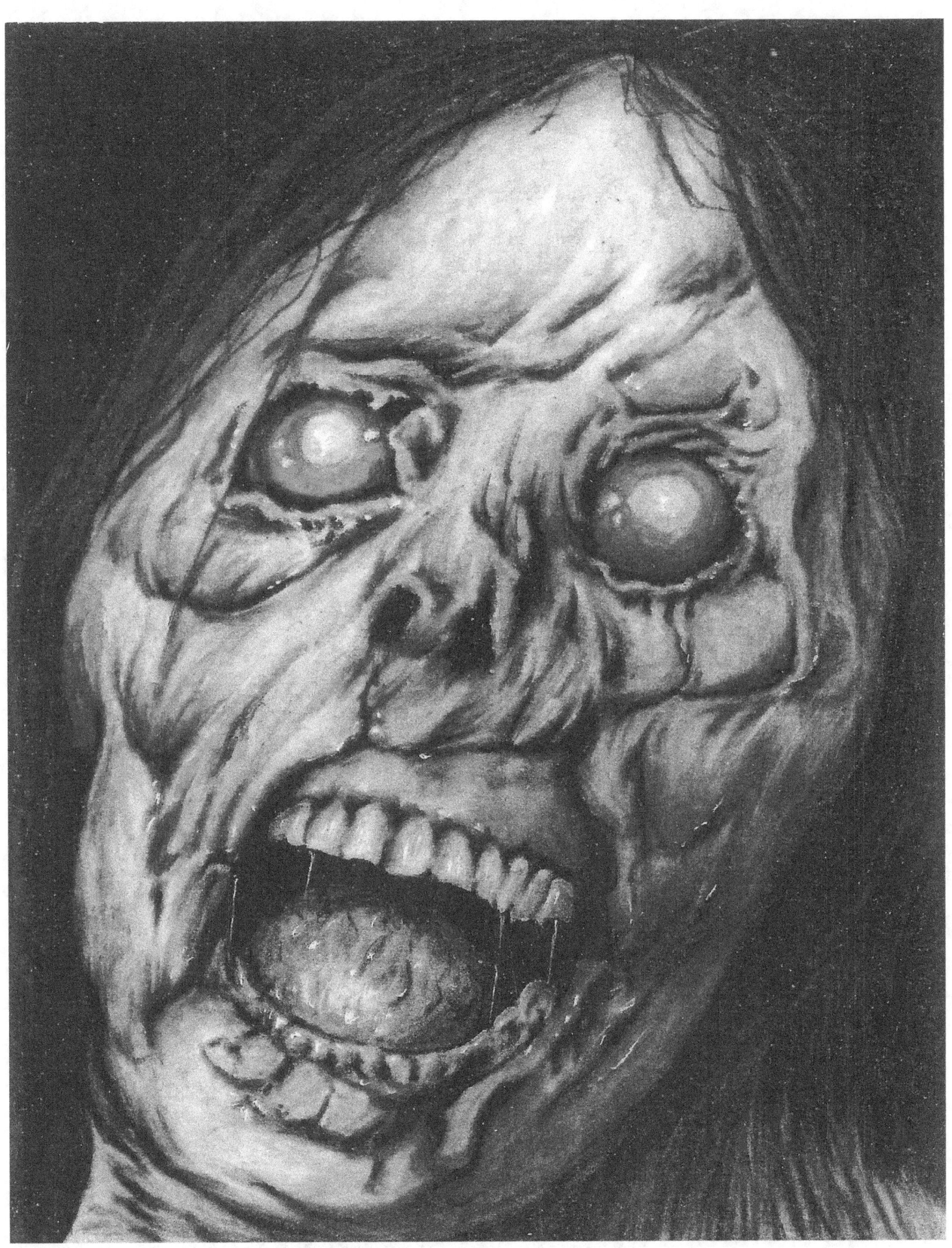

Part One

The Enduring Monster Culture and Its Fandom

Gary J. Svehla and Forrest J Ackerman meet for the first time and exchange magazines at a New York City convention.

Celebrating the 1950s, the 1960s and 50 Years of Gore Creatures/Midnight Marquee

Monster-Mania Walks Among Us

by Edmund G. Bansak

We have been immersed in worlds of fantasy, science fiction, horror and terror for quite some time. As far as pop cultural movements are concerned, the current predominance of these related genres—in literature, cinema, and television—cannot be overstated. They are the waters through which we long-time fans have been swimming for well over 50 years, so much so that we have sometimes forgotten—or perhaps become inured to—just how drenched we really have become. Saturated, yes, but perhaps like me, not *nearly* as satisfied as I would have imagined I'd be in this bloated dream-come-true of ours. But of course I should not complain.

The year 2013 continues the decades-long trend of big-budget genre productions—on screens both big and small—a prospect we long-time fans had been anticipating ever since Forrest J Ackerman, keeper of the gate, unlocked his doors in February 1958 with the first publication of *Famous Monsters of Filmland* and bid us welcome to his realm of monsters. Over the last five decades, the evolution of this ongoing deluge of monster-mania has rendered the world a very different place than it had been back in 1963, when Gary J. Svehla wrote, created, and distributed both hand-written and typed carbon copies of his first issue of *Gore Creatures*.

Since this cultural phenomenon of monster indulgence has been such a long-time unfolding (resulting in an environment where Hollywood appears to have complied with our every wish and catered to our every whim), it is easy to lose sight of how mainstream our beloved genres have become. Back in 1963, we may have been hoping that something significant would come of our rabid fanaticism with monster movies (then, a shorthand term for horror, science fiction and fantasy releases), but we had little foreknowledge of the dizzying heights that would be achieved in a field of cinema that was, at the time, largely disparaged by our elders. Some fans, me included, have become disenchanted by the film industry's shamelessly derivative methods of making a profit but, really, whom are we kidding? Have we forgotten the gimmicks and moneymaking schemes dreamed up by William Castle, Samuel Arkoff and Roger Corman? Perhaps these earlier cult filmmakers—hacks though they often were—enjoy more credit today because of their unabashed pride in their inventiveness, their enthusiasm, their methods and, of course, their level of hype. Castle, Arkoff, Corman and others achieved fame and a welcome level of autonomy by bargaining their way into the big time, doggedly turning out memorable hit movies—some huge moneymakers—without a big layout or an embarrassingly inflated bottom line. I suppose a large amount of my respect for the work of these pioneers of schlock cinema has something to do with their fortitude and survival in a relatively unsympathetic Hollywood environment, but I also must admit that I continue to enjoy the body of work that came from their combined efforts. So, too, do I continue to satisfy my cravings for their 1930s and 1940s antecedents—those earlier, often more respected genre films of Universal, Paramount, Warner Bros., RKO, Columbia and 20th Century Fox, as well as the cut-rate productions of Monogram and PRC. I would like to say that genre films have never been better than they are today—and technically that would be true—but I've become more cynical and less enthusiastic over the years.

For better or for worse, an all-too-common impetus to "think big" prevails, which is why a *single* T-Rex or a *single* brontosaurus (or just a *few* of the creepy-crawlies at the bottom of the ravine/chasm) were not good *enough* for Peter Jackson's remake of *King Kong*. Jackson is a marvelous filmmaker and I truly enjoyed his sincere homage to the original, including his wonderfully realized characterization of the new Kong. Still, I find it difficult to appreciate the industry's propensity for excess, coupled with non-stop-action that would satisfy the staunchest of video gamers—but such overkill severely strains a film's credibility for the rest of us. This is nothing new, of course; Hollywood has always gone for the "socko" appeal of big box-office returns, having been an investor's market from the very beginning. Can we today imagine a Hollywood that would deliberately ignore a blockbuster's copycat appeal and resist taking bandwagon rides into the land of profit? I can't. Like the snake eating its own tail, box-office bonanzas form franchises that, sequel after sequel, give customers what amounts to a bottomless cup of more of the same.

Since horror/terror, fantasy and science fiction are bigger today than they have ever been, I suppose I should keep my grumpiness to myself. But at times that is not easy, in spite of my sincere enjoyment of so many modern releases. In the 1950s and 1960s, genre films thrived but were less commonplace than they are today. I would never have *thought* of turning down the opportunity of viewing whatever film—no matter how derivative—that featured aliens, werewolves, dinosaurs, vampires, monsters of *any* variety. But today, I *do* turn down a majority of such opportunities. Given the overwhelming number of genre releases (especially those that up the ante in torture and dismemberment), I couldn't do *otherwise* and still have an operable life.

First, we have the cult-like *subgenre crazes* that ebb and flow to meet box-office demands. Recent trends—some bigger than others—have showcased vampires, zombies, werewolves, post-apocalyptic futures, cybernetic nightmares, serial killers, ghosts, aliens from space, time travel, robots, dinosaurs, sword and sorcery—the list goes on (and the next in line, according to the 2013 "Summer Issue" of *Entertainment Weekly*, would be witches).

We also have the succession of *remakes* of the films we have long treasured: first, the crown jewels of Universal's original 1930s horror boom (*Dracula, Frankenstein, The Wolf Man, The Mummy*, et al.), first remade abroad by England's Hammer Film Productions in the 1950s and 1960s, then more recently reinvented stateside, with major budgets and star power: *Bram Stoker's Dracula, Mary Shelley's Frankenstein, The Mummy, The Wolfman*.

Somewhere along the way, a later generation of genre classics became ripe for the big-budget remake grist mill—*War of the Worlds, The Time Machine, Invasion of the Body Snatchers* (three remakes, here), *Invaders from Mars, The Day the Earth Stood Still, The Thing* (two remakes), *The Blob, The Little Shop of Horrors, Village of the Damned, Psycho, Godzilla, Mighty Joe Young, The House on Haunted Hill, 13 Ghosts, The Haunting, Cat People, King Kong* (two remakes), and I am sure I missed a few. This is not to say that said remakes are inferior to the originals (though several are), just that the former versions, after all, *were* original.

Famous Monsters of Filmland, debuting in 1958, ushered in the baby boomer love for monsters in the wake of the *Shock Theater* TV package.

And then there are the *franchises* (*Star Trek, Star Wars, Halloween, Friday the 13th, Alien, Indiana Jones, Gremlins, Poltergeist, Paranormal Activity, Resident Evil, Nightmare on Elm Street, Saw, Texas Chainsaw Massacre, Evil Dead, Blade, Hellboy, The Matrix, Scream, Scary Movie, Harry Potter, Jurassic Park, Lord of the Rings, Night of the Living Dead, Chucky, Twilight, Final Destination, Terminator, Transformers*—please continue the list if you have an hour to spare). Note that these films usually have two titles and a number: the franchise title, a chapter title and a numeral, be it Roman or Arabic. Several of these franchise groupings are so well loved by their audiences that we must respect the magic hold they have on their fans. Today it would be difficult to imagine a cinematic landscape without the presence of such filmic bundles, some based on an actual series of novels (*Potter, Rings, Jurassic Park, Twilight*), and others conceived out of whole cloth (*Halloween, Alien, Gremlins, Star Wars, Indiana, Poltergeist*) by filmmakers who grew up "cutting their fangs" on *Famous Monsters of Filmland*. So, far be it from me to deny the excellence of a film that is so momentous as to inspire a franchise, but I am sorely missing the creativity and novelty that lies outside the territories of franchise filmmaking, an enterprise that, aside from such excellent

A red flag appeared when Universal remade the classic *The Wolf Man* as *The Wolfman* (2010), signifying that a younger generation of filmmakers had no clue as to what made the originals such endearing classics.

The quality of economic filmmaking can be found in *Burn, Witch, Burn* (1962); Margaret Johnson uses black magic to make sure her professor husband advances.

sequels as *Aliens* and *Terminator 2*, often veers dangerously close to fan-fiction.

And, finally, if derivative choices in filmmaking had not already crowded the field, here come the equally ubiquitous and franchise-driven "boots" and reboots of what we may dub—for lack of a better term—comic book-superhero-mania. It is at this point where—tents, sleeping bags, and sidewalk camping-gear notwithstanding—readers need to compile their *own* long and exhaustive list of comic book superhero movies, the keepers and the losers. Again, there is no denying the merits of a great many of the films in the superhero category but, really, do we need to have so *many*?

I respect economic filmmaking, whether I find it in vintage classics (like Don Siegel's *Invasion of the Body Snatchers*, Sidney Hayer's *Burn, Witch, Burn*, Jacques Tourneur's *Curse of the Demon*) or in modern examples (like Wes Craven's wonderful Hitchcock homage *Red Eye* or Duncan Jones' brilliant second feature, *Source Code*, both of these latter-day films, by the way, clocking in at under 90 minutes). I admire a film where every shot, every image, every exchange of dialogue becomes essential to the progression of *story*. We tend not to get that in films where massive budgets ensure that audiences see a stultifying amount of on-screen wreckage and non-stop action. If I want a wild and crazy ride, I'll go to the amusement park instead of wasting my money on 21st century remakes of *The Mummy* or *Journey to the Center of the Earth*. Thankfully, we have freedom of choice.

In this State of the Union of genre filmmaking, artistry is far from being extinct; it's just that we have to look around harder to find it. To quote Talking Heads' David Byrne, it is the "same as it ever was." Thanks to the current industry's hype-driven efforts in the direction of box-office returns, however, we are too often led astray in our search for excellence. It is very similar to our modern pop music culture: the *Billboard* charts no longer reflect the vast number of brilliant artists who are making great music *without* becoming household names. David Bowie's "Changes" never made a dent in the charts when released in 1971, although the song is, today, one of the famed singer's most well known. The Velvet Underground never enjoyed immediate fame, even though they have, arguably, become one of the most influential bands in modern music. In whatever venue of artistic endeavor, it appears that dark horses must bite the bit and that "sleepers" must be wakened by the kiss of a world catching up.

Show me a modern film historian who has little cognizance of the tremendous significance of William Castle, Roger Corman, and Samuel Z. Arkoff, and I will show you an imposter. In film, as in music, it is often the underdogs who weather through inauspicious beginnings only to rise to cult status—and beyond. This is why, from low-budget/underground origins, determined neophytes like Stanley Kubrick, Don Siegel, Francis Ford Coppola, Peter Bogdanovich, Martin Scorsese, James Cameron, Oliver Stone, Sam Raimi, the Coen Brothers, Peter Jackson, Danny Boyle, Katherine Bigelow—and a wide array of others—eventually find their way into the big time. If it appears that I have been dismissive of current trends and over-hyped movie events, it is with no disrespect to the well-deserved success of such powerhouse filmmakers as those listed above. Hollywood's current tendency to exploit fantastic cinema is still the "same as it ever was," only *more* so.

At the present, it is truly difficult to take it all in, the magnitude of genre blockbusters that have formed, *in*formed, and *re*formed our modern entertainment culture, year after year, decade after decade. However, we can be very grateful, as we go along with our daily lives and practical means of employment, that fan writers *among us* have taken the time to share their thoughts about what they have embraced—or discarded—in tracking this phantasmagorical media journey of ours. Were it not for the two generations of monster movie periodicals we have sought and read with considerable enthusiasm, it is doubtful that we could have ever kept tabs on the genre's inevitable conquest of mainstream culture.

Now, at least, we can rest assured of our convictions; we need *no longer* defend our questionable genre preferences to scoffing elders and befuddled authority figures. Long ago, we took the opportunity to foresee the future of popular culture and we were given a veritable blueprint for the shape of things to come. At the cutting edge was Forrest J Ackerman's *Famous Monsters of Filmland* and, following in its wake, countless issues of like-minded publications—both professional and amateur—with mostly one thing in common: an absolute love for the field of inquiry—*monsters*

By 1958's premiere issue of *Famous Monsters of Filmland*, it was apparent that Forrest J Ackerman had already laid claim to a territory he knew would strike it big. Given his long-time fan status, coupled with his interest in the evolution of the film fantastic, Ackerman shined a light upon the pioneers of the silent era, the 1930s horror boom and its continuation into the early 1940s, the '50s science fiction film bonanza and the September 1957 television premiere of *Shock Theater*. Forry (as fans affectionately dubbed him) had the prescience of mind to examine the pop culture of the period and predict a widespread proliferation of what was yet to come. And in the pages of his groundbreaking magazine of which he was both editor and primary writer, he held the attention of hordes of younger fans eager to discover more.

Today, looking back at that first issue of *Famous Monsters*, we can see that

Ackerman's presentation was actually more *adult* than many fans remember. The cover—a chesty blonde in a *very* low cut black gown, standing in front of a well-dressed man in a Frankenstein monster mask—was one I most certainly had to hide from my parents. The magazine clearly had our undivided attention, introducing younger readers to a nightmare world they had previously only dreamed about. After Forry's avuncular welcome, claiming that "Monsters Are *Good* For You" (say what?), he next gave us a surprisingly esoteric—if brief—history of cinema's monsters and the actors who played them ("Alice in Monsterland"). An engagingly academic article followed called "The Frankenstein Story," which not only included the obvious Mary Shelley origins, but also gave a historic account of a real-life Castle Frankenstein. We are thereafter provided with a portion of *Mad Magazine*'s comic-book parody of Universal's *Frankenstein*, as conceived by artist Jack Davis (who would soon be responsible for the best monster bubble gum trading cards ever). Then, taking his cues from the '50s science fiction movie boom, the editor-in-chief offers his avid readers an article, "Out of this World," which showcases a "modern" crop of some distinctly novel monsters (including top-notch photographic reproductions of the wildest-looking creatures imaginable—Saucermen, Crab Monsters, a Black Lagoon Creature, Monsters both Metaluna and Robot, an "It" that Conquers the World, et al.). As the issue nears its end, readers are introduced to several ladies in peril (a Gothic movement mainstay) by way of "Scream Test." Finally, the last article ("Monsters on Television") tackles the subject of the *Shock* package of classic horror monster movies that were currently being ushered into the living rooms of America (readers here being provided with a large list of the national television stations participating in the *Shock Theater* syndication).

Forrest J Ackerman may have mapped out the territory in his premiere issue, but this garden of ghoulish delights was already tilled and ready for the planting to come. Before that historic first issue, a youth-driven fascination with monsters of all shapes and sizes existed, a movement that turned out to be as significant to baby boomers as the introduction of the 45-rpm single and the popularization of rock 'n' roll. Looking back today, creeping through the well-worn pages of the wondrous magazines and fanzines that heralded the monster-mania yet to come, we can begin to appreciate the quandary of those

An ad for Baltimore TV's Channel 11 *Shock*, hosted by Dr. Lucifer (Richard Dix)

self-proclaimed *responsible parents* who were trying to avert whatever *dangerous* influences were believed to be undermining the values and purity of their children. Fortunately for us, they-who-protested-too-much would prove to be no match for the likes of Forrest J Ackerman, Calvin T. Beck or a certain 13-year-old Baltimorean named Gary J. Svehla.

Let's step back to the early 1950s when conservative adults, school teachers and "experts" in the field of child psychology were voicing concerns about the negative effect popular culture was having upon the nation's children. These concerns, bolstered by Dr. Frederic Wertham's 1953 anti-comic-book expose *Seduction of the Innocent*, culminated in 1954 with a virtual banning of horror comics, creating a Comics Code that altogether eliminated the word *horror* from the titles of said publications. Still, the younger generation's morbid fascination with monsters refused to die; it was a fascination that would withstand the pressures of the myriad claims of the credible experts (including Dr. Wertham)

50th Anniversary Issue [1963-2013]

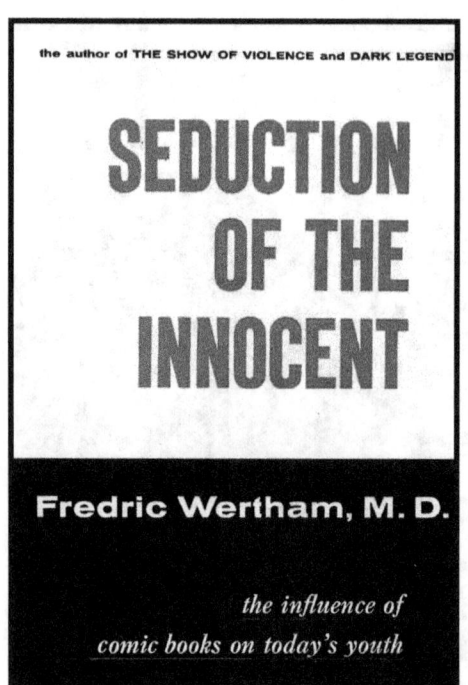

Dr. Wertham's book, published in 1953, led to the Comics Code one year later, virtually banning all horror comic books.

who told mainstream America that comic books were somehow sowing the seeds of juvenile delinquency. In the 1955-produced *Rebel Without a Cause*, Jim Stark—played by James Dean—reacts to having his tire slashed by a juvenile delinquent by telling the culprit, "You know what? *You* read too many comic books."

So where did all this morbid fascination originate and *why*, in the ensuing years, did it appear to take on a life of its own? We will continue seeking answers to these questions for years to come. But for now, let it suffice that the children of the 1950s grew up in a world so permeated by fear that it should come as no surprise that they would be preoccupied with a metaphorical embodiment of their parents' own greatest anxieties. Our national fears were many and they kept close company with each other, like a loud, well-attended party that refused to call it a night. The list is an exhaustive one: fear of Communism, fear of juvenile delinquency (and the peer pressure that feeds its flames), fear of abnormalities and non-conformers, fear of the bomb (later, accompanied by phobic concerns over the effects of *radiation*), fear of polio and other illnesses (both physical *and* mental), fear of criminals (the Kefauver Hearings accentuating concerns about juvenile delinquency and organized crime), fear of race, ethnicity and cultural differences (the amorphous "melting pot" of old—growing, moving, and changing—with unfamiliar traditions trickling into the *safe* neighborhoods of middle-America), fear of the effects of rock 'n' roll (which, for a time, was called "race music," since many adults were *already* aware that "rock 'n' roll" was an African-American euphemism for sex), fear of the findings of the Kinsey Report (and the perversions it uncovered), fear of the effects of television (and the vast wasteland it signified), fear of losing the space race (and the dire possibilities of the Soviets having the upper hand in outer reaches) and fear of keeping up with the growing pace of everyday life (as if keeping up with the Joneses was not enough). But finally, and perhaps most significant of all, given the younger generation's sudden and undeniable worldliness in regard to all things new and popular, was a looming fear of being woefully left behind. This was, after all, the first generation of parents to take their pop cultural cues—in fashion and hairstyles, in music and popular dance, in current fads and entertainment, in lifestyle, too—from the habits of a younger generation, a new demographic with money to spare.

Looking back, I believe most *Midnight Marquee* readers would admit that the monster magazines they grew up reading proved to be more beneficial than harmful to the vast spectrum of young people who, rather obsessively, pored through their photo-filled pages. Gary Svehla and I—lifelong English teachers both—were not the only monster fans whose *junior* critic ambitions within the realm of the fantastic (upon the page *and* the screen) played a large part in the intellectual growth and sincere hunger for knowledge that, rather quite naturally, led to gaining a foothold in public education. A list of our youthful counterparts whose parallel interests evolved into spectacular *Hollywood* careers is nothing less than mind-boggling. Add to that the number of monster magazine readers who became published writers/novelists in related genres of the fantastic—several among them household names—and the jaw drops. So go stand in the corner and sulk, Dr. Fredric Wertham.

As Gary Svehla and I—both having been born in 1950—grew up in our separate locations (Baltimore, MD and Fairfield, CT respectively), we were prime material, sitting ducks, for the lure of monster fandom. Gary's operational sources were the Baltimore and Washington, D.C. television broadcasts; mine were the broadcasts coming from nearby New York City. At the theaters during the 1950s science fiction films had become the latest big thing, although they were mostly of a variety that led many to view them as, really, a *space age* equivalent of the horror film (with monsters to spare, sometimes even hordes of them). In fact, *actual* science fiction writers, Damon Knight being a particular example, renounced 1950s sci-fi films as horror movies in disguise, given that so many of them featured monsters from space (pejoratively termed BEMs—Bug Eyed Monsters) or, just as often, ordinary Earth creatures that had undergone monstrous metamorphoses from exposure to atomic radiation.

Although a veritable mother lode of science fiction films were released in theaters during the 1950s, most of these '50s titles (excepting a few maverick quickies like *Rocketship XM, Lost Continent, The Man From Planet X, Cat Women of the Moon, King Dinosaur* and others) would not find their way to the small screen until the early 1960s. When that time came, most of these, combined with a selection of '50s horror titles, would arrive in packages, like gifts waiting to be opened.

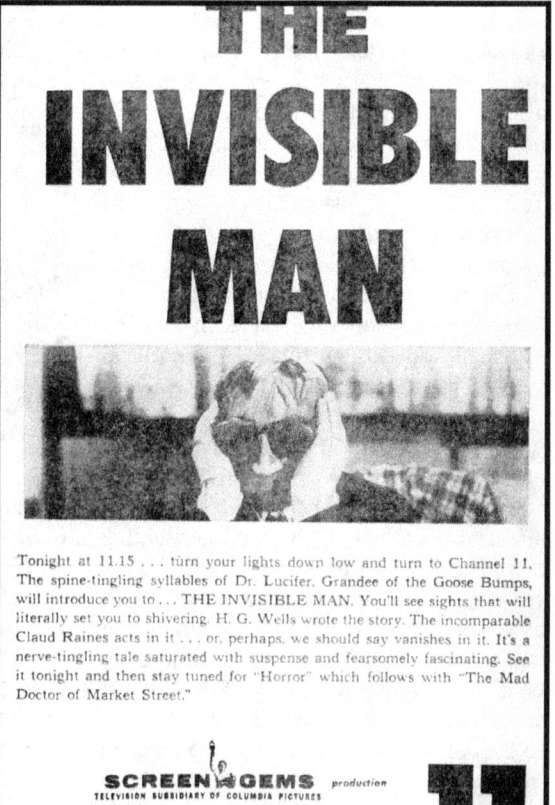

TV'S NIGHTMARES

TARANTULA GHOUL pokes morbid fun at everything within range of Portland's KPTV

Nobody, but nobody, is safe from the witty but acid tongue of Tarantula Ghoul, a cross between the Charles Addams woman and a "road company" Tallulah Bankhead, who welcomes viewers to her *House of Horror* in Portland, Ore., on Wednesdays (10:30 P.M., KPTV). She attacks the Highway Commission for removing the few decent death traps left, assails the City Zoo Commission for not exhibiting prehistoric animals, kids the D.A.R. with her own organization, the D.S.W.T. (Daughters of the Salem Witchcraft Trials). She's active in the Black Cross, lectures on Second Aid and keeps her finger in the political pie through her party, The Cemeterians (which boasts more ex-presidents than any other political group). With an occasional assist from Milton, a retired grave-robber turned gardener, Suzanne Waldron clowns up the Tarantula role enough to win family acceptance for the show. Taranch, as she's known off camera, introduces the films either with a special set or from her "home"—a weirdly-decorated room overlooking a run-down cemetery (which she refers to as the neighborhood) and a patio where she and Milton "plant things." For *Frankenstein* pictures the lab was recreated for her entrance from the operating table. For the *Mummy* films she made her entrance from a mummy case. For *Murders of the Rue Morgue* she did the show in French with English sub-titles. *King Kong* was presented as a satire on *This Is Your Life* with a large studio audience of costumed monsters paying tribute to a live chimp, Kenya, an alleged great, great grandson of Kong. A native of Portland, Suzanne describes herself as having been "depressingly tall, thin and shy" during high school. But at Highland University in Las Vegas, New Mexico, she discovered the value of individualism—which she had. Ironically, her first dramatic appearance was as one of the witches in *Macbeth*. After college, stock and touring shows, she returned to Portland to do radio commercials. Since the horror show started in October, 1957,

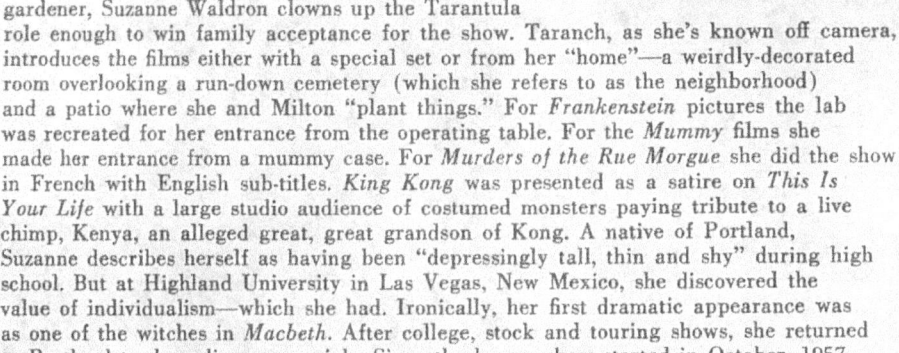

Suzanne's been carted around in coffins, appeared with gorillas, held press parties in cemeteries, etc. Her most embarrassing moment—she fell asleep in a coffin and did NOT arise as scheduled for half-time ceremonies of a nationally-telecast football game. Her most frightening time—appearing on stage with an 11-foot boa constrictor which, at the last minute replaced the smaller, less active snake she was used to. In her free time Suzanne reads and listens to hi-fi in an apartment she shares with an overly-friendly Great Dane named Frankenstein. She likes people, all kinds of music (she made two R 'n' R records—*King Kong* and *Graveyard Rock*), dancing, art, skiing, riding, and surf-swimming. She still does commercials and spoofs the *Movie of the Month*, looking ahead to the day the horror craze joins Davy Crockett, but the way things look now, that may be a long way off.

DR. LUCIFER... Baltimore's bumbling bogeyman haunts on WBAL-TV

A macabre figure who comes off more mocking than menacing is Dr. Lucifer, a tremendously popular fellow in Baltimore, Md. In his laboratory at WBAL-TV (1 A.M. Sat.) his fiendish brain is constantly at work experimenting and creating—but his experiments usually backfire and his creations are harmless, making him a bumbling sort of a bogeyman. As a terror he's all thumbs, and that's just the way Richard Dix, who breathes life into the luckless Lucifer, plans it. For instance, the bear trap he set to catch Santa Claus (just to prove there *is* a Santa Claus) caught the good doctor instead. His attempt to recreate a baby sitter from a 3,000-year-old mummy (because the label said she was young and beautiful) resulted instead in an unhappy 350-pound weight lifter in the Egyptian princess' clothing. One night Lucifer dropped a marble slab on a bill collector who was hounding him. At various times during the show he'd lift the marble and ask the man if he'd give up. Each time the answer was no, so the slab would drop again. When the collector finally gave up Lucifer let him have it again—because he hates quitters! Though Lucifer works mostly

40 FEBRUARY, 1959

solo he is occasionally joined by the rest of his video family—his wife, Grace; a daughter, Lucretia, and Baby Borgia. The formally attired doctor is also aided—or victimized—by a Great Dane who's addicted to showing up on camera with dismembered arms and legs of neighborhood children. For this Lucifer chastises him publicly as not being neighborly. And, believe it or not, the whole thing is handled so amusingly that it comes off more "grin" than "grim." Years of acting, directing, producing and studying the dramatic arts are behind the 33-year-old Mr. Dix's week-after-week characterization. A native of Baltimore, Md., he attended City College of Baltimore and Johns Hopkins University. In addition he received a scholarship to the Institute of the Theatre in Williamsburg, Va., in 1948 and again from 1950-52. His career was interrupted by service in the U.S. Air Force from 1944-46 and 1950-51. A veteran actor, Dix has some 200 roles to his credit, including off-Broadway productions and a five-year run as lead in *The Common Glory*, a historical pageant staged annually at Williamsburg. A versatile performer, Dix has run the gamut of professional acting from such deep drama fare as *The Glass Menagerie* and *Petrified Forest* in legitimate theater, to the role of *Officer Happy* on WBAL-TV. His favorite role is that of *Scrooge* in Dickens' *Christmas Carol*, which he did on network television in 1948. At present he's a director of the Children's Theatre Association of Baltimore and president of the local AFTRA chapter. So when things go wrong on Baltimore's *Shock Theatre*, the viewers needn't get too upset, for Dr. Lucifer knows what he's doing—every stumble of the way.

GORGON brings the bizarre to Fort Worth's KFJZ-TV

Authentic, bizarre, Camfield—that's the ABCs that make a horror show popular during a prime time spot (8-9:30 P.M. Sat.) down Texas way. Taking that in reverse there's Camfield, first name Bill, the man behind the soft-spoken, ominous-sounding, borderline maniac Gorgon, who hosts *Nightmare* for KFJZ-TV in Fort Worth. In addition to hob-nobbing with both monsters and viewers as the menacing but polite Gorgon, Bill also writes the show and directs special effects—which brings us to the bizarre and authentic. When *The Invisible Man* was featured, Gorgon labored with a chemistry problem in his lab. At the end of the show he removed his smock, leaving only his head and hands; then his gloves, leaving only his head. With invisible hands he raised a test tube to his lips, sipped the formula, and his head slowly faded away! Once a camera was embedded in a coffin to give a "corpse's eye view" of the world. Another time, while demonstrating the game of "headball," Gorgon place-kicked a human head into the camera lens. And viewers will be a long time forgetting his effects for the *Daughter of Dracula*. A full-size replica of the movie's funeral pyre was constructed and a life-size dummy was sent up in flames. Then Gorgon mounted the burning pyre, too— or so it looked on the home screen! A lifelong resident of Fort Worth, 29-year-old Bill is married, a graduate of Texas Christian University, has been on the KFJZ-TV staff since the station signed on in 1955. Bill is also sales promotion director and plays three other on-the-air characters—Hoover, a life-size puppet dog; Binky Beaver on *Saturday Cartoon Clubhouse*, and Mr. Tapioca on *JoJo's Funhouse*—insurance policies for the future should the monster madness pass.

But we are getting ahead of ourselves.

The original monster packages—*Shock* and *Son of Shock*—were introduced to television in 1957 and 1958, respectively, in the very midst of the burgeoning rock 'n' roll craze. Those were glorious years for the younger generation; for the first time in American history, corporations and merchants were catering to the needs and buying power of a generation of minors who were intoxicated with rock 'n' roll, movies, television and, of course, monsters. It is both ironic and fortuitous that it was an *older* generation of monsters, the horror classics of the 1930s and 1940s, which eventually spawned the monster craze of the 1950s, as well as the subsequent monster magazine boom which inspires this article. No doubt there were countless concerned parents who found monster magazines to be even more of a threat than the horror comics that were earlier under fire. In place of those lurid renderings, illustrated by comic book artists—of walking corpses, stalking vampires, misshapen monstrosities, deranged killers, murderous shape shifters, angry aliens from beyond and scantily clad and wonderfully built women in peril—monster magazines offered the youngsters *actual* photographs of the same. And oh, how we loved them.

The first professional—and surely most prototypical—of these notorious magazines, *Famous Monsters of Filmland*, was set into motion largely in response to the widespread availability and *extreme* popularity of the two groundbreaking film packages—*Shock* (August 1957) and *Son of Shock* (May 1958). Columbia's television arm, Screen Gems, had bought and syndicated the batch of pre-1948 shockers and, for the first time, released them to the small screen. They were, most of them anyway, true monster classics of the 1930s and 1940s, several whose reputations had long achieved mythic status, and they were predominantly Universal productions along with a few minor, if noteworthy, Columbia films up for grabs by their Screen Gems affiliate.

But this was not the first instance of packaging Hollywood feature films for television, nor was it the first to bring monster movies into our homes.

Although the infamous 1948 anti-trust court ruling prohibited the major film studios from continuing their previous ownership and management of theater chains, eliminating the "block booking" that had a stranglehold on independent theater-owners, this turn of events presented little interference with a film studio's influence upon the growth and development of the burgeoning medium of television. By the mid-'50s, television stations (national network as well as regional independents) were often—right down to their call letters—carry-overs from radio's Golden Age. Hence, RKO's Radio Pictures, a major Hollywood studio with true New York City origins, wound up gaining an early foothold in the regional television industry, founding several syndicated television stations that would provide opportunities to showcase films from the RKO vaults. Columbia formed Screen Gems, under whose banner the studio not only released film packages to television, but also created network and syndicated shows made exclusively for television (often—but not always—for CBS network affiliates). Warner Bros. Television (aka Warner Bros. Presents) had what appeared to be an exclusive contract with the ABC network and made several extremely successful Western shows (*Cheyenne, Maverick, Lawman*, etc.). ABC, this time with connections with Paramount (ABC-Paramount), was also a player in the record industry, as was NBC, then owned by RCA, a major industry in the production of records, radios and televisions. Desilu Productions bought RKO when it went under, and (due to the unprecedented success of the early television sitcom, *I Love Lucy*) Desilu filmed a considerable volume of productions exclusively for television. We can go on and on with the changing of hands between Hollywood film studios and television production, but as they say, *we get the picture.*

Around the time that Howard Hughes sold RKO's Hollywood studio to Desilu Productions, regional independent television and radio stations primarily on the East Coast absorbed the remainder of the RKO management. New York City's WOR-TV (Channel 9) was one such regional station, and a very significant one it was, bringing to the "greater New York area" the beloved *Million Dollar Movie*. When Forrest J Ackerman, in an early issue of *FM*, boasted that the television debut of *King Kong* was so popular in New York City that it was televised 18 times in a single week, he was absolutely correct. But what he did *not* say is that WOR-TV's *Million Dollar Movie* (which premiered *King Kong* in the pre-*FM* days of 1955) televised *every* feature 18 times per week—two back-to-back screenings on each of the five weeknights, and four back-to-back matinees on both Saturday and Sunday.

I was not quite five when I saw *King Kong* on the Monday it premiered and,

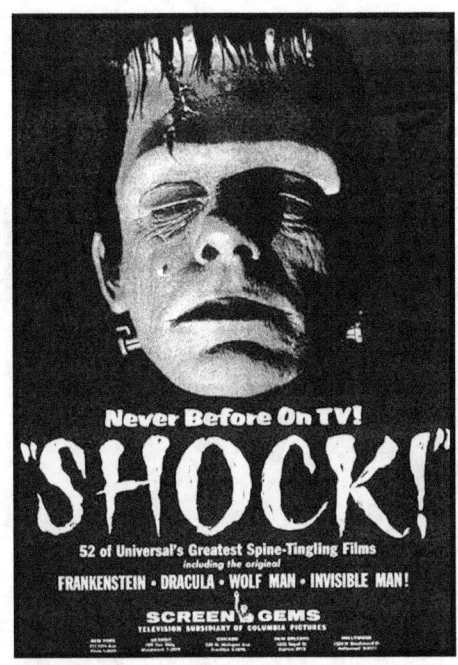

because of the *Million Dollar Movie*'s theater-like weekly multi-screenings, I managed to talk my parents into allowing me to view it a couple more times, including the weekend matinees of course. It was my introduction to the monster movie and the rest was history—or, rather, *pre*history, since I developed a dinosaur obsession shortly thereafter. In the years to follow, *Million Dollar Movie* came through with such monster classics as *Godzilla, Mighty Joe Young, Son of Kong, One Million B.C.* and *The Thing From Another World.* During these early years of television, missing (or falling asleep during) a single showing of a monster movie was tantamount to a tear-rendering disaster, so *Million Dollar Movie*'s multiple offerings received the sincere blessings of future monster fanatics like me. Where else could baby boomer film historians analyze a single film in such a meticulous way? Martin Scorsese also credited *Million Dollar Movie*'s multiple showings of *King Kong, Citizen Kane, The Third Man, Stromboli* and myriad others as having a considerable impact on his future filmmaking career.

I didn't know Gary Svehla at the time, but we were blood brothers then, just as we are blood brothers today. Both of us were fortunate to have been born in 1950 which, by my calculation, was the ideal year of birth if one were to take advantage of the youth-driven zeitgeist of an encroaching monster-mania that was aggressively laying claim to our collective imagination. My hometown of Fairfield, Connecticut was close enough to New York City to pick up all the pop culture it had to offer. The predominant media, both television and radio, came by

An ad from inside the pages of *Famous Monsters* for the Magnajector, one of Ed Bansak's favorite presents from Christmas of 1960 and one that sparked his creativity.

way of the Big City which, at the time, was still the broadcasting entertainment capital of the country. And so, for me, it was *Million Dollar Movie* that had the earliest impact on my cinematic leanings. I was not quite old enough to get on board with the after-hours weeknight programming of *Shock Theater* on WABC-TV (Channel 7), but when I saw their photo-advertisements in the *TV Guide,* it was like looking over the fence into someone else's backyard. That backyard happened to belong to my older cousin, Ronnie, who was then twice my age and who managed to be my most immediate eyewitness to the *Shock Theater* presentations. I am sure I was a pest, grilling him about those old Universal classics whenever I could. Although I had heard about those mythic movies—*Frankenstein, Dracula, The Wolf Man, The Mummy*—I had no idea (until I saw evidence in the *TV Guide*) that there was such a thing as a *Bride of Frankenstein,* a *Son of Frankenstein,* a *Dracula's Daughter,* a *Son of Dracula,* a *Frankenstein Meets the Wolf Man* or a *Mummy's Hand.* As if to give me further proof, it was also my cousin Ronnie who let me look at his first two issues of *Famous Monsters of Filmland,* both of which took my breath away. Consider my exhilaration, some months later, when I discovered that—by *popular demand*—WABC-TV had been persuaded to run a double-billed *Shock Matinee* every Saturday from 1:00—4:00 p.m. The first offering was the back-to-back combination of *Frankenstein* and *Werewolf of London.* I remember to this day what a revelation this was for me.

Famous Monsters of Filmland continued to roll off the press and into my cousin's hands; the well-dressed-playboy-in-a-monster-mask gag covers of the first two issues were now replaced with truly scary covers: *Phantom of the Opera* (issue 3) and an artistic rendering of the one-eyed Martian from George Pal's 1953 *War of the Worlds* (issue 4). By this time, we were well into 1959 and I realized that it wasn't just my cousin and my friends that were "monster crazy," but rather an entire country. I found out much later that the likely impetus for the *Shock* and *Son of Shock* film packages was, in part, the groundbreaking success of the first *Frankenstein* film to be shot in glorious Technicolor: 1957's *Curse of Frankenstein,* produced by a fledgling British production company known as Hammer. However, if *that* film lit the match, it was *Shock Theater* that fanned the flames and spread the fire. Like rock 'n' roll, it turned out to be a connecting link to the desires of children as well as teenagers. Moreover, monster-mania made its presence known within the parallel world of rock 'n' roll. Aside from an array of 1957 sci-fi novelty hits by Buchanan & Goodman ("Flying Saucer," "Flying Saucer 2," and "Santa's Satellite"), whose spoken comedic narratives were broken into by snippets of actual hit songs, fully performed original songs were also part of the sudden monster craze. Three of them, in particular, were hits in 1958: "Dinner With Drac" (a March release by John Zacherle who, billing himself as "Roland," was the host of Philadelphia's *Shock Theater*), "Witch Doctor" (an April release which, performed by David Seville, became a #1 hit) and "Purple People Eater" (a June release that also rose to #1, as performed by Sheb Wooley). Yes, monster-mania was upon us. This may be a good time to remind older readers of the running gag on 1959's new hit television show, *The Many Loves of Dobie Gillis,* where any given character who was heading to the movie theater would announce, without fail, that the feature was *The Monster Who Devoured Cleveland.*

I was delighted when I saw my cousin's sixth issue of *Famous Monsters* (February 1960) featuring *King Kong* on the cover. It was evident that my interest in monster movies had gone full circle. The contagion of monster-mania was not

The first two gag covers of *Famous Monsters* were replaced with truly scary covers, beginning with issue #3.

to be deterred; in fact, the televised *Shock* packages had already delivered a final, triumphant thumbing-of-the-nose to Dr. Fredric Wertham. Inspired by the EC horror comic-book tradition of providing a "Crypt Keeper"-type master of ceremonies, *Shock Theater* programming across the country had created a market for EC-styled horror hosts to introduce and comment upon the particular feature being shown, always, mind you, with an *un*healthy dose of ghoulish humor. In one fell swoop, horror hosts were as plentiful as the walking dead in a George Romero film.

In 1959 New York's WABC-TV had managed to steal Philadelphia's tried and true model, Roland (aka John Zacherle), whose move to the big city was treated with the kind of spectacle and fanfare usually reserved for royalty as he, now under the name of Zacherley, claimed the throne as the undisputed king of *Shock Theater* hosts. And that is no exaggeration. He appeared on *American Bandstand* fairly regularly and was a huge ratings conduit whenever and wherever he appeared. And, yes, he was the only horror show host to have a hit record, "Dinner With Drac." In June 1960 Zacherley finally made the cover of *Famous Monsters* (#7) that advertised his new paperback horror anthology for Ballantine Books: *Zacherley's Midnight Snacks* (soon to be followed by *Zacherley's Vulture Stew*). As if that were not enough, Zach also made a mock run for President in 1960. "Zacherley For President" signs, buttons and bumper stickers were noticeably present in political gatherings in the New York/New Jersey/Connecticut areas around the time John F. Kennedy and Richard M. Nixon were having their media-groundbreaking debates. Zacherley was likely the first horror show host to include "break-ins" during the playing of the film. Although other horror show hosts would follow his lead with this ingenious comical device, Zach's "break-ins" were the most original, the most iconoclastic and by far the most hilarious (in my highly biased opinion). By the time he appeared on the cover of *FM #7*, Zach had already moved to WOR-TV, where he was given greater air time between movie segments in the new format, *Zacherley At Large*. In the "greater New York area" in the early 1960s, Zacherley had become nothing less than a household celebrity. Everyone—young and old—knew who he was; when his name was dropped during a social occasion those who overheard his mention would volunteer a long list of favorable "Zach bits," many being his movie "break-ins," but also his wild, funny and always very hip shenanigans during the in-betweens (which, as his New York television career progressed, were often as long or longer than the feature segments). His legions of fans followed him from station to station. (In the fall of '63, he would move again, this time to WPIX's *Chiller Theater*, where he would be at his very best. But that would come later.)

On Christmas day, 1960, just after my 10th birthday, my parents would really come through with the gift I had been mooning over for months. It was something called a Magnajector, and I discovered it in an advertisement in *Famous Monsters*. Basically, it was a black plastic rendition of what the teachers in school called an opaque projector. With the Magnajector, all we needed to do was screw in a standard light bulb, plug in the device and, as a result, we could turn movie stills—like those found in *Famous Monsters*—into a projected image (of variable size) upon the wall (provided the room was dark enough). Just tape a sheet of white paper where the image is, and go to work with a pencil, drawing your own monsters. After approximating the image, along with the appropriate dimensions (the latter was vital), we could take the drawing to a well-lighted desk, with the magazine photo in tow, and *embellish*. Following this plan with the addition of some self-styled spooky lettering, I designed a number of would-be monster magazine covers. The name of my proposed venture was *Gothic* and the first cover that made me feel a modicum of pride was a very good facsimile of Oliver Reed's lycanthrope from *Curse of the Werewolf*. My embellishments included exciting blurbs ("SEE ... a normal man turn into a fiendish wolf ... SEE ... a gorgeous woman fighting for her life ... SEE ... a full moon that beckons death ...") about the wondrous articles within. However, perhaps because I had not actually *seen* the movie, I never quite got around to writing the articles themselves. I designed at least a half dozen covers, all of which I was very proud of, but the articles remained unwritten. Alas, it was as close as I got to the creation of my own fanzine. Fortunately for all of us, Gary Svehla and others like him kept with it longer than I did.

The first three years of the new decade continued to fuel the growing appetites of monster mavens, with film packages being doled out with great regularity. At the end of 1962 (according to Kevin Heffernan's excellent book, *Ghouls, Gimmicks, and Gold: Horror Films and the American Movie Business, 1953-1968*) the major Hollywood studios had 3,350 feature films

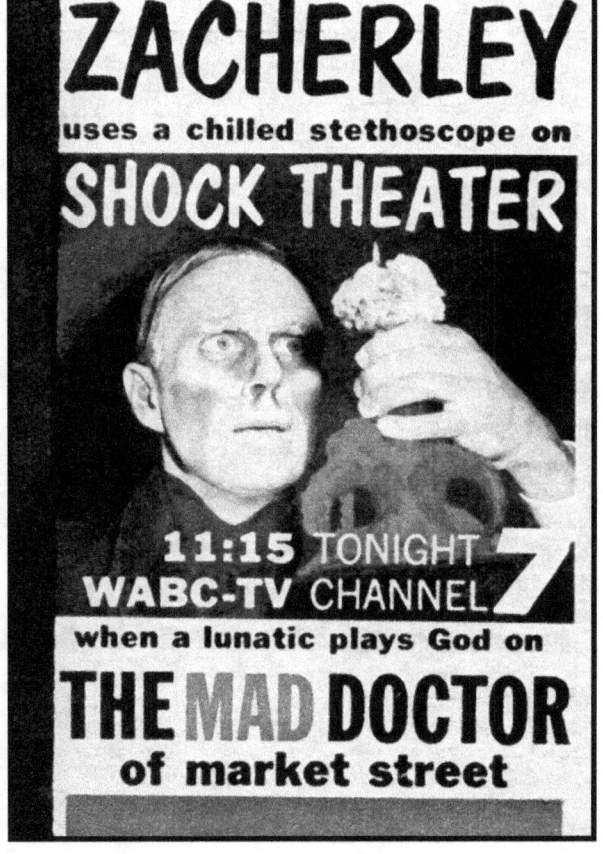

Monster-mania made its presence known within the parallel world of rock'n'roll with parodies coming from Buchanan and Goodman.

(of mixed genres) that were yet unsold to television. Just one year later—the year of *Gore Creatures'* debut—the number of unsold features had dwindled to 1,400. So, over the course of 1963, the feature films that *were* released to television amounted to a hefty total of 1,950. Clearly, monster fans were reaping the benefits of a large assortment of syndicated film packages, several of them targeting the horror/science fiction market. This would include, in the fall of '63, Screen Entertainment's eagerly awaited American International package of 69 formulaic films made-to-order by the budget-conscious team of James Nicholson and Samuel Z. Arkoff.

As stated, my early exposure to horror and science fiction films came to me courtesy of New York television stations including three network affiliates (Channel 2 WCBS, Channel 4 WNBC and Channel 7 WABC), all of which provided a wide selection of feature films during their network off-hours. But it was the independent station venues that appeared to go out of their way to contribute to the rising tides of monster-mania. The independents were Channel 5 (WNEW), Channel 9 (WOR), Channel 11 (WPIX) and Channel 13 (WNTA), but National Education Television usurped the latter. The programming in other major cities would vary, but the nature of the syndicated packaging should offer some recognizable continuity, regardless of location.

For example, in New York, the Screen Gems' *Shock* packages were aired on the ABC network affiliate while, in Philadelphia, they were aired on the city's CBS affiliate, but their duration—as a televised package of features—was fairly uniform from city-to-city and state-to-state, in spite of varied playing order. When *King Kong* debuted on New York television in 1955, it also premiered in different locations across the country at roughly the same time. Wherever one happened to live, the first screening of *King Kong* was looked upon as a major television event of 1955. Hence the syndicated release of other film packages on other television stations across the country corresponded, more or less, with the release year of the package. When Associated Artists Productions (one may remember its lower-cased acronym a.a.p.) jumped upon the *Shock* bandwagon, in October 1957, with its release of a direly misrepresented *Horror Feature* package (52 Monogram releases, only four being horror features, the rest low-budget mysteries whose titles simply *sounded* scary), it was brought to viewers courtesy of WPIX, where it remained for years to come.

Because of *Million Dollar Movie*, it was WOR-TV that provided the most intense exposure—18 screenings per week—of genre films, particularly those with giant monsters, either simian *or* reptile. In addition to RKO releases, however, WOR-TV would soon be laying claim to monster movies from a wide array of sources, even from studios abroad. By the early 1960s, *Million Dollar Movie* had become more studio-diversified, with such offerings as *The Crawling Eye, Attack of the Crab Monsters, Rodan, The House on Haunted Hill, Not of the Earth, The Brain from Planet Arous, The Giant Behemoth, The Beast From 20,000 Fathoms, Forbidden Planet, World Without End, Cosmic Monsters, War of the Satellites, Gorgo, Queen of Outer Space, Frankenstein 1970* and many others, all with the multiple-screening format that would be *Million Dollar Movie*'s claim to fame (although one viewing was, perhaps, more than enough for *Queen of Outer Space* or *Frankenstein 1970*). Significant to the purists among us, it should here be noted that *Million Dollar Movie* screenings were often edited to conform to a 90-minute format (only years later expanding to two hours). Most annoying was WOR's misguided decision to lop off the title and opening credits of *all* their screenings, often making further cuts within the first reel. This was why my first viewing of *King Kong* began with Carl Denham and company examining the map of Skull Island in the captain's quarters. I had no idea why Ann Darrow was aboard but, for a small kid seeking some monster action, the edited version quickly got down to business.

By 1960, Zacherley had made a move, as formerly stated, to WOR's *Zacherley at Large*. No longer was he screening Universal horror classics; instead the

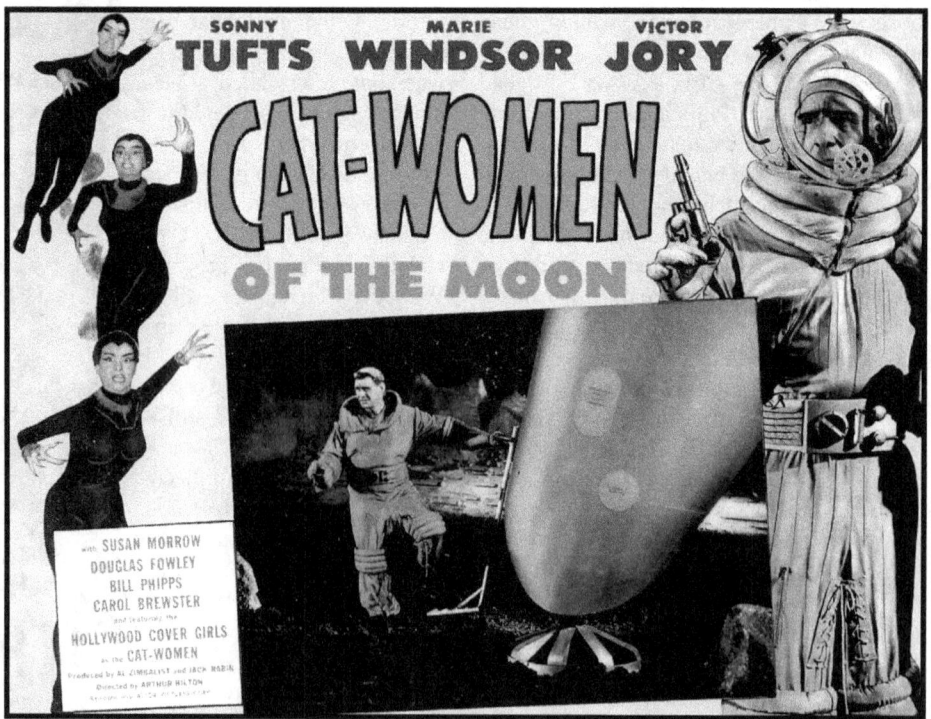

Horror genre fare such as *Cat-Women of the Moon* started to appear on WNEW's Channel 5 on Saturday mornings, where a limited number of films would be constantly rotated.

films being readied for Zach's signature lampooning were drab quickies like Wheeler and Woolsey's *Mummy's Boys* or the horror spoof *Zombies on Broadway*, along with truncated screenings of *Son of Kong* or *Mighty Joe Young*. On *Zacherley at Large* these films were, again, very heavily edited and occasionally not even shown to completion. No matter, since it was Zacherley who was always the main attraction. More serious WOR genre offerings would be found later on the short-lived, but more studio-diversified, Sunday night movie showcase, *Now Fear This* (where I caught Universal's *The Invisible Man*, Warner's *The Beast with Five Fingers* and Columbia's *The Face Behind the Mask*), and later still, Saturday night's *Supernatural Theater* which, along with the usual WOR staples, premiered more esoteric fare: *Carnival of Souls, Terror Is A Man, Macumba Love, The Manster, Black Orpheus* and *The Horror Chamber of Dr. Faustus*.

It was on WNEW's Channel 5 that I could tune to a varied but severely limited number of genre films—*Cat-Women of the Moon, Gog, Riders to the Stars, Lost Continent, Rocketship XM, Magnetic Monster, King Dinosaur, Project Moonbase, The Man from Planet X, Donovan's Brain, Cry of the Werewolf, Return of the Vampire, The Vampire's Ghost* and a few others I cannot recall. On Saturday mornings, this small batch would be rotated with great regularity over the course of several years (talk about static programming).

WPIX's Channel 11 was the bargain basement channel and appeared to be the landing site for all low-budget film packages. The Monogram and PRC films were right at home there. When Atlantic Television, in 1961, released a notoriously bad handful of *five* low-budget films—*Frankenstein's Daughter, Missile to the Moon, She Demons, Giant From the Unknown* and *Plan 9 from Outer* Space (marketed by their arithmetically challenged execs as a "Six-Pack" Special)—it was WPIX that welcomed them with open arms as part of their Saturday night programming. The next year, when Allied Artists Television released a package called "Science Fiction for the 60s," the heavily rotated "Six-Pack" found its brethren in such films as *Attack of the 50 Ft. Woman, The Indestructible Man, The Cyclops* and *The Daughter of Dr. Jekyll*, all of which were also added to the playlist of their Saturday night lineup, now being showcased under a new banner, *Chiller Theater*. The quality and/or quirkiness of the *Chiller Theater* offerings jumped at least a notch or two when United Artists Associations (UAA) released their 1963 package, "Science Fiction-Horror-Monster Features," comprised mostly of UA's Vogue, Gramercy or Bel-Air productions. We had read about—or seen photos from—some of these films in *Famous Monsters* and were eager to welcome the following to the program's roster: *The Black Sleep, It! The Terror From Beyond Space, Neanderthal Man, The Vampire, The Pharaoh's Curse, Voodoo Island, Four*

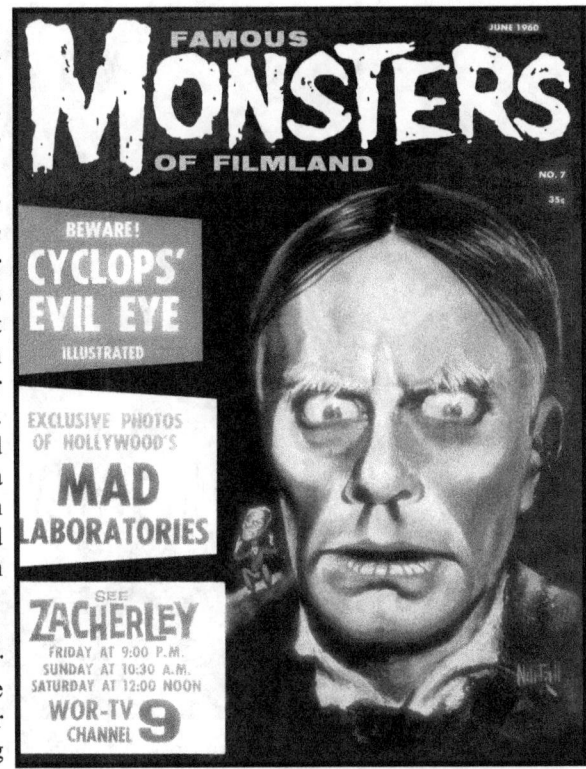

Zacherley, on the cover of *Famous Monsters* #7, had a great time laying waste to films that deserved his scorn, while playing the horror host on his live TV shows.

Skulls of Jonathan Drake and *Curse of the Faceless Man*. Shortly thereafter, in the late fall of '63, great news appeared: Zacherley, who had already moved to WPIX, hosting an awful package of *Hercules* cartoons, would soon become the official horror host of *Chiller Theater*, affording opportunities for the "Cool Ghoul" to be at his very best. Some old Warner Bros. classics (*Doctor X, The Walking Dead, Mystery of the Wax Museum*) were added to the rotation, intermixed with independent cheapies like *Killers From Space, The Hideous Sun Demon, The Monster From the Ocean Floor* and *The Monster From Piedras Blancas*. If only we had DVR back then, I'd have lasting proof of the hilarity that accompanied every *Chiller Theater* presentation hosted by Zacherley. It was glorious. And it was live. Zach had a great time laying waste to films that deserved his scorn: *Plan 9 From Outer Space, Attack of the 50 Ft. Woman, King of the Zombies, She Demons* and other mock-worthy features.

Although this most satisfying format lasted about a year, alas, as the story goes, the station and the sponsors were not happy with Zach's irascible on-air conduct, like when he told viewers to switch the channel to *Jackie Gleason's American Scene Magazine* (which occupied the same time-slot on CBS) because the movie to be shown was too awful to behold, or the numerous

Another one of the B films shown regularly on WNEW was *The Man from Planet X*.

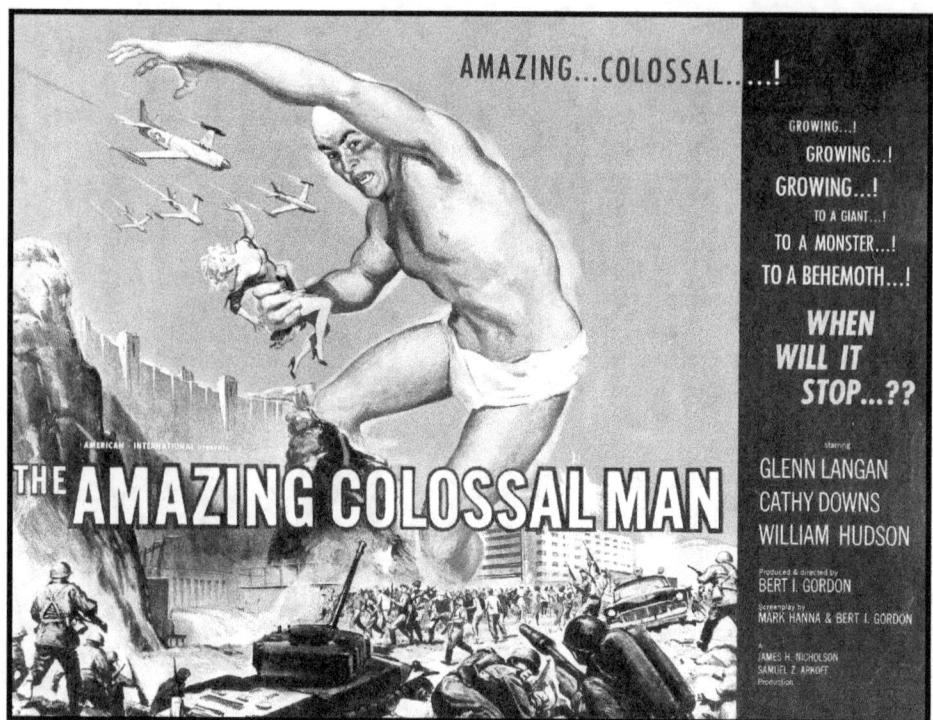

times he "set up" his commercial sponsors, unexpectedly transforming the forthcoming advertisements into targets of ridicule. It was so typical of Zach to announce, on his very last show—and in his devil-may-care fashion—the management had fired him ("They sent me the black spot!"), only to suddenly feign an on-air collapse, immediately followed by a commercial break.

WABC's Channel 7 had a late night movie spot called *Best of Broadway* that on Fridays tended to favor horror films. It was through this venue that I saw such classic fare as *The Hound of the Baskervilles* (Hammer's 1959 version), *Black Sunday, Terror in the Crypt, Burn, Witch, Burn* and *Curse of the Demon.* Of course it was WABC that had earlier started the ball rolling with their presentation of the *Shock* and *Son of Shock* packages. It thus came as no surprise, in the fall of 1963, that this particular network affiliate would soon begin airing Screen Entertainment's AIP package of 69 films, Monday-Friday, settling into a more accessible 5:00-6:30 p.m. slot rather than the late-night hours of the earlier *Shock* packages. This local ABC affiliate dubbed the event *The Big Show* and each day of the week, as initially planned, was reserved for one of the short list of genres inherent within the bulk of AIP's catalog. While I cannot recall the days of the week upon which such specified programming would fall, the general idea was that one day would be reserved for horror films, another day for Westerns, another day for war films, another for teen movies and another for science fiction. This routine would be dropped when the war films and/or Westerns failed to draw an adequate audience. For a while the station played around with other genre ideas as replacements for the failing time-slots, giving the green light to a series of late-1940s "hillbilly musicals" starring Judy Canova (yes, *The Big Show*'s actual classification of this new weekly "genre" was, in fact, "The Hillbillies"). I was genuinely puzzled by the choice of the Judy Canova films because, one, they were painful to watch and, two, they were not even AIP films but low-budget late-1940s programmers from Monogram, likely grouped together in the ill-advised hope of capturing the attention of the, admittedly, large number of city dwellers who were currently going *plumb loco* over rural sitcoms like *The Andy Griffith Show, The Beverly Hillbillies* and *Petticoat Junction.* Eventually, *The Big Show* would drop its obsessively compulsive weekly schedule and settle for whatever they thought would fly on any particular day. It amounted to heavy portions of the horror, science fiction and teenager films (however with AIP most likely *all three* would appear in one feature), with an occasional foray into the war or Western genres. Most importantly, the policy of choosing particular genres for particular weekdays went out the window (or, in the case of the Judy Canova pics, out the barn door).

When all was said and done, the AIP horror and science fiction films proved to be more than a little disappointing; the wonderful photographs as presented in *Famous Monsters* had given many of us high hopes. We also remembered some of those delectable television ads that had earlier promoted AIP films when they hit the theaters and drive-ins (the most frequent of these, I remember, being the ad for the double-bill of *Attack of the Puppet People* and *War of the Colossal Beast*). To further whet the appetites of monster fans, a series of bubblegum trading cards devoted exclusively to AIP films had been marketed months before; each black-and-white card consisted of three different "tall" rectangular images divided by perforations, like stamps, just waiting to be torn asunder by avid collectors like me (we just have to admire the well-oiled publicity machine that *was* AIP). By the time we saw the actual films, however, let's just say that we had to be more than a little forgiving.

The first to be presented, *The Amazing Colossal Man*, started off well enough with that memorable atomic bomb blast that destroyed the uniform and hair of the title character (taking no chances of being *less-*than-memorable, the sequence is repeated twice, via flashbacks, in the same film, as well as turning up again for its sequel). Unfortunately, by the time the tortured protagonist lived up to the promise of the title, the special effects became laughably inept, with matte-lines visible, resulting in a film that could have just as accurately been titled, *The Amazing Translucent Man.* The Las Vegas scenes were unwatchable to *this* 12-year-old, and the positioning of the giant's body as he fell off the Boulder Dam was probably the worst special effect I had ever seen (and I already had *The Attack of the 50 Ft. Woman* under my belt, as it were). Regardless of this initial experience, there *were* films within the package that I would remember fondly (though not always for reasons of quality and excellence): *Earth vs. The Spider, The Killer Shrews, The Screaming Skull, I Was A Teenage Werewolf/Frankenstein, Attack of the Giant Leeches, It Conquered the World, How to Make a Monster, The Beast with a Million Eyes, Day the World Ended, The Brain Eaters, The Giant Gila Monster, Beast from the Haunted Cave* and *War of the Colossal Beast* (which I liked much better than the original, no doubt because of the great make-up job and endangered school bus finale). I also got a really big kick out of the horror/comedies *Bucket of Blood* and *The Little Shop of Horrors,* along with the guilty pleasures of the rock 'n' roll flicks (*Rock All Night, Rock Around the World, Shake, Rattle and Rock, Daddy-O*) and, of course, the juvenile delinquent pics (*Motorcycle Gang,*

The Loew's Theatre chain sponsored a spook show float that paraded through New York City to promote the double feature of *Curse of the Demon* and *The Revenge of Frankenstein*.

Dragstrip Girl, High School Hellcats, Hot Rod Gang, Reform School Girl, Dragstrip Riot, others).

Although it never had its own monster-film showcase, my favorite movie channel was network affiliate WCBS; the station delivered the goods with the choicest films of *all genres*, including horror and, especially, science fiction. Like many CBS affiliates across the country, Channel 2 provided the best of all worlds whenever network programming was off the air. On weekdays viewers had *The Early Show,* which aired at the pre-news 90-minute dinner slot at 5:00 p.m. and withstood heavy movie competition (in the same time-slot) from three other channels (4, 7, & 9). But it was the late-night hours that turned the city's programming into a virtual movie-war and WCBS always came out on top. Other stations offered double-billed films, but Channel 2 gave its viewers all-night movie programming. Starting with *The Late Show* and continuing with other films, all of which were aired (unedited) as *The Late, Late Show,* WCBS would provide up to five different—and quite varied—selections until the early morning hours. Eventually, movie showcases from other channels would follow suit with extended programming. But I most fondly remember the Saturday night version of *The Late Show*, the edition that most often featured the blurb, "New York City Television Premiere." For such premieres, WCBS would run enticing full-page ads in *TV Guide.* Channel 2 would also present films from a variety of studios: Paramount, Warner Bros., MGM, Columbia, United Artists, 20th Century Fox, Allied Artists, and, yes, Universal-International—basically, every studio except RKO, whose vault remained with WOR-TV.

A small list of my most fondly remembered WCBS offerings (in no particular order): *Invasion of the Body Snatchers, Abbott and Costello Meet Frankenstein, Creature from the Black Lagoon, The Incredible Shrinking Man, The Creeping Unknown, The Beast from Hollow Mountain, The Abominable Snowman of the Himalayas, Revenge of Frankenstein* (my first color Hammer film), *It Came From Beneath the Sea, The Blob, House of Wax, Enemy From Space, The Haunted Strangler, Fiend Without a Face, The Black Scorpion, Corridors of Blood, The Maze, It Came From Outer Space, Them!, Face of Fire, First Man Into Space, The 4D Man, Twenty Million Miles to Earth, The Uninvited, Ghost Breakers, Revenge of the Creature, The Haunting, This Island Earth, Earth vs. the Flying Saucers* and many, many more.

If certain genre classics are conspicuous by their absence in the above list, chalk it up to prime-time network film programming, whose execs had first dibs on unsold films. It started in 1961 as NBC's *Saturday Night at the Movies,* followed the next year by ABC's *Sunday Night Movie* and shortly thereafter by CBS as well; within a short time, there would be a 9:00 p.m. network television premiere movie (be it on NBC, ABC or CBS) offered every night of the week. Obviously networks were seeing gold in those mountains of movie reels. *The Day the Earth Stood Still* was the first genre biggie to come our way in March 1962 on NBC. After that, I lose

Famous Monsters #21, now 100 pages in size, sported a Basil Gogos cover, heralding the first photo Filmbook on Bride of Frankenstein.

track of who screened what, but a partial list of genre films premiering on network movie programming is as follows: *Journey to the Center of the Earth, War of the Worlds, The Time Machine, Mysterious Island, The Seven Faces of Dr. Lao, The Power, The Pit and the Pendulum, The Lost World, Atlantis, the Lost Continent, Jason and the Argonauts* and eventually even a couple of severely edited Hammer films were aired (*Kiss of the Vampire* as *Kiss of Evil*, for instance) with entirely new shots and sequences filmed and inserted to lengthen the running time to fit the two-hour time-slot.

Television at large had also been invaded by monster-mania, with such weekly shows as *The Twilight Zone, Thriller, Way Out, One Step Beyond, Science Fiction Theatre, Outer Limits, The Addams Family, The Munsters, Lost in Space* and *Star Trek*, all of which aired during my formative years (assuming everyone remembers the Wonder Bread commercial). By early 1965, Zacherley would be appearing—in his full, ghoulish garb—on New Jersey's UHF's Channel 47, where he hosted *Disc-O-Teen*, Zach sometimes calling it "Transylvanian Bandstand" (check YouTube for a long clip featuring The Box Tops, with Zach interviewing singer and future cult rock icon, Alex Chilton). Note: By the late 1960s John Zacherle (sans costume, make-up and spooky patter) would become one of NYC's pioneer FM-radio progressive rock deejays, starting in 1968 on WNEW and continuing through the 1970s on WPLJ, at the time, the two most popular radio stations in the Greater New York Area.

Lest we forget, among the greatest boosters of monster-mania were, of course, the monster magazines. My cousin, Ronnie, had bestowed upon me his early issues of *Famous Monsters of Filmland* (I still have them) and I began to seek out the new issues on my own. The magazine continued to thrive and improve throughout the early 1960s. Famous author/fan Robert (*Psycho*) Bloch would grace many an issue with his erudite explorations about what made movies scary, including chilling moments within *and* without the genres cherished by readers. In the 18th issue (July '62) Forry Ackerman included an article called "Dante's Inferno," which gave capsule reviews of the 50 worst horror films ever made. Written by a teenaged future-monster-movie-director Joe Dante Jr., this article was something of an epiphany for future monster film critics, giving the kind of incentive that led to a glorious number of fanzines, including the one you are holding in your hands. Another *Famous Monster* benchmark was the 100-page February '63 issue, featuring the first of many Filmbooks (i.e., extensive analysis and production history of a major classic). Rather appropriately, it was with the 21st issue that *Famous Monsters* had finally come of age. The first monster classic to receive this Filmbook coverage was *Bride of Frankenstein*, and the colorized photo (rendered by artist Basil Gogos) that adorned the cover was very exciting to a readership that only knew the black and white version of said photo. The expanded length and Filmbook coverage continued in future issues; selected Filmbooks included *Dracula, Werewolf of London,* and, yes, *King Kong*, the last being quite a landmark of information for years to come, well before the numerous volumes of books on the subject became available to us. Forry was able to make his Filmbooks so successful because he had the tightest connections with the faces behind the films as well as the faces behind the make-up.

By 1963 some competition existed in the professional monster magazine field, although most were vastly inferior to *FM*. Many only lasted an issue or two and were often unavailable in my area. The worst of these were from Charlton Publications (in nearby Derby, Connecticut). Charlton also published the worst comic books, so it came as no surprise that their twin publications—*Horror Monsters* and *Mad Monsters*—would leave much to be desired. Particularly egregious were the newsprint paper stock and the terrible photo reproduction, coupled with uninspired writing (long-winded and dull film summaries) and funny photo captions. These Charlton magazines suffered from a dearth of personality and an absence of pride. It is rather surprising that both publications lingered on for 10 issues each over a span of four years (1961-1965), but at the time, such was the desperate nature of monster-mania. I'm not proud of it, but I still own my copies of *Mad Monsters* and *Horror Monsters*. Several notches better was *Fantastic Monsters of the Films*, which was, at least, created by genuine fans of monsterdom. The covers were excellent (seeming to favor Paul Blaisdell's monster creations) and the pages and writing were colorful, well produced and sincere. Seven issues appeared from 1962-1963 and I don't know what happened to my three issues; I wish I had them now.

Aside from *FM,* the monster film prozine that had the largest impact on my life was (you guessed it) *Castle of Frankenstein* which, from January 1962 to June 1975,

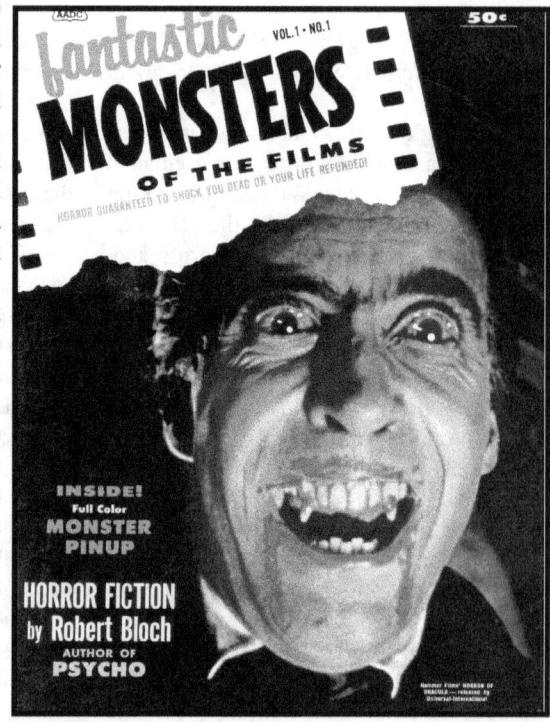

Fantastic Monsters of the Films #1, one of the best professional monster magazines, features a colorful photo of Christopher Lee from Horror of Dracula.

published 25 issues and a *Fearbook*. Editor Calvin T. Beck (aka Charles Foster Kane) actually started this labor-of-love with a 1959 one-shot called *The Journal of Frankenstein*. I'm a bit obsessive about *Castle of Frankenstein* so I'm not even going to get started on the subject. But I *will say* that although I owned most of the issues, it took me 14 years after it ceased publication to finally assemble a complete set. On the same victorious day that this was realized, (at Albany, New York's 1988 FantaCon), I met Gary Svehla for the first time. Gary was the editor of a wonderful fanzine, *Midnight Marquee*, which I had just discovered (and of which I immediately purchased back issues, including the very thick one celebrating the magazine's 25th anniversary which was being premiered at the Albany show with Gary, wife Susan and father Richard as special guests). Eventually, things fell into place. I went to a panel where the editor of *Midnight Marquee* was going to appear/participate and recognized Gary's uniquely spelled last name. It didn't take too much longer to make the connection. This was the very same Gary Svehla who, upon my request way back in 1970, mailed me issues of a very impressive fanzine called *Gore Creatures* (#'s 15, 16, 17, and 18, to be exact, as I have them in front of me). Needless to say, I caught word of the publication's existence from *FM*'s continual coverage of monster fanzines. Upon the opportunity of talking with Gary, I discovered that the two of us had a disproportionate number of things in common: we were both born in 1950, we were both proud veterans of monster-mania, we were both avid rock 'n' roll freaks who (unlike most of our peers) had never stopped listening to new music (in '88 we were mutual fans of vintage underground, punk and post-punk, including The Replacements and The Pixies), we were both high school English teachers for the *same* number of years and we were both loyal to the undying spirit of *Castle of Frankenstein*.

Gary and I were in agreement in so many things that this meeting-of-minds appeared nothing less than serendipitous. And serendipitous, it was. Around this time, I was teaching American Cinema at my high school and, with my newly purchased Apple 2e, I had been writing articles for my students on every film screened in class. Yes, I finally found my captive audience; students were responsible for reading and commenting upon the articles I had written. (In retrospect, I can now see that I was finally fulfilling the promise of those *Gothic* fanzine covers that the Magnajector and I

The Maze appears on the short list of fondly remembered films shown by WCBS.

had designed some 28 years before.) I told Gary that I would like to show him some of my work, thinking of the lengthy articles on *Frankenstein* and *Bride of Frankenstein* that I had written for my students. I did, and I was quite ecstatic when Gary gave me the green light to write an article for *Midnight Marquee*. This would be my first opportunity to actually be published. I proposed an article—on the Val Lewton films—that became so long it needed to be published in *four* separate issues. When the first installment came out in *Midmar* #40, I sent the magazine to McFarland Publishers with a chapter-by-chapter proposal for a book to be called *Fearing the Dark: The Val Lewton Legacy*. I waited a long time, was told that "no news was good news," and a little over a month later was given the green light and a McFarland contract to sign. It was McFarland's idea to change *Legacy* to *Career* and I was never comfortable with their insistence, but so be it. It seemed somehow appropriate given that Val Lewton had little power over the titles selected for his movies.

I'm just speaking for myself but, had it not been for Gary Svehla and *Gore Creatures/Midnight Marquee,* one less title would have appeared in the McFarland catalog. I realize Gary and his fanzine did not exist in the field alone, but a half-century of such devotion is a wondrous thing to behold.

Thank you, Gary, for your 50 years of service to our collective cause.

It All Started in 1963
Two Amazing Life-Long Journeys Through Monsterland

by Richard Klemensen

Indeed, it did start in 1963 for *Gore Creatures* and me. Was I a monster movie fan before that? Of course I was. I was born in 1947 in the little Iowa burg of Mason City, the original home of Meredith Willson and site of his *The Music Man*—the world premiere of the film occurred there during the North East Iowa Band Festival. Shirley Jones, Robert Preston and others rode in the parade. I can't remember for sure what first fantasy or horror film I may have seen—memories of the original *Invaders from Mars* on television remain. I do know the "Id" monster in *Forbidden Planet* petrified me, and seeing the black stocking creature from *Fire Maidens of Outer Space* gave me nightmares for weeks. After sitting through the double feature of *The Giant Gila Monster* and *The Killer Shrews* three times, I saw killer shrews in the bushes everywhere as I walked home in the dark. Knowing my mom and dad were going to kill me, I left early that Saturday morning and it was now nearing 10 p.m. at night when I returned. I lived ... but *just* barely. My parents did understand the need for this goofy son of theirs to see these films more than once—such as sitting through a double feature of some Sophia Loren soaper to see Toho's *Battle in Outer Space* three times. What a fool I was—now I would be more inclined to stare at Sophia's cleavage!

But by April 1963, I have memories of viewing with great youthful pleasure *Gorgo, The Brides of Dracula, Phantom of the Opera* (the Hammer version), *Night Creatures, Curse of the Werewolf, Black Sunday* (boy, did that wreck me for weeks—the mask of spikes—yikes) and all the Disney animation features—and falling in love with Janet Munro. Discovering girls was a revelation—watching Annette Funicello's sweatshirt expanding week after week on *The Mickey Mouse Club* (rest in peace dear Annette. You ushered in puberty in a nice way for a lot of baby boomer boys). But why do I remember April 1963 so vividly? My father had gotten notice the dairy he worked for was shutting down and he had the choice of transferring to Los Angeles—the Watts area (just before the riots, so you can imagine we were glad he didn't make that choice)—or a short ways south of Mason City—Waterloo, Iowa. And Waterloo is where we ended up. I had two months of 9th grade to finish, then a summer in a new town where I didn't know anyone. That summer I shot baskets by myself at the local basketball court, listened to music on the radio and read, read, read. And hoped some sort of cool monster flicks might show up on television. They seldom did. That same summer, 13-year-old Gary Svehla was putting together his first issue of *Gore Creatures*. I know changing the title to *Midnight Marquee* was a good business move, but I still miss that old-school name.

I had my own publishing history, but not about films. I envisioned myself as some sort of comedy writer—some sort is

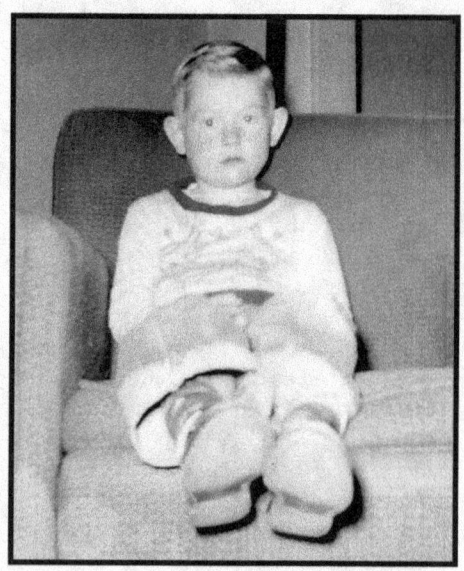

The young Dickie Klemensen

Little Shoppe of Horrors #2, focusing on Amicus Productions, was printed by Associated Services, a small offset printing company in Iowa run by two invalid brothers.

right. I wasn't very good, or very funny. I published, I think, five or six issues of *Fleabit* with a couple of Mason City pals—Don Silby and Jim Whetzel—then two issues in Waterloo, with Allen Brumbaugh. This gave me a chance to present my cartoons. I think I could have been a pretty good cartoonist, by the way. But 50 years later that particular train has really passed me by. After those issues, the thought of publishing any kind of magazine, let alone one about monsters and horror movies, was far from my mind. All I thought about was girls and getting a driver's license so I could get my first car (a 1947 Plymouth) so I could get girls. Puberty *does* sort of focus a boy's mind with a testosterone-driven force.

During high school at East Waterloo I made a number of really fast friends, some of whom I'm still close to this very day. I fantasized that Alice Flehner or Kathy Griffith would be my girlfriend. (In a case of "geez, I wish I'd known," the luscious Alice F. approached me at a recent high school class reunion and asked me why I hadn't asked her to the senior prom. I looked at her and said, "Man, you were so much out of my league." Ahh, what could have been.) I fantasized about being a better basketball player than I was. I could shoot but just could not jump. Nature and my family doomed me to never getting any taller than 5'9"—an inch of that I've now lost. Oh, did I mention girls?

Off to college in Cedar Falls, Iowa in 1966—the school then was called State College of Iowa. A year later it became The University of Northern Iowa. I expanded my horizons and met some cute girls from upper Iowa such as Laurie Swenson. I used to make out with Margot Herman while drinking the frozen daiquiris she would prepare for us at her parents' home (while they were gone, which was often, bless 'em). I did *terrible* in college grade-wise—under 2.0 at the end of four years. I was on probation every year, but I lived for basketball and girls—do you see a monotonous line there?

In September 1969, I was 21 years old. I had one more year of college ahead of me before my four-year deferment ran out and I knew I'd get drafted into the Army during the Vietnam era. I had mono that summer. Towards the end of August I went out drinking with my pal Ralph "Butch" Clements and got so sick I vomited on the wall beside my bed, while still asleep (as my mother, who had to clean it up, pointed out to me). I went to the drive-in, mid-week, to see a triple feature of *The Valley of Gwangi, Godzilla vs. The Thing* and Hammer's 1968 *Dracula Has Risen from The Grave*. As I caught my breath with a "wow, what an ending" as Dracula squirmed on the cross, I then rushed home and in the early morning (with work just a few hours off) I dug out the issues of *Famous Monsters of Filmland* and *Castle of Frankenstein* that my mother had carted along with us from Mason City, but now I devoured them in a new light. Discovering there were magazines named *Gore Creatures, Photon* and *Horrors of The Screen*, I sent off for all of them, back issues of *FM* and *CoF* (which never arrived until over a year later when I was in Army

Little Shoppe of Horrors #10/#11, 172 pages of offset printing wonder, featuring the first of five covers by Steve Karchin.

Little Shoppe #5 became *The Hammer Journal*, intending to publish a Hammer newsletter four times a year. The new Hammer owners were not too happy about this, so the magazine returned to its old ways.

boot camp at Ft. Leonard Wood, MO). For the rest of 1969 and up to May 1970, it was like a whole new world opened up for me. My younger brother Terry and I went to the drive-in all the time (no girls around to interfere with watching the films, just lots of junk drive-in food … the best!). I bought books; I bought more magazines; I sent off a little ad in an issue of *Gore Creatures* asking for info on other fanzines, as I wanted to do a magazine where I would rate the various fanzines. The Draft Board, sadly, called my name May 1970 and off I went to boot camp and AIT (Advanced Individual Training). I became a clerk/typist—aka "Remington Ranger." Hey, I could type 50 words a minute on a manual typewriter and this skill saved my white Iowa ass from combat in Southeast Asia.

I spent October 1970 to January 1972 in Richmond, VA as the induction clerk for the State of Virginia, at the AFEES station (Armed Forces Entrance and Examining Station). If anyone got drafted in Virginia during that time, he would see me before going off to boot camp (or I would have to witness those refusing to take the step forward, then send them home, letting the powers that be take care of them later). I attended every drive-in theater in the area. Being sort of in the South, I caught up on films that would have never made it to Iowa—Herschell Gordon Lewis, etc. I continued to order and read horror movie fanzines and prozines. During the end of my time in Missouri, I got the first issue of *Cinefantastique* and the vampire-themed

50th Anniversary Issue [1963-2013] 31

The Brides of Klemensen: (top to bottom): first wife Karla; second wife Espie; third wife (and the love of his life) Nancy

issue of *Photon*, forwarded to me by my mother. What revelations they were. What crystallized in my mind was the burning idea that when I was discharged, I wanted to do one of those, I wanted to be a horror 'zine publisher/editor.

Driving home from Richmond in January 1972, through horrible snowstorms across Ohio, I saw my GTO slide from lane to lane, in the wind, without me even touching the steering wheel. Time to find a place to stay and watch some TV in warmth while everyone else was hitting the ditches. I was back in college within a week of my discharge, with plans afoot for the first issue of *Little Shoppe of Horrors*. To this day, I'm not exactly sure why I chose that title. I'm sure it related to the Roger Corman comedy/horror of the same name, but I just thought it sounded neat. I've never regretted the choice. I like to think that, in a small way, my *LSoH* is as well known as Corman's cult classic. By that time Gary Svehla was in college, or rather nearing the end of his college days. My first issue would appear in June 1972. Gary's 21st issue came that July, along with his B.A. in English. Gary was by then down to one issue a year, something I could only envy later on when I was lucky I could manage one issue every three or four years. But at this point, I had such high hopes for *LSoH*.

That first issue of my mag pulled in early friendships for contributions. I had gotten to know former Hammer films make-up man Roy Ashton, and he gave us a short interview. The "infamous-to-be" Gary Levinson wrote about American-International, while my longest-time pal, England's "el bummo" Gary Parfitt, told of his visit to Bray Studios during the making of Hammer's 1965 *Plague of the Zombies*. Famous fan names of the period contributed, such as Alan Dodd (now no longer with us) and Chris Fellner, one of the original writers for the Gloria Lillibridge-sponsored *Christopher Lee Fan Club Bulletin*. This was one of the best fan clubs ever. My first ever-published article was on Hammer in one of the bulletins. It was also with *LSoH* #1 that I established a minor friendship with Milton Subotsky, co-owner of Amicus Films.

That first issue did well enough to get plans in motion for a #2. I was still in school while working at ESCO Auto Supply, in Waterloo, to finance the cost. During that period, I helped out a friend named Rudy Petra, who also worked at ESCO. On the side, he had started up a booking agency for Go-Go Dancers and strippers. I would ferry them to this town and that, sometimes go out bowling or whatever with the strippers between gigs. I've never been around so many women willing to take off their clothes, and it was a bit of hetero heaven. Except almost without an exception, the Go-Go dancers were immature and often not too bright, and they often lost whatever money they were paid (I was making $120 a week and they could make up to $400-$600 a week). Time and again I would have to drive to pick them up at some little burg or get them out of jail. The strippers, on the other hand, were often college students and sharp as tacks. They had nothing to do with the customers of the bars after hours. I enjoyed their company (knowing the odds of getting between their legs was about nil) because just being seen in the company of such drop-dead gorgeous women was a plus for my ego. Gary Svehla hit us with *Gore Creatures* #22 in August 1973. My #2 was March 1972, 8 months since the last issue. It would be *many* years before I published that regularly again. Two invalid brothers in Janesville, Iowa, who had a little offset press business called Associated Services, printed those early issues (1 through 3). They lived with their mother and were fascinated by the materials I'd bring to them (it was a shock a few years later, when I wanted to reprint those first three issues, to call their mother and find that both of them had died before they were 30 years old). An actual offset house in Waterloo (Curt Craft) would do the pages with photos on them. Then my mother and I would spread the pages around my bedroom and, one by one, we'd sort them out and I would use an industrial stapler to put them together. My mother made me a movie fan, got me into reading and would help me in any way she could. My father was the same sort of person. The kind of parents a kid could only dream of having. What a privilege that I had two parents supporting my obsessions. *LSoH* #2 had our first real in-depth feature, where I interviewed Amicus' Milton Subotsky, director Freddie Francis and screenwriter Robert Bloch about Amicus. Who knew that such celebrity interviews would become the meat and potatoes for *LSoH*. More names from fandom history joined the magazine— Jean-Claude Michel, Stephen Pickard, Hector Pessina, Saki Hijiri, Gary D. Dorst (my dearest friend, who died earlier this year) and Alain Schlockoff.

1974—what a year. I got my B.A. degree in Art and Education. I went to work full time for ESCO Auto Supply/Central States Distributors Warehouse. My second convention (the first was in 1973, the World Science Fiction Convention in Toronto,

In 1984, at Elstree Studios, Klem met with the current head of Hammer, Roy Skeggs, during the shooting of *The Hammer House of Mystery and Suspense*.

The Klem meets Melissa Stribling—Dracula's victim in *Horror of Dracula*—at the Horror Elite Convention, London, 1977.

Posing at the Horror Elite Convention from 1977: Morag Fisher, the Klem and Hammer's ace director, Terence Fisher.

Canada) was the Crystal City, VA World Science Fiction Convention. I started going with and living with the woman who would become my first wife, Karla Minard Burt. AND *LSoH* #3 finally showed just what the magazine could, and would, become (Gary Svehla missed an issue of *GC* in 1974). Contents included the first major English language interview with Hammer's star director, Terence Fisher, by Gary R. Parfitt; the Films of Eiji Tsuburaya by Saki Hijiri; Andre Morell: Actor, an interview by Professor David Soren (we combined his magazine *Fantastic Worlds* with *LSoH* for this one issue); Gary Dorst's tribute to Lon Chaney, Jr. with the transcript of his *Tonight Show* interview with Johnny Carson; etc. More famous fandom names came to us— Sam Irvin, Jr., Chris Knight, Dave Ludwig, Hajime Ishida.

It was a great issue, but one I thought would be the end of *LSoH*. I was now totally caught up in my real life world, with Karla and our sons, Tom and Pat. Work and family ruled supreme. I still was seeing every movie that came to town and continued playing basketball. A stern talking to by Mark Frank of *Photon* and Frederick S. Clarke of *Cinefantastique* made me decide I *did* need to continue. But publishing once a year was now darn impossible. And what exactly did I want *LSoH* to be? Did I want to continue as a general interest horror zine (last issue had Japanese Giants, Universal horror and Vincent Price, as well as extensive British coverage)? No, my real love was British horror—especially that of Hammer films. So although I had some other minor features and a David Prowse (bathing in his *Star Wars* fame) interview, 1978's #4 was totally devoted to the history of Hammer. It was the first issue where two of my dearest friends from England, Susan and Colin Cowie, joined to help us in a million different ways, with some truly exclusive interviews (producer Anthony Nelson Keys, special effects man Les Bowie and many more). When #4 came out in 1978, it was acclaimed everywhere. Hammer's former head producer, Anthony Hinds, called it "bloody brilliant." It was professionally printed, typeset and featured a color-cover. At that point the magazine's template became pretty well set and I adhered to that format from then on.

While I was spending those four years putting *LSoH* #4 together, Gary Svehla would pump out a yearly *Gore Creatures*. Or would for a while, because in September 1977 that old warhorse title went by the wayside. Trying to find a name that didn't sound so "gory" for want of a better term (a more mature title to replace an immature one?), jotting down titles on a filing folder while showing a film to one of his high school film classes, he came up with the title *Midnight Marquee*. And the rest is that history you've all been hearing about. It was the heyday of highlighting original art covers every issue— Bill Nelson, M. Squidd (Dave Ludwig), etc. *GC/MM* was the finest fanzine being produced at the time—that is, having a real fannish feel as well as featuring great articles and boosting a nice physical look.

The years started to move along. *LSoH* #5 actually was re-named *The Hammer Film Productions Journal* in August 1980. I thought I could publish a fanzine newsletter devoted to Hammer four times a year, 28 pages, simply done. But at that time, Michael Carreras had lost Hammer, and the new owners, Roy Skeggs and Brian Lawrence (actually they were just leasing the name. It was later that they would actually buy the Hammer name from the debt holder), weren't too keen on the idea of my doing a quarterly Hammer journal. So we returned to the *LSoH* drawing board. Surprisingly, later, in 1994, Brian Lawrence would call me part of the Hammer family. Lawrence had been Hammer's long-time business manager.

It was at this time that my sister Kris Mraz really became part of the *LSoH* family. She worked for a small company in Clarion, Iowa called Allen Printing. Starting with *The Hammer Journal*, Allen would print the magazine for over a quarter of a century. The return of the real *LSoH* #6 occurred in July 1981 and featured our tribute to Terence Fisher, who had just passed away. I was coming in contact with more and more of the old time Hammer staff, such as Jack Asher, and with most of them no longer with us, I'm very glad we pursued their stories and memories.

With *LSoH* #7 in December 1982, I was struggling to get on a once a year basis again. I changed jobs and was now Parts Manager for the Chesley Company, a Freightliner truck dealership, in Waterloo.

A dapper Mr. Klemensen meets with the head of Hammer, Michael Carreras, in 1977, at Hammer House, Pinewood Studios, England.

Long days and nights and most weekends were occupied by work. Waterloo was in an economic mess and I had to take care of my family—so I did what I had to do. My father-in-law, the late great Big Bill Minard, built me an office in the second home Karla and I occupied. It was amazing and my boys used to just come down and stare at the posters on the wall. With #7, the main theme was Quatermass. It was our first feature by Bruce G. Hallenbeck, who would become the backbone of the *LSoH* authors. Hallenbeck also interviewed director Val Guest and writer Nigel Kneale, as well as actress Barbara Shelley, music composer Harry Robinson and *Dracula A.D. 1972* producer Josephine Douglas. *Midnight Marquee* was up to Issue #31. And Gary's days as a *single* magazine tycoon were nearly ended, as Sue Miller entered his life.

My own *LSoH* #8 came along a year and a half later in 1984 and once again demonstrated the evolution of *LSoH*. I never had a concrete idea of what I was doing or where I was going. At that point, I was always amazed if I got another issue out. Our first Karnstein issue represented both the best and worst. The best—we featured dozens of rare (for the times) interviews. The worst—the reproduction in the issue was terrible. The quality of the materials overcame the lousy physical look, but just barely. This was the first time I really griped to a printer and they even reprinted more issues, free, when the first print run ran out.

1986 was a cataclysmic year for me and the magazine. That year I was fired from my job at Chesley and went through two other jobs before moving to Des Moines, Iowa in December 1987. *LSoH* #9 in March that year was one of our greatest issues, before or since (and it would be four years before another *LSoH* would appear. I thought at this time the magazine was finished). The inside story of the last days of *Famous Monsters of Filmland* by its final editor, Randy Palmer, appeared. We also published the story of Hammer's Bray Studios, our first feature on *Vampire Circus* and dozens of rare interviews. However, in December 1987, just as I had made my move south, hoping to bring Karla and the boys to our new place the next summer, she sprung: "I'm unhappy and I've been unhappy for a long time" on me. The long and short of it, she left us and moved to Kansas City. Tommy was struggling with a failed marriage. Patrick was just trying to finish his last few months of high school. I was losing our last Waterloo home to foreclosure, and I didn't have two nickels to rub together. *LSoH* was a long, long ways from my mind. Back in Baltimore-land, Gary and Sue, now married for two years, were going great guns on *MidMid* as plans for the legendary FANEX conventions starting to form in their imaginations.

The period from the end of my marriage in January 1988 until marrying Esperanza Santos Mallari was as unusual as any in my life. I had never been really heavy during that period (my knees still allowed for sports and jogging), but after the divorce I really hit the workouts hard. I even got tanned. My hair was blonde on the way to turning white (bless men's hair dye). While I'd never been either popular or unpopular with the ladies, this period was ridiculous. Women at the Laundromats, with their gaggle of ankle-biters, would approach me while I was doing my own load of clothes ("Hey ladies, he's straight and has a job. He's for me!"); at 7Flags, where I worked out, I'd spend a number of evenings when finished exercising chatting with one lovely lady or another in the juice bar. For a period, I was dating three women at the same time—Mary, Jane and Edie. Mary even wanted to take me to her little Iowa town where she was from to introduce me to her friends. I hated playing the game and, one by one, we broke up; I felt a sense of relief. One lovely lady and I had what I would call a very "vigorous" physical relationship. Then one night she pulled out a scrapbook that showed she had had major back surgery a while back, the surgeon bracing her spine between metal plates. She spent almost a year in bed while it healed. She called it a miracle. And I could just envision the headlines—"Des Moines Man Cripples Miracle Woman!" I hooked up with a drop dead cute Filipina, Espie. We married and honeymooned in Hong Kong; were together for three years; had the marriage annulled. And that's all that needs to be said. Except during the last year or so I put together, with my sister, what would prove the ultimate edition of *LSoH* at that time, our double issue #10/#11, in July 1990. Steve Karchin provided our color cover painting (one of five he would do for us, with his upcoming *Demons of the Mind* planned for *LSoH* #31). Professionally typeset, the issue was the kind of presentation we would only have imagined back in the 1970s. Our feature article/interviews covered Hammer's 1962 *Kiss of the Vampire*. The issue contained 172 pages. Woof!

The 1990s are kind of a blur for me. My knees started to go, and I had the left knee scoped twice during the decade (leading up

Bray Days, 1999. Klem, in the middle, poses with The Brides of Dracula—Andree Melly (left) and Yvonne Monlaur (right).

to the left knee replacement in December 2012). My retina in my left eye detached in 1998, almost leaving me blind except for the surgical wizardry of Dr. Scott Heilskoff. I suffered the effects of a hernia ... man I was falling apart fast. *LSoH* #12 came out *four* years later in 1994. Another brilliant Steve Karchin cover from Hammer's *The Devil Rides Out* appeared, as we explored the three films Hammer would make from Dennis Wheatley's novels. Our first Christopher Lee interview, courtesy of his friend (and our late, dear pal Bill Kelley), appeared. The issue filled 132 pages. And a lot of topless British actress shots were on display in "Horrors of the Black Nylon Museum" by Jimmy Zero. Interviews with Raquel Welch, Valerie Leon, Stephanie Beacham and a career article on Yutte Stensgaard brightened the issue. That April I visited England and attended the final supper for the late Hammer headman, Michael Carreras. All the Hammer big shots were there and it was quite amazing to be included with Anthony Hinds, Jimmy Sangster and Kenneth Hyman, etc. I also spent a lot of time with former Hammer actress, Suzan Farmer. After a rough start we had become very close friends and remain so to this day, although after I married Nancy, we aren't quite as "close" as we used to be.

Only two years passed and our massive Hammer Dracula issue #13 featured the most comprehensive interview by Christopher Lee about all his Dracula performances. We investigated the making of *Dracula Has Risen from the Grave, Taste the Blood of Dracula* and *Scars of Dracula*, the last Gothic gasp for Dracula before the

The FANEX gang after hours: Gary J. Svehla, is in the middle, surrounded by (left to right) Bryan Senn, Klem, Mark Miller, Harvey Clarke and Paul Jensen

modern Hammer films hit. Even a color centerfold section appeared, courtesy of Ted Newsom. For me, during this period, other than my time with Suzie Farmer, I met, dated and broke off with a string of very nice ladies. I felt I wasn't good at the marriage thing, and when they get to a certain age, most women want more than just dating and a good time. I look back now and saw myself becoming quite happy with the single geezer lifestyle. Gary Dorst and I went to England in 1999 for the second Bray Days Hammer celebration, spent time with Sue and Colin Cowie, then journeyed to Paris with our friend Alain Schlockoff. With Gary's unexpected death this year, it makes those two weeks even more precious.

LSoH #14 in 1999 marked more changes and improvements in the look of *Little Shoppe of Horrors*. The photos were now being scanned digitally rather than resorting to the old cutting, pasting and gluing of PMTs that gave less than perfect reproduction. We dropped the page count to 100, as Allen Printing complained it was becoming too difficult to bind 132 pages. The new issue also ushered in Jeff Preston as another of our premier cover artists. Nothing before or since has come close to what we achieved in our coverage of *The Brides of Dracula*. It still remains my favorite Hammer film. By this time, too, I had attended, with Gary Dorst and my other friends, most of Gary and Sue's FANEX conventions, as well as the massive *Famous Monsters* World Convention sponsored by Ray Ferry and the new *FM* crew in Crystal City, VA.

2001—what a monumental year. Everything that was good in my life came together. Nancy Emdia entered it! For most of 2000 I had been dating a very cute girl I had known for years, Nikki Halverson. But as she had two small boys, at my age I wasn't up to raising younger kids, so we broke up at Christmas that year. Around the same time Nancy broke up with her boyfriend, Bob. We had mutual friends, Mike and Winnie Rye (who now only live two houses away from us), who were just waiting for both of us to become available. They had never hooked me up with a woman before—well, I was always with one or another lady anyway. But they said, "Boy, do we have a girl for you." It was supposed to start with a dinner at Mike and Winnie's, but Winnie became very ill. Finally, after a number of weeks had passed, I called and asked if I could contact this lady myself. I did and we went to see *Enemy At The Gate,* with Mike Rye making sure we didn't hold hands or anything. That was March 2001.

More of the FANEX gang: Steve Vertlieb, Gary D. Dorst, Richard J. Svehla (Gary's father) and the Klem

50th Anniversary Issue [1963-2013]

Ingrit Pitt posing with Klem's wife Nancy at Monster-Mania. Nancy is the main reason why two issues of *Little Shoppe* are released every year.

By the second date, I had fallen head over heels in love with her. After the horrors of 9/11 we decided life was too short and got married in October that same year. Twelve-plus years later, the greatest 12-plus years of my life, Nancy remains a total delight and the true love of my life.

The first issue we did as man and wife was *LSoH* #15, and Nancy has been hands-on totally involved with the magazine from day one, reading, proofing, helping me chose photos and doing the boring work from which she never shirks. Another knockout Jeff Preston cover illustrated *The Curse of the Werewolf*. What other mag has a Veronica Carlson painting as their *back* cover? Our interview/article on Oliver Reed was enough to send chills down one's spine. Better it was handled by Denis Meikle rather than me (Denis Meikle came to me for help with his Hammer book around the time of *LSoH* #12. Since then, he is another backbone of *LSoH*—writing a few articles, doing interviews, designing our headers and selling hundreds of copies of each issue through his Hemlock Books).

It would be 2004 when *LSoH* #16 appeared, but once again the format changed. Slick (glossy) enamel paper appeared and the brilliant comic artist Bruce Timm designed his first of many covers for *LSoH*. We decided that since our previous Karnstein issue had been such a poor job of presentation, we'd re-do it with better layout, photo reproduction, more interviews and better articles. Discovering Kirsten Lindholm (Betts), who appeared in all three of the films, she told her story, as did the potential successor to Christopher Lee, Mike Raven. This issue really took off and placed *LSoH* back on the fandom map once again.

During that period of 2003, we bought our current home, only to prove that two collectors should never marry. Even with four floors and over 2,500 square feet of space, we've managed to pack it to the ceilings with books, posters and movies—and Winnie the cat. I also think we had it in our minds that we could do one issue of *LSoH* a year now. The digital age allowed us to make quick contacts where previously much time had been wasted using snail mail. We could locate people much faster overseas where before we wouldn't have had a clue where to start looking. #17 in 2005 combined our interviews with producer John Temple-Smith, director Peter Graham Scott (done at Bray Days, with an additional Patrick Allen interview by Sue and Colin Cowie and Tom Johnson, a friend that I inflicted upon them). Once more we were focusing on one specific film or series of films per issue, but

At James Bernard's London home in 1999, left to right, are James Bernard, Klemensen and writer Gary Smith.

we also tried to publish features outside that sphere for those who might not be enamored with *Captain Clegg/Night Creatures*.

Shortly after Nancy and I married, I lost my job with Power Brake/Transcom (with whom I'd been employed for 14 years) when they went bankrupt. Expecting a few weeks of down time, I went for a last breakfast with my old co-workers. When I got home, Nancy gave me a list of people who had called who wanted to offer me jobs. Short story—I was back to work with a fabulous company called Midwest Wheel a week later. Heading toward my 12th year with them, I will continue to be with them until I turn 69 and our house is paid off. Worse ways to spend a day; these are nice people I work with. *LSoH* #18 came out in 2006—a year of pain for Nancy and me. We both lost our fathers during the Christmas season. But we did celebrate the 60th wedding anniversary of my mom and dad shortly before his passing, with everyone together posing in a huge family portrait. It was hard to believe that my dad would be dead three months later. #18 featured Brian Clemens at Hammer with *Dr. Jekyll and Sister Hyde* and *Captain Kronos—Vampire Hunter*. This issue offered a chance for cool interviews and hot photos of Martine Beswicke and Caroline Munro. Again, the issue did well and Bruce Timm knocked it out of the park with his color cover (William Hobbs, who played the head vampire in *Kronos*, said when his family saw his image on the cover, they made fun of him all day).

Best buds for over 40 years—Klem stands arm-in-arm with the late Gary Dorst, the consummate fan.

Director Terence Fisher was the only film celebrity I ever really wanted to meet. I had that privilege in 1977 at the Horror Elite Convention in London at the Kenilworth Hotel. I sat in the bar and drank with him, watched *The Curse of the Werewolf* with him, and walked out on the screening of Jesus/Jess Franco's *El Conde Dracula* after one too many zoom shots. So doing a full issue devoted to Fisher was always a dream of mine. I thought by now the Alan Frank biography of Fisher would have appeared, but such was not the case. So this was the chance for Nancy and me to became friends with Fisher's daughter, Micky Harding. Neil Barrow's Rondo-award winning bio of Fisher became the lead article of the issue, with wonderful interviews with Fisher by Jan Van Genechten, Tony Dalton and Paul Jensen augmenting the feature article. The issue contained 100 pages, all Terence Fisher, all the time. And besides Steve Karchin's wonderfully hand-created collage cover, it was our first issue to feature the magnificent artwork and paintings of Mark Maddox, now our close friend and another backbone of the issue. Micky Harding loved Bruce Timm's back cover tribute to Terry.

2008 offered what no one (least of all, me) would have imagined happening. Two issues published in one year, and as we are currently in 2013, this is our 6th successive year meeting that goal. Philip Nutman became the featured writer for *LSoH* #20. Nutman had written an unpublished book on Amicus back in the 1980s, working with producer Milton Subotsky. But fear

The Rondo Awards come to FANEX—(left to right) Neil Vokes (holding an extra Rondo for Robert Tinnell), Richard Klemensen and Gary J. Svehla receive their Rondo Awards.

of a lawsuit from the other partner, Max Rosenberg, had put the manuscript into a bottom drawer. We convinced Phil to pull it out, dust it off and provided him more research to go along with what he had collected in over 20 years. One hundred pages on Amicus, with Nutman and my sister/designer Kris working on this together. I was an interested bystander. I did arrange the two magnificent Mark Maddox covers, along with art from Tim Hammell and the talented Bruce Timm and his EC homage on the back. Again, this was one of our most popular issues. As soon as we finished that, off we went on Hammer's 1956 *The Curse of Frankenstein*, the movie that started the Gothic revival. It becomes more difficult to do something new on the older Hammer horrors because so many of the people involved are dead. I had a head start on this issue because Fred Clarke of *Cinefantastique* had been after me to do a feature on *The Curse of Frankenstein* for his magazine. It didn't come off then, but I had interviewed Jack Asher, Phil Leakey, Anthony Hinds, among others. Also our second major feature coverage on *Night/Night of the Demon* appeared, written by Denis Meikle (the first coverage appeared in issue #18 by Elstree film historian, Paul Welsh).

In the area of "you can't keep a good monster magazine down," we figured if we could do two issues in 2008, why not two in 2009. Issue #22 appeared with coverage of "Dracula Today! Hammer's Vampire in 1970s London." I can't say the two modern-day Dracula films are everyone's favorites, but they are colorful, lots of fun and populated with eye-catching gorgeous ladies. Again, we were able to latch onto interviews I didn't think were possible (thanks to Jonathan Sothcott and Mark Redfield. Hey, we even talked to Stoneground!). Mark Maddox, Frank Dietz, Norm Bryn and Bruce Timm produced real eye-catchers of covers. Halloween that same year saw the release of #23, one of my all-time favorite issues featuring coverage

Monster Bash 2011—(left to right) Dave Davey (*Undying Monsters*); Dick Klemensen; Dennis Druktenis (*Scary Monsters*) and Jim Clatterbaugh (*Monsters from the Vault*)

Klemensen and Svehla catch up at FANEX. *Little Shoppe of Horrors* and *Gore Creatures/Midnight Marquee*, the two longest-published magazines in the horror film genre, with a combined 91 years between them. Long may they reign!

of *Plague of the Zombies* and *The Reptile*; Michael Carreras remembers *10 Seconds to Hell*; David Del Valle wrote on Michael Gough. The ultimate career interview with director John Gilling appeared courtesy of Gilbert Verschooten. Bruce Timm, Adrian Salmon, Neil Vokes and Mark Maddox delivered the four covers.

We were on a roll—2010 saw #24 and coverage of the four Hammer Mummy films (and Peter Cushing's diary of his time in Hollywood); #25 became one of our most popular recent issues because of the coverage of the making of *Blood on Satan's Claw* (in no small way because of the nude Linda Hayden shots featured throughout).

Our 2011 output saw the end of the long-time arrangement with Allen Printing. The owner died at age 100 and his daughter-in-law tried to run the company, but she ended up selling out to another local company. The new regime let go their best employees (including my sister) and the final two issues done there had awful printing quality. Issue #26 was an example of exceptional material including the making of *Hands of the Ripper* (covers by Mark Maddox, Jim Salvati and Bruce Timm) and a rare interview with the late Angharad Rees, plus the first of our Hammer character actor interviews by David Williams (interviewing Alan Wheatley), but poor printing diminished the issue's overall effect. Constantine Nasr, a young friend from the past, joined us with this issue and now has become another of those backbones I've been discussing. The list of interviews and articles he has done for us since is astounding! Constantine was friendly with the actor/son of Freddie Jones (Toby Jones) and we got an amazing in-depth interview with this terrific performer (I saw him last night in an older episode of *Midsomer Murders*). So issue #27 necessitated locating a new printer, and our pal and the Rondo-winning publisher of *Monsters From The Vault*, Jim Clatterbaugh, hooked us up with his Baltimore printer, Consolidated. For the next three issues (until, sadly, they went out of business) they gave us superb work. #27 shows what you can do when you don't give up—like getting Roman Polanski (thank you, Constantine Nasr) to talk for an hour about *The Fearless Vampire Killers*. Incredible paintings by Mark Maddox, Belle Dee (Shana) Bilbrey and Jim Salvati (his Sharon Tate is breathtaking) appeared as covers. Some people say *The Fearless Vampire Killers* is their favorite horror film ever. Others compare it to watching paint dry, with not a laugh or chuckle in sight. Sometimes a publisher has to make a decision and run with it.

We got the chance in 2012 to cover Hammer's first new Gothic horror movie since *Frankenstein and the Monster from Hell* in 1972. *The Woman in Black* was covered in depth—we talked to the star Daniel Radcliffe, the director, the producers, the music composer, the designers and more. We interviewed the author of the original novel, Susan Hill. We analyzed the 1989 British TV version (and featured an interview with the star, Adrian Rawlins) and the long-running stage play. I never really plan, initially, to go so overboard on these subjects. But someone will say "how about this?" or someone else asks, "What if we interview so-and-so." Before you know it, you've got 100 pages of coverage that no one else can touch. A good ego boost occurs between selling greasy truck parts to greasy old truckers and delivering the goods intellectually with each issue of *Little Shoppe of Horrors*. Even the WIB production people said the job committed by Constantine Nasr and everyone else was so good that they didn't bother reinventing the wheel with other magazines. Hammer even kept copies of the issue in their offices. I like that!

Who wouldn't want a chance to feature the ultimate article on the making of the two Vincent Price Dr. Phibes films? When Justin Humphreys offered us his long-in-the-works behind the scenes study of *The Abominable Dr. Phibes*, we jumped at it. Again, who expected it would take up so many pages, or that we would include a career article on

Vulnavia #1? (played by Virginia North). Heck, at this time in the history of *LSoH* I should have known! We got directors Frank Darabont and Tim Burton on board. But big names, small names, no names (like me!) do not matter when desiring to do the best coverage ever done on a particular film or film series.

Our current issue (as I write this) shipped this past June 9, 2013. I had my left knee totally replaced on December 17 last year. At that time I had a vague idea we could do something on *Vampire Circus*. We had a decent feature in *LSoH* #9, but I love this film and it seemed that there should be more available information. During his visit to England (with his wife, Mandy), Constantine Nasr did a long interview with *Vampire Circus* director Robert Young, conducted at the British Film Institute. I had Bruce Timm's cover rough next to my bed in our guest bedroom as I waited for my titanium knee to start healing. I did not have a clue where this issue would lead us. Now six months later, it led to a fact-filled making-of-feature by Bruce G. Hallenbeck. Interviews with performers Lalla Ward, Robert Tayman (Count Mitterhaus), John Moulder-Brown and Anthony Higgins (Corlan) appear, among others. And a heartfelt remembrance of the late Domini Blythe appears by her long-time companion, director Jean Beaudin. It is still the early days of the magazine's release as I write this reflection, but we have high hopes for it. *Demons of the Mind* and *Trog* coverage appears in issue #32, released Halloween 2013. We touched the opposite ends of the quality spectrum in this issue. Steve Karchin is back on our front cover and Frank Dietz gives in to his guilty pleasure for *Trog* on the back cover.

I turned 66 October 2, 2013. It has been an amazing journey through monsterland for this less than *famous* Monster Kid. That I should arrive at this point in life with a wonderful, gorgeous, monster-loving wife at my side is way beyond belief. I have two great sons that I adore and five grandchildren that keep me busy. My mother, sister and brother are still around to give me grief. It has been a great ride. I wouldn't change it for anything. I don't think we'll see 100 years of publication out of Gary and Sue and *Midnight Marquee*. But I am happy that the end hasn't arrived yet for *Midnight Marquee*. Just as I hope *Little Shoppe of Horrors* can mope along for a few more years. This long, strange, twisty, interconnected trip shared by Gary and me might just carry on for a little while longer. Let's wait and see where it takes us.

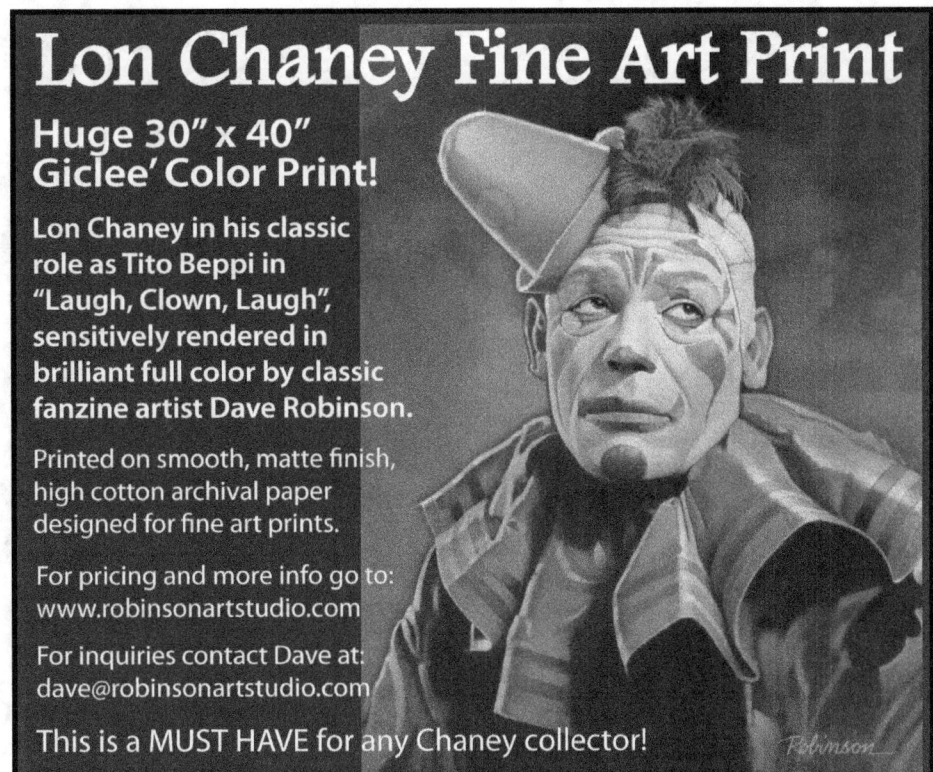

The Monster Magazine Family Tree—
50 Years of Gore Creatures/Midnight Marquee

by Jim Clatterbaugh

As do many of you who are reading this, I fondly remember the first time I caught a glimpse of a monster magazine at the local newsstand. It was 1967, and while looking at the comic books, I turned and locked onto the image of Frankenstein's Monster doing battle with the Wolf Man. The magazine was *Famous Monsters of Filmland* #42, and I was hooked!

It wasn't much before then when I discovered my first Universal monsters on TV (courtesy of my two older brothers), and here was a magazine featuring so many monsters; I could look at these magazines over and over and not have to wait until the following week for a new film on TV. Fortunately for me, my mother was very understanding of my wants and had no problem letting me take the magazine home. With this purchase, a new routine started—I would hit the two newsstands in my small town almost weekly, as I accompanied my mother downtown nearly every Saturday. We would visit my sister, who worked at the local Woolworth's, and then it would be off to the newsstands in search of the newest monster magazine.

This ritual continued for years, and soon a double feature at the local theater and a stop at the nearby hobby shop (in search of the latest Aurora monster model) were part of the day. As the years went by, new TV shows appeared that spotlighted the classic monsters. In my area, they were *Shock Theatre* on WXEX-8, hosted by The Bowman Body, and *Sir Graves Ghastly Presents* on WTOP Channel 9, hosted by Sir Graves, of course. Also, each trip to the newsstand uncovered more titles, such as *Castle of Frankenstein*, *Creepy*, *Eerie*, *Monsters of the Movies*, *Monsters Unleashed* and a slew of others. I was in heaven, but little did I know that fanzines devoted to classic horror and sci-fi films were popping up all over, with the granddaddy of all of them, *Gore Creatures*, premiering in 1963.

As I now realize, I missed out on many of the best monster publications because they weren't readily available to me. While they could be ordered from small ads in the publications I was reading or through word of mouth from one fan to another, I was all about instant gratification, and waiting for a mail order was not on my agenda. My first glimpse of a fanzine, or more importantly, *Midnight Marquee*, didn't happen until many years later.

As I entered high school, I became more focused on music and girls than on monsters. The monster photos that once covered my bedroom walls were replaced with photos and posters of bands clipped from *Circus*, *Hit Parader* or *Creem* magazine. While I still loved horror movies and checked out the latest ones at the local theater, the classic monsters and all things related were packed in boxes and stored in the garage, and my thoughts of them would be buried for almost 10 years.

Immediately upon graduation, I joined the Air Force and spent the next 20 years serving my country. It was in 1983 or '84, after returning from a three-year tour in Italy, when I discovered *Fangoria* magazine at a local drugstore in Altus, Oklahoma. Home video was just starting to take off. I remember seeing an ad in *Fangoria* for Marshall Discount Video and I ordered their catalog. I also joined Columbia House (who didn't in the 1970s and '80s?), and two of the introductory VHS tapes I chose were *Dracula* and *Frankenstein*. I waited with great excitement for the movies to arrive, as it had been more than 10 years since I saw either one. Once they arrived and I watched them, I felt the same feeling I had at that newsstand in 1967. Soon I ordered more classic titles from Marshall Discount Video and cruised the local mom and pop video stores looking for films from my past that would rekindle those feelings I was experiencing. I was hooked again, except this time it was for good.

Fast-forward six years (when I was stationed at Scott Air Force Base) to that fateful day when I scanned the shelves of a new comic book shop in Belleville, Illinois for the latest issues of *Fangoria* and Forrest J Ackerman's new magazine, *Monsterland*, and I again caught a glimpse of an old friend

Jim Clatterbaugh first meets Forrest J Ackerman in 1987

on the shelf. This time it was Boris Karloff as the Mummy, and the magazine was *Midnight Marquee* #39. This was the first fanzine I had ever laid eyes on, even though they had been available for decades— in *Gore Creatures/Midnight Marquee*'s case, 25 years. After purchasing the issue and reading it, my first thought was, how could I have missed out on this fabulous publication for a quarter of a century? It didn't seem possible. Soon I discovered another fanzine, *Little Shoppe of Horrors* (issue #9), at the same shop, located in the back issue boxes, along with many other titles of which I was never aware. Some were new and disappeared quickly; others stuck around. Also at this time, I discovered Fantaco in Albany, New York, a mail order company that specialized in horror. Soon, I was ordering books and magazines from them regularly; my first order included *Midnight Marquee* #37, which was the trade paperback 25th anniversary issue of *Gore Creatures/Midnight Marquee*. If I wasn't already hooked on *MidMar*, once I read Gary's fascinating article, "25 Years of Gore Creatures/Midnight Marquee: A Biased History," he had me hook, line and sinker. I just couldn't believe that a single person could produce a magazine on his own for over 25 years. Of course, Gary didn't do it totally alone, as his late father Richard handled the mail order part of the business, along with other duties, and then Sue became his *MidMar* partner once she and Gary were married. Last but not least, there were all the artists and writers who

Jim Clatterbaugh and wife Marian hawk the latest issue of *Monsters From the Vault*.

Ballyhoo and The Bride of Frankenstein—The cover page from a recent issue of *Monsters from the Vault* demonstrates the magazine's creative layout design.

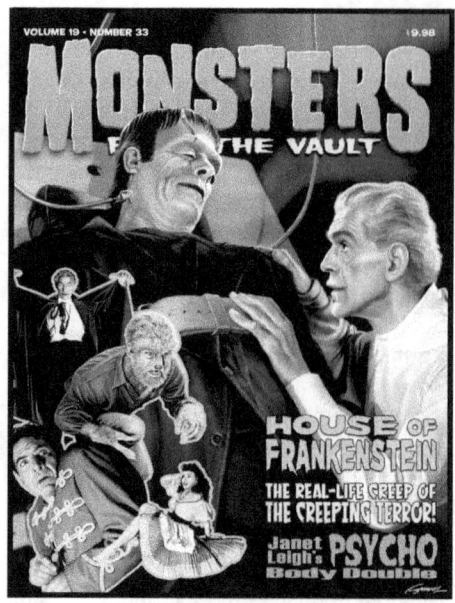

Kerry Gammill (top) and Daniel R. Horne (bottom two) cover art for *MFTV*.

contributed over the years, a who's who of today's genre experts. But no doubt about it, Gary was the main man, and without him there would be no *Gore Creatures/Midnight Marquee*. After that fateful day in 1989, I began obtaining back issues of the magazine from various sources, and over the years I've been able to acquire a complete run of *Midnight Marquee*. Unfortunately, the limited availability and high prices that back issues of *Gore Creatures* demand have prevented me from obtaining a single copy, even though I've held many of them in my hands.

Fast-forward again to summer 1992 and the first time I heard of FANEX. I had recently been stationed at Andrews Air Force Base in Maryland, and, while checking out the latest issue of *Filmfax,* I saw a small ad for a convention being held in Baltimore called FANEX. Having previously attended several West Coast Fangoria Conventions (run by Creation), I decided to call the number and find out more about the show. Little did I know that I would be conversing with Gary. After talking for well over a half hour about the show, I decided to give it a try. Unfortunately, the hotel was sold out, but I managed to find one nearby, so off I went for the weekend to my first FANEX Convention (FANEX 6).

If you think you have a hard time deciding what events to attend when you go to Monster Bash, Monster Mania, or any of the other conventions currently held, FANEX had them all topped: a dealer's room; two movie rooms (one running 16mm, the other video projection) with films running nonstop through the wee hours of the morning, sometimes even all night; a guest talk room; and two or three panel discussion rooms, where many of the genre's best writers held court before a captive audience and discussed a wide variety of topics (it was FANEX 6 where I first learned about McFarland books). "So much to see, so little time" was never truer than at FANEX. I never missed another FANEX from that point on and was even a chairperson for several of the shows. It was during this period that I met Michael and Steve Kronenberg, and with the guidance of Gary Svehla, *Monsters from the Vault* was hatched and premiered at FANEX 9 in the summer of 1995. Both Gary and Sue were magnanimous with their time and walked me through the process of creating a magazine. They provided contacts for distribution, hooked me up with the printer and tutored me on Photoshop, and Gary generously contributed an article to my first issue. It was also at FANEX where I met most, if not all, of my longtime regular contributors to the magazine. In short, without FANEX, and more importantly, without Gary and Sue, there would be no *Monsters from the Vault*. Years later, when Michael Kronenberg stepped down as the Art Director of *MFTV*, I was at a crossroads with the magazine. I either had to call it a day after seven years or figure out how I could continue, since I had no design skills. It was then that Gary and Sue again showed me so much kindness and offered to provide me a design program (Pagemaker) and some lessons so I could attempt the design and layout myself. Apparently, they're both really good teachers, as *Monsters from the Vault* is now in its 18th year. Many other publishers would have never shown the generosity Gary and Sue did—others would have viewed it as helping the competition. But for Gary (like me), there could never be too many monster magazines out there. A few years ago, I found myself offering the same kind of help to a longtime *MFTV* reader when he decided he wanted to publish a monster magazine. To date he's published five issues of his magazine (*Undying Monsters*). I figured it was the least I could do after the kindness I was shown by Gary and Sue.

Another reason Gary and Sue and FANEX will always hold a special place in my heart is that it was through FANEX that I met my lovely wife, Marian. I also know several other couples who met through FANEX. Thanks to FANEX, I get to spend

Jim Clatterbaugh poses behind his display showcasing *Monsters from the Vault*.

the rest of my life with my soul mate, who I never would have known if it weren't for the efforts of Gary and Sue—and for that I'm most grateful!

So, was *Gore Creatures/Midnight Marquee* a major influence in my desire to publish a monster magazine? You bet your life it was, as I'm sure it was for tons of other editors/publishers. Undoubtedly, *Famous Monsters of Filmland* was a major influence on Gary 50 years ago when he started his journey. For me, the monster magazine family tree has many branches and hundreds of leaves, but the trunk is made up of a limited number of rings. Those rings are named *Famous Monsters of Filmland*, *Castle of Frankenstein*, *Gore Creatures/Midnight Marquee*, *Photon*, *Cinefantastique*, *Little Shoppe of Horrors*, *Starlog*, and *Fangoria*. And carved on the trunk are the names Ackerman, Warren, Beck, Svehla, Frank, Clarke, Klemensen, Jacobs and O'Quinn. It's that strong foundation that has allowed the tree to flourish over the past 50 years, and new leaves continue to be added as new print publications pop up. But for fanzines, one name has stood the test of time, and that's *Gore Creatures/Midnight Marquee*. Having the same editor and publisher for 50 years is a feat that has never been duplicated in the genre magazine/fanzine world and won't be surpassed—except by Gary and gang in 2014, when *Midnight Marquee* enters its 51st year. Congratulations to Gary, Richard (RIP) and Sue on 50 years of excellence, and here's hoping for many more to come!

by Gary J. Svehla

How the Cult Culture of Horror Film Fandom Changed Over Five Decades

Many baby boomers see the writing on the wall. As children and young adults we were raised on classic horror movies and the mushrooming monster culture that erupted during the late 1950s and 1960s. If we did not originally stay up late to watch the *Shock Theater* TV package upon its original release in 1957, we were reared on some sort of local late-night TV horror host or monster movie package. We rushed to newsstands to buy pristine, non-smudged copies of the latest movie monster magazines and comic books, stopped off at drugstores or hobby shops to buy the latest Aurora Monster Model kit and, if any money remained, purchased packs of monster bubble gum card sets. We ordered monster movie novelties from the back pages of *Castle of Frankenstein* and *Famous Monsters of Filmland*. Many purchased Castle Films super 8mm condensations of classic horror and science fiction movies, edited down to 18-odd minutes. Of course Saturday horror movie matinees were playing at neighborhood movie theaters allowing children to stay all day and watch a monster double-feature complete with cartoons and perhaps a movie short or two (hopefully The Three Stooges would be included). We stocked up on our big bags of popcorn and candy bars (the combination of salt and chocolate would prevent us from getting too thirsty, since the soda machine policy did not allow patrons to take drinks to theater seats, at least not in Baltimore). Evenings, if we could stay up late enough, we were able to see our monster and alien buddies on network TV, thanks to television shows such as *Thriller* (with host Boris Karloff), *One Step Beyond*, *Science Fiction Theatre*, *The Twilight Zone*, *The Outer Limits*, *The Addams Family*, *The Munsters* and *Lost in Space*. The 1950s and 1960s became the perfect generation to be a Monster Kid.

But recently as Sue and I mail out books, magazines flyers and DVDs to customers, many of whom have been with us since the early days, we hear from more and more relatives informing us of the death of their mother or father or uncle, all of whom were long-time patrons. Many heirs write heart-felt letters telling Sue how much Midnight Marquee Press meant to their late relative or friend. While some younger folks enjoy the classics and the horror film culture, we must admit that watching Universal horror classics, Hammer films, the classic B movies, the giant monster and alien invasion films of the 1950s, the blobs, the little green men, the crawling vegetable monstrosities, the rotting corpses returning from the dead, etc. was primarily a focus for members of our generation. Today, people born after the 1960s just do not hold the same love, in the same way, for the nostalgic cinema that we hold. When the baby boomers pass, most of the Monster Kid culture will also pass away. It's just the way things are.

But after 50 years of publishing *Gore Creatures/Midnight Marquee*, some trends have shifted and radically changed. Just thinking back about the birth, development and evolution of the monster culture since the 1950s, I see many changes that cry out to be analyzed. So let's reflect upon such changes to horror film fandom and its cult culture over the course of the past 50 years. See if you agree with my assessments.

The Paper Has Gotten Better—
Back in the late 1950s, monster magazines were printed on cheap pulp paper (currently popular *Scary Monsters*

John Newland was the host of *One Step Beyond*, one of TV's early supernatural series.

magazine is a testament to such low-end printing and proud of it). While the quality of *Famous Monsters of Filmland* and *Castle of Frankenstein* seemed to be slightly better, seams easily cracked on covers as edges split from the staples and inferior interior paper became brittle and yellowed. Edges of pages would often flake and crumble. Today's magazines and fanzines are generally printed on coated enamel stock (what we call glossy) that is thicker and more durable. Perhaps we all suffer from OCD, but today's aging boomers fear that their 35-cent monster magazines will rapidly decay and disintegrate after decades of re-reads, so publishers today produce magazines with the quality to last intact for generations. However, while publishers make magazines longer lasting, human beings still have a relatively short shelf life, so perhaps now our magazines will outlive us. Isn't that a pleasant thought?

The Paper Has Disappeared—

Now that most publishers today manufacture magazines with heavier glossy paper stock—magazines having less a chance of yellowing, cracking, drying out and turning to dust—hard print publications are rapidly becoming a relic of the past. More and more newspapers, magazines and books are no longer being published as hard print copies. Today the operant word is digital, with the hard print copy slowly fading away. Even though a digital copy online looks as pristine and colorful today as it will look 50 years from now, Monster Kids are fearful that digital copies can vanish overnight from hard drives and servers existing in The Cloud. Can such digital editions become even more temporary than hard print editions of beloved monster magazines? Even when Warren Publications and others went out of business, their stock of remaining out-of-print magazines were warehoused so that near mint copies could still be acquired decades later. The fear today is that digital copies will only exist as long as the original publisher is alive and well and paying to offer the product online. When publishers do not pay their bill for web or Cloud storage, that publication will disappear and be gone forever, in the flick of the virtual switch. However,

it must be remembered that digital files still exist potentially, even if not posted on the web. Perhaps future generations will develop an archival digital online museum where out-of-print publications can still be maintained long after publishers cease publication or go out of business. Let's allow publishers to die but *not* their art—the books and magazines.

The Movie Palaces Are Not The Same—

As a young child, say between 1959 and 1965, I spent most weekends at the neighborhood Waverly Theater, not far from the original Memorial Stadium where the Orioles and *Baltimore* Colts played. My father could drop me off at the theater around 1 p.m. and pick me up around 5 p.m.. I would have at least two features to watch (roughly three hours of programming) with about another half hour of movie trailers, cartoons and shorts. Kids could stay the entire day since theaters were not cleared after each showing. We had clean bathrooms and a candy concession area to keep us fed (if not healthfully at least our appetite and thirst were sated). Also in the same block as The Waverly, a huge outside newsstand existed that sold science fiction paperback novels and short story anthologies, monster magazines and comic books—all the reading material that any kid could possibly desire. I always made sure I allowed at least 20 minutes to browse before my father returned to pick me up and transport my big bag of goodies from the newsstand to our home. The neighborhood theaters were friendly places; usually the older man or woman who sold tickets at the box-office was kindly and the people at the concession stand equally outgoing and chatty. Only the teenage ushers were sometimes the villains, asking kids to quiet down or take their feet off the seats. But mostly they just circulated and left us alone. What was nice was that The Waverly showed movies that were not current. That meant in 1962 I could see older films such as *Forbidden Planet* (from 1956) and all the great AIP teenage monster classics. All the monsters created

---

12—NEWS-POST   Baltimore, Sat., Jan. 18, 1958

Aldine Bird

'Black Cat' On Tonight

Dr. Lucifer is in trouble.

Just for added atmosphere on the WBAL Saturday night "Shock" show a couple of weeks ago, he talked about such succulent dishes as fried grasshoppers, smoked octopus, roasted caterpillars and lily bulbs soaked in honey, to say nothing of a delicious beverage made with sauerkraut and champagne.

After eulogizing their delicacy, Dr. Lucifer who actually is WBAL's Richard Dix, offered

DIX as DR. LUCIFER

to send the recipes for any or all of these dishes to anyone who would write and ask for them, together with a stomach pump!

He figured no one would really care a whoop about such ghoulish dishes — but he figured wrong.

LETTERS began rolling in and the bald truth of the matter is, Dr. Lucifer has no such recipes ... now he wants to try and figure a way out that looks logical and will satisfy his viewers.

Dr. Lucifer, of course, is the Satan-ish character who introduces the terrifying shows which really aren't so terrifying at all each Saturday evening.

You see him come out of his casket ... a real last-ditch box (!) by the way ... and begins making your flesh creep.

If you think Richard Dix has any qualms about getting in and out of a real casket before his time, you're dead wrong. He's not that superstitious ... neither is his dog. That canine loves to crawl in and snooze—it's that soft inside ... but his wife, Nancy Lee, and daughter, Landra May? No thank you ...

A WEEK AGO, when Dix was ill and couldn't appear, Mrs. Dix took over ... remem-

actor ... goes to Williamsburg, Va., each summer to appear in the famous colonial play, "Common Glory" ... would like to develop a sort of Charles Adam family situation on TV ... but perhaps you, or the children, or both, remember him best as "Officer Happy," he with the Irish accent, instead of a ghost ... tune in and watch how Dr. Lucifer leads you unsuspectingly into commercials in a ghoulist sort of way ...

Tonight's offering will be on "The Black Cat," starring Boris Karloff and Bela Lugosi ... here's a tip: Lucifer's offerings will be on music ... taking you from primitive to modern types, starting with the jungle tom-toms, through the Indian drums, on up to classical and then modern ... but watch out for that modern ... it'll be a shocking surprise ... moreover, Lucifer will lift his own scalp, smash someone's head in, and end up with ... boy, you'll have to see for yourself ... I feel kinda funny ...

Big doings here tonight on WBAL and NBC—a full camera crew is in town, with Art Baker, and they will do the second of the network shows on "End of the Rainbow" from here ... Someone in Baltimore will be the recipient of a pot of gold, almost, like Ralph Edwards does on This Is Your Life ... Can't tell you who it will be before show time, but if you tune in WBAL at 10 P. M., you'll find out ... Baker is the new emcee of the show ... he has given up his role on "You Asked For It" as of January 26.

Gail Patrick Keen On Home

It's Gail Patrick Jackson's quote re her executive producer activities on the "Perry Mason" show:

"I can't afford me as an actress, even if I wanted to work on the show. Besides, if I took an acting part, I couldn't keep the hours I want—getting home in time to get dinner for our two children and finding out what

Frankensteinia: The Frankenstein Blog is one of the superior horror film online blogs that are rapidly replacing print magazines. Created by Pierre Fournier, the blog offers plenty of interesting text and graphics.

by atomic radiation were still regularly screened, as were Hammer movies and 1950s B productions such as *Frankenstein's Daughter*. For a monster movie lover, spending one's Saturday or Sunday at the Waverly was a perfect way to grow up. And it did not matter if I brought along a friend or two or attended alone, for it was the movies themselves that served as the principal attraction. The Waverly was my happy place.

Today, movies in malls are not the same. Even with larger screens, higher-tech sound and stadium seating, movie theaters are run with a spirit of crowd control first and foremost. The object is to squeeze the crowds in and get the crowds out rapidly after the show is over. No more lingering or watching a movie for a second time, as the auditorium is cleared and often a good amount of time exists between one show ending and the next show beginning. Theaters are no longer welcoming and cozy…they are no longer exotic palaces but mass-produced multiplexes where every theater interior looks similar to the next (perhaps a few more or few less seats). The same previews are shown, as are the same commercials. The only advertising in the movie palaces of our youth was the public service announcements for finding the exits in case of fire.

B Films Were Loathed Back In The Day—

As a child weaned on the classic Universal, MGM and Paramount horror movies, it was an entirely different experience to watch *Blood of Dracula, Return of Dracula, The Vampire, The Brain From Planet Arous, How To Make A Monster, Monster From the Ocean Floor, The Amazing Colossal Man* and *Earth vs. The Spider*. These were the exploitation, teenage drive-in theater fare, the grade-Z movies mass-produced during the 1950s. Even though baby boomers learned to ultimately love this ilk of cheapjack cinema, I can go back and re-read early issues of pro-zines and fanzines to discover that many of the beloved 1950s exploitation movies were reviewed negatively. Only in the light of nostalgia and childhood reflection did these B productions shine a lot brighter. Even the better B movies such as *Tarantula, Creature From The Black Lagoon* and *Them!* were not revered in the same way they would be by the middle or end of the 1970s. Take a classic such as the original *Invaders From Mars* (1953). True, the film's premise and cinematography (including art direction and set design) was inspired, but the stereotypical manner in which military personnel, the police and scientists were displayed is almost laughable today. And, boy oh boy, those green giant Mutants running like cartoon characters with zippers up their backs, carrying the majestic little Martian head in a glass globe, were rather silly. Even stern parents appear larger than life. Is it plausible to believe that our friendly neighbors that walk out on the sand dunes behind their homes and disappear, only to return the next day with glazed eyes and a new attitude, are actually alien controlled? But while as kids such movies worked for us, what is amazing is that upon our maturation, education and exposure to higher quality movies, we still held a special place in our hearts for such juvenile, teenage-oriented product. As a kid I loved Sheb Wooley's 45-rpm hit "The Purple People Eater," but when I got a little older, I saw the record as a novelty and its charm quickly wore off. But shockingly, without any logic, a Monster Kid's love for all movies schlocky—*The Blob, Invaders From Mars* and *I Married A Monster From Outer Space*—continues into adulthood. Instead of leaving childhood favorites by

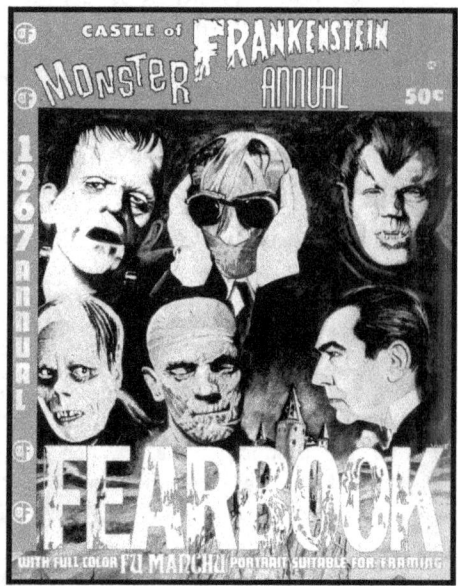

My home away from home. The Waverly Theater back in 1963, showing *X, The Man With X-Ray Eyes*, as one of Baltimore's famous electric streetcars passes by.

the wayside and reassessing a film such as *Attack of the Crab Monster* for exactly what it is, somehow that film's sense of nostalgia overpowered our good sense and elevated it onto a temple of greatness that should never have been. Today, I would rather see *It! The Terror From Beyond Space* for the 20th time than watch avowed classic *The Day The Earth Stood Still* one more time. While critics lambasted *It! The Terror from Beyond Space* back then for its silly rubber-suited monster and less than convincing special effects, featuring a cast populated by merely adequate players, 20 years later critics were citing the film's claustrophobic sense of terror as the monster busted through and occupied each successive level of the ship as being one example of how well the little B film operates. Good cinema was no longer dependent upon star power (of course B actors such as Marshall Thompson, John Agar and Kenneth Tobey became stars in their own right by commanding attention within the niche subgenre), big budget or the most convincing acting or special effects. Instead, our generation could enjoy the eccentricity of non-mainstream moviemakers or fast-working B directors who could mount an entertaining little production in record time. For us movies were either good or bad, they resonated and stuck to our ribs like hot oatmeal or they passed rapidly through our system to be quickly forgotten. But a movie that stuck, that resonated, that become part of our identity did not have to be produced by mainstream Hollywood or made with millions of dollars. Our generation appreciated great B productions.

Remember, it was our generation who elevated lowbrow comedians The Three Stooges to the same status as The Marx Brothers and Laurel and Hardy.

But my point is this. Read a review of *It! The Terror From Beyond Space*, *Tarantula* or *Attack of the 50 Ft. Woman* back in the day and compare that original review to reviews written at least 20 years later. The differences in critical acceptance will knock you out!

The Rise and Recognition of the Val Lewton RKO Horror Factory—

Back in the 1950s and 1960s, the *Shock Theater* TV package, featuring mainly Universal horror classics, mysteries and 1940s programmers, ruled late-night television airwaves. On the other extreme television offered the emerging packages from American International and Allied Artists of cheap horror exploitation movies such as *Attack of the 50 Ft. Woman*, *From Hell It Came* and *It Conquered the World*. These low-budgets appeared on TV alongside *Bride of Frankenstein*, *The Mummy* and *The Wolf Man*. Back in the 1960s B productions were called grade Z and lambasted with little affection. These movies, especially the teenage monster exploitation drive-in theater fodder, were not well received initially.

But just like PRC's cheap little film noir *Detour* made film noir lovers realize that many of the B productions were as good as the Hollywood mainstream, the Val Lewton B RKO unit had the same effect on horror. Back in the late 1950s and early 1960s, the Lewtons were broadcast

This was Gary Svehla's bedroom at 5906 Kavon Avenue around 1967 to 1969. Notice the posters, the lobby cards, the movie stills—Monster-Mania at full obsession.

Val Lewton classics such as *The Body Snatcher* were not esteemed when shown on local TV stations during the 1960s in scratchy, re-release prints.

never be rid of me," as the flashing lightning illuminates the creepy corpse. This sequence holds up as effectively as the best of the Universal monster classics.

What Val Lewton taught an entire generation of Monster Kids was that classic horror movies did not necessarily have to be produced on a Hollywood mainstream budget and that horror movies did not have to feature an iconic monster such as Dracula, Frankenstein's Monster or The Wolf Man. Sometimes generic zombies, re-animated corpses, fiends with knives and satanic cults in New York City were enough. While it was nice to see horror stars such as Boris Karloff appear in a Val Lewton movie, such celebrity power was not always necessary to produce a winner. The story, the exceptional acting by an unknown cast, the cinematography, the direction and editing (ah, the joy of those spooky Val Lewton walks and buses) were more than enough.

The slow progression from loving Universal classics to savoring the B classics produced by Val Lewton led to, say, appreciating 1957's classic Columbia low-budget *The Curse of the Demon*, whose director Jacques Tourneur also directed a few of the Val Lewton classics such as *Cat People* and *I Walked With a Zombie*. And even that terrifying puppet demon, either loved or loathed, brought home the horror to an emerging generation of Monster Kids. It was not that big a leap to admire *Curse of*

in scratchy re-release prints on evening or late night television. Mainly four titles appeared—*Cat People, Curse of the Cat People, I Walked With a Zombie* and *The Body Snatcher*. Val Lewton movies such as *The 7th Victim, The Isle of the Dead, The Leopard Man* and *Bedlam* were shown far less frequently and without much fanfare. *Cat People* was considered Lewton's finest film, his production company's debut, so it and its direct sequel received plenty of airtime. *I Walked With a Zombie*, for most children an absolute bore (although its mood and creepy atmosphere made it of slight interest for kids), gained critical momentum as time went on. But it was the dynamic Boris Karloff performance that fueled *The Body Snatcher*, and it did not hurt that the movie also featured Bela Lugosi in a supporting performance. While kids loved the horror concept of medical science experimenting on human specimens freshly retrieved from the grave, *The Body Snatcher* resonated mainly with children because of the plot device of using a sympathetic, crippled little girl who was intimidated by the surly and insensitive doctor, a plot device pushing the juvenile audience toward liking the kinder Cabman Gray (Karloff) and his horse, even though he was the conniving body snatcher of the title who held power over the respected Dr. MacFarlane (Henry Daniell).

But for me these low-budget productions offered high-budget chills, often featuring excellent sets, cinematography and performances. The climax of *The Body Snatcher*, where the rain-soaked carriage carrying the cold corpse of Cabman Gray appears to come to life, bouncing around and almost cuddling the terrified Dr. MacFarlane, terrifies me to this day. Karloff's booming voice threatens, "You'll

Grade Z movies such as *The Brain from Planet Arous* were dismissed as dreck back in the 1960s, until connoisseurs of *le bad cinema* emerged to sing praises of low-budget cinema.

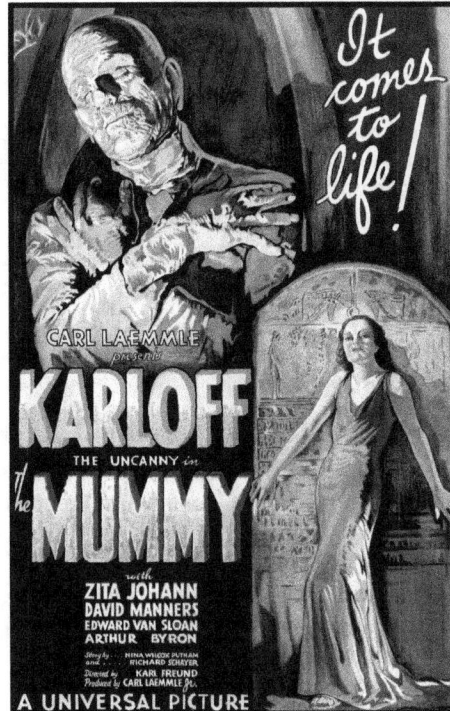

What a difference 30 years make! Go back 31 years from today and we arrive in 1982, watching *The Thing*. In 1963, the year *Gore Creatures* debuted, *The Birds* played in theaters. Go back another 31 years and we can watch Universal's *The Mummy* in 1932.

the Demon and also enjoy *The Giant Claw, The Monolith Monsters, The Monster That Challenged the World, From Hell It Came* and all the other B productions that were appearing in theaters or on television. Of course very few B productions managed to hit the artistic heights of *Curse of the Demon*, but that leap of faith allowed lovers of the classics to go wild over *House on Haunted Hill* and *The Tingler*. The fine line was becoming more a blur. Kids knew that *Son of Frankenstein* was a much better production than *Frankenstein 1970*, but it was nice seeing a modern version of an old classic that also starred the iconic Boris Karloff.

Children could discriminate and tell the differences between *Horror of Party Beach, The Flesh Eaters* and *Carnival of Souls* and the true classics produced 20 and 30 years earlier, but remember, both types of movies were being written about side-by-side in *Famous Monsters of Filmland*, whose mantra that "Lon Chaney Shall Not Die" now also included coverage of the rock 'n' roll horror film as well. James Nicholson and Samuel Z. Arkoff were mentioned almost as often as Tod Browning and James Whale in their pages, and kids learned, even if these newer films were not as good, that most horror movies were worth watching.

The Val Lewton productions became essentially a bridge between artistic horror classics and lower-budgeted ones, soon allowing the floodgates to open even wider as more and more exploitation and cheap programmers entered the fray to be accepted as the bastard child of classic horror. Like a seedy cousin or down-on-his-luck uncle, with these movies, the horror movie fan began to include and accept every type of horror movie—the good, the bad and the ugly. They all were part of the family.

What A Difference 30 Years Make?

When *Gore Creatures* debuted in the summer of 1963, the current theatrical horror fare included the latest AIP Poe picture (*The Haunted Palace*), the latest Mario Bava import (*Black Sabbath*) and the latest Hammer horror (*Kiss of the Vampire*). Our fanzine celebrated both the current and especially the classics of horror cinema, the cherished early Universal icons. Back in 1963 these earliest of the Universal horror classics were only 30 or 31 years old; that's three decades of history separating the old and the new. Today, in 2013, if we traveled back 30 or 31 years we would be in 1982-83. The classics of that era included: 1982—*Basket Case, Poltergeist, The Thing, Tenebre* and *Creepshow*; 1983—

The Hunger, Videodrome, The Dead Zone and *Cujo*. When I first wrote about *Bride of Frankenstein, The Invisible Man* and *Dracula* way back in 1963, those Universal classics seemed as though they existed in some mystical, magical portal to the ancient past. Today when reflecting back on *Videodrome, The Thing* and *Poltergeist*, remembering that 30 or 31 years separates them from 2013, these older films seem much more contemporary. When comparing the craft of filmmaking of Alfred Hitchcock's *The Birds* or Robert Wise's *The Haunting*, both released in 1963, to the early Universal horror classics of the early to mid-1930s, the craft of movie-making seems so radically different. Perhaps the horror movie genre arrived slightly after the sound era debuted, reminding us that in 1931 movies were still in their infancy and film grammar was still based upon the silent film era and the American theater, with the subtlety of film still being discovered and defined. Compare the 30 years separating *Frankenstein* and *The Mummy* from *The Haunting* or *The Birds*, and then compare the 30 years between then and now—*The Woman in Black, Cabin In the Woods* and *Prometheus* (I use 2012 as my reference point as it is too soon in 2013 to include all movies released in 2013).

On one hand we ask, could it only have been 30 years separating all these movies? Yet at the same time, the evolution of cinema between 1931 and 1963 was more startling than the progress that occurred between 1963 and 2013. In a world of ever-changing technology, it is evident that the changes

A recent photo of Andrew Porter, who formerly edited and published the s.f. fanzine *Algol*.

that occurred in the past 30 years involving movies have not been as radical or earth shaking. Perhaps the most groundbreaking technology is the digital evolution, replacing movies shot and projected in 35mm (or 65mm or 70mm film) with digitally photographed and projected movies. Even today's digitally photographed movies more closely resemble movies made 30 years ago than films of the early 1930s resemble movies made in the early 1960s.

Anger Management As A Concept Ruled Fandom—

Fandom has always been a hotbed of egos and arguments that sometime become nuclear. I will never forget when I attended LunaCon (the regional science fiction convention held in New York City) for the first or second time. Andrew Porter, four years older and more experienced than the wet-behind-the-ears Gary Svehla, was the editor and publisher of a very slick science fiction fanzine with huge s.f. fandom cred, *Algol*, and my mimeographed fanzine was inferior by nature of its paper stock and less mature (at the moment) writing. When I happily introduced myself to Porter, thinking our friendly knocks via the mail (more accurately, his relentless knocking of my fanzine) would not interfere with a friendship, he roared with laugher and gathered his surrounding cronies, announcing loudly to one and all that here was Gary Svehla—"he publishes a true crud zine!" Most rude and unkind, but fandom was filled with this big fish in a small fishbowl mentality, where being in the right clique gave one a false sense of power. Perhaps such venom was slightly less potent in the newly emerging horror film fandom created by Forrest J Ackerman and Calvin Beck, but pure science fiction fandom was often mean spirited. It was in the so-called "lettercol" or letter columns of fanzines that such poisoned pens festered in the most scattergun manner. If a reader did not enjoy an article, the resulting critical letter was usually over-dramatic in describing just how and why the piece came up short. Soon the criticism morphed from the content of the article to the author who penned such words. Ultimately it was the writer who was taking the heat and not just the words he wrote. Feuds between personalities became the rule and sometimes science fiction and horror film fandom could not wait to receive the next issue of just about every fanzine published to dig into the lettercol and see just how far the insanity was spreading.

But one positive thing existed about fandom and lettercols. Fanzines were usually published quarterly or bi-monthly, so that meant a lapse of at least 8 weeks or more between issues. In other words, people had time to compose, think things over, crumple up the paper and start over again, allowing common sense and reason to rule. Fandom's authors and publishers still had plenty of opportunity to be uncivil toward one another, but with months to compose a reaction, the responses were generally well thought out, supported factually and at times fair-minded, if not frequently over-zealous and over-reactive.

Cut to horror film fandom today. On the message boards and blogs (with limitless

On the opposite page is a reproduction of an actual letter Christopher Lee sent me in 1970, commenting upon a recent interview published in *Gore Creatures* conducted by David Soren. The interview was accompanied by a fantastic art portfolio of the actor designed by artist Dave Ludwig. Is the art of letter writing a lost cause?

comment space beneath) people criticize, over-react and respond immediately, within the hour if not within the minute. Emotion (not logic) rules with little time mandated before reaction. Even the most polite, intelligent and responsible people get caught up in the moment and fire off a half-baked reaction without giving it time to simmer in the cool light of reason. Not that everyone flies off the handle, but if people remembered two months existed before their reaction saw the light of day, no longer would these writers feel they had to fire off an *immediate* response. Time would exist to read and re-read the original letter, settle down, rethink and then respond. Back in the old days fewer letters were written but each meant a great deal more than the short bursts of negativism that pummels today's message boards.

People in fandom today are too quick to react and I am sure a few might compose an email that, in hindsight, they may later regret. Sometimes being forced to ponder, wait and then respond is a positive thing.

When horror classics such as Universal's *Frankenstein* (1931) were released to the mass market on VHS cassette tape, suddenly all those rarely seen movies became less magical.

12th February, 1970.

Gary J. Svehla, Esq.,
5906, Kavon Avenue,
BALTIMORE,
Maryland, 21206,
U.S.A.

Dear Gary Svehla,

Many thanks for your letter and the enclosed magazine. I would like to compliment you and your staff on the degree of devotion that you show in your work and it is a source of great satisfaction to me that so many people throughout the world are interested, like yourself, in what is after all an essential part of the history of the cinema. I am always hoping that bigger and better films in this genre will be made in the coming years, but alas there seems to be no sign of this as yet.

You and your associates have produced a magazine which is intelligently presented and has an obvious universal appeal. I wish you every success now and in the future.

I am glad to note you approve of my appearance in the so called definitve version of "Dracula", as I do feel that I am now the only actor who has ever presented this character on the screen as the author conceived it.

I have read with interest the interview that David Soren had with me and I would say that is generally accurate and a fair representation of what I said. However, in all fairness to myself, I must protest the description "a trifle ill at ease"! I am not a particularly nervous person and I greatly enjoy meeting people as a general rule. Mr. & Mrs. Soren were no exception to that rule. I think the truth of the matter was that I was behind time for my next meeting and I must confess that I don't greatly enjoy the process of being interviewed as I can never really bring myself to believe that so many people are deeply interested in what I have to say!

Sincerely,

Christopher Lee

P.S. I am greatly impressed with the outstanding drawings of David Ludwig, he is a remarkable artist. I may well be in the market for these drawings myself. My only comment is that the picture of 'Sherlock Holmes' might confuse people if they don't appreciate that this was 'Holmes' in one of his disguises.

In the BaltiCon screening room during the 1970s ... Local Baltimore director Don Dohler (the intense man behind the projector, leaning above the bearded man) is about to screen a movie entered in the 8mm amateur film competition.

The Accessibility of Movies Makes Them Far Less Magical—

Even before VHS hit the market in the 1970s (a machine sold for around $1,000 and a blank two-hour VHS tapes cost around $25 each), fans attempted to capture televised programming memories. For instance, many of my friends owned reel-to-reel audio tape decks (not cassette but actually tape wound around a large plastic reel) and they often hooked up these tape decks to their television sets so they could record movies broadcast on TV. True, this did not allow watching the movie, but for fans of the dialogue and especially movie musical scores, this was the way to go. If *Bride of Frankenstein* was broadcast one snowy Saturday night in January, the film might not be broadcast again for 9 months to a year or longer. By playing reel-to-reel tapes, fans could capture and relive the film experience. I remember seeing *Pat Garrett and Billy the Kid*, featuring a supporting appearance and musical score by Bob Dylan. I just had to have access to the musical score so I snuck a cassette recorder into the theater, hidden inside my coat, and set it to record. The music varied in tone and volume, sometimes slightly muffled, at other times crystal clear, but since the soundtrack album was not expected to be released for quite some time, this method allowed me the opportunity to enjoy the Dylan music at home.

At times I wanted to write articles on movies not readily available for personal consumption, so I had to go to the movies or drive-in theater and actually take notes while watching it in the dark. It was impossible to copy down all the dialogue verbatim, but such viewing allowed me to get a few phrases and lines down intact. Of course getting the visuals and order of the story correct was always a challenge, but this was the only way to write detailed articles about movies before the advent of home video. I can remember how upset Sue was on one of our dates when I spent the entire evening in the car at the drive-in theater watching the movie without flinching, taking notes with my pad and pen front and center.

But in 1976 the emerging technology of the VHS audio/video recording technology arrived upon American shores and changed the world of home entertainment forever. Two-hour cassette tapes could be used to record any type of television broadcasts. Now when *Bride of Frankenstein* appeared on TV, we could record it and watch the movie anytime we desired. Pretty soon the major studios and distribution companies released professionally mastered versions of feature films to audiences at hefty prices. It was certainly cheaper to record movies at home, but the quality was generally not as good and the recorder had to accept broadcast logos and commercials. Although the improved quality of the laserdisc remained a niche product that never found mainstream acceptance, the DVD came to America in 1997 with improved resolution in both the audio and visual components. We won't even mention Blu-ray discs or digital HD streaming.

The bottom line advantage of owning movies at home is accessibility, but that magical quality of rareness and anticipation is immediately lost. When the classic *The Texas Chain Saw Massacre* arrived in 1974, the only option to watch it outside of theaters was to invest in an expensive 16mm setup that involved splicers, take-up reels, projector screens, shipping expenses, Vitafilm chemical cleaners and spare bulbs. And the cost of 16mm movies was not cheap. Purchasing discarded movies from local TV stations or worn and discarded film rental prints was considered illegal. Current movies did not arrive immediately on the marketplace, and when they did, most of the prints were copies of original prints, many produced in bathtubs and backrooms. Such "dupes" were generally of inferior quality where the color, contrast, clarity and sound were compromised.

But, if you were a true fan or, worse yet, a reviewer or historian, any means of acquiring and watching movies was accepted. One of the reasons I got involved with running the film program for

Anyone remember when a top-loading VHS video recorder cost $1,000 and was a status symbol, allowing the owner to record and watch TV shows or movies anytime desired?

conventions such as BaltiCon was the fact that films were delivered to my house and I could screen them privately before the convention started and take my notes. Let's say I wanted to do an in-depth review?of George Romero's *Night of the Living Dead* (1968). Of course I could watch the film at the drive-in or theater when the film played Baltimore. But then what? After the film left town, suppose I became fuzzy about incidents that occurred or my memory started to get sloppy? Other than 16mm and perhaps a re-release or revival house screening at a local college, I had to wait perhaps years until the movie showed up on television. Universities were the hotbeds of sponsoring innovative film festivals and theme-based screenings, but far too often the films selected were foreign art films or non-mainstream offerings. However, by the end of the 1960s horror and science fiction cinema was becoming outré enough for colleges to offer horror film festivals and related screenings.

Film criticism at that time depended upon recreating detailed plot synopses because films were infrequently screened and getting the story right became invaluable for film scholars who used the synopses as a means to jog fading memories. Film cast and crew credits were minimal since references such as the Internet Movie Database did not exist. The closest we had were thick reference books published by McFarland and Scarecrow Press where credits for horror and fantasy films were reproduced in dull but essential lists. Thank you Donald Willis and Harris Lentz (and others) for your dedication to creating such lists for the film fan and scholar.

Gary cuts the cake as Sue, in the back, prepares the glasses of bubbly for the 40th anniversary *Midnight Marquee* party held at FANEX.

Today just about every existing film is available at a moment's notice, at the push of a button (including foreign films in unedited editions). Many feature films are available on YouTube for free (the PD or public domain titles). For people who care about the tactile ownership experience, they can purchase beautifully packaged DVD and Blu-ray discs or box sets. For others who want the option of watching everything at home there is cable/satellite's VOD or Video on Demand, or, the two largest streaming services (Amazon.com and Netflix) allow movies to be passed to your television monitor digitally from that large Cloud in the sky via Wi-Fi. Other movies can be downloaded directly to your computer and watched on large monitors.

In other words, anyone willing to pay a reasonable fee can pretty much watch any film on a personal computer/tablet or home TV monitor. Movies are no longer rare or a true event. Decades ago when highly sought after movies such as *Abbott and Costello Meet Frankenstein* played on television, every neighborhood kid who loved monsters anticipated this event for a full week or even longer. Forget about the phone, the visiting relatives, walking the dog or any type of disruption (no DVRs existed to pause the action) ... if you snoozed you losed! If your mother asked you to run an errand, you missed seeing a large section of the film. And once the movie was over, we had absolutely no idea when that it might be broadcast again. Movies were rare. Movies were special. Movies were not just another common commodity.

Today anyone who wishes to watch *Abbott and Costello Meet Frankenstein* can do so anytime and anywhere. That special magic of anticipation no longer exists. Making movies accessible has been both a blessing and a curse, but the availability of movies at home is one of the most dramatic changes in horror film fandom in the past 50 years.

The Rise and Fall of the Horror Movie Convention—

When Sue wanted to bring the pages of *Midnight Marquee* to life in the mid-1980s, science fiction and comic conventions were the only regularly sponsored shows. A few horror film conventions were held in the past, but having spent so much time helping with the annual Baltimore Science Fiction Convention, it seemed time to sponsor a

Ingrid Pitt and international star Christopher Lee relaxing behind the scenes during the FANEX sponsored MONSTER RALLY weekend in 1999.

John Agar, one of the most enthusiastic and kind FANEX celebrity guests, accepts his award from Gary J. Svehla. For those early guests, it wasn't about making money signing autographs, it was all about being appreciated and remembered.

to be the major guests of honor, but problems of raising finances and agreeing to all the creative decisions caused the core group to disintegrate before the convention was finalized. Sue and I realized that we had to take the bull by the horns, so we subverted the recently renamed Horror and Fantasy Film Society (formerly the Dracula Society of Maryland) into becoming the manpower needed to run the FANEX conventions. Our first show was held at the Howard Johnson's Motor Lodge on Route 40 West; author and film historian Greg Mank was our only guest that first year, 1987. The convention reigned for 19 years, achieving its artistic pinnacle with our two expanded mega-shows held in Arlington, VA in 1999 and 2000. The first show, called MONSTER RALLY, hosted Christopher Lee in his only American convention appearance (other than a brief hour "Q&A" at a *Fangoria* show to promote *Gremlins 2*), where he debuted the American edition of his autobiography (of course published by Midnight Marquee Press). The two mega-shows were artistic triumphs but financial disasters, some of the problems caused by over-enthusiasm and over-reaching, but most of the problems resulted from the efforts of others who worked overtime to sabotage the project. But that's another story.

FANEX conventions were held with the idea that many classic horror stars and celebrities of the 1950s and 1960s horror and science fiction genre were forgotten by their fans, and we wanted to fly them to Baltimore for a party weekend to let them feel the love they instilled in Monster Kids all over the country. Our purpose was to honor them, show their movies, allow them to speak to the assembled and give them an award of appreciation. During this period of time the guests were simply happy to attend the show and be adored. Of course celebrities, who became stars because of the fans, would willingly meet and greet people and sign autographs. FANEX was a convention sponsored for fans by fans to honor the movie heroes of our youth. And all those early FANEX guests were happy to attend.

But several things happened all at once to shake things up. Sports memorabilia shows occurred where iconic athletes (granted, some of the old-timers were not well paid) charged fans to have their baseballs, footballs, jerseys, bats and bubble-gum cards autographed. Other film conventions rose in our creative wake, most noticeably the Chiller Theatre show in New Jersey, sponsored by Kevin Clement. However, his purpose was to evolve the fan

local Baltimore-sponsored classic horror film convention. The first aborted attempt was chaired by a conglomerate of close knit friends including filmmaker and publisher Don Dohler and wife Pam, fanzine publisher/bassist Charlie "Dave" Ellis and wife Natalie and Sue and Gary Svehla. The convention, to be called FANEX (for Fantasy Film Expo), lined up ultimate fan Bob Burns and 1950s director Jack Arnold

Gary J. Svehla and Susan hawking Midnight Marquee Press books and magazines in 1998, setting up at one of numerous conventions.

convention into a profit-making concept, and if he made money, his guests would most definitely need to make money as well. Borrowing the idea from the sports memorabilia shows, Chiller allowed guests to set up tables and sell their movie photos and charge for autographs. Of course the purity of FANEX became remodeled as a vibrant cash cow in the hands of other entrepreneurs. At the same time eBay was becoming a major factor in the memorabilia hobby where people were selling celebrity autographs for whatever the market would bear. Of course I am sure some autographs sold were acquired for free at shows such as FANEX and celebrities began to notice. Pretty soon the mindset was, and it made sense, why should celebrities sign posters and stills for free when the very same fans can place autographs for sale on eBay and make money?

FANEX believed in the non-profit fan experience and we maintained the policy that guests were not allowed to charge for signing autographs. Our guests respected that wish until about FANEX 10 when the writing was clearly on the wall. Pretty much all the other film conventions allowed guests to profit from their appearances (in fact retired movie stars were now acquiring agents to negotiate appearance fees and guarantees that they would be paid a minimum amount of money for the weekend) and celebrities were pretty much saying they would not attend FANEX unless they could charge and make back their expenses (even though we were flying them in, paying for their hotel rooms and covering their meals). Soon FANEX capitulated and allowed guests to charge fees for autographs. The tide had obviously turned, but FANEX was never the same.

About that point in time the entire relationship between FANEX and our guests changed radically, and for the worse. Before we were the sponsoring fans who wanted to honor the guests and demonstrate they had not been forgotten, that their fans still loved them and appreciated their professional work. For most of our celebrity guests, this was more than enough. These guests appreciated their fans and left Baltimore at the end of the weekend feeling overwhelmed and humbled. However, when guests were allowed to charge for autographs and had agents arrange their appearances, the guests began to see Sue and me as the boss/sponsor and the convention became a working get-away weekend. I will never forget seeing actor Ben Chapman (the Gill Man) talk to a young fan at a Chiller Theatre convention as he entered an elevator, telling the youngster, "Boy, you can really make a lot of money at these shows!!!" Of course, making a profit is never a sin, but it just rubbed Sue and me the wrong way to see horror film celebrities, whose careers were based entirely upon a small fan base, now profit further from this same fan base. Even if such celebrities never became rich as Hollywood mainstream stars frequently did, it never seemed right for such cinematic heroes to profit from the people who made them famous. Watching early FANEX guests bask in the glory at early shows and then comparing them to celebrities appearing later on who worked overtime to hawk their photos and sell autographs just sucked all the fun out of the FANEX experience for Sue and me. Somehow it just did not sit well watching our personal heroes milk that final dollar from their fans. When Sue and I began FANEX, we imagined the stars being above such monetary lust, but as the convention *hobby* became the convention *business*, we learned differently.

In 1957 Gary saw his first horror movie, The Monster That Challenged the World, at The Earle Theater. Thirty years later The Earle was a porno theater. And today, it has been transformed once again into a church (using the same building).

Monsters on the Loose from The 1950s

captured by Robert Knox

Part Two
The Midnight Marquee Legacy

Forrest J Ackerman, surrounded by Susan and Gary J. Svehla, receives the Laemmle Award.

Early Tales of Gore Creatures

by David Metzler

Preliminary drawings of Dave Metzler's art for the very first issues of Gore Creatures

Recently I received an email from my old pal Gary Svehla. He asked me to write something about the early days of *Gore Creatures/Midnight Marquee* and the production of our first epic monster movie. It's my pleasure to recall those idyllic times.

As I recall I first met Gary on the school bus when we were in the first grade. He was a quiet kid, didn't say much. Naturally I sat next to him. I think there were other seats vacant, but perhaps not. That's just how I am. And as I write this, I realize our meeting was 57 years ago. Has it *really* been that long?

Eventually we learned that we lived less than three blocks apart and visiting Gary became part of my routine. Early on I discovered that Gary was a big comics collector. And he loved science fiction and monster movies. He was really impressed with a Japanese movie he recently saw called *The Mysterians*. So we rigged a sliding board next to a huge blooming cherry tree, and that became our spaceship, complete with a ladder to climb aboard. Add one Steve Canyon jet helmet and one Colonel McCauley space helmet ($2.98 at Read's Drugstore) and we had everything needed to fight off invading aliens. It was only three years ago that I finally saw the Toho space opera that so influenced Gary all those years ago. So Gary directed all of our play-acting. I had no idea what I was doing but had a good time doing it. I was Hobbes acting in Calvin's plots.

Eventually Gary began to focus specifically on monsters, but how and why that occurred is Gary's tale to tell.

Around that same time, my dad started a business venture involving the transformation of a waterfront property into a marina. He actually had a pier built that was 500 feet long. Every summer my family would move down to the beach to pitch in. I am sure, motor mouth that I was, that Gary and I talked about the place, but the next part of the story has always eluded me. I was wandering the grounds, about three and a half acres, when I realized I saw Gary's dad (Mr. Dick) working on his small runabout. Gary's dad bought a boat and decided to dock it at my dad's place. This marina, Holly Beach, was 10 miles from home and hundreds of similar tiny marinas operated between Baltimore and Annapolis. To this day I am amazed that out of all the possible marinas in the area, Mr.. Dick found Holly Beach.

On many summer evenings Mr. Dick would arrive after work and go fishing or cruising along the Chesapeake Bay. And eventually Gary appeared—once again I have no idea of how or why—and we would walk the grounds and talk while his dad fished. As best as I can recollect, Gary and I were sitting on an ancient picnic table and talking about monster movies. You expected Tolstoy? We both knew Gary's dad owned a 8mm camera. And my dad owned a 10-acre lot across the road from the marina. A field was mowed and became a small baseball diamond, but most of the

The very same Frankenstein Monster mask purchased from the back pages of *Famous Monsters* and worn in our 8mm classic, *Frankenstein Vs. The Wolf Man*.

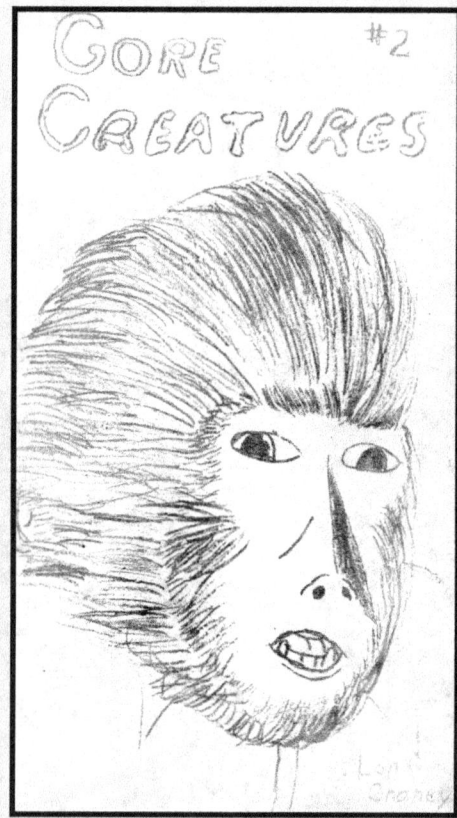

The Metzler cover of GC #2 that was used for most of the copies of issue #1.

Metzler and Svehla made the Svehla backyard cherry tree into a rocket ship manned by two little boys wearing the Col. McCauley and Steve Canyon helmets.

property was wooded and wild. Our city homes were not so much different from the neighborhood in the film *A Christmas Story*, and while safe and warm, not much there could be substituted for a movie set. And an idea was born—let's buy some monster masks from the back pages of *Famous Monsters* and film a movie using the woods for outdoor shots and Gary's unfinished basement as the mad lab. Gary wrote the story, of course. It was going to be a tale of Frankenstein's Monster confronting another classic Universal monster, this time the Wolf Man. Completely original! But we all know the template had been cemented decades ago.

A year in the making! We would tramp through the woods. Our family dog thought it was great fun and he would follow along, completely oblivious to our efforts to keep him out of the shots. So there are random moments in the film when a dog just walks into the field of view. Frankenstein's dog! Of course!

Having had a life-long extreme allergy to poison ivy, poison oak and sumac, I would catch a rash every time we filmed. Sometimes the position of the rash would change slightly over the course of filming. Cue cards provided narration—Magic Marker on white cardboard. No expense was spared. We had not learned stop motion effects so the Wolf Man's transition, so to say, was rather abrupt—from a werewolf rubber mask to a kid who could not stop grinning, not even for a two-second shot. I never was much of an actor. Gary played two roles. Who could have guessed the same actor played both the doctor and the Monster (a third friend, athletic Keith Vinroe, played the Monster for action or stunt sequences, such as the climactic fight to the death).

All good things must end and the film was completed. A lot of fanfare occurred. But since this was the era before the days of esteem building, I heard lots of, "Oh, that's my idiot brother. He makes monster movies."

And I believe it was in 1962 but, it could have been 1963, that I was visiting Gary one afternoon and we spent the afternoon scrutinizing Forrest Ackerman's *Famous Monsters of Filmland*. The feature articles had been totally digested hours before and we ended reading the classified ads. There just was not enough of *FM* to go around. One ad appealed to us and we decided to buy the product—what is called a fanzine today. The magazine sounded great in the ad. The big day arrived when the package arrived. It was always special for me to get something in the mail. Gary called me and told me of its arrival.

I was really excited when I arrived, but then I saw … it. Time has dimmed my memory but I recall a two-page piece of drivel. It was truly pathetic. And we paid good kid money for it!

And that was the Eureka moment—Gary and I looked at one another and said simultaneously—I could do better than that! And that is how *Gore Creatures* was born.

As anyone anywhere who starts something new knows, use what we have. The only mechanical method of reproduction that Gary or I knew was a typewriter and carbon paper. So Gary handwrote *Gore Creatures* issue 1 and I typed it out. I also hand inked a solid black bat for the cover (none of these covers exist today and Gary does not even remember them). I could

This Teenage Werewolf mask became our Wolf Man in the horror movie filmed at Holly Beach.

manage three or possibly four pages from each carbon. I think the first issue was possibly eight or 10 pages long and we produced perhaps 20 copies. I am guessing. It was tough work considering Baltimore suffered through another hot August and no air conditioning existed at my house. That just about killed my enthusiasm.

But Mr. Dick, our in-house high-tech guy and chief *rah-rah* VP, came to the rescue. Over the next years, Mr. Dick found a succeeding series of technical improvements beginning with a super basic method of reproduction involving purple ink, and soon that changed to mimeograph and finally culminated in professional offset printing. *GC* kept getting better and better. My role evolved to artist. Eventually in school I took more than 30 credits in art. But at that time, I was 12 years old or so. I was not exactly Duerer or Picasso. I did my best to render Mr. Hyde and various other monsters, but eventually Gary was approached by an out-of-towner named Dave Ludwig. His craft was light years ahead of mine. I never met him and never learned his age difference (Gary tells me Ludwig was five years or so older than we were). But he seemed to be a nice guy and he kept producing a lot of really top-notch artwork. I continued to contribute the occasional piece, slowing down as school and work demanded their due.

I never did make it in art. But I still dabble. I have learned that it is not the end of the world to learn you are not as good as you thought you once were. It is the end only if you stop trying. I followed my own path and made my way in the world (as a C.P.A., who runs his own accounting firm). Life is good.

Gary kept plugging away at *GC/MidMar*. He is a true Energizer bunny. He has created his own monument to himself. Gary is truly a unique guy. He and I have traveled different paths over the decades, but we are still pals. And I hope we are still pals for another 50 years.

Midnight Marquee Memories

by Gary J. Svehla

Reflecting back upon those 50 wonderful years of publishing *Gore Creatures/Midnight Marquee*, I wanted to come up with those shining, defining moments in a lifetime of being an obsessed horror movie fan, to recall those memories that spark the brightest flame. Of course these pivotal reflections are not in any type of order, but they are moments (some lasted one brief day but others lasted much longer) that branded me as a lifelong horror and monster movie lover. Even if the name, dates and locations change, I think that all baby boomers can relate to the following universal experiences.

The Night I saw My First Horror Movie (1957)

On that fated night I accompanied my brother Dickie (I was 7 and he was 16) and father Richard to go, on a school night, to the neighborhood Earle Theater to see *Bop Girl Goes Calypso* (my father and brother were into music) and second feature *The Monster That Challenged the World*. I was never the same. At such an impressionable age, I never before experienced slowly mounted cinematic fright, the type created by a manipulative director who played the audience like a violin. I did not know what to expect. But I still remember fidgeting in my theater seat, closing my eyes yet forcing myself to open them a quick second or so, darting my eyes left and right of the center of the screen. I held my fingers up to my eyes, spreading my fingers so I could sneak-peek, protecting myself if the sequence became too intense. When the giant sea mollusk suddenly appeared after a slow buildup, I jumped and spilled my popcorn. I was frightened out of my wits, but at the same time I felt energized and thrilled. When the movie eventually returned to the part where we first entered (in those days patrons went to a show and saw movies from

Our neighborhood theater *The Earle*, back in 1959 (notice the streetcar passing by), two years after Gary first saw *The Monster That Challenged the World*.

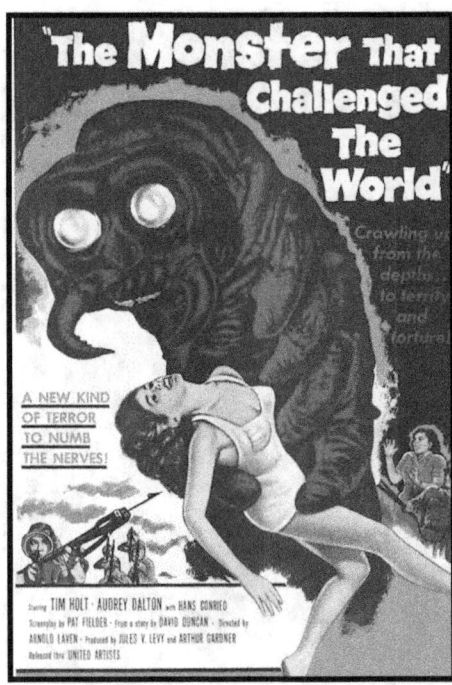

the beginning, middle or ending and could remain as long as they wanted), I wanted to sit through the movie again. Of course school and work arrived early the next morning so my father had to get me home, but I just knew I wanted to experience that adrenalin rush again and again. While *The Monster That Challenged The World* was not the greatest creature feature ever made, it was the movie that hooked me and made me a horror movie fan forever. I never imagined a giant mutated mollusk from the Salton Sea could be so terrifying.

The Night I Saw My Favorite Horror Movie of All Time

Accompanying my father Richard one evening to the Colony Theater in Parkville (actually not far from where I currently live, but the theater is now a VFW hall), we saw *Horror of Dracula* upon its initial theatrical release in the summer of 1958. "Who will be his bride tonight" the newspaper movie ads asked, and in one glorious evening I was introduced to Hammer films, Christopher Lee, Peter Cushing and dazzling Technicolor. What a life-altering experience. Because I became so fearful once my father got me home, vomiting in my sleep during the night, my mother Ann banned me from watching horror films in theaters ever again. Fortunately, one year later I was allowed, on a trial basis, to return to the movies to get scared out of my wits once again. But I remember the summer after I first experienced *Horror of Dracula*. I would prance around the backyard wearing a white sheet that served as my regal cape, spreading my arms wide, making a long wooden bench from the picnic table my coffin, where I would lie with arms folded across my cross during hot afternoons. Dracula was my hero and horror movies my passion. I can only imagine what the neighbors must have thought.

One Year Later, The Day I Was Allowed to See Horror Movies Again

I knew I could not muck it up this time. No vomiting, no night sweats, no screaming, no tossing and turning. Absolutely no nightmares! My mother was allowing me, one sunny Sunday afternoon in March or April 1959, to once again go to the movies and watch a scary horror movie. And this was a special occasion. Our neighbors on Kavon Avenue were the Penn family, a wonderful family of Baptists who were the kindest of people. My mother Ann and Margaret Penn were more than neighbors, they were close friends. Daughter Elaine Penn was four years older than me (I was 9 at the time) and she asked me if I wanted to go on the streetcar with her to the Vilma Theater to see *House On Haunted Hill*, a movie where she heard a skeleton flies out into the audience. Perhaps her friends did not enjoy scary movies or perhaps she was just being nice, but I accepted pronto. Boy, any chance to see another creepy movie was just fine with me. My mother made me dress up extra fancy with a spiffy hat and sports jacket, since my mother wanted me to learn to show respect for my "date." All I can remember is being delightfully scared out of my seat several times, and when the glory that was Emergo occurred, and a skeleton actually did fly over the heads

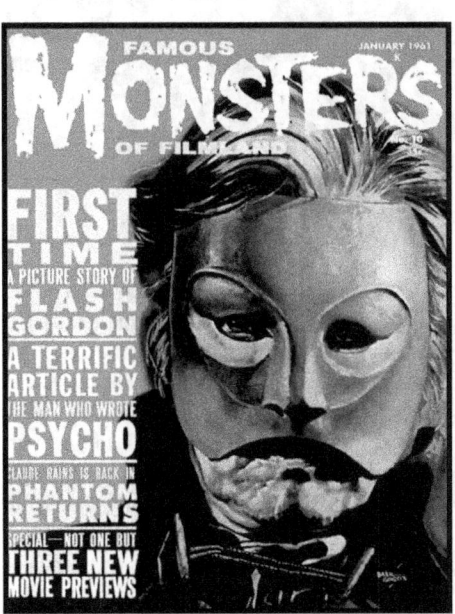

Famous Monsters of Filmland #10, the very first issue of a monster magazine I ever saw.

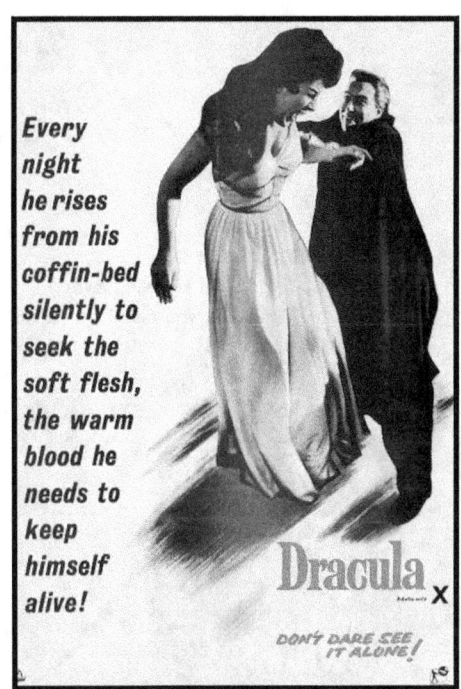

A British ad for *Dracula*, released in the U.S.A. as *Horror of Dracula*.

of the audience, I knew I would be okay. No screams that night, no nightmares, no sickness ... at 9 years old I was old enough for the world of horror. And to this day I still thank Elaine Penn for convincing my mother to allow me to once again see the type of movie I most enjoyed.

The Day I Saw My Very First Monster Movie Magazine

One day on the walk to school in 1961 one of the guys had something that I never saw before, a copy of the just published issue of *Famous Monsters of Filmland*. It was the Claude Rains cover, issue #10. My jaw dropped as I asked to leaf through the pages, seeing for the first time every monster passion that was contained in my heart. What *Playboy* and the mysteries of the naked female form meant for most young males, this issue of *Famous Monsters* meant to me. Loving horror films and wanting to learn more about the classics, here, in my hands, was the Bible, the answer to all my prayers. After school I asked my mother if I could walk up to the drug store on Belair Road that had a large magazine rack and a very cosmopolitan selection of periodicals and comics. There I found the same issue of *Famous Monsters* and plunked my money down and walked home, a smile on my face. At this young age of 11, it took me a while to know that a magazine published quarterly meant it came out every three months or that bi-monthly meant one issue every two months. So when it was about time for a new issue to arrive, I frantically

A publicity photo that emphasizes the "Emergo" gimmick for *House on Haunted Hill*.

walked to my drug store newsstand to hope and pray that the new issue was available. Often just the anticipation that I might be returning with an issue of *Horror Monsters* or *Mad Movies*, let alone *Famous Monsters*, *Modern Monsters*, *Fantastic Monsters* or *Castle of Frankenstein*, was better than buying and reading the issue itself. Mostly *Famous Monsters* and *Castle of Frankenstein* never disappointed, but some of the inferior periodicals sometimes left me wishing for more. Such disappointments pushed me to the idea that if I wanted to read a truly masterful classic horror movie publication, I just may have to write and publish it myself.

The Day I Purchased My Very First Horror Movie Poster

In the winter of 1963, shortly after John F. Kennedy's assassination, I was checking out the "Haunt Ad" section in the back of *Famous Monsters* and saw an ad by some character named Bill Obaggy, who sold original movie posters. That ad and a flyer I recently received in the mail from Dalton Film Exchange, another company that sold movie posters, prompted me to start a new hobby. I now wanted to collect and display horror movie posters in my bedroom, just like the ones I saw at the theaters. To me owning a movie poster from a film I saw in the theaters such as *House on Haunted Hill* and *Black Sunday* meant as much to me as the Universal classics of old that I saw on late night TV. So for my first order I bought an insert (a standard 14 by 36 inch poster … I had a preference for that size, printed on heavier card stock) from *Return of Dracula* and another original insert from Universal's 1943 *Ghost of Frankenstein*. I probably had the opportunity to purchase more of the classic Universals, but I opted mostly for the newer American International and Hammer releases, as these were the movies I had seen recently in theaters. So, you might ask, what was the price for both of these treasures? Well, they cost $3 to $4 each with $1.50 for shipping. Universal's *Ghost of Frankenstein* featured a huge close-up of Lon Chaney, Jr.'s stoic face as the Monster, and I would constantly stare at the image while lying on my bed. If I were wiser and had the ability to forecast the future, I would have asked my father to stop saving for my college fund and instead use all his disposable cash to invest in Universal horror movie posters. I still managed to amass a sizeable collection, many posters of which I still own to this day (including that poster from *Ghost of Frankenstein*, on today's market worth roughly $5,000 to $8,000). *Return of Dracula*, well, I wasn't quite as lucky with its investment value. But to me owning the poster and lobby cards (11 by 14 inch colorized photos embellished with border art, created as sets of eight, including

Another publicity photo showing the Emergo skeleton in action overhead theater patrons during a showing of *House on Haunted Hill*.

a title card that was actually a mini-poster) meant more to me than watching the movie. Just having posters to thumbtack on my bedroom wall was thrilling and allowed me to create a monster den like no other.

The Day I First Met the Father of Horror Film Fandom, Forrest J Ackerman

An unusually "suited" Gary Svehla points to his latest movie poster of *Ghost of Frankenstein*, right beside the insert poster to *Horror of Dracula*.

My father and I attended NyCon3, the 25th World Science Fiction Convention in New York City, in late August 1967. Some of the guests in attendance included Robert Silverberg, Harlan Ellison, Fred Pohl, Roger Zelazny, Michael Moorcock, Isaac Asimov, Fritz Leiber and Lester del Rey. But the person that I met there for the first time was none other than Forrest J Ackerman, who was the dean of horror film fandom, the editor of *Famous Monsters of Filmland* and *Spacemen* and the man who inspired me to create my fanzine *Gore Creatures*. Being shy, but then so was Forry, it took me a while to build up the courage to approach him, introduce myself (he bought my very first copy of issue #1 of *Gore Creatures*) and give him a copy of my latest issue. We of course posed for photos, with Forry always cuddling the latest issue of *Famous Monsters*. His running gag was always to hold both magazines for posed photos, his and mine, but he always was sure to hold *Famous Monsters* a little higher or on top of the others. It wasn't arrogance or a power trip; Ackerman was simply pulling a little boy's prank, with devilish glee, carrying out the supreme gesture of one-upmanship. But meeting Forry for the first time was like journeying to Mecca. NyCon3 may have been the World Science Fiction Convention, but for me, it was a shrine to horror film fandom with the editor of *Famous Monsters* as special guest.

The Day-by-Day Ritual of Waiting for the Mail

This ritualistic occurrence was a constant during summer vacation (and beyond) between the ages of roughly 11 and 17. Summer was a time of rest, spending time with friends and family, writing and printing the new issues—but here it comes—it was mainly a time of eager anticipation for the mailman to arrive. The mailman arrived within a two-hour window, and I generally sat out on the front porch (right outside my bedroom) or I stayed within the bedroom and watched and waited for his appearance. He always started the long trek on Kavon Avenue directly across the street, walking the entire way down our long block before crossing over and making his way back to our house (second house from the end). Generally, I was awaiting a package of 8-by-10 glossy photos from Movie Star News, a poster to arrive from Dalton Film Exchange or the latest Castle super 8mm condensation of a Universal classic such as *Bride of Frankenstein* or *Frankenstein Meets the Wolf Man* to arrive from *Famous Monsters*' Captain Company (or perhaps this week it may have been a record album such as *Themes From Horror Movies* or *Lights Out* or perhaps Forry Ackerman's *Music for Robots*). But just

One of the truncated Castle Films 8mm versions of Universal's *Frankenstein Meets the Wolf Man* that boomers loved to watch.

50th Anniversary Issue [1963-2013]

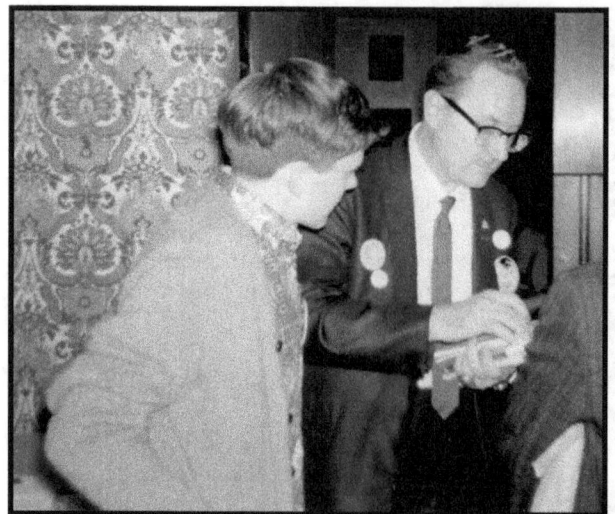

Above: At NyCon3 *Gore Creatures* columinist Robert Hancock meets Forry Ackerman and gets an autograph as Gary Svehla takes the photo; Right: A page of delicious "monster" ads from the back pages of *Mad Monsters*.

more!" In this way if the wind blew, it would not throw off reception until after the movie was over. Remember, in those non-digital days, receiving a broadcast signal in Baltimore from Washington was rough going, and the best reception was always with ghost images and "snow" with a less than stellar image. But this was how I first encountered *Bride of Frankenstein*, and, even with less than perfect picture quality, I knew I had watched a classic. My little mind was blown.

The Pleasure of Meeting Long Distance Friends

Before the FANEX conventions, before we brought a community of authors, historians, fans and celebrities together, there existed the rare face-to-face meeting with people involved with the magazine who traveled across the U.S.A. to meet me (or vice versa). One of my columnists and publishing buddies was Robert Hancock, a guy my age who lived in Roosevelt, New York and published the fanzine *Mystification*. After corresponding via the mail and cassette tapes (oral letters, so to speak, embellished with music), we finally meet several times at the New York City science fiction conventions. I remember eagerly anticipating the arrival of some of these packages (hey, it might even be one of my favorite fanzines such as *Horrors of the Screen*) made my day. And boy, if the mailman did not bring my hoped for bounty, I was dreary and depressed for the rest of the day. Literally, all my childhood days were built around waiting for the mailman and praying that he would bring me a package of unlimited joy. I can remember my mother telling me, "Gary, it's okay, your package will probably arrive tomorrow." But at that age tomorrow seemed so far away.

The Joy of Watching Horror Movies on Saturday Nights (thanks Mom!)

It was Saturday night and of course a horror movie would be shown on late-night television. Basically Baltimore channels did not show many monster movies; instead, it was the Washington, D.C. stations, channels 5 and 9, which featured late-night horrors. I was too young to stay up late in 1957 to watch the debut of *Shock Theater!*; instead I came on board around 1961 or 1962. Washington's Channel 5 had its *Chiller Theater* program of classic and (mostly) not so classic horror movies. But channel 9 broadcast the Universals, Val Lewtons and older stuff that I most admired. It was always time, about 15 minutes before broadcast (at alternating times between midnight and 1 a.m.), to ask my mother to don her robe and coat and venture out back to adjust our antennae which was mounted, not on our roof, but in our backyard, making it easy for mothers to "turn it a little bit more to the left, no, no, a little bit more; no, turn it back to the right, okay, just a little

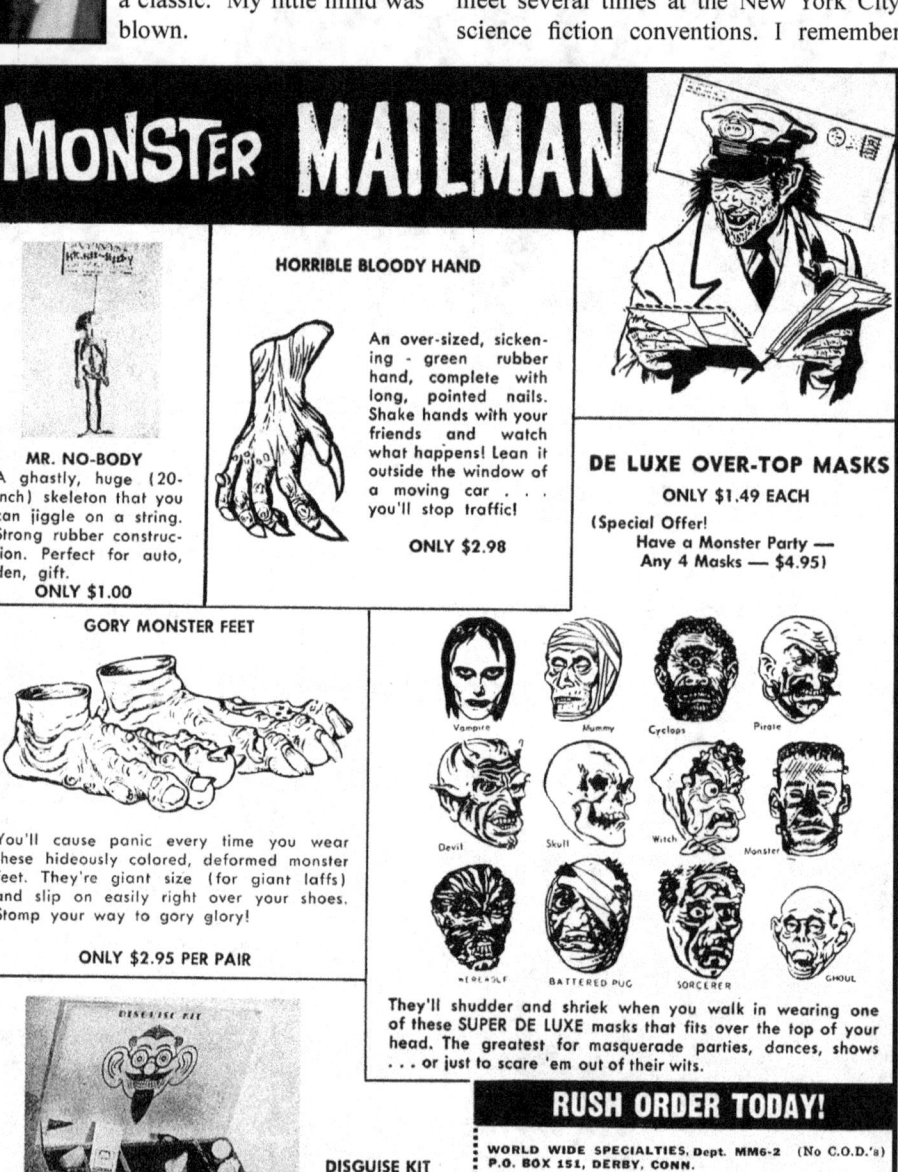

those times where Rob took me on a tour of his NYC, always telling me the great places to get the best burgers and restaurants that sold orange juice that was not sugared up and watered down. He took me to the location where the latest Clint Eastwood movie was filmed (*Coogan's Bluff* I believe). We even saw *A Clockwork Orange* together when it was first released.

At these conventions I also met Gene Klein, who published *Cosmo Stiletto*, another fanzine of merit. Klein, who would soon change his name to Gene Simmons and become a rock 'n' roll icon, first fronting the band Wicked Lester and soon thereafter KISS, was a person who campaigned that fanzines should be given away for free, that publishers should not be greedy and charge money for them.

Early on in the early seventies David Soren and his lovely wife Noel visited me once or twice and we bravely ventured into downtown Baltimore to attend mostly all-black theaters to see blaxploitation movies such as *Blacula* and others. Dr. Soren became one of the most renowned archaeologists of his time and a giant in his field (he is also the producer of many documentaries for various cable TV channels), but he continues to teach film courses at the University of Arizona, his home base for decades. Midnight Marquee Press provides most of the textbooks for his classes.

Dennis Cunningham, renowned editor and publisher of the underground comic oriented *Weirdom*, came to visit me in October 1969, traveling all the way from San Jose, CA. Together we ventured down to Baltimore's Civic Center to see a live concert that evening, Iron Butterfly (of course they played *In-A-Gadda-Da-Vida*), but the opening act Spirit owned the night by providing the best performance and songs of the evening (anyone remember *Nature's Way*?).

I will never forget that one of our enthusiastic custumers from Japan came to visit me one Saturday afternoon. I don't even remember his name. While he did not speak English very well, he was extremely polite and bowed a great deal and enjoyed seeing my collection of monster goodies. He did not stop smiling during the entire visit.

One day I even got a phone call in 1968 from two strangers my own age, Charlie "Dave" Ellis and Bill George, two enthusiastic locals who discovered my magazine and decided to simply organize a meeting. While Bill George went on to become editor of *Femmes Fatales* magazine, working for Frederick S. Clarke, Charlie Ellis (who worked on many Don Dohler films) remains a close friend. He and his wonderful wife Natalie and their kids are very special people to both Sue and me.

Simply remembering all the people we met who wrote for us—even a letter—or the fans who purchased the magazine was always very special.

The Legacy of George Stover's 16mm Shrine

What is Baltimore's oldest shrine to classic horror movies? I would say George Stover's basement (or living room) 16mm home theater. I first met Stover at a New York science fiction convention around 1967, learning that we both lived 20 minutes away from one another. The following year we accidentally met once again at Baltimore's Town Theater at the Cinerama Roadshow premier of *2001: A Space Odyssey*, where star Keir Dullea was special guest. We finally decided to get together. George invited me to his parents' Towson suburban home to watch 16mm features and shorts in his basement theater (where he served drinks in little round glasses with big hunks of ice). Other film-obsessed friends attended the screenings as well. And before long a Baltimore tradition was born. Over 40 years later I still spend many Thursday evenings traveling to George's home to watch 16mm on a small beaded screen with squeaking metal reels rubbing against celluloid, where the roar of the projector motor threatens to drown out dialogue. Hell, in the world of digital perfection where today's state-of-the-art home theaters blow analog and one-channel 16mm projection audio out of the water, experiencing such an antique is akin to

Bill George, future editor of *Femmes Fatales*, points as Charlie "Dave" Ellis pokes his head through the window.

During summers, the theater moved outdoors. Left to right: Ralph Kirchoff, Polly Lynn and Gary Svehla watch a movie.

Gary Svehla chats with Forry Ackerman in George Stover's 16mm basement theater. Forry was in Baltimore attending a FANEX show at the time.

playing old 78s on turntables connected to analog tube amplifiers. Something remains quite pure about the experience of seeing celluloid projected in a communal setting. Besides, where else can one view 16mm television programs such as *Amos 'n' Andy, Beulah, Mr. Wizard, The Pendulum* (a British anthology crime series that featured a gaunt Christopher Lee as special guest in 1955) and *Dick Tracy* (the Ralph Byrd TV series, not the serial or features)? George, who formerly tried to own as many 16mm feature films as possible, today collects feature films and mainly early TV shows not available on home video, concentrating on rare and unavailable programming. Of course lots of what he collects fits into the horror and science fiction genre, but there's something to be said about watching obsessive Warner Bros. TV-series fan Barry Murphy stand at attention and salute the Warner Bros. logo at the beginning of a *Lawman* or a *77 Sunset Strip* episode. In Stover's home theater we all have something to salute and remember every week. Unfortunately, over the course of four decades friends have come and gone, several esteemed attendees have died (R.I.P. Bernie O'Hare, Don Leifert, Rick Neff) and new cliques of friends replace the old, sometimes because people simply grow tired of the weekly commitment. But for those of us Baltimore boys (although a few women such as Leanna Chamish attend) who truly enjoy the camaraderie beneath the afterglow of the projector bulb, a night at Stover's is a rocketship back to the past and one shared amid the laughter of a lifelong friendship.

George Stover, in his 16mm theater, April 14, 1963

The Daddy-O's Go To The Movies

What is Baltimore's newest shirine to classic horror movies? I would say Gary Svehla's Guru Bijoux or Charlie Wittig's Charles Theater East, both 1080p HD home theaters. Even though most agree 16mm is wonderful once in a while, for pure cinematic experience nothing beats a 1080p (Well, 4k is right around the corner, right?) 7-channel audio digital home theater presentation on a 120-inch screen (that's nine feet wide). Whether we are watching Blu-ray restorations of the classics such as *Dracula* or *Frankenstein*, or viewing more current demonstration quality Blu-rays such as *Prometheus, Ben-Hur* (beautifully restored) or *Hugo*, the experience of watching theatrical movies at home that look and sound just as good as they do in actual theaters is cause to celebrate. And even more important than the technical specs and presentation are the life-long friendships nurtured over a decade of band-ing together, screening two features, going out for dinner, etc. The memoires just keep going on and on: Vince Dileonardi getting one last orange soda before he falls into the swimming pool, Bill Littman's rage when we premiered the Blu-ray version of *King Kong* (1933) and I accidentally pushed the wrong icon and started playing Peter Jackson's recreation of the spider sequence to Bill's vocal screams of outrage, Tom Proveaux's happy place corner seat cuddling with our dogs Buddy and Lambchop, John "Bags" Weber's constant hauling of sacks of memorabilia over to the house to share with the assembled, Charlie Wittig's constant stream of various comic asides to augment the movie experience and Buddy (our dog) barking at the absolute worst time as Bill puts his fingers in his ears. The movies just become the excuse for friends to gather, and the 1080p theater becomes the perfect man-cave to frame such gatherings.

Mr. Robert T. Marhenke's Movie Shop: A Communal Hangout

Spending a Saturday afternoon at Marhenke's Movie Shop near downtown Baltimore (on Wolfe Street near Monument) was stepping back in time. Mr. Robert T. Marhenke, former theater manager, was a true Baltimore character. Referred to in the *Baltimore Sun* as a "political gadfly" and the person who sparred most frequently with The State Board of Motion Picture Censors, Marhenke was known for drawing scathing political cartoons and distributing them around Baltimore. When he managed a Baltimore movie theater during the 1940s, he screened a movie clip at the end of the program warning patrons to be aware of a "speed trap" located on North Point Road approaching the bridge on Route 40 and was threatened with arrest for daring to tip off his patrons. But now retired, getting older and crankier, still as feisty as ever, the cigar-chomping Marhenke, towering above all of us, owned a shit hole shop that sold lobby cards, posters and even rented rare (but splicy and well-worn) 16mm prints to the public (as a small-time distributor, he traded as Cinema Films and all his prints were stored in the shop's basement). The store was open only to the public on Saturdays, but it became a hotbed of activity around 1970 when everyone in Baltimore who loved movies (this is how I met close friends Rick and Monica Neff) congregated at the shop to shoot the breeze and get into classic arguments with "The Chief" Mr. Marhenke (not good with remembering names, Marhenke called everyone "chief"). But Marhenke was never a one-man band, as he brought along his bevy of Baltimore underlings. First there was "The Sarge," Marhenke's right-hand man, meaning he was the guy who always asked, "Where do you want it Mar-hank … What, I put them there, Mar-hank … No, we never had that one, Mar-hank … What kind of sandwich did you want again? Mar-hank, I'm going to need some money," etc. Besides being the grunt (the Sarge was the Sarge, but "Mar-hank" was the General), the Sarge was filled with wonderful stories that he told in a rapid-fire hiccupping manner where the words poured out of his mouth like lava overflowing a volcano. Another mysterious and almost non-verbal member of the troupe was gray-bearded Dantini the Magnificent

Robert T. Marhenke, in a photo courtesy of the *Baltimore Sun*, holds a movie poster and looks for a 35mm movie.

("He Knew Houdini!" always appeared on his promotional posters), the elderly but famous Baltimore magician who formerly dazzled audiences at local hangouts such as the Peabody Bookshop and Beer Stube. Marhenke would constantly tease Dantini, but Dantini appreciated all the attention. I was one of the closest of the movie gang to Mr. Marhenke because teaching buddy Wayne Shipley and I rented 16mm films from him to stock all the classes in Anne Arundel County Schools that were teaching either "The Art of the Motion Picture" (for the honor students) or "The World of Movies" (for everyone else), and he saw Shipley and me as a source of steady income. Once in a while Marhenke would simply find something rare under mounds of dusty piles of posters long forgotten. His tack was to show the piece off and state he would never sell the item, that it meant too much to him. Soon someone would approach me, off to the side, and ask, "Do you think Marhenke would sell the piece for this or that amount?" I typically said, well, ask him. Of course he always said no, that piece was too valuable. I said, "I think I know a way to get him to sell." Perhaps in those salad days the rare piece was worth $200, but I told the third party here is how we will play it. The next week I took Marhenke aside with the third party and said, this guy is serious about buying the poster. Marhenke would protest and refuse to discuss it. I nodded to the guy, who passed me a wad of 20-dollar bills. I said, "Mr. Marhenke, look here." I plopped

The Svehla Guru Bijoux—back row (left to right): Vince DiLeonardi, Tom Proveaux; front row (left to right): movie hound Buddy, Charlie Wittig and Bill Littman

Gary Svehla (center) speaks to fans at BaltiCon in the 16mm movie room between features. Noted science fiction author (on Gary's immediate right) Samuel R. Dulaney joins in.

down one 20 dollar bill, then another and finally *another*. I said, "Mr. Marhenke, this guy has 60 bucks *cash*. Look" and I plopped down another 20, making it $80. Marhenke, getting more interested, keep saying, sorry, I just don't want to sell it, no way, I won't sell. By the time I smacked down 5 or 6 twenties, Marhenke, without missing a beat, without changing his expression, went from saying "I don't want to sell the poster" to "Chief, SOLD!!!!!!!!!!!!!!!!!!! The poster is yours!" The old poop would always say he would not sell, but if you put the cash money on the table, he caved *every* single time. The only poster (which I wanted as trade bait for horror movie material) he would not let go was a one-sheet original from *Hell's Angels* (1930), starring his favorite star Jean Harlow. The poster never made it to the shop, but was mounted on a door with thumbtacks in the basement of his home. I could have easily turned that piece around for some pretty sweet classic horror paper. Eventually Marhenke's health failed and he had to abandon the shop, eventually dying from the complications of diabetes (he lost a leg to the disease and developed cataracts). Near the end his grandson helped him along and it was very evident that the grandson would inherit the poster and film collection, or what was left of it. But going down to Marhenke's shop on a Saturday was the highlight of the week, where the small gathering met to dicker over poster deals, discuss the latest new theatrical films and just watch the show with the Chief badgering the poor underdog Sarge. They were true Baltimore characters, and watching that generation fade away was akin to watching the passing of the old Baltimore neighborhood theaters and the time when theater managers were true independents, colorful characters from Baltimore's past.

Running BaltiCon's Film Program, or, Sue Svehla Notices That Flashing Blur Buzz Past

I ran the film program (sometimes along with Charlie "Dave" Ellis and the late Don Dohler) at BaltiCon (the Baltimore Science Fiction Society's annual convention) for over a decade. During the 1970s until the early 1980s, I organized and projected the 16mm film program at BaltiCon, which ran Easter weekend at the Hunt Valley Inn, just north of Baltimore. During this time DVD did not exist and VHS was actually just getting started. If anyone wanted to watch classic and current movies, 16mm rental was the only way to go, and at the time the BaltiCon 16mm screening room was huge, one large ballroom at Hunt Valley Inn, because the movies really packed them in. Since I was virtually trapped for 2 ½ days and nights projecting, I soon learned to move one of the hotel's lobby overstuffed easy chairs in back of the projector so I could sit and watch movies in comfort. This is how my future wife Sue Miller got to know who I was. The movies were generally stored in my hotel room and I had no more than 15 to 30 minutes between features to unload the reels, package them up, rush rapidly and carry the projected films back to my hotel room and run back down with the next two features and shorts to be projected. Sue remembers me during those frantic times as the guy rushing by carrying the packages of movies at breakneck speed in and out of the movie room, through the crowded hallways, waltzing to the elevators and repeating the process several times a day. Being young, energetic and having the power to select and schedule the movies (with the approval of the club's board) was a special treat. Once in a while I had to deal with blown projector bulbs and speakers that distorted or cut out all together. But the world of analog projection was fraught with bad cabling, troublesome speakers and projectors that sometimes caused sprocket hole damage. Ultimately the film program's huge success (s.f. types call it "media") was my undoing. The film program was one-upping the literary focus of the convention and tying up too much function space, so the club president Sue Wheeler told me that I was being relieved of my duties and that another film geek, Mark Owens, would be running the film program the following year. In other words, they no longer had the luxury of devoting that much function space to the world of movies, so they turned the program over to Owens, who had a far more esoteric and less

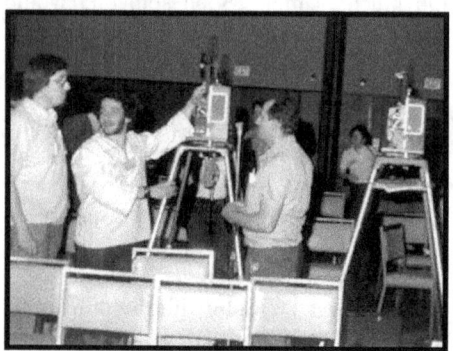

Gary Svehla (left) speaks to Larry Reichman (a *Gore Creatures* columnist and friend) and onlooker in the BaltiCon movie room.

Gary Svehla and personal hero John Agar bond at FANEX.

At The Monster Rally Convention in 1999—Gary and Susan pose with Laemmle Award-winning Christopher Lee, with wife Brigit.

mainstream concept of what films to show. Within a few years movies were relegated to a dark nook in the corner hallway after being downsized from a small function room. But my vision was clear. At first I was insulted and felt my firing was a slap in the face, but then I appreciated it as the kick out of the womb that I needed. Deciding that it was time for Baltimore to sponsor its own horror and science fiction film convention (mainly through the motivation and creativity of my by then wife Sue), my firing from BaltiCon lead to the creation of FANEX, the ultimate horror film convention that reigned strong for 19 years. If it were not for my apprenticeship at BaltiCon, most likely FANEX would never have been born. What hurt at the time became a blessing.

Making It Real: FANEX (thanks Sue!)

Sue and I hope to publish a FANEX history in 2014 recounting all the wonderful memories that occurred over 19 years, so we will need to save most of these reflections for that book. But I just had to mention a few of the wonderful celebrities I met at the shows that left long-lasting impressions. Too many stars and innovators attended the show for me to list here. But meeting John Agar was, believe it or not, one of the greatest experiences ever. We all know that Agar was handpicked as a potential new movie star with heavy studio promotion and hopefully a quick rise to the top, being "introduced" in major John Ford productions back in the late 1940s. But his meteoritic rise crashed and burned after alcohol waylaid his career, which was further blemished by a messy divorce from child star Shirley Temple. Relegated to (at best) Universal B monster movies such as *Tarantula* or (at worst) low-budget independents such as *Zontar: The Thing From Venus*, John Agar never failed to impress, not even in his lowest-budgeted productions. Agar always submitted a performance of interest. But what impressed me in meeting Agar was the fact that Agar kicked the booze and found faith in religion and music and was always one of FANEX's classiest guests. He refused to badmouth his ex-wife Shirley Temple (although she badmouthed him); instead, he quietly remarried the love of his life, Loretta. During his twilight years Agar saw a re-sparking of his movie career and did himself proud in films such as *Miracle Mile*. He never regretted what could have been, as he always enjoyed the blessings of now. He was honored and humbled when FANEX remembered him for all his work. During one award stunt, masterminded by committee member John Freyer, an alien-type monster bursts through Freyer's shirt, leaving his entire chest a bloody mess. Agar jumped up out of his audience seat ready to run up on stage and save the day one more time. He was not part of the act (neither were Sue and I); Agar was simply concerned for Freyer's health. Meeting genuine, decent people like John Agar and Loretta made the convention very special and provided a lifetime of memories.

Meeting Christopher Lee was another high point. True, he was sometimes a high-maintenance guest, beckoning with pointed finger for Sue or me to be at his disposal, but he was also a delightful guest who constantly entertained with intelligent repartee and kindness. He provided so much more for the convention than was originally agreed, and all these extras acts were offered from the heart and with a sense of humility. He was adamant that he did not wish to autograph any personal memorabilia and set strict rules for his appearance, agreeing only to autograph copies of the new American edition of his autobiography and perhaps pose for a quick photo (at first he did not even wish to pose for photos, but Sue and I softened him up). But I remember that first vision of seeing the very tall Mr. Lee with his wife arrive at the train station and climb into the limo together—it was the experience of a lifetime. Delivering the Lees up to their hotel suite and helping them settle in allowed Mr. Lee and myself some private time to talk about ancestry, tea and being a fan of his work. Since this was the only American film convention ever to feature Christopher Lee as Guest of Honor, that makes it all the more special. Sue's grand scheme to get Christopher Lee to come to FANEX/MONSTER RALLY was the coup of a lifetime, one that has never been topped by any other convention.

A Technological Fanzine Odyssey 1963-2013
by Gary J. Svehla

When I was 10 or 11 years old, I fancied myself a writer. I often pulled out lined notebook paper and wrote, in one long unedited draft, fictional horror tales that were generally based upon television programs or movies I saw. Short stories of space flights to other planets or more Earthbound battles with parasitic creatures I dubbed "Eviltons." I rarely had an original bone in my body when it came to plotting, but I enjoyed writing these stories and sharing them with my friends and parents. As a writer I was supposed to only be interested in the manipulation of words, the creation of character conflict and the plot that resulted. In other words, fine-tuning my writer's craft.

But when I fell in love with monster movies, I desired to write heart-felt appreciations, analyses and histories of all the films I saw on TV and at the movies. I now found myself dreaming about becoming a publisher and graphic designer as much as desiring to be a writer. After discovering *Famous Monsters of Filmland* and falling in love with the idea that a bi-monthly magazine existed devoted to the appreciation of horror cinema, I knew I would just have to create my own personal variation. And that would involve not only writing, but also gathering articles and art, designing the look and layout, and finding the most affordable means of printing and distributing the magazine.

The writer is an artist, a wordsmith, and a person who engages in the manipulation of language. But the publisher is a person who is half artist (one who crafts the look of the magazine) and also half businessman and techno wizard. My first attempt at a magazine (created in 1962 when I was 12 years old), *Facts About Monsters*, was a scrapbook-style magazine where I wrote cursive text on notebook paper and stapled the pages onto larger, colored bulletin board

FACTS ABOUT MONSTERS

VOL 1
number 1
copyright 1962 by Gary Svehla

    This book is written on what I know about monsters. It is based on fact and opinions of me and opinions of many people.

                              Gary Svehla

CONTENTS

Page one	Famous Monster I Frankenstein
Page three	Hail to the King, Boris Karloff
Page four	Famous Monster II Wolfman
Page five	The New Hope Christopher Lee
Page seven	Mr. Dracula, Bela Lugosi
Page eight	Famous Monster III Vampire
Page nine	Miss America
Page ten	Famous Monster IV The Mummy

Famous Monster I

Frankenstein

Ever since Mary Shelly wrote the story that is famous all over the world. For 40 years people are bring back the famous story.

The first real movie of Frankenstein was a great hit. People beleved it was too scary for children to see. Bela Lugosi was asked to play the monster but he turned it down and Boris Karloff was given the role.

After Karloff played the monster in 3 movies Lon Chaney was given the role for one movie. Then Bela Lugosi was to play the monster and he was a real ham as the monster! That is a fact. It is a good thing he turned the role down in the first place. Then came Glenn Strange. He was the only person to play the monster as many times as Karloff.

Strange was the last of the famous Frankensteins. Lately there have been many Frankensteins but none could compare to the good old ones.

← moder Frankenstein

end

Hail to the King

Boris Karloff

As a boy Karloff lived a regular life. When he grew up he became an actor and had small parts. But one day he was asked he if he wanted a part in the movie Frankenstein and he said yes. We did not think he would play the monster but he did. When he found out he was playing the monster he said it is a part in a movie so I guess I will take the part and over night the movie was a big hit movie. The set for the movie cost in the thousands but the movies made in the high millions. After his first big hit he made so many more hit movies it is impossible to name them all. A few are The Mummy, The Black Cat, The Raven, Before I hang, The Mask of Fu Manchu, Son of Frankenstein, Bride of Frankenstein, The Walking Dead, The Man they could not Hang, Bedlam, Tower of London, The Body Snatchers, and Frankenstein 1970. These are just few of his many movies

His newest movie is called the Raven and will be out soon. His real name is William Henry Pratt. So hail to the king.

  Boris Karloff

   End

Famous Monster II

The Wolfman

Ever since Lon Chaney first played the wolfman in the forties he has been famous for the role.

Chaney played a man who was bitten by a werewolf. When the moon was full he would turn into a thing halfman and halfwolf and kills. Only one thing could kill him. That is a silver bullet. There have been about 6 movies with Lon Chaney as the wolfman. In the last 6 years there have been many new werewolf movies like The Werewolf, I was a teenage Werewolf, and The Curse of the Werewolf but none could compare with the Lon Chaney version.

End

— The New hope

— Christopher Lee

Chris Lee is the new hope for horror movies. People say the old movies were the best and that is right but men like Lee can make people say the new horror movies are great too. Chris always plays the monster. Ever since his first movie, The Curse of Frankenstein (see page 2) He had hit after hit. He played the Tong terror in Terror of the Tongs. He played a mummy in the movie The Mummy. He played an average man in House of Fright. He played in many more but I think and so do many people that the best movie in about 15 years in the movie Horror of Dracula. He played the Count and the Movie was a masterpiece. A truly tr great movie of our time. Our new hop, Chris Lee

end

Mr Dracula

Bela Lugosi

Bela was born in Lugos Hungary in 1888. When you hear his famous name you think of Dracula. He has won world fame for the part of Count Dracula. Karloff had his Frankenstein, Chaney had his wolfman, but Lugosi had his Dracula. Bela wasn't only famous as Dracula but he played in many Karloff films and films of his own. Just a few of them are H.G. Wells Island of Lost Souls, The Black Cat, Return of the Vampire, Son of Frankenstein, Black Friday, Return of the ape man, Voodoo Man, Murders in the Rue Morgue, The invisible Ray and of course Dracula. He died August 16, 1956.

End

DRACULA

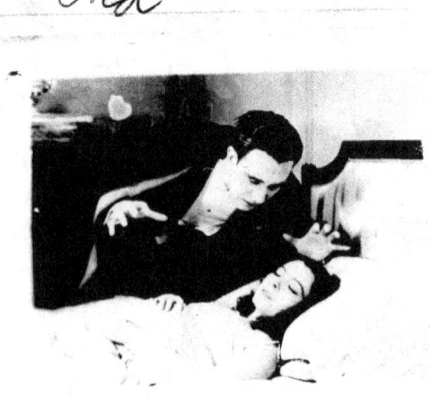

— Famous Monster III —

Vampires

No true monster lover doesn't know about Vampires. The Vampire is a think that sleeps in a coffen in the day and roams at night. Finding a person (most of the time a girl) the vampire will draw the blood of out of the person and drink it. A vampire cannot stand daylight, it will kill the poor theng. The Vampires worse ~~enemy~~ foe is the cross. The Vampire cannot stand it. The only way to kill the Vampire and to stop the curse. A person must drive a wooden stake thought the ~~Vamp~~ Vampires heart at dawn and the Vampire can rest in peace.

End

Mess America

What would a movie be without a girl. Don't say if would be good because it wouldn't. A girl can die a monster in a movie or a thing the hero saves. A horror movie would not be good without a girl. Think of the movie The Bride of Frankenstein. The hole movie was based on a dead girl who was brought back to life. She became the Bride of Frankenstein. How about King Kong. Without the girl screaming and yelling it would have been a bad movie. So a movie wouldn't be any good without a Mess America.

End

Famous Monster IV

The Mummy

There have been many stories about the mummy. Boris Karloff was the first to play the famous role. The story always goes that men find an old mummy case and one night the mummy comes back to life and kidnappes the girl and the hero saves the girl but the movie is always good. Lon Chaney was famed for his famous role as the mummy. The most famous mummy was Kharis. A few of the mummy movies were The Mummy, The Mummy's hand, The Mummy's curse and The Mummy's ghost

End

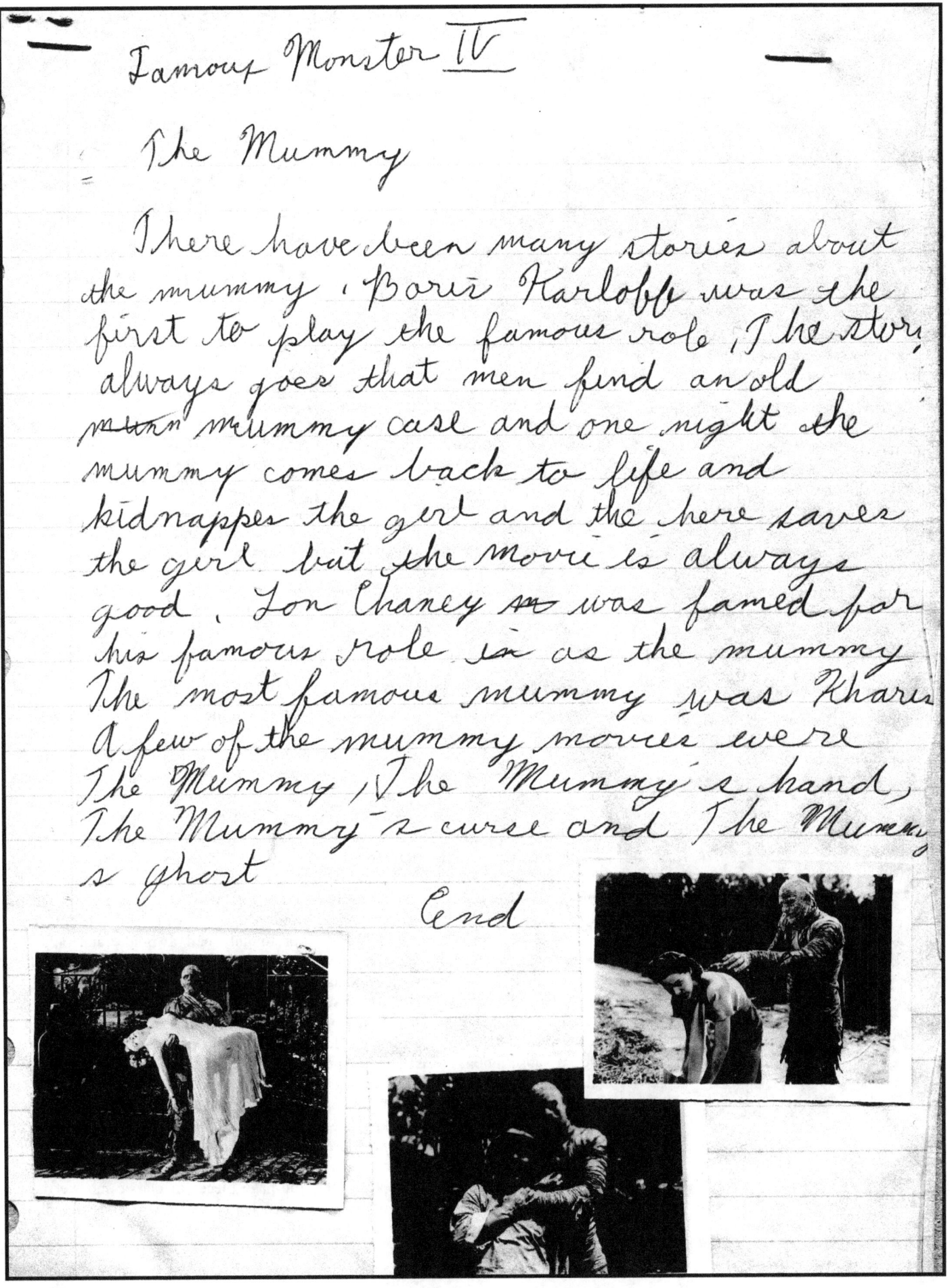

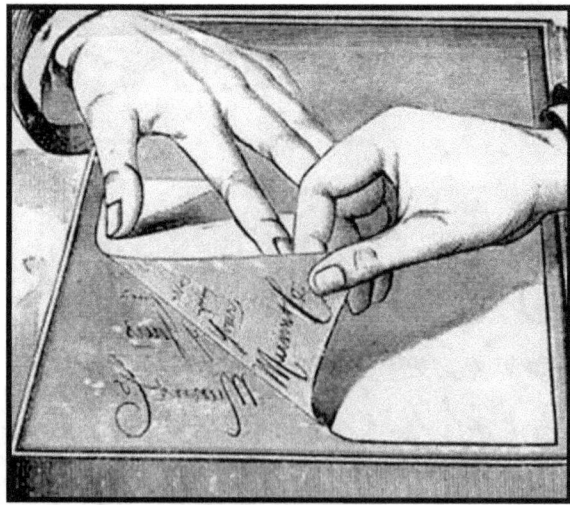

Hectograph was a simple printing method that did not change, as we can see from an ad in 1876.

An ad for carbon paper appeared in 1940, but who would notice the carbon with the lovely secretary front and center.

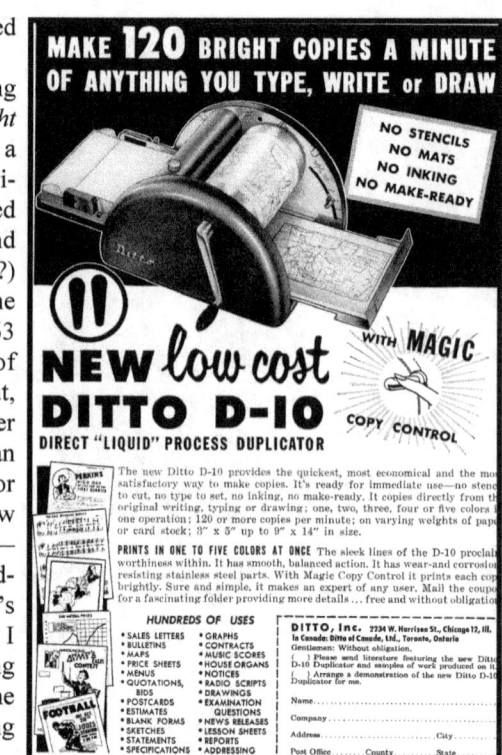

An ad for a ditto machine that boosts a person can crank out 120 copies a minute.

the actual fanzine that I created the following summer in 1963.

In the 50 years of publishing *Gore Creatures* and *Midnight Marquee*, I evolved from a cut-and-paste scrapbook quasi-magazine to a magazine designed with an expanded print run and national (perhaps international?) distribution in mind. That same 13-year-old child is now 63 years old, and his discovery of the technology of design, layout, printing and distribution over five decades might become an interesting history of how horror film fanzines evolved and how the ever-changing technology—incredible, exploding and mind-blowing—shaped the magazine's direction as much as any creative mind. I thought sharing a history of the evolving technology of producing the magazine might be a novel way to share this young boy's odyssey from boy to man.

Gore Creatures issue 1 existed in two formats. The first copies (including one that Forrest J Ackerman purchased when he bought our very first copy of the fanzine) were written in blue ballpoint pen on what we called digest-size sheets (the size of national magazine *Readers' Digest*). All we did was take a typical 8.5 by 11 inch white sheet of paper and cut it in half. Thus *Gore Creatures* issues 1 through 12 were basically size 5.5 by 8.5 inches. That's digest size. After growing sore from recopying several copies of issue 1 in long hand, my baby-sitter and friend Joan Jewell (still going strong at almost 84 years old) offered to type up the magazine using carbon paper to produce multiple copies in black ink. Friend David Metzler also typed up copies. Even in that manner, the magazine only produced about 4 to 8 legible copies from the carbon copies. Issue number 1 never even had a cover. It wasn't until my good friend Dave Metzler was designing a cover for issue 2 that we decided to use that cover for the remaining copies of issue 1 as well. Since we foolishly sold a year's subscription, six issues for one dollar including postage, we had to go straight into the writing and production of issue 2. But we were now thinking big. No more hand-written copies; no more typed carbon copies. Thanks to my father, whose boundless energy and support kept us going, I discovered a new means of reproduction, hectograph.

Hectograph looked exactly like the dittos we received in public school when the teacher needed multiple copies of a handout. The print was purple where the first 20 to 30 copies were dark and sharp and all the copies afterward got lighter until they were basically unreadable. But ditto was too expensive and sophisticated for my father and me at the moment. Hectograph involved typing or drawing on the ditto master (a coated white paper attached to a second sheet of purple ink or another colored ink—the purple produced the most copies) that left a printable impression on back of the white page on which we typed or drew. That side was pressed down on small, clear gelatin pads that would hold the inky impression. Then white sheets of paper were pressed down onto the gelatin sheets for roughly half a minute and pulled up slowly (always curling, never staying flat). The printed impression would copy onto the paper. If we got 30 good copies from the one ditto that was superb, as each copy pulled off the gelatin pad was lighter and fuzzier than the one before. Issue 2 only had Dave Metzler's werewolf art on the cover. The rest of the magazine was pure text, typed in all caps, and printed on only one side of the paper. Issues 3 through 5 continued in the same manner, with generally two Metzler full-page pieces of classic monster movie art each issue. However, in the editorial of issue 5, I announced that issue 6 would feature the art of Dave Ludwig, a young college student from outside Chicago.

With issue 6 things were already evolving, and with our discovery of older and art-schooled Dave Ludwig, Dave Metzler was replaced (but his art would return several issues later). Being a bratty kid, I am sure I was not very tactful in telling my life-long buddy that his art could not compare to Ludwig's, but the truth was that Ludwig, drawing on a purple ditto master, produced some incredible renderings of all the classic monsters. My father had his friend, a local printer, create heavy-stock covers that featured our *Gore Creatures* logo in bold red with the 25-cent price tag listed in the upper right-hand corner. At the bottom appeared "Published by Gary Svehla, Baltimore, Maryland." The entire middle section was left blank, allowing ample space for Dave Ludwig's cover art to be printed in the center. The magazine was still hectographed, but now we printed on full-size 8.5 by 11 inch white sheets that were folded in half and stapled. The text was now typed using upper and lower case letters. And for the very first time printing appeared on the front and back of every page, and the magazine was stapled, saddle-stitch style, in the center fold of the magazine (we purchased a special elongated stapler that reached the center of the magazine). *Gore Creatures* actually looked like a magazine. Especially since with issue 7 we started adding art to our back covers.

With issue 8, with the increasing page count, we threw out the hectograph and my father bought me a used ditto machine. The resulting purple print looked about the same, but placing the ditto master on the round drum of a hand-cranked machine into which white sheets of paper were fed was much, much easier than pressing our ditto master onto messy gelatin pads and peeling each sheet off individually. The only problem was that at times the sheets, which were fed underneath the ditto drum, become too saturated by the ditto fluid and this resulted in the purple ink on some pages smudging and smearing. But actually ditto reproduction was superior to the outmoded hectograph technique. By issue 9 I was using bright alternate colors for some of our title page headings, and to include an additional splash of color, we printed some of our pages on goldenrod paper, which actually reproduced the purple text in a more readable manner.

With issues 10 and 11 we ran out of the original heavy-stock yellow covers, so we ordered new covers, but this time we replaced the bright, colorful yellow covers with drab green ones, and we printed the title in bland black (instead of red) and

Cowboy star Gene Autry appears in an ad for a Smith-Corona manual typewriter, much like the one used to type early issues of *Gore Creatures*.

neglected to put any text on the bottom of the page (allowing cover art to be larger).

Issue 12 returned to using heavy-stock yellow cover stock, but artist Ken Lodge developed his own title logo (very psychedelic) and cover art. We were using heavier stock interior paper by this time, so the problem with show-through ditto printing was eliminated. For the first time we included a two-page centerfold *Kong of Skull Island* montage by Dave Ludwig, but we reproduced the art via offset printing in stark black ink. It was our first flirtation with professional printing, but offset printing was still several issues away.

Since even the best ditto printing could only reproduce at most about 130 legible copies and our subscription base was increasing, it was time for us to turn to mimeograph as our new mode of printing.

A mimeo master was a thin plastic sheet placed in a typewriter. As we typed, the hard metal keys would cut an impression into the master. A mimeograph was another round drum hand-cranked or electric-driven machine. The drum was filled with gloppy (and terribly messy) black ink that stained fingers and clothes alike. When the mimeo master was placed on the black inky drum, it would reproduce text in solid and fairly sharp blacks and was capable of printing hundreds more copies than ditto ever could. However, the problem with mimeo was under- or over-inking. If too much ink was used, then the text would smear and letters would fill in. If we did not use enough ink, the text would be light, with parts of letters failing to print legibly. Art was always a problem with mimeo, but taking line drawings to be processed

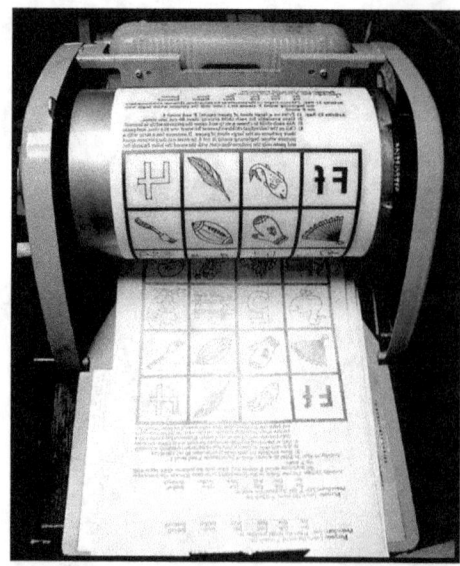

A ditto machine in action. Notice the copies reproduced from the purple master.

and electro-stenciled at local office supply stores solved the problem. Art could then be printed with all the dots and fine lines carefully reproduced. Issue 13, our initial mimeo issue, was the first issue of the magazine to be published 8.5 by 11 inches, so the new double-column layout proved to be a challenge in keeping the width of each column consistent. But with issue 14 and 15 the printing became darker, sharper and clearer and the layout improved. Issue 14 also heralded a cover price increase to 30 cents from 25 cents.

With issue 16, we abandoned mimeo for professional offset printing, reducing our page count from 40 pages (larger type printed on thicker white paper) to 20 smaller size print offset pages. Maintaining our 30-cent price, we delivered a magazine that was painfully thin when compared to the former mimeo version. This fact did not please many people. However, because of the smaller page count, we started to eliminate fiction and poetry, and while many of our feature articles had literary themes, we were morphing toward becoming the pure classic horror zine we always strived to be. Instead of printing on double-sized paper allowing us to use saddle stitch binding when the paper was folded, we instead printed on regular 8.5 by 11 inch paper with two big staples on the left margin edge. This was our first endeavor with Arcade Press (September 1969), our printer for decades. The humble little printing company was located off Harford Road in the heart of Hamilton, in a brick building behind the Arcade Theater. Arcade Press printed the theater preview programs distributed by the Durkee movie theater chain. Arcade Press and Bob Gehring are still in operation today.

In what might appear to be a step backwards, issue 17 (now 35 cents) combined offset printing with mimeo, to produce a thicker, bulkier and 36-page issue. At least people felt they were getting their money's worth. And I felt great that Dave Metzler at last got a front cover opportunity, and his ghostly specter art was superb. Issue 18 returned to an all offset format, but the page count was steady at 30 pages, so the issue was thick-feeling enough and had the content necessary to make it well balanced. With issues 19 and 20 (the cover price went up to 50 cents) we added a splash of red to the front covers, but our means of reproduction remained the same. With issue 20 Bill Nelson created a bold logo that seemed tailor-made for the magazine, and since we never maintained a consistent title logo before, I felt it was about time to establish a professional identity. Dave Ludwig submitted the smaller and subtle "GC" logo that deemphasized our title as an alternative choice to Nelson's splashier logo. Nelson's bold, 3-D-style logo won out. By issue 22 the page count was up to 50 pages, but the cover price was now 75 cents.

The next major format change was issue 23, our first offset issue to be printed on 17 by 11 inch paper, thus allowing us to print the issue double-sized and bind it by folding the printed page in half and stapling right down the middle (saddle stitch). Such improvements came at a cost, as the cover price was now $1.00. Dave Ludwig, working as his alter ego M. Squidd, delivered one of his finest covers, the nightmarish dream sequence from *House of Usher*. For the first time since our earlier hectograph days, we once again looked like a true magazine. The front and back cover was printed on a heavier stock paper, while the interior paper was regular #60 offset stock. Instead of using the standard manual Royal typewriter on which most of the earlier issues were typed, my father

A crank-operated mimeograph machine. Notice the messy black ink on the drum.

A can of A.B. Dick mimeograph ink, the can outside rusting and the ink inside staining.

invested in an IBM Selectric typewriter that allowed us to purchase different font typeballs to vary the look of text, and the typewriter was fully electric, which made a uniform typed impression and created a professional typeset look. This format, our most professional appearing at the time, continued virtually unchanged through issue 25, the last of the *Gore Creature*-titled issues. Issue 24 had a $1.25 cover price, while issue 25 sold for $1.75.

Foolishly changing printers for one issue, simply because Arcade Press could not print on glossy paper, we debuted our new title *Midnight Marquee* (Bill Nelson designed our new title logo, incorporating a full moon) as issue #26. Since it was only the title that was changing, everything else remained the same. But the new printer, Holliday Press, made a huge mistake, one that necessitated our return to the more sympathetic and nurturing Arcade Press. The issue was printed erroneously slightly oversized and the printed text and graphics spread dangerously close to the inner and outer edges of the paper. The pressman told me he assumed the layout grids were to be shot actual size, but that was never the case. We always created oversized layout grids that would be shot and reduced by about 20 percent. At this point we knew immediately I made a mistake leaving Arcade Press, and with the dreams of glossy paper stock a one-issue failed experiment, we happily returned to our friends at Arcade. Perhaps in recent years when our competitors all "evolved" to using thick, glossy enamel paper, we happily remained with nice white offset paper, since the pain of switching to glossy paper would haunt us for decades.

When doing the magazine's layout cut-and-paste style on layout grids, owning a graphic design drafting table was essential.

By this time, as previously stated, we were laying out the issue on large boards that allowed us to paste two oversized pages side-by-side on a giant two-page grid. Using oversized layout grids allowed the negatives to be slightly reduced to the printed size of 17 by 11 inches (which when folded in half became 8.5 by 11 inch pages), allowing reduced print to be used in the layout. In other words, if we laid out pages the actual printed size, the photos and print would appear a little too large. By laying out 20% larger, we could squeeze more photos and text onto every page of the magazine. But just imagine all the frustration of typing up strips of text and using Wite-Out to cover up and correct any typos. Often I would type up two lines of text that I would carefully cut out and glue overtop the original error, as most errors were not found until the final proofreading stage when the layout boards had already been finalized and glued. We had to use a proportion or ratio-sizing wheel to figure out the percentage of reduction for photos and pressbook ads to be shot and then fitted into the blank space on the layout sheets. If the ratio was in error, the photo would be photographed and slotted in either being too big or too small. Not very professional, but if readers look at the issues produced around this time, they will notice photos that do not quite fit the allotted space in the layout. Working with these grids and doing the physical cut and paste layout was frustrating but also rewarding. When the issue was officially done, I could flip through these huge oversized sheets and see a reasonable approximation of how the final magazine would appear. I would carefully slide the layout grids into a huge brown folder which I would present to Bob Gehrig at Arcade Press. I would methodically show him the layout, page by page, and he would examine the grids for any errors that might have slipped by me. If he caught anything, I would have to redo that two-page spread and then return the layout sheets later. Once Bob approved the layout, it was out of our hands and entirely in his. It usually took about three weeks for Arcade to print and bind the issues and box them up.

With issue 27, our first issue back at Arcade Press, we wanted to do something bold. Our Bill Nelson front cover, for the first time, had a bright red background—we now printed two-color covers. Returning to the thick cover stock and bright white interior pages, we were home again. Issue 28 (cover price now $2.00), featuring our final Dave Ludwig cover, reduced the title logo (remember Ludwig's "GC" logo, the one that lost the vote to Nelson's, was small as not to overpower the art's dominance, a concept that Ludwig maintained on all his covers) so it fit above the Ludwig art and was printed in a second color, a brown, so the two-color effect was far less dramatic and achieved a quiet subtlety. But when Bill Nelson's cover for issue 29 ($2.50 cover price) appeared, a Yoda portrait, the yellow background really snapped and drew attention. Perhaps this dual color effect reached its pinnacle of impact with *The Howling* cover by Nelson on issue 30 (bearing a $3.00 cover price), where the second color was placed directly over the face of the beast, so the art appeared to be magenta and black and was very dynamic. Bill Nelson, I believe, convinced us to change our logo to a more modern style and he had his graphic design buddy Ed Paxton design our new logo, one that was distinct but perhaps not best suited to a classic horror film magazine. Bill Nelson's former Gothic logo was better suited to *Midnight Marquee* and what we represented. For issue 31 Nelson was at his most experimental, creating an *E.T.* cover that featured brown (for the alien) but shades of purple were used for the background (no black ink was used at all). Also, issue 31 was the first issue where we had Arcade Press do the typography for us, so we typed up the text, gave it to Bob, and a week later he handed us columns of typesetting that we glued to our layout boards. Besides looking more professional, it allowed us to reduce the page count and contain the same amount of copy, due to the reduced size text. Nelson used the same two-tone color effect on his *John Carpenter's The Thing* cover on issue 32 (creating an eerie green alien head). Our cover price was now $3.25. For the following issue 33, Nelson employed the far less distinct shades-of-black for the Michael Jackson *Thriller* cover, featuring Jackson as a zombie fiend from his classic music video.

For *Midnight Marquee* 34, even though the typesetting created by Arcade Press looked terrific, it was sometimes frustrating to find errors and spend a week awaiting new text to be generated to fix multiple errors. So I finally purchased a Royal Alpha 700-D electronic typewriter that allowed me to type up all the text and use interchangeable font heads. The typewriter could store almost one page of text in memory, so I could proofread and correct what I typed before committing it to a final print out, which then became permanent. For the time such technology was state-of-the-art, but the small viewing screen and limited memory, while superior to sticky and messy Wite-Out corrections, was still clunky and problematic. I have to admit that the text appearance of issue 34 was inferior to the wonderful typesetting used in the three previous issues, but we were saving a little money and the electronic typewriter gave us a greater sense of freedom in manufacturing our text and layout design. Issue 35 (with cover price of $3.50), our first to use cover art by dear friend Allen Koszowski, continued our experiment with the electronic typewriter, this time using a different font to generate

The popular IBM Selectric electric typewriter, with the interchangeable font ball to vary the look of the type.

50th Anniversary Issue [1963-2013]

Left: An IBM Selectric font ball; Right: A typical font wheel used on many electric typewriters to change the look of type (switch from Times to Aria to Optima)

a different look. Still, our layout looked inferior to the typeset text. But I simply liked having complete artistic control. Now if I caught a textual error I could fix it in minutes.

But with issue 36 another change occurred, one that vastly improved the look of our typography. Electronic typewriters were nice, but they only mimicked what was possible with the advent of the personal computer. Although it was very crude in design and technology, Sue and I purchased our first computer, a 64K Kaypro that operated on a CP/M operating system (soon MS-DOS exploded upon the computing world and put CP/M to rest). Kaypro became just about the only affordable home computer in the early 1980s. But what made home computers desirable for fanzine production was that we were able to type and save text on the old-style large floppy discs, which allowed us to save and manipulate text. Of course we had to enter text codes for italics, bold and capital letters, but once an article was composed, it could be saved and edited and altered later. I did not know it at the time, but our special 208-page anniversary issue could not have been produced in the allotted time without the Kaypro computer. Still, the Kaypro allowed us to generate strips of print that continued to be cut and pasted onto our oversized layout grids. This computer was too simplistic for us to create layout within the computer itself.

Twenty-five years in, Tom Skulan, of FantaCo Enterprises, bankrolled the production of our 25th anniversary issue as a trade paperback, 208 8.5 by 11 inch pages with a whopping $14.95 cover price. While I had total artistic control over content and design, producing such a massive undertaking in the old-school manner (doing the layout as usual on oversized grids, cutting and pasting text, using the reduction wheel to figure out the sizing of photos and pressbook ads) and working to a firm deadline (Skulan was premiering the oversized anniversary issue at his annual FantaCo Convention, flying my father Richard, wife Sue and me to Albany, New York as guests) was more than grueling. If we were not working with the electronic typewriter, it would have been impossible to produce a magazine four times our usual size in the 10 months or so we had to complete the issue. The final product was the dream of a lifetime, the ultimate book-a-zine anniversary issue that highlighted our first quarter century of publication. That final product was more than a little responsible in getting the Svehlas interested in publishing books, but our book publishing company would not arrive for another seven years.

One thing would never change though. Issue 37 was the first issue to feature a full color front and back cover, printed on laminated cover stock, and after working with two-color covers on non-laminated stock, we decided we were never going back. Full color glossy front covers became the new normal for the magazine (full color *back* covers took a few more issues to arrive).

After producing the super-sized anniversary issue, it was almost humbling to return to our regular format for issue 38, but now the 50-page issue felt heftier with the addition of covers printed on thicker, glossy stock (and readers loved the return to our former $3.50 cover price). A new air of professionalism was upon us. This format continued with issue 39, with the fabulous cover art of David L. Daniels. Many readers consider these Daniels-designed covers to be among the best that fandom ever produced. But then again, *Gore Creatures* and *Midnight Marquee* featured so many gifted artists that it would be difficult to pick favorites. Issue 40 dramatically upped the cover price to $4.50, but at the same time we offered a two-issue subscription of $8.00 to encourage readers to buy directly from us. Issue 41 was the first issue to offer full color front and back covers.

The next technological change was only hinted at in issue 42. The entire issue continued to be produced by the Kaypro computer, but the title page, one that stood out dramatically from the rest of the issue, was produced on our new Apple Macintosh computer. That one page, an experiment, was addressed in the editorial as the shape of things to come. I don't see why at the time I just did not throw out the rest of the

The Kaypro II 64K computer was the first home computer for many fanzine designers.

magazine and compose the entire issue on the Mac, even though the issue would arrive much later than it did. That one page simply speaks volumes of heightened technology to come. However, one change did occur in this issue—we changed to a three-column format from a two-column one. And we did introduce a new logo, designed by Ted Bohus, incorporating both the full moon and a bat. And it survived for six issues (including one variation for our Hammer-themed issue). However, our first all-Macintosh-produced issue arrived, issue 43, one that brought a new level of sophisticated typesetting, layout and design to the magazine. It would take a few issues for us to become comfortable with composing on the Mac (and those monitors were so small back in the day), but a new professionalism had arrived. Issue 43, I believe, contained the first digital frame grabs we ever employed to illustrate an article. In the Don Willis-composed "The Fantastic Asian Video Invasion," we had to use frame grabs because these direct-to-video releases arrived with very little promotional materials available. But as we all realize, frame grabs quickly became a common tool to help illustrate articles by reproducing an exact moment from the film under discussion. With issue 44 the cover price jumped from $4.50 to $5.50 per issue, but in our editorial we pleaded for people to subscribe and buy directly from us, where each issue would cost only $4.00. With issue 45 we produced our 30th Anniversary issue (the summer of 1993) and the cover featured a blood-soaked and nearly bare-breasted Yutte Stensgaard as the vampire fiend from *Lust for a Vampire*, a rather sexual cover for the times. The issue more than doubled in size, featuring 100 pages of content (at a $5.95 cover price). But we wanted to celebrate 30 years of publication properly. In issue 46 we featured a few

Once you go Mac, you ain't never looking back! Here is the technologically Earth-altering Macintosh Classic, one of the most important home computers ever designed. We continue to use Macs for all our computer needs (video editing, business and design/layout).

photos taken at the 30th anniversary party which we hosted at the *Famous Monsters* Convention, held in Virginia, which was attended by many of our staff writers and film director John Landis.

Although the format and technology remained the same with issue 47 (100 pages of three-column text with full-color covers), this turned out to be our first theme issue with our tribute to Hammer. Instead of featuring a David L. Daniels cover, Michael Kronenberg, the man who would soon go on to design all the earlier issues of *Monsters From the Vault,* painted the front cover illustrating a dramatic sequence from *Curse of Frankenstein*. With issue 48, our latest *Midnight Marquee* logo was inaugurated and remained for a total of seven issues. Issue 49 returned with our second theme issue, this time our "All Vampire Issue," featuring a Lorraine Bush cover depicting Bela Lugosi as Dracula.

Radical changes arrived with issue 50, our first issue printed by Kirby Lithographic, the same company that was printing our line of Midnight Marquee Press books. Arcade Press was a small mom and pop offset company and they were not equipped to do large print runs

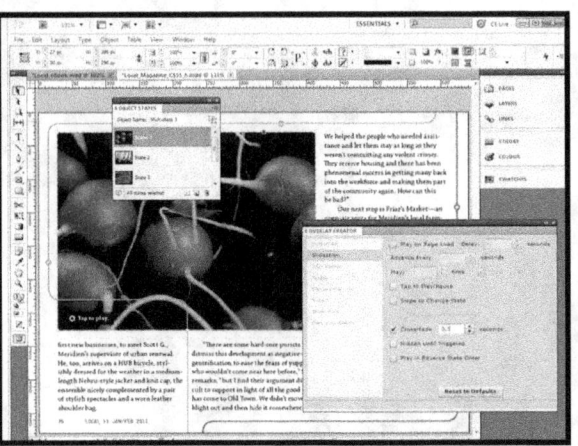

Aldus PageMaker became Adobe InDesign, the leading computer-generated graphic design/layout program.

of trade paperbacks, with film-laminated covers. And they had to send product out to be perfect bound (square bound). So we gave all our business for several years to Kirby, but the only drawback was that they were not able to deliver a standard-trim size 8.5 by 11 inch magazine. Instead our issue shrunk to the odd size of 7 ¾ by 10 ¾ inches. Due to Sue's suggestion, our interior font size enlarged to 12 point (the failing eyesight of aging baby boomers?) but the layout still remained 3 columns. The text was now output at a higher resolution, and, for the first time, we scanned photos into our layout using PhotoShop software to further improve image quality (sharpening, taking out scratches, lightening or darkening contrast). Using the equally impressive PageMaker layout and design software, the entire magazine was created digitally on the Mac. I could happily throw away my photo resizing wheel and was now able to crop, enlarge, shrink and tweak graphics in any way I desired, right on the computer screen. Those over-sized layout grids were also tossed, as was my can of adhesive cement that made everything near its spray sticky for months. For the first time an entire issue was completely designed on the Apple Macintosh computer and I had total artistic control. The only old-school thing that remained was the return of a David L. Daniels *Frankenstein* cover.

Actual copies of George Stover's *Cinemacabre* waiting to be cut, collated and bound at John D. Lucas Printers in Baltimore.

Issue 51 was significant for a variety of reasons, but mainly it inaugurated the first use of a photo-generated front cover in lieu of art. We had become known for our stunning front cover paintings, but we decided to change our look for two reasons. First, our current artists had many magazines pulling at their coattails and artists were finding it difficult to meet deadlines with the increased demands on their work and time. A few artists (none of the major players I must add) were becoming quite demanding. One artist threatened us because we dared crop one piece of art he submitted. Loving the total artistic control that computer-generated publications offered, Sue felt it was about time to move on and leave old school art behind. She felt that photo-generated covers were more modern in design and allowed creative freedoms that painted covers did not. For better or worse, we forged ahead and this started the era when Sue designed all of our covers, with a few exceptions. Attempting to produce three issues per year, we decreased the page count to 68 pages but lowered the cover price to $5.00 (from $5.95). Because we felt that our print was too large last issue, we decreased the font size to 11 point.

For issue 52 our logo remained the same but the actual type became thinner (and remained so for issue 53 and 54). We decided that even 11-point type was still too large, so we felt that 10-point print would become the ideal compromise, not too big and not too small. Issue 53 changed in one distinctive way. While our front and back covers were printed on heavier stock paper, we could not afford the shiny coating that film lamination provided. To avoid covers getting scratched while packaged in boxes, we had the issues varnished where a thin powdery layer would protect issues from getting marred while sliding in the storage cartons. But with issue 53 we started to film laminate our front covers, making them super slick and glossy. The change in cover quality was like day and night. Issue 54 featured our second specialty theme issue on Hammer, as the first Hammer issue sold like hotcakes. And both issues were tie-ins to our Hammer-themed FANEX film conventions.

Issue 55 featured another theme issue, cinema's favorite psychos, and to attempt to create something fresh in the cover design, Sue approximated a tabloid cover, something that *The National Enquirer* or any one of the scandal sheets might produce. The cover was imaginative and generated a sense of fun, with Norman Bates front and center. Tag lines appeared declaring, "Dracula—My children are a disappointment to me!" and "Depraved teenage monsters roaming U.S. cities!" However, our readership, raised on classic Basil Gogos *Famous Monsters* covers, just did not appreciate the satire or the off-the-grid design. It was one of Sue's biggest disappointments when that cover design did not go over. Issue 56 returned to the stark red, green and black coloring featuring Dr. Pretorius ready to throw the laboratory switch in *Bride of Frankenstein*, a much more classic, horror-oriented cover that was sure to please the fans. Also, we premiered our new title logo, one that still survives to this day. Issue 57 and 58 continued the same format, technologically settling into a groove, creating the same style cover design and interior layout. There's no need to fix what isn't broken, right? However, the cover price once again rose from $5.00 to $6.00.

Issue 59 became an extra special issue. It was an experimental issue that worked artistically but not financially, as Sue and I learned we could never predict what the readership wanted. The issue was perfect bound and contained 100 pages, but instead of using typical 60 pound white offset paper, we upgraded to expensive matte finish paper (thicker coated paper but without the ultra shine that creates glare, something I felt was counter-productive to photo reproduction with so-called glossy enamel paper). This was our first all-photo theme issue of classic movie monsters from Hollywood's Golden Age. The issue was captioned but the bulk of the space was

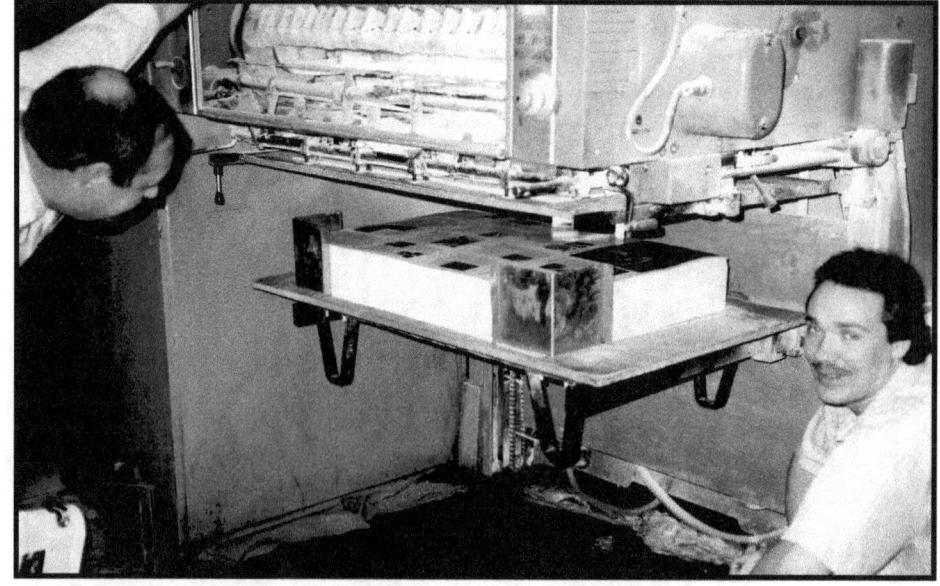

An issue of *Cinemacabre* is about to be collated and bound at John D. Lucas Printing.

devoted to large reproductions of classic movie photos from the 1930s and 1940s. We felt fans would appreciate movie stills reproduced at high resolution and large size. When the issue premiered, sales disappointed. We felt the $10 cover price was more than fair for the quality within, but perhaps the four-dollar cover price jump was too much for some fans. However, to drive home the point of what we were all about, we incorporated our current *Midnight Marquee* logo into a smaller size while we started to use *Monsters* in larger print, just so fans understood what *Midnight Marquee* was all about. Besides our knowledgeable fan base, we were distributed nationwide to people who were not familiar with our brand.

Issue 60 and 61 returned to the $6.00 cover price and 68-page format, printed on standard white offset paper. But issue 63 made one more attempt to present the photo-themed over-stuffed issue, this time focusing upon monsters from the 1950s (and early 1960s). The page count returned to 100 pages and a $10 cover price, but this time we used standard offset paper instead of the much more expensive enamel stock with the matte finish. In spite of the downgrade in paper quality, the issue still snapped and looked very impressive. But sales were underwhelming once again. This time we gave up on the photo concept.

Issues 63 and 64 returned to the format we had been using for the past few years, and while the quality continued, the sales were slipping. We found it more and more difficult to continue publishing three times a year, especially with less money coming in (and we lost more money than I care to remember with our major Virginia-based conventions in 1999 and 2000). So our publication schedule slowed up and we got behind schedule.

With issue 65/66 we embarked upon our first major change in several years. We had been distributed nationally to bookstore chains such as Borders and Barnes and Noble, and Ingram Distribution handled this for us. However, because Ingram returned more books than they paid for, Ingram claimed we owed them money (the point of distribution is that Ingram would pay us, not the other way around) in the amount of slightly over $5,000. We basically settled by paying them $2,500, after proving that their so-called accurate accounts were in error. To be honest, Ingram almost put us out of business because of their practice of returning books when payment was due, and then, within weeks, re-ordering the *same* books they had recently returned, allowing

When it comes to the finest quality offset printing, most claim the Heidelberg Offset Press rules supreme.

the company even more time to pay us—and eventually return most of them (always shipped back to us beat to hell). This way of doing business seemed simply unethical. So we limited ourselves to Diamond distributors (who sold to a national chain of comic book stores), our website, our subscription and mailing list. Because we stopped our national distribution via national chain stores, we stopped calling the magazine *Midnight Marquee Monsters* (hoping originally to avoid confusion with our line of books) and returned to calling the magazine *Midnight Marquee*, again using our standard logo but printing it large size. However, we decreased publication from three 68-page issues per year to two 128-page *double* issues per year (thus labeling the issue with two numbers, such as 65/66), decreasing the size to a book-like 7 by 10 inch format and carrying a $10 cover price, since the magazine was now a small trade paperback each and every issue. This altered the layout of the magazine, and, because of the smaller size, we returned to a two-column format. Financially, the company had struggled over the past year and a half and we were attempting to weather the storm and remain on course. These 7 by 10 inch format issues actually added a look of eloquence and style and I am quite proud of them.

The new format continued with our next double issue 67/68 and our 40th anniversary issue, number 69/70. Double issues 71/72 (another specialty theme issue dealing with mad doctors of cinema) and 73/74 followed. Growing tired of numbering 128-page-issues as double issues, we finally settled on calling issue 75 simply issue 75. Sue felt we needed a tagline for our product and we started using the line "At Midnight Marquee we know movies" on our covers and in our advertisements. The format of the magazine decreased slightly from 128 to 96 pages, a more manageable format. The work involved with our books and film production unit pushed the publication of the magazine back even further, but our readers understood that the magazine being late only meant the anticipation for the next issue was greater.

With issue number 76, we made our most radical technological move yet. Sensing that digital magazines, so-called online publications, were the future of publishing, Sue and I returned subscription money or extended credit to our subscribers to buy other Midnight Marquee products, and we decided to continue publishing the magazine as a digital online magazine, for free. In this manner we could produce a PDF format magazine, in color, with a limitless page count (the magazine could be as long as it needed to be) as a true labor of love. No charge existed to us and so no charge was passed on to our readers (not even the fee we paid to host the website). Free meant free. Only one little problem occurred. We did not realize just how many baby boomers did not own computers and were no longer able to access our issues because the magazine was online. People began offering us money to actually print out the color issue, have it bound at Kinkos or Office Depot, and send them the physical

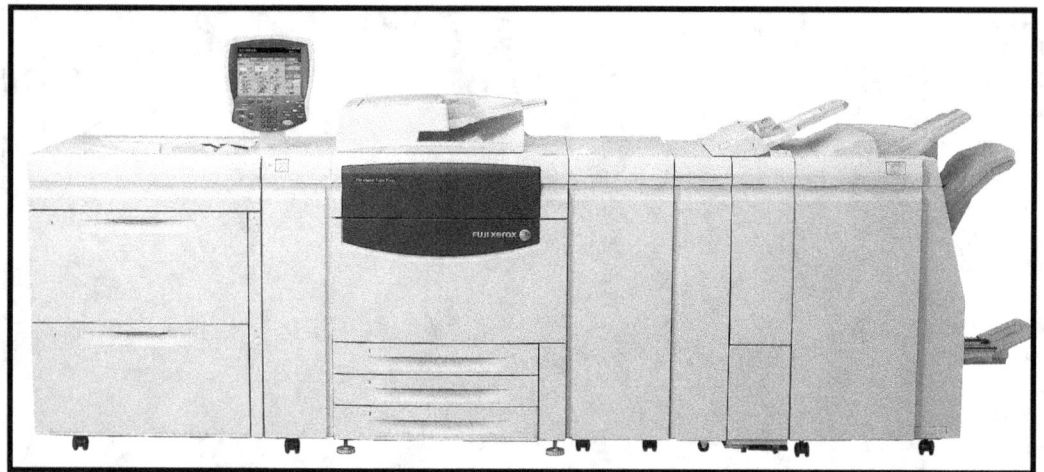
While many consider offset printing an art, the printing technology of the future involves digital printing, where offset printing ink is replaced by electronic toner.

magazine. Well, it become so unwieldy for us to have to print off these issues and go to have them bound. It was literally easier for us to return to hard print publication and let the professionals do the printing and binding of the issues. Even though we were technologically advanced, our stop-gap method of transforming digital issue 76 to hard print issue 76 was very similar to what we did back in the 1960s, when we printed, collated and stapled issues of the magazine in my father's basement. So guess what, we reformatted and re-designed the entire magazine, now in black-and-white (except for the front and back covers, of course), and sold it as a regular hard-print magazine. This was our first experiment embracing digital print on demand (POD) and forsaking offset printing, allowing us to manufacture only the number of copies that we sold. Even though I was excited to transform *Midnight Marquee* to an online classic horror film magazine, our readers just were not ready for that adventure, at least not yet. Unfortunately, many of our dedicated subscribers never returned to the fold. And with our irregular publishing schedule, it has been a hard-fought battle to win their loyalty back.

With issues number 77 and 78 we again expanded our trim size to the awkward 8.25 by 10.50 inches (Create Space, at that time, did not print 8.5 by 11 trim size), and since we were no longer using offset printing, we had Create Space, owned by Amazon.com, continue to be our digital print on demand (POD) printer. The major difference between offset printing and digital is that offset is basically ink on paper while digital is toner on paper. With digital we have a setup fee and a cost per book that does not vary if we order one copy or 100 copies. In this way we could manufacture copies only after they sold, so we could avoid the huge expense of warehouse storage of books and magazines that might sit on the shelves for decades. And warehouse storage rates were monthly and always went up annually, causing us to lose more and more money paying for product that did not sell. Digital printing became a boon to the small press publisher, allowing us to only print as many copies of books and magazines as needed and the books and magazines would be available indefinitely. This was a win-win situation for both the customer and the publisher. Even though the issues cost much more, issue 77 and 78 were published in full color. We had to decrease the page count to 38 pages to be able to afford color printing, but the readership once again preferred a larger format magazine and did not feel color reproduction was essential. For a $10 cover price, readers wanted at least 68 or more pages. We listened and adapted.

And this brings us back to the just-released 50th anniversary issue. This 8.5 by 11 inch trade paperback/magazine won't be the normal thickness of regular future issues. We will most likely continue the larger-size format, but regular issues will be under 100 pages (the exact format to be figured out later). Once again, we depend entirely upon reader support and sales to continue publication.

But technologically, what is the next logical step? I can envision *Midnight Marquee* being available as an e-magazine formatted for Kindle Fire, the iPad and other e-readers. Most likely we will continue the print format and experiment with a digital version as well, so we can grow and appeal to both markets. And I am sure the technology of publishing will evolve in ways that even I cannot foresee at the current time.

But I have to smile. Those days of messy hectograph purple ink on my fingers seem like only yesterday. The even worse black ink smudge of mimeo seems merely a blink of time away from the present. I still own my electric typewriter (although it lies ignored in our crawl space), and while the Kaypro computer was consigned to the garage heap decades ago, I still remember my first Apple Macintosh computer, with the small black-and-white built-in monitor. Those layout boards, as messy as they were, reeking of that stinky adhesive spray, were testaments to individual creativity, with the cut and paste strips of text and layout symmetrically assembled. And when magazine layout design could be created on the computer, becoming digital, that was a science fiction dream of the far, distant future becoming reality. Amazingly I still own a manual typewriter that sits in my home theater, a contrast of technologies. It is utterly amazing to consider just how rapidly technology changed since 1963 and how much more it will continue to evolve, even in the next decade. Still, while this editor/publisher is amazed by the advancement of technology, I still have to smile at the old-school magazine collector who loves the smell of a freshly printed issue, with a color painting on the cover, reminding them of the Basil Gogos-created covers of the old *Famous Monsters of Filmland*. These marvelous collectors just love the feel of flipping carefully (so not to dent or smudge any page) through every magical page of the latest issue of some classic horror magazine. I've been there myself and still get emotionally stimulated by the look and feel of actual magazines that I can hold in my hands. But as a creative adult, I am just as stimulated by the look and feel of the future where magazines will most likely not exist as hard print editions much longer. Perhaps a determined old-school publisher may keep such niche products alive (if not well) until the last of the baby boomer generation expires. But I remain curious to see where the future of publishing leads, ready to accept change and embrace a new world of gods and monsters. That's exactly what I've been doing since I was a little boy in 1963, transfixed and transformed by my cherished collection of *Famous Monsters* and *Castle of Frankenstein.* I continue, 50 years on, to embrace the spirit of that young boy who had a dream to communicate using available technology.

The Evolution of Horror Film Fanzine Art:
The Dave Robinson Portfolio

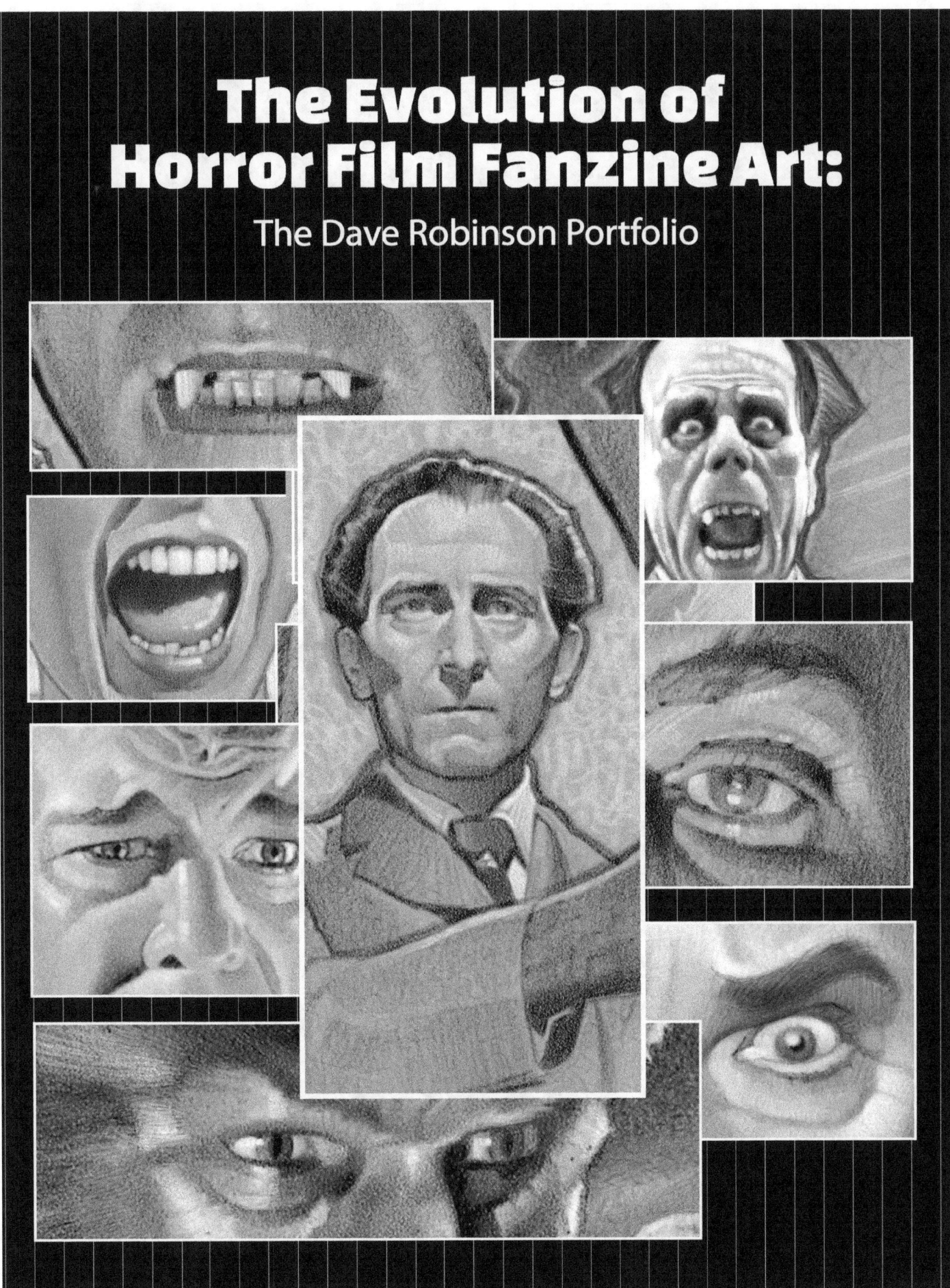

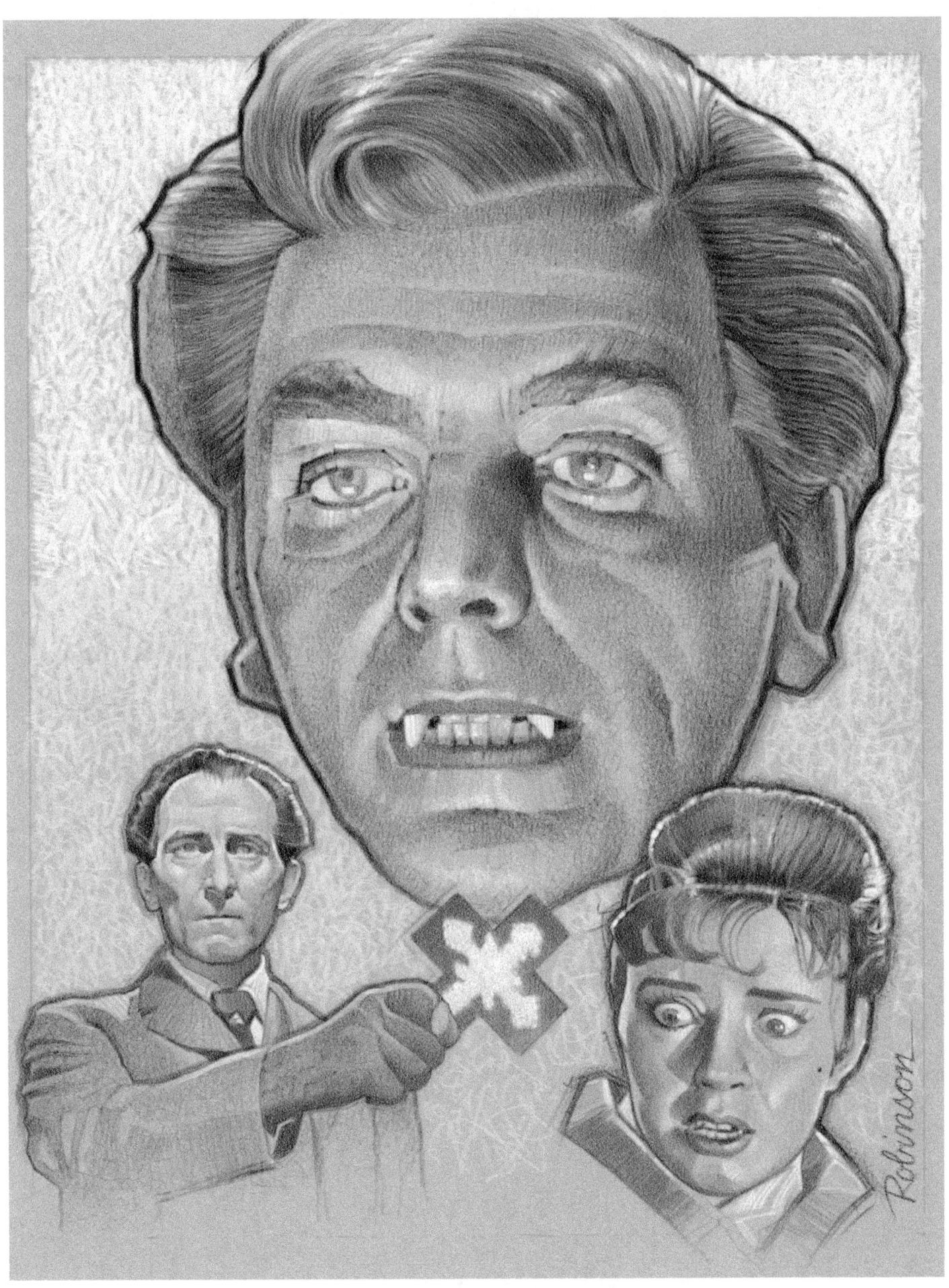

Part Three
It's the Movies that Matter

TOWER OF LONDON
POMP, PAGEANTRY AND THE MACABRE

by Greg Mank

Tower of London ... might have been written by Bill Shakespeare after a joust at the Mermaid Tavern with Boris Karloff and Fu Manchu.
   Variety, November 18, 1939.

Well, they finally dug up the old devil.

The skeleton of Richard III, whom Shakespeare poetically described as that "foul lump of deformity," has been resting all these centuries in Leicester and was exhumed September 2012—incongruously, but definitively—from beneath a parking lot. With a respectable pomp and ceremony re-interment set for 2014, Richard's ghost, finally unleashed from its all-too-humble grave, is currently free to enjoy a world tour.

Perhaps he'll spend it performing the atrocity of his choice upon the graves of others who have done so much, for so long, to blaspheme his royal memory.

Maybe he'll drop by Holy Trinity Churchyard in Stratford-upon-Avon and desecrate the resting place of Shakespeare (who penned his pejorative *Richard III* in 1591). Perhaps he'll visit Westminster Abbey and profane the tomb of Sir Laurence Olivier (who played him so diabolically in his film version of Shakespeare's play in 1955). And certainly Richard's vengeful specter would want to visit Universal City, California ... and despoil the back lot site of 1939's *Tower of London*.

It was perhaps the most indelicate of the Richard III tales, instantly impressive today due to its Unholy Trinity of horror powerhouses: Basil Rathbone as a bloodthirsty Richard, Boris Karloff as the monstrous executioner Mord, and Vincent Price

"Bottled Spider": Basil Rathbone, in the prime of his stardom, as the diabolical Richard III

as the simpering Duke of Clarence. If ever Richard spun in his Leicester grave, it was during the blistering midsummer shoot of this mad, medieval melodrama, an eerie extravaganza that boasted a beheading, a drowning in a wine vat, the killing of two young boys, two gory (for the time) battle scenes, a bombastic musical score lifted partially from *Son of Frankenstein*, a bevy of torture instruments almost a match for those in MGM's *The Mask of Fu Manchu*, and virtually all the sadism and bloodletting that could escape the 1939 censors.

Of course, if Richard III's ghost does visit 2013 Universal, he'll find that the Tower, a venerable site of the Universal back lot for nearly 50 years, is long-gone—razed in the late 1980s to make room for the *Earthquake* ride. And he's already had plenty of time in the afterlife to scold the also dearly departed Rathbone, Karloff and Price (who played Richard in the Roger Corman-directed 1962 *Tower of London*).

At any rate, this *Tower of London* retrospective is dedicated to Richard III, who, we hope, was hardly the "hedgehog," "bottled spider," "poisonous bunch-back'd toad," "abortive rooting hog" and other sinister soubriquets Shakespeare devised for him.

Trade advertisement for Universal's *Tower of London* (1939)

"To you, sir!
Crookback. Dragfoot. Misfits, eh?"
   Basil Rathbone as Richard, talking to Boris Karloff as Mord about their respective deformities in *Tower of London*.

It was, poetically, a production seemingly cursed with troubles.

Humpty Dumpty from Hell: Boris Karloff as Mord, the bald-pated, club-footed, bloodthirsty Tower executioner.

Saturday, August 13, 1938: Rowland V. Lee, director of such films as *Zoo in Budapest* (Fox, 1933) and *The Three Musketeers* (RKO, 1935), begins shooting *Service De Luxe* at Universal. He's signed a producer/director contract with the studio and his first film is this screwball comedy starring Constance Bennett and, in his film debut, Vincent Price. M.F. Murphy, whose job it is to troubleshoot Universal productions and report weekly to the front office, will write precisely five weeks later, September 17, 1938:

> With all credit to Rowland V. Lee, this picture finished up Thursday, September 15, and can be considered the most commercially handled big picture we have had on this lot in many years. The total shooting period consumed 27 days ... We figure the probable final cost will run to approximately $350,000—this being $25,000 under estimated budget.

Meanwhile, Basil Rathbone comes to Universal on a multi-film contract. Lee had directed the actor in the British *Love from a Stranger* (1937), in which Rathbone played a raving mad wife-slayer with an escalating, bravura intensity. Lee sees Rathbone as *his* star. As a team, he hopes they will do big things at Universal.

Wednesday, November 9: Lee starts shooting *Son of Frankenstein*. Rathbone plays the title role, Boris Karloff is the Monster, Lugosi acts old Ygor and Lionel Atwill portrays one-armed Inspector Krogh. Lee and his writer Wyllis Cooper virtually make up the horror saga day-to-day. M.F. Murphy, who'd so admired Lee's efficiency on *Service De Luxe*, wails in his production report about the $420,000 final cost (about $120,000 over budget) and the 46 shooting days (19 days over schedule). Lee finishes at 1:15 a.m. January 5, 1939, and Universal releases the horror epic only eight days (!) later.

March 14, 1939: Lee starts *The Sun Never Sets*, a purple paean to the British Empire. The heroes are Rathbone (who, since *Son of Frankenstein*, played Sherlock Holmes for the first time in 20th Century Fox's *The Hound of the Baskervilles*) and Douglas Fairbanks, Jr. The villain (an ant-studying madman, hell-bent on starting a world war) is Lionel Atwill. Shooting begins with only 30 pages of revised final script. It wraps up May 3. Lee announces the film needs a prologue and montage sequence and resumes shooting May 10. The final cost is $586,000, more than $60,000 over budget.

All of which indicates that Rowland V. Lee has become rather a problem child at Universal. He's a talented director, no doubt, who daubs the screen with lavish production value; *Son of Frankenstein*, for example, has a wonderful fairy tale aura. Universal has always excelled at melodrama, and Lee appears destined to launch such studio fare into a new, prestigious realm. Yet, after his good behavior on *Service De Luxe,* he's prone to running wildly over schedule and budget.

This is dangerous at a studio that dreams of its first profitable season in several years.

Horror Crown Prince: Vincent Price, fated decades later to reign as Hollywood's horror king, as the Duke of Clarence—doomed to perish in a wine vat.

Epic Scoundrels: Basil Rathbone as Richard III and Ian Hunter as King Edward IV

Monday, April 17: As *The Sun Never Sets* is shooting, *Variety* headlines, "U Adds $5,000,000 This Year On Big Schedule." Announced in the report is *Tower of London*. The producer/director is Rowland V. Lee; the star is Basil Rathbone.

Tuesday, June 20: *Variety* runs this item:

> Universal has the world's easiest casting job in *Tower of London*. For executioner—Boris Karloff.

Wednesday, June 21: "Give 'Em the Axe," headlines *Variety*:

> Rowland V. Lee gets the directing chore on Universal's *Tower of London*, with Basil Rathbone as Richard III and Boris Karloff as the executioner. Picture rolls about August 1.

Richard III is an ideal role for Rathbone. Hollywood has only offered the movie public Richard once before: John Barrymore, carrying a severed head atop a mountain of corpses, delivering the soliloquy in an episode of Warner Bros.' *The Show of Shows* (1929).

> Why, love forswore me in my mother's womb ...
> She did corrupt frail nature with some bribe
> To shrink mine arm up like a wither'd shrub;
> To make an envious mountain on my back,
> Where sits deformity to mock my body ....

Meanwhile, Mord, the tower executioner, is a made-in-heaven (?) role for Karloff. Since *Son of Frankenstein*, Karloff's stardom had spiked, and on April 17, Alta Durant, in her *Variety* "Gab" column, ran this amusing news:

> Fans [are] no longer willing to take Boris Karloff straight since horror make-up reached [a] new high in *Son of Frankenstein* ... 500 autographed photos of thesp[ian] showing natural rather than monster mien having been returned by recipients in [the] last three weeks ... with requests for art showing him as [the] public rather than [as] Hollywood knows him.

Writing the script is Lee's brother, Robert N. Lee. Universal even plans to erect a facsimile of the Tower of London on the back lot. Then, as production approaches in July 1939, there's a major problem:

Basil Rathbone is overbooked.

First of all, Rathbone is busy working this June at 20th Century Fox filming *The Adventures of Sherlock Holmes*. Universal has scheduled him for *Rio*, a saga in which Rathbone will portray an escapee from a French penal colony. Meanwhile, RKO has baited Basil with the role of Frollo, the wicked chief justice of *The Hunchback of Notre Dame*. Indeed, as the July 6 shooting date for *Hunchback* comes near, *The Hollywood Reporter* lists Rathbone in that film's cast list, along with Charles Laughton as Quasimodo and Maureen O'Hara as Esmeralda. Then supposedly comes *Tower of London*, which will also conflict with *Hunchback*'s shooting schedule.

Storybook lovers: John Sutton as John Wyatt and Nan Grey as Lady Alice

Karloff's Mord merrily showing off his mighty axe to admiring wenches as the Tower looms above them.

Although Rathbone can hardly voice his feelings publicly—and probably doesn't want to offend his friend Rowland Lee—he surely must prefer to do *Hunchback*. It is to be one of 1939's biggest productions, a spectacular budgeted at $1,826,000; the combined costs of Universal's *Rio* and *Tower of London* will only approximate half of what RKO will invest in *Hunchback*. Also, the role of Frollo, the anguished, black-robed zealot, "bewitched" by Esmeralda, climactically trying to kill both her and Quasimodo, will likely be the richest film villain role Rathbone has ever played—and as directed by the masterful William Dieterle, maybe even more dimensional than "Crookback" Richard.

Universal and RKO try to arrange a schedule where Rathbone can make both *Rio* and *The Hunchback of Notre Dame*. It will be a daunting challenge, no doubt exhausting for the star, but Rathbone is eager.

Saturday, July 8: *Variety* headlines, "Rathbone May Leave *Hunchback* for *Rio*":

> Overlapping assignments probably will take Basil Rathbone out of RKO's *Hunchback of Notre Dame* in favor of Universal's *Rio*, slated to start next week. Both studios have endeavored to work out schedules to accommodate, but prospects for Rathbone in *Hunchback* yesterday seemed to have gone glimmering.

Glimmer away it does.

Thursday, July 20: Universal begins shooting *Rio*. Rathbone co-stars with Sigrid Gurie, the Samuel Goldwyn discovery promoted as an Aphrodite from Norway. (The truth will come out eventually that she was actually born in Brooklyn.) John Brahm (fated for 1944's *The Lodger*) directs. M.F. Murphy soon predicts that *Rio* will likely extend beyond a 30-day schedule and the approximated $450,000 budget.

Meanwhile, *Tower of London* is set to start shooting come early August. Rowland V. Lee decides he better consider a new Richard III.

On July 18, Paramount's *Beau Geste* had a gala premiere at the Carthay Circle Theatre, and Brian Donlevy is a sensation as the Foreign Legion's scar-faced Sgt. Markoff. Lee decides to test Donlevy for Richard III. It's a bit daunting to imagine Donlevy (who would never play a medieval role in his 90-plus films career) in 15th century wig and a hump on his back, lurking as Richard III; nevertheless, he's game.

Saturday, July 29: George Phair writes in his "Retakes" column in *Variety*:

> Universal is cooking up something extra-special in the horror line. How would you like to meet Boris Karloff and Brian Donlevy in *The Tower of London* on a foggy night?

Friday, August 4: Six days after Phair's notice, *Variety* reports that Lee has cast Nan Grey and Barbara O'Neil in *Tower of London*'s "top femme roles." Ms. Grey (who played the victim of Gloria Holden's lesbian-tinged attack in Universal's 1936 *Dracula's Daughter*) will play Lady Alice, the heroine; Ms. O'Neil (who'd

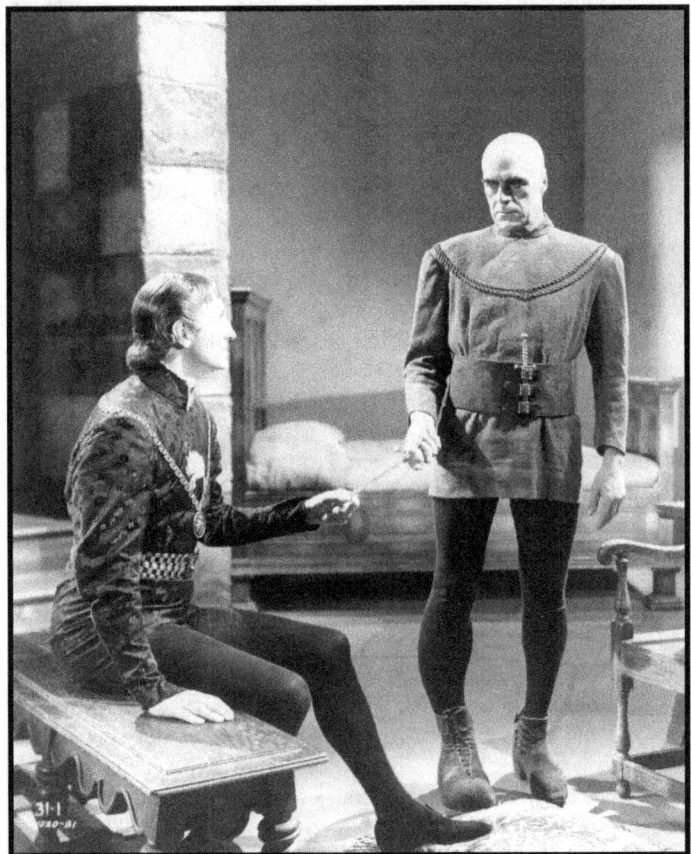

Rathbone's Richard assures Karloff's Mord that this cross-shaped dagger will "insure the thrust and bless the wound."

Rathbone's Richard and Rose Hobart's Anne Neville; Hobart played Muriel in Paramount's 1931 *Dr. Jekyll and Mr. Hyde*.

just played Scarlett O'Hara's mother in *Gone with the Wind* and had been one of the leading ladies in Lee's *The Sun Never Sets*) will play Queen Elyzabeth (as the film's credits spell it). The same *Variety* notice writes that Lee has cast George Sanders and John Sutton. Sanders is to play Edward IV, Richard's compatriot in crime; John Sutton will play the heroic John Wyatt.

The news in this notice is definite—these actors will appear "in support of Basil Rathbone and Boris Karloff."

At any rate, the final roster of *Tower of London* creates a whirlwind of cast changes, affecting several studios.

Sir Cedric Hardwicke replaces Rathbone as Frollo in *The Hunchback of Notre Dame*.

Since Hardwicke had been committed to playing a British officer in RKO's Revolutionary War saga *Allegheny Uprising*, George Sanders leaves *Tower of London* and comes to RKO to replace Hardwicke. Sanders also lands a featured role in James Whale's *Green Hell*, to begin shooting at Universal on August 21.

Ian Hunter, borrowed from MGM, will play (very well) Sanders' vacated role of Edward IV. Brian Donlevy, who also appears in *Allegheny Uprising* as a heavy, fulfills his Universal commitment as the villain in the Marlene Dietrich–James Stewart Western *Destry Rides Again*, which will start shooting September 7.

Basil Rathbone will have to work in *Tower of London* as he's finishing *Rio*. Vincent Price, cast as the Duke of Clarence, will have to go back and forth between *Tower of London* and *Green Hell*.

Still, all looks promising. Jack Pierce provides Karloff a nightmarishly vivid Mord make-up—a shaved head, a clubfoot and eyebrows that look like gorged caterpillars. Then there's the Tower—a foreboding 75-foot structure looming above a back lot lake. Set designer Jack Otterson has designed the set, so Universal claims, after examining the Tower's original 13th century blueprints. In some ways, the Tower is a more impressive set than RKO's *Hunchback* Notre Dame Cathedral, which stands on the flats of the RKO Ranch in Encino, without the two towers that will be matted in to complete the effect.

Friday, August 11: *Tower of London* began shooting, with an estimated budget of $490,000 and a schedule of 36 days.

An interesting camera angle that captures Karloff's Mord and his army of beggars.

"While it is somewhat early to make predictions," writes M.F. Murphy the next day, "we feel, if encountering any sort of good luck, it will be quite possible to finish up within just a few days of this schedule."

> "I've never killed in hot blood!"
> Boris Karloff as Mord, begging
> Basil Rathbone's Richard III to
> allow him to go into battle, from
> *Tower of London*

It's hot that summer in the San Fernando Valley—very hot.

As temperatures soar, *Tower of London* wins plenty of attention at Universal City. Basil Rathbone is a sly, beguiling serpent of a Richard, his "Crookback" wearing a very modest "hump," the real deformity the one in his soul. He acts with a splendidly vile majesty, royally wicked in speech and action. At one point he sends Mord into an alcove to kill the senile old King (Miles Mander), as the graybeard is praying, handing the executioner a dagger that resembles a cross.

The blasphemous weapon will, Richard promises, "insure the thrust and bless the wound."

The star runs back and forth from *Rio* to *Tower of London*, changing from the contemporary hairpiece and wardrobe he wears

The Tower rises on Universal's back lot.

in the former to the 15th century Richard wig, silk tights and leather shoes that adorn him in the latter.

"I know now," jokes Rathbone, "what it's like to be a glamour girl!"

The wig, which photographs silvery in the black-and-white film, is actually reddish blonde in color, and it earns Rathbone a nickname on the Universal lot: "Harpo."

Then there's Karloff as Mord. With his bald head, the star evokes a Humpty Dumpty from Hell appearance, gaunt, deformed and loping about on his clubfoot, carrying an executioner's axe almost as tall as he is. Now and then he sports a hat with a peaked brim; in a nicely perverse touch, he goes through most of *Tower of London* wearing dark tights, which are fetching with his mini-skirt of a tunic and built-up shoes.

"There, my pretty," leers Boris' Mord as he captures John Sutton's fey hero Wyatt. "Let that be a lesson to you. Don't try to escape from old Mord!"

Amused by his own shaved head, Boris decides it will be fun if he shaves the head of his nine-month-old daughter Sara Jane, so they can be "baldies" together. Unfortunately, he proceeds without clearing the idea with his wife Dorothy.

"Boris, how *dare* you!" wails Dorothy.

Vincent Price, as the Duke of Clarence, scents his foppish role with a whiff of lavender, much as he perfumed several later roles; if there had been Gay Pride parades in 15th century England, one can easily imagine Price's Clarence straddling the lead horse. He also wears a heavy left eyelid (courtesy of Jack Pierce) to accentuate the sinister. It's intriguing that Price (who had wed actress Edith Barrett in April 1938) had been previously engaged to Barbara O'Neil, who's a wide-eyed eyeful as *Tower of London's* spirited Elyzabeth. The more prurient might well wonder how many lunches "Vinnie" and Barbara enjoyed together in the Universal commissary during the shoot.

George Robinson, cinematographer of Lee's previous three Universals, is cameraman again. He enjoys the film's pictorial flair; the *New York Daily News*, in its *Tower of London* review, will write that Robinson "gives every indication of having apprenticed on *Dante's Inferno*."

Monday, August 21: Harrison Carroll writes in his column in the *Los Angeles Evening Herald Express*:

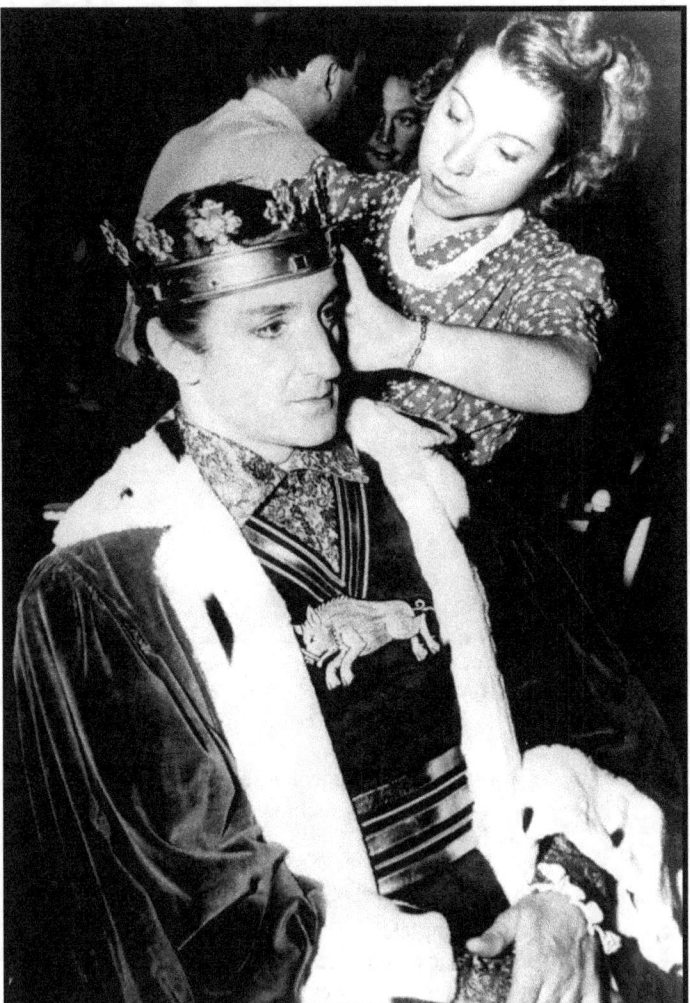

Rathbone joked that he learned what it was like to be "a glamour girl," due to his wig dressing and fancy costumes in *Tower of London*.

> For drama, Hollywood sound stages have offered nothing recently to top the scene in *Tower of London* where Basil Rathbone as Richard III sat in a royal box and watched executioner Boris Karloff chop off the head of a young man who the tyrant had condemned to death.
>
> It took all day to photograph the grimly realistic scene and, by the time it was over, impressionable Rathbone was ready to collapse from nerves.
>
> He had a special reason. The actor portraying the executioner's victim was his 25-year-old son, Rodion Rathbone.

Rodion had previously acted in *The Dawn Patrol* (Warner Bros., 1938), in which his father had co-starred with Errol Flynn. These were Rodion's only two films.

Tuesday, August 22: Harry Mines of the *Los Angeles Daily News* reports his visit to Universal:

> By far the most exciting point of interest is the ghastly set where Boris

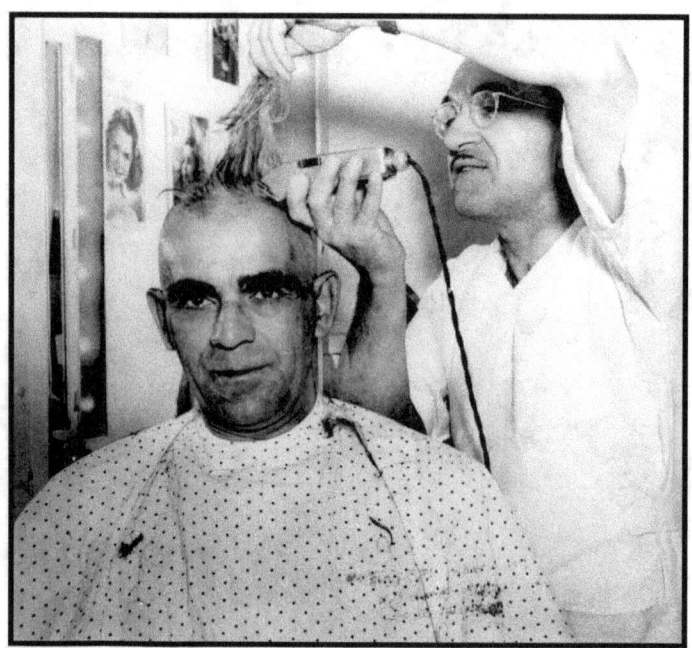
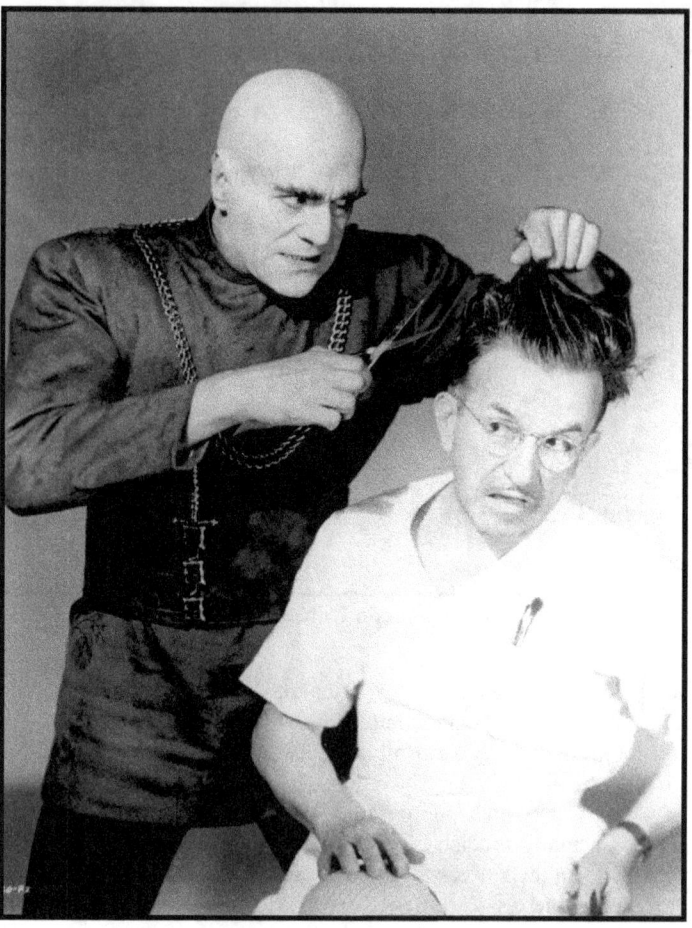

Above: Dedicated actor Boris Karloff sacrifices his hair (it grew back) to portray Mord; Right: Karloff pretends to get tonsorial revenge on make-up artist Jack Pierce in this studio shot.

Karloff, new horror make-up to his credit, plots further chills for avid fans in his role of the executioner in *Tower of London* …

For his role Karloff has had his head completely shaved, his ears pinned back to his head, a hump put on his nose and wears a clubfoot. His disguise is arranged so as to accentuate the superhuman strength of the man.

Friday, August 25: Alta Durant, in her "Gab" column in *Variety*, writes words that, considering the very hot weather, seem to prophesize possible disaster:

> Pre-dawn procession of 450 extras trekked out to Universal this morning in answer to 4 a.m. studio call … stars of *Tower of London* fared no better as studio … in search of realistic battle scene which necessitated foggy dawn brawl … ordered 6 a.m. shooting near Tarzana … film, laid in 14th (sic) century, has all players wearing chain mail and armor … [the] makeup department demanded two hours to stuff players into suits and fit wigs … plans are for washing up battle scene in one day's shooting.

The result, indeed, is a debacle. As Murphy bemoans in his August 26 *Tower of London* report:

> We are greatly concerned over the cost of this picture … We encountered a very serious setback yesterday with a crowd of 300 extras who left the studio at 4:00 a.m. to work at a nearby ranch location. Difficulties [occurred] with a special fog effect which we could not control because of wind, the breakdown of a pump when we switched to a rain sequence, a particularly hot day, plus a group of unruly, uncooperative, and destructive extras clothed in helmets and armor, all added to make this one of the most unsuccessful days we have had with a large crowd of people in many years.

Tuesday, August 29: "Extras Refused Work After Alleged Sabotage," reports a page one *Variety* headline:

> Fifty of 200 extras working in battle scenes for Universal's *Tower of London* were removed from [the] callback list yesterday after [a] protest had been filed with [the] Screen Actors Guild over [the] asserted lack of cooperation by players.
>
> Rowland V. Lee, producer-director in charge of picture, notified Antrim Short, SAG representative, that [a] big percentage of players were not cooperating, although they were being paid above Guild scale. Was claimed many of them tossed away equipment,

Rodion Rathbone, Basil's son, relaxes during the shooting of his execution scene with his famous father and a cigarette-smoking, axe-wielding Karloff.

"My kingdom for a whore": Rathbone cavorts with Marlene Dietrich, who was starring at Universal as saloon queen "Frenchy" in *Destry Rides Again*, while he was starring in *Tower of London*.

including spears, helmets and cordage breastplates, during shooting of [an] important scene.

Studio officials claimed [a] property truck which followed shooting was piled high with equipment that had been discarded by "soldiers" during [the] march up [the] hill to [a] battle scene. Was said action interfered with [the] shooting schedule and lowered [the] morale of [the] entire company.

Executives pointed out extras were receiving $11 day, although SAG scale for soldiers is only $8.25, with [a] uniform furnished. Pay was tilted, officials said, because [the] task was difficult, "soldiers" being required to wade [in the] stream. Was understood that by paying above scale [the] company expected to get more experienced players, who would be willing to cooperate during shooting.

The *Variety* article (which gives the number of extras as 200, as opposed to Martin Murphy's 300) intimates that the problems waged both Friday and Saturday, August 25 and 26, had been "ironed out" by Monday "after approximately 50 of [the] extras were removed and others substituted." The story went on:

> Film executives pointed out last night ... such action as that ... was causing companies to go outside [the] SAG zone to shoot important battle and crowd scenes. [The] situation is being investigated by SAG, and if evidence warrants, players who were reported will be called before [the] trial board where conviction might result in indefinite expulsion.

There are other problems:

Saturday, August 26: Murphy writes in his *Rio* report that, with Rathbone needed for *Rio* and *Tower of London*, *Rio* will have to trim its script's closing scenes.

The same day another problem arose. Distraught over costs on *Tower of London*, Murphy suggests the front office cut *Tower of London*'s St. John Chapel scene, in which, via the chicanery of Richard, two children of royal blood marry: five-year-old Donnie Dunagan (from *Son of Frankenstein*) as the "Baby Prince," and seven-year-old Joan Carroll as little "Lady Mowbray." Murphy argues this would cut $10,000 from the budget; "While this carries a certain air of pageantry and color," he writes, "as far as production values go, and although the sequence may be historical, it definitely has no bearing or development on the story."

Lee, fortunately, disagrees.

Friday, September 1: Hitler invades Poland. Anxiety overtakes the world and, naturally, the *Tower of London* set is no exception.

Saturday, September 2: *Rio* finally completes shooting. M.F. Murphy freshly assesses *Tower of London*:

> While the results of this production look unusually big and particularly

A production shot of the fight arena—note Vincent Price on the sidelines

promising, the progress is far from our schedule plans.

The film is four days behind schedule, will probably take a total of 42 days to complete (rather than 36), and Lee has fortunately won the battle about retaining the St. John Chapel episode. The sight of Master Dunagan and little Miss Carroll getting married is one of the most vivid episodes of *Tower of London*, both funny and shocking as the kiddies take their marriage vows.

"Ah will," promises Donnie Dunagan in his Texas accent, the two words—due to the incongruous drawl—among the film's most memorable. In a 2004 interview with the author, Donnie Dunagan chuckled about his royal casting.

"I was Junior Redneck number one!" he laughed.

Dunagan, who "had a ball" on *Son of Frankenstein*—going for ice cream with Rathbone, playing Checkers for quarters (and winning!) with Karloff—recalls that Rathbone wasn't always in comparable high spirits during *Tower of London*:

> I think Basil Rathbone was responsible for me being in *Tower of London*. He was angry that they kept cutting scenes out of the script. Not angry like rednecks get angry—he was a gentleman, always—but he was disturbed about the script.

Donnie remembers Karloff, whom he affectionately called "the Giant" after *Son of Frankenstein*, talking about the war that was looming on the horizon:

> Mr. Karloff made some remarks that I paid attention to, when we were sitting there, in different places with other adults. He was talking to some people who had European backgrounds, and he was very concerned about the recklessness, callousness and stupidity—he had great enunciation—of politicians and senior people ... how this thing was going to blow up and involve everybody for a long time.
>
> Somebody said, "No, it'll be over in a month." And he scolded them! Oh, he had his homework done! He was rattling off places, geo-political

Tower of London producer/director Rowland V. Lee adds sooty make-up to Nan Grey for her chimney sweep disguise.

Fast friends: Karloff becomes chummy with Universal's Baby Sandy, who burst into tears when taken away from Boris and back to her own set.

places in central Europe, places that I wouldn't have known at the time if they fell on me.

Mr. Karloff was extremely sensitive to what was happening, and he kept talking about the poor and defenseless people, the ones who couldn't protect themselves against what he perceived, and what ended up being ... World War II.

"You mention a word of this outside these walls ... I'll tear your tongues out!"

Boris Karloff as Mord, *Tower of London*

War is looming, but the stars are professionals, and high spirits are necessary for morale on a movie, especially one with a runaway budget, hot wigs, heavy costumes, corseted actresses and brutally hot weather.

Friday, September 8: *Variety*'s Alta Durant reports in her "Gab" column that Baby Sandy, Universal's 20-month-old star, has met Boris Karloff:

With trepidation, Universal flacks took Baby Sandy to meet Boris Karloff ... [the] latter in hideous executioner's costume for *Tower of London*'s initially scared babe, but Karloff's shaven pate attracted [the] gurgling youngster ... followed [by] Karloff's treating [the] kid to ice cream and [their] friendship was clinched with [the] "heavy" feeding youngster ... [the] babe's cry came when she was taken off Karloff's lap and [taken] back to [her] own set.

Of course, Vincent Price loved telling the story of his terrific *Tower of London* demise— drowned in the vat of Malmsey wine by Rathbone and Karloff. The wine Rathbone and Price quaffed down in the drinking duel was actually Coca-Cola. As for the wine vat, Price told *Cinefantastique*:

Boris and Basil, knowing I was new to the business, thought it was great fun to throw everything into that vat of wine—which was actually just water— old Coca-Cola bottles, cigarette butts, anything they could find to dirty it up. They knew at the end of the scene I had to get into it! They had fixed a handrail at the bottom of it, so I could dive down and hang onto it. I had to stay under for

50th Anniversary Issue [1963-2013] 115

Basil Rathbone, out of character, holds hands with Donnie Dunagan and Joan Carroll during the shooting of *Tower of London*.

a full 10 count, and then was yanked out by my heels. When I came out I got a round of applause from the crew, but I was disappointed not to see Boris and Basil. Then a few minutes later they reappeared. They congratulated me for playing the scene so well for a newcomer—and then they presented me with a case of Coca-Cola!

Saturday, September 16: Murphy reports:

Considering the type of work this company has been doing during the past week, they have made very good progress, averaging better than three pages each day. To accomplish this they have worked beyond the usual 6 p.m. each evening and [worked] two nights as late as 7:30 without dinner. We have concentrated on [filming] Karloff during this week and will succeed in finishing his role tonight, thereby eliminating $3,750.00 weekly from the payroll.

Monday, September 18: The hot weather goes berserk. The official top number this week will be 107.2, although some reports insist that Burbank registered 117 degrees, while Universal reportedly hit 130.

Thursday, September 21: *Variety* writes that, due to the record heat, Charles Laughton had lost six pounds in a single day while playing the Hunchback at the RKO ranch. The trade paper also reports that, on the saloon set of *Destry Rides Again*, Universal has "attached kegs of real beer to spigots, and told cast and crew to help themselves. Free beer has been assured until thermometers do [an] about face."

Lee cancels any *Tower of London* exterior shooting. His progress on stage sets that week, according to Murphy, is "consistently good."

Sunday, September 24: As the rains finally arrive, Carl Laemmle, Sr., Universal's founder, who had lost the studio to usurping new management in 1936, dies of a heart attack. He was 72. The funeral will be Tuesday, September 26. All Hollywood studios observe two minutes of silence, and then work continues, including *Tower of London*, which is now behind schedule.

> Karloff can't be taken seriously—else he would drive one insane of fright.
> Frank S. Nugent, *New York Times* review of *Tower of London*, December 12, 1939

The rain cools off Universal. Hedda Hopper writes that the "funniest sight of the week" is Basil Rathbone taking a break from the *Tower of London* set and joyously running about in the rain "in his short-shorts."

Wednesday, October 4: Production unofficially closes on *Tower of London* after 46 days of shooting—10 days over schedule. The estimated final cost is $533,000.

However ... production isn't over yet. Scenes are still needed to be shot of beggars ("no members of the cast—all extras and bit players," reports Murphy). Also, due to the farrago with the battle scenes, Lee feels he needs to embellish the sequences, with, as Murphy writes, "small groups of soldiers against process plates."

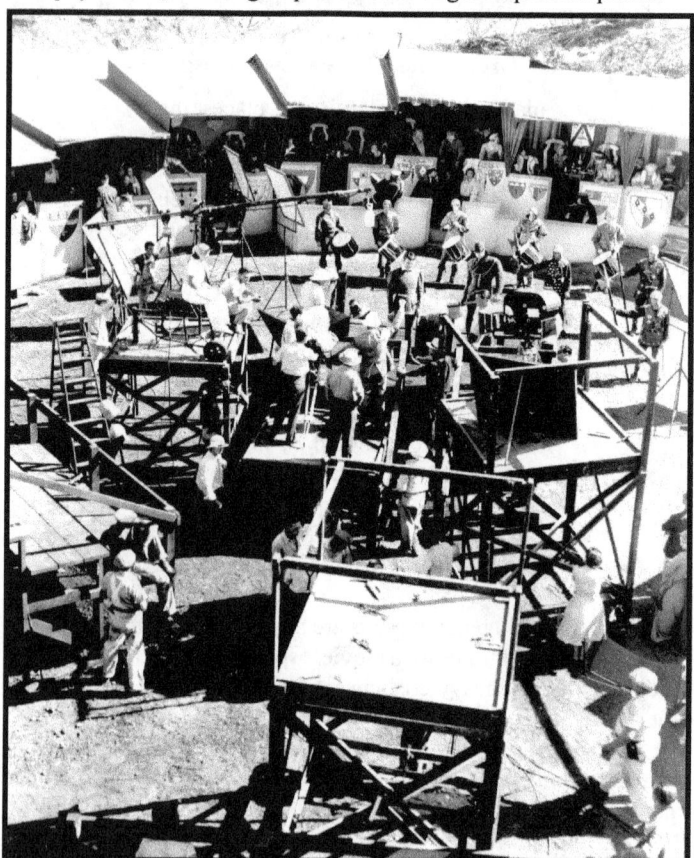

An aerial view of the Tower's execution area

Macabre mayhem reigns as Karloff's Mord swings his axe, the mob seethes and royalty watches from atop the Tower.

Tuesday, October 17: *Variety* reports:

> Adds for *Tower* —
> Principals in Universal's *Tower of London*, which Rowland V. Lee produces, were recalled yesterday for [one] day's shooting of added scenes. Basil Rathbone, Boris Karloff, John Sutton and Nan Grey check back on lot this morning.

As for the battle scenes ... the "embellishment" job goes to Ford Beebe, who directed such Universal fare as the 1939 Bela Lugosi serial *The Phantom Creeps*. Beebe will die on his 90th birthday in November 1978; in March of that year he writes a letter to Richard Bojarski (author of *The Films of Boris Karloff* and *The Films of Bela Lugosi*, and who died in 2009), recalling *Tower of London*. The letter is now in the archives of collector John Antosiewicz, who graciously shares its never-before-published content:

> Rowland V. Lee was a splendid director, but his forte was not what we know as "action" films. Fortunately he knew this and when he saw the first cut of *Tower of London*, he was the first to realize that its battle scenes lacked action. So he appealed to Martin Murphy, the production manager, to find one who could supply what the film lacked; and since I had been making nothing but action pictures for most of my life, Murphy suggested that he turn the job over to me.
>
> So we met and Lee told me to go the limit, that expense was no problem. "Just look at the film," he said, "and do anything you choose to liven up the battle scenes." It turned out to be one of the most enjoyable assignments I had ever had. The studio gave me everything I asked for, the best stunt men, and at the suggestion of my assistant (Charlie Gould), they gave me half a dozen horses clad in armor. The crew and I had a field day! They even let us work with a number of the actors to add a touch of reality to the stunts, Basil Rathbone, Boris Karloff and Ralph Forbes, and they all cooperated beautifully.
>
> As for Karloff ... To me the strangest bit about him is that of all the heavies in the business, it would have fallen to Boris to play the heaviest roles. In my experience I have never worked with a man who was so essentially gentle and so courteous as he. What made it even more astounding was that it was not the courtesy of a man of his standing ... trained to be so. It was a courtesy that was an inherent part of the man's character. He was not acting it; he was living it, and a greater compliment I cannot conceive.

Saturday, October 21: Murphy writes:

Esteemed character actor Leo G. Carroll as Lord Hastings

Execution! Rodion Rathbone, as Lord DeVere, loses his head to Karloff's Mord.

Since last Tuesday (October 17), we have been shooting additional scenes for this picture and encountering great difficulties in obtaining the various members of the cast [who are] at present occupied in other productions. Lee will finish up all his work tonight. Ford Beebe, shooting a second unit for the past two days, will finish up his work on Monday—all of this making a total shooting period for Lee of 51 days ... in addition to three days of second unit work. We figure these additional scenes will cost approximately $25,000 and our probable total final cost on the picture will run approximately $558,000.

Friday, November 23: It's Boris Karloff's 52nd birthday, and Universal hosts the first preview of *Tower of London.* Presumably it's not an overwhelming success, as M.F. Murphy writes the next day, "We believe a musical score will help this show considerably." Actually, the film already has a musical score. Charles Previn is the film's musical director. However, composer Hans J. Salter, Previn's associate on the film, told Preston Neal Jones in an interview in *Cinefantastique* (Vol. 7, No, 2, Summer, 1978):

> I remember *Tower of London* very well. What we tried to do there was to record music of that period, Dowland and other early English composers' music, without regard to the scene, just for sort of a mood. And we used harpsichord and flutes and viola da gambas—all those old instruments. But when we went to the preview with this, it didn't work out. The executives were somehow startled. They didn't like it. They couldn't make heads or tails out of that sound. I think I had orchestrated some of that old music for strings and harpsichord, and I think I wrote a few sequences, too, in that style. It was a good idea, but it didn't work. So, after the preview, all this music was replaced by other music, and some of it was from *Son of Frankenstein*.

Pageantry! Ian Hunter, Barbara O'Neil (as Queen Elyzabeth), Vincent Price and Frances Robinson; Price and O'Neil had been romantically involved prior to this film.

Intrigue! Karloff, Rathbone and Rose Hobart

Actually, music such as Salter described does appear here and there in the film, including the scene that climaxes with the murder of the two princes in the tower.

Tower of London's final cost is approximately $577,000. The average cost of a Hollywood feature film in 1939 was $275,000.

Thursday, November 16: *Tower of London* previews at the Alexander Theater in Glendale. *Variety*, aware of Universal's troubles with the film, is a bit extravagant in its review the next day:

> A horror picture designed to end all horror pictures ... while *Tower* is a chiller in the fullest sense of the word, it is something more ... It is a parade of pageantry and trappings as they actually existed in medieval times. It is a gripping cinematic offering, and, above all, a highly entertaining one.
>
> [The] Production and directorial achievements of Rowland V. Lee will zoom his professional stock to a new high, while the brilliant portrayal of his star, Basil Rathbone, definitely makes the latter a contender for Oscar consideration.
>
> Boris Karloff, heading the support as Mord, misshapen chief executioner and tool of Rathbone, never has had a role so befitting his talents for silver sheet gruesomeness. Beside it, his previous Frankenstein characterizations are dwarfed.

Friday, November 24: "RKO After Rowland Lee As Producer/Director," reports a page one *Variety* headline.

> Rowland V. Lee is being dickered by RKO on [a] producer/director deal. He returns Monday from Palm Springs, where he has been since the preview

of *Tower of London*, the final picture under his Universal contract.

Thursday, December 7: Universal, eager to give the film a splashy L.A. opening, presents *Tower of London* at Hollywood's 3,595-seat Paramount Theatre, with Glen Gray and his Casa Loma Orchestra live on stage. Erskine Johnson critiques in the *Los Angeles Daily News*:

> It's all pretty strong and morbid stuff, but if you like that sort of thing, you'll find it good melodrama. There is some fine acting by Rathbone, as No. 1 plotter for the throne, Karloff as the sinister chief executioner and Barbara O'Neil as Queen Elisabeth [sic]. The battle scenes, too, are exceptionally well-staged ... The wine "duel" between Rathbone and his younger brother, Vincent Price, is probably the best sequence in the film and provides its only bit of comedy.

The show plays a week, and *Variety* reports the take as "Nothing to get excited about at around $15,000."

Monday, December 11: *Tower of London* opens at New York City's 750-seat Rialto—and is a smash hit. *Variety* reports:

> Opened sensationally Monday (11) and should have a big week of around $14,000, kickoff being $2,300. This is the biggest Monday this small-seater has ever had, which is all the more remarkable in view of the time of the year it's done. House ran 10 full shows, grinding a total of 21 hours.

Tower of London actually hits over $15,000 at the Rialto, the second best week the theater ever had, and the movie is held over.

Friday, December 15: *Tower of London* enjoys its biggest ballyhoo as it opens at the 2,680-seat Warfield Theater in San Francisco. Appearing on stage in person are the film's stars Boris

Universal's *Tower of London* played up the horror more than the history.

Karloff, Nan Grey, and John Sutton, hosted by Mischa Auer—and featuring, as a bonus, Bela Lugosi!

It sounds terrific, but at least one disappointed patron attended. One B.J. Smith will write a stinging letter about the show to the editor of *Variety*, which publishes his lament January 10, 1940:

> The recent personal appearance of five Universal players in conjunction with the opening of *Tower of London* at the Warfield here stands as a glaring example of poor showmanship. Described at the opening by the m.c. Mischa Auer as, "Just a little something we knocked together on the phone on the way here—confidentially, it stinks," the show lived up in every way to Auer's statement.

Actually, "Confidentially, it stinks" was a paraphrase of Auer's line as the ballet teacher in Frank Capra's *You Can't Take It With You*, Columbia's Best Picture Oscar winner of 1938. Nevertheless, B.J. Smith wrote of the Universal contingent, "Equipped with poor material and in one case with none at all, it would seem that the picture might have had a better chance without their efforts." Then he itemized the ways the show did indeed "stink":

1. First there was Mischa Auer, who, Smith wrote, "offered two or three Hollywood jokes that the audience applauded out of politeness."

2. Then Auer introduced John Sutton, "a personable young man who stooged a minute or two" for Auer. Then Sutton walked off stage, "holding his belly." As Smith added, "We can understand that."

3. Then came Karloff, who as Smith reported, "got a big hand." Smith wrote that Karloff "proceeded to dish out a lot of 'up the years from the Majestic to the Warfield'," which presumably meant Boris told old theater stories, maybe about his struggles as an actor. Karloff also pleased the crowd by saying he'd "overheard there's a better than even break" that the San Francisco Fair of 1939 would reopen in 1940.

4. Bela Lugosi followed. Unfortunately Smith didn't describe what Bela precisely did; he merely wrote that he "tried hard for a while."

5. Finally, Bela introduced Nan Grey, who drew the sharpest criticism from Smith: "A great disappointment indeed. She is of the hand-kissing, arm-flinging I-love-you-all-my-public variety."

As Smith concludes, "All this might appear to be offset by the fact that the show was packed from noon till midnight by one pushover audience after another, mostly kids." At any rate, *Tower of London* was, as *Variety* called it, San Francisco's "best bet" that week and predicted it would take in a "nice" $14,000.

Tower of London does sporadic business. *Variety* reports vary; it was "getting some action" (as the trade paper expressed) in Baltimore, "oke" in D.C. and "brutal" (meaning very bad) in Chicago.

January 3, 1940: *Variety* headlines "Hollywood Toppers" on page one, listing 1939's biggest grossers from the major studios. Universal's list:

> *That Certain Age* (a Deanna Durbin vehicle, actually released in the fall of 1938, directed by Edward Ludwig)
> *When Tomorrow Comes* (starring Irene Dunne and Charles Boyer, directed by John Stahl)
> *You Can't Cheat an Honest Man* (W.C. Fields with Edgar Bergen and Charlie McCarthy, directed by George Marshall)

An ad heralding the personal appearance of Boris Karloff, Bela Lugosi, John Sutton, Nan Grey and emcee Mischa Auer at the opening of *Tower of London* at San Francisco's Warfield Theater, December 15, 1939. At least one spectator was disappointed.

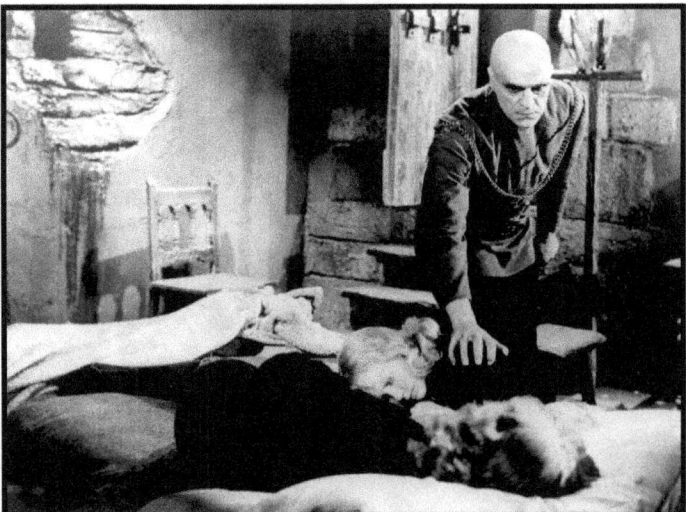

Karloff's Mord is ultimately unable to carry out the cinema's most horrific atrocity, the killing of children, in *Tower of London*.

East Side of Heaven (starring Bing Crosby, directed by David Butler)

Three Smart Girls Grow Up (another Durbin vehicle, directed by Henry Koster)

Destry Rides Again (Marlene Dietrich and James Stewart, directed by George Marshall)

None of Rowland V. Lee's four Universal films make the studio's "Topper" list. Nevertheless, with *Son of Frankenstein* and *Tower of London*, he'd bequeathed Universal two of its most majestic melodramas.

> [Boris Karloff was] one of the few (very select) of my Hollywood life I'd even care to mention. Boris came into it early on—my second or third film, *Tower of London*, and he and Basil Rathbone introduced me to a kind of joyousness of picture-making I too seldom encountered in the 100 films that came later …
>
> Vincent Price, letter to Cynthia Lindsay, author of *Dear Boris* (1975)

Seen today, *Tower of London* has its problems. Lee never excelled at pace. Rathbone has a less-than-stellar demise, killed in a climactic, sadly perfunctory sword duel with Henry Tudor (Ralph Forbes); he deserves a far more bloodthirsty come-uppance (see Olivier's chillingly violent death throes in his *Richard III* as an example of how an epic villain *should* die).

Nevertheless, *Tower of London* has plenty to offer. Here are my personal Top-12 episodes/moments from the film:

Meet Mord: A hellish hoot of an introduction, as we see Karloff's Mord in his torture chamber, sharpening his axe with a raven perched on his shoulder. "Razor sharp!" he exults.

The Execution of Lord DeVere: Morbid pomp and pageantry as Rodion Rathbone's Lord DeVere processes to his death, with a tolling bell and many extras. A nice touch is when DeVere tips the executioner, giving the hooded Mord the smallest of coins with the words, "Do your worst." Karloff spits on the coin and tosses it. Fadeout shot: Rathbone grinning.

Rathbone's Puppetry: Throughout the film, Richard slyly peeks at his closet of doll-like figures, all representing the powers-that-be who stand between him and the throne. He tosses his latest victims into the fireplace.

The Battle Scenes: Despite those 50 jackass extras, the rainy battle of Tewkesbury and the foggy climactic fight at Bosworth Field are both loud, nightmarish and look almost Expressionistic, with the dark figures and their weapons on the hill and horizon.

The Marriage Scene of the Two Children: One of *Tower of London*'s prize sequences. A singing choir of altar boys, the stunning entrance of the two children, Joan Carroll taller than Donnie Dunagan, the straight-faced crowd … Thank Heavens Lee fought Universal not to cut the episode!

The Drowning of Clarence in the Malmsey Vat: Truly a highlight, with Price's wild-eyed, boisterous laughter as he thinks he's won the drinking contest. A nice touch occurs when Price reaches over and spitefully rubs Rathbone's hump. (Incidentally, the original script had called for the character of Edward to pat Richard on his hump, but the censorship office nixed it, claiming it was "apt to give offense to people suffering from physical deformities.") Another nice touch is that huge splash that soaks Rathbone as Karloff slams down the vat lid on poor Price.

Boris Karloff (note the club foot) managed to get a bizarre pathos into the role of Mord, despite the character's nightmarish savagery.

Mordant Humor: At one point, Mord, while chatting with a minion, opens his iron maiden. A bleeding figure—corpse?—falls out. Mord barely notices, leaves the victim on the floor and runs off to perform some new perfidy.

Torture: Mord at work is a force of nature ... we see Karloff torturing John Sutton's Wyatt with whip, red-hot pincers and the rack. It's strong stuff for 1939.

Wyatt's Escape: Cinematographer George Robinson captures Wyatt escaping down the tower's face at night, the lake water shimmering on the wall, with a Romantic storybook charm.

Mord's Conscience: Karloff gets peculiar dimension into his role when he can't bring himself to carry out Richard's directive to kill the teenage princes in the tower. He recruits other killers and then watches the murders, his face a mix of both repulsion and fascination.

Richard's Aftermath: His death scene isn't much, but there's the nice barbaric touch of Rathbone's Richard's corpse, hooked to a horse, dragged off the battlefield as his enemies shout and spit at the cadaver—the corpse on its way, presumably, to the Leicester parking lot.

Mord's Demise: Finally allowed to kill in "hot blood" at Bosworth Field, Karloff's Mord sees Richard dead on the battlefield, killed by Ralph Forbes' Henry Tudor. "You're a god to me," Mord told Richard early in the film. Now, in a God-Is-Dead panic, Mord flees, battles a pursuing Wyatt, suffers a hacking, falls into a tree that hangs from the edge of a cliff and both Mord and the tree tumble down the cliff. In a vivid irony, Karloff's Mord dies screaming.

A bonus 13th fine moment, and my personal favorite: After Mord asked to accompany Richard to the Battle of Tewkesbury, and has been rather brusquely denied, we see the bandy-legged executioner, sadly watching the soldiers riding and marching off to glorious battle, as he slowly stalks back through an archway, alone and seemingly heartbroken. It's a weirdly sad vignette, reminding us what a splendid actor Boris Karloff was.

A real star of the show is the Tower itself. It later appeared in too many films to mention, but just one here—it's Karloff's "Mad Doctor" castle in 1944's *House of Frankenstein*, where Glenn Strange's Monster throws J. Carrol Naish's Hunchback (actually his double, Billy Jones) through a skylight, and he topples from the Tower roof for a crowd pleasing demise.

Of course, Golden Age horror fans will most enjoy *Tower of London*. Many familiar faces and forms abound to enjoy: Rose Hobart (from 1931's *Dr. Jekyll and Mr. Hyde*) as Anne Neville; Leo G. Carroll (*Tarantula*) as the faithful Hastings; Lionel Belmore (from 1931's *Frankenstein*) as Beacon, a florid old attendant who announces demises; Harry Cording (from 1934's *The Black Cat*) as one of the killers who slay the princes in the tower. The *Son of Frankenstein* musical score works effectively. And best of all, there's Rathbone, Karloff and Price, 24 years before they'd team up again (and with Peter Lorre) in American-International's *The Comedy of Terrors*.

Finally, as Vincent Price wrote, there's a joy in *Tower of London*, amidst the beheading axe, torture rack, and marriage and killing of children. Despite the film's many production travails we have a happy camaraderie of actors, clearly enjoying a merry romp in this crazy melodrama, fated to make indelible impressions in the horror genre.

So ... with Richard III's skeleton facing re-burial in 2014, *Tower of London* might be Universal's classic melodrama of the hour. Indeed, in its star trio, the film boasts a boisterous Hollywood Horror Royalty, and a command performance encore is in order for all who pay homage in their realm.

Greg Mank's new book, *The Very Witching Time of Night: Twists and Tangents in Classic Horror*, is forthcoming from McFarland.

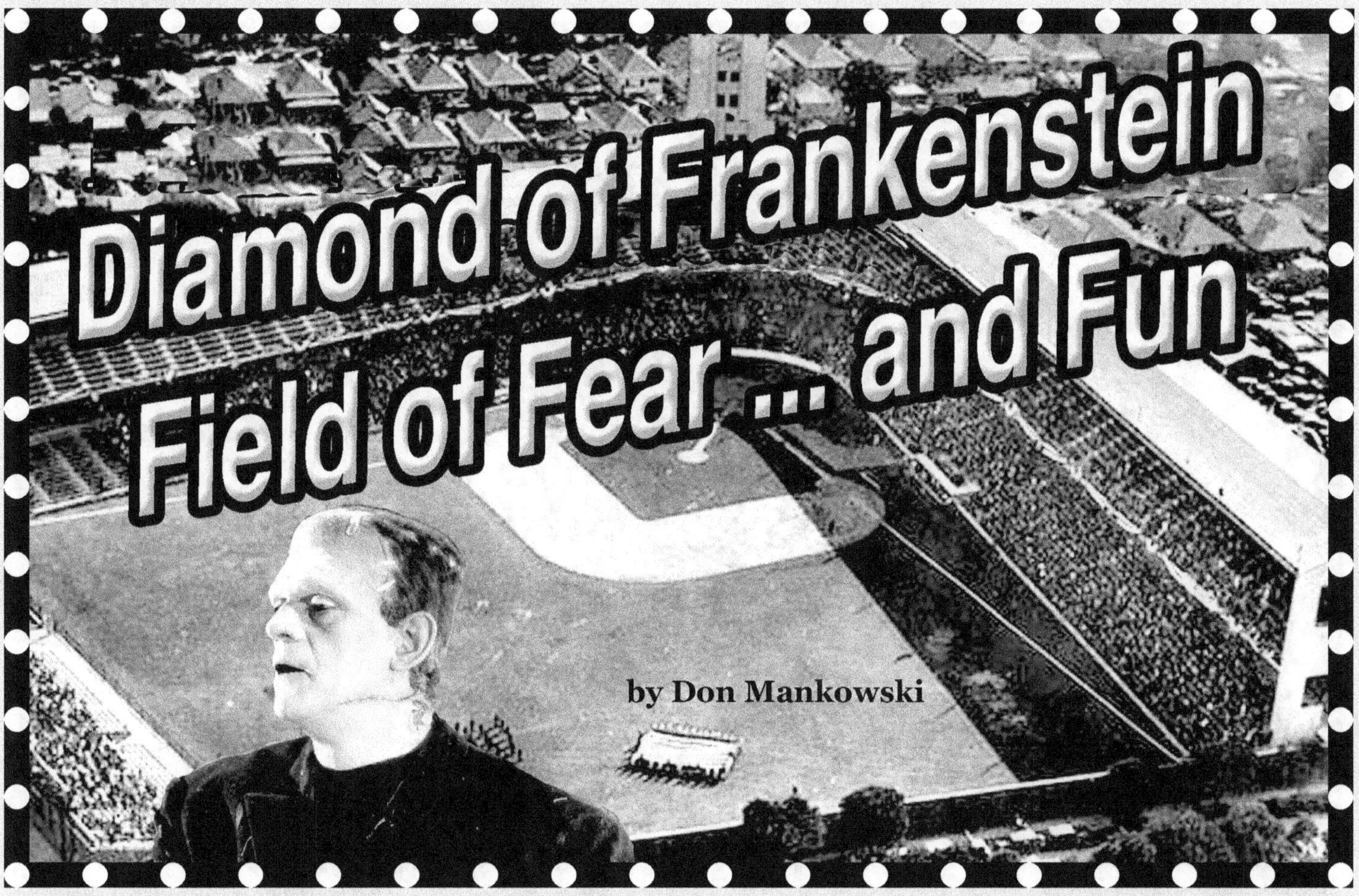

Diamond of Frankenstein
Field of Fear ... and Fun

by Don Mankowski

They say that one day in 1954, when Marilyn Monroe returned home after entertaining U.S. troops in Korea, she told her husband about appearing before an appreciative crowd of 60,000. "Dear, you never heard such cheering!"

"Yes, I have," replied Joe DiMaggio.

It's not your typical family story, but it does suggest the public's passion for the silver screen and the national pastime. For a really big event, combine the two.

It all started in 1935 when Hollywood annually provided the talent for a couple of very unusual competing baseball teams. Whether or not they could play the game, one of the teams would certainly *look* good out there, and the other could promise some *action*. It would be the Leading Men versus the Comedians. All heroes, please note, no villains, as it was all for a good cause. Mount Sinai Hospital and Free Clinic would be the beneficiary.

The 1940 game was scheduled for August 8, a Thursday night, at Wrigley Field in Los Angeles. Our interest in this game stems from one remarkable appearance—featuring the Frankenstein Monster, the real one.

Today, the name *Wrigley Field* at once conjures up memories of the bucolic ivy-lined shrine incongruously situated deep within the City of the Big Shoulders—and of its hopeful but hapless tenant team. But once long ago a doppelganger appeared. In 1925, Cubs' owner and chewing gum tycoon William Wrigley, Jr. built a smaller version of the Chicago edifice for his minor league team, way out West, in South-Central Los Angeles.

In point of fact, this park was the *first* Wrigley Field. The Windy City version was built as Weeghman Park in 1914 for the Chicago Whales of the short-lived Federal League. The Cubs took it over in 1916 when the Feds folded. It was Cubs Park in 1925, and it wouldn't be known as Wrigley Field until 1926. The smaller park, which played host to the Los Angeles Angels and sometimes the Hollywood Stars as well, had a lighting system as early as 1931; the Chicago field wouldn't support night baseball until one night in 1988 (coincidentally 48 years to the day after the event under discussion here).

No major league baseball would exist on America's left coast until 1958. Teams in the thriving Pacific Coast League had to represent the great cities that had grown here—San Diego, Los Angeles, San Francisco, Oakland, Sacramento, Portland and Seattle. Joe DiMaggio and Ted Williams broke into organized ball with PCL teams. On a lesser scale, slugger Steve Bilko of the Angels was a 1950s PCL star. Actor Phil Silvers swiped that man's surname for his television character. By the 1950s, the PCL was regarded as the strongest minor league ever. It was undercut only when the major leagues moved into its best cities, though it survives to this day with a reduced profile.

Hollywood studios often used Wrigley West to film baseball action. Some on-field scenes from the following productions were shot here: *Alibi Ike* (1935), *Pride of the Yankees* (1942), *Whistling in Brooklyn* (1943), *It Happens Every Spring* (1949),

Above: Los Angeles' Wrigley Field, the site of the celebrity baseball game in 1940; Below: Inside the Wrigley Field stadium

One year after playing the bulkier Monster in *Son of Frankenstein*, Boris Karloff (in make-up created once again by Jack Pierce) as a skinnier Monster terrifies catcher Buster Keaton in the 1940 celebrity charity baseball game.

Kill the Umpire (1950), *Rhubarb* (1951), *The Winning Team* (1952), *Pride of St. Louis* (1952), *The Kid from Left Field* (1953), *Damn Yankees* (1958) and many television shows, such as sitcom episodes and the sports challenge show *Home Run Derby*. Be on the lookout for a pretty park with double decks around home plate but no seating at all behind the left field wall. Of course, some of the films utilized footage taken at other parks for certain scenes. In the finished movie, a ball struck in one park might be fielded in another, thousands of miles away!

L.A.'s Wrigley was notoriously hitter-friendly, with freakishly short power alleys. A record number of homers were bashed there in 1961, the one year it played host to a major league team. Appropriately, Steve Bilko, then with the American League's new version of the Angels, was the last man to sock one at Wrigley.

It was on August 8 that press releases announced the names of stars as they were added to the rosters. Several practice sessions were held during July at Hollywood Ball Park. By July 21 readers had learned that Marlene Dietrich and Paulette Goddard would serve as honorary captains of the "heroes" and the "buffoons," respectively. Randolph Scott, Fred Astaire, Gene Raymond and Lee Tracy signed onto Dietrich's squad. Goddard would have the services of Mischa Auer, Billy Gilbert, Edgar Kennedy, Henry Armetta, Guinn "Big Boy" Williams and the Ritz Brothers.

On the comedians' side was African-American tap dancing legend Bill "Bojangles" Robinson. Imagine the sight of him playing second base and executing the pivot on a double play. Incredibly, this was seven full years before another player named Robinson integrated the major leagues. Men of their race were not welcome on a major league roster at this time, though you'll find several on the "star" squads.

Curiously missing was Joe E. Brown. One of Hollywood's greatest baseball fans, Brown had participated in all of the earlier games, even suffering a broken finger in the 1937 contest. Also absent were Richard Arlen, John Boles, James Cagney and Glenn Morris (Olympic decathlon champion and star of *Tarzan's Revenge*), who had played in previous contests. It's unfortunate, because according to reports, these fellows could actually *play* some baseball!

As the stakes went higher, the charmers added Preston Foster and the funny guys countered with Hugh "Woo Woo" Herbert. This was to be the first night game in the series, and Louella Parsons wrote that tickets were at a premium.

Hedy Lamarr would be grand marshal of a "parade of stars" before the game, which would begin at eight o'clock. In between innings features on a portable stage entertained the assembled. Child star Jane Withers signed on to lead the cheering section for both sides.

One writer proclaimed it "the most expensive aggregation of *baseball talent* ever gathered together on a diamond." Expensive talent it was. (Detailed lists of the participants are provided. Certainly, some men were qualified for either team. It's not certain how many participated as players and how many appeared only in supporting acts.)

Hedda Hopper described Paulette Goddard's on-field attire as "The Sarong That's All Wrong," but she conceded that it was a popular item with the fans. When the game began, Milton Berle was performing announcer duties on the stadium's public address system. The umpires were Kay Kyser, Jackie Gleason, Chico Marx (do you detect a Comedian bias here?) and Thurston Hall.

The name of one very special participant had been withheld, as there was to be a memorable pinch-hitting appearance.

Karloff's Monster passes his true creator, make-up artist Jack Pierce (far right), as he moves through the stadium crowd.

A Leading Man, we are told, should be tall, dark and handsome. Two out of three isn't bad. Thus did The Frankenstein Monster make his appearance, embodied by Boris Karloff. It must have been the highlight of the game.

Based upon the sketchy details, one might have *imagined* Karloff working a terrified pitcher, perhaps Mantan Moreland, for a walk, then taking a cautious lead off first, wary of a hidden ball trick involving Jerry Colonna's mustache. Gary Cooper then steps into the batter's box in his *Pride of the Yankees* uniform, the one with the backward "4" on it so that he can hit right-handed and be reversed into a facsimile of Lou Gehrig. Catcher Buster Keaton gives the secret sign for "high and inside" by pointing to the batter's skull. Coop, undaunted, smashes a grounder to the mostly Stooges infield, becoming a perfect double play for Howard, Fine and Howard. But Boris breaks up the play with a hard slide, knocking Curly into left field! Of course, Shemp has to come off the bench to replace him. A big inning looms as John Wayne steps in. Is that Bela Lugosi in the dugout, brandishing a Devil Bat?

Didn't happen. Not quite that way.

News accounts are very sparse with regard to the game itself. Frustratingly, they all boil down to the tried-and-true "a good time was had by all." The Comedians won by a 5-3 score. According to *The Los Angeles Times*:

"Jack Benny, with two bodyguards and two scriptwriters, appeared on the mound to hurl to Fred Allen, who was accompanied by three bodyguards. Allen asked Benny, 'Did you warm up?' Benny replied in the affirmative, whereupon Allen parried, 'I thought I smelled ham burning.'"

Karloff's Monster takes a swing at the ball with catcher Buster Keaton behind home plate.

Jack took umbrage, and it wasn't even raining. Additional bodyguards appeared and things got rowdy. It took the crowd control skills of The Keystone Cops to restore a semblance of order.

Lucien Littlefield (somehow) pitched disappearing baseballs. Kay Kyser's umpiring was praised for its consistency: They said he "called *everything* wrong." Not only did Karloff ("In Frankenstein costume") homer, if we are to believe the account, so did The Invisible Man. No details exist of the latter stunt. Perhaps it involved some shadow ball, with effective pantomime by a pitcher (Fred Astaire comes to mind) serving up an elaborated phantom pitch, and then gracefully spinning about to watch the mighty but nonexistent drive leave the park.

Don Glut's 1973 book *The Frankenstein Legend* has the site of the game as Gilmore Stadium, which is a reasonable, though incorrect, guess. We are indebted to him for this tantalizing description of the Karloffian at-bat. When The Monster lurched out of the dugout and toward the batter's box …

"Catcher Buster Keaton did a backward somersault and feigned unconsciousness. The Monster swung his bat at the ball and hardly tapped it due to the restraining clothing. Then he stalked toward first base. The first baseman fainted on the spot. At second base, all Three Stooges fainted. The same happened at third base, allowing the Frankenstein Monster awkwardly to make a home run."

Accounts vary as to how hard, or rather how soft, Karloff hit the ball. He may have missed it entirely, but surely the umpire would have ignored so trivial a nicety as contact for the sake of the stunt.

The few surviving photographs show the 52-year-old Karloff, in Jack Pierce make-up, looking much like his slimmer Monster of *Frankenstein* and *The Bride of Frankenstein*. It appears that he had sweated off much of the added bulk that we perceived in *Son of Frankenstein*. It was surely his biggest live audience in the immortal role. (Close inspection of the photos reveals eyeglasses on the Monster!) Given the built-up boots and leg braces, the terror-assisted home run must have featured the slowest circuit of the bases ever witnessed.

Five to three? That's a rather sedate score for a game that had promised so much. Based upon accounts of previous games, they probably played only enough innings to provide for an appearance by everyone. Surely the between-innings agenda consumed a lot of time. It would be wonderful to find a play-by-play account, but it would certainly be confusing.

Apparently, these games always bordered on diamond anarchy, featuring funny clothes, exploding bats, doctored

Even without showing the heads, one can easily see Karloff stomping on the catcher's foot as the Monster touches home plate.

The intense Boris Karloff (apparently wearing glasses) takes another swing at the ball.

baseballs and various vehicles on the field. The corpse of General Abner Doubleday (incorrectly credited with inventing baseball) probably required annual reburial back at Arlington National Cemetery after having spiraled to the surface. In 1936, gangster player Jack "Trigger" LaRue safely ran out a short home run by *shooting* (with blanks, of course) all the infielders in turn with his pearl-handled .45. The previous year, he had shot the umpire after two called strikes.

In 1937, LaRue refrained from shooting anyone (perhaps because Ty Cobb was an umpire and might have fired back with live ammo), but the Leading Men snuck a real ballplayer, Ernie Orsatti of the Cardinals, into the game as a ringer for Paul Muni. ("I knew that Muni was a great actor, but look at him in center! He sure can pick it!") If that name is somehow familiar to you, it's probably because Ernie's son and namesake would be a prolific movie stuntman. The score of the 1938 game remains unrecorded. Chaos ensued after the Ritz Brothers took over the umpiring duties.

The 1940 attendance was announced as 37,700, the largest crowd in Wrigley Field history. As the official park capacity was but 20,500, clearly standing room only occurred with the overflow crowd standing in roped-off sections of the outfield, according to an old custom. Box seat patrons included Jeanette MacDonald, Basil Rathbone, Nigel Bruce, Fredric March, Frank Capra, Samuel Goldwyn. Darryl Zanuck, Busby Berkeley, Howard Hughes and Will Hayes.

Hollywood, My Home Town, a 1965 documentary compiled and hosted by Ken Murray, features approximately eight seconds of The Monster leaving the dugout (Jack Pierce is briefly evident to one side) and approaching home plate, certainly from the 1940 event. Unfortunately, Murray's narration describes Karloff as "the umpire," and said clip is inserted amidst footage from other Hollywood charity games of ensuing years featuring Burt Lancaster, Frank Sinatra and Mickey Rooney in uniform, and so the documentary is useless as a historical item. "I was never one to spoil a good story by the lack of a few facts," says Murray a few moments later.

Mount Sinai Hospital opened its Free Clinic for the sick and needy of East Los Angeles on November 3. Rabbi Edgar F. Magnin and Edward Arnold, president of Screen Actors Guild, spoke at an outdoor dedication. Arnold paid tribute to the movie stars who had taken part in the annual baseball games that funded the clinic.

For the 1941 game, the Comedians announced plans to extend their winning streak by using scooter bikes to "run" the bases. The Leading Men would counter with nails and tacks along the baselines. Olson and Johnson (guess which team) planned to use long-handled butterfly nets in the field, in further degradation of a great sport. A football version of the rivalry was set for October of that year.

"For screwy stuff on the diamond Los Angeles doesn't need the Brooklyn Dodgers—it has the annual Comedians' and Leading Men's baseball game … " wrote a *Los Angeles Times* writer. It was just a lucky guess that Los Angeles *would* get the Dodgers one day. The team rumored most likely to move to California had been the St. Louis Browns. Their planned exodus was spoiled by WW2 and its necessary travel restrictions.

The last widely reported Leading Men versus Comedians game was the 1943 contest, though sporadic attempts to revive the custom occurred in later years. Ronald Reagan reportedly broke a leg in a 1949 match against a squad of comedians.

It would be nice, in a *Field of Dreams* sort of way, to make a pilgrimage to that cozy ballpark in the City of Angels and stand on its pitcher's mound on a warm summer night as the witching hour approached, feeling a Pacific breeze on one's face. It wouldn't be the spirits of Shoeless Joe Jackson and Buck Weaver that we'd sense, but rather those of Paul Douglas, Ray Milland, Gary Cooper, Dan Dailey, William Bendix, Ray Walston and Gwen Verdon. And a certain hulking figure who appeared surprisingly in the batter's box.

Alas, Los Angeles' Wrigley Field was razed circa 1966. A public park and community health facilities occupy its footprint.

However, Gilbert Lindsay Park *does* feature a small baseball diamond.

Following is an alphabetical list of participants in the 1940 charity game.

I cannot vouch for who showed up, or what role he played.

Comedians: (Paulette Goddard, Captain): Fred Allen, Eddie "Rochester" Anderson, Mischa Auer, Jack Benny, Charles Butterworth, Leo Carillo, Jerry Colonna, Broderick Crawford, Andy Devine, Wallace Ford, Billy Gilbert, Hugh "Woo Woo" Herbert, Allan Jenkins, Dickie Jones, Bobby (Dead End Kid) Jordan, Buster Keaton, John Kelly, Edgar Kennedy, The Keystone Cops, Arthur Lake, Jack LaRue, Lucien Littlefield, Keye Luke, Ken Murray, The Ritz Brothers, Bill Robinson, George E. Stone, The Three Stooges, Guinn (Big Boy) Williams.

Leading Men: (Marlene Dietrich, Captain): Frank Albertson, Desi Arnaz, Edward Arnold, Fred Astaire, Sidney Blackmer, Johnny Mack Brown, John Carroll, Gary Cooper, Robert Cummings, Errol Flynn, Preston Foster, Cary Grant, John Hubbard, Buck Jones, Rod LaRocque, Peter Lorre, Adolphe Menjou, Dennis Morgan, Wayne Morris, George Murray, Edward Norris, Denis O'Keefe, Tyrone Power, Robert Preston, Dick Purcell, Gene Raymond, Roy Rogers, Cesar Romero, Randolph Scott, Robert Stack, Lee Tracy, John Wayne. And, if he had been listed … "? (**KARLOFF**)!"

Umpires: Kay Kyser, Jackie Gleason, Chico Marx, Thurston Hall.

The *Other* Lionel Atwill
Sinister, Vengeful and Perverse

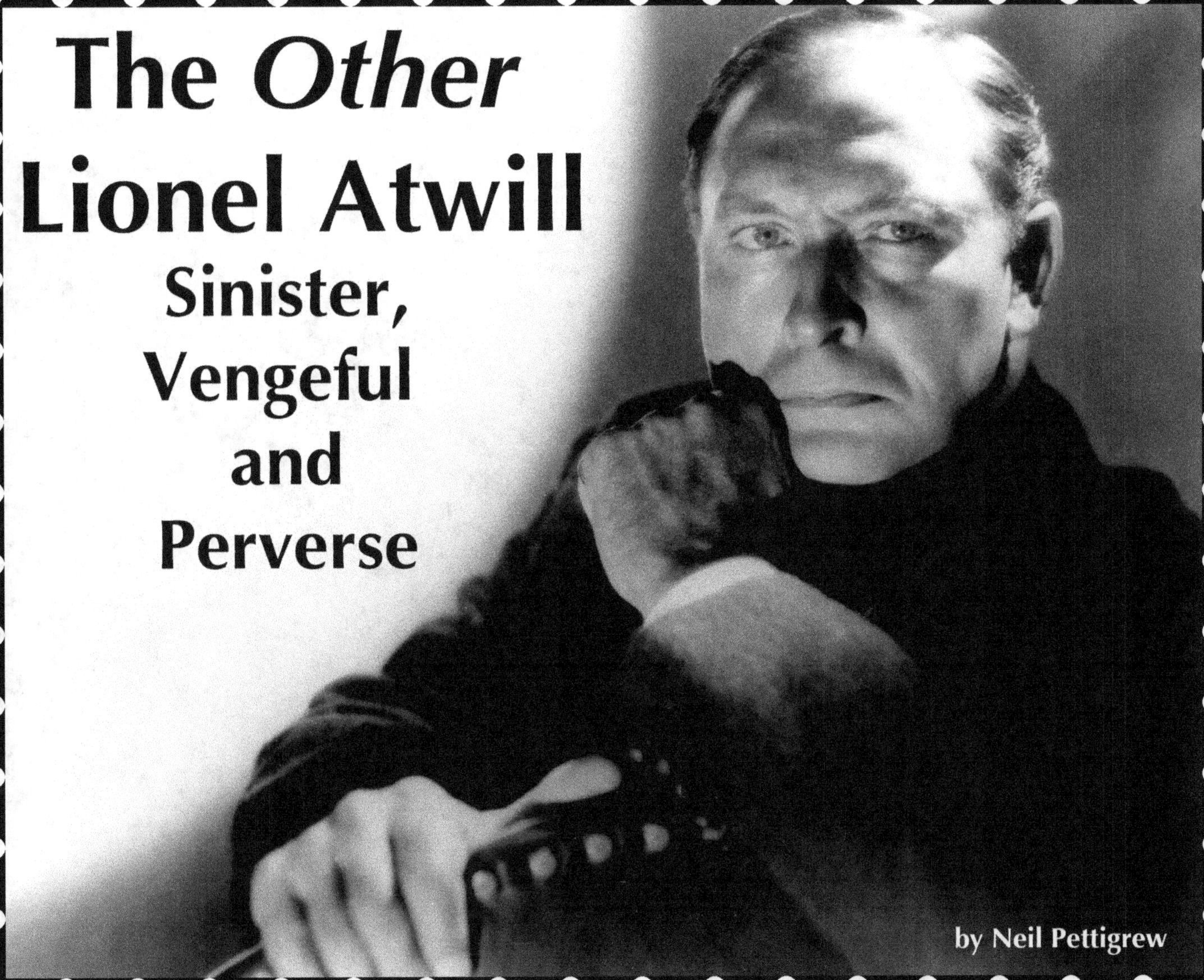

by Neil Pettigrew

Lionel Atwill is one of the most entertaining character actors of the 1930s and 1940s. He is one of those actors who have a special charisma: Once he is on the screen, viewers can't take their eyes off him. All fans of vintage horror films know him for unforgettable roles, such as the scar-faced madman in *The Mystery of the Wax Museum* (1932) and the crazed scientist of *Man Made Monster* (1941). Others know him for a notorious court case in which it was claimed—according to the press—that he held wild orgies at his house. Of course the reality was much less salacious.

But the horror films and the court case overshadow other important aspects of his career. For example, contrary to his sinister screen persona, he was a warm-hearted man who often went the extra mile to give generous support to worthy causes and charities. And long before *Dr X* (1932) or *The Vampire Bat* (1933) launched him to horror stardom, Atwill had already been acting on the stage to great acclaim for over a quarter of a century. In fact, he first acted on the stage as early as 1904 and received glowing newspaper reviews as early as 1906.

This article is going to explore some aspects of Atwill's early stage career, partly because it has never before been examined in any depth, and partly because it is full of ominous and intriguing hints that point toward the kind of menacing persona that would eventually become his trademark. Additionally, my long-time research has uncovered lots of hitherto unreported details of his early life. Some of these details are the result of my having made the acquaintance of Atwill's great-niece, Leslie Dale—the granddaughter of Lionel's brother Stanley, and a charming lady who has shared with me some of her many memories of the Atwill family.

I made contact with Leslie after several years of detailed detective work. After learning that Lionel left three brothers behind when he moved from Britain to the United States, I felt sure that a number of his relatives might still be here in England. I researched the family histories of his two brothers, Clarence and Herbert, but found no living descendants. However,

A striking image of Lionel Atwill in a half-page ad for *Mystery of the Wax Museum* in a 1933 issue of *Film Weekly*, a British film magazine.

A visually striking full-page feature on *Mystery of the Wax Museum*

The south London house where Lionel Atwill was born—Number 2 Upton Villas, the white-painted house in the middle, as it looks today, complete with broken cooker in the front garden.

the other brother Stanley, two years younger than Lionel, married and fathered two daughters, Diana and Daphne. Diana married in 1946 and Leslie is her daughter. So Leslie represents the only surviving line of Lionel Atwill's relatives in England, and she is custodian of various family heirlooms, including many old photographs.

During the 1930s in England, Leslie's grandparents and their daughters made sure that they never missed one of Lionel's films at the cinema. Each trip was eagerly anticipated and they were understandably proud of having a relative who had become successful in Hollywood. Leslie's grandmother Ethel compiled a large file on brother-in-law Lionel, including newspaper clippings, programs, photographs and memorabilia sent to the family by Lionel. Imagine my excitement on hearing about this priceless treasure trove of material. "Whenever I visited my grandparents," Leslie told me, "I remember Grandma saying, 'Come and have a look at the pictures of Lionel' … but she threw it all out before she died."

As well as looking at Atwill's early life and stage career, this article will also discuss another important but neglected aspect of Atwill's career—his many roles in non-horror films. Throughout the 1930s he was very highly regarded by the Hollywood studios and was given some choice roles in non-horror films. Atwill appeared in roughly 20 horror films and his fine performances in all of them reward repeated viewings. But he was also featured in around 50 non-horror films: spy melodramas, crime films, costume dramas, war films and even a musical. In many of these he was either the star or had a very prominent role as the chief villain or some other important supporting role.

Some horror purists will watch only Atwill's horror films, but such fans miss the chance to enjoy some never-to-be-forgotten Atwill performances that are loaded with sinister overtones, cold stares, vengeful scheming and even some juicy hints of sexual perversion. And among these non-horror appearances is one role in particular which may well be the finest performance of Atwill's screen career. This character is a thoroughly revolting brute, and Atwill plays it to the hilt.

Whether performing in horror films or mainstream productions, Atwill excelled in villainous roles. Few other actors could match him when it came to portraying cold and sinister characters. Certainly, no other actor could *stare* quite like Atwill. It was a stare that could kill at 20 paces. As soon as a victim became the target of a stare from Atwill's blue-gray eyes, he or she knew that they wouldn't last beyond the next reel.

Surprisingly, Atwill's non-horror films contain some of the most horrific, cruel and perverse scenes of his career. Even fans who would not normally watch non-horror films will derive huge pleasure from Atwill's performances in these films. They include, for example, the most gruesome moment of his film career, when molten steel is deliberately poured onto his legs, burning them away. They contain also the most perversely erotic scene of his career, when he examines Myrna Loy's discarded underwear in great detail, chuckling indecently as he does so. This article will take a look at a select few of these non-horror performances, characterizations that overflow with the best elements of his horror film work.

Atwill's Early Years and His Rise in the British and American Theater

Let's begin at the beginning and find out the truth about Lionel Atwill's early years. Most articles about him state that he was born into a wealthy, privileged family. Atwill himself was happy to promote the public image that he came from a vaguely aristocratic background. His wonderful voice and his imposing manner seemed to bear this out, and up until now, this version

The earliest known surviving photo of Lionel Atwill, in costume for the stage play, *The Flag Lieutenant*, in 1908.

Lionel's parents, Alfred and Ada Atwill, seen in a grainy old photo from 1918.

Imagine being a London pedestrian in 1915 and seeing this grand sight coming racing toward you—Phyllis Atwill in the driver's seat and husband Lionel in the side car of a Royal Enfield motorbike.

of events has been generally accepted. My research, however, suggests otherwise. His grandfather, William Atwill, was a postmaster and pawnbroker (as shown by old government census documents). His father, Alfred Atwill, was a clerk (and later inspector) at the Board of Education. When Atwill was born in 1885, the family was living in a very modest two-bedroom house in the London suburb of South Norwood. This locale was hardly the aristocracy.

Not much is known about Atwill's very early years, but an article that appeared in a New York newspaper, *The Fulton Register* (May 17, 1924), gives us some clues. "He declares that even as a child, he wanted to go on the stage. He began acting in his nursery days and at 14 years of age was doing plays in drawing rooms." Atwill's great-niece told me how her grandfather Stanley remembered appearing on the school stage at age 8 with his 10-year-old brother Lionel as part of a blackface minstrel troupe. What a sight it must have been.

The *Fulton Register* also relates that when Atwill was 18, "In his leisure hours, he formed a dramatic society, which still exists and with which he often played." But where did he get this interest in acting? Certainly not from his father: "On the paternal side he is descended from a long line of seafaring men, all of who were in the British Navy." More likely, he inherited his artistic leanings from his mother, because, as the article claims, "His relatives on his mother's side leaned to painting and music." His three younger brothers, Clarence, Stanley and Herbert, could not have been more different, and all ended up with careers in insurance.

One of Atwill's most appealing qualities is his fine voice, and he spoke his lines with a grand theatrical resonance and impeccable diction. And yet, growing up where he did, the young Atwill may have started out with a South London accent—which, for those unfamiliar with the area, is not very dissimilar from a Cockney accent. The explanation lies in an old *Who's Who in the Theatre,* which informs us that very early in Atwill's career, he attended elocution classes given by S.L. Hasluck, a gentleman who around 1900 produced a series of books with titles like *Hasluck's Recitations for Boys and Girls, Recitations from Dickens* and *Recitations for Ladies.* The teenage Atwill would have traveled up to Hasluck's school on Regent Street in London's West End on a regular basis. There he would have practiced his diction and projection until finally developing that incisive voice which served him so well throughout his career.

It is difficult to be exact, but some time in either late 1904 or early 1905 Atwill made his first professional appearance on stage, aged 19 or 20. It was a minor role as a footman in a production of *The Walls of Jericho*, staged at the Garrick Theatre in London. Alongside Atwill in the cast was, among others, O.B. Clarence, who many years later provided the benevolent voice of Dr. Dearborn—alter ego of evil maniac Bela Lugosi—in *The Dark Eyes of London* (1939).

After this, the young Atwill spent a number of years touring around Britain's provincial theaters. All that remains of these early stage performances are a few tantalizing photographs and some theatrical reviews that make reference to him. These are enough to fire our imaginations and make us realize what a loss it is that no filmed record of Atwill on stage exists. Not only that, but very probably no one remains today who can claim to have seen him on stage. Even so, it is fascinating to look at some of these roles in detail, because in several of them we can see premonitions of his horror typecasting of many years later.

Phyllis Relph, whom Lionel married in 1913, is seen in costume for the stage play *Anthony and Cleopatra.*

Lionel is about to plant a kiss on Esme Hubbard in the hugely successful stage play, *Milestones*, in 1912.

He acted in several Ibsen plays during this period, including *A Doll's House*. A 1906 newspaper reviewer of the play wrote (in *The Manchester Courier*): "Mr. Atwill played Dr. Rank with distinction, toning down the gruesomeness of the part most acceptably." An ironic comment, to say the least, given that Atwill spent most of his later career doing all he could to *emphasize* "the gruesomeness." In *A Doll's House*, the gruesome angle is the fact that Atwill's character professes his love for a married woman, while at the same time, admitting that he is in the terminal stages of syphilis.

From 1908 to 1909 Atwill toured successfully in *The Flag Lieutenant*, playing the leading role, and the play helped to bring him to the notice of the British public. Fortunately, two stills of Atwill in this part have survived. They show him in military costume, a dashing foretaste of all the uniformed roles he would play later in his career, as military men and police inspectors, such as one-armed Inspector Krogh in *Son of Frankenstein*. What a shame, though, that no photo seems to have survived of one scene in particular from this production, because Atwill's character, in order to sneak across enemy lines, dresses up as a bashi-bazouk, an elaborately costumed and turbaned Turkish soldier. A reviewer in *The Western Times* wrote, "Mr. Lionel Atwill, who takes the title role, has acted with success in many prominent and well-known plays, and nothing could excel his fine treatment of the part of *The Flag Lieutenant*."

The screenplay of *The Flag Lieutenant* contains an uncanny foreshadowing of the court case that was to have such an impact on Atwill's life in the 1940s. The title character, Richard Lascelles (Atwill), lies to protect the reputation of a friend on a battlefield. As a result, Lascelles finds he is accused of cowardice in action. Only at the last minute does the truth come out, and Lascelles is saved from a court martial and his honor upheld. Many years later, when Atwill was in court charged with perjury, he would say, "I lied like a gentleman to protect friends." (Anyone unfamiliar with the details of the court case should read the detailed account of it in Gregory William Mank's excellent book, *Hollywood's Maddest Doctors*.)

If only a time machine could be invented so that we could go back over a century to watch Atwill in *The Prisoner of the Bastille*, in which he toured in 1909. A 1909 review in the Hull *Daily Mail* suggests the grisly tone of the play: "The Bastille may always be relied upon for giving us a thrill of horror. As the symbol of everything that is terrible and cruel, it is always effective." This is the famous *Man in the Iron Mask* story, and it would have been a treat for Atwill fans because he played the dual roles of King Louis XIV and his twin brother Philippe. *The Daily Mail* continued: "Mr. Lionel Atwill plays with intelligence and force, and at times with distinction." In those scenes in which Atwill's face was concealed by the iron mask, how wonderful it must have been to hear that distinctive voice booming forcefully into the auditorium. And no doubt a climactic scene occurred in which Atwill, as the imprisoned king, screams and batters on the walls of his cell, slowly becoming mad. *The Manchester Courier* praised Atwill's performance and observed that he had "a keen sense of the value of reserve force." This astute comment tells us that, even this early in his career, Atwill had developed some of the stylistic nuances that would characterize his later acting in horror films.

Acting alongside Atwill in *The Prisoner of the Bastille* was

Digby Mansions in Hammersmith, the exclusive riverside apartment block where Lionel and Phyllis lived from around 1913 to 1915.

Phyllis Relph, a young lady who would soon become very significant in Lionel's life.

Then in February 1910, Atwill played the Chevalier de Mauprat in *Richelieu* at London's Strand Theatre. *The Times* didn't think much of the play but thought "Mr. Atwill is an agreeable Mauprat."

Lionel Atwill in 1913

Rare photo of Lionel Atwill and Constance Collier in *Monna Vanna*, in 1914.

Atwill as the foul Baron, sporting a monocle and wearing a sepctacular Hussar's uniform, including skull-and-crossbones hat.

plans to produce many others, even though many of them never came to fruition. A 1910 issue of *The Daily Express* provides the earliest record of this, informing us that, "*The Fourth Kiss* is the name of a tragic little play by Mr. W. Douglas Newton—the short-story writer—which Mr. Lionel Atwill produces on Friday at the Peckham Hippodrome." A few days later, the same paper wrote, Atwill "gave evidence of great tragic power" in this play. We would be able to see exactly what the writer meant years later in many of Atwill's non-horror films, because in scene after scene, as tortured lovers or humiliated husbands, he emotes real tragic force from just a gaze.

In the spring of 1910, Atwill sailed to Australia with a theater company. There he toured in a number of plays including *The Whip*, *Henry of Navarre* and *Via Wireless*. In an age when long-distance travel was not common, it must have been a real adventure for the 25-year-old actor who had never left Britain before. Not much is known about this episode in Atwill's life and it would be wonderful if an Australian researcher could do some delving and perhaps turn up newspaper articles, theater reviews or old photographs of this tour. Old passenger lists show that the young Atwill certainly made the most of the return journey. After leaving Sydney in October 1911, Atwill spent two months getting back to Britain, stopping off for a week's vacation in Honolulu and then heading for Vancouver, Canada, before eventually arriving back in Liverpool in December 1911.

Atwill was far more than just an actor: He also wrote, directed and produced several plays and always seemed to have

Back in London, he landed a part in *Milestones*, a three-act play which was indeed a milestone in Atwill's career. He played a romantic role as a young engineer in the second act, returning in the third act as the same character but much older and now the head of the Labor Party. Highly popular at London's Royalty Theatre in the West End over a period of a year and a half, the play ran for an impressive 600 performances. The respected newspaper *The Times* considered that "there is some clever acting from … Mr. Lionel Atwill."

On April 14 of 1912, the Titanic, the largest ship afloat, sank on her maiden voyage to New York. Atwill was one of many actors who helped raise money for those affected by the tragedy. On May 10, he gave his acting services for free in a special matinee performance of a new play called *Kynaston's Wife*, which was performed at London's St. James's Theatre to support "sufferers from the Titanic disaster." All proceeds went to the fund, as they did five days later, when an extra matinee of *Milestones* took place. A special program for the event appeared "with autographs and portraits of all concerned in the play." Have any of these survived, I wonder?

The extremely successful 18-month run of *Milestones* kept Atwill busy until

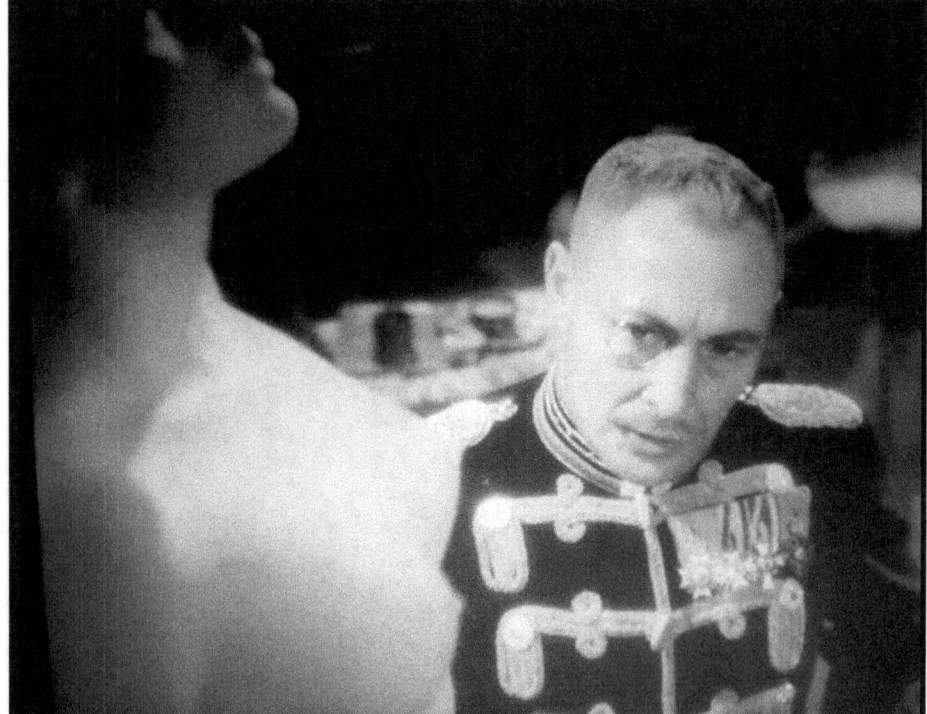

The depraved Baron von Merzbach plots his seduction of Marlene Dietrich, beneath a statue of the actress naked, in *The Song of Songs* (1933).

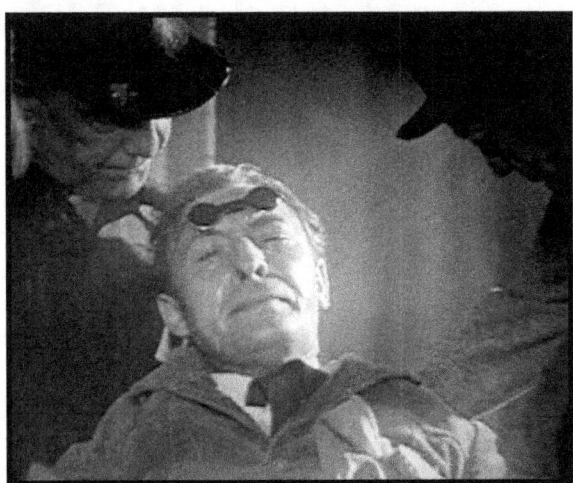

A frame enlargement of Atwill's expression of pain after his legs have been burnt away by molten steel, in *Beggars in Ermine* (1933).

August 1913, but he did find time, in March, to act in a one-off matinee performance of *The Cradle* at London's Court Theatre. The following month he found time for something rather more significant. *The Observer* reported an important event in Lionel's life. "A large number of actors and actresses attended the wedding at St. George's Parish Church, Bloomsbury, yesterday, of Miss Phyllis Relph to Mr. Lionel A.W. Atwill, who is well known to theatergoers as the impersonator of the engineer in Mr. Arnold Bennett's play *Milestones*. Miss Relph is equally known by her performance in the part of Margaret Knox in *Fanny's First Play*."

What a shame that no audio recording of *Years of Discretion* exists, staged at London's Globe Theatre in the latter half of 1913. The reason: We would have been treated to hearing Atwill adopt an Irish accent. According to *The Gloucester Citizen*: "Mr. Lionel Atwill made a good Michael Doyle, the Irishman." Playing alongside him was C. Aubrey Smith, another able Englishman who would uproot and move to Hollywood. Smith went on to become one of the most familiar supporting actors in Hollywood, and in fact he and Atwill appeared together in four films in the 1930s.

In December 1913, Atwill was in *The Poor Little Rich Girl* at London's New Theatre, starring Helen Hayes. Atwill played a money-obsessed father who ignores his daughter. The play was later filmed twice by Hollywood, once starring Mary Pickford (in 1917) and then starring Shirley Temple (in 1936) ... and both times without Atwill.

Also late in 1913, Atwill had the bright idea of producing a play inspired by H.G. Wells' *The Invisible Man*. Described in newspaper ads as "a Farce suggested by the Story by H.G. Wells," it probably bore very little relation to the original novel. It was a sketch (a one-act play), and the play probably lasted no more than half an hour. It contained "illusions by Leslie Lambert." *The Observer* found it "of exceptional interest" and "notable." *The Manchester Courier* was impressed: "Some of the effects are very cleverly contrived, and it is indeed a weird sight to see a suit of clothes walk about with apparently no one inside."

Atwill appeared in *The Invisible Man* "twice daily" at London's Coliseum Theatre in Charing Cross. (Advertisements for the play show that also on the bill was a young comedian named W.C. Fields.) In January 1914, the sketch moved to the Hippodrome in Manchester, and Atwill continued to appear twice nightly. Twenty years later, the distinctive voice of Claude Rains made him a superb choice for James Whale's 1933 film version of the story, but one cannot help but think that Atwill would also have been outstanding in the role.

The year 1914 was a busy one for Atwill, and he appeared in a number of plays in both London and the provinces.

In February he was at London's Palace Theatre, acting in *Rivals For Rosamund* (by Arnold Bennett). *The Manchester Guardian* thought that all "the players did their part high-spiritedly and gave the piece the right rapidity, Mr. Atwill doing wonders with an Irish accent." Again!

In June 1914, Atwill was in *Getting Out of It*, a one-act sketch. He was certainly putting in the hours: This was staged twice nightly at the Hippodrome in Manchester, with an additional three matinees during the week, and later in the month Atwill traveled with the play when it was staged at the Manchester Gaiety Theatre.

In *Monna Vanna*, at London's Queen's Theatre from July to August 1914, Atwill co-starred with Constance Collier in a controversial play that contained some early hints of the more depraved elements that would characterize his best non-horror

Frame enlargement of a moody shot of Atwill as spymaster Von Sturm, taking a voyeuristic delight in watching an execution by firing squad in *Stamboul Quest* (1934).

parts in 1930s films. In fact, the play was so controversial that it had been banned in England for 12 years. Atwill plays Prinzivalle, the commander of an army that is about to destroy Pisa. But he gives an ultimatum. He will spare the city only if Monna Vanna, the beautiful wife of the commander of Pisa, will spend the night with him in his tent. And moreover, she must come wearing only a cloak! The thought of all that near-nudity had been too much for the delicate British censor, who feared that audiences' morals would be permanently corrupted. Atwill must have lapped up all the notoriety.

The legendary Atwill stare—the moment he realizes that his wife (Verree Teasdale) has been unfaithful to him, in *The Firebird* (1934).

Frame enlargement of Atwill planting his deadly stare on Binnie Barnes in *Rendez-vous* (1935),

His back is broken and his face is bleeding: Atwill's death scene in *Till We Meet Again* (1936).

The Manchester Courier thought, "Mr. Lionel Atwill, if I mistake not, is no stranger to the part of the general Prinzivalle." Am I reading too much into this remark by inferring that the reviewer is suggesting that in real life Atwill was also no slouch when it came to demanding sexual services? It is almost certain that the writer was referring to a newspaper report that had appeared in *The Times* just six days earlier (July 6, 1914) in which Atwill's name had been mentioned in a high-profile divorce case. Elsie Hissey, an actress, was charged with adultery by her aggrieved husband and accused of frequenting London nightclubs such as the Cave of the Golden Calf and the Cabaret Club. The husband reeled off a list of actors known by his wife, including Sir George Robey and several in the theater company of which his wife was a member. It was implied that she "knew another actor in the company, a Mr. Lionel Atwill." "You seem to suggest," the husband says, "that I accused her of misconduct with every actor we knew." The lawyer replies: "That is precisely what we do suggest you did." Of course, no evidence that anything happened between Elsie Hissey and Atwill exists, but the suggestion is most definitely there.

Despite this, the reviewer from *The Manchester Courier* was full of praise for his performance. "He made a picturesque figure and endued his lines with an appealing forcefulness that commanded attention." This apposite phrase could just as well be applied to every one of Atwill's later film roles.

In September 1914, Atwill started a three-month run of a play by *Peter Pan* playwright J.M. Barrie. It was called *The Little Minister* and ran successfully until mid-December at London's Duke of York Theatre. *The Times* found an "ugly vindictiveness" in Atwill's character, Captain Halliwell. Playing alongside Atwill was Donald Calthrop, who was so memorable 22 years later when he co-starred with Boris Karloff in *The Man Who Changed His Mind*.

In November of 1914, Atwill was in *The New Shylock*, "a comedy of New York ghetto life." *The Observer* thought that "Mr. Lionel Atwill as the young Gentile did good work."

In December 1914, *The Poor Little Rich Girl* was taken to Manchester's Gaiety Theatre. This time Atwill starred alongside his wife Phyllis. *The Manchester Courier* described this work as, "A play of fact and fantasy … from the synopsis it would appear the play is full of delightfully whimsical and beautiful conceptions" and called it "a Christmas play for children." The review continued: "The cast is a strong one and includes … Phyllis Relph and Lionel Atwill."

By the end of 1914, life was good for the 29-year-old Lionel Atwill. He was happily married to Phyllis. In June that year he became the proud father of a baby boy, John Atwill. Now that he was a well-regarded actor on the London stage, the money was rolling in. He could afford to rent a swanky riverside apartment in Hammersmith. It was situated in a prestigious Victorian apartment block and had a balcony that overlooked the landmark River Thames. Not only that, but he could afford to buy a car. In 1914, few people owned cars. What a sight it must have been to see West End stage star Atwill and his wife driving around the streets of London, which in those days were still full of horse-drawn cabs and carriages.

Atwill recalled one such occasion (in an interview in a 1938 issue of the British film magazine *Picturegoer*): "The film actor recalled the days when he lived in Kensington. 'Motorcars were then just coming into fashion,' he declared. 'I remember I bought a car for £200 and felt a terrific dog. I was so proud of it that the first Sunday morning I had it I decided to drive over to Bromley, where my parents lived, and give them a treat. Naturally I could not drive very well, but undaunted I sailed along merrily till I turned into the road in which my parents lived. But then disaster came. I tried to swoop into the kerb and to pull up in style outside the old folks' home. But I had become too confident. I collided with the trunk of a chestnut tree and ripped the mudguards off!' He laughed heartily at the recollection."

On other days, an even more remarkable sight could be seen on London's roads: Lionel Atwill sitting in the sidecar of a Royal Enfield motorcycle ridden by his wife Phyllis. Both husband and wife were keen motorbike riders and they were even featured in a 1915 edition of *Royal* magazine.

Atwill's sadistic Colonel Bishop in full fury: "Now I'll take this rod to you until there's not an inch of hide left on your dirty carcass!" From *Captain Blood* (1935)

Lionel Atwill AND HIS PICTURES

With Joan Bennett in "The Man Who Reclaimed His Head."

(On left) With Myrna Loy in "Stamboul Quest."

With Irene Hervey in "Absolute Quiet."

(On right) "Murders in the Zoo."

"The Murder Man."

"The Devil is a Woman."

An impressive full-page article from a 1936 issue of Picture Show, a British film magazine.

LIONEL ATWILL, who is to be seen in two new films—"Absolute Quiet," which was generally released last week, and "Lady of Secrets," which is one of this week's films—is an Englishman. He was born in Croydon, on March 1st, 1885, and he was educated at the Mercers School in London.

When the time came for him to make a decision as to his future career, he thought that he would study architecture, but at the end of three years' study he changed his mind, and decided to become an actor.

His stage début was made at the Garrick Theatre, London, in 1904, when he played in "The Walls of Jericho." Other London productions followed, and he also had engagements with touring companies. After that he had leading rôles in a series of melodramas, and then played leading rôles in "The Prodigal Son," "Bondsman" and other productions.

Then came an opportunity to go to Australia and he played leading rôles in a number of plays there, including "The Whip" and "Henry of Navarre."

It was in 1912 that he returned to London, and appeared in "Milestones," which ran for eighteen months. Following this, he signed a contract with Charles Frohman, and appeared in the revival of such plays as "The Little Minister" and "Poor Little Rich Girl."

In 1916 Lionel Atwill went to the United States to be Lily Langtry's leading man. He then starred under his own management in "The Lodger," which ran for a year in New York. Various other New York stage engagements followed, and then in 1919 he made a couple of silent films—"The Marriage Price" and "Indiscretion." He found that he did not care very much for screen work, and after these two films he returned to the stage and it was several years before he tried the screen again.

In his stage experience that followed he acted with Nazimova, Katherine Cornell, Helen Hayes, and other famous actresses of the American stage, and the productions in which he appeared included the works of Shakespeare, Ibsen, Galsworthy and Shaw. In was in 1925 that he created the rôle of Julius Cæsar in Bernard Shaw's "Cæsar and Cleopatra" at the Theatre Guild's opening of its first owned theatre, and Helen Hayes played the feminine lead.

IN TWO EXPERIMENTAL TALKIES

It was in 1927 that Lionel Atwill had his second experience of film work. This was in two experimental talkies made for the Fox company. During the same year he appeared in a musical play and also played the leading rôles in a couple of straight plays.

Then came one of his greatest stage successes, his starring rôle in "The Silent Witness." When the run of this play came to an end he was approached by Fox Films, as they wanted him to portray the same rôle in the screen version. He accepted this offer and a contract was signed. He reported at the Hollywood studio in December, 1931.

This time film work must have appealed to him, for he has been on the screen ever since. Here are some of the films in which he has played—"The Secret of Madame Blanche," "The Mystery of the Wax Museum," "Murders in the Zoo," "The Vampire Bat," "The Sphinx," "The Song of Songs," "The Secret of the Blue Room," "The Solitaire Man," "Lady of the Boulevards," "Beggars in Ermine," "Stamboul Quest," "Over the River," "The Firebird," "The Age of Innocence," "The Man Who Reclaimed His Head," "The Devil is a Woman," "Mark of the Vampire," "The Murder Man," "Rendezvous," and "Captain Blood."

Lionel Atwill has dark brown hair, grey eyes, and is five feet ten and a half inches in height. His pastimes include yachting, golf, swimming and other outdoor sports. He is the owner of two yachts, and whenever possible he gets away to his estate, which is twelve miles from Baltimore in Maryland, because there is a bay close to it where he can sail his yachts. This estate of his, by the way, has a very delightful name—"Rainbow Hills." His house in Hollywood is set high on a mountainside and has a marvellous view across to the Pacific twenty miles away.

He breeds prize cattle on his farm, and has taken four blue ribbons at Maryland fairs. He is a lover of animals and owns several dogs. He has a very unusual hobby; it is attending murder trials.

A rare insert poster from *High Command* (1937), with Atwill looking on intensely.

Said Phyllis: "My six-horse-power Royal Enfield is simply delightful. Together with my husband, Mr. Lionel Atwill, I have made many long trips, and I always take my turn in driving. I am sure that I have found great pleasure in motorcycling, and the sidecar combination is ideal—so easy to drive and so very dependable. We could not want anything better."

For Atwill, 1915 was just as busy as the previous year. In January he was acting alongside his wife again in *She Stoops To Conquer*, and *The Manchester Evening News* thought he acted "with much spirit." In February he played in *Blue Stockings*, and *The Manchester Evening News* reported that for "Mr. Lionel Atwill, nothing but praise is due." In the same month he played in *The One Thing Needful* at the Gaiety. *The Manchester Courier* wrote: "Mr. Charles Groves and Mr. Lionel Atwill gave charming character studies as the two fathers."

Across the English Channel, war was raging. Atwill was quick to do his bit to support the war effort. In February, he and Phyllis arranged a special matinee of *She Stoops To Conquer*, and £130 was raised for the Arts Fund, which was created "to relieve distress due to the war" to those working in the arts.

In March, Atwill was in *Whimsies*, again at the Gaiety, Manchester, and again co-starring with his wife. *The Manchester Evening News* considered that Atwill and Phyllis were "worthy of special mention." He received more good reviews for his parts in *The Walls of Jericho* and *The Fugitive*, both in early 1915.

In June, the Atwills were back in London and once again showing their charitable side. At the Playhouse Theatre they appeared in *Mater*, all proceeds going to the Actors' Orphanage Fund. It was a comedy in which "a mother is mistaken for a daughter by an eager suitor" (Atwill being the eager suitor).

During this period, happily married Lionel and Phyllis were having the times of their lives. They acted together again in *One Summer's Night* at the Manchester Gaiety in August 1915. *The Manchester Guardian* wrote: "Mr. Lionel Atwill is as complete and elegant a sentimentalist when it is his will as any on the stage. Miss Phyllis Relph can be as fascinating as flashing eyes and shrugs can make anyone."

In September Atwill was back at the Gaiety for *The Two Virtues*, a comedy by Alfred Sutro. *The Manchester Evening News* was impressed: "No greater praise could be given to Mr. Lionel Atwill, who carries the new Sutro comedy *The Two Virtues* on his shoulders ... It was a wonderful study of a lovable man—always pleasant to play, but often difficult to deal with because of the complexities... The outstanding success belonged to Mr. Atwill."

The Walls of Jericho was revived for another successful run at the Gaiety in September and October. In early October, Atwill was again supporting the war effort. As part of a recruitment drive, a large rally was held in Manchester followed by an evening of entertainment at the Hippodrome Theatre. Atwill was one of numerous performers donating his services, and Eva Moore joined him on stage. Seventeen years later she turned up in James Whale's *The Old Dark House*.

During this period, the Atwills were planning a radical change to their lives. In July 1915, Lionel had acted alongside Lily Langtry (infamously a former mistress of Prince of Wales, Edward VII) in a play called *Mrs. Thompson*, but it had not been a success. Langtry liked the play and thought it had a better chance of success in America. She suggested to Atwill that he travel with her to the States, and he decided to seize the opportunity, taking Phyllis with him.

First, though, he had to conclude his commitments at the Gaiety Theatre. *The Manchester Evening News*: "The Gaiety will rely on *The Walls of Jericho* for another week—a safe card to play with such fine acting as that given by Lionel Atwill and Miss Phyllis Relph in the leading parts. These two players, by the way, are unfortunately nearing the end of their Gaiety engagement. *The Two Virtues* will be put on again on Monday for their special benefit, after which they leave for America to appear there with Mrs. Langtry." So great was the popularity of the couple that the local paper ran an advertisement every night for a week announcing the "farewell performances" of Lionel and Phyllis.

When, on October 16, 1915, Atwill, Phyllis and their son John sailed for New York, they could afford to do it in style—they traveled first class. For Lionel it was

Mad scientist Dr. Hugo Zurof is quite dead in this frame from *The Sun Never Sets* (1939), but the Atwill stare lives on, as an ant crawls across his forehead.

the end of a decade of success on the British stage, and, he hoped, the beginning of an even brighter career in America.

In America, life for Lionel and Phyllis began well. Atwill's theatrical career started out promisingly, if modestly. Despite bringing up a two-year-old boy, the couple was even able to continue its occasional on-stage partnership when, in 1917, they acted alongside one another on the New York stage in *The Lodger*, based on the novel about the notorious Jack the Ripper by Marie Belloc-Lowndes. But the happy marriage was destined to come to an end. Exactly what happened is unknown, but a shipping passenger list tells us that in November 1919 Phyllis sailed back to England, taking young John with her. In 1919 divorce carried a stigma, so it cannot have been easy for Phyllis to make the drastic decision of taking her son away from his father and returning to face perhaps disapproval and embarrassment back home. Something major must have happened. Had Phyllis perhaps caught Lionel with another woman and walked out on him?

Despite this personal upheaval, Lionel triumphed in the theater and during the next 15 years became one the great stars of the Broadway stage. This is a significant period in Atwill's career, but it is not a tale that I will tell here. That period in Atwill's life is covered in some depth in *Hollywood's Maddest Doctors*. I am now going to jump to the early 1930s, when Atwill—now in his mid-40s—was finally tempted by the lure of Hollywood.

Atwill in the Golden Age of Hollywood

Let's start by discussing the film that contains what may well be the standout performance of his entire career. If fans watch only one of Atwill's non-horror films, then make sure it is *The Song of Songs* (1933). His Baron von Merzbach is a bully, a brute, a drunkard and a letch—and he steals every scene in which he appears. He looks magnificent in his Prussian hussar uniform, his hat emblazoned with a skull and crossbones. And he lives in a huge chateau that is straight out of a horror film, complete with gargoyles, giant statues and Expressionistic ceilings. Who can forget the lascivious way he blows cigarette smoke over a sketch of the nude Marlene Dietrich? Or the way he giggles indecently like an excited schoolboy as he waits outside Dietrich's bedroom on their wedding night? Or the cruel way he mentally torments Dietrich and her former lover Brian Aherne, across a dinner table, boasting of how he has enjoyed Dietrich sexually? Without a doubt, this pre-Code melodrama is one of the most erotic films of the period, and Von Merzbach is one of Atwill's kinkiest roles.

I would suggest entirely quite seriously that Lionel Atwill deserved an Academy Award nomination for his performance in *The Song of Songs*. But the Academy members probably found the role too distasteful. They overlooked him, too, for a very strong performance in *The Firebird* (1934). One of Atwill's great strengths was his ability to look tortured. He made a string of films in which his lovers or spouses cheated on him or humiliated him, and this is one of them. Here he does some of his finest tortured acting as he first suspects that his wife (Verree Teasdale) has been up to no good with Ricardo Cortez, and then again when he realizes in fact that it is his daughter who has been doing the dirty deeds. At crucial moments of realization, Atwill's eyes seem to stare off into a world of nightmarish possibility. Delicious acting!

Beggars In Ermine (1934) is a rare starring role for Atwill in a non-horror film. Non-horror it may be, but the plot of this obscure low-budget melodrama reads like a combination of elements from *The Mystery of the Wax Museum*, *Freaks* and one of the old Lon Chaney/Tod Browning melodramas involving cripples and amputees. At the start of the film, Atwill, who plays the boss of a steel plant, loses both legs when a disgruntled employee pours molten steel over them. Now a wheelchair-bound cripple, Atwill spends the rest of the film plotting his revenge, surrounding himself with other cripples, most of whom are played by genuine amputees—armless men, one-legged men and a legless man who wheels himself along on a trolley, etc. Although this isn't a horror film, the scene

Atwill nears the end of his career, seen here in a tussle with Dennis Moore in *The Raiders of Ghost City* (1944).

Amazing proof that Lionel Atwill did not actually die aged 61—but carried on making films until his late 70s, or so his performance in *The Great Waltz* (1938) seems to suggest.

Two original lobby cards from *The Devil Is A Woman* (1935), featuring the second teaming of Atwill and Dietrich. Atwill plays a character utterly obsessed with the Dietrich character and she destroys him.

in which Atwill's legs are burnt away is one of the most horrific in his career. And at one point in the film, Betty Furness comes out with a magnificent line that pithily sums up Atwill: "Did you see the hate in his eyes?" She adds, "It frightens me."

Despite the fact that it was released a few weeks after the Hays censorship code was enforced, *Stamboul Quest* (1934) nevertheless managed to sneak some very risqué moments into its engagingly convoluted counter-espionage plot. In fact it gave Atwill the kinkiest scene of his whole career. He plays Von Sturm, a monocle-wearing German spymaster, immaculately dressed in long coat and spats. Slinky Myrna Loy plays his favorite spy. When she tells him she needs a bath, Von Sturm generously offers his own bathroom. Just why a room with a bath adjoins his office is unclear, but it certainly makes for a memorable scene. "We can talk while you scrub," he says.

She does a sexy striptease while she talks to Von Sturm, throwing items of her clothing and underwear in his direction. Von Sturm picks up each item of clothing, including a lacy slip, and examines each article with great enthusiasm, sniggering filthily. It turns out that the reason he is so interested in the clothing—or at least one of the reasons—is that code words are hidden in the garments.

I have mentioned the legendary Atwill stare earlier in this article. Lionel Atwill could *stare* like nobody else. It might be a sinister stare that could freeze our blood. Or it might be the tormented stare of a man who has just realized his wife has been cheating on him. Or it might be the desperate stare of a man who feels that a sudden turn of events has humiliated him. Whatever the cause, Atwill had a repertoire of stares that suited the moment. He was a master at donning an expression that suggested hidden layers of thought and emotion. An intensity of feeling existed behind his blue-gray eyes that few other actors have ever matched, and this is one of the characteristics that make him such a watchable actor, even today, over a half-century after his death. Among his non-horror films, a wealth of roles exists allowing fans to enjoy this aspect of his talent.

A question for all horror film experts: In what film does Karloff shoot and kill Atwill? No such film, you say? In *Rendezvous*, a 1935 spy drama starring William Powell and set during the WWI, Atwill plays a code-breaker who is having an affair with a woman called … Olivia Karloff. Atwill suspects she is a spy. To expose her, he pretends his briefcase is lost but then arranges for her to find it. This is a long and well-staged sequence entirely devoid of dialogue or music. Atwill finds the empty briefcase and realizes that Barnes must have taken out a classified document. Full of menace, he slowly crosses the darkened room, opens a door to the kitchen and catches her red-handed, steaming open a letter. He gives her one of those legendary Atwill stares, then, with his back to the camera, stalks toward her, entering the room where she is standing and closes the door behind him with great portent. The sound of a gunshot is heard. We assume he has shot her … but moments later we see Barnes walking away, and the truth is revealed. It is "Karloff" who shot Atwill! The film also features a Russian character with the first name Boris. The picture was based on a 1931 book; had the author just seen *Frankenstein*, I wonder?

Atwill was reunited with Marlene Dietrich in *The Devil Is A Woman* (1935), directed by Josef Von Sternberg. After Atwill's vile treatment of Dietrich in *Song of Songs*, this time she gets her revenge and the roles are reversed. Atwill, giving a strong performance, is hopelessly obsessed with her and in return she utterly destroys him. By 1935 the Hays Code was being rigidly enforced, as reported by Atwill in an interview in a 1936 issue of Britain's *Film Weekly* magazine, in which he talked about the film's characters: "They were all perverts—but we couldn't show this. Will Hays' representative was there all the time to see that we didn't stray."

Atwill's last film in 1935 was the spectacular swashbuckler *Captain Blood*, starring Errol Flynn. Atwill was third-billed as Colonel Bishop, the vicious owner of a sugar cane plantation in Jamaica. His flamboyant costumes—long coats and feathered hats—hide a nasty sadist who enjoys thrashing his slaves at every opportunity, then branding them with a hot iron. When he finally gets the chance to tie Flynn to a whipping post, he grabs a five-foot rod and exclaims: "Now I'll take this rod to you until there's not an inch of hide left on your dirty carcass!" In an interview in a 1936 issue of *Film Weekly* magazine, Atwill himself described Colonel Bishop as "a hateful beast" with a "lust for thrashing people." No wonder he was able to say, with considerable relish, at this point in his career: "I have been in 23 films altogether, and I have been responsible for some very black acts!" *Captain Blood* gave Atwill a major role and the film is essential viewing for his fans.

Till We Meet Again (1936), starring Herbert Marshall, is another obscure Atwill film set during the WWI. He plays Ludwig, a plain-clothes German spymaster, sporting a monocle and flamboyant moustache. It's a significant role and he is stern and cold throughout, forever barking orders to his underlings. The ending is particularly gruesome. He has fallen from a train and broken his back. In his dying moments, his face is bleeding and dripping with sweat. He is clearly in pain as he barks his final orders before expiring.

In October 1936, Atwill sailed to England and made his only film there, *The High Command* (1937). Little could Atwill have known that this film's climactic courtroom scene would prefigure his own court case a few years later. In this powerful scene, Atwill is in the witness box, implicated in a murder in which he did nothing wrong. The prosecutor makes a veiled reference to an earlier crime of which Atwill *was* guilty. Atwill gives him another

Monogram's *Beggars in Ermine* (1934) plays up the exploitation angles, as Atwill portrays a wheelchair-bound man plotting revenge for crimes committed against him.

of those legendary cold stares and tells him, with aggressive intensity in every syllable, "I must decline to follow you into such vague speculations." There isn't another actor, alive or dead, who could have spoken the line with such force.

A few months after completing *Son of Frankenstein* in 1939, Atwill was in *The Sun Never Sets*, and it was something of a reunion for cast and crew. Basil Rathbone is the star of both, and the two films share the same director (Rowland V. Lee), cinematographer, set designer and musical director. Although not a horror film, it nevertheless gave Atwill a chance to really chew up some scenery as mad scientist Dr Hugo Zurof. He gets one of his most memorable death scenes. He is found stone dead in his chair, eyes wide open, killed by extreme concussion from overhead bombing. Rathbone looks at Zurof's wide-eyed corpse closely and sees an ant walking over his forehead. It's a satisfyingly dramatic image in light of Zurof's earlier ranting that he wants to rule the world's entire population, whom he regards as mere ants that need to be dominated. And it's a deliciously macabre touch that even in death the legendary Atwill stare lives on!

By the late 1930s, Atwill was living the good life. He had married again (to multi-millionairess Louise MacArthur), owned two large houses, two Rolls Royce cars and a 65-foot yacht. But then it all startled to unravel rather cruelly. He separated acrimoniously from Louise in 1939. In 1940 a 16-year-old girl threatened to tell the press that Atwill was holding "orgies" at one of his homes. Even worse, in April 1941 Atwill received a telegram informing him that his son John, a flying officer in Britain's Royal Air Force, had been killed by enemy action. Just when he thought it couldn't get any worse, he was indicted on a perjury charge. He finally admitted that he had previously told an untruth in court, declaring that friends of his had not been at a party even though they had in fact been present. He summoned all his wonderful theatrical presence and told the courtroom, "I lied like a gentleman to protect friends." How I would have loved to hear him utter that legendary line in the courtroom.

He was found guilty of perjury. The Will Hays censorship office, which had been so disapproving of the subject matter of *The Song of Songs, Stamboul Quest* and *The Devil Is A Woman*, now jumped on this opportunity to get revenge on Atwill. They instructed all the major Hollywood studios not to hire him. For five long months he was unemployable and thought that his career was over. But eventually the court exonerated him of all charges and he found work at Universal, where he appeared memorably in some of their horror sequels such as *Frankenstein Meets the Wolf Man* (1943) and *House of Frankenstein* (1944). Although in later decades these films have come to be regarded as classics, at the time accepting such roles was, in terms of status and financial reward, a great comedown for the former Broadway theatrical legend and esteemed 1930s film star.

A recent visit with author Neil Pettigrew and Lionel Atwill's great-niece, Leslie Dale

For an example of just how far Atwill had fallen, take a look at Universal's 13-part serial *Raiders of Ghost City* (1944). The budget is low, the script is muddled and Atwill's role, as a villainous Prussian stealing gold in order to buy Alaska, is highly forgettable. The saddest thing of all is to see that the spark has gone out of those marvelous eyes. The legendary Atwill cold stare is no more. Atwill looks weary, brought low by the series of harsh blows that fate had dealt him. Cruelly, fate had an even harsher blow in store—lung cancer was starting to eat away at him. In mid-1944, when he filmed this serial, the cancer had not yet been diagnosed and Atwill was probably unaware of it. In fact, he is seen puffing away on a fat cigar in most scenes, oblivious to the fact that he had less than two years to live. In one scene it almost appears that for some reason the scriptwriter wished to make Atwill suffer even further. Atwill's character is asked how he feels about the news that Confederate soldiers are surrendering. "A soldier should fall in battle," he responds, somehow managing to conceal the painful memories the line must have brought back about his son John.

We have looked at some of the many faces of Lionel Atwill on-stage and in non-horror films. In fact another face of Lionel Atwill exists. It's the Lionel Atwill we never got to see. The Atwill who lived until his 80s and carried on playing character parts in horror films, in the way that Karloff and Carradine carried on professionally into their 80s. But regrettably chain-smoker Atwill succumbed to lung cancer at age 61, depriving his fans of possibly another 25 of filmmaking.

One way exists, however, to watch the elderly Atwill in action. *The Great Waltz* (1938), a biopic about the life of Johann Strauss, concludes with a final scene that takes place "43 years later." Here we see Atwill in a very credible old-age make-up, made to look as though he is in his 70s or 80s. Is this how Atwill might have looked had he lived another 20 years? In this scene, he has a brief dialogue with Emperor Franz Josef—played by the *Werewolf of London* himself, gravel-voiced Henry Hull, also in an effective old-age make-up and sporting some flamboyant whiskers.

One thing is clear to me from watching Atwill's non-horror film roles. Of all the stars who became typecast in horror films, including Karloff, Lugosi, the Chaneys, Price, Lee and Cushing, Atwill was the finest *actor*. He had learned and refined his craft thoroughly on the stage over a period of 27 years, so that by the time Hollywood beckoned him, he knew his trade thoroughly.

Too often, what has been written about Atwill has either concentrated solely on his horror films or else has dwelt with excessive interest on one short and unfortunate episode in his life that ended in court. I hope this article has done something to redress the balance and get his whole life and career into a truer perspective. The records show that he was a warm-hearted man who gave up his time to help the relatives of those lost in the Titanic disaster, helped to raise money for the Actors' Orphanage Fund and did what he could to aid the WWI war effort. Let us also remember the fine stage actor who shone brightly on both the British and American stages. And let us remember the superlative screen actor who starred opposite Marlene Dietrich, Myrna Loy and other fine stars of the Golden Age of Hollywood. Many different faces existed for Lionel Atwill, and some of them were flawed and got him into trouble. But above all let's remember that some of those faces were made of nobler stuff and were those of a man who acted, in his finer moments (to use the actor's own words), "like a gentleman."

The 13 Most Influential Horror Movies
The Grand Finale!

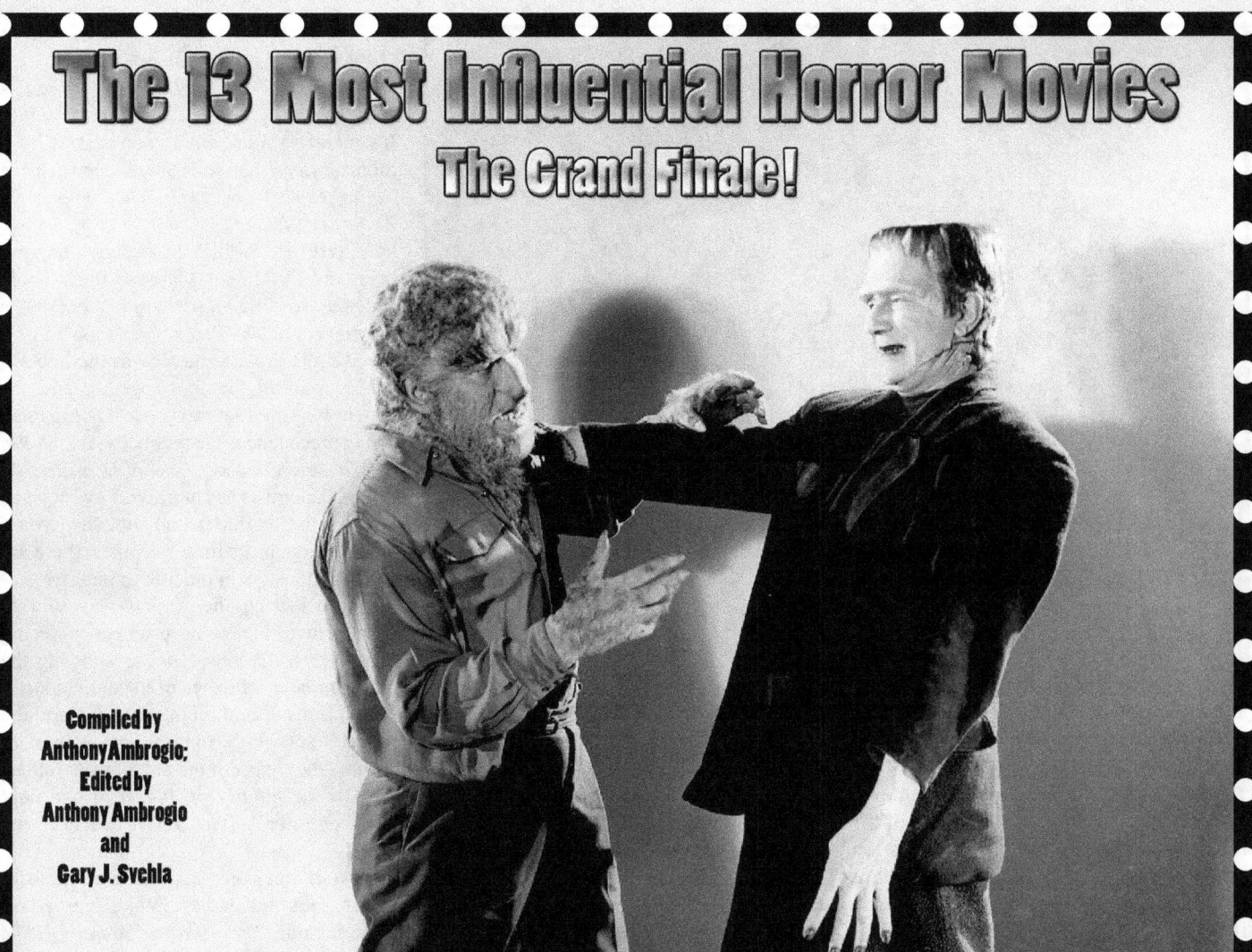

Compiled by Anthony Ambrogio; Edited by Anthony Ambrogio and Gary J. Svehla

Our story so far: You may recall that Gary Svehla touched off a storm of controversy when he introduced his list of the 13 Most Influential Horror Films (see "Groundbreakers," *Midnight Marquee* 75 [2006]). His list included—*Frankenstein* (1931), *King Kong* (1933), *The Black Cat* (1934), *Cat People* (1942), *Frankenstein Meets the Wolf Man* (1943), *The Thing* (1951), *I Was a Teenage Werewolf* (1956), *Horror of Dracula* (1958), *Black Sunday* (1960), *Night of the Living Dead* (1968), *The Exorcist* (1973), *Halloween* (1978), and *Ringu* (1998). Some members of *MidMar*'s gang of contributors took issue with the fact that *Psycho* (1960) was not on the list, which caused a considerable dust-up. (See *Forum/Against 'Em, Midnight Marquee* 76 [2008].)

After that little fracas, the dust settled, and Gary, Mark Clark, Brian Smith, Bryan Senn, Steven Thornton, Jonathan Malcolm Lampley and Anthony Ambrogio raised it again, this time arguing about several of Gary's other choices. (Neil Vokes and Bruce Dettman offered a couple of comments, too.)

1. Steven Softens the Blow before Lowering the Boom

Steven: None of this is meant to be a rap against you, Gary. "Groundbreakers" was a fun article and one of the strongest pieces that I have seen in *Midnight Marquee* in quite some time. Very thought provoking. But I submit that the limit of 13 titles is an arbitrary number. It makes for a snappy title for the article, but it has no real meaning beyond that. Horror cinema is well into its eighth decade, so why limit the list to only 13?

Gary: Arbitrary is right. I could have included the top-100 most influential, but that lessens the impact of only focusing on the top-13 (13 allows a top-10 list with a few extras overflowing) or the most essential titles. By selecting the arbitrary number 13, I am forcing myself to confront the top contenders, and it is always harder to narrow the list to its bare-bone essentials.

Brian: If we're going to limit ourselves to 13, Gary asked us what movies we would take off his list to make room for the films we'd want to add. Here are my modifications to Gary's list (my changes are in bold):

Frankenstein, The Black Cat, King Kong, Cat People, The Thing, I Was a Teenage Werewolf, Horror of Dracula, Black Sunday, **Psych**o, **Rosemary's Baby**, *Night of the Living Dead, The Exorcist* and *Halloween.*

It seems to me that both *The Exorcist* and *Rosemary's Baby* deserve to be on the list, for different reasons. They both contributed to the major trend in satanic/occult films of the 1970s and 1980s, but each had a wider influence beyond that. I decided to take off *Ringu*, not because I disagree with Gary's analysis, but because I think it's too early to include any film from the 1990s on a list of the most influential horror films of all time.

So, after all the sound and fury, I basically made two changes to Gary's list. That means we're mostly in agreement.

Boris Karloff, David Manners and Bela Lugosi toast one another in *The Black Cat* (1934), one of the 13 most influential horror movies from Gary Svehla's list.

Mark: I, too, would consider removing *Ringu* from your list. I'm well aware of the recent vogue for J-horror but think it's too soon to assess how significant that will turn out to be. J-horror has waned as we speak. If someone prepares a similar list in 20 or 30 years, perhaps *Ringu* (or something else like it) will make the cut. But, right now, no.

Gary: Okay, Brian; okay, Mark. You might be right about waiting a while to see if *Ringu* actually "sticks." But I placed it on the list not merely because it started the J-horror movement, but mainly because it encapsulated horror movies based upon "found footage" (*The Blair Witch Project* followed a year later) and urban myth as well. Also, *Ringu* turned horror movies away from the splatter and gore to a return of slowly building atmospheric chills. *Ringu* was placed on my list for *many* reasons, not just because it fueled a creative resurgence in Asian horror cinema. *Ringu*'s influence was felt immediately in other ways.

2. *Frankenstein Meets the Wolf Man*: Part of the 13 or Not?

Gary: Mark, you were in the forefront of those clamoring to include *Psycho* among my list of groundbreaking horror films. So, would you remove *Ringu* to make way for *Psycho*?

Mark: Perhaps. For starters, I'd be inclined to remove *Frankenstein Meets the Wolf Man*. I'm not necessarily arguing that *Frankenstein Meets the Wolf Man* and some of these other films were *un*influential. I'm arguing that *Psycho* had much greater influence. The "monster rally" concept led to a few films (*House of Frankenstein* [1944], *House of Dracula* [1945], *Abbott and Costello Meet Frankenstein* [1948] and maybe *Return of the Vampire* [1943]) but proved to be a dead end. Perhaps its greatest influence was that it inspired Paul Nashcy's entire Waldemar Daninsky series! Even so, none of those films strike me as a particularly important development in the overall context of the genre.

Brian: Hey, I have to agree completely with Mark's assessment of *Frankenstein Meets the Wolf Man*. The monster rally is just not that important a development in the history of the horror film. I can only think of a handful of such movies since the 1940s: *How To Make a Monster* (1958), *Freddy vs. Jason* (2003) and *Alien vs. Predator* (2004). Eight movies over 60 years do not make a subgenre.

Arthur: I might like to add *The Jungle Captive* (1945) and *The Black Sleep* (1956)—at least for its stars.

Mark: *The Black Sleep* is *not* a "monster rally." Sorry, just can't see it. It's merely a film with a good cast. If it's a monster rally, then so is *Scream and Scream Again* (1970)—or even *The Whales of August* (1987).

Arthur: Well, according to my invaluable Midnight Marquee Press book, *Bela Lugosi: The Film Actors Series* (1995), the makers of *The Black Sleep* thought of it precisely in those terms. It was the impetus behind putting the film together and the way it was sold to its audience. Giving them some precedence, the publicity for *House of Frankenstein* and *House of Dracula* sold its mad scientists as "monsters" every bit as much as the Wolf Man and Dracula. Even if we don't count its mad scientists, there are enough monsters in the film to qualify.

Considering the way it was sold to its audience, I have no problem in seeing *Scream and Scream Again* as showing the 20-years-later influence of the old "monster rally." Indeed, one might even include the Amicus anthology films as an attempt to harness the cachet of the old monster rallies.

As for *Whales of August*, it had only one "monster." Two, if we count Bette Davis.

Neil: Let's get back to true monster rallies, lads and lasses. Which means we must include *The Monster Squad* (1987). And several Euro-horrors used multiple monsters.

Brian: Okay. Eight or 10 or a dozen movies over 60 years do not make a subgenre.

Maria Ouspenskaya, Ilona Massey, Patric Knowles and Lon Chaney, Jr. from *Frankenstein Meets the Wolf Man* (1943)

Besides the monster rally aspect of *Frankenstein Meets the Wolf Man*, this Universal classic deserves to be remembered for its studio-bound set decoration, which erupts with visual atmosphere.

Gary: True, monster rallies are all about the sizzle, the sell, the poster. All the monsters need to do is wrestle for 30 seconds or so to justify the poster art. And the wonderful ad campaign for *Frankenstein Meets the Wolf Man* was iconic and masterfully executed. But, behind every great movie, there exists a great campaign. We can separate the two, but simply as a movie, *Frankenstein Meets the Wolf Man* is influential. The movie is more than just its ad campaign.

Brian: I love *Frankenstein Meets the Wolf Man*. It's one of my favorite Universal horror films from the 1940s. But I don't see it as a particularly innovative movie. It's basically a rehash of earlier Frankenstein and Wolf Man movies. A very good rehash, but a rehash nonetheless.

I think this is a movie where you can say the poster art was more influential than the movie. It promised a battle royal between two classic monsters. But it didn't deliver on that promise. *Abbott and Costello Meet Frankenstein*'s climactic battle between Dracula and the Wolf Man was more satisfying. But since you're counting Japanese giant-monster movies, then the

Mark: Certainly, the number of films spawned by *Psycho* dwarfs the number of multiple-monster movies spawned by *Frankenstein Meets the Wolf Man*. So, even by your yardstick, Gary, *Psycho* remains *more* influential than *Frankenstein Meets the Wolf Man*.

Brian: If you count as monster rallies any movie with more than one monster in it (rather than movies that take monsters from two different movies and bring them together), there are more. But those kinds of movies were being made long before *Frankenstein Meets the Wolf Man*. *Werewolf of London* (1935) has two werewolves in it. *Bride of Frankenstein* (1935) has the Frankenstein Monster and the Bride. *Son of Frankenstein* (1939) has two monsters in it, if you count Ygor as a monster (which I do: The inability to kill Ygor by normal means—hanging, shooting—puts him in the category of being not quite human, to my mind).

Frankenstein Meets the Wolf Man did have a significant influence on the giant Japanese monster movie, as Godzilla, Mothra, Rodan, and Ghidorah all started meeting each other. But the Godzilla movies aren't really horror films.

Gary: Sure they are! Besides the obvious Universal choices, besides the Spanish and Mexican *rallies des mostros*, we have all the Japanese monster rallies with Godzilla, Baragon, Mothra, Gamera, etc. So many people added so many titles that I think *Frankenstein Meets the Wolf Man*'s justification has been made and well supported.

Brian: Only if *Frankenstein Meets the Wolf Man* truly is the first monster-rally movie. What sets *Frankenstein Meets the Wolf Man* apart from earlier films with multiple monsters?

Gary: Here is what sets it apart. Universal used it as a marketing ploy to create a series of like-minded monster-rally films for the remainder of the decade, and beyond. In fact, most of the more successful Universal horror movies of the 1940s were monster-rally films. It was a creative formula that worked.

Brian: Fair enough—but, if the significance of the movie is how it was marketed, wouldn't it be more accurate to say that *Frankenstein Meets the Wolf Man* had one of the most influential *ad campaigns* in horror-movie history? Especially considering that Frankenstein and the Wolf Man only meet for a frustratingly brief period in the movie—just a couple of minutes of screen time together before they're washed away by the flood waters.

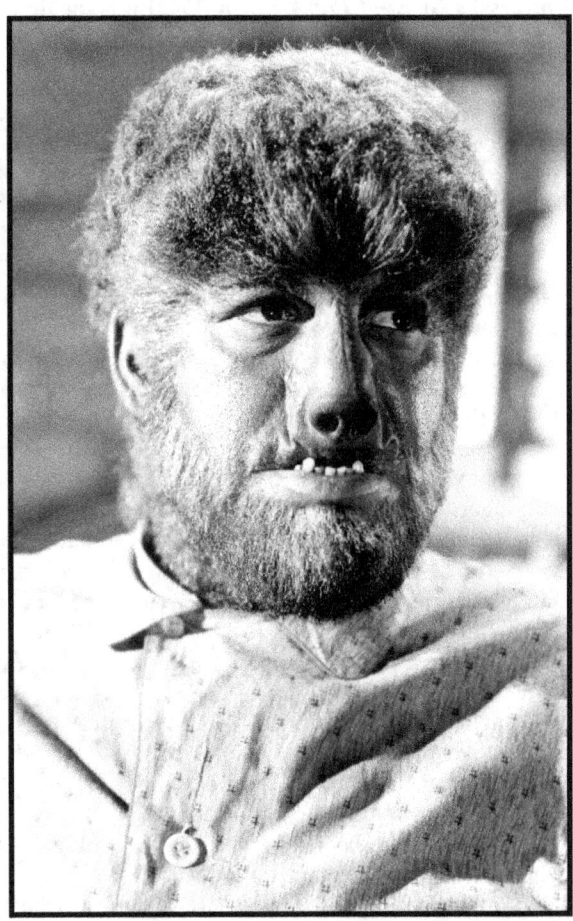

Even though this still makes it seem that the Wolf Man is wearing pajamas, Lon Chaney Jr.'s iconic characterization is among the classics of horror cinema.

Universal's *Ghost of Frankenstein* (1942) was the first Frankenstein entry to not get the big-budget A-movie treatment.

Steven: Valid point. But, if only by pure chance, *Frankenstein Meets the Wolf Man* seems to represent a pivotal moment in big-studio opinions of the horror film. How many big-budget horror movies were released in the remainder of the decade? *Phantom of the Opera* (1943) was pretty much concurrent with *Frankenstein Meets the Wolf Man*. Paramount released *The Uninvited* (1944). MGM had *Dorian Gray* (1945). I don't recall any others.

Maybe it's more accurate to call *Frankenstein Meets the Wolf Man* the confirmation of a new trend rather than the influence that establishes one.

Brian: A trend that probably began with *Ghost of Frankenstein*, the first Frankenstein film not to get the big-budget, A-movie treatment.

Anthony: Years ago, Paul Severn, in an article on *Ghost* for *Fantastic Monsters of the Films* (vol. 1, no. 5 [1963]) praised the film and lamented that, if they'd only taken more care (i.e., spent more money) on the picture, it "coulda been a contender," like *Son of Frankenstein*.

[Anthony is met with stony silence.]

3. Mark Makes His Mark …

Mark: Do you still want me to continue with my "process of elimination," Gary?

monster rally really didn't take off until *King Kong vs. Godzilla* (1963).

Arthur: Well, *Frankenstein Meets the Wolf Man* may not have had the battle royal, but it did have the magical scene where Larry Talbot frees the Monster from the ice. What more could a monster rally need to offer?

Brian: Ygor freeing the Monster from the sulfur in *Ghost of Frankenstein* (1942)? I'm beginning to think that *Ghost of Frankenstein* is one of the most influential horror movies. It even has three monsters in it: Ygor, the Monster and the Ghost of Henry Frankenstein. (I'm joking here.)

Arthur: Awwwwww, the sulfur scene ain't near as magical as the ice-cave scene. Though, if you combine the sulfur scene with the subsequent lightning scene, it comes closer.

Gary: Well, gentlemen, it seems to me that everyone here has made the point loud and clear that the monster-rally film, which began as a marketable concept with *Frankenstein Meets the Wolf Man*, continues in horror cinema to this generation, and not only in America. From Godzilla to Mexican horrors to *The Monster Squad*, the monster rally film became a significant horror film subgenre.

Steven: I suppose one could make an argument that *Frankenstein Meets the Wolf Man* had an influence of a *different* type. It's the moment where the majors begin to classify the horror movie almost exclusively as a formula-driven, B-movie commodity. That is very much an influence, I'll grant you, although I sure don't see it as a positive one.

Mark: I must admit that I view *Frankenstein Meets the Wolf Man* as more symptomatic of Universal's declining seriousness of intent with regard to its horror cycle than the active cause of that decline. I don't believe *Frankenstein Meets the Wolf Man* actually *caused* Universal to begin thinking of its horror films as second-rate commodities. Rather, it reflects the reality that Universal had *already* begun thinking of its horror films as second-rate commodities.

Lon Chaney, Jr. as the Monster and Cedric Hardwicke as Ludwig Frankenstein carry on the monster rally tradition in *Ghost of Frankenstein*.

Gary: Yes, by all means.

Mark: Okay, then. Much as I love it, I'm not sold on *The Black Cat* as one of the most influential horrors, either. Certainly it's not *more* influential than *Psycho*.

Arthur: *The Black Cat*'s one of my favorite films, but I am hard pressed to come up with many (or any) films that show its influence.

Most importantly, the supernatural horror in the film explicitly flows from recent history in the real world. I don't think that other films started doing that for at least 20 years.

Anthony: Well, Gary wrote that "*The Black Cat* established the concept of horror-film celebrity and forwarded the sense of gruesome unspeakable horrors," so he's saying its influence is two-fold. Certainly, the teaming of two (or more) horror-film icons began with *The Black Cat*. In that case, its influence was enormous. *The Black Sleep*, which was mentioned previously as a possible "monster-rally" movie influenced by *Frankenstein Meets the Wolf Man*, is a movie that shows the influence that Gary finds in *The Black Cat*: a "monster rally" in terms of its all-star horror-film-icon cast.

Mark: Removing *Ringu* and/or *The Black Cat* would enable you to include *The Cabinet of Dr. Caligari* (1919). Really, any

Edgar Ulmer's quirky and depraved *The Black Cat* (1934) demonstrates the concept of horror-film celebrity, as well as creating distinctive art decoration to depict satanism in the modern world.

list of this type without *Caligari* is, in my mind, unthinkable. Frankly, I'd be tempted to remove both *Ringu* and *The Black Cat* to make room for the Chaney *Phantom of the Opera* (1925), as well.

While I'm at it, let me say that *Eyes Without a Face* (1959) is another film that should be given serious consideration (perhaps in place of *Frankenstein Meets the Wolf Man*). Although it didn't make a big impact here in the U.S., it was very influential overseas, in terms of Euro-horror films and even art films like Teshingura's *The Face of Another* (1966). And *Eyes* wasn't completely without influence in the U.S.—witness Frankenheimer's *Seconds* (1966). Moreover, I think *Eyes* influenced many American films in a secondary way, especially in the way the films it spawned amped up the gore factor.

I'd make several other changes, too: I'm of the opinion that, while *Halloween* is a magnificent and influential film, *Friday* was *more* influential in the overall development of the slasher subgenre. If *Friday* had flopped, the slasher cycle would have wilted on the vine. But it was a smash—and, moreover, it proved that a film of this stripe didn't have to be good to make money. The hallmarks of the slasher films of the 1980s are excessive gore and indifferent craftsmanship. Neither of those qualities apply to *Halloween*. Both begin with *Friday*.

Thus, I would remove *Halloween* and (reluctantly) replace it with *Friday the 13th*. Similarly, I would replace *The Exorcist* with *Rosemary's Baby* (1968), the film that introduced Satan as a bankable screen villain and ushered in a bunch of films dealing with the devil and devil-worship. *The Exorcist* followed, and its enormous box-office spawned countless rip-offs, but it's a branch, not the root.

I understand your arguments for *Teenage Werewolf*, *Horror of Dracula* and *Black Sunday*. All three were definitely influential and should be in the Top 13, but I'm not sure I would put any of them ahead of *Psycho*, *Caligari*, or the '25 *Phantom*—or even *Eyes Without a Face*.

I agree with you entirely regarding *Cat People*, definitely one of the most influential chillers ever made. And *King Kong*, *The Thing*, and *Night of the Living Dead* are also definitely in that class.

My revised list would look like this:

The Cabinet of Dr. Caligari, *The Phantom of the Opera*, *Frankenstein*, *King Kong*, *Cat People*, *The Thing*, *The Horror of Dracula*, *Psycho*, *Eyes Without a Face*,

Bela Lugosi as Vitus Werdegast in *The Black Cat* prepares to skin Boris Karloff's Poelzig alive.

Black Sunday, Night of the Living Dead, Rosemary's Baby and *Friday the 13th*.

4. Everyone and His Brother Make Suggestions, Too

Bruce: The term "horror" might preclude this from being on the list, but I would think that Harryhausen's *The Beast From 20,000 Fathoms* (1953) was very influential in giving birth to all the giant-monster films of the 1950s, unless you think that distinction goes to *Them!* (1954) since it was the first to introduce the atomically altered nature wrinkle into the mix.

Arthur: *The Beast from 20,000 Fathoms* didn't just thaw out. He was released by the use of nuclear weapons. That's close enough to the atomically altered wrinkle for me. *Them!* and *Godzilla* (1954) took the idea one step farther, but all the parts were already in place.

Neil: As *Beast* was the direct influence on *Godzilla*, I'd say you're on the right track.

Steven: I think an argument can be made for the inclusion of one of the AIP Poe films too. That was certainly one of the most notable horror trends of the 1960s.

Jonathan: If I had to list the top-10 most influential horror films (notice that I'm arbitrarily stopping at 10, rather than 13), my list would look like this (in chronological order):

The Cabinet of Dr. Caligari; *The Phantom of the Opera*; *Dracula* (although I prefer to list this and *Frankenstein* together, as they really are the one-two punch that kick-starts the Golden Age. We have debated which is the more influential film, but I would have to go with the one that came first if I can cite only one); *I Was a Teenage Werewolf* (how many prior horror films featured teens as the primary protagonists? How many have done so since?); *Curse of Frankenstein* (1957; again I would co-list with *Horror of Dracula*, but see my logic above); *Psycho*; *Night of the Living Dead*; *The Exorcist*; *Halloween*; *The Sixth Sense* (1999).

Films that would almost make the cut would include *Nosferatu* (1922), *King Kong* (1933; if you consider it a horror film, that is), *Son of Frankenstein*, *The Wolf Man*, *Cat People*, *House of Wax* (1953), *Repulsion* (1965), *Rosemary's Baby*, *The Texas Chain Saw Massacre* (1974), *Friday the 13th*, *A Nightmare on Elm Street* (1984), *Silence of the Lambs* (1991) and *Scream* (1996).

You will all note the lack of non-English films. Not to be a jingoist, but I honestly don't think any foreign language film has yet had the influence of the American/English films listed above. I don't count the Toho giant-monster movies because (like Brian and unlike Gary) I am not defining them as horror films, although you could make the argument that they are as much horror as science fiction. But the films of Bava, Argento, and now the recent Japanese horrors would be the most influential foreign-language horror films, I think. Del Toro's films may also join those ranks, particularly *Pan's Labyrinth* (2006), but I think it will be a few more years to accurately ascertain their status.

Gary: I see giant monsters as being an integral part of the horror film genre; *King Kong* is definitely a horror movie starring an iconic monster and, to me, the movie influenced numerous movies made during the 1930s and 1940s, finally influencing the giant animal/insect films of the 1950s and beyond. Even if based upon some of the tenets of science fiction, I see giant monsters as components of horror cinema.

5. Gary Considers It

Gary: Such thoughtful challenges make me think more about my choices and whether they deserve to remain or not. I don't intend to argue these "suggestions" point-by-point ... this is all opinion, and we all have different ways of examining the same influences. But I did want at least to address Mark and Jonathan's revisions to my list and to make a few comments, telling why I selected the films I selected.

First of all, in answer to Mark and Jonathan's nominations of *Caligari* and the Chaney *Phantom*, you must remember

A case is made for *The Beast from 20,000 Fathoms* (1953) being worthy of consideraiton as an influential horror movie, inspiring the giant-monster films of the 1950s and beyond.

The Cabinet of Dr. Caligari (1920) might deserve consideration as being worthy of joining the list of most influential horror movies by virtue of it jump-starting the Golden Age of horror. Werner Krauss is front and center as Dr. Caligari.

that I limited my influential list to the talkies. Silent movies are a different animal altogether, and if I wanted to include them, I would have upped the number of films from 13 to 15. I set the parameters to include only sound movies and created a list of the top-13 (not 10). But Mark and Anthony insist upon rewriting the parameters.

Anthony: The silent-film aesthetic *is* different; one could argue that the nature of influence is therefore different. And then there's the thorny issue about when horror films became known as "horror films." The horror films of the silent era were generally called something else.

Gary: Exactly. Let's keep the playing field level … apples with apples, so to speak. Now let me speak to Mark and Jonathan's apples, if I may …

I would select *Horror of Dracula* over *Curse of Frankenstein* because *Curse of Frankenstein* did not resonate with the American public as much as *Dracula* did. While *Dracula* was not a huge moneymaker (it was a *horror* film hit and did well as a genre film), it did better box-office than *Curse*. *Dracula* created the buzz. And that created the influence.

Jonathan, I am glad to see you agree with me about *Halloween*, and don't want to jettison it for *Friday the 13th*.

The Sixth Sense … perhaps this is still too current, but I don't see the influence on other movies that followed. Perhaps you can enlighten us? It was a huge moneymaker and critical darling, but other than subsequent films made by the same director, what creative movement arrived in its wake?

Runners up … quite an interesting list of also-rans. But I don't see the influences that *Son of Frankenstein* created (it seems more like an end to a movement than a beginning) or that *The Wolf Man* or *House of Wax* created. And I was disappointed to see such an influential film as *Cat People* off your main list. Perhaps you would justify the above three films for all of us?

Jonathan: Universal's *Son of Frankenstein* is influential for a number of reasons, including the fact that *Young Frankenstein* (1974) is a parody of *Son* even more so than it is of *Frankenstein* and *Bride of Frankenstein*. Most young people don't seem to be familiar with the original Karloff films, but the number of students in my film classes who know Mel Brooks' comedy classic staggers me. Hell, if we were doing an article on most influential horror comedies, *Young Frankenstein* might get my vote for most influential.

But let's get back to *Son of Frankenstein*. The single most important reason why it ranks so highly in my view is the incorporation of the Ygor character. Even people who don't know a lot about horror films or horror history know that a hunchback named Ygor (or even Igor) helped Dr. Frankenstein and other mad scientist characters.

Gary: Then shouldn't we consider Fritz in *Frankenstein* to be the original "mad doc's crippled assistant"—a character that happens to be renamed Ygor two films later? After all, isn't Ygor's character influenced by and cut from the same cloth as Fritz, followed by Dwight Frye's similar Karl in *Bride of Frankenstein*?

Jonathan: While the hunchback assistant is introduced in *Frankenstein*, few people outside of horror fandom know that the character was named Fritz. Everybody knows Ygor/Igor, which is a testament to the influence of *Son* and Lugosi's performance in particular. It is significant that Ygor appears in only two movies, yet we find references to him in everything from *House of Wax* (this time as a murderous deaf mute, not a hunchback) to television's *The Munsters* (Grandpa's pet bat) to popular songs like "The Monster Mash." Again,

Besides the iconic Karloff Frankenstein Monster, *Son of Frankenstein* (1939) becomes influential for introducing Bela Lugosi's conniving and crippled Ygor character.

Horror of Dracula (1958), Hammer's classic, resonated with audiences to a far greater degree than the earlier *Curse of Frankenstein* (1957) did.

I am talking about the impressions of the general public, and Ygor/Igor is still very familiar to many people, and that familiarity is what supports my claim for the influence of *Son of Frankenstein*.

Gary: I *like* your point about Ygor/Igor from *Son of Frankenstein*. But isn't that like saying *The Mummy* (1932) is influential because it introduced the character of the monster mummy? If we follow your logic to its logical conclusion, *any* film that introduced a recurring character can now be called an influential film, such as the Alien monster in *Alien*, and I don't think that's the thrust of my list or what is meant by influential. I proclaim that introducing influential characters in a movie is not the same as creating an influential film, let alone a groundbreaking one.

Now, what about *The Wolf Man*?

Jonathan: As for *The Wolf Man*, I include it on the list because that movie, more than anything that came before or since, established the iconography of the werewolf in film and popular culture. That by itself would justify inclusion. So would the establishment of Lon Chaney, Jr. as a major figure in horror films. But it's not just that the werewolf is finally established in movies, it is the specific way that he is killed. A werewolf's vulnerability to silver is entirely the product of the movies—specifically, this movie. Werewolves were not, in fact, "wolf *men*"; they were

Author Curt Siodmak created a modern folk tale with *The Wolf Man* (1941); Lon Chaney, Jr. as Talbot tries to warn lady friend Evelyn Ankers (Gwen) of impending danger as her father (J.M. Kerrigan) looks on.

largewolves, often with human intelligence, that could be killed like any regular wolf—including using regular bullets. In essence, screenwriter Curt Siodmak created a modern folk tale in *The Wolf Man*, one that has become the wellspring for most people's assumptions about the werewolf legend. It's really quite fascinating, for it proves that movies are a source for the folklore of contemporary times.

Gary: Your claim that *The Wolf Man* is influential because it created the werewolf mythology is both true and false. It did create the mythology that carried on within the Universal Wolf Man series (I mean *Werewolf of London* featured the full-moon mythos and some other aspects, didn't it? And Henry Hull was a wolf *man*, not a man who turned into an actual wolf), but it was part of a series, and, as such, that series played by specific rules. Influential as I defined it is different from saying that one film within the same series influences another. Of course it does, but that's not the point of my article. That's as simplistic as saying aspects of *Alien Resurrection* (1997) were influenced by the original *Alien*. You're missing the point. That's not what I meant by influential. (People need to go back to my original article to get the principles correct. Back issues *are* available!)

What have you got to say about *House of Wax* on your list of runners-up?

Jonathan: *House of Wax* makes the runner-up list for several reasons, most significantly because it is the true beginning of the establishment of Vincent Price as "Mr. Horror." True, Price made horror films before *House of Wax*, and, in my own book on Price (*Women in the Horror Films of Vincent Price* [McFarland & Company, 2011]), I trace the gradual association of the actor with horror, pointing out that it is not until *House of Usher* (1960) that he truly becomes a bona fide "horror star." But only the most determined film fans would remember Price's pre-1953 horror films had he not done *House of Wax*. It and *The Fly* (1958) are the two movies most often cited as representative examples of Price's work, and I doubt William Castle or Roger Corman would have thought of Price for their own horror films had they not recalled his work in *House of Wax*.

Gary: Saying *House of Wax* is influential because it started Vincent Price's horror-film run is not what I intended by "influence." Then we would have to put *Frankenstein* on the list because it started Karloff's horror career. What about *Man-Made Monster* (1941) for starting Chaney, Jr.'s horror film run or *Curse of Frankenstein* because it debuted the horror

Vincent Price as now crippled Henry Jarrod from *House of Wax*, the film that established Price as "Mr. Horror"

run of Cushing and Lee? That is not how I defined *influential* horror movies. That's not the point of my influential list, is it?

Jonathan: Then try this. Perhaps more significantly, *House of Wax* was a major box-office hit; Warner Bros. continued to re-release the film for years, even as late as the 1980s, and it kept generating revenue for the studio. Indeed, Phil Hardy in *The Encyclopedia of Horror* includes a list of the genre's box-office champs, and *House of Wax* is second only to *Jaws* (1975) in money earned as of 1985. (Come to think of it, shouldn't *Jaws* be on our lists somewhere?) Add to that all the 3-D films made in its wake, and how the 3-D films that are all the rage now can be traced back to the 3-D fad of the 1950s, and we see more evidence of how influential *House of Wax* truly is. Finally, there have been relatively few wax museum/chamber of horror movies since 1953, but all of them—including the unfortunate 2005 remake with Paris Hilton—exist because of *House of Wax*.

Gary: Hmm, a huge box-office and inspiring a remake is not influential as I defined it. The 3-D craze born in 1953 was dead by 1954 and wasn't resurrected until the 1970s, when it died a second time. What about *Cat People*?

Jonathan: I put *Cat People* on the runner-up list because, while it is a great favorite of horror fans and critics (especially

Cat People (1942) belongs among the 13 most influential horror movies because it started the subgenre of psychologically based horror movies; Alice (Jane Randolph) finds her robe shredded to pieces after emerging from her swim.

critics who hate horror films), I don't think that by itself the film has really influenced that many movies or is particularly well-regarded by the general public. The Val Lewton films as a whole have certainly been influential, of course, and, if any one film in that series is the most influential, it would be *Cat People* (heck, it's the only one to get a sequel of sorts and a remake). So it is influential but not quite influential enough to make my top-10 or even top-13 list.

Gary: Jonathan, I hate to say it (or maybe I *don't* hate to say it), but you are *mistaken* to downgrade *Cat People* to runner-up status, as the movie started the entire subgenre of psychologically based horror movies. Its influence is among the most significant of any single horror movie. It even influenced *Psycho* and Norman Bates.

Jonathan: Well, I don't know about that. Upon further reflection—and at the risk of adding oranges back to your bunch of apples by insisting that silent films should be included—I would have to promote *Nosferatu* to the main list and downgrade *The Cabinet of Dr. Caligari* to the runner-up list.

We always hear about how influential *Caligari* is, but, honestly, how many films can you name that clearly and specifically show its influence? Even major critics have pointed out how few films can be deliberately and specifically traced back to *Caligari*. As Arthur Knight in *The Liveliest Art* says, "One can point to no films that derive from it directly." I think *Caligari* may be more important as a film that made the general public take movies more seriously as an art form than anything else—and as our discussion is focused on what movies made other movies change their approach or their point of view, I just don't think *Caligari* ranks quite as highly as I once did.

Nosferatu, on the other hand, really did influence pretty much every vampire film that came along. It established the vampire genre in cinema, and the iconic look of Count Dracula/Graf Orlok has been copied, stolen and parodied over and over again, particularly in the last decade or two. By contrast, nobody makes a reference to poor old Dr. Caligari, although some have claimed that the not-so-good hypnotist influenced the look of Danny DeVito as the Penguin in *Batman Returns* (1989). In particular, *Nosferatu* established the idea that sunlight destroys vampires. In previous tales and in folklore, vampires either don't come out at all during the daylight hours

Nosferatu (1922) established the vampire genre in cinema and the iconic look of Count Dracula. But it remains a silent film and thus stands outside our parameters.

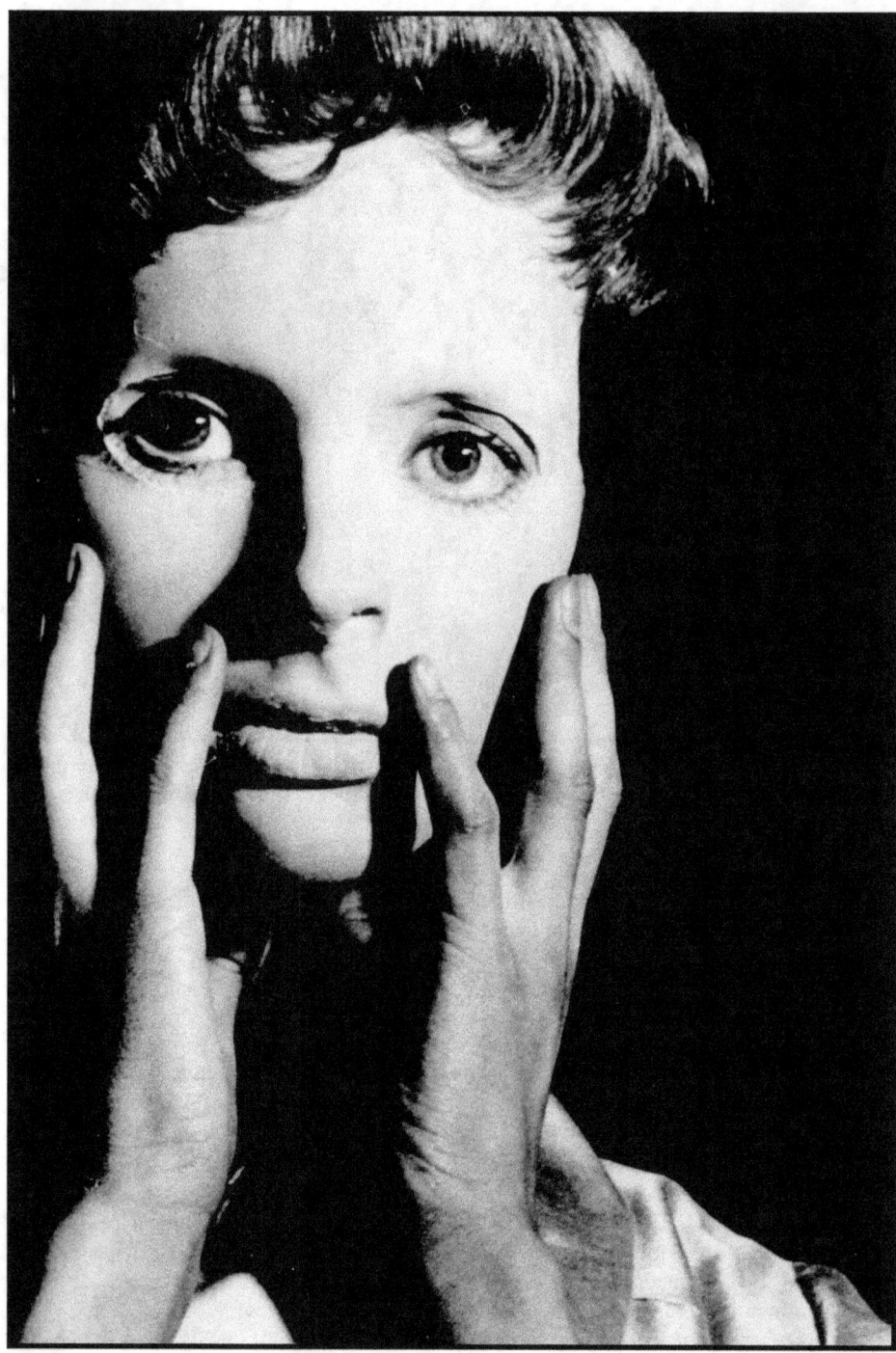

Eyes Without a Face (1960) influenced European filmmakers to amp up the gore factor rather than focus upon the poetic visuals and sensitive characterizations; Edith Scob as Christiane awaits a successful face transplant.

or they are unharmed by sunshine. Even Count Dracula in Stoker's novel is seen in daytime, but he doesn't have his vampire superpowers and clearly prefers the nighttime. Just as I claimed with *The Wolf Man* that establishing what kills a monster is a significant contribution to folklore, then by that logic *Nosferatu* has to make the cut.

Gary: Sorry. No matter what you say, it's *still* a silent film. It's just the first film version of a novel that was filmed again (as a *sound* film) in 1931.

Jonathan: You're a harsh man, Gary.

6. On the Influence of *Eyes Without a Face*

Gary: Mark, *Eyes Without a Face* has always been a favorite of mine, and I've been writing about its merits for decades. But is it influential? I see it as more of a stand-alone classic of the genre (much like I see *Psycho*). I don't see it as starting a new creative movement. Art-house horror films never caught on.

Mark: *Eyes Without a Face* was certainly influential, but more so overseas. Unfortunately its influence was mainly that it inspired European filmmakers to amp up the gore factor rather than focus upon the poetic visuals and sensitive characterizations that Georges Franju employed to counterbalance the gore. In my write-up on this film for *Sixties Shockers: A Critical Filmography of Horror Cinema, 1960-1969* (McFarland Books, 2011), I note, "Along with Henri-Georges Clouzot's *Les Diaboliques* and Alfred Hitchcock's *Psycho*, *Eyes Without a Face* profoundly influenced the subsequent generation of European horror movies. Too often, however, its imitators would duplicate only the copious gore of *Eyes Without a Face*, never realizing that what made the original film special was the beauty that accompanied its ugliness."

Anthony: I confess that I've yet to see *Eyes Without a Face*. That's how influential it is for me. I can see how one could say it started a trend toward operations-to-restore-damaged-females movies, and—until I see it—I can't begin to say how much later movies may have taken from it. But a subgenre of the horror film that deals with the mad scientist obsessed with restoring his beautiful wife (or daughter or sister) exists, isn't there, going back at least as far as Lugosi's Monograms, *The Corpse Vanishes* (1942) and *Voodoo Man* (1944) specifically. Many people's cult favorite *The Brain That Wouldn't Die* (1962) is such a picture. What follows? Cushing in *Corruption* (1967), *Mansion of the Damned* (1977) with Richard Egan and Gloria Graham and that Franco film *Faceless* (1987), which is an *Eyes Without a Face* rip-off, and … what? Certainly, when it comes to a poetic cinematic treatment of the subject, we must include Almodovar's *The Skin I Live In*, my pick for best film of 2011.

But I'm probably selling Mark short because he is suggesting that *Eyes* was influential for more than just its operating-room plot.

Mark: Pretty much. *Eyes*' influence was not in its story elements but in the way it approached those elements. As you say, the basic storyline goes back to *Voodoo Man* and its ilk, if not further back. Its "face-lift" scene was one of the goriest things audiences had ever seen at that time, and other European filmmakers took note of this and began using more graphic violence and gore in their films, much more readily (as a rule) than in the U.S.

Gary: Perhaps I will have to re-read your book to understand the Euro influence of *Eyes Without a Face*. Wouldn't the early

Bava films (his *giallo* ones) have been more influential in defining the trend for Euro-violence in horror films, even going back to 1956 for his *I, Vampiri/Lust of the Vampire*? Maybe even the earliest Jess Franco movies such as *The Awful Dr. Orlof* (1962) were more influential, as *Eyes* was something of an art film, wasn't it? But for me it's too much of a stretch to say *Eyes Without a Face* influenced Euro-splatter to that extent. Wasn't it a tad too high-brow to be a major influence on the down-and-dirty Eurotrash cinema?

7. On the Influence of *Friday the 13th*

Gary: Here's my main argument why *Halloween* should be included on my list and not *Friday the 13th*.

Go back to Lou Gaul's groundbreaking article on *Halloween*, published in *Midnight Marquee* a lifetime ago, and remember Gaul's major point that *Halloween* was, at that time, the highest-grossing independent production of all time. After *The Exorcist* fired up the mainstream big-budget Hollywood filmmaking machine, *Halloween* swung the pendulum in the other direction by jump-starting the trend of indies making *beaucoup* bucks. (*Night of the Living Dead*, a cult midnight-movie/drive-in movie experience, did not generate enough money to ignite the trend by itself.) *Halloween*'s box-office influenced not only the slasher movie but also *any* independent horror movie produced during the 1980s and even beyond. That's why I believe it belongs. *Halloween* started the trend of independently produced horror movies, so independent productions flooded the market.

Friday the 13th arrived two years later from major-studio Paramount. My point is this: Paramount wanted to show that the majors could produce low-budget horror movies that could ape and appear similar to the ever-evolving indie horror movies saturating theaters. It was *Halloween* that influenced Paramount to make a copycat film featuring teens and slashers. So, to me,

P.J. Soles thinks she is about to have sex with her boyfriend, but it is the monstrous "Shape" in a sheet that is about consummate the situation differently, from *Halloween* (1978).

Friday the 13th was directly influenced by the success of the indie giant *Halloween*. The big boys were simply cashing in and imitating the low-budget cash cow.

Anthony: Gary makes a good case and may yet convince me to go with *Halloween* instead of *Friday the 13th* in terms of influence.

I think the killings are gorier and more explicit in *Friday* than in the first *Halloween*, but *Halloween* does introduce one element (to its detriment, I think) that many later slasher movies pick up on. Gary has alluded to this: the unstoppable, seemingly supernatural slasher. One of the things that I objected to when I saw *Halloween* upon its theatrical release—I thought it was an excellent exercise in style but lacked a great story—was the "shifting" nature of the villain. He *seems* to be a psycho kid who grew up in a mental institution, escaped and started killing again. But in the end, for no good reason that I could see, he suddenly becomes "the bogey man," a supernatural creature who disappears after being "killed" several times over. That character is *not* in *Friday the 13th* (as the killer in *Scream* makes clear to initial victim Drew Barrymore): It's *Mrs*. Voorhees who's committed all the crimes. Of course, *Friday* does adopt a moment from *Halloween*—and a bunch of other 1970s horror films—by having the surviving camper attacked by the drowned corpse of the child Jason. (This is a moment that gets conveniently forgotten in the *Friday* sequels, when Jason, who somehow *didn't* drown but survived

The teenage body count mounts as a dangling corpse with a knife plunged into the heart becomes a dominant image in *Friday the 13th* (1980).

Jamie Lee Curtis as Laurie, the babysitter and survivor, from *Halloween* ...

out in the woods or something, becomes the unstoppable killer that Michael Myers was.)

Gary: You make a good point, Anthony. Since Mrs. Voorhees was the murderer, *not* Jason, the supernatural knife-wielding psycho that became an icon in the 1980s appears as the result of the *Halloween* imagery and not *Friday the 13th*. I forgot about the identity of the true killer. Thanks for understanding the thrust (so to speak) of my *Halloween* argument, Anthony.

Anthony: Well, I hope I don't twist the knife and disappoint you now, Gary, but, on further consideration, I think I've decided that, when it comes to *Halloween* vs. *Friday the 13th*, I have to give the edge (ha-ha) to Mark's reasoning. True, there might not have been any *Friday* without *Halloween* (but there might not have been any *Halloween* without *Psycho*, which is another title we're dickering over). But *Friday* opened the floodgates for the slasher films that followed more than *Halloween* did. And, to reinforce that claim of mine, I'd point to *Halloween II*, which upped the gore factor—*in response to* what was going on in *Friday* and its ilk. (If it had been a more popular success, I suppose we could have pointed to the 1974 *Black Christmas*—recently remade—as a slasher-film precursor; it certainly has a stupid-enough downbeat ending.)

Gary: Anthony, I am getting weary of stating the obvious. *Halloween* featured a faceless fiend with a knife, a supernatural killing-machine that stalked and slaughtered teens in gruesome ways. People who argue for *Friday the 13th* try to make a point that *Halloween* avoided extreme bloodshed and gore, which *Friday the 13th* embraced, so slasher films were influenced more by *Friday* and not *Halloween*. When was the last time anyone here watched *Halloween*? It is intense and gruesome yet contains subtle gore brushstrokes, mainly due to director John Carpenter's inspired handling. Remember the sequence in *Halloween* where one male victim is stabbed through the belly and left hanging from the kitchen door impaled? Carpenter did incorporate intense gore in *Halloween*. Obviously, *Halloween II* was a cash-in product (it was made and released by Universal Pictures, no longer handled by an independent) directed by a hack, not Carpenter, so without the artistry of a John Carpenter, the film opted for the lowest common denominator. Both *Friday the 13th* and *Halloween II* demonstrate major Hollywood studios jumping on the indepen-dent bandwagon, slumming and trying to make a quick profit. Why? *Halloween* managed to get the attention of the majors who were cashing in on a financially successful but relatively cheap bandwagon. The influence demonstrated that the independent production influenced the major studios (specifically Paramount and Universal) that made quick and cheap product to take the profits away from independents.

Mark: I *do* believe that *Halloween* was influential, and I certainly concur that it is an excellent film. I simply disagree with those who credit it with launching the slasher cycle of the 1980s. Stylistically, and in just about every other way, those films play more like *Friday the 13th* than *Halloween*. As Anthony notes, even *Halloween II* is closer to *Friday* than to *Halloween*! The sequel lacks the subtlety and restraint of the original.

All of these points are debatable, of course. But—I'm sorry—I simply do not believe that there are 13 horror films more influential than *Psycho*. I'm not even convinced there are four more influential films.

Gary: Mark, again, it's not the quality of the product but the creation of the new subgenre or artistic trend that defines influential films in my article. (Certainly, the rash of slasher movies in the 1980s is not quality cinema in any sense, but it was a new subgenre influenced by *Halloween*.)

I agree, given our trickle-down theory, that more 1980s slasher films were similar in style to *Friday the 13th*, but my point is that *Friday* was directly influenced by—indeed, *made* as a result of—*Halloween*. So the influential credit reverts back to *Halloween*. It's very simple logic. Would *Friday the 13th* have been made without *Halloween*? NO! And as Anthony made clear, the model for the slasher psycho was not a deranged mother but specifically the type of killer ("The Shape") introduced in *Halloween*. For *Halloween II*, its sequel, Carpenter was out as director, replaced by Rick Rosenthal, which could further explain its more violent shift. Mark, using your flawed logic, I can conclude that the rash of *Psycho*-clone films produced during the 1960s were not directly influenced by *Psycho* but were rather influenced by *Homicidal*, the sleazy William Castle cheap cash-in. By your logic

Betsy Palmer, as the fiend Mrs. Voorhees, has a bigger knife than Jamie Lee Curtis, from *Friday the 13th*.

Michael Myers, aka "The Shape," melds the psycho-killer and supernatural in *Halloween*. Myers might just well have the biggest knife of all.

most of the resulting psycho-movies of the decade were closer in spirit, style and tone to *Homicidal* than they were to the artistic *Psycho*. But no one would agree that *Homicidal* was the more influential film, just as I find it just as ludicrous to say that *Friday the 13th*, not *Halloween*, was the more influential film.

Mark: Let's stick to *Halloween* for the moment. Nevertheless, I maintain that in this case the second film of the cycle, *Friday the 13th*, proved more influential than the first. I also think this was true of the 1930s horror cycle—and you seem to agree with me, since you selected *Frankenstein* for your list and not *Dracula*. Would *Frankenstein* have been made without *Dracula*? NO! But so what?

Bryan: I'm thoroughly enjoying your thoughtful back-and-forth on this, guys. I just wanted to jump in here and say I'd have to side with Mark on this particular issue. While you're dead right, Gary, that there'd be no *Friday* without *Halloween*, coming first does *not* necessarily translate into being a greater influence. It was *Friday* that codified that voluminous subgenre that became the slasher film, for it was *Friday*, not *Halloween*, that became the blueprint for the umpteen gazillion slay-and-spray flicks that followed in its wake. More than that, Paramount (a major film company) distributed *Friday*, not an independent, therefore adding corporate legitimacy to the exploitation market.

Gary: Bryan, your logic is absolutely wrong! The codification of the slasher film involved the masked or demonic slasher, not a psycho-mother. It involved sexually liberated teens who isolate themselves from oppressive adults, with the teens having sex and getting killed in gruesome ways. The rules involve, usually, the most innocent girl surviving while sexually experienced girls die horrible deaths. We experience the elevation of the psycho-killer to supernatural larger-than-life status. We usually find the horror in small town America. And many slasher films occur on or near a specific holiday (even *Friday the 13th* copied this concept from *Halloween*). While it was artistically handled, *Halloween* did contain its fair share of blood and gore. Bryan, to me, all of these codes appeared first in *Halloween*. How many rules of the slasher subgenre did *Friday the 13th* introduce? Perhaps some were modified, but most occurred originally in *Halloween* and were copied in *Friday the 13th*. Open your eyes, guys!

Bryan: Well, by that reasoning, you should have included *Dracula* on your list instead of *Frankenstein*, as there would not have been the latter without the former. Pride of place is not enough in and of itself.

Gary: The most controversial choice of my top-13, and one I debated with everyone here on these forums, was whether *Dracula* or *Frankenstein* should be included on my list. Many people, even here, disagreed and thought *Dracula*, being first, should be included. Pride of place is not really the issue here. My argument was (and I'll give the simple version) that *Dracula* was made as a Dark Romance with a Byronic-style leading man, a mysterious stranger from Europe. The film was released on Valentine's Day, and Lugosi was promoted as the dark Valentino. Check out the promotion for *Dracula*. It wasn't advertised as a horror movie. *Frankenstein*, which did come in the wake of *Dracula*, was promoted as an example of the newly emerging horror-film genre. So I see one *literary* adaptation influencing another *literary* adaptation, and the second *literary* adaptation influencing the birth of the horror-film genre. To me, it wasn't pride of place because both were not

At the very end of *Friday the 13th* audiences are lulled into falsely believing the horror is over, but in a few seconds Jason Voorhees will make his appearance.

promoted or sold as horror movies. Only *Frankenstein* was. Just because the second film in the series was more influential in this *one* case does not mean that the pattern occurs all the time. Determination must be considered on a case-by-case basis.

Bryan: *When* did the slasher subgenre suddenly take off? That occurred in 1980-81, after a *major* studio ("legitimizing" the concept) distributed *Friday the 13th*, then every producer in Hollywood without an original idea in his head suddenly jumped on the slasher bandwagon, letting a sea of slasher cinema spray out. This did *not* happen in the two years after *Halloween*, an anomalous *indie* hit. *Friday* took what it could from the well-crafted, not-very-gory *Halloween* and lowered its common denominator to begin the slay-and-spray subgenre in which the kills became the be-all and end-all, the gorier and more fantastical the better. Personally, I think it's pretty obvious which film was the blueprint, despite *Halloween* being an excellent, cleverly crafted thriller and *Friday* being a poorly crafted gore-fest.

Gary: Bryan, look at the box-office gross of each film. The original *Halloween* grossed $47 million while the original *Friday the 13th* grossed only $37.5 million (from IMDb). With all the promotional power the major studios bring to distribution, *Friday the 13th* with big studio promotion did not sell as many tickets as the indie classic *Halloween*. By this time the subgenre was already teetering toward a financial decline. "Legitimacy" is measured only one way in Hollywood—money grossed. *Halloween* features a supernatural killer who wears a mask that hides his face, has superhuman strength, uses a blade to kill and slaughters teenagers who are having sex. Bodies pile up but virgins seem to survive. Both killers have a back-story as troubled yet sympathetic children. And, bottom-line, the independent film influenced majors Paramount and Universal to attempt to repeat the artistic success of the superior little film that could. Remember, *a major studio also released Halloween II*, but in this case the majors were following the influence of the charmed independent.

Betsy Palmer's Mrs. Voorhees is made to appear even more horrifying by spreading her arms, opening her mouth wide and attempting to burst through plastic.

The only thing that *Friday the 13th* changed was the quantity of blood and gore ... more a statement about the quality of the moviemakers and *not* the influences here. At Paramount, getting a project off the ground, filmed, and released in two years is damn good. That's how long it took a major studio to be influenced by and follow up on *Halloween*. The first film influenced by *Halloween* was *Friday the 13th*, and then the floodgates opened for the inferior copycats.

My point is that *every* codification first appeared in *Halloween*—except the amount of gore shown, and gore came long before *Friday the 13th* (say, in *Night of the Living Dead* and others). One of the chief codes is that virgins live and sluts die. Where did that originate? We see it first in *Halloween*! It was copied in *Friday the 13th*, thereby supporting my claim.

Mark: I personally believe that these so-called slasher codes are greatly overstated. Many slasher films violate some or all of the codes.

Gary: Okay, let's change the rules again! No, let's not! Codification does matter in our discussion here. *Halloween* introduced the supernatural psycho that does not have to play by human rules. And this is just a start for codification.

Mark: I would challenge that assertion. For most of the film, first-run audiences accepted Michael Myers as simply a lunatic with a knife. Sure, Donald Pleasence as Sam Loomis has some lines about him being pure evil, blah, blah, blah. A serious hint of any potential supernatural element does not appear until the end, when Michael miraculously survives/disappears. The supernatural element doesn't come fully into flower until *Halloween II*, which operates under the influence of *Friday*.

Gary: Remember that sequence in *Halloween* when we think that Michael Myers is dead but he suddenly rises back up behind babysitter Jamie Lee Curtis, who fails to see his re-animation? I'd say that gave a strong supernatural hint *before* the very end. And other supernatural hints occur throughout the movie. Subtle little bits employed throughout that explain the shocking ending. How can people say *Halloween* is a stand-alone film and that *Friday* influenced the slasher film genre and set the rules? This is simply wrong. *Halloween* came first and pretty much created the template for inferior films to

Every codification of the slasher film genre first appeared in *Halloween*, including the one where virgins live and sluts die.

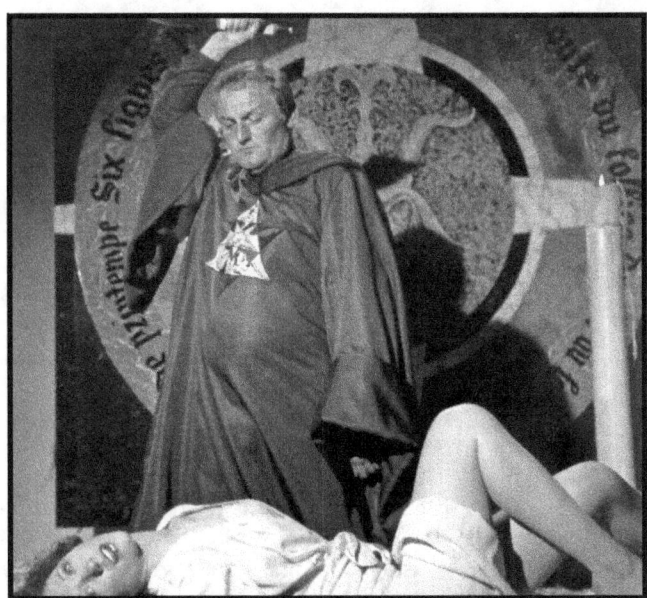

Charles Gray as satantist Mocata is prepared to sacrifice another female in *The Devil Rides Out*.

follow. *Friday* refined and developed rules of its own, but it was clearly influenced by those rules or codification established by *Halloween*.

Mark: I'm not saying that *Halloween* was without influence. I simply think its influence on the slasher genre is overstated. *Friday* was *more* influential. (Alas—the genre would have fared much better had it sought to emulate Carpenter's subtle classic.)

Gary: But *Halloween* was crafted skillfully in the hands of creative filmmaker John Carpenter. Those psychos-with-knives films that followed in the influence wave were helmed generally by hacks, so the lack of subtlety shows through. The same pattern occurred in the wake of *Psycho*, where inferior films about psychos with knives littered the screen, but again without the artistic execution of the originator. Influencing the proliferation of a subgenre does not mean that subgenre produces good movies. But keep in mind brutal violence does appear in *Halloween*—where are people getting the idea that this "R" rated film is bloodless?

8. On the Influence of *Rosemary's Baby*

Gary: I was watching *Rosemary's Baby* only the other night, and I thought long and hard about whether that film should bump *The Exorcist*. And I concluded, "No way." Mark's point was that *Rosemary's Baby* inaugurated the Satan-as-main-character horror movie. I did some checking and discovered that *The Devil Rides Out* (aka *The Devil's Bride*), one of the finest horror movies featuring Satan, was released in July 1968, exactly one month after the better-known *Rosemary's Baby* was released. Both films appeared concurrently, so to speak. And both featured the devil in leading roles. So who deserves the credit here for starting the devil movement?

Arthur: Honestly, I was thinking about this very point the other day. Here's what *Rosemary's Baby* does that changed horror movies: The devil in *Rosemary's Baby* is the actual Satan that we are taught about in Sunday school. The devil in *The Devil Rides Out* is a kind of a comic book, Never-Never-Land devil. Never when watching *The Devil Rides Out* do we have that sense of unease that we are resurrecting our childhood fears of the return of the actual, Old Testament Satan into the world of today. That is the fear offered by *The Exorcist* and *The Omen* (1976) and their ilk right up to this day.

Mark: Please, no offense, Gary, but *Rosemary's Baby* was a blockbuster hit and became a sort of cultural touchstone. *The Devil Rides Out*, although it turned a profit and is well remembered by fans of the genre, had nowhere near that kind of impact on the mainstream.

Brian: *Rosemary's Baby* was the huge mainstream hit. *The Devil Rides Out* was basically just another Hammer film. It's one of their better efforts, and, I imagine, was a successful film from Hammer's perspective. But it didn't cross over to an audience wider than the typical Hammer-film audience. Although the two movies may have been released concurrently, the Satan trend began as a result of studios trying to capitalize on the success of *Rosemary's Baby*.

Gary: Ah, let's examine your logic here, Mark and Brian. Since *Rosemary's Baby* grossed more than *The Devil Rides Out*, that means it is more influential? You agreed that *Horror of Dracula* belongs on my list, a Hammer film, and everyone considers it very influential. Neither were the Val Lewton movies mainstream hits, but they remain influential. Remember, Ira Levin's best-selling novel *Rosemary's Baby* was more of the cultural phenomenon than was the movie.

Anthony: Speaking of *Horror of Dracula*, I think I would take issue with the point Gary makes about the business of box-office. I do believe that a film has to be popular to be influential—either an immediate hit or (like *Night of the Living Dead*) something that has "legs" and keeps going and going. If nobody sees a movie, it can't really be influential, can it? Unless

Left to right: Ruth Gordon (Minnie), Sidney Blackmer (Roman) and Mia Farrow (Rosemary) from *Rosemary's Baby* (1968)

As downbeat as the ending of *Rosemary's Baby* may be, the ending to *The Seventh Victim* (1943), focusing on modern satanism in Greenwich Village, is even more depressing. A gloomy Jean Brooks stares down a glass of poison wine that the cult wishes her to drink.

a famous filmmaker sees something that influences him and he makes a movie influenced by it, which becomes a *huge* hit. The influential film is actually the "small" picture that inspired the director, not the director's resulting blockbuster, which everybody then tries to emulate/imitate/improve on.

But I believe (and we can check this) that *Horror of Dracula* was indeed a big hit when it came out. And so was *Cat People*. (I don't know about the other Lewtons, but *Cat People* raked it in. That's what made the other Lewtons possible—that's why RKO forced Lewton to make the others—and he of course undermined their expectations, taking the exploitation titles and making non-horror horror films that connoisseurs enjoy but that disappoint a lot of the rest of us.)

Am I making any kind of sense here?

[Anthony is met with stony silence, which sort of answers his question, doesn't it? And everyone goes on with the discussion at hand.]

Gary: If I subscribed to Mark's defi-nition (and in another framework and article I very well might), I might say that *The Seventh Victim* influenced *Rosemary's Baby*. Both occur in modern-day New York City. Both involve secret satanic cults trying to control the lives of their members. People in both movies are punished for saying too much or revealing the cult's inner secrets. And *The Seventh Victim* has perhaps an even more downbeat ending than *Rosemary's Baby*—the heroine commits suicide in utter mental despair at the movie's end. *The Seventh Victim* has so many parallels to *Rosemary's Baby* (even right down to an innocent heroine and men, not to be trusted, who pretend to be helping her). The sex in *Rosemary's Baby* was more blatant, but that just wasn't allowed back in the Lewton era. Now, according to my definition, too much time passed between the first and second movie for me to say that *Victim* directly influenced *Baby*. However, as defined by Mark, that would be fair game, right?

Mark: No, that makes sense to me, and it's a very astute observation. Many of the Lew-ton films were widely influential, especially *Cat People*. In fact, I would rank *Cat People* the third most influential horror film of all time, behind *Caligari* and *Frankenstein* and just ahead of *Psycho*.

Gary: The more I watch and reflect upon the Lewton movies, the more influential I consider these films. I see parallels between *The Seventh Victim* and *Rosemary's Baby*. I see parallels between *Isle of the Dead* and Corman's *House of Usher*. I think *Cat People* is a horror-movie classic. I think that *The Leopard Man* is a vastly underrated and ignored horror masterpiece waiting to be discovered (and one that features a psycho killer that influenced Hitchcock's Norman Bates).

Brian: Gary, you point out some very interesting parallels between *The Seventh Victim* and *Rosemary's Baby*. *The Seventh Victim* may very well have had an influence on Ira Levin when he wrote *Rosemary's Baby*. Or maybe he never even saw *The Seventh Victim*, and the similarities are just coincidental. The time lapse isn't the real factor, in my opinion. It's the relative obscurity of *The Seventh Victim*. I don't believe it was a particularly big hit when it came out, and I don't remember it ever playing on television until relatively recently. The first time I saw it was at a screening at a museum, and it was a big deal because this movie had been unavailable for so long.

Anthony: Well, *The Seventh Victim* did play (rarely) on Detroit-area TV. I saw it in the early 1960s and again in the 1970s. Not that that makes it any less obscure.

Brian: On the other hand, it is simply not conceivable that the people who made *The Exorcist* were not familiar with *Rosemary's Baby*. If they hadn't seen the movie, they read the book. If they hadn't

This one-sheet from *The Devil Within Her* (1974) demonstrates direct influence from *Rosemary's Baby*, from the banner at the top of the poster.

The Exorcist (1973) did not introduce demons, profanity or sexuality, but it did convince Hollywood that the big-budget horror movie was profitable ... for a while.

read the book, they read the *Mad* magazine movie satire. The basic parameters of the story had become part of the culture.

Gary: I would certainly grant you that *Rosemary's Baby* influenced more movies about Satan than *The Devil Rides Out*, but how many movies featuring Satan were made in *Rosemary's Baby*'s wake (in the five years between its release and the release of *The Exorcist*)? Remember, in 1968 *Rosemary's Baby* was a smash best-selling *novel* and, perhaps, like *The Da Vinci Code*, the book was more influential than the inferior movie released in its wake. I read and liked the novel and saw and disliked the movie. The movie's success was mostly due to its literary success (it was huge!). But the movie, at least to me, failed to live up to its literary source.

The Exorcist did not introduce demons, profanity or sexuality to the horror film, but what it did do that was groundbreaking was convince Hollywood that the big-budget horror movie was profitable. And, in its creative wake, mainstream horror films became the norm, and B units such as Hammer, Amicus and others floundered and died. Perhaps because I hated *Rosemary's Baby* even more than I hated *The Exorcist*, I find it difficult to see any groundbreaking trends in that movie. If Mark's point is that *Rosemary's Baby* influenced *The Exorcist*, well, there's a five-year gap between the release dates of both movies—too long, for me, to be a *direct* influence.

Brian: I agree with your first point, that *The Exorcist* is important because it essentially killed off studios like Hammer and Amicus. When Richard Burton and Gregory Peck started showing up in big-budget horror films, the market for mid-budget horror films with stars like Christopher Lee and Peter Cushing dried up. I disagree that the five-year gap between *Rosemary's Baby* and *The Exorcist* obviates a direct influence of the one on the other. *The Exorcist* is based on a novel that was published in 1971—just three years after *Rosemary's Baby*. The success of *Rosemary's Baby* had to have some bearing on William Peter Blatty's decision to write a satanic horror novel. Blatty was not previously associated with the horror genre (earlier credits include the screenplay for comedies like *A Shot in the Dark* [1964], *John Goldfarb, Please Come Home* [1965] and *What Did You Do in the War, Daddy?* [1966]).

Anthony: When it comes to all the Satan/possession movies, I am torn between agreeing with Mark (and Brian) about *Rosemary's Baby* and Gary about *The Exorcist*. It's nice that *The Devil Rides Out* came out almost simultaneously with *Rosemary's Baby*, but—despite the fact that many of us like Hammer and Christopher Lee and that Dennis Wheatley was a best-selling novelist—any "devil-made-me-do-it" influence has to come by way of the much-better-known *Rosemary's Baby*, which was a blockbuster hit as a book and a movie, whereas *Devil Rides Out* hardly made any ripples.

Certainly, *Rosemary's Baby* initiated the devil-as-villain monster movie, but *The Exorcist* made *possession* big box-office, and the devil movies that followed in its wake were all based on possession. (Well, maybe not *The Omen*.) I think that Gary is right when he says that *The Exorcist* (more than *Rosemary's Baby*, which also originated at a big studio) started the horror-movie-as-A-product trend and certainly did raise the bar (for better or worse) on special effects. Plus, *Rosemary's Baby* is a cerebral thriller, creepy as heck—whereas *The Exorcist* is scary as hell.

Gary: Gentlemen, let's talk again about that term I like, "pride of place."

Bryan: Let's. How can you use it to bolster your claim of influential supremacy for *The Exorcist* over *Rosemary's Baby* when *Rosemary's Baby* takes pride of place in this instance?

Gary: I remind you again: *Five* years existed between the release of *Rosemary's Baby* and *The Exorcist*. Isn't that *too* long a time in movie land for one film to influence a creative trend?

Arthur: Not really—in my opinion, anyway. For example, when I argue that *Psycho* was so influential, the next film to carry on the trend is *The Birds*. I don't think the next film in the trend comes along until

Mia Farrow and John Cassavetes play husband and wife and appear to be madly in love, before all Hell breaks loose, in *Rosemary's Baby*.

In the 41 years between the release of *Flash Gordon* (1936) and *Star Wars* (1977), are we observing influence or synthesis?

Night of the Living Dead (I'm sure I could be wrong here), and only then does the ball start rolling. I just think in this case it takes a while for the people who saw *Psycho* as kids to grow up and start making their own mark in moviemaking. The gestation period may have taken a while to make major mainstream changes, but I don't think that anyone could argue that the influence isn't there.

Gary: An interesting theory, Arthur. But this long-gestation theory would, like a dream, blend many diverse and influential films together to create something totally new and different. When I speak of influential films, I am talking about the profound effect of *one* movie's release that others were made fairly immediately in its wake, made as a direct consequence of that influential movie.

Tell me, how many big-budget Hollywood horror movies were made in the wake of *Rosemary's Baby*? Exactly *none*, right? *Right*! Now, how many big-budget Hollywood horror movies were made in the wake of *The Exorcist*? Lots! Pride of place holds here—two years vs. five. I can see evidence of influence two or three years later. *Five* years later, a film becomes a stand-alone.

Mark: I reject the idea that there's a time limit on how long a film can influence another film. How many years elapsed between *Flash Gordon* (1936) and *Star Wars* (1977)? Yet the former certainly influenced the latter.

Gary: Isn't this a stretch to say this, Mark? *Flash Gordon* influenced the *Buck Roger*'s serial and perhaps a few others. But when George Lucas made *Star Wars,* wasn't he actually synthesizing a slew of many favorite films from his past? By the same logic can we say that *It! The Terror From Beyond Space* influenced *Alien*? I see *Alien* as a synthesis of many movies that the filmmakers loved.

Arthur: As for *Rosemary's Baby*, I'd go back to my earlier point that its innovation is in making the devil in the movie the very devil that we feared from our religious upbringing. *The Exorcist* took that fear and made the entire movie about it. But the inspiration was *Rosemary's Baby*.

Gary: Again, you are taking a personal statement and making it a collective one. All our religious training about the devil comes from different places. Your reference is obviously Catholic doctrine while others may be influenced by Jewish or Protestant teachings. And what about all those a-religious people out there? One man's devil is not necessarily another's.

Mark: Let us look at *Rosemary's Baby* and *The Devil Rides Out* from another perspective. I think it's clear that I'm not basing my argument for *Rosemary's Baby*'s major influence on its box-office alone. Over 40 years later, *Rosemary's Baby* is a film many casual film fans know, are familiar with, joke about when their wives are pregnant. It's a film that regularly shows up in mainstream books and cable television shows about horror movies. On the other hand, you have to be a fairly committed horror-movie geek to have even *heard* of *The Devil Rides Out*.

Gary: Mark, I'll agree that *Rosemary's Baby* was a pop-culture phenomenon. But many of the pop-cultural references to *Rosemary's Baby* evolved from the Ira Levin novel and not necessarily the movie, as the novel was a blockbuster. Movies are not the only pop-culture reference points, and the Levin novel was a monster! Also *The Devil Rides Out* was more successful in the U.K. where its literary source material was much better known and very popular. Here in the States who knows author Dennis Wheatley? But over the Pond he is a revered author.

Anthony: On the issue of *Rosemary's Baby*'s influence, Gary, I've got to give the edge to Mark. I can think of a number of horror films post-1968 that were inspired by *Rosemary's Baby*. As you'll all recall, since you have no doubt read and probably embossed on your walls my Rondo-nominated article, "Tell Me When It's Over: The Rise and Fall of the Downbeat Ending," an essay about the excesses and abuses of the post-*Rosemary's Baby* shock ending in horror films (*Midnight Marquee* 67/68 [Spring 2003], pp. 34-43), every other low-budget filmmaker after *Rosemary's Baby* was convinced that "the bad guy wins" was the way to go for box-office success. Evil triumphing over good can be directly traced to *Rosemary's Baby*, and—for good or ill (mostly ill)—it had an effect on the horror

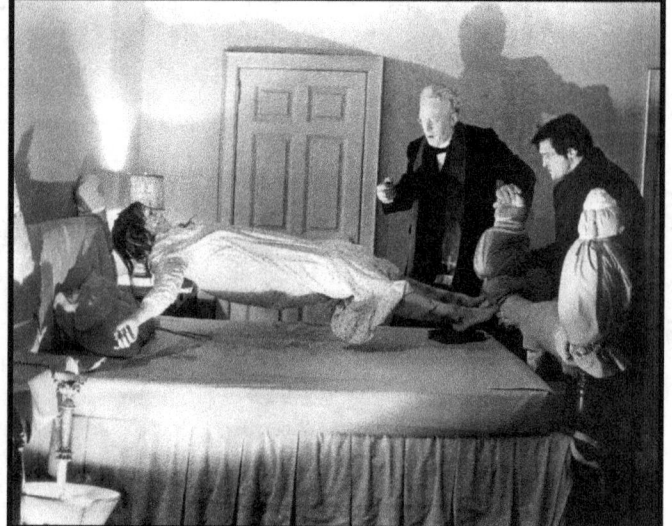

The question arises, in the wake of *The Exorcist*, were satanic movies still influenced by the earlier *Rosemary's Baby*, or had the baton passed to the new satanic blockbuster?

films that followed, codifying the downbeat anti-climax, whether the story warranted a "heroes lose" ending or not.

Gary: Anthony, wasn't Romero's *Night of the Living Dead* made the same year as *Rosemary's Baby*, and when it comes to downbeat endings, you must agree that *Night of the Living Dead* might be just as influential for the downbeat ending trend as *Rosemary*? You have me thinking as well, Anthony. I think the first step is for people to list all the movies that came before *The Exorcist* that they feel were directly influenced by *Rosemary's Baby*. That's a five-year span. Let's see what exactly *Rosemary's Baby* wrought. Let's list the titles. The proof is in the pudding.

Brian: I'll leave it to Anthony to identify movies with anti-climactic or downbeat endings inspired by the ending of *Rosemary's Baby*. But here are a few additional films that may have been inspired by *Rosemary's Baby*. I haven't seen all of these, so I can't swear that they all have a *Rosemary's Baby* influence. But I would say that they are likely candidates: *The Dunwich Horror* (1969), *Blood on Satan's Claw* (1970), *The Virgin Witch* (1970), *The Mephisto Waltz* (1971), *The Other* (1972), *The Possession of Joel Delaney* (1972). Also, a number of made-for-television-movies in the early 1970s had satanic themes—such as *Crowhaven Farm* (1970)—which fairly

When it comes to the advent of the downbeat ending in horror cinema, does *Rosemary's Baby* alone or *Night of the Living Dead* (1968), made the same year, deserve recognition for starting that far-reaching trend?

closely mirrors the plot of *Rosemary's Baby* (the couple adopts a teenage girl who is part of a witchs' coven, as I recall).

Arthur: One might add Polanski's own *Macbeth* (1971) to the list (naked witches and such). Also there's *Night of the Witches* (1970), a hilarious comedy that I haven't seen in over 30 years. How about that Roy Thinnes television movie where he is a minister who goes to a town and is seduced over to the dark side—*Black Noon* (1971)?

A science-fiction variation on *Rosemary's Baby* was *The Stranger Within* (1974).

Brian: I did a search on the IMDb on *ABC Movies of the Week*. Sure enough, they have them listed. *The Stranger Within* was on the list and made me think that *Rosemary's Baby* spawned (ha-ha) an entire movie subgenre: the demonic/alien/mu-tant pregnancy movie. *It's Alive* (1974) and its many sequels. Also, wasn't there a movie called *Xtro* (1983) with that theme? Here's a list of ABC movies of the week that may have had *Rosemary's Baby* influences, to one degree or another: *Crowhaven Farm* (1970); *The House That Would Not Die* (1970); *The Devil and Miss Sarah* (1971); *Satan's School for Girls* (1973); *Don't Be Afraid of the Dark* (1973); *The Devil's Daughter* (1973); *The Stranger Within* (1974); and, of course, *Look What's Happened to Rosemary's Baby* (1976).

Anthony: In my article on downbeat endings, I think I mention the Count Yorga films, *Witchmaker* (1969) and *Murders in the Rue Morgue* (1971) as examples of downbeat endings that—to my mind—stemmed from a misreading of the ending of *Rosemary's Baby*.

Brian and Arthur do a good job of mentioning movies—both theatrical and made-for-TV—that featured Satan/witchcraft themes and/or downbeat endings. One could add *Brotherhood of Satan* (1971), the Strother Martin movie, to the list (which has both witches *and* a downbeat ending, if I'm remembering right).

I wanted to mention *The Devil's Rain*, *The Devil Within Her*, and *Race with the Devil*—which all turn out to be 1974/1975 productions (and thus could be argued to be *Exorcist*-inspired, since they're post-*Exorcist*).

Besides downbeat endings, witch/devil movies with scary children were a direct outgrowth of *Rosemary's Baby*, wouldn't you say? This is why *The Omen* (1976), although it follows *The Exorcist*, owes a debt to *Rosemary's Baby*, too.

Gary: I would eliminate all the movies made in the wake of *The Exorcist*, but

Does it take two films to create a trend? In other words, if *The Black Cat* established the horror film celebrity subgenre, does this mean that *The Raven* (1935), made one year later, was needed to validate that subgenre's existence?

Jess Franco's *The Awful Dr. Orlac* (1962) perhaps influenced Euro-splatter more so than *Eyes Without a Face*.

the list of movies created in the wake of *Rosemary's Baby* supports the theory that *Rosemary's Baby* was influential. I have finally come around. But satanic movies made after *The Exorcist* become connected to that iconic production.

Anthony: Thanks, Gary, for that open-minded assessment.

Where does this leave us? Well, precisely where we started, I'm afraid. If one feels that *Rosemary's Baby* started the trend, one can point to the movies that Arthur, Brian, and I have mentioned. If one feels that *The Exorcist* started the trend, one can point to a number of the movies listed above, plus a rash of possession films that followed in its wake. Certainly demonic possession as central action in the horror film was so rare as to be practically nonexistent before *The Exorcist*.

Arthur: Hmm. Pre-*Exorcist* demonic possession. Well, offhand, I could think of *The Dybbuk* (1937). They're not exactly demonic, but there was possession in *Supernatural* (1933) and *The Mummy* (1932). There are lots of science-fictional possession movies, but those are probably too far removed to have influenced *The Exorcist*. There may be others ...

Anthony: So did *Rosemary's Baby* beget a bunch of films, including *The Exorcist*, which then begat all these others? This influence business gets tricky because, as has been written, everything influences *something* else.

9. Does It Take Two to Make a Trend?

Brian: I would argue that it generally takes two films to really set off a major new subgenre. An earlier film, whose runaway success takes people by surprise, and a second film, which may be made several years later, proves the success of the first film wasn't just a fluke. If the second film is as big a hit as (or bigger than) the first, the studios really jump on the bandwagon. *Rosemary's Baby/The Exorcist* follows this pattern, as does *Halloween/Friday the 13th*.

Bryan and **Steven** together: So does *Dracula/Frankenstein*. That's a very clever observation, Brian.

Anthony: Tellingly, Leonard Maltin's *Movie Guide* calls the Joan Collins starrer, *Devil Within Her* (aka, *I Don't Want to be Born*), "another idiotic *Rosemary's Baby/Exorcist* rip-off." By pairing *Rosemary's Baby* and *Exorcist*, Maltin unconsciously lends credence to the one-two theory about influence that Brian has put forward.

Gary: Brian's idea that it takes two influential films to create a true cinematic influence is a good theory, but I don't buy it. And here's my reason.

Whenever films are influential, the first film influences many more that follow. So we can always list a second film to go with the first, right? If we take the first two films in any influential line of films, be they *Halloween/Friday the 13th* or *Cat People/I Walked with a Zombie* or *The Black Cat/The Raven*, we can always say, as Brian insists, that it takes two to start an influence. But the second film that appears points back to the originator, the first film, being the dominant, influential one. The second film only shows that the influence has occurred.

Brian: I think I said "generally"—not "always." To better state my argument: I think it's frequently the case that a new trend in films is sparked by two movies, not just one. The first movie is a huge hit. A second movie, which could arrive several years later, draws on that first film, and is also a huge hit. After the second movie, the studios jump on the bandwagon, and a flood of imitators comes out.

Ringu (1998) turned horror movies away from the splatter and gore to a return of slowly building atmospheric chills.

Anthony: It's a filmdom truism that, in Hollywood, everyone wants to be first to be second. (Does that reinforce Brian's position and undercut Gary's—or vice-versa?)

Brian: It's true that almost any film has precursors and influences on it. It's a film-geek parlor game to find some obscure B-movie that influenced a later blockbuster. But I'm talking more about the behavior of movie studios than the behavior of filmmakers. An individual filmmaker might be influenced by an obscure B-film. But a trend usually starts when you have a couple of wildly successful A-films.

Gary: But does it?

This simply weakens the argument that one film is so influential that it started a trend. If you list films like *The Black Cat/ The Raven* and argue that they started the concept of marketable horror-film stars, well, the second film, *The Raven*, carried on the influence started by *The Black Cat*. *The Black Cat* was the influential one, and *The Raven* was proof of *The Black Cat*'s influence. *The Raven* wasn't influential ... it was first in line of influences created by *The Black Cat*. But it takes *one* film to start a trend. The second film, the third, etc. are the films crafted in the creative wake of the first, thus proving only that the first film was influential. That's what makes a trend-setting film unique. It stands alone. It lacks this "two-ness."

Let's go back to *Halloween*. It was the originator and the one that influenced all the rest. As soon as it made big money, Universal was negotiating to bring a direct sequel to the market, but at the same time, Paramount was concocting a way to exploit the indie success of *Halloween* with a low-brow version of its own, to be called *Friday the 13th*. Both influences most likely occurred at the *same* time but in different Hollywood offices (where one office was unaware of what was occurring in the other office). So one film influenced two others (planned concurrently) and many more.

Anthony: As with all arguments, this one about influential films turns on semantics. I think that Gary did define his terms in his article (which I'll have to go back and reread), but we'll have to see if we agree with all the points he raised.

For example, to count *Eyes Without a Face* as influential (a possibility that Mark raised), we'd have to decide what we mean by "influence." Does it have to be "operation" movies? Or is it something else—a style, a mood, certain techniques?

Ditto *Psycho*.

[Anthony is met with stony silence. Again. Undeterred, he doggedly presses on.]

Anthony: When it comes to influence, it's a matter of carefully defining terms. Almost every movie has some influence on *some* movie that comes after it. For example, every guy who pitched a slasher film to a studio from 1981 on probably claimed "It's *Halloween*, it's *Friday the 13th*" (probably in the same breath) but with the novelty, the gimmick of offering—"New Year's as the date"; "Valentine's Day as the date"; etc. It's just a matter of determining the *most* influential, as per Gary's title, right?

Gary: Absolutely correct! As my original article made clear, I was never referring to *one* film influencing another one thematically or stylistically. I was dealing with the 13 *most* influential and ground-breaking horror films in the *entirety* of the sound era. With all the nit-picking, semantics and breaking apart the parameters set forth in my original article (such as the list of 13 would only cover films made during the sound era), many here lost sight of the forest by concentrating on specific trees and personal agendas. I loved our discussion, and many comments voiced made me think long and hard, but I still stand by my original list of 13 "groundbreakers" (listed at the beginning of this discussion). I accept the obvious fact that not all genre fans will agree with my list. But creating and defending such lists is precisely what makes the love of horror films so stimulating and fun.

Anthony, let the stony silence end.

[Readers, feel free to suggest the next topic for our *Forum/Against 'Em* discussion.]

Favorite Top-50 Horror Movies of the Sound Era [1931-1999]

by Gary J. Svehla

1. *Horror of Dracula/Dracula (1958)*
2. *Bride of Frankenstein (1935)*
3. *Curse of the Demon (1957)*
4. *Cat People (1942)*
5. *Invasion of the Body Snatchers (1956)*
6. *Alien (1979)*
7. *Black Sunda/Mask of the Demon (1960)*
8. *The Haunting (1963)*
9. *Brides of Dracula (1960)*
10. *Frankenstein (1931)*
11. *Dracula (1931)*
12. *Dr. Jekyll and Mr. Hyde (1931)*
13. *The Black Cat (1934)*
14. *The Mummy (1932)*
15. *Son of Frankenstein (1939)*
16. *Aliens (1986)*
17. *The Thing (From Another World) (1951)*
18. *The Uninvited (1944)*
19. *The Seventh Victim (1943)*
20. *Night of the Hunter (1955)*
21. *Eyes Without A Face (1960)*
22. *Curse of the Cat People (1944)*
23. *Quatermass Xperiment/Creeping Unknown (1955)*
24. *Quartermass 2/Enemy From Space (1957)*
25. *It! The Terror From Beyond Space (1958)*
26. *The Invisible Ray (1936)*
27. *Revenge of Frankenstein (1958)*
28. *Halloween (1978)*
29. *The Body Snatcher (1945)*
30. *Suspiria (1977)*
31. *Invaders From Mars (1953)*
32. *Abbott and Costello Meet Frankenstein (1948)*
33. *House on Haunted Hill (1958)*
34. *John Carpenter's The Thing (1982)*
35. *Night of the Living Dead (1968)*
36. *The Wolf Man (1941)*
37. *Psycho (1960)*
38. *The Crawling Eye/Trollenberg Terror (1958)*
39. *I Was A Teenage Werewolf (1957)*
40. *The Tingler (1959)*
41. *Silence of the Lambs (1991)*
42. *Deep Red (1975)*
43. *Doctor X (1932)*
44. *Ringu (1998)*

45. *Monster That Challenged the World* (1957)
46. *The Vampire* (1957)
47. *Curse of Frankenstein* (1957)
48. *The Mummy* (1959)
49. *House of Usher* (1960)
50. *The Howling* (1981)

Considerations for the Top-50

1. Does the artistic craftsmanship and cinematic vision (merging performance, direction, art direction, set decoration, cinematography, editing and script) place the film above the rest?

2. Does the film, perhaps even more than its vision or message, manage to entertain?

3. Does the film encourage repeat visits? Is this a film that audiences can watch regularly without growing weary? Even if compromised as a low-budget production, is its vision revealed in multiple onion-like layers allowing the viewer to see something new in each subsequent viewing?

4. Is the film one that has influenced the genre, allowing others films to fall within its shadow, by forging a new creative direction?

5. Does the film elicit one or two strikingly powerful moments? Is there a classic scare or memorable genre performance that stands the test of time? Is the cinematography or editing so nuanced and mesmerizing that some of the film's other flaws can be ignored?

6. Does the film resonate on a personal, emotional level? Does each viewing bring us back to a specific place and time or perhaps remind us of an experience from our past that connects us to the movie in a powerful way? Does the film strike a chord or bellow some personal truth that we cannot shake?

Overall Rationale for the Top-50 List

I did not wish my top-50 list to only include the so-called classics. Some of my favorite horror films are B productions. While the lower-budgeted, double-feature programmers often contain flaws, they still include creativity, a sense of entertainment and a desire for return viewings. When I think of film noir, I love *The Big Sleep, Out of the Past, Double Indemnity* and the other classics. But I also like the Bs such as *Detour* and *Narrow Margin* almost as much. The same goes with Westerns. The classics such as *The Searchers, Rio Bravo, Red River, The Man Who Shot Liberty Valance* and *Once Upon a Time in the West* are among my favorites. But I find myself also loving the Budd Boetticher and Anthony Mann B Westerns a great deal. When we accept the Bs for what they have to offer, understand their budget limitations and formulaic approach, we start to appreciate their ability to do so much with so little. When it comes to top-50 lists, many B productions simply must be included.

The following is my top-50 list, along with a brief explanation of why each title has been included. My choices and reasoning are personal, although I have confidence in my selections since my list is based upon 50 years or more of repeat viewings. If I left your personal favorites off my list, tell me why they should have been included (please keep those letters and emails coming my way).

The 1930s

Frankenstein (1931)

Iconic and original, this classic casts a compelling story amid marvelous performances, stunning art direction and shiver-inducing cinematography. Boris Karloff's performance as the re-animated Monster is one of great subtlety, giving a classic mime/silent film performance in an early sound production. The template created here would influence generations of horror movies to come and it remains one of the most influential movies of all time.

Dracula (1931)

Bela Lugosi's performance is the reason why *Dracula* is a classic. The feral

beast only emerges in brief snippets (when Edward Van Sloan opens the cigarette box with the mirror), Lugosi's true evil remaining hidden under foreign, romantic intrigue as the European stranger woos naïve America. As seen in the recent Blu-ray restoration, the film's cinematography and set design embellishes Lugosi's performance, and Dwight Frye's Renfield adds a quirkiness and splash that further elevates the production's eccentricity.

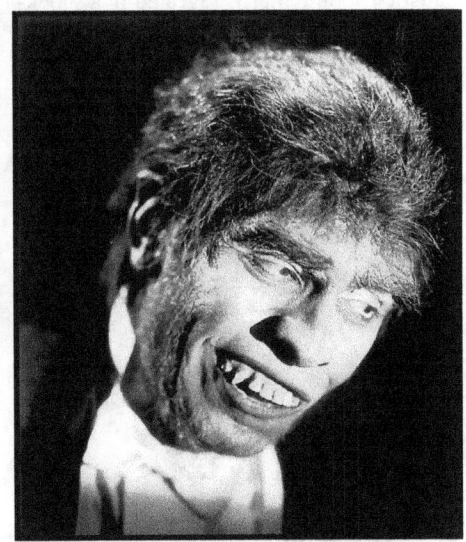

Dr. Jekyll and Mr. Hyde (1931)

Paramount answered Universal's call to create Gothic literary horror with its classic interpretation of the battle between good and evil, or perhaps, civilized man vs. his bestial ancestor, in this wonderfully photographed version of Robert Louis Stevenson's story. Some of the acting is stiff, but Fredric March's Mr. Hyde and Miriam Hopkins' whorish Ivy are two performances that remain gripping, exposing Victorian lust lying just beneath the prim and proper surface. The shadowy cinematography and detailed art decoration brings this vision to vivid life.

Doctor X (1932)

Synthetic flesh and a lunatic who reshapes his body to gain strength to kill transforms the old dark house mystery genre into a new variation—a place where the mad lab exists *inside* an old dark house. Sassy dialogue (the tone never gets too serious) and performances (courtesy of Lionel Atwill, Fay Wray, Lee Tracy and Preston Foster) anchor this whodunit as the cannibalistic Moon Killer is revealed in a shocking climactic sequence that influenced John Carpenter decades later in his remake of *The Thing*.

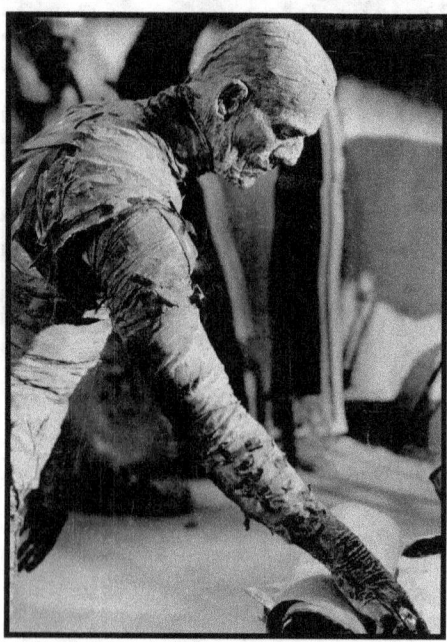

The Mummy (1932)

Creaky and somnambulistic are generally negative terms when describing movies, but Karl Freund's *The Mummy* is a creepy classic woven together from slow-building chills through a depiction of time's slow-moving hands. Boris Karloff submits another classic performance (under heavy make-up as the human Ardeth Bey, let alone the actual gauze-wrapped Mummy) where his crumbling, decaying flesh is conveyed by his deliberate slow-motion movement and sleepy dialogue line readings. The Mummy cleverly combines horror with romance, revenge and reincarnation, where time is the ultimate enemy.

The Black Cat (1934)

A delightful sexually twisted horror classic pits icons Boris Karloff and Bela Lugosi against one another. Karloff's ultimate evil satanist casts Lugosi's revenge-obsessed character as the hero (even when he skins the shackled Karloff alive). Director Edgar Ulmer's art-deco futuristic set design, juxtaposed with Gothic-flavored underground catacombs where beautiful corpses are displayed in glass cylinders, creates a new kind of Modernistic Gothic horror. Hampered by Universal's hatchet editing job, the film still emerges as one of the most perverse horror movies made in this or any decade.

Bride of Frankenstein (1935)

James Whale remakes/remodels his Gothic horror classic *Frankenstein* as a darkly horrifying yet absurd black comedy with Boris Karloff molding perhaps the finest performance of his career, taking the newly born re-animated Monster from Whale's original and maturing him into adolescence. The addition of dialogue to Karloff's performance only adds to the complexity of character, and Karloff truly demonstrates to Dr. Pretorious why—"We belong dead."

The Invisible Ray (1936)

Too often neglected, this sweeping Universal horror classic again pits Lugosi vs. Karloff, but this time Karloff is the warped yet sympathetic loner with mother issues who sacrifices himself to the cause of totally mad science. Moving from Eastern Europe to Africa and Paris, the movie maintains an epic scope absent in most of the more claustrophobic Universal canon, and even with science fiction wrappings, this is most definitely a mad scientist-turned-monster on the prowl movie. Thank goodness!

Son of Frankenstein (1939)

No longer in eccentric director James Whale's hands, Rowland V. Lee takes the helm of the most expensive edition of the *Frankenstein* series, but artistically the

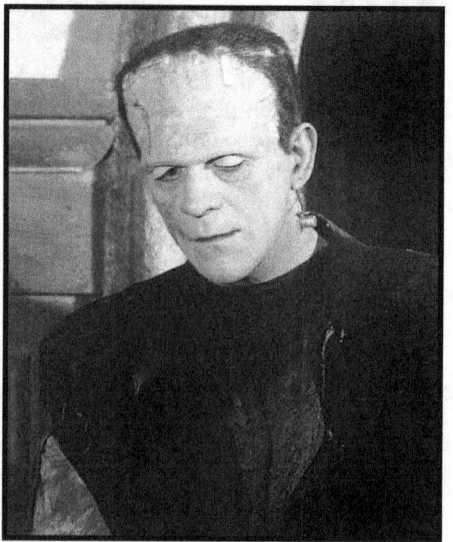

porting role), the dialogue crackles with wit and intelligence.

The 1940s
The Wolf Man (1941)

Undeniably Universal's finest horror movie of the decade improves upon repeat viewings and Blu-ray restoration. The film's creation of iconic monster mythology becomes its strongest suit, and the fog-shrouded forest set creates the perfectly twisted fairy tale mood. The Wolf Man himself is a classic Universal monster, yet the film's script meanders in sections and Lon Chaney, Jr.'s inability to tap into the inner psychological subtlety of his character ultimately undermines the production.

Cat People (1942)

The Val Lewton RKO B factory's first production, derived from the success of Universal's *The Wolf Man*, improves upon the more expensive Universal hit. Under director Jacques Tourneur's inspired handling, Simone Simon conveys weariness and inner conflict as she finds herself falling in love with a bland architect. Once sexually aroused, she believes she will transform into a leopard that will tear her lover apart. So she sits lonely and naked in her tub, crying, as the beautiful snow falls outside her window. Metaphor has never been put to better use in horror cinema. Tourneur's classic taps into the deep-seated horror buried within the human psyche, demonstrating that the greatest monsters often lurk within, not externally.

The Seventh Victim (1943)

Satanic cults, grisly murders and knife-wielding fiends lurking in Greenwich Village equal horror in my estimation, even though the supernatural is nowhere to be found. Val Lewton's horror thriller remains one of the most depressing films of all time, concluding with the most downbeat ending ever (Jean Brooks commits suicide offscreen). Director Mark Robson maintains an air of mystery and suspense as naïve Kim Hunter comes to the corrupt city to find her missing sister. And that same city becomes the ultimate evil and the symbolic *monster* that consumes all.

script is by the numbers, the film excelling mostly because of three fine performances (Boris Karloff as the Monster, Basil Rathbone as Frankenstein and Bela Lugosi as Ygor) and the imaginative set decoration and cinematography that suggest German Expressionism. Even with a mediocre story (with the Monster relegated to a mere sup-

The Uninvited (1944)

Paramount, influenced by the RKO Val Lewton B unit, created a Val Lewton-style psychological horror classic of its own, considered one of the greatest ghost stories in horror film history. Director Lewis Allen, working with Ray Milland, Ruth Hussey and Gail Russell, weaves a mesmerizing tale of damaged people with haunted pasts who try to solve the unsettled mystery of why the house still remains possessed by supernatural elements. The film's script is very literate and the direction and performances make it easy to believe in things that go bump in the night.

Curse of the Cat People (1944)

Robert Wise, directing his very first movie for Val Lewton, creates one of the most indefinable horror classics ever. The film is a child's fantasy; it's a sequel to the chilling *Cat People*; it's a human drama of aging, dementia and parent/child abandonment; and it's a powerful ghost story that probes the need for human interaction. Ann Carter as the young child drives the movie and becomes its heart and soul. The problematic relationship between Elizabeth Russell and her mother Julia Dean, who suffers from dementia, contrasts nicely to Ann Carter, also existing within a fantasy world, and her troubled relationship with her father and ghostly mother. Such dysfunctional relationships define *Curse of the Cat People*.

The Body Snatcher (1945)

Robert Wise, again directing for Val Lewton, creates another classic. Boris Karloff is at his absolute best as Cabman Gray, the smiling, soft-spoken yet sinister man who loves to wield power over the celebrated Dr. Toddy MacFarlane (the equally wonderful Henry Daniell). The film deals with the struggles of MacFarlane to become free of the clutches of the lower-class cabby. More a character study, *The Body Snatcher* deals with corpse snatchings, cold-blooded murder and perhaps even re-animated bodies ripped from the grave. It is one chilling movie that is character driven. But that rain-soaked, lightning lit, wild carriage ride finale becomes an iconic and chilling horror film moment.

Abbott and Costello Meet Frankenstein (1948)

The ultimate Monster-Rally Universal classic, *Abbott and Costello Meet Frankenstein* shines because it happens to be one of Abbott and Costello's funniest movies, but it also remains faithful to the spirit of the original Universal classic monster series.

The movie reprises a surprisingly energetic Bela Lugosi as Dracula and Lon Chaney, Jr. as The Wolf Man (with Glenn Strange returning as the robotic Frankenstein Monster). Plenty of monster sequences abound, and Abbott and Costello have never been better.

The 1950s
The Thing (From Another World) (1951)

The heart of the 1950s horror film genre is the inclusion of science fiction into the mix. And *The Thing* was the innovator that re-invented the Frankenstein Monster as a vegetable from outer space. Created within a frigid and isolated claustrophobic military setting, populated with interesting and intelligent characters that spew clever dialogue, *The Thing* features multiple pulse-pounding moments that linger long after the mantra of "keep watching the skies" fades.

Invaders From Mars (1953)

Outer space invasion is one of mankind's most paranoiac fears, but suppose the Martian invasion were told from the eyes of a little boy (brilliantly, the film's target audience) where no one believes that his parents, looking the same but sporting little probes embedded in the back of their necks, are now alien controlled. And the film's riveting horror generates from the fact that beneath our neighborhood are alien-infested hives where humanity is under attack. While the film is hampered by far too much military hardware stock footage, William Cameron Menzies' vision is mesmerizing and his nightmarish dreamland fascinating.

Quatermass Xperiment/The Creeping Unknown (1955)

While Hammer is best remembered for its color Gothic horror classics, I find myself returning to their black-and-white science fiction fare frequently. Intelligence in the script (by Nigel Kneale) and total dedication in the execution (thanks to director Val Guest) make this tale of an astronaut's return to Earth and his biological merger

with plant life gripping, simply because Richard Wadsworth's subtle performance makes it so. Even the gruff-as-nails Brian Donlevy maintains attention. But Richard Wadsworth's silent stares and rigid movement, whimpering yet never saying a word, terrifies. This film proves little subtleties often count the most.

Night of the Hunter (1955)

Another classic psycho-thriller, but *Night of the Hunter* becomes horror by nature of its Gothic set pieces. When we watch as the children evade the demonic Robert Mitchum preacher character as they run up the cellar stairs, the fiend's clutching hands inches away from their feet, we know we are in horror genre-land. The waterlogged corpse of Shelley Winters, her blonde hair wavering in the underwater tide, no longer can protect her children, who flee to the swampland near the river (by the light of the moon no less) to continue their escape from this human predator that wants them dead as well. The direction (by Charles Laughton), art direction, cinematography and performances make this a gripping cinematic experience, American Gothic at its finest.

Invasion of the Body Snatchers (1956)

Iconic and innovative, Don Siegel's *Invasion of the Body Snatchers* creates the ultimate fear—the loss of our human identity—as seedpods from space grow into exact human duplicates, minus emotion and the capacity for kindness. Something as simple as a kiss can determine the moment when our loved one becomes "one of them." The invaders, working as a secret hive community, look exactly the same as their human hosts, minus a soul or sense of individuality. The true horror is that our humanity can be yanked away in the split second when we fall asleep, that our essence is erased suddenly without protest.

Curse of the Demon (1957)

Val Lewton was dead by 1957, but one of his outstanding directors, Jacques Tourneur, made this Lewton-inspired gem as homage, a Gothic horror classic about modern-day satanism, curses passed on parchment and fiery demons from Hell. Tourneur controls the crescendos of horrific "walks" in the mansion and woods that always manage to terrify. The cast, headed by Dana Andrews and Niall MacGinnis, is superb. I love the inclusion of the puppet demon, but the ambivalent depiction of evil surrounding wizard Karswell (who loves his mother and neighborhood children and

only demands his privacy) makes him both complex and sympathetic. And MacGinnis' performance steals the show.

I Was a Teenage Werewolf (1957)

American International and director Herman Cohen got it all right when they made their teenage monster classic that started a drive-in movie craze. The talented Michael Landon helped, as he plays the psychologically damaged rebel who falls into the hands of evil scientist Whit Bissell, who transforms the troubled boy into a werewolf. What makes this programmer so cap-

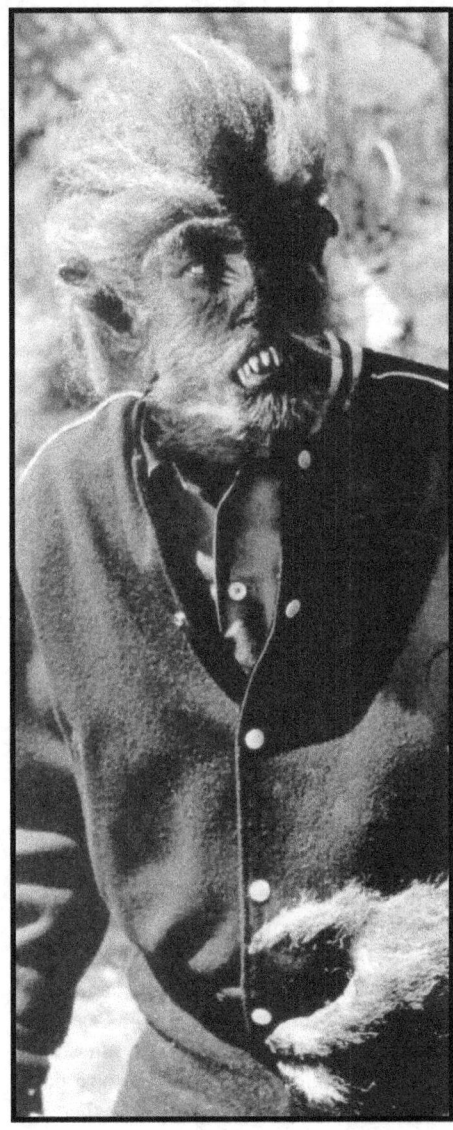

50th Anniversary Issue [1963-2013]

tivating is the sensitive focus on the boy's damaged psyche, existing side-by-side with the far more exploitative foaming-at-the-mouth werewolf sequences. Science-fueled technology meets teenage hormone-driven passions in one of drive-in cinema's finest moments.

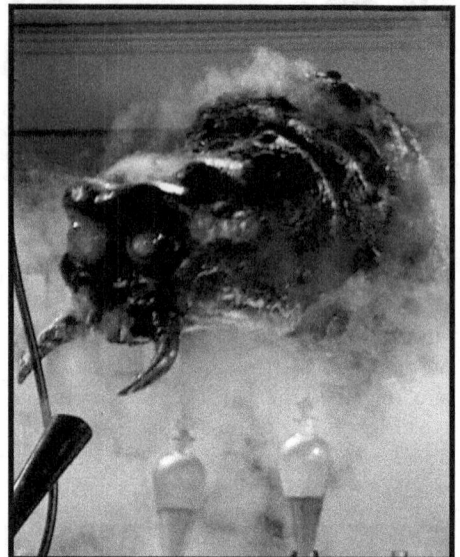

The Monster That Challenged the World (1957)

I admit my total bias here. This was the very first horror movie I ever saw back in 1957, along with my father and older brother. The movie mesmerized me. But as an adult I still marvel at the effectiveness of the film's pacing, the marvelous (effectively photographed and edited) execution of the sea beasts, and director Arnold Laven's ability to generate so many slowly building sequences that pay off with a jolting scare. For me horror film B pictures do not get much scarier than this one. Unlike most 1950s horror programmers that keep the monster hidden until the last reel, *The Monster That Challenged the World* maintains monster action and creepy suspense constantly throughout. And the explosive finale with the child endangered by the hatching baby monster is superb.

Quartermass II/Enemy From Space (1957)

After the excellent *Quatermass Xperiment*, was it too much to ask that its sequel be as good? In many ways *Quatermass II* is slightly superior to the original, although its premise borrows noticeably from *Invasion of the Body Snatchers* with meteorites (not seedpods) falling to Earth and emitting mind-controlling gas, turning the locals into alien-controlled zombies. The alien community is building an industrial size dome full of writhing space amoebas that will

feed on human flesh and blood. The sense of mystery, paranoia, chills and loss of human identity prevail. But it is once again the direction by Val Guest from an imaginative script from Nigel Kneale that fuels this classic.

The Vampire (1957)

I enjoy Gothic horror that occurs in small-town America, circa the 1950s. And Paul Landres' chill-a-minute *The Vampire* (with an effective script by Pat Fielding) is probably my favorite B production of the period. With a solid cast featuring John Beal, this variation of the Jekyll-Hyde theme makes an old chestnut original once again. Beal's performance as the beloved small-town doctor who accidentally takes the wrong pills and retrogresses into a vampire beast is played as a full-blown tragedy. He is a caring father raising a cute young

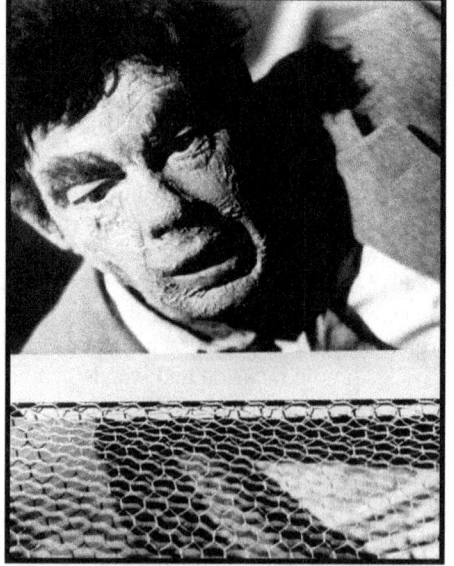

daughter alone, and we pull for his salvation as he descends into the Hell of monster-regression pill addiction.

The Curse of Frankenstein (1957)

The first full-color, gore-ridden, period Hammer, *The Curse of Frankenstein*, presenting the debut of the creative trio of director Terence Fisher and stars Peter Cushing and Christopher Lee, was only a warm-up for the classic *Horror of Dracula*. But this first Gothic Hammer remains a horror classic. With excellent sets and costuming mounted at Bray Studios, we have the superb Peter Cushing as the obsessed and single-minded Baron, and long and lanky Christopher Lee dominating as the gruesomely patched-together Creature. Jimmy Sangster's script breathes life with powerful dialogue that nurtured the creative palette that we now call Hammer horror.

The Crawling Eye/The Trollenberg Terror (1958)

While American horror fare of the 1950s was often exploitative or slightly tongue-in-cheek, the Brits always took their low-budget horror very seriously. Hampered by limited finances, *The Crawling Eye* rises above to produce an original concept of alien invasion while generating intensity and mystery, often utilizing the suggestion of the alien presence (invisible in thick, crawling mist) for the film's betterment, before the monsters are actually depicted during the film's explosive climax. The gigantic eye monsters with tentacles

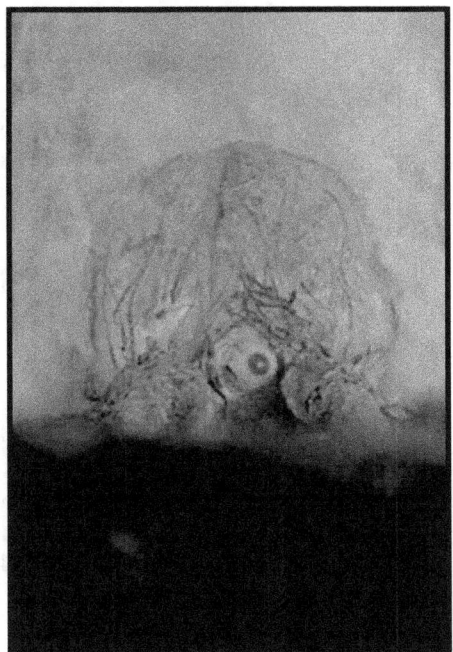

writhing are horrifying and original. But all this would be for naught if a superior script were not front and center.

Horror of Dracula/Dracula (1958)

For this 8-year-old little boy, *Horror of Dracula* was the movie that made me a horror film fan for life. Not the fastest paced or the most gruesome film ever made, *Horror of Dracula* rises to classic status by virtue of creating a creepy, mood-inducing, darkly mythological look (filmed in marvelous Technicolor) at the soul-destroying cult of vampirism as it never before had been visualized. Here the Undead exude evil. Christopher Lee's short performance as Count Dracula manages to dominate the production. But Peter Cushing's energetic turn as Professor Van Helsing is iconic and remains one of the most intense horror film performances ever.

It! The Terror From Beyond Space (1958)

This tidy little B production, directed by Edward L. Cahn, borrows from *The Thing* (1951) and yet was creative enough to influence the decades-away *Alien*. Ray Corrigan in a rubber Martian alien suit never looked more terrifying. Working within a claustrophobic multi-leveled spacecraft returning from Mars (carrying an unwelcome cargo), the set design and shadowy cinematography manages to make this low-budget bone-chiller frightening. With a committed B cast headed by Marshall Thompson, this popcorn thriller keeps the audience spellbound for 69 terror-filled minutes as the alien beast forces the human crew into smaller and tighter quarters with nowhere left to run.

Revenge of Frankenstein (1958)

A superior sequel to *Curse of Frankenstein*, *Revenge of Frankenstein* returns Peter Cushing to embellish his performance as the not-so-evil Baron Frankenstein (this time out). In Hammer's original the Baron was evil to the core, but here his obsessions are tendered with sympathy, making his character ambivalent. Breaking further away from the Universal Pictures mold, Hammer forges its own depiction of the Frankenstein Monster (played effectively by Michael Gwynn), rendered brain damaged and sympathetic, after he is severely beaten by a cruel barkeep shortly after his operation. The Creature's brain transplant is savagely undone as his twisted and crippled stature returns, but even more horrifyingly so. For me this is the series' best entry.

The Mummy (1959)

This casual remake of Boris Karloff's Universal classic comes up short when compared to the original, but the Hammer remake becomes more of a full-tilt monster-on-the-loose popcorn epic, allowing towering Christopher Lee to stomp and ravish where Karloff simply crept. Forget the human, reanimated Ardeth Bey character, for Lee's Mummy stays wrapped and dangerous. Peter Cushing manages to elevate the John Banning archaeologist character to full-blown hero by exercising so much spunk and bravery in battling Lee's rotting corpse hand-to-hand. The creative use of set decoration and color photography only enhances the ominous Gothic mood.

House on Haunted Hill (1959)

Film noir meets supernatural ghost cinema, with the emphasis on broad performances and a playfully frightening tone. William Castle works from Robb White's inspired script, with the added gimmick of a skeleton flying above our heads in the audience (Emergo), producing a truly frightening ride that features a falling chandelier, acid baths in the cellar, a woman hanging from the ceiling, dismembered heads, the sudden appearance of a witchy servant and cute little pistols in mini-coffins. Add to the mix a truly malevolent Vincent Price performance, with Elisha Cook, Jr. thrown in for good measure. This is a chilling film I can watch over and over again. And it features one of the scariest moments in all of horror cinema.

The Tingler (1959)

Now buzzing our butts with vibrating motors, William Castle follows up his wonderful *House on Haunted Hill* with another outrageous monster-mash that works far better than it should. Once a person is frightened, spinal cord scorpion creatures

grow within our bodies to kill us unless we scream, and scream is exactly what the theater audience does after Vincent Price cuts this living "tingler" from a formerly mute (she could not scream) corpse and the monster runs loose in a small movie theater. When the on-screen theater audience screams, so do we. Vincent Price is once again at his scene-crewing best and this outrageous story of LSD, delusion, deception and mayhem entertains.

The 1960s

Black Sunday/Mask of the Demon (1960)

The classic originator of Euro-horror (at least to the American mainstream), the dank and masterfully photographed *Black Sunday* creates a bleak sense of lethargy and soul-numbing depression where the vampires actually liven things up. Barbara Steele, in her dual role of vampire witch and virginal innocent, creates a performance that shines not merely by what she says but how she looks decorating her surrounding scenery. Blending mythologies of witchcraft and vampirism, director Mario Bava crafts a macabre world that remains consistent throughout. *Black Sunday* remains one of the greatest visual horror films ever produced.

Psycho (1960)

The master of suspense produced a little cast-off production on the cheap, very fast, after coming off *North By Northwest*, one of his most expensive, sweeping epics. The black and white production, resembling his weekly TV series more than any of his recent theatrical features, became an iconic classic. He kills off his heroine early on, makes his leading lady a criminal and presents the deadly psychopath of the title with a sense of the comedic, the quirky and

emotionally damaged. The twisty and taut screenplay sizzles. Hitchcock created one of his finest films without trying too hard, or so he makes it seem.

Brides of Dracula (1960)

This is a worthy sequel to *Horror of Dracula* and one that is faster-paced and perhaps even quirkier. Instead of distinguished Christopher Lee as Count Dracula, we have the flamboyant carrot-top Teddy Boy David Peel as Baron Meinster, whose first conquest is his mother, the Baroness. Framed with excellent set design and color photography, *Brides of Dracula*, under Terence Fisher's inspired direction, flies from one sequence to another, making the victims of the Undead appear more sensuous and lustful than ever before. And Peter Cushing's second appearance as Van Helsing is equally inspired. Hammer has *never* delivered a better one-two punch.

Eyes Without A Face (1960)

First released to American audiences cut and dubbed in 1963 as *The Horror Chamber of Dr. Faustus*, the uncut, original French *Eyes Without A Face* is an intense study of an obsessed mad surgeon who sacrifices the lives of beautiful young females when trying to restore his daughter's mangled face, caused by his driving error. The juxtaposition between a graphically gory facial transplant operation and the lonely daughter's solitary existence in her opulent house, wearing a china-doll mask that reminds everyone of her lost beauty, creates the framework for a gruesomely poetic horror fairy tale. The movie is ultimately a contradiction, in that its visual subtlety rubs against its gore and mayhem.

House of Usher (1960)

This is the only AIP Poe adaptation that really matters. Though *House of Usher* lacks the bombast of *Pit and the Pendulum* and the pseudo-poetry of *Masque of the Red Death*, the spirit of Poe and the ghastly horror that exists within the confines of our minds is best explored in this initial Poe entry, starring an oddly white-haired Vincent Price. The quiet intensity of Price's restrained performance fascinates, his inner torment mirrored by a Gothic house of horrors (with a ghastly burial vault). Instead of trying to over-power the audience, Roger Corman (in what I consider to be his finest film) gets under our skin. Vincent Price's performance cuts deep and resonates. What felt meandering as a child now seems masterful and nuanced upon repeated viewings as an adult.

The Haunting (1963)

This was one of the first adult psychological horror movies; director Robert Wise handles a superb ensemble cast to execute one of the most terrifying movies ever made. Like all effective ghost stories, the central character is psychologically damaged to the point where the ghostly manifestations are actual external extensions of her inner turmoil. Wisely, supernatural apparitions are never shown but instead we see doors breathe, feel a ghostly chill that infects the air, and discover that the hand holding our own is not actually a human one. Inspired cinematography of the manor house produces non-stop goose bumps.

Night of the Living Dead (1968)

Independent films suddenly appear with remarkable results. George Romero's terrifying zombie classic shows what an industrial film crew can do when they get

inspired. In 1968 *Night of the Living Dead* was one of the first splatter epics that raised the bar of graphic cinematic violence. While the movie boasts only adequate acting and a tried and true B script, the film's visceral shocks and take-no-prisoner tone simply demonstrates what great direction, editing and cinematography can produce when gonzo filmmaking replaces safe, formulaic Hollywood templates.

The 1970s

Deep Red (1975)

Dario Argento is the greatest director of horror in the final quarter of the 20th century. Whether working within the suspenseful *giallo* subgenre or the supernatural horror one, Argento always manages to creep his audience out. Here a twisty and involving plot is presented via an impressive aura of gaudy colors, elaborate set design, intense murder sequences and slowly building hold-your-breath walks down dank, rotting corridors. When it comes to visual unease that gets under the skin and festers, Argento is the master.

Suspiria (1977)

Working within the supernatural horror subgenre, *Suspiria* is both subtle and bombastic, sometimes at the same time. Featuring a throbbing musical score by Goblin, director Dario Argento beefs up the body count with a series of visually stunning orchestrated murders. Most of his victims are beautiful women who die in various stages of undress, but his twisty mayhem always remains artistic, building stylistically, ultimately becoming orgasmic in his payoff of violence. More so than presenting classic performances or intelligent scripts, Dario Argento's strength is cinematography, editing and direction. His creation of mounting tension and an aura of doom is unsurpassed. *Suspiria* shocks audiences senseless every single time.

Halloween (1978)

John Carpenter opened the door for the creative independent during a time when Hollywood was losing its mojo. Even though *Halloween* inspired a generation of inferior slasher movies, *Halloween* downplayed the graphically gruesome. Instead of grossing out his audience, Carpenter terrified it by pitting the nameless and faceless embodiment of ultimate evil against the goodness of a nerdy teenager. Guess what, the babysitter kicks ass, even if we learn at the end that evil cannot be destroyed, only vanquished in the short run. Crafting intense murders that are often as clever as they are shocking, Carpenter created a horror classic of both style and substance.

Alien (1979)

When asked what is the scariest horror movie ever made, I would have to answer Ridley Scott's *Alien*. Built brick by brick from the remains of schlocky B science fiction monster movies of the past, *Alien* is imbued by Scott with a slick artistic pretense and style that earlier B movies could not afford. Even if a man in a monster suit sometimes plays the alien, the cinematography and editing make this slimy phallus from outer space decidedly non-human and totally alien. Add a marvelous ensemble cast headed by kick-ass heroine Sigourney Weaver and we have a classic monster movie for all time.

The 1980s
The Howling (1981)

Even though *An American Werewolf in London* received the most accolades, *The Howling* is superior. Both movies boast a semi-comic tone infused with pure terror, but *The Howling* is far more intense and frightening, and its satiric homage to B werewolf directors of the past is touching. Rob Bottin's werewolf execution might be slightly inferior to Rick Baker's, Bottin's werewolves become the living nightmare of our childhood. In *American Werewolf* we spend far too long appreciating the craft instead of believing the character. Director Joe Dante manages to infuse every sequence of *The Howling* with tension, and his werewolves are the most unsettling in movie history.

John Carpenter's The Thing (1982)

Not as iconic as the original version of *The Thing*, but John Carpenter's take comes much closer to the John W. Campbell story on which both movies were based. Carpenter's claustrophobic Antarctic military base and its eccentric cast allow the alien infestation to create a sense of dread slowly but steadily. Audiences realize that every sequence features at least one member of the human crew that is actually an alien, the parasite hopping from one human host to another. This concept builds in suspense until audiences are manipulated to jump at every edit or sound. Once again Rob Bottin's alien creature effects remain terrifying, and the movie's climax is gripping and unnerving. Carpenter's classic only gets better with time.

Aliens (1986)

James Cameron's sequel to *Alien* is a different style horror film classic. While Ridley Scott's *Alien* was equivalent to being a haunted house in outer space, always remaining a horror movie, Cameron's sequel is more a science fiction epic war movie, with the emphasis on action and suspense. Instead of one monstrous alien fiend, we now have a colony/army of alien drones whose mission is to protect the hive's queen. Sigourney Weaver's Ripley, finally front and center, becomes one of the greatest warriors in film history. The monster thrills come flying at break-neck speed and the rapid-fire direction never lets up. And supporting player Bill Paxton's comic hijinks are just about perfect—"game over!" … indeed!

The 1990s

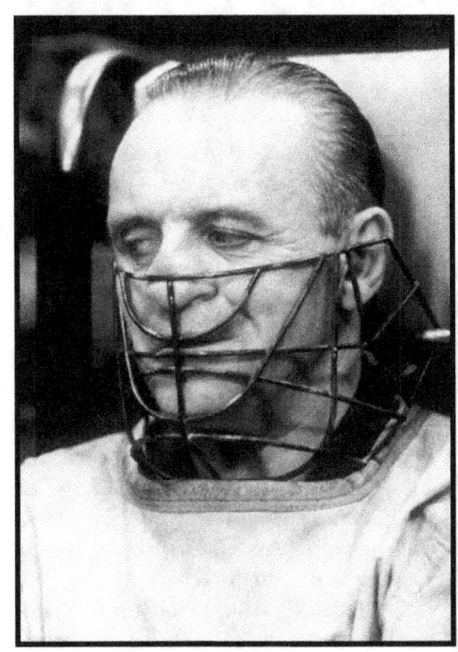

Silence of the Lambs (1991)

The psycho-killer of the 1970s and 1980s was merely a killing machine with a blade, not ever a fully meshed character. Enter Hannibal Lecter, the ultimate serial killer who would serve as the template of where horror cinema was heading in the 1990s. Director Jonathan Demme creates an absolutely terrifying look at the horror created by human monsters, and Anthony Hopkins' portrayal of Lecter won him an Academy Award. The actor's ability to morph from the shyly cultured connoisseur of the arts to the maniacal Hannibal the Cannibal is both inspired and totally terrifying. Add Jodie Foster's equally inspired performance as an F.B.I. agent and we have a classic that grabs audiences by the throat and refuses to let go.

Ringu (1998)

Even if the J-horror explosion evaporated much too early due to familiarity and lack of creativity, the earlier classics such as *Ringu* infused the horror genre with a shot of creativity and adrenalin. Fusing a "found footage" scenario with a classic ghost story wrapped in urban-myth, *Ringu* becomes one of the creepiest horror movies of the modern era. Just the image of the herky-jerky demon child crawling out of the television monitor, entering the real world, creeping toward its victim, is simply mind-numbingly scary. *Ringu* deserves raves for turning the horror genre away from gore and splatter, returning it to atmospheric chills.

Lists are basically opinions and should be seen only as the means for initiating discussion. I called my list "favorites" and not "greatest" because the movies I enjoy the most and wish to view repeatedly are more about me and not the genre as a whole.

It was tough to select my favorite horror film. *Bride of Frankenstein* and *Horror of Dracula* were almost tied as #1 choice, but I gave the top spot to *Horror of Dracula* since it was the movie that affected me profoundly when I was 8 and branded my love for the horror film genre for the rest of my life.

Is Anyone There?

by Arthur Joseph Lundquist

An Iconic Doomsday Moment

Harry Belafonte, the lone survivor of nuclear holocaust, in The World, The Flesh, and The Devil *(1959).*

Historians may debate whether or not the nation actually panicked during the classic 1938 Orson Welles broadcast of *The War of the Worlds*. But there is no denying it contains one sequence of incredible power that echoed in popular culture for decades after.

This moment in the Mercury Theatre's radio play occurs just after we have heard live reports of the nation's armies and air force having been wiped out by heat rays and poison gas from the invading Martians. With no remaining defense, amid reports of Martian cylinders landing across the nation, we cut to a reporter on the roof of "Broadcast Building" (i.e., Rockefeller Center) who describes in you-are-there fashion the approach of Martian war machines, advancing on Manhattan "like a line of new towers rising on the city's west side." Behind his voice we hear ships' horns howling in the Hudson.

"*Now they're lifting their metal hands. This is the end now. Smoke comes out, black smoke, drifting over the city. People in the streets see it now. They're running towards the East River, thousands of them, dropping in like rats. Now the smoke's spreading faster, it's reached Times Square. People are trying to run away from it, but it's no use, they, they're falling like flies. Now the smoke's crossing Sixth Avenue, Fifth Avenue, [coughs] a hundred yards away, [coughs] fi-fi-50 feet.*"

Orson Welles directs a radio play at CBS studios for his Mercury Theatre.

We hear the sound of his final exhalation, then of a body hitting the floor. For several seconds, only the sounds of boats in the river are heard. Then we hear a voice we'd heard earlier, a short wave operator searching for other stations.

"*2X2L calling CQ. 2X2L calling CQ. 2X2L calling CQ, New York. Isn't there anyone on the air? Isn't there anyone on the air? Isn't there anyone? 2X2L.*"

Silence. Then an announcer reassures us that we are listening to an adaptation by the Mercury Theatre of H.G. Wells' *The War of the Worlds*. Of course, by this time, an indeterminate percentage of America had fled its radios in panic.

This is an amazing piece of radio, and if you weren't one of the people who heard it then, you had the chance later on, when it was re-broadcast and re-recorded and sent out on record albums. In the mid-60s I heard it for the first time one Saturday night on Baltimore radio, and the reporter's speech haunted me so much that in high school I was dumb enough to use it to audition for the class show. (Jesus, that was not pretty.) Well, it reassures me now to know I was not alone. One of the people originally fooled in 1938 was a little boy who would one day grow into radio personality Steve Allen. When in 1988 the Mercury script was re-recorded by NPR to commemorate its 50th anniversary, Allen lobbied for and got the role of that lonely reporter on the rooftop. Lucky bastard.

And so in 1938 that moment vanished into the American imagination. But from time to time its memory would surface, finding new life in the movies of doomsday.

The first time is in *When Worlds Collide* (1951). After the approach of the planet Zyra has devastated America with earthquakes and tidal waves, from a radio we hear a shortwave appeal for help:

"This is emergency channel 9 again. Is anyone left? Can anyone hear us? ... Repeating, we are remaining on the air. Repeating, can anyone hear us? We need drinking water and medical supplies .... Is anyone left, can anyone hear us?"

In *The World, The Flesh, and The Devil* (1959), the last survivor of a nuclear holocaust goes to a radio studio and listens to a tape of officials attempting to coordinate responses to the doomsday crisis. Amid reports of cities going off the air as clouds of radioactive fallout sweep the world, we hear chatter in the newsroom. One by one the other stations fade out, as voices in the background vanish until one last voice can be heard:

"Listen, what do I do about the equipment here? The generation room is still operating. Do I leave it or what? Frank. Frank? Anybody there? Anybody?"

In the Year 2889 is a 1967 remake of Roger Corman's 1955 sci-fi thriller *The Day the World Ended*, about survivors of World War III battling radioactive mutants. But it begins with a sequence not in the original. Over its opening credits we hear a radio reporter's last broadcast:

"The Geiger counter here in the studio reads 632 roentgens. That's six times more than enough to kill a man ... Maybe there's no one left to hear my voice. No living human being to record the end of the world. Now, this is Ted Johnson for [his voice falters] *KGBE Radio*."

Then his voice fades with a final exhalation.

The celebrated 1983 television drama of World War III, *The Day After*, chose to end on this note. After a closing shot of Jason Robards, Jr. huddled on the smoking rubble of Kansas City, the screen goes black, and just before the closing credits run, we hear the voice of a University of Kansas science student (John Lithgow) calling out on a short wave set:

Hello? Is anybody there? Anybody at all ... ?

To this day you can still hear Orson Welles' *War of the Worlds* on radio stations here and there on a Halloween night. As we continue into the 21st century, it would sadden me to think of children not having the chance to experience that bit of 1938 radio. Especially that scene and its ending, with its lonely appeal to the silence.

The Day After, TV's 1983 depiction of World War III, came complete with nuclear devastation and a lone voice over the airwaves.

PANIC!

THIS IS THE ORSON WELLES BROADCAST THAT HOAXED AMERICA

Thriller's Classic Horror Episodes Season One

by Gary J. Svehla

Sometimes our creative limitations become strengths. Television, the bastard child of mainstream Hollywood, suffers from downsized budgets, time restraints, available talent and censorship. Back in the day it was a comedown for an actual movie star to do more than a guest appearance on network television, as TV actors were most likely the best of all the minor Hollywood supporting players that were not quite good enough for the movies (perhaps the talent was visible but the overall physical package was lacking by Hollywood standards). Horror film icon Boris Karloff, in the final decade of his life, agreed to host (and in a few rare instances even star in) an American-produced crime-horror anthology series that would feature taut 50-minute episodes based upon some of the best horror and crime fiction written by authors including Donald S. Sanford, Robert Bloch, August Derleth, Barre Lyndon, Cornell Woolrich, Charles Beaumont, Robert E. Howard, and Philip MacDonald. The series, by its very title *Thriller,* was conceived basically more as a crime drama anthology series than as an actual horror anthology series. Mystery (*Perry Mason, Alfred Hitchcock Presents*) and crime dramas (*Mike Hammer, The Untouchables, The Naked City, M Squad, Peter Gunn*) ruled television airwaves during the late 1950s and early 1960s. So a show dedicated to thrillers would fit into this environment. *Thriller*, after it debuted in September 1960, got off to a slow ratings start, so a new producer, William Frye, was hired to turn the series around. His initial contribution was a series-defining one that arrived as episode seven, *The Purple Room*, the first balls-out horror episode and one that remains a critical favorite to this day. Written and directed by Douglas Heyes, who helmed some of the better episodes, *Thriller* exhibited a creative burst of energy that jump-started the series and resulted in establishing a new direction—half of the episodes being thrillers of crime and mystery and half being supernatural horror episodes of the jump-out-of-your-seat variety. I am sure studio executives considered it far easier to produce crime episodes that could imitate the same type of stories presented on the highly successful *Alfred Hitchcock Presents* television series, also produced by MCA/Universal. In fact rumors persist that Alfred Hitchcock's dissatisfaction that his own studio was producing a competing series similar to his, one that invaded his creative turf, may have been partially responsible for *Thriller*'s

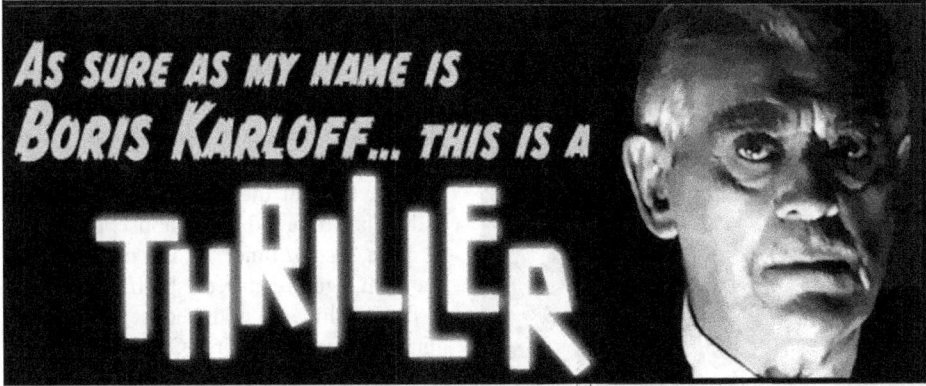

sudden cancellation after only two complete seasons (broadcast from 1960 to 1962).

But it was the horror-themed episodes—grisly tales dealing with family curses, a painting of Death coming to terrifying life, ghostly spirits pulling humans into a haunted world, demons possessing human beings and turning them into monstrous murderers, the evil powers of witchcraft convincing the unconvinced of its dark power—that pushed the creative envelope and challenged the production staff. Back in 1960, horror on the theatrical screen was subdued compared to today, and even more restrictive was violence allowed on television, which was controlled by a tough governing censorship board. But instead of abandoning the idea of bringing the horror genre to mainstream television, producers, writers and directors had to think outside the box. Nightmarish cinematography, the creation and redressing of Gothic sets (mansions, prison houses, cellars, attics, mist-shrouded exteriors), dramatic music scores (by some of the greatest film music composers including Jerry Goldsmith, Morton Stevens and Pete Rugolo), slowly mounted chills relying on atmosphere and suspense rather than grisly mutilation and gore, and bone-chilling scripts that depended upon dialogue and performance that allowed audiences to believe in the world of the supernatural became the challenges for the creative minds behind the series. Network television had to work within the confines of producing 50-minute mini-movies that managed to tell complex stories. And since violence had to be downplayed, the establishing of goose bumps and slowly mounted scares within the confines of a tight script took time to deliver. Horrifying mood had to be created via cinematography, performance and dialogue quite rapidly within the confines of 50 minutes. The production schedule was most likely quite tight with little time to build or redress sets. And the series had to deliver over 30 episodes each season (exactly 37 for season one and 30 for

From *The Purple Room*'s pre-credits sequence, a subjective shot of a frenzied wife about to shoot her innocent husband.

season two). So the mere fact that on such limitations classic horror episodes resulted from season one including *The Hungry Glass, Parasite Mansion, The Cheaters* and *Pigeons From Hell* is utterly amazing.

Even though the best *Thriller* crime episodes are receiving coverage in our companion magazine *Mad About Movies*, it is the horror entries that usually attract attention and are most fondly remembered, as scores of fans that grew up terrified sitting in front of television sets in darkened living rooms can testify. So allow me to select my personal favorite horror episodes of the first season of *Thriller* and attempt to analyze why they've become such classics.

The first horror entry was broadcast October 25, 1960, a few days before Halloween. It was *The Purple Room*, written and directed by Douglas Heyes, starring a virtual three-person cast—Rip Torn, Patricia Barry and Richard Anderson. William Frye entered as new series producer and his emphasis was on introducing supernatural horror tales amid the crime and mystery ones. Tales of people having to sleep one night in a haunted house to collect an inheritance were not new, but *The Purple Room*'s spin was original and effective.

The episode works because of its simplicity. The story can be broken down into the setup, the delivery and the twisted surprise ending. The fact that the exterior of Universal's *Psycho* house becomes our iconic haunted house only ups the chill quota. And the dank interior photography (by Bud Thackery) creates thrills and chills.

Richard Anderson, standing left, is framed by Universal's still fresh *Psycho* house, which created an aura of horror for *The Purple Room*.

The half drunk and drugged Duncan is frightened to death by this grim figure of death in the middle of the night, from *The Purple Room*.

The setup: Mr. Ridgewater (Alan Napier), attorney, tells Duncan Corey (Rip Torn) that in order to become legitimate heir, he must occupy his late eccentric relative's house for a year to be able to sell the house and make a tidy profit. However, the will states that he must first sleep overnight in the house to know if the house is the right one for him. One night is all the time the house or he will need. The house's legend tells of a married couple—she's up in the bedroom and he's rushing downstairs to investigate noises. It turns out that a prowler stabs the husband, who in desperation uses his last drop of strength to stumble back up to the bedroom to receive medical attention from his wife. But the ambling and zombie-like husband seems more like the intruder to the terrified wife. She, scared to death, shoots her own husband dead. And the shock of what she has done drives her insane.

The delivery: Nasty and untrusting Duncan arrives to sleep at the house and is greeted by the current tenants, the couple who will inherit the house if Duncan forfeits the yearlong residence. Duncan, arrogant, negative and unlikeable, suspects the couple, Oliver (Richard Anderson) and Rachel (Patricia Barry), are already planning trickery to frighten him out of his inheritance. And he's simply too smart to fall for any such pranks. After the couple helps Duncan settle in, they announce they cannot spend the night and leave. However, in the middle of the night, a figure, dark and gloomy, that wears an ornate rubber mask (resembling Lon Chaney's Erik from *The Phantom of the Opera*) and gloves approaches the now half drunk/drugged Duncan. Duncan suffers a heart attack and apparently dies. Of course Oliver and Rachel are behind the scare tactics, but they never assumed such a young man would die of heart failure. They plant his corpse in his car and drive it off the side of the road, making it appear that Duncan suffered the heart attack while driving to the home. Rachel and Oliver return home to spend the night, when another prowler is heard downstairs and Oliver leaves Rachel in bed while he goes down to investigate. Of course occult history is repeating itself.

The twist ending: The house's urban legend plays out again, this time with Oliver as the intended victim as we discover that Duncan did not die of heart failure at all and he has returned to the house, only soon to die a *second* time. In the midst of this mayhem, good-natured sheriff Ray Teal arrives, rushing up to the house, as he hears gunshots from upstairs. Oliver buries his head in his hands, realizing the jig is up.

More so than featuring an iconic story premise, *The Purple Room* becomes such an effective horror entry by nature of its campfire-tale direction, its dark and moody photography and effective acting by a small cast in tight, claustrophobic locations. The episode's main flaw is that each of the three major cast members is unlikeable and the audience does not care who lives or dies. But *The Purple Room* was one of the most terrifying hours ever to reach network television and headed the MCA series in an entirely new direction. Only hinting at the supernatural, this crime episode was played strictly for horror, and its urban legend myth and haunted house setting only fuel that premise.

Surprisingly, host Boris Karloff only starred in one episode during season one and it was, of course, a horror entry, produced by William Frye and directed by veteran John Brahm (with a script by Donald S. Sanford), entitled *The Prediction*. The best thing about the entry is Karloff's

Boris Karloff as mentalist Mace, horrified that he suddenly has the power to predict the future, from the only episode in which he appeared in season one, *The Prediction*.

performance as kindly, good-hearted (but fake) mentalist Mace. As the headlining star attraction for 10 years, Mace has the theatrics down and the dramatic dialogue to draw in the English customers. He is surrogate father to his young and beautiful assistant Norine (Audrey Dalton), who dresses in exotic attire and plays the harp to punctuate the action onstage.

But of course, things begin to go awry. Norine has a secret boyfriend, Grant (Alex Davion), and the relationship is getting hot and heavy. Norine thinks that Mace will disapprove so she keeps her relationship hidden. Effectively moody John L. Russell photography augmented by special effects-enhanced pulsating facial shots create the illusion that Mace actually begins to have visions of the future, all dire predictions involving life and death. He first learns that a local prize fighter will die in the ring, and when he pleads with Norine's abusive and worthless father Roscoe (Alan Caillou) to speak to the boxer's manager, Roscoe neglects to see the manager, but he places a bet on his opponent. When the fighter dies and Roscoe collects, we see just how father-like Mace has become to Norine, whose real father is killed soon after in a dark alleyway after a bar tramp lures him outside, knowing he collected a bundle of money. Of course Mace received another vision and tried to warn the betting man of imminent danger.

By the show's end, Mace retires due to his uncontrolled visions of the future, and Norine and Grant leave to be married and go on a honeymoon. Mace has another

Mace is kind and gentle toward his beautiful assistant Norine (Audrey Dalton), who dresses in exotic attire to punctuate the action onstage.

desperate vision warning the couple to turn back if they see a twisted road sign directing them to Edinburgh. Brahm's creepy, rain-soaked direction, augmented by Russell's spooky photography, results in the couple almost ramming into the rear of a truck cleaning up debris spewed all over the highway after an accident. After Grant admonishes the driver, telling him to place a flare behind his truck, the lovey-dovey couple continues their journey, but immediately afterwards the trucker picks up the twisted Edinburgh sign as the couple drives away. Only Mace has the chance to save the lives of the younger couple, as he and his friend speed in their car to intercept the doomed couple before it is too late.

Karloff's performance is simply wonderful. He gets to act very theatrically when he is onstage performing his mentalist act, but in contrast, he gets to be the caring father figure whenever he is with his young assistant Norine. And we get to observe Karloff as the frantic out-of-his-mind mentalist who suddenly begins to receive actual warning flashes about the fates of people he knows. This haunted, supernatural angle makes Boris Karloff's performance a magnificent one, transforming what might have been an average *Thriller* into something extra special. Now in his seventh decade, Karloff proves he still has the enthusiasm and energy to deliver a standout performance.

Two days after Christmas, 1960, *The Cheaters* premiered, directed by John Brahm (who directed *The Lodger* and *Hangover Square*) with a screenplay by Donald S. Sanford based upon the Robert Bloch short story. Cleverly, most of the earlier horror-oriented *Thriller* entries were basically crime stories with supernatural overtones. The title *The Cheaters* refers to old-time slang for eyeglasses, but it also describes the sinister morality that surrounds each person who possesses the glasses ... each mini-story involves "cheaters" or dishonest people who are

Mace, out of costume, warns Norine's boyfriend Grant (Alex Davion) of the dangers facing Norine and him, building to the climax of *The Prediction*.

Salvage operator Joe Henshaw (Paul Newlan) puts on the glasses to learn that his wife is having an affair with the young character played by Ed Nelson, from *The Cheaters*.

revealed because of the truth that the wearer of the glasses experiences. *Thriller* was very effective at presenting mini-episodes within the hour-long presentation, a type of TV anthology where three or four smaller stories make up the hour-long episode. This episode both begins and ends at the eerie mansion where Dirk Van Prinn (the always wonderful Henry Daniell) concocts special yellow-gold glasses with the Latin word "veritas" or truth etched across the bridge. In the show's prologue, Van Prinn puts on the glasses and stares into a mirror, as the camera zooms in closer on the old man's grimaced face. As a look of total terror climbs over his face, as his eyes bulge open, Van Prinn tries to scream aloud but only a silent one erupts, as we fade into the title card. At the end of the episode, another man will don the very same glasses and stare into the very same mirror, but this time we will see what he sees, and the episode will end with one of the starkest images of horror that ever erupted on the home television screen.

Even though *The Cheaters* contains one continuous story, it is framed in the same way that the movie *Winchester '73* was framed. Instead of focusing upon just one set of characters, each story focuses on the people who inherit and possess the supernatural glasses. In the first segment the glasses come into the possession of salvage operator (or junk store owner) Joe Henshaw (Paul Newlan), who placed a bid and now owns Van Prinn's abandoned mansion. Next, after Henshaw's violent death, the glasses come into the possession of eccentric old lady Miriam Olcott (Mildred Dunnock) when she visits Henshaw's old shop, now under new management. Finally, after Miriam's death, the glasses pass to her nephew Edward (Jack Weston), and when he dies the glasses come into possession of unpublished author Sebastian Grimm (Harry Townes), who literally takes the glasses off Edward's cold body. And the story ends with Sebastian confronting himself in that same mirror into which Van Prinn stared at the story's beginning.

All the mini-episodes involve victims wearing the cursed glasses and hearing the thoughts of close friends and relatives who are supposed to be friendly and supportive of them. But he or she who wears the glasses hears malicious thoughts from loved ones, then a few seconds later the words pop out of their mouths and paint a distinctly more pleasant picture. Before long the episode forwards the idea that everyone close to us has self-serving and violent thoughts about us. At least that's how it seems to everyone in the story. Junkman Joe comes home to find his formerly shrewish wife suddenly all peaches and cream and cooking a romantic dinner. Of course she has intercepted the mail and discovers that his property can be sold for a major amount of money, so everyone is planning to bump off old Joe to collect the money. Even affable, youthful employee Ed Nelson is having an affair with Joe's wife Maggie and they cannot be together until old Joe is gone. When Joe catches the couple on the couch going at

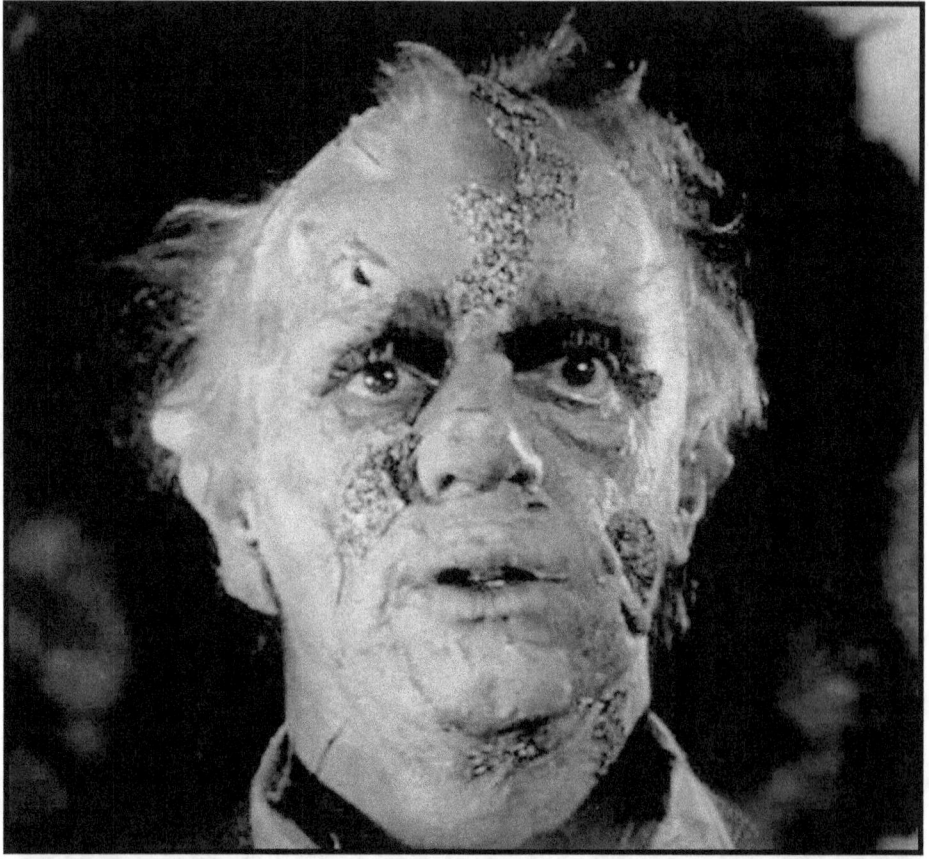

Harry Townes as Sebastian Grimm looks into the mirror, discovering the horrible truth about himself, from *The Cheaters*.

it, he beats them to death with a tire iron. When the local cop arrives on the scene, Joe tries to smash the cheaters lying before him on the table, but the cop thinks that Joe is attacking him, so he shoots Joe dead.

Similar stories of deception occur with elderly Miriam Olcott sneaking out of her home to visit little shops where she shoplifts small trinkets (since she does not have any money). When she returns home she overhears her caregivers, Edward and Olive Dean, along with good friend Clarence (Dayton Lummis), plot to get her drunk to push her down the stairs to get her money. While she manages to stab Clarence, she, unfortunately, drinks the wine, falls asleep but spills the wine that causes fire to spread from the fireplace, ultimately killing her. Soon her evil nephew Edward gets involved with sleazy society types that play a crooked game of cards during a costume party, which Edward attends dressed as Ben Franklin, wearing the supernatural glasses and overhearing all the negative chatter. Even though Edward is now wealthy, he is an unworthy inheritor of *old* wealth. In a rage Edward stands up and rants, but another guest beans him over the head, killing him accidentally. To be honest, we do not regret his death for one moment. But in attendance is god-awfully pretentious author Sebastian Grimm, who swipes the glasses and, during the next year, writes a book on their history. Before writing the final chapter, Sebastian must travel to Van Prinn's fallen-into-ruin mansion and he finally wears the glasses (something he learned *not* do from the get-

Host Boris Karloff, always interesting in his on-air openings, introduces *The Hungry Glass*, one of the series' most terrifying episodes.

go) and gazes into the mirror. Grimm sees himself as a corpse-like fiend with decaying skin and bulging eyes. The horror of his inner-self made tangible causes the man to tear at his face with his fingernails and descend into a state of insanity. The truth is too much to bear, and this ghastly and unnerving ending to one of *Thriller*'s first horror entries is classic television. Even today the make-up horrifies and the rhythm of the ending leaves us feeling disoriented. Of course we want to scream as well.

To me, *The Hungry Glass* is the classic horror entry of the series, the hour that I remember most vividly from my youth. The show utterly terrified me, and seeing it again, the episode still creeps me out. Horror specialist Douglas Heyes adapted the story (based upon a Robert Bloch story) and directed, and the episode stars William Shatner (Gil), Joanna Heyes (Gil's wife Marcia), Russell Johnson (Real Estate agent Adam) and Elizabeth Allen (Adam's wife Liz). Heyes, who directed *The Purple Room* episode, builds upon the creative decisions he made for that earlier episode. First, the hour story occurs at night, at first during a storm and then moving to a huge mansion without electricity. When the power finally gets turned back on, the glaring overhead lighting only accents the harshness of the house and illuminates the spooky shadows. The mood of the episode is unnerving, whether the action occurs in the house's cellar, main floor or attic. Each room is carefully dressed with shadows featuring antique furniture covered with dust and dirt. In a house without mirrors, mirrors become the prime focus. During the prelude we have a wonderful establishing pan as the beautiful Donna Douglas (as self-absorbed and beautiful Laura Bellman) parades in front of a roomful of mirrors, smiling at herself. Even when the camera reveals her to be an old hag, she still sees herself as young and desirable when she peers into a mirror or a reflective window. She even dances dizzily through one such mirror, smashes the glass and dies. When we cut to

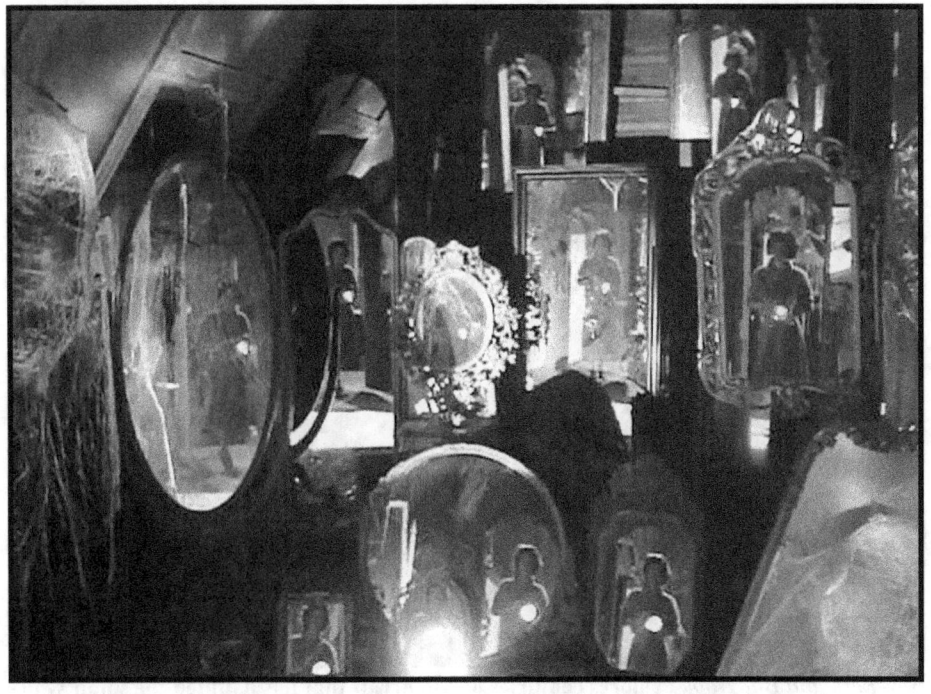

The haunting, other-worldly room of mirrors from *The Hungry Glass*

50th Anniversary Issue [1963-2013]

Gil (William Shatner) shields his wife's (Joanna Heyes) eyes from the ghostly apparation appearing before him in *The Hungry Glass*.

current times, Liz discovers the mysterious locked attic room that now houses all the missing mirrors, and when she enters the room of glass, Heyes cuts to a dramatic shot showing Liz reflected in all the mirrors at once. It is similar to the opening Donna Douglas shot, but this one is photographed in blackness with the mirrors, and a strange flash, becoming the only light source.

What makes the episode an intense horror classic is its slowly mounting horror. When young couple Gil and Maria celebrate their first night together in the new home (in the dark), Real Estate agent Adam and wife Liz help them celebrate, Adam uncorking a bottle of bubbly. However, the camera hones in on Liz' terrified face as she screams and points, causing Adam to cut his hand on the bottle that he accidentally breaks. The audience never sees what she sees, but we get a ghastly description. As soon as the couple leaves, Gil and Marcia get all cuddly as we zoom in on Gil's terrified expression, but this time we see the ghostly image he sees hovering in the distance inside the room. He shields his wife's eyes from gazing upon the ghostly figure. But the director makes sure we remain focused on William Shatner's intense stare.

Adding to the horror, Gil's back story involves the fact that he was a walking wounded of the Korean War, a soldier who suffered a mental meltdown, and that the illusions he sees might be a figment of his own relapse into mental illness. But after finding the room of mirrors, with Adam revealing the story of the Bellman tragedy to Gil, the audience pretty much patches all the pieces together. During *The Hungry Glass*' final act, we have the exciting climax featuring Marcia, who like Laura Bellman before her, gravitates toward the mirror room, becoming its unwary victim. When the men race upstairs hearing Marcia's screams after she is left alone in the room, Gil arrives and finds ghostly figures pulling Marcia into the netherworld. Reacting more instinctually than rationally, Gil smashes the mirror with a sharp metal object, shattering the glass all over the attic. Adam arrives and pulls him aside, telling Gil to look down at his feet. On the floor, bloodied and lifeless, is Marcia, the victim of the attack. Whether Gil murdered a defenseless wife or saved her from being taken by force to the parallel universe, he will never truly know. The only thing that is certain is that the house and its ghostly occupants claimed the life of his wife, much like a century before it claimed the life of Laura Bellman.

Amazingly, star William Shatner, pushing 30 in 1960, would 50 years later be starring in his own situation comedy on television, not looking much worse for wear half a century later. He even turned up on this year's Oscar Awards, revisiting Captain Kirk in a broad spoof with Seth MacFarlane. The often ham-fisted actor, disparaged unfairly for far too long, submits a very effective performance as Gil, the shell-shocked veteran who faints dead away in the middle of the episode. Yet his high-strung character wins our sympathy and earns our respect, even after he breaks the mirror and is most likely responsible for the death of his wife. *The Hungry Glass* demands we keep the lights on and reminds us, over 50 years later, what is means to be frightened by effective photography, art direction and directorial style. This one still curdles the blood today.

One of the best examples of Old World vs. New World ethics is illustrated in *Hay-Fork and Bill-Hook*, the second episode in the series directed by Herschel Daugherty, for me *Thriller*'s most consistent director

Hay-Fork and Bill-Hook explores centuries of witchcraft that has haunted the small Wales community of Dark Falls. In the opening, a hedge-cutter becomes the first new victim.

Nesta (Audrey Dalton) finds the omnipresent homeless dog to be her best friend in discovering the truth of the horror in *Hay-Fork and Bill-Hook*.

of the horror episodes. Working from a screenplay by Alan Calilou, who also plays Sir Wilfred in the episode, the tale takes place in the rural outskirts of Wales in the not-so-quaint village of Dark Falls and focuses upon the perceived horrors these villagers project upon the big, evil city. As village constable Sir Wilfred reveals, Dark Falls thrives within the dementia of witchcraft where the ancient Druids carried out their ritualistic sacrifices over 1,000 years ago. Half of the villagers had relatives who were hanged for burning so-called witches, or had relatives burned alive in wicker baskets as witches. So within this demented little hamlet we have warring factions of people who fear the return of witchcraft to their rustic community. The story starts as a loony hedge-cutter is brutally murdered by an unseen assailant who wields a hay-fork (pitch fork), ramming it through the elderly man's chest, finally finishing the job using another tool to carve an "x" in his throat. People of Dark Falls recognize this as the ritualistic murder of witches. Shortly thereafter newly married Londoner Detective Harry Roberts (Kenneth Haigh), and wife Nesta (Audrey Dalton) arrive to find another old woman burned to death within the still-standing Druid altar, her smoldering body found inside a wicker laundry basket stolen from the home of Sir Wilfred.

The complex family histories reveal grandparents who died in similar manners and whose heirs carry on the curse. Into this mix comes the realization that Sir Wilfred's father, an aristocrat who died in an insane asylum, had a love affair with a commoner, but he was never allowed to marry her. But he fathered a child by her, and the current village policeman Constable Evans (Alan Napier) is unaware that he is both a bastard and the brother of Wilfred. The elderly Mother Evans (Doris Lloyd) knows this secret but rightfully keeps it quiet. In the village of Dark Falls, city dwellers are pitted against country folk, the commoners against the aristocracy, and the modern scientific ways (using fingerprints to solve murders) vs. the old ways (people who mock scientific police investigation).

Detective Roberts puts the military on the case, having them scan the rural grounds to find the murder victim's watch using headphones and metal detectors. When the watch is found, the detective pretends to ship the watch off to Scotland Yard, to dust for fingerprints. He announces to all the locals that the watch will be held safely at the local post office overnight. Of course the detective knows that the murderer will strike by attempting to steal the watch. While Roberts sneaks into the bushes and awaits the killer's arrival, his wife Nesta remains alone at the Inn (where she has now seen a ghostly black cat twice, an omen of death). When Mother Evans arrives to visit Nesta, her son the Constable follows close behind, the audience quick to figure out that Constable Evans is the murderer (in his initial dramatic entrance at the beginning of the episode, he is wielding a hay-fork, so this disclosure is none too surprising). Evans and his mother lock Nesta in a wicker basket that they drag outside to the Druid ruins, planning to burn her to death as a witch. However, Sir Wilfred, wielding a bill-hook (a scythe), battles the hay-fork-wielding Constable in a battle to the death. At the conclusion a mysterious black dog leads Detective Roberts to his wife, but will he arrive in time?

Thriller's limited budget (the moody backdrop displaying the Druid stones is obviously a matte painting) resulted in producing an episode thick with darkness and mood, as the white mist rolls in over the Stonehenge-like Druid altar. Surrounded by dense woods, the setting was tailor-made for horror cinema. Even with the use of the matte painting, director Herschel Daugherty weaves a marvelous visual blend accented by Jerry Goldsmith's musical score. *Hay-Fork and Bill-Hook* is devilishly entertaining and contains enough suspense and mystery to maintain its web of horror. It's a terrific entry.

Moving on, remember how Hollywood negated the supernatural element from many horror movies of the 1920s and even 1930s, explaining away all the ghostly or undead elements in the film's final moments?

The giant Master Styx (Richard Kiel) terrifies in *Well of Doom*.

Master Styx and Henry Daniell as the silent film-inspired Squire Moloch, from *Well of Doom*, one of the series' darker and yet surprising episodes.

Perhaps *Mark of the Vampire*, the 1935 MGM horror classic starring Bela Lugosi, is the best example to illustrate that trend. The audience believes that Lugosi and his bat-like daughter are actually vampires, until in the film's final moments we observe that Lugosi was merely a stage performer who removes his make-up and speaks of how he was hired to frame the actual murderer and frighten him into confessing. One excellent *Thriller* follows this same thread, but instead of the gimmick lessening the episode's impact, it only enhances it. We are referring to *Well of Doom*, directed by John Brahm from a screenplay by Donald S. Sanford, based upon a short story by John Clemons. This episode clearly illustrates the strengths that made *Thriller* the classic TV series it became. First, using studio sets for exteriors, the soundstage is covered in dark shadows with eerie fog rolling over the scraggly trees and shrubs approaching some sort of decaying structure that houses evil. We also have *Thriller*'s outstanding supporting player Henry Daniell in perhaps his best characterization, as Squire Moloch, in a make-up resembling Lon Chaney's make-up from *London After Midnight* (the original version of *Mark of the Vampire*), even wearing a similar hat. Added to the mix is monstrous giant Richard Kiel as Master Styx, Moloch's cutthroat assistant. And to add even more villainy, we have Torin Thatcher as the haughty servant Mr. Teal. With basically a five-person cast, interest is maintained in a tense story of deception and revenge.

The story concerns playboy aristocrat Robert Penrose (Ronald Howard) accused of squandering the family fortune, who finally promises to settle down by marrying Laura Dunning (Fintan Meyler). He has been estranged from the family butler Mr. Teal, but the two reconcile and Teal attends the pre-marriage "stag" party to keep Penrose from embarrassing himself. Along the nightmarish journey, passing through part of the estate that is off-limits, the car is waylaid and the driver killed by the sudden appearance of giant Styx and his master Squire Moloch (who also resembles any number of characters from silent Germanic cinema). While Moloch declares himself the devil and exercises magic powers (torches light with the snap of a finger and his pointing a finger at the fleeing Teal results in his death), he later declares that he was the man who originally owned the Penrose property and was murdered by Robert's father, who drowned him by throwing him down the well of doom in the family block prison house. Moloch wants Robert to sign over the family estate and fortune, or he will have Master Styx murder the also kidnapped bride-to-be. In every haunting sequence Henry Daniell has never been better. With a blacked out missing tooth, fright-wig hair and sagging, wrinkly face, he is the very image of corruption and evil. His sourpuss grimaces and leering smiles, accented by deep-throated enunciation, makes him one of *Thriller*'s greatest villains ever.

As soon as Penrose signs over his estate, instead of freeing the captive, Moloch has Styx pick up the victim and throw him down the well, hopefully killing him. But Penrose prepared for such deception by erecting a cloth rope held by steel spikes to allow him to climb up out of the well and rescue Laura. After emerging from the well, dripping wet, battered and bruised, Penrose hears laughter and discussion above. While hiding in the shadows, he finds Teal alive as Styx and Moloch are removing make-up and demanding payment for their little ruse. When Moloch demands the pay-off money, Teal shoots and kills him, but as he lies dying, Moloch fires his own gun killing Teal. When Penrose appears from the shadows, Styx is terrified that the man has returned from the dead and the giant falls down the steep stone steps to his death. Penrose, of course, rescues Laura and they make good their escape.

The make-up used for Squire Moloch reminds the viewer of Lon Chaney's make-up from *London After Midnight*, and for good reason.

Yes, Styx and Moloch turn out to be actors, much like Lugosi and Carol Borland in *Mark of the Vampire*, but Daniell's performance as Moloch is a stunner and one that drips with malice and otherworldly evil. Before the eventual reveal, audiences would have loved to see a series of movies starring Daniell as Squire Moloch. His performance is that good. And with the creepy fog-shrouded woods and the prison housing the well of doom, *Thriller* has produced a gripping horror episode that resonates long after the end credits. For 1961, horror television could not get any better than this first season of *Thriller*.

Though it is not as easily recognizable, *The Devil's Ticket*, directed by Jules Bricken from a script by Robert Bloch, based upon Bloch's own story, is one terrific tale of terror and ambivalent morality. Macdonald Carey, with those bugged-out eyes and hangdog expression, is perfect as our corrupted hero Hector Vane, a poor but struggling artist whose wife Marie (Joan Tetzel) stands by his side. He goes to the pawn shop to try to get $10 for one of his latest paintings, but he finds the regular shop owner gone, replaced by a flamboyant new owner (John Emery).

This change in ownership is depicted in the episode's pre-credits sequence, where a sneaky Mr. Spengler (Robert Cornthwaite) closes his shop early so no one will knock, any would-be patrons believing that he already left for the evening. Spengler is counting thousands of dollars on his countertop. Hearing a bell tinkle at his door, Spengler throws the door open to a storefront of billowing fog and a stray cat who enters the establishment. In a sequence similar to one in *Alien*, the cat at first recoils in fear but then hisses with aggression, looking at the other door, the rear one. A satanic voice echoes the pawnbroker's name and states that it is time. The door flies open and Spengler reluctantly walks to meet his fate out the back door, which slams shut as fog flows beneath the door's bottom and a scream erupts outside. Of course actor John Emery becomes the new shop owner, a man we soon recognize as the devil himself.

The irony of the ending of *The Devil's Ticket* is telegraphed by the large sign in the pawn shop; artist Hector Vane (Macdonald Carey), right, approaches the flamboyant pawn shop owner, played by John Emery.

The new pawnbroker admires a realistic shoe painting done by Vane, but he refuses to offer the artist-at-wit's-end any money, instead saying he will offer the painter fame and financial success in exchange for his soul. Vane has less than one month to paint a portrait of the person whose soul will go to the devil, or the devil will claim Vane's soul. The screenplay always manages to inform the audience of exactly how many days are left until April 5 arrives, when he must deliver the painting no later than sunset. The story develops in an interesting direction. Vane, who is loved by his beautiful wife, is now tempted by one of his artist's models, a true temptress Nadja (Patricia Medina), who seduces the artist and insists they go off together to Mexico. Of course we discover that she is the devil's plaything and accomplice, trying to blacken Vane's soul before the devil claims it. Director Bricken juxtaposes many sequences where Vane and his wife embrace, and suddenly we cut to Vane and Nadja embracing. But pathetic Hector Vane is fooled before resigning himself to giving up his own soul or sacrificing the soul of an unaware wife.

The day of April 5 arrives and the proud Vane has his painting covered as he and his wife commit to one another all over again, Nadja becoming a rejected relic of the past (although she does destroy Vane's painting of his wife before the breakup). Almost oversleeping, the pawnbroker comes to Vane's home at sunset to claim his prize. Vane is very proud of himself for painting the devil himself, outsmarting ultimate evil, or as he says, giving the devil his due. Even the pawnbroker admits that he has been

John Emery's demonic stance reveals him to be Satan, the taker of human souls, from *The Devil's Ticket*.

In the creepy *Parasite Mansion*, Lollie (Beverly Washburn) is believed to be possessed.

cleverly outsmarted, but not quite … The devil demands that his pawnbroker ticket be delivered to him personally to officially pay off the debt, but wife Joan admits that she burned her husband's old coat and bought him a new one. The devil breaks into laughter while Vane, again outsmarted, recoils in fear, as the devil spreads his hands high, ready to claim another victim while Joan, forced out of the room, listens and watches in horror as the fog billows out from beneath the door!

The Devil's Ticket does not receive the buzz or acclaim that the better known *Thriller* horror entries garner, and the episode is definitely not the scariest one by far, but what this entry offers is a minutely detailed character analysis of a man desperate to make ends meet financially. When he feels caught between a rock and a hard place, he sells his soul to the devil and then wages the internal battle of whether to allow himself to burn in Hell or select some bystander to take his place. In a plot filled with subtle humor and irony, the intelligence of the script and the performances make *The Devil's Ticket* a standout in the series.

The very next week *Thriller* offered another outstanding horror entry, *Parasite Mansion*, directed by Herschel Daugherty from an adapted script by Donald S. Sanford (based upon a short story by Mary Elizabeth Counselman). This is one of those excellent claustrophobic *Thriller* entries where the action occurs on only a few sets and the cast is minimal. This is the type of template for which *Thriller* won accolades and is best remembered today. Just take the pre-credit sequence. We watch a car driving at night in the heart of a tremendous thunderstorm, the background illuminated by lightning streaks. The car, moving woefully slowly, still manages to drive down an embankment, injuring the female driver who falls into unconsciousness. In the misty background's flickering lightning we observe the haunted mansion that holds terrible secrets. The rain erupts in wind-blown torrents as the car headlights provide ominous lighting. What outstanding cinematography and mood has already been generated, and this is before the story even begins.

Members of a creepy, dysfunctional family appear at the scene of the car crash. The father figure Victor Harrod, a man frenzied and heavily boozing, carries the beautiful blonde, Marcia Hunter (Pippa Scott), inside the mansion, keeping her sedated. Members of the family decide her fate. The always-reliable Jeanette Nolan plays Granny Harrod, in heavy make-up and white fright wig. The children include Tommy Noland as frightened and gun crazy Rennie, the renegade brother who takes pop shots at Marcia to keep her from leaving the household. Hidden away in an attic bedroom we later find Lollie (Beverly Washburn), the barefoot child who is either the victim of violent stigmata or possessed by demons. She is the one family member that causes the others to decide that Marcia can never leave the household alive.

The Harrold clan has been plagued by a curse for generations and Lollie is the latest family member to be a victim of unexplained bloody gashes that suddenly appear on her face or limbs. And at the same time small objects float around her, seemingly without rhyme or reason. The family assumes that the resident demon possesses her and the family believes that Lollie must be sequestered in the attic room, the family forced to protect their "sin" at any cost. Only the livewire Granny cackles and breaks into hysterical laughter during these haunting events, giving the audience

Lollie appears terrified by her innate ability to levitate objects and fling them through the air, but the question arises, is Lollie controlling such powers?

The always reliable Jeanette Nolan plays Granny Harrold, who holds the ultimate secrets of *Parasite Mansion*.

the most unsettling and visually horrifying manner possible, where set design, direction and cinematography mean more than plot. But when it comes to visual storytelling, *Thriller* does not get much better than *Parasite Mansion*.

Thriller frequently investigated the inherent horror to be found when looking into a mirror, and everyone references *Thriller*'s classic episode *The Hungry Glass* as the perfect example of exploiting such horrors. But, to be honest, *The Prisoner in the Mirror*, although not as masterfully crafted, is still an exceptional episode. Directed by the too often unheralded Herschel Daughtery from a screenplay by Robert Arthur, *The Prisoner in the Mirror* builds upon a very haunting premise. One of the episode's flaws is that its money shot occurs in a pre-credits sequence and nothing in the episode quite lives up to that initial shock. However, the show does contain many well-crafted, terrifying sequences. The episode starts as Marquis Robert de Chantenay (David Frankham) wines and dines a beautiful blonde 200 years ago. Presenting her with a beautiful necklace, his arms extending to place it around her neck, the Marquis' expression turns deadly dangerous, as his face becomes an illuminated skull and his extended arms bones. Within seconds the girl is dead, strangled to death, but this horrid deed is not the action of the Marquis but of the evil Count Cagliostro, whose spirit possesses the body of the Marquis. Cagliostro is on a murdering rampage and he has found a way to both protect himself from prosecution and to live perhaps eternally. The secret lies in

more than a hint that all the problems lie within her.

As was usual with the haunted house episodes that *Thriller* excelled at, *Paradise Mansion* is wonderfully photographed by John L. Russell and scored dramatically by Morton Stevens (in an era where Jerry Goldsmith earned most of the praise for *Thriller*'s marvelous musical scores). The set decoration by John McCarthy, Jr. and William Stevens must also be noted. The house is dripping in visual horror. Poor hostage Marcia earns our sympathy and we feel for the innocent teacher who is told more than once that she will never leave the house alive. Even if she does escape, odd duck Rennie is usually lying in wait to ambush her at unexpected times. But the reveal is a creepy one where we learn that Granny is the one with the special powers of levitation and that she makes it appear that Lollie is the poltergeist-possessed "bad seed" to enact revenge for wrongs committed against Granny's side of the family. In a wonderful frightening sequence, Granny makes objects around her levitate, including a dagger on the floor that floats right into her open hand. During this creepy course of events, Granny's make-up becomes even more horrific while her wrinkles deepen and her eyes become black slits as the old woman rants, while she is about to stab Marcia to death. Only the intervention of Rennie saves her as a lantern catches Granny's dress on fire and the old hag runs down the mansion's huge staircase, eventually burning to death.

Paradise Mansion excels by virtue of its visual decadence and mood. This episode does not feature any marvelous performances, except perhaps Jeannette Nolan's Granny. The story is rather predictable and the episodes rather stereotypical. But just like those wonderful campfire ghost stories from the days of our youth, this *Thriller* is nothing more than a creepy ghost story presented to perfection in

The body-hopping Count Cagliostro uses a supernatural mirror to keep himself alive eternally, from *The Prisoner in the Mirror*.

the full-length mirror that the Marquis peers into before he jumps off the balcony to his death. Before taking his life, he paints over the mirror's surface with black paint.

In modern day America Professor Harry Langham (Lloyd Bochner), a scholar studying the antics of serial killing Count Cagliostro, finds the Count's mirror in France and has it delivered to his home in America. With it still blackened and painted over, Langham scrapes some of the paint away and is startled by the appearance of a beautiful brunette staring at him from the other side of the mirror. Langham keeps the secret from his fiancée Kay (Marion Ross) and her brother Fred (Jack Mullaney). As Langham sits in his chair before the mirror, a mysterious man within the mirror's reflection does a chant with a candle and beckons Langham to enter the mirror (while his unconscious body remains seated in the chair). Once he traps Langham inside the small black room within the mirror, the old man reveals himself as Count Cagliostro (Henry Daniell, in another classic villainous performance), stating once he snares a human victim inside the mirror he is able to possess that man's physical body outside and thus continue his killing spree. Whenever the authorities threaten, Cagliostro can return inside the mirror and allow the possessed human to face all the consequences.

The Cagliostro-possessed Langham gives Marion the physical attention that she desires but did not receive from the workaholic Langham. But even more powerful than his sexual drive is his lust for murder, and Marion faces the sequences of being seduced, not by her actual lover, but by fiend Cagliostro inhabiting Langham's body. And of course brother Fred gets involved in the mayhem. By the story's end people are dead and the mirror is smashed. With a rather abrupt and not clearly resolved end, the audience is never sure if the real Langham is freed from the mirror or

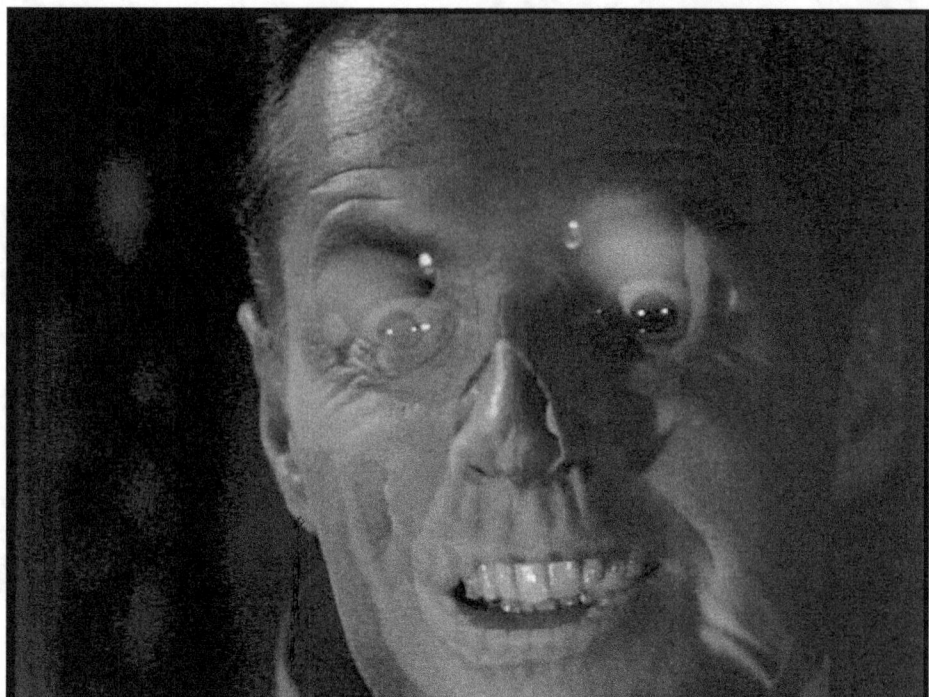

Stellar performance is merged with well-crafted make-up and superimposition photography to achieve the effect of demonic human possesion in *The Prisoner in the Mirror*.

remains trapped inside forever. Unlike the superior *The Hungry Glass*, *The Prisoner in the Mirror*, while wickedly inventive, never quite smoothes out some of the rough screenplay edges that would produce an even more satisfying story.

But Lloyd Bochner in a dual role—playing the repressed and obsessed professor and his hedonistic, Id-driven double—creates two diverse and thoroughly believable characters. As always the magnificent Henry Daniell plays Count Cagliostro as he needs to be played—deadly serious, manipulative, seductive and evil to the core. Wearing period costume and wig, it is always Daniell's stone cold face that carries his performance, that and his deep rhythmic voice. Director Herschel Daugherty effectively conveys the claustrophobia of being trapped within a mirror, and the suspense builds as Bochner watches his evil twin commit horrible acts that he is powerless to alter. This sense of helplessness goes a long way to amp up the tension to classic, horrific dimensions. Even though *The Prisoner in the Mirror* is generally not noted as one of the classic *Thriller* episodes, it is indeed a superior entry and one scary ride.

Season one of *Thriller* ended with a one-two knockout punch, the first episode being the fan favorite *Pigeons from Hell*, directed by John Newland (creator of TV's *One Step Beyond*), from a screenplay written by John Kneubuhl based upon an

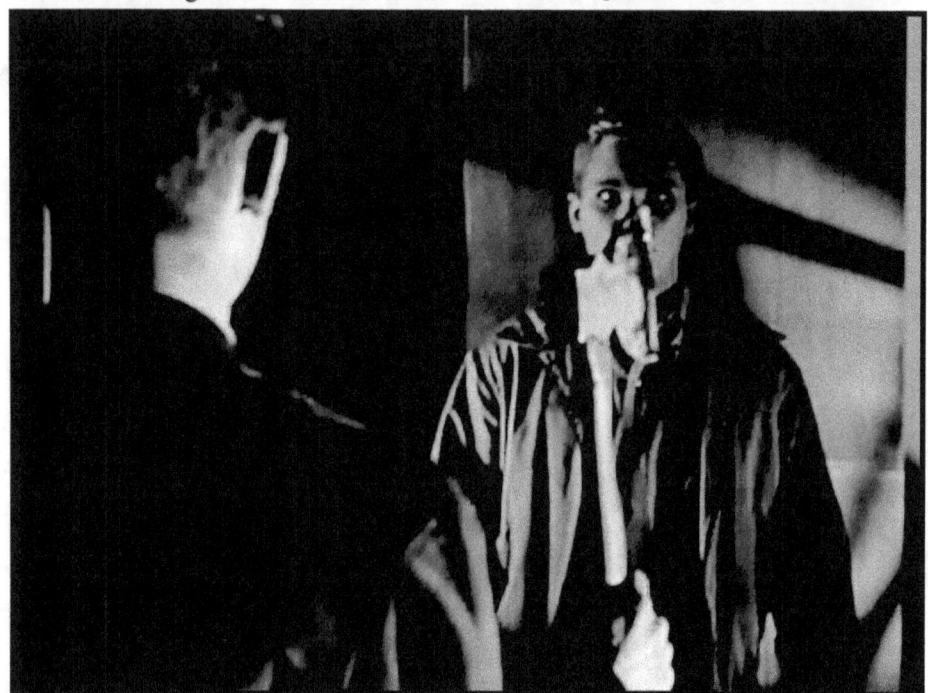

Brother Tim (Brandon De Wilde) confronts axe-wielding Johnny (David Whorf) in the middle of the night, from *Pigeons from Hell*.

One of the rotting, decaying sisters whose ghost holds the secret of the evil mansion, from *Pigeons from Hell*.

original story by Robert E. Howard. The screenplay, from my point of view, is a tad busy and more complex than it need be, but when it comes to the cinematography of Lionel Lindon and the direction by John Newland, this classic haunted house episode is perhaps the best entry in the series, along with *The Hungry Glass*. When it comes to black and white atmospheric horror, this 50-minute episode chills the blood most effectively. The visually told tale concerns two young college-age brothers, Tim (Brandon De Wilde) and Johnny (David Whorf), traveling the South exploring swampland plantation history. When their car breaks down, the boys yank their sleeping bags to the seemingly deserted Blassenville plantation mansion, where they bed down. In the middle of the night young Tim hears a scream upstairs, and when he ventures up, he sees brother Johnny in a trace-like state, holding an axe in hand, with blood running down his head. Tim runs out of the house and collapses, as Sheriff Buckner (Crahan Denton) comes to his aid and takes him to a dilapidated shack to regain his senses. Returning to the mansion, the duo find Johnny dead, face down in his sleeping bag. When he is turned over, in a clever creepy moment, Johnny's hand seems to grasp the axe in death. Of course the sheriff at first blames Tim for his brother's death, but as the supernatural events unwrap at the mansion, the sheriff realizes Tim is also a victim. The duo venture back up the stairs armed with one gun (the sheriff's) and one lantern, and TV's most pulse-pounding sequences unfold in a suspenseful slow-building manner. As the pair moves from the hall into one of the inner rooms, the lantern dims and dies out. No draft exists and the lantern's dimming seems to be nothing more than a supernatural occurrence, creeping out the audience. A great deal of the episode deals with such nocturnal wanderings. The story becomes overly complex when we learn of three sisters, two who left the house, with one remaining, and a family curse involving a half sister that was never acknowledged as being a family member. This evolves into a zombie sub-plot involving an old black man who lives in another dilapidated shack who reveals the dark powers lurking in the mansion, since he once worked there. In a brief yet quite impressive tour-de-force performance, Jacob Blount (Ken Renard) explains the family curse quite dramatically and dies a sudden death when a snake emerges from the fireplace to bite him, as he screams his head off in pain and fear. The entire episode is bathed in darkness and John Newland maintains a sense of dread and foreboding.

The final time the sheriff and Tim return to the mansion the secret of the mansion is solved, involving the discovery that one of the sisters has remained living in the mansion and that it is she who wields the axe and commits murder. And in a most iconic moment, the episode closes by focusing on the demented, ancient face of a crazed old woman. For me the story is too busy for its own good, but when the episode creates chills and a sense of visual fear, *Pigeons from Hell* is landmark television. Even the initial sequence of Johnny approaching the mansion, seeing flocks of pigeons on the front lawn, and finally being attacked by the birds, foreshadows Alfred Hitchcock's *The Birds* by a good two years.

The season's final episode, *The Grim Reaper*, is another excellent entry, sending season one home in dandy style. *Thriller*'s ace-in-the-hole director, Herschel Daugherty, returns with a story by Harold

The climax of *Pigeons from Hell* involves the discovery of the axe-wielding surviving sister who wants to claim one more victim.

Paul Graves (William Shatner) displays blood on his fingers after touching the portrait of *The Grim Reaper*.

Lawlor, adapted for the series by Robert Bloch. Once again the pre-credits sequence rivals the climax for its gripping sense of dread. In this tense prologue, we have father Pierre Radin (the always exciting Henry Daniell) looking for his missing artist son. The artist is infamous for painting monsters and creatures from the supernatural, and when the father and landlord open the son's locked apartment, they gawk at the shadow of him swinging in death from the rafters.

Once again, as *Thriller* tends to do after introducing the action in the past, the story moves to the present, as the huge Gothic painting of the skeletal Grim Reaper, shouldering his scythe, has found a home in the house of eccentric mystery writer Bea Graves (Natalie Schafer). The incredible painting commands the room in which it has been hung, lumbering overhead as an angel of death. Bea's only living blood relative, Paul Graves (a nicely high-pitched William Shatner), comes for a visit because he loves his aunt. Or so he says. Bea has recently married smarmy Gerald (Scott Merrill), and Paul thinks Gerald only wants Aunt Bea's money. Bea's beautiful secretary is Dorothy (Elizabeth Allen) and it seems Gerald has his eye on her and she in turn might be attracted to him. Gerald is many years younger than the elder Bea. Soon the tone darkens as we learn that the formerly kooky and comical Aunt Bea is in fact haunted by her bad marriage and she gradually slips into alcoholism.

Overly dramatic Paul shares the grim history and curse of the painting, stating whenever the Grim Reaper is ready to claim another victim that actual blood forms on the scythe in the painting. To prove his point Paul appears to touch the blade in the painting and pulls his hand away, revealing blood dripping from his fingertips (as the musical score swells). Soon Aunt Bea is found dead, a victim of a terrible drunken fall down the stairs. And the mystery intensifies as the audience struggles to figure out who among the three remaining dwellers in this creepy house is good or evil. Gerald, of course, will inherit everything, but he seems to lust after Dorothy more than over the estate and all its wealth. We wonder if Dorothy and Gerald were plotting Aunt Bea's death. However, the real bastard turns out to be Paul, who says he created the curse of the painting (and later admits to faking the dripping blood appearing on the scythe) to set up his aunt's death. Now Paul admits to poisoning Gerald realizing that he, the last living heir, will inherit Gerald's wealth. However, at the episode's end, the Grim Reaper literally disappears from the canvas, and in a subjective point of view finale, the camera becomes the Reaper as Paul, in livid horror, backs away but is trapped in the room as the Reaper approaches. As Paul finally stumbles and falls, we see a quick flash of metal as the blade dives downward toward Paul, his throat slashed by the Reaper, who now returns to the painting, but with fresh blood dripping from his blade.

The effective over-the-top performance by William Shatner, aided by the wonderful point-of-view cinematography by Bud Thackery, further enhanced by minimal sound effects and a gushing musical score by Jerry Goldsmith, makes this climax a chilling one. For TV family audiences in 1961, episodes such as *The Grim Reaper* were cutting edge and very adult in nature. But thankfully, in this gore-less era of visual filmmaking, the suggestion of a slit throat is so much more powerful than showing it to audiences. Atmosphere, lighting, music, sound effects and acting weave the web of horror that permeates this claustrophobic household of terror, making *The Grim Reaper* another exceptional supernatural episode of *Thriller*.

What is amazing is the utter force of execution that saturated each supernatural episode. This was not the monster-less television of *Men Into Space* or the straight science fiction or fantasy-satire-symbolism of the more cerebral *The Twilight Zone*. Nor was it the twisted fantastical presented as fact in both *Science Fiction Theatre* and *One Step Beyond*. Negating the mystery/crime episodes for the moment, when *Thriller* went the full-throttle horror route, the show delivered the majority of the time. Not only was the writing crisp and lean, but also the direction and cinematography produced a mood of unrelenting terror, buoyed by television veterans or Hollywood cast-offs that fully committed to their performances. The best horror episodes of season one of *Thriller* were dark, shadowy, haunting and passionate. No other primetime (or even syndicated) television program created the intense malaise that *Thriller* delivered. For children like me who were 10 to 12 years old when the series aired originally, *Thriller* was nightmarish, get-under-the-skin horrifying, and its images of horror stick to this day. The tone of the series wasn't Hammer (with classic monsters returning in bright and gaudy Technicolor) or even Poe/American International (with its iconic Vincent Price acting amid colorful cobwebs and decaying, antique furniture). If anything *Thriller* approximated, on a budget, the tone of Robert Wise's black-and-white classic *The Haunting* (to arrive about one year after the series' demise) with its character-driven stories (written or adapted from or by the best horror fiction writers of the time) of ghostly possession and haunted psyches, making the internal horrors of our broken lives external in ways that only ghosts, demons and the devil can. Though it lasted only two seasons, *Thriller* remains iconic television, still terrifying, over half a century later.

Lost Innocence, *Blood Demon* and Christopher Lee

by Stephen Mosley

It's the summer of 1967. The Beatles release their phenomenal *Sergeant Peppers' Lonely Hearts Club Band* album and hippies descend upon Haight Ashbury. But it isn't all peace and love, as race riots explode across America, giving the so-called Summer of Love another moniker—The Long Hot Summer.

While all this is going on, British actor Christopher Lee, now an international star (thanks to his mesmerizing roles in several Hammer horror films), is cramped in some small Munich studio, taking direction from Harald Reinl. They are filming *Die Schlangengrube und das Pendel*. The literal English translation of this title is *The Snake Pit and the Pendulum*. U.K. and U.S. audiences will eventually see the film as *Blood Demon*.

Someone may be reading this, scratching his or her head, thinking, "Hmmm, I think I've seen that one"—and it's very possible that they have, but under a different title. On DVD, in both the U.K. and U.S., the film is known as *Castle of the Walking Dead*, not to be mistaken for another Lee venture, Luciano Ricci's *Castle of the Living Dead* (1964). Readers may also have seen it as *The Snake Pit*—definitely not to be confused with Anatole Litvak's 1948 classic on the perils of mental illness.

Or maybe audiences tittered at its tame tortures and grotty photography when it came out disguised as *The Torture Chamber of Dr. Sadism* on late-night television? Actually, it's more than likely that I've just confused everyone now. Such are the vast array of title changes accorded to European Christopher Lee vehicles of the early-to-mid 1960s, making it easy to grow confused ... but that's another article. To avoid further confusion, I shall refer to the film herein under its original English-language title, *Blood Demon*.

The film is one of a clutch of atmospheric horrors Lee made in Europe during the early '60s, a list which includes Mario Bava's *The Whip and the Body* (1963), Camillo Mastrocinque's *Terror in the Crypt* (1963) and the aforementioned *Castle of the Living Dead*. It is also the first Gothic horror film to be made in Germany since the 1930s. This is fairly surprising, not only because the country was slow in joining the Gothic horror revival sparked by Hammer's late 1950s hits, but also because—with influential Expressionist classics such as *The Cabinet of Dr. Caligari* (1919), *The Golem* (1920) and *Nosferatu* (1921) hailing from there—Germany is arguably the birthplace of the horror film. And during that summer of 1967, as those Teutonic cameras roll, Lee must be experiencing a terrible sense of *déjà vu*, for not only is he draining virgins and muttering lines like, "The blood is the life," but the film itself plays like a virtual remake of superior genre entries.

Blood Demon opens as Lee's sinister character of Count Regula awaits judgment in some dank cell for killing 12 virgins. (More than one commentator has mentioned the name of Count Regula sounding like some kind of grim suppository aid, so I'll refrain from doing that here.) As Lee perches in his tiny cell, it being barely large enough to contain him (his knees almost touch his chin), the judge, played by former Tarzan Lex Barker in a wig and false moustache, pronounces sentence. Mere decapitation is too good for Lee, so only total dismemberment will do. He will be drawn-and-quartered in the village square. Naturally, Lee spits out a curse. He will take revenge, after-death, on the families of his prosecutor and families of his 13th would-be victim (played by the lovely Karin Dor). Logically, Barker and Dor assume the roles of their ancestors later on.

Once Lee has said his piece, a bulky chap in a red hood slams a spike-lined gold mask into his face. Because the mask has a weird smiling face on it, it looks faintly absurd. But it also looks disquieting; such

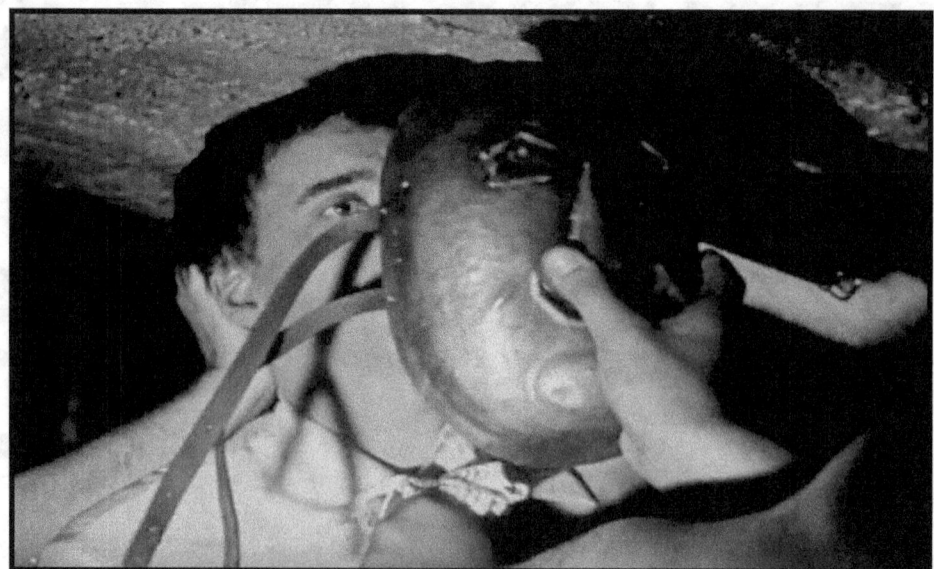
Count Regula (Christopher Lee) has the metal mask lowered on his face.

A German poster for *Blood Demon*

is the nature of many an image from our favorite horror films. The title credits roll superimposed over a shot of Lee being escorted to his fate. Pumping from the soundtrack is a delirious organ dirge full of pounding drums and scratchy brass. The credits inform us that what follows is based on Edgar Allan Poe's novel *The Pit and the Pendulum*. Ahem ... surely, they mean *short story*. Actually, it would make more sense to have a credit announcing: based on Terence Fisher's *Dracula, Prince of Darkness* (with additional bits inspired by Mario Bava's *Black Sunday* and Roger Corman's *Pit and the Pendulum*). But, hey-ho, let's get on with the show.

Ruddy-faced locals crowd around the village square, peering perversely as Lee lies tethered to four horses, squirming in hopeless frustration, raising his mask to the pale gray sky. The horses are released and run their separate ways. We cut politely to a crude illustration of the resulting dismemberment. We are now 35 years into the future and it's Good Friday, of all days. A one-legged chap, who looks like an aging Donald Pleasence in heavy character make-up, is standing in the same village square, declaiming the curious legend of the evil Count Regula and his grim execution. This nightmarish Hans Christian Andersen character type notices our hero Lex Barker among the spectators and hobbles after him to present an invitation to the Count's castle.

Like any good movie hero, Barker's character, bearing the typically heroic name of Roger, knows nothing about his family, where he came from or the place of his birth. So he's naturally intrigued by the letter's ominous promise that, if he accepts the invitation, he will learn more about his heritage. Besides, it doesn't look like he has anything better to do. He clambers into a carriage at once. Reflected in murky pools, the coach rattles across a deserted landscape. Arriving at a gloomy village, a bearded priest, Pater Fabian (played by Vladimir Medar), joins Barker. They set off together as a grimly staring crowd of hatchet-faced villagers watch on, their features clenched like punching fists. The carriage winds its way along more desolate vistas, up winding paths flanked by crumbling rocks, through autumnal forests of skeletal trees and picks up two female travelers—a Baroness (Karin Dor once again) and her servant Babette (played by Christiane Ruecker).

As it happens, the ladies are also en route to Count Regula's castle, but merely as thrill-seekers. They've heard old Donald's stories in the square and, much like certain film fans, are keen to visit the locations of these terrible crimes. With the girls in tow, the coach delves deeper into the haunted forest as thin mists gather by the horses' legs. The driver looks up to see blue-gray human limbs and heads poking from the gnarled, crow-infested trees like bizarre growths. Night deepens, darkness falls and the carriage rolls along. Above, a profusion of limp, hanging bodies descends from the trees. It's enough to give the driver a heart attack as he falls from his perch, clutching his chest. As the carriage halts, the gents climb out and see their dead driver lying in the dirt. Nonplussed, they witness their strange surroundings for the first time. As the men ogle the corpse-filled forest, a waxen-faced fiend with red-rimmed eyes lurks in the shadows, watching. He takes possession of the carriage. With the girls inside, the fiend escapes, thrashing the horses.

Before being drawn-and-quartered in the village square, the defiant Count Regula spits out a curse.

Aboard the coach we encounter Roger (Lex Barker) and the Baroness (Karin Dor)

The men pursue on foot. Traipsing through a graveyard of crooked tombs, they arrive at Count Regula's castle and enter the feared building. Inside, the men are greeted, if that is the word, by the Count's candelabra-clutching manservant Anatol (played by Carl Lange). As we've probably guessed, Anatol is the waxen-faced, red-eyed bloke who stole the travelers' carriage.

Reunited with the ladies, the chaps are offered refreshment—which turns out to be acid. This so enrages Fabian, the bearded priest, that he tears off his cassock and produces a pistol. In fact, he's so irate that he reveals (surprise!) that he's not really a Monsignor but a crafty thief. Nonetheless, Anatol knocks back a goblet of the acidy stuff without complaint. It doesn't seem to do him any harm. And then he sneaks away with Babette down some shadowy passage. Our heroes give chase and find poor Babette gagged and bound to an X-shaped frame, her screams muffled. She is slowly being lowered toward a floor lined with spikes.

Barker, remembering his Tarzan days, saves the girl in the nick of time and they make their way down deep-throated caves, along walls studded with skulls. The sinister servant Anatol reappears and tries to strangle Babette. She is saved, for the second time that evening, by the sudden appearance of Fabian. This time he's brandishing *two* pistols. He fires at the creepy servant, but the bullets have no effect. After a bout of maniacal laughter, Anatol says he'd like to introduce his estranged guests to the master (hooray!). They pass through a roomful of 12 nude women on slabs. These bloodless virgins are Lee's previous victims (the ones that *didn't* get away) and the straps that bind them to their slabs do double duty by tastefully concealing their exposed breasts.

We are led to a big glass coffin with a purple coverlet. The servant pulls the cloth away revealing the body that lies within. It's you-know-who at last. The Count is resurrected (more on this later) and Anatol takes his chance to shove Karin Dor into a conveniently placed Iron Maiden that stands nearby. Lee halts the proceedings. Apparently, an Iron Maiden is too good for Dor (it was certainly good enough for Barbara Steele). Lee is more interested in inflicting a slow, painful and lingering death. That's the spirit, Sir Christopher!

Lex Barker, meanwhile, has wandered off and succumbed to bursts of choking gas spat from the walls. He falls to the ground, teeth clenched, clutching his throat. In the Count's secret laboratory, Karin lies strapped to a rack, gasping, writhing and moaning. Above her, Lee looms. "It will be an agonizing death," he offers assuredly.

Then she is untied to witness Barker being tortured. This is the second time that Dor's long-awaited death has been halted by the Count. He reasons that he is inflicting fear by doing so. But my mind can't help drifting to the bungling criminal incompetence of Mike Myers' Dr. Evil character in the *Austin Powers* movies. Spying through a stone mask that affords a view of the chamber below, Dor sees Barker bound by ropes. A pendulum swings from above.

This is too much for Dor. In a gesture reminiscent of Gaston Leroux's Erik in *The Phantom of the Opera*, Lee allows her to run to Barker's aid, through a passage lined with horrors. She runs off screaming "Roger!" as vultures lurk and squawk within the rocks, picking at bloody carrion. Ungallantly thrown into the shot comes a vulture, obviously tossed by an off-screen hand.

The re-animated Count, Christopher Lee, now bears the marks left by his death mask.

The body of Count Regula lies in a glass coffin, the smiling mask still hammered onto his face, shortly before his resurrection.

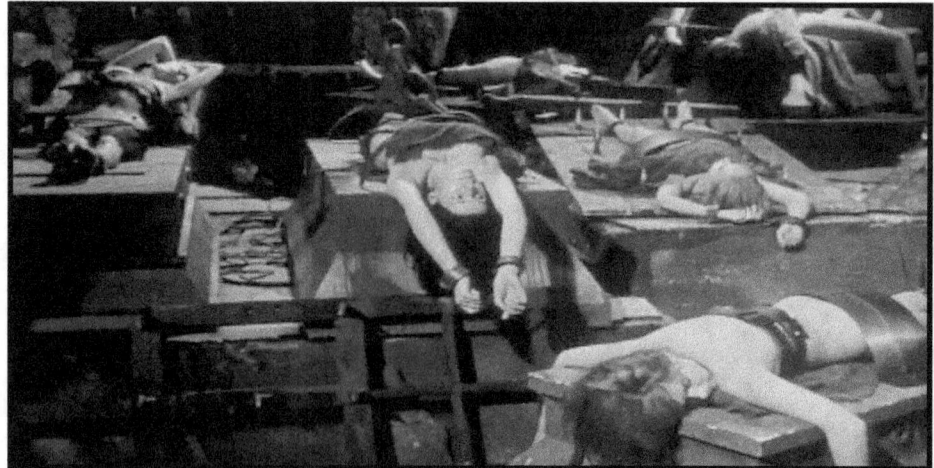

The roomful of 12 nude women on slabs, Regula's previous victims

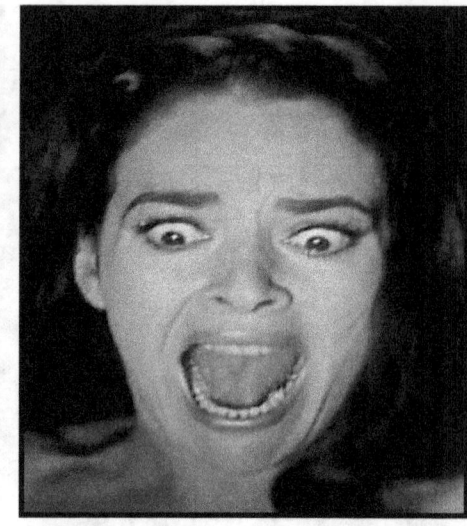

The Baroness (Karin Dor) screams during many sequences during the movie.

The poor bird thuds clumsily to the floor, spraying up clouds of dust and feathers. As if cruelty to birds of prey wasn't enough, Dor also has to contend with lizards on her bosom and tarantulas up her dress. She brushes them away, her dark eyes wide and peering, breasts heaving. Scorpions crawl down the walls as roaring mists of gas squirt through the fetid air, but onward she runs. She arrives at a snake pit. The reptiles' thick coils writhe slowly in the dirt, slithering among skulls and detached gray limbs—the remains of their previous victims. Dor finds herself standing on an ingenious plank above the pit. It slides away beneath her feet. She is just a hair's breadth from plunging when Anatol suddenly drags her from the edge. Her fear suitably increased, Dor is returned to Lee. Surely she's ripe for slaughter now?

Nope.

The Count just needs "a few more seconds" to complete his (slow) revenge. With Dor yet again strapped down, Lee lugubriously prepares the correct procedure for her death. The draining of her blood will be done, but not by sinking his teeth into her neck. No. That's child's play. Lee will instead use fiddly long tubes and a green liquid "concentrate" in a beaker to bleed her dry (the tubes I understand, but don't ask me what the green fluid does). As Lee and his assistant muck about with tubes and green potions, Barker has all the time he needs to escape the pendulum. He does this by using a rock (I could tell you how, but you wouldn't believe me). Such a rock also proved to be Lee's undoing in his final Hammer horror, *To the Devil, A Daughter* (1975). But the less said about that *grand* finale, the better.

Fabian, meanwhile, has caught up with Barker and they rush to save Dor. At Lee's laboratory, spiked iron shutters slam down as our heroes' approach. But thanks to a nifty bit of snaffling earlier in the evening, the thief has one thing that can save them—a crucifix. They waggle it in Lee's face and, inexplicably, the laboratory explodes. Through the parting smoke Lee comes at Barker with an axe. But it's all too late. The power of the cross has worked its magic. Like any good fairy tale, good has triumphed over evil. The corpses of Lee's victims finally become the skeletons that they ought to be after 35 years lying draped over slabs. Lee and his sinister manservant are reduced to slimy, putrid globs on the castle floor. Then the walls cave in. Showers of dust and rubble rain to the ground. The castle collapses.

The hero and heroine stand on the dying grass, embracing each other. Fabian links arms with Babette (where did she come from?) and they take the reins of a carriage. Barker and Dor climb inside to smooch. As the coach rumbles away, mists gather over the corpse of a dead black tree, its branches reaching out in failed capture of the receding vehicle. The film sputters to a close. The End.

So, other than the fact the film's not very long, why view *Blood Demon* again? Well, although by no means a classic, the film is often overlooked. Precious little has been written about it, and what has is mainly disparaging. For instance, the kindest comment Christopher Lee ever accorded the film, in his entertaining memoir *Lord of Misrule* (Orion Books, 2004), is that it is "perfectly dreadful." Steady on. Is it really that bad?

Well, it's not as bad as we are led to believe. A florid, offbeat fairy tale, it plays like a veritable greatest hits package of familiar Gothic imagery and, as such, if caught in the right mood, is a very worthwhile and entertaining late-night treat for genre fans, with many points of interest along the way.

Roger (Les Barker) prepares to escape the hideous swinging pendulum.

The Baroness, demonstrating a wide range of emotions, seems fascinated by the snake that she holds in her hand.

Foremost among those points of interest is the sumptuous production design of Gabriel Pellon and Werner Maria Achmann, which constantly reminds us we are in fairy tale land, dark, strange and elegant. The voyage to the castle is a justly celebrated example of their work. In a triumph of surreal Gothic imagery, the corpses that hang from the phantom trees are like strange decorations—gruesome, macabre and oddly beautiful. And there's not just one or two, the forest is *full* of them. The dark world in which the drama enfolds is convincing enough. For example, the Count's castle is overflowing with creaking gates and slamming shutters, everything lined with spikes. The gloomy chambers are more like caves. Torches burn from the walls, spreading dim light across the cracked stone floors. The walls are also festooned with paintings, fabulously grotesque, depicting oddly beaked figures involved in horrible acts, namely, the consummation of pale, naked figures. Vincent Price's Roderick Usher would love to stand back and admire such art. The decorative scheme is extended to the rest of the building. Similarly beaked figures haunt the castle's many dark corners as cobwebbed statues, thin-limbed and angular. A skeleton in a suit of armor guards one of the shadowy passageways and is just one of the slightly more normal accoutrements of Count Regula's castle. Such imagery is *Blood Demon*'s major attribute.

The movie is also worth watching, as is true of many films from this era, for its cast. We know all about Christopher Lee, but Karin Dor and Lex Barker are also more than watchable. A German actress, Dor (born 1938) made her name in such native, self-explanatory fare as *The Carpet of Horror* (1962), *Hotel Where Guests Are Killed* (1965) and *The Dismal Monk* (1965). Yes, these are real films, mostly based on Edgar Wallace stories. Best remembered by mainstream audiences as Helga Brandt, Dor was the redheaded she-villain of the 1967 James Bond caper *You Only Live Twice*. In one unforgettable scene she straps Sean Connery to a chair. Purring out threats, she slaps him, holds a surgical blade to his gulping throat and then finally seduces her prey. Memorably, Bond cuts the straps of her dress with the very knife that once imperiled him. Just as vivid, Donald Pleasence ends up feeding her to his piranhas. Dor resurfaced for her next assignment, *Blood Demon*. Perhaps she appeared as a favor to her husband Harald Reinl, the film's director?

Before the screams of nepotism ring out, however, it must be stated that Dor has a rightful place among the cast. She makes an appealing heroine, her dark-lined eyes and sensuous features are well-suited to the genre and I, for one, think it a shame that she graced no further Gothic productions, especially as the alluring villainy she displays in her one James Bond outing is a perfect illustration of the Hammer philosophy—what Terence Fisher termed "the attraction of evil." *Blood Demon* was a reunion of sorts for the actress. She had previously starred alongside Christopher Lee in *The Face of Fu Manchu* (1965) and collaborated with Barker and Reinl on the Fritz Lang-inspired thriller, *The Invisible Dr. Mabuse* (1961). After divorcing her director husband in 1968 (I hope *Blood Demon* didn't have anything to do with it), Dor returned to play the Cuban mistress of a French agent in Alfred Hitchcock's ill-received *Topaz* (1969). From Hitchcock she next worked with Paul Naschy, starring as Michael Rennie's alien lab assistant

The power of the crucifix results in Count Regula's slow, agonizing death.

Count Regula confronts Roger with his axe, as manservant Anatol (Carl Lange) looks on.

in *Dracula vs. Frankenstein* (1970, aka, *Assignment Terror*). In this movie, she was the girl fated to romance Naschy's El Hombre Lobo (well, someone had to do it). Dor's film appearances became less frequent from the late '70s onwards, where she mainly worked in television. In 2008, she returned to the stage in a play entitled *You Only Live Thrice*.

Lex Barker (born 1919), on the other hand, succeeded Johnny Weissmuller in the role of Tarzan at RKO. The actor reportedly offered an interpretation of the character that won approval from its creator Edgar Rice Burroughs. Barker played the yodeling vine-swinger in five films, beginning with *Tarzan's Magic Fountain* (1949) and culminating with *Tarzan and the She-Devil* (1954). Not only did Barker make five Tarzan movies, but he also married five times. One of those wives was Lana Turner, to whom the actor was married from 1953 to 1957. Barker had a second wind of fame in the 1960s in several European features, mainly Westerns and thrillers. By the time of *Blood Demon* in 1967, his steely, rugged demeanor was still on proud display. Unfortunately Barker died of a heart attack in 1973.

Another point in *Blood Demon*'s favor is that Christopher Lee's famous rumbling baritone is retained. As those who have seen English-language dubbed versions of his other European efforts will attest, this has not always been the case. Take *The Whip and the Body*, for example, where he speaks with someone else's American accent, or as the title character in Terence Fisher's German opus *Sherlock Holmes and the Deadly Necklace* (1962), where it's almost comical to see the ubiquitous, gaunt features of Christopher Lee speaking in a voice that is ... well ... slightly less robust. As for the actor's characterization, it pretty much falls into the mold of what we would expect at this interminable stage of his career. As is true of his 1960s movie persona, he drains virgins of blood, is wary of crucifixes and is concerned with vengeance and eternal life.

However, one startling moment occurs during the climax. When the Count is faced with the dreaded crucifix, he hisses impressively: "Destroy the cross! Throw it away; *throw it away!*" The effect is alarming as Lee rasps in a hoarse croak that we rarely hear him use, an instance of the actor trying to bring something new to his limited dialogue.

Also limited is the star's screen time. The movie is more than halfway over before Lee rises from the grave. *Blood Demon*, I'm afraid, follows the grand tradition of making audiences wait for our favorite monster's entrance (it takes half the movie to assemble Lee's Creature in *The Curse of Frankenstein;* there's a good deal of weird locals and nude dancing before he pops out from behind a chair in the 85-minute version of *The Wicker Man* [1972], and just think of any number of Dracula sequels in which we wonder impatiently at what point the star will make his first appearance). When he is finally resurrected, Lee's pale gray face looks extra long, almost as lengthy as the black frockcoat he dons (cloak-like enough to remind us of a certain Transylvanian nobleman). A fringed black wig sits on his head. Indeed, with his long nose, sad and dark eyes and furrowed brow, Lee reminds me somewhat of Peter Sellers, or rather, Sellers taking on Christopher Lee in a reverent spoof. (Incidentally, whether intentional or not, Sellers' silver-haired, mustachioed Nayland Smith character in his final film *The Fiendish Plot of Dr. Fu Manchu* reeks strongly to me of Lee, though, curiously, not his Fu.)

To get back on track, genre fans unfamiliar with *Blood Demon* may have fun observing its borrowings. We behold the first of the film's liberal echoes of previous genre entries in the pre-credit sequence when that odd, smiling mask is pushed onto the Count's face. Needless to say, this is a direct steal from the fantastic opening scene of Mario Bava's *Black Sunday* (1960), with Lee taking the place of genre favorite Barbara Steele. However, whereas in that classic film the mask was *hammered* into place, here the executioner merely slams it onto Lee's features with a single thrust of his bronze, well-muscled arm. Presumably the budget wouldn't stretch to include a mallet? (When the mask is finally removed, we expect to see Lee's familiar visage dotted with holes, like the golf courses that made the making of these films so worthwhile to the actor, but there's just a few marks visible.)

As already stated, I feel the film's biggest influence seems to be Terence Fisher's *Dracula, Prince of Darkness*. This influence extends to the characters: Count Regula is Dracula in all but name. Indeed, the odd-sounding name of Regula sounds suspiciously to me like scriptwriter Manfred Kohler's laziest way of finding a name that sounds slightly like Dracula, as if Regula will do for now and "I'll think of something better later." Only he never did. Similarly, Kohler's dialogue for the Count is just as lax and Draculean. "Welcome to my house," Lee intones to his guests, explaining that he needs to drain maidens because, "The blood is the life." And we've all heard that one before. Vladimir Medar's irreverent priest character, Pater Fabian, is obviously inspired by Andrew Keir's Van Helsing substitute Father Sandor character from Fisher's Dracula sequel. The personas of *Blood Demon*'s two female characters echo those of Suzan Farmer and Barbara Shelley from the same sequel. To put it bluntly, Karin Dor's Baroness is engaging and Christiane Ruecker's blonde serving girl is prim.

An illustration of their respective characters is best typified by their treatment on arriving at the castle. Karin Dor is revealed behind a revolving oil painting; seated at a piano, her graceful fingers run up and down the keys as she relaxes in a charming, décolletage-revealing dress. She

Les Barker and Karin Dor strike a dynamic pose in the cave of human skulls.

rises, fanning herself, and dips her arms willingly into snake-filled urns. One of the blighters entwines itself about her pale flesh (before she comes to her senses and flings the reptile away). She's quite happy to do such things, as Anatol has administered a "soothing" drug to her. Babette, on the other hand, has no such luck. She clumps into the room, clutching a tray of drinks. She merely remains a serving girl. No elegant gowns or musical instruments for her. Oh no. Nor does she deserve such finery, as she clumsily spills the proffered wine. But it's a good thing that she does, as, once spilled, this particular wine smokes and corrodes whatever it touches. This is one of Anatol's little jokes.

And speaking of Anatol, Carl Lange's sinister manservant is more than reminiscent of the character Klove, portrayed by Philip Latham, in yet another nod to Lee's second Dracula film. But whereas Klove, despite his idiosyncrasies, was most definitely human, the same cannot be said for Anatol. He mopes and stares from shadows—his eyes evil glint—and has a penchant for downing acid to no ill effect, a fierce dislike of crucifixes and a resistance to bullets. When Fabian shoots the old ghoul, Anatol just laughs, revealing the creamy square bones of his teeth. He proudly tears open his frilled shirt to display the ripped holes in his flesh as a thick green goop seeps out in place of blood. Then the wounds gradually heal, leaving the surface of his waxy skin smooth and unblemished once more. (Again, I think back to Christopher Lee's vampire pulling open *his* frilly shirt so that Suzan Farmer can lap up his blood, in one of *Dracula, Prince of Darkness*' most erotically charged scenes, one that many seem surprised to find intact in Bram Stoker's original 1897 novel.) Nowhere are Anatol's similarities to Klove more apparent than in the resurrection scene—the most deliberate of all of *Blood Demon*'s steals from Fisher's Dracula opus.

Remember the scene in *Dracula, Prince of Darkness* when the king vampire is finally revived? Anatol's Hammer equivalent Klove stabs one of the guests from behind and hangs the dead weight over Lee's stone sarcophagus. Then Klove slits his throat. An outpouring of stodgy crimson splashes out over the ashes, mixing with the powdery embers like some kind of revolting milkshake. *Et viola*—instant vampire. It's interesting to compare the equivalent scene in *Blood Demon*. Here, Anatol slits his wrist with a mangy-looking blade, dripping yet more of his thick green blood. It spatters across Lee's mask, and that's all it takes. The Count's limbs twitch to life (and reattach themselves, I assume). Karin Dor backs away, her hand on her breast. The Count's own chest rises, followed by his shadow on the wall. We are thus spared the gruesome sight of that spiked mask being plucked from his face.

Elsewhere, homage is paid to Fisher as the *Blood Demon* credits roll—Lee, arms bound behind his back, donning a frilly white shirt, is led to his execution in

Christopher Lee (left), as the Count, receives his sentence by the judge (Lex Barker), as the red-hooded executioner stands by holding the spike-lined gold mask, which will be shoved into his skull.

shots reminiscent of Peter Cushing's Baron being escorted to the gallows at the close of Fisher's *The Curse of Frankenstein* (1956). Likewise, the bubbling beakers that fill the Count's laboratory wouldn't look out of place in any of Fisher's Frankenstein sagas. On the journey to the castle, the carriage rolls and bumps over corpses, lying in dank leaves, like Michael Ripper's vehicle at the outset of *Brides of Dracula* (1960). Only the corpses in *Blood Demon* are real and not deceiving tree trunks (fans know what I mean when viewing *Brides of Dracula*).

Blood Demon's next major influence is the work of Fisher's American counterpart Roger Corman. The wasted vistas and decayed vegetation on which the coach journeys owe more than a nod to Corman and the opulent designs of his art director Daniel Haller. (The only thing that kills the mood is the inappropriately jazzy music that plays over these scenes. In the grand tradition of Euro Horror, where incongruous music always plays, the score wouldn't be out of place in a seedy British sex comedy.) And it's not just the barren landscapes and gloom-soaked graveyards that reek of Roger Corman (if you'll excuse the expression). When Anatol steals the travelers' coach early on in the film, his thin lips peel back from square, gnashing teeth; one is reminded instantly of the possessed young Jack Nicholson in an identical moment from Corman's *The Raven* (1963).

As *Blood Demon* nears its climax, the influence of *Dracula, Prince of Darkness* is abandoned, and the film begins to ape Corman's popular A.I.P. thriller *Pit and the Pendulum* (1961), most tellingly in its torture sequences. As hero Lex Barker lies strapped beneath a lowering pendulum, rats squeak and scurry at his sides. Water drips and splashes from the slimy walls as cogs crank and creak. The sound is as horrific as the images. A fantastic painted tableau of beaked figures with watchful eyes and snapping jaws frowns down from the walls. Images of flashing teeth and thin, one-eyed goblins blur as the pendulum's sharp, glinting blade jolts ever lower toward the hero's torso. All of this is, of course, familiar to any one who saw the Vincent Price movie when hero John Kerr awaits a similar fate. A brilliant, frightening mural overlooking Kerr appears in the Price film. It depicted hooded beings with glowing eyes. Finally, a sequence occurs in which the castle eventually caves in on itself, falling much like the *House of Usher*—or, indeed, any house inhabited by Price's tormented anti-heroes in Corman's Poe series.

And *Blood Demon*'s influences don't end there. Homage is even paid to the works of James Whale. Like Whale's *Bride of Frankenstein* (1935), images of crucifixes are dotted throughout the early parts of *Blood Demon*, reinforcing the locals' fear and need for protection from the bogeyman. And when the men first exit their carriage, after the death of their driver, they pause to climb a gibbet-like tree to cut down a hanging skull-faced corpse. I don't know why, but the only explanation I can conjure is to remind the viewer of Dwight Frye committing a similar deed in *Frankenstein* (1931). Further influence of Universal horror can be found not only in *Blood Demon*'s brisk running time, but also once the castle explodes, the hero and heroine stand clasped in each other's arms, just like Colin Clive and Valerie Hobson did in the final moments of *Bride of Frankenstein*, or David Manners and Jacqueline Wells did at the conclusion of *The Black Cat* (1934). Universal knew this was the perfect way to end their ventures into the fantastic, with the power of love prevailing, even if love had shown no evidence of rearing its head in the previous six reels.

Indeed, *Blood Demon* is infested with nods to horror movie folklore from the genre's illustrious past. On his way to the castle, Barker stops at a gloomy German village, the kind of place where Max Schreck's *Nosferatu* would be proud to scuttle. But no sign of Count Orlok exists. Instead, amid murmured chants and tolling bells, a funereal procession makes its way through the dingy, cobbled streets. Barker asks the locals if they know where Count Regula lives. They react in typical fashion, scampering away in terror at the mere mention of elusive castles. All of this is, of course, pretty familiar stuff to anyone who's ever viewed a horror film.

But before we dismiss the derivative nature of *Blood Demon*, I also discovered, on glimpsing the movie again, moments that look *forward* rather than back. For instance, the spectacle of Babette plunging toward the spike-lined floor is reminiscent of a would-be witch falling headfirst into roaring flames in the yet-to-be-filmed *Witchfinder General* (1967). Also, kudos must go again to the art direction team for creating the skull-studded walls of Count Regula's subterranean dwelling. The effect is really quite stunning, anticipating the similarly blue-lit crypt walls of Robert Young's Hammer classic *Vampire Circus* (1971). Incidentally, Count Regula's bone-filled walls thrilled again as an eerie highlight of the montage playing beneath the credits of the 1986 TV series, *Stephen King's World of Horror* (remember it?).

Summing up, *Blood Demon* is a luridly colored bogey story (as Boris Karloff preferred to describe his horror films) in which we see the influence of fairy tales everywhere—in the haunted forests, ghoulish castle, stoic hero and distressed maiden. This motif is also evident in Lee's slightly ridiculous garb of gray wool tights and buckled shoes. The use of a glass coffin for Lee's resurrection further emphasizes such imagery, though the Count is no *Snow White* (but rather a purplish gray). The uniquely Germanic quality of *Blood Demon*'s fairy tale feel is what sets it aside from the raft of Hammer-inspired epics swamping European cinemas in the mid-1960s. Sadly, it was a quality that was beginning to seep from the genre.

On its eventual release in May 1969 (in England, it was double-billed with Barbara Steele's equally lurid *The Faceless Monster*—aka, *Nightmare Castle*, 1965), the horrors of *Blood Demon* would seem very tame and tatty indeed in the wake of *Rosemary's Baby* and *Night of the Living Dead* (both 1968). The horror film was losing its innocence. The genre was growing up. *Blood Demon* is a crystallization of that fading innocence—or so it seems now—the last vestige of a transformational genre. Indeed, had *Blood Demon* been less flatly directed and imbued with more inspired photography, we could be looking at an archetypal minor classic. As it is, despite its low-brow aspirations to Gothic grandeur, we have only hazed colors and blandly dubbed voices.

But *Blood Demon* is still worth a midnight peek, and for anyone who hasn't seen it, I hope this review inspires fans to do so. After all, what are our favorite Gothic horror films if not dark and slightly strange fairy tales for adults? They offer a distorted mirror to the human condition in which we see our own lives and fears reflected and, through cathartic viewing, we face such fears and, even if we don't exactly exorcise them, they are certainly eased.

But enough of the psycho-babble and zeal these films inspire in me. What of Count Regula? When filming was complete, the ever-restless Christopher Lee returned to England. His next Hammer assignment reunited him, happily, with Terence Fish-er, one of *Blood Demon*'s undoubted inspirations. The film was *The Devil Rides Out*, an outing that, unlike *Blood Demon*, every horror fan seems to like. Even Mr. Lee rather likes it. And, as his fans all know, that's a very rare thing indeed.

A lifelong lover of movies and monsters, Stephen Mosley played the monster in the movie *Kenneth* (www.kennethmovie.com). His book of strange tales, *The Boy Who Loved Simone Simon* (which he also illustrated), is now available and was selected by *Entertainment Focus* as one of the 10 Best Books of 2011. His film-related articles can be found on the Spooky Isles website (www.spookyisles.com). He is also one half of the music duo Collinson Twin. This is his first article for *Midnight Marquee*.

Steel bars cannot keep the judge, symbol of justice and goodness, away from Count Regula, the evil murderer who cast a spell on generations of innocent people.

Seduced by Small-Town America, 1950s-Style

by Gary J. Svehla

The horror and science fiction movies of the 1950s sometimes appear to be a contradiction of tone and ideas. For baby boomers who matured during this relatively quiet decade, these movies became cozy friends reminding us of a simpler, peaceful and comforting world. Perhaps the reality is that Hollywood, even when indulging B movies made by MGM, United Artists, AIP, Allied Artists and Universal-International, crafted a storybook American suburbia that never existed, but this cinematic vision was a consistent one that provided safe haven for audiences who returned to the well time and time again to catch a little peace of mind from Hollywood's depiction of small-town America. Yet remember these quaint communities were populated with mutated monsters, invaders from space, human beings transformed into something utterly horrible and trusted authority figures who became society's worst villains (be they doctors/scientists, the military or the police). In such subversive cinema, children cannot trust their neighbors, their parents or the police. When subversive evil enters an idyllic and nurturing world, our guard is let down and our defense mechanisms forgotten. So 1950s American horror movies, on one hand, became the comfort food that nurtured our inner soul, providing the respite needed to escape, if even momentarily, the stress of a far less innocent modern world. Yet, at the same time, such comfort movies made us fail, for instance, to see the horror of alien seedpods duplicating our loved ones, replacing them with an alien mentality that sought to destroy humanity. We failed to recognize that those around us, looking exactly the same, have changed and

The small town depicted in *The Vampire* is inviting until the monstrous murders begin.

become one of *them*. We failed to see that even our visiting European cousin, a kindly father figure in a father-less home, was in reality the iconic vampire king seeking to steal our life's blood.

In the spirit of such dichotomy, two diverse looks at American horror movies of the 1950s are offered. The first analyzes their ability to provide comfort, reminding us of a kinder and gentler world of the past. The second analyzes the same movies, but we now see them for their subversive themes, lulling us into comfortable submission, failing to see how absolute evil permeated our formerly safe environment. Just like the Big Bad Wolf (deviously disguised as Grandma) invited Little Red Riding Hood into the cozy cottage, sometimes horror erupts violently in the very same place where we seek comfort and feel the safest. The billowing smoke from grandma's chimney might not always represent the folksy environment we crave.

A. The Seductive Power of Small-Town America

My wife Susan loves to cook "comfort food" in the winter months, because she feels such long-cherished childhood meals renew the spirit and feed the soul.

Old movies do that for me. Especially those made during the decade of the 1950s, when I was a kid growing up.

Sometimes I love to watch a movie such as *Return of Dracula*, *The Vampire* or even *The Monolith Monsters* because I love the depiction of small-town America where everyone knows everyone else and most people get along just fine and dandy. Everyone greets one another with a smile. Young kids deliver prescription medicine from the local drug store on bikes, usually to houses that are not locked and where the customer invites the delivery boy to share a glass of lemonade, just to be hospitable. People buy groceries on a personal tab and neighbors trust one another. Even in films such as *I Was a Teenage Werewolf* or *Blood of Dracula*, where there's trouble in paradise (psychologically and physically damaged teen protagonists with anti-social behavior manipulated by powerful adult predators who take advantage of such situations), life at high school was depicted as being a nurturing environment, with kids rocking out at the high school hop, having fun indulging in innocent flirtation in the science lab, in the parking lot or at the soda shop after school. Back in the mid-1950s such a depiction of tranquility was a dream created by Hollywood, but enough of the truth of such times shines through these and other movies, reminding us of a world and society that no longer exists. America in the 1950s was far more innocent than today's America.

Sometimes I watch movies such as *Earth vs. The Spider* and *Invaders from Mars* because that world is where I would love to spend a little time. Hey, I would not wish my parents to be transformed into thought zombies by Martians that surgically implant little probes into the base of their brains that could later cause fatal strokes, at the discretion of the alien overseer. But wouldn't it be wonderful to play in those sand dunes in back of your house where the wooden planks end? Wouldn't it be ideal to live in a neighborhood where everyone becomes friends and all the children play with one another? When such children venture downtown they are on a first name basis with the police. During the decade of the 1950s our teacher not only challenges us but is our friend, and we are willing to help our teacher in any side projects requested, even if that means exploring uncharted caves that house a deadly giant spider or conducting science labs involving sulfuric acid. The world was much safer back then, so the occasional threat of mutated monsters was even more frightening because the horrors created a far greater contrast. In this world young people were not subjected to violent street crime, drive-by shootings, gang violence or home invasions. Yes, of

The innocence of small-town America being invaded by the giant crystal rocks that approach from just outside the town's borders, in *The Monolith Monsters*.

I Was a Teenage Werewolf makes the werewolf, Tony Rivers (Michael Landon), a metaphor for anti-social, psychologically damaged teenagers who are dominated by adult predators.

Movie heroes of the 1950s, such as John Agar, were depicted with chiseled good looks and were self-sacrificing and willing to die for their community.

course crime existed, but it occurred on a smaller and more civilized scale.

In those films of our youth we encountered heroes with chiseled, good-looking features, heroes who were not morally conflicted and who always took the higher ground. Heroes were self-sacrificing, willing to die to keep their community and friends healthy, safe and happy. Thus we grew up looking at smiling faces such as John Agar, Robert Clarke, Arthur Franz, Kenneth Tobey, Ed Kemmer, Grant Williams, Richard Denning, and Gene Barry. Most of the characters played by these actors did not have complex histories or troubled pasts. They were good-natured working or professional people who were productive citizens of their community, people who tried not to stand out but willingly gave back and made a difference.

They were well liked and well known within the community. They were heroes in whom we immediately could place our trust. And how did such stereotypical protagonists defeat the enemy? They prevailed by using common sense, intelligence/creativity (most of these heroes were doctors, military men, scientists or officers of law enforcement) and courage. Such characters were usually ordinary in one sense but superior in another—the community usually looked up to such people as being slightly more knowledgeable, even if they occupied the role of average common people. But such characters made children feel safe and protected.

And when it came to defeating the enemy, it usually took a team, either a small community of people or the entire community working together. Think of the quaint independent production (smartly gobbled up by mainstream Paramount) *The Blob* (1958). Yes, the hero played by Steve McQueen was a belligerent and flip high schooler (looking as though he were on the 10-year graduation plan), but at heart he was a good kid who was a team player (he even called the town's adversarial cop by his first name and, through his actions, McQueen's character Steve shows respect, even if he is apt to indulge in teenage hi-jinks such

In the world of *Earth vs. The Spider*, life was much safer, so the threat of mutated monsters was even more frightening.

Rebel Steve (Steve McQueen, second from left), along with girlfriend Jane (Anita Corsaut), seem very comfortable with the small town's police force, from *The Blob*.

as drag racing on public streets). When Steve needs multiple fire extinguishers to deep-freeze the alien invader, he rallies not only his fellow high school buddies but teachers and the principal as well, and they all cooperate to destroy this monster from space. Even when the monster invades the town's Colonial Theater, it takes teamwork and intelligence to survive (but only after all hell breaks loose initially and a panicking mob rushes out of the theater). When Steve and other citizens are trapped in the diner, it takes communication and cooperation to defeat the blob. The community pulls together to stay alive. What starts as a low-rent version of *Rebel Without a Cause* soon becomes something else altogether, a testimony to young rebels and mainstream society working together to defeat the common threat. And in the last frame the monster is carried away by airplane, the "cancer" isolated symbolically from the quaint Pennsylvania burgh, restoring order and safety because opposing personalities came together to fight a common cause, both rebellious youth and entrenched old-timers alike.

And what makes these old 1950s movies so endearing is ultimately those set pieces that become iconic vestiges of the nostalgic past. Many movies of this era spend quality time in the local doctor's office, one filled with a waiting room of only 1 or 2 people where the doctor knows everyone by their first name. Doctors or employees deliver medicines directly to the home. People walk down main street U.S.A. and seem to know everyone they meet, and everyone has a smile and friendly comment or two. People in drug stores or grocery stores never seem rushed and everyone cooperates. We observe high school science classrooms where the respected teacher oversees laboratories conducted by star pupils. High schools seem fun and safe where dances fueled by rock 'n' roll are always high energy with the kids having a blast. The police are authority figures, but they are also nurturing and friendly, as are teachers, ministers and members of the military and federal agents. Shopping seems to be more like an excuse to socialize and visit friends then it is to rush through aisles, in frenzied stress, and plunk down money to buy unnecessary products. Neighbors always have time to visit and be visited by other neighbors, and everyone has a cup of sugar or tool to loan. Families sit down and eat and speak together in kitchens or dining rooms. Family picnics and family togetherness become the norm. Sidewalk streets are safe and neighborhoods have well kept homes and lawns that always seem bright and inviting (exceptions exist—remember what happens to the little old lady who was out too late on the streets in *The Vampire*?). The streets are populated (never crowded) with roomy gas-guzzling automobiles whose drivers never give a worrisome thought to how much gasoline costs. Community comes always front and center, with socials and picnics (either school or church related) bringing people together in bright spirits and camaraderie.

Even though as a child I focused on the creepy menaces to society, those monsters, alien invaders or perversions of ego-driven science, but now, as an aging baby boomer, I best remember that idyllic world, those sleepy communities that no longer exist. Perhaps they never did and probably never will again. While Hollywood never tells the total truth, it does create an emotional palette on which to paint our collective yearnings about a particular time in our lives, a time when life was simpler, comforting and emotionally renewing. When I now watch

The Blob becomes a testimonial to young rebels and mainstream society working together to defeat the common threat.

all the *I Was a Teenage …* or *Invasion of … * or *Attack of …* B movies, I enjoy the monsters and mayhem, but I find myself noticing the community backdrop and societal interaction more. I might enjoy a monster-caused riot in the high school gym, but I find myself noting how the teens acted before and after the riot. I might enjoy a giant fiend prancing through small-town America, but I notice what people were doing before that monstrous rampage begun. I might enjoy the fact that the once regal Count Dracula was now living in small-town America, and while I appreciate the sequences with coffins, wooden stakes and mist, I find myself becoming more mesmerized with the quiet parlor sequences and the family interacting.

It is no longer only about the monsters, invaders and giant atomic-fried creations: it is just as much about that perfect little community that is about to be invaded and the aftermath of that invasion and restoring peace to the community. After watching these movies for over 50 years, perhaps 10 to 20 times, isn't it about time avid viewers find some new chestnut to feed upon, a different slant to intrigue our imaginations and play to that "comfort food" mentality? For me revisiting the former small-town cinematic America creates a warm and fuzzy feeling of which I can never get enough. And the best thought is the idea that as we age we watch the movies that we enjoyed in our youth, but we look at them through aging eyes and focus on different aspects that continue to justify our obsessions of watching them over and over again.

The Subversive Power of Small-Town America

In 1957's *I Was A Teenage Werewolf*, teen predator Tony Rivers (Michael Landon) gets an instant migraine when standing too near the school bell that signals the change of class. He has been eying up a sexy young gymnast who is working out on the parallel bars, and Tony soon morphs into a foaming-at-the-mouth werewolf, becoming a visual metaphor for every adolescent male's sexual yearnings. He does not rape her; his hormone-fueled passions cause him to rip out her throat. While President Eisenhower's bland, strait-laced 1950s is generally pictured as American as apple pie, horror cinema casts this innocent era in an entirely different light. As seen in the drive-in movies crafted by American-International and others during this period, the J.D. emerges, the rebel without a clue, the leather-garbed punk who is motivated by breaking rules, rock 'n' roll and the fairer sex. Tony, raised by a single parent father who loves but does not understand him, tries to suppress an uncontrollable inner rage where his lycanthropic transformation becomes the perfect metaphor for deep psychological fragmentation and loneliness. While all the other cookie-cutter generic teens at school seem to be carefree and enjoy the socialization that their high school provides, Tony is the troubled outsider who basically does not fit. And the beast that emerges reflects his emotional disconnect raging inside, fueled by hormones, chemicals and the fear of authority (instead of evolving and maturing into adulthood, Tony is a product of de-evolution and regression). Becoming what singer Paul Westerberg would label the "bastards of young," Tony rejects his loving father and instead puts his

In movies such as *I Was a Teenage Werewolf*, the J.D. emerges, the rebel without a clue, the leather-garbed punk who is motived by breaking rules, rock 'n' roll and the fairer sex.

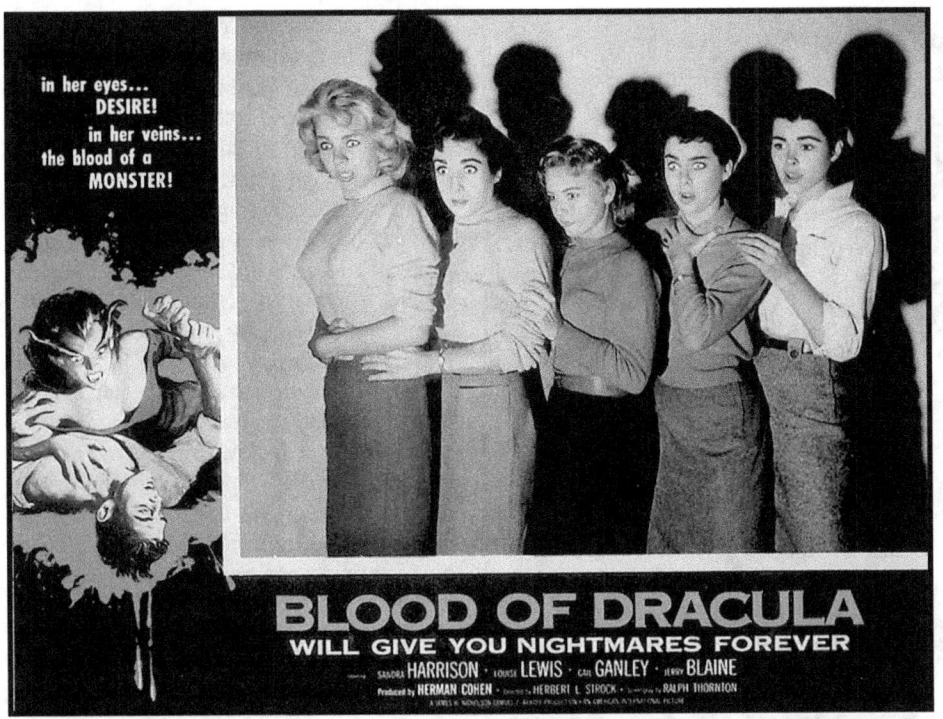

In this publicity posed lobby card, the "Birds of Paradise" clique bullies the new girl Nancy, soon to be transformed into a modern vampire and causing the fear on their faces.

faith into the hands of the very manipulative scientists who will destroy him. [As Westerberg sings, "The ones who love us least are the ones we'll die to please."]

Damaged psyches and the disintegration of the nuclear family become the focal point of classic AIP drive-in fodder, *Blood of Dracula* (1957). Picture Tony Rivers re-imagined as a similarly despondent female rebel. Imagine a father who, six weeks after his wife's death, remarries and relocates to another city, placing his rebellious and confused 18-year-old daughter Nancy (Sandra Harrison) into a private girls' school, where the snotty chicks who run the powerful "Birds of Paradise" clique bully her immediately. No wonder that Nancy gravitates into the orbit of powerful but eccentric chemistry teacher Miss Branding (Louise Lewis). Hoping to become Branding's chief student assistant, replacing the teacher's current pet Myra (Gail Ganley), leader of the clique, Nancy tries to bond with the chemistry teacher since she needs an adult advocate and mother-figure to help appease the violent rage boiling inside her. Too bad the evil chemistry teacher first manipulates her (setting Nancy up to be burned by acid during a classroom lab, then telling the injured student that her feelings of hate and revenge are healthy when properly directed), using an ancient Carpathian amulet to hypnotize and transform her into a gruesome vampire who slaughters her classmates. [Basically the plots of *Blood of Dracula* and *I Was A Teenage Werewolf* are quite similar, one movie occurring at a public school and the other at a private one, but both movies show evil, self-serving scientists hypnotizing and self-servingly transforming troubled teenagers into predatory beasts.] Not yet fully grasping the implications of such transformations, Nancy asks Branding to release her from the power of the amulet after the first few killings, but the teacher tells her that she must finish the experiment (Branding is writing her scientific thesis and must observe all conclusions first hand). Of course when the victimized vampire student directs her monstrous rage against Branding, killing her savagely, that request is granted. Unfortunately, Nancy is also impaled and destroyed as well. Whether her father cares or not, we will never know. But Sandra Harrison's performance as an abandoned young girl, unloved by both her family and peers, becoming the sacrificial, experimental victim of a cruel teacher, makes her character fairly sympathetic, even while appearing as a masterfully depicted bloodthirsty fiend (her camera-enhanced monster make-up is spectacular). Even within the safe confines of a meticulously run private girls' school in a small-town community, vampire women can run just as buck-wild as the fellas.

From a different direction comes Don Siegel's *Invasion of the Body Snatchers* (1956), taking an idyllic American town, Santa Mira, and recasting it as ground zero for alien invasion, as mysterious alien seedpods replicate human beings. The newly formed pod person becomes just like the original human being in every way ... except his or her humanity has been replaced by a hive mentality, where emotions are eliminated and a survival-based consciousness emerges. Pod people walk down the town's main street with a vacant gaze, never showing emotion, not even when a car is about to strike a dog. The horror created by quick-cut editing—low-angle shots that show the shadowy, non-expressive dead eyes of Becky (Dana Wynter) after she awakens from her sleep, cutting to her lover Miles' (Kevin McCarthy) totally frenzied emotional reaction realizing she is now one of *them*—is riveting and cuts deeply. Former friends and neighbors become transformed

Tony Rivers (Michael Landon), from *I Was a Teenage Werewolf*, does not rape the female of his desires. Instead, he rips out her throat.

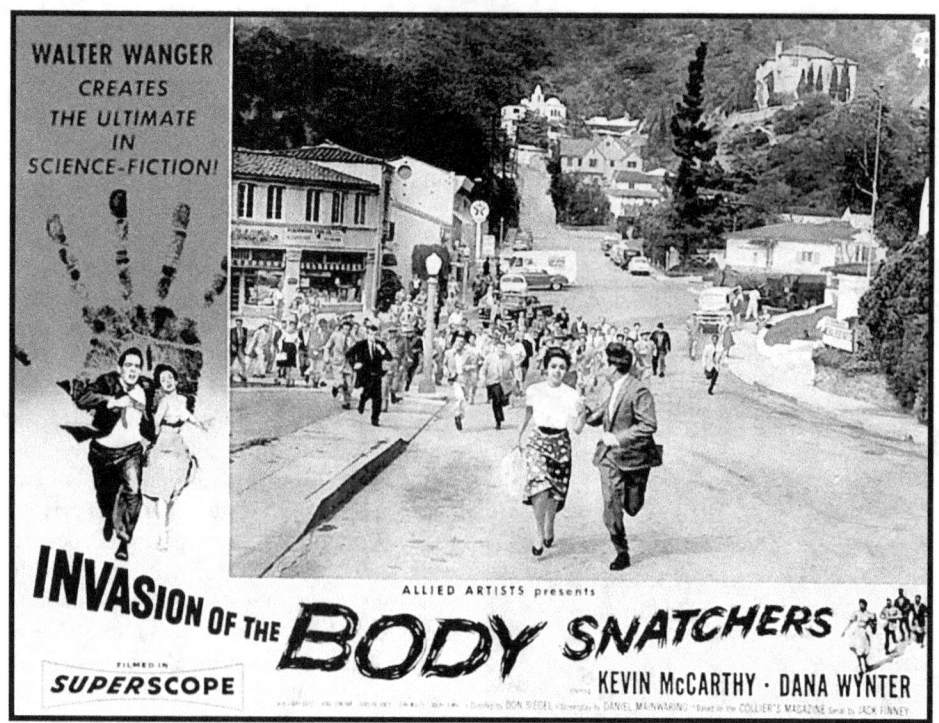

Invasion of the Body Snatchers takes an idyllic American town, Santa Mira, and recasts it as ground zero for alien invasion.

overnight into this alien consciousness that demands compliance. And such insidious horror makes Miles' solo flight (into a world being invaded by truck loads of alien seedpods being delivered everywhere) even more profound.

In movies such as Paul Landres' *The Vampire* (1957) we have a single parent struggling to raise a perhaps too precious daughter and maintain his small-town medical practice, even going so far as to allow the child to practice her ballet right outside his office. The pressures of modern life have caused the doctor to experience migraines, but when he accidentally sub-stitutes his headache medicine for pills that make human beings revert to their primordial state, all hell erupts and little old ladies no longer are safe walking the town's streets after twilight. The post-WWII American dream has quickly transformed into a nightmare. Even when the sympathetic doctor is forced to go "cold turkey" and is denied access to the regression pills by a protective friend, the doctor's addiction to the pills still transforms him into the ravenous beast.

The sly contrast of transforming the middle-aged small-town doctor into the monster, his scientific intelligence reduced to animalistic snarls and snorts, demonstrates how savagery lies just slightly beneath the surface, one pill removed, transforming the most trusted and wizened elders among us into fiends.

In Paul Landres' similar and equally important *The Return of Dracula* (1958), the European Count journeys to America in search of fresh blood, assuming the identity of a kind artist who escaped repressive Communist Eastern Europe for the freedoms of small-town America. Once again we encounter a fragmented family, a single mother raising a daughter, who welcomes the fatherly Cousin Bellac (Francis Lederer) to live in their home and become their badly needed male authority figure. But unfortunately Bellac spends his days either sleeping in his casket or hidden away, while at night he always extends his regrets, explaining how circumstances prevent him from assuming his intended responsibilities. However, sexy daughter Rachel Mayberry (Norma Eberhardt) takes a more than fatherly attraction to Bellac and wishes him to share all his worldly experiences with her and help her embark upon an artistic career designing clothes. Meanwhile, across town, not even the sickly and blind young woman who lives in the church home is safe from the curse of the undead, as Bellac/Count Dracula makes her his victim, inviting his prey to step from the darkness into the light. Among silhouetted sidewalks, quaint railroad depots, church socials, rolling rustic countryside and a house filled with comfort and love comes absolute horror, with the naïve community never realizing until the end that the supernatural has invaded them.

American-International's *Earth vs. The Spider* (1958) demonstrates a different variety of lurking horror waylaying the charms of small-town America. On the

John Beal, as the sympathetic town doctor, gets transformed into the blood-sucking monster in *The Vampire*.

A foreign movie poster for *The Vampire*

Francis Lederer stars as the infamous Count in *Return of Dracula*. Notice how the overcoat draped over his shoulders becomes cape-like in 1958 small-town America.

eve of her birthday, perky Carol (June Kenney) and boyfriend Mike (Gene Persson) discover the wreckage of her father's car on a deserted back road, but Dad is missing. In the car Carol discovers her wrapped birthday present (a bracelet) and card. Deciding to search the nearby caverns for a potentially injured father, the reckless couple discovers a huge spider's web containing human bones. Before long a giant spider attacks and the kids escape. In this rustic community of River Falls, the science high school teacher Professor Kingman (Ed Kemmer) becomes the titular leader, the egghead able to defeat the monster with DDT and electricity. Unfortunately the not-quite-dead creature is foolishly placed on display in the high school gym, the authoritarian adults assuming the creature is dead. Soon the local teenage rock 'n' roll band asks the high school janitor if they could rehearse in the gym, and during their rehearsal the music attracts a large crowd of energized fans. The supposedly dead spider comes back to life, running amok in the community. Sometimes these movies demonstrate that stupidity is spookier than giant, mutated monsters. But not even young love, rock 'n' roll music, team work, authoritarian adults or the security of the local high school can save this community from the wrath of nature's unfettered and mutated giant spider.

In a very similar vein, Universal-International's *Tarantula* (1955) shows what happens when biologist Leo G. Carroll fails in his efforts to concoct a safe synthetic food source to feed the world's ever-expanding population. Instead, he produces a serum that destroys the entire research team when they inject themselves with the experimental drug, at first morphing into mutated monsters. The team manages to transform the fuzzy little tarantula in the experimental laboratory into gigantic proportions. Luckily the lazy desert Arizona town of Desert Rock has humble hero John Agar as local doctor Matt Hastings, the man instrumental in saving his community from destruction. Once again an innocent creature that mutates to monstrous size threatens a dusty small-town community, a failed experiment in the cause of curing world hunger.

In Universal-International's too often neglected programmer *Monster On the Campus* (1958), directed by Jack Arnold, the quaint college's Professor Blake (Arthur Franz) is transformed into a Neanderthal beast when the blood from a recently found prehistoric fish contaminates him. In the ultimate battle between nurture and nature, the monster deep within emerges as the dominant personality. The monster continues to kill until the weaker-willed symbol of intellectualism, the college professor, is killed (but so is the beast, since they share the same body). In this metaphor both prehistoric beast and modern intellectual share a symbiotic relationship where each needs the other in order to survive. In yet another variation on the Jekyll and Hyde premise, the tainted human possesses that which is both intellectual and

In *Earth vs. The Spider*, a supposedly dead giant spider escapes from the high school gym and runs amok in the community.

In *Tarantula*, biologist Leo G. Carroll mutates an innocent creature to monstrous size, causing the gigantic beast to threaten the community.

savage; he is both planner and predator and sharer and thief. And the college professor can revert to pre-history's savage beast at any moment, since the beast is dominant. The small-town university campus, filled with inquisitive students, will never be the same.

Young David MacLean (Jimmy Hunt) becomes the archetype 1950s kid in *Invaders From Mars* (1953), the innocent exposed to the horrors of Martian invasion in his small American town. A head with tentacles in a bottle controls the invading Martian army, whose zombie mutants carry out the tunneling and physical work, submitting to the will of the dismembered head. Humans are captured when they step out into the sand dunes that cover the backyards of their safe neighborhood houses (the Martian saucer is embedded there below the surface). Once lured out back, neighbors disappear beneath the sand, where they are implanted with mind-controlling devices attached to the back of their heads. Once programmed, these humans do the bidding of the invading aliens, and once their job is finished, they too are finished when the devices are exploded causing cerebral hemorrhages. Young David finds that not even one's parents or the local police can be trusted, for the alien invaders now control them as well. A way of life that seemed so pastoral and safe is infested by evil. Who can we trust? In a world where the police, authority figures and even our parents are monsters, how can innocent little boys survive? Only the collaboration of brain (the pipe-sucking scientists) and brawn (the weapon-heavy military) can bring down the insidious invasion that is waged beneath the surface and imagery of suburbia's American Dream.

Eisenhower's America with its housing boom (thanks to the ending of World War II) and exodus to the 'burbs seems so peaceful and safe. Yet the horror and science fiction movies made during this era always go out of their way to shatter the illusion. Even during the 1950s science was growing too reckless, destroying the natural environment little by little with nuclear testing, DDT and the rush to overstuff landfills. In these movies scientific mutations created for good causes (such as world hunger) suddenly run amok and work against the very reasons for which they were created. Invasions from space occur, but usually not with the invading war machines introduced in George Pal's *The War of The Worlds*, but more insidiously, with invasion erupting from beneath our own backyards (metaphorically, we all have dark and twisty sand dunes and worm holes beneath our perceived safe reality ... for instance, in the reality of 2013 a sinkhole, 30 feet wide, opened up beneath a home in Florida, swallowing up an innocent man as he slept in his bed, furthering the premise that we aren't safe anywhere, not even in the security of our own beds). The movies demonstrated that often those we love (mother and father in *Invaders From Mars*; friends and lovers in *Invasion of the Body Snatchers*) can no longer be trusted, for the monstrous threat to our quiet community lies in the perversion of everything that makes us feel safe. Even our visiting cousin

Arthur Franz (or his stuntman) plays a college professor who is transformed into a Neanderthal man in *Monster On the Campus*, terrifying Joanna Moore in this PR shot.

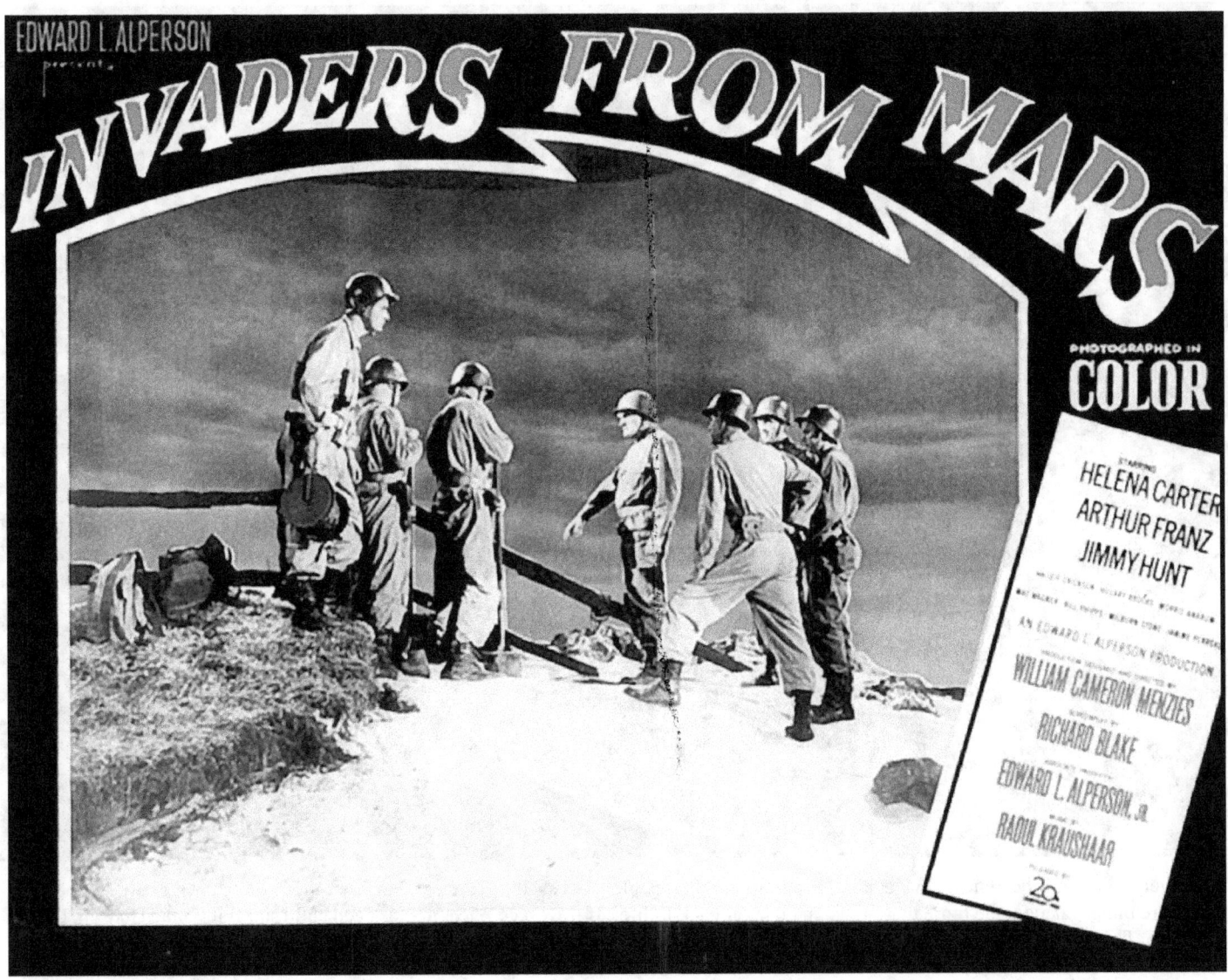

Be careful the next time we go out back and venture beyond the unknown area where the wooden planks end and the sand dunes begin.

from far away Europe might be a bloodsucking vampire. Even the town's loved doctor, self-sacrificing and caring beyond a fault, might himself be twisted to commit harm against the very people he protects and serves because of his addiction to monster-inducing pills. The bastion of civilization, our nation's high schools, may become the experimental pool for devious adults who seek out psychologically damaged or emotionally needy children as their experimental guinea pigs. *Blood of Dracula* (1957) shows how daughters rejected by parents are prone to bond with teachers, educators who see them as expendable experimental subjects. *I Was a Teenage Werewolf* (1957) shows how disconnected males with anger-management issues can be easily manipulated into becoming willing subjects.

Horror cinema of the 1950s shines the fictional light of truth on the decades' façade of peaceful perfection. It shows the 1950s society to be a hidden hotbed of twisted science gone wild, revealing it to be the breeding ground for serial killers and monsters created either through superstition or science. When held up to close inspection, the sanitized America of the 1950s is revealed to be a world where even our own relatives can be working to do us in. And those bastions of societal security, the police and the middle classes, can be subverted and made the enemy.

Recast by horror movie moviemakers, America of the 1950s no longer appears to be such a Utopia. It instead becomes a world where innocent workers, parents, uncles and children put their guard down and become too trusting in the inherent good of the government, the military and the world of science. Instead of keeping one's guard up, in these and other movies, 1950s America becomes the Disneyland (that amusement park first appeared during the 1950s) that desensitizes its citizens and forces us to feel safe in a feel-good community that apparently is superficial and empty. Just when we sigh collectively and think all the horrors of World War II and Korea are behind us, the new enemy (from outer space, from the military, from science, from those Red Commie bastards) sneaks in the back door and gets us when we are not looking, while we sit with a smile on our face, our feet propped up on the sofa, eating an easy-to-heat TV dinner, oblivious to any of these dangers, hypnotized by the magic oval television screen. The children, in the other room, are preoccupied listening to their 45-rpm records or transistor radios.

What a wonderful life, right?

The cinema of the 1950s teaches us a totally different reality. Be careful the next time we go out back and venture beyond the unknown area where the wooden planks end and the sand dunes begin. What's unseen just beneath the surface will get us every time.

Deja vu Boo!

by Steven Thornton

A haunting face from Paranormal Activity 2

Everything old becomes new again. The more things change, the more they stay the same. The point is that, as I go along in life, I am struck by the realization that many so-called "new" experiences are actually old experiences dressed up in a bright, shiny wrapper.

And nowhere is this more so than in the world of contemporary cinema. On the surface, the movie industry of today gives lip service to the notion that creative thought and artistic vision are held in the highest esteem all along the Hollywood food chain. But far too often, the industry falls back on copycat ideas, recycled concepts and "been there, done that" gimmicks that are as old as the double-feature and as stale as last week's popcorn.

Horror cinema, which has always typified the underbelly of the Hollywood dream machine, is where this tendency most often reveals itself. Promotion is the name of the game and the goal is to grab the audience's attention any way possible. And in today's corporate-driven world, this means falling back on time-tested strategies to put butts into seats. A quick survey of the following trends shows that, in the minds of today's filmmakers, no decades-old attention-grabbing ploy exists that cannot be bought back to life. If it worked once, it can work again and again and again.

Star Power

Whether it's Al Pacino in *Devil's Advocate*, Robert De Niro in *Angel Heart* or Robert Downey, Jr. in *Zodiac*, big-budget releases often use star power to bolster the box-office chances of a horror film. For a vintage example of this trend, check out the eerie, estrogen-fueled extravaganza, *What Ever Happened to Baby Jane?* (1962), featuring Hollywood legends (and real life rivals) Bette Davis and Joan Crawford.

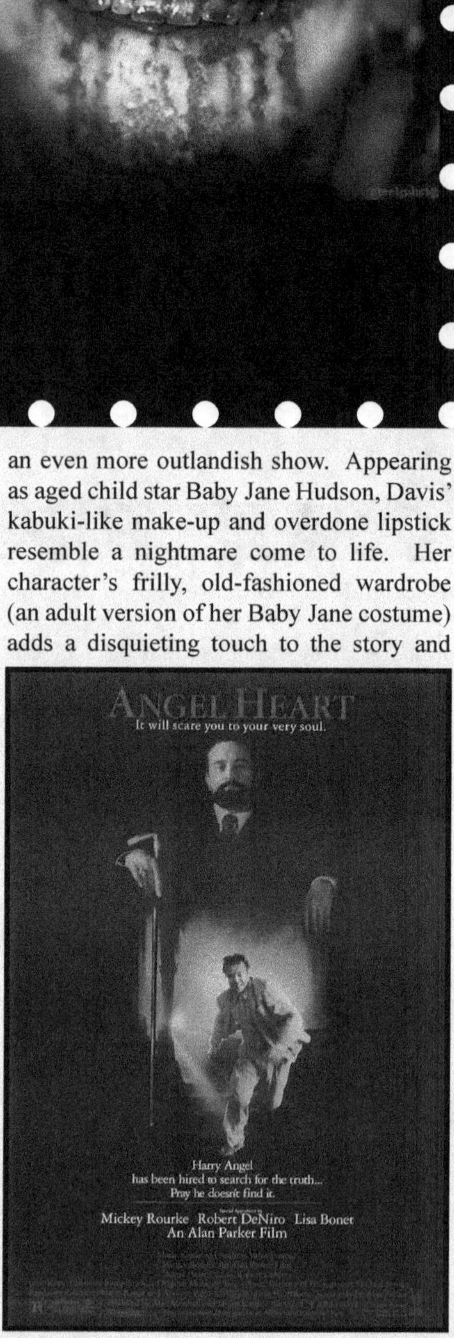

Much of the fascination of seeing *What Ever Happened to Baby Jane?* on its original release was the delirium of seeing the films' headliners so far out of character. In contrast to their carefully crafted screen profiles, Crawford and Davis willingly go the extra mile to appear as unglamorous as possible. Crawford, portraying former movie queen Blanche Hudson, is costumed in a frumpy frock and sports an unattractive "hair don't." Her character's handicap—she is confined to a wheelchair as a result of an auto accident—also adds to the pitiful aura of her role. Incredibly, Davis puts on an even more outlandish show. Appearing as aged child star Baby Jane Hudson, Davis' kabuki-like make-up and overdone lipstick resemble a nightmare come to life. Her character's frilly, old-fashioned wardrobe (an adult version of her Baby Jane costume) adds a disquieting touch to the story and

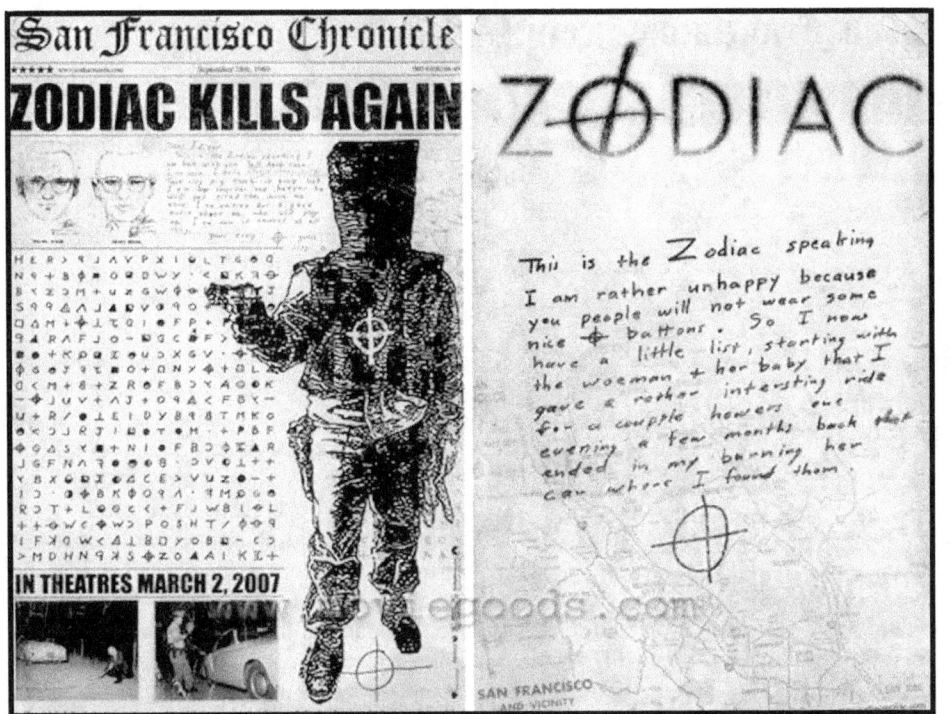

visually illustrates the unbalanced nature of her character. Seeing these two headliners in roles that were 180 degrees removed from their glory days at Warner Bros. and MGM is part of the bizarre fascination of this sordid little thriller.

As the film progresses, the tense relationship between the has-been sisters grows more twisted. Blanche comes off as a suffering saint, compassionate and always willing to overlook her sister's compulsive, self-centered behavior. In spite of (or, perhaps, because of) Blanche's forgiving nature, Jane relishes each opportunity to belittle her sister, taunting her, slapping her, verbally abusing her and always reminding her of her utter helplessness. Like scorpions in a bottle, the pair is locked in a lethal battle of wills, fueled by failed careers and resentments that have festered for decades. Viewers who know of the real-life animosity between Davis and Crawford can take a perverse pleasure in seeing these two screen dynamos act out their well-documented professional jealousies in full view of the camera.

Jane and Blanche's toxic rivalry takes an abrupt turn for the worse at the film's midpoint. The catalyst is the daily mealtime ritual in which Jane brings a dinner tray to her wheelchair-bound sister. Over time, this ritual has become a test of nerves, with each tray carrying the threat of something unspeakable. Jane tips her hand when she casually mentions a problem with "rats in the cellar." The music builds, the pace quickens and everyone in the audience can see what's coming when clueless Blanche lifts her tray to reveal a plate of rodent surprise. Jane squeals in delight as the hysterical Blanche cries out and spins her wheelchair in a helpless, never-ending dance of horror.

It has become commonplace for today's stars to include a horror title or two on their resumes. Whether it's the challenge of a villainous character role or the chance to rejuvenate a flagging career, the stigma of appearing in a tawdry terror tale is largely a thing of the past. But before it became oh so fashionable, Bette Davis and Joan Crawford dared to strip away the veneer of Hollywood

Bette Davis plays aged child star Baby Jane Hudson, wearing kabuki-like make-up and overdone lipstick, dancing away in *What Ever Happened to Baby Jane?*

Bette Davis (left) and Joan Crawford both appear unglamorous in *What Ever Happened to Baby Jane?*

50th Anniversary Issue [1963-2013]

Horror movie franchises, such as *Paranormal Activity* (2007), are marketed almost exclusively to adolescent and young adult audiences.

glamour and turn *What Ever Happened to Baby Jane?* into something more than just an average horror film.

Youth Appeal

Today's mainstream movies are marketed almost exclusively to the adolescent and young adult audience, horror films especially included. The *Paranormal Activity* and *Final Destination* series are typical examples of this. But that wasn't always the case. Once upon a time, adults were targeted as the primary audience for nearly every Hollywood film. It was considered a bold and risky gambit for a filmmaker to focus exclusively on a potentially profitable but unpredictable segment of the movie-going public, the teenager.

This strategy began to change in the 1950s. Innovative upstarts like American International Pictures and others recognized the opportunities offered by the growing youth market and began to tailor their releases accordingly. Wild werewolves, giant spiders and marauding Martians gamboled side by side with lovelorn teenagers, not so street legal customized muscle cars and wanna-be rock 'n' roll bands. One of the more extreme examp-les of this "kids meet the monsters" trend was the 1964 independently produced but 20th Century Fox released *The Horror of Party Beach*.

Director and co-producer Del Tenney spices up *Party Beach* with strong doses of sex appeal and rock 'n' roll to maximize the film's fun quotient. The latter is pro-vided by the Del-Aires, a regional surf band that never hit the big time, while the former is provided by—well, just about everyone. Teens and 20-somethings gyrate in time with the heavily reverbed guitar twang, outfitted in the sexiest swimsuits that the early 1960s cinema would allow. Girls neck with their boyfriends, then trade off with new partners and continue the game of lip wrestling without missing a beat. And "wink, wink, nudge, nudge" asides add predicable but welcome chuckles to the proceedings. "Do you like bathing beauties?" asks one bikini-clad female hopeful. "I don't know," replies the wannabe teenage Romeo, "I never bathed one!" The hormone-infused sensibility captures perfectly the racy yet essentially innocent atmosphere that prevailed before the sexual revolution made everything so very complicated.

The film's catch-as-catch-can plot quickly establishes its innate youth appeal. It all starts with the end of a romance—Hank (John Scott) and Tina (Marilyn Clarke) have grown apart and decide to throw in the towel on their youthful fling. Tina takes the breakup hard and, to get even, announces her intention to let the world see "Tina swing." And swing she does, her bare tootsies dancing in the sand to the sound of the local beach party. Soon she catches the eye of a local bad boy/gang leader who offers to show the beach bunny a thing or two about life on the wild side. Hank takes exception to Tina's new best friend and the two men engage in short-lived but energetic fisticuffs. Feeling vindicated, Tina celebrates with a solo swim in the local bay. But danger lurks nearby—the local waterways have become

The Horror of Party Beach, heavily hormone infused, caters to sexy girls, horrible pollution-created monsters and rock 'n 'roll.

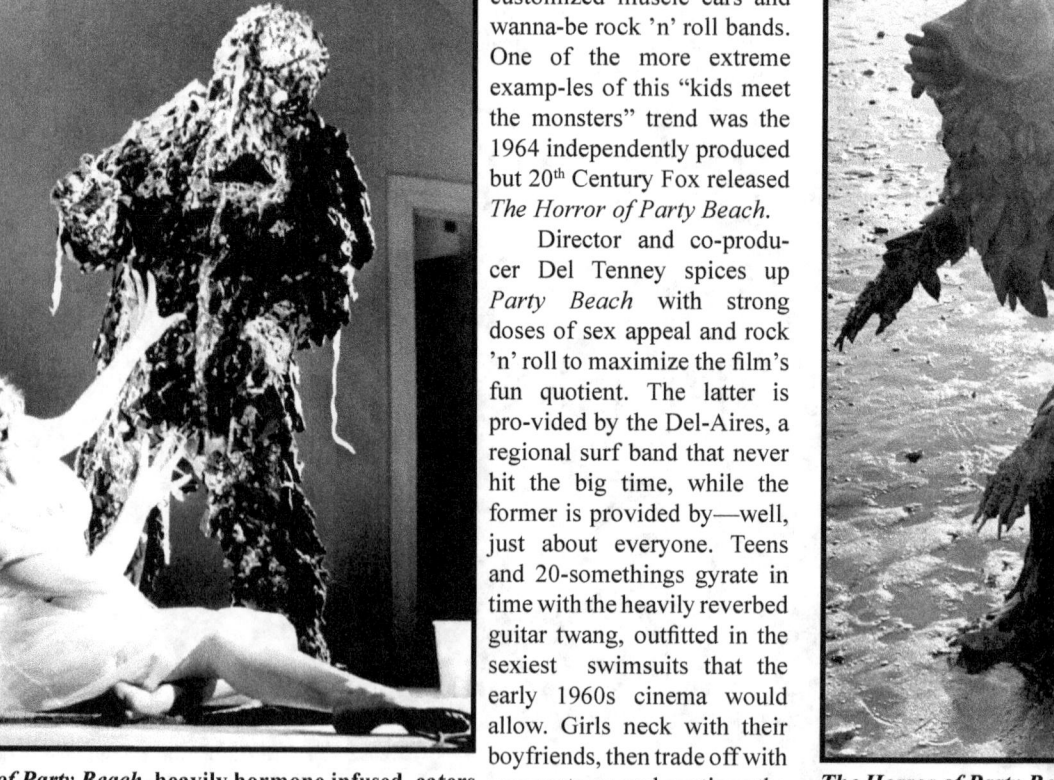

The Horror of Party Beach is one of the first low-budget monster movies that champions concern for our natural resources.

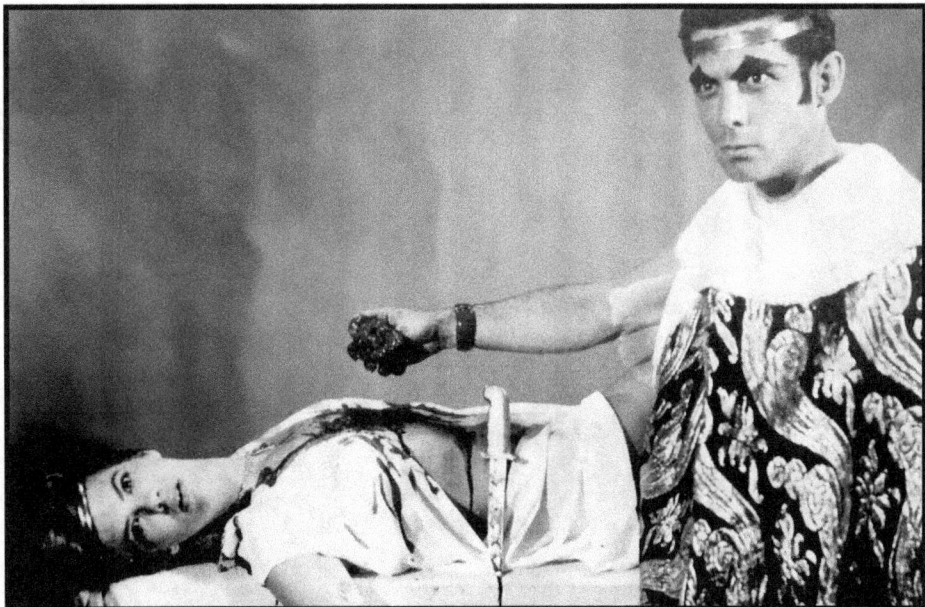

Faud Ramses (Mal Arnold) commits a series of grisly murders to harvest body parts in hopes of recreating the Feast of Ishtar, from *Blood Feast*.

infested by a deadly mutated life form. The beastie attacks and Tina's beautiful body quickly becomes a bloody pulp. The catalyst for the monsters' birth, incidentally, is the dumping of radioactive waste by a local manufacturer, making the film rather prescient in its environmental awareness. Consider this: *Horror of Party Beach* is a low-budget monster movie that champions concern for our natural resources—who'da thunk?

The movie will never show up on any critic's best films list, but for a 70-minute time-killer, it has its moments. And as a time capsule of the sexual mores of the early 1960s, it's a regular Kinsey manual. Anyone interested in the evolution of Hollywood's youth-oriented marketing focus should give *Horror of Party Beach* a look. If nothing else, audiences will get to see Tina swing, and that alone is worth the price of admission.

Gore

Gore is an essential ingredient of cutting-edge horror films like *Dead Alive* and the ongoing *Hostel* series. But among fans of gore cinema, the name Herschell Gordon Lewis holds a place of special esteem. Making films at a time when the dictates of the Production Code were loosening but still in place, Lewis combined tawdry, threadbare narratives with violent sequences that delivered the shock of a blunt force hammer blow. Whether we consider it a high point of creative freedom or the nadir of exploitation cinema, Lewis' work has lost none of its power, especially his magnum opus, the 1963 stunner *Blood Feast*.

Blood Feast eschews subtlety in its pursuit of all things grisly and gory. The film's lurid plot concerns Faud Ramses (Mal Arnold), a caterer, who by coincidence happens to be a modern day disciple of the Egyptian god Ishtar. Devoted to the point of fanaticism, Ramses commits a series of murders to harvest body parts in hopes of recreating the legendary Feast of Ishtar—a multi-day orgy of debauchery and cannibalism. The police are baffled by the crimes that have no apparent motive and common denominator outside of the savage way they were enacted.

Lewis' skill as a film director would never earn him a place on any critic's top-10 list. Individual scenes are flatly lit and indifferently staged. Dialogue is delivered

Gore and torture porn go hand-in-hand as we watch the bloody chair from *Hostel* (2005).

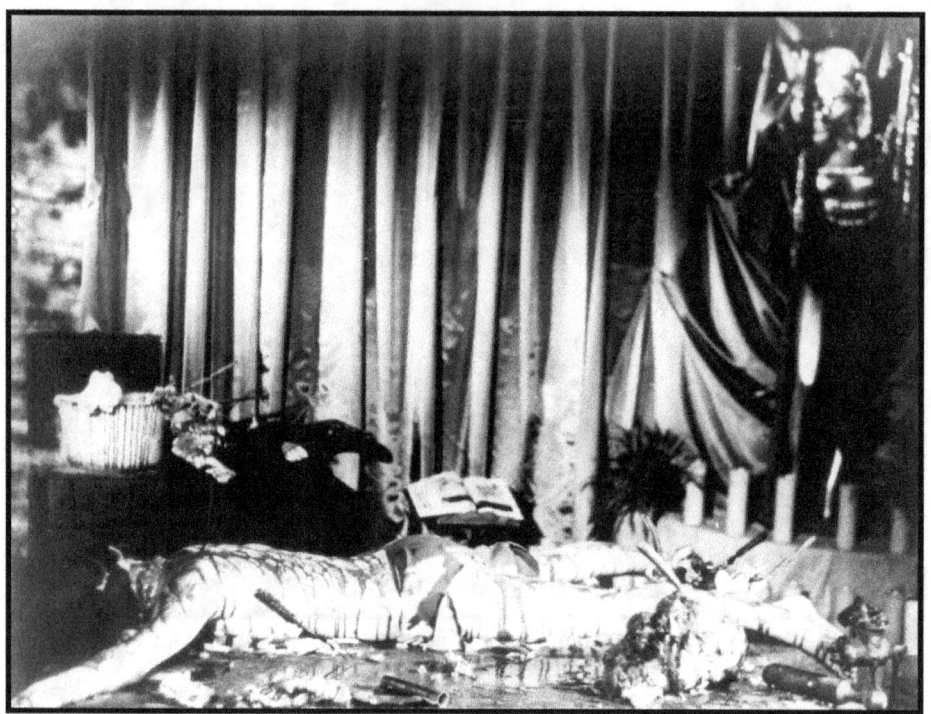

The moments of gore in *Blood Feast* are so over-the-top that they can easily induce laugher in contemporary audiences, 50 years after its release.

in matter-of-fact fashion, reflecting a paucity of talent both in front of and behind the camera. Even the money shot murder sequences have a "let's get on with it" quality that undercuts any real sense of suspense. If not for the eyebrow-raising nature of its death scenes, *Blood Feast* would be considered forgotten fodder for the drive-in market.

But my, do those murder scenes pack a punch! In the film's opening moments, a statuesque blonde strips to her bra and panties as a prelude to her evening bath (yet another treat for the prurient-minded viewer). A radio announcer who warns the populace of another brutal slaying helps set the stage. As our lady friend reclines in the comfort of soap and bubbles, a shadowy figure approaches. Out comes a knife—a BIG knife. With sudden and unsuspected savageness, the attacker begins hacking away, decorating the bath fixtures with a snail trail of blood. He soon focuses on the object of his quest and plucks out the poor girl's eyeball. The squirm-inducing luridness of this sequence is heightened by the overly saturated color intensity of the film stock, a quality that renders the gooey body parts and copious blood smears all the more vivid.

Blood Feast's moments of gore are so over-the-top that they can easily induce laughter in contemporary viewers. Some evidence exists that the risible quality was quite intentional—Ramses' plan to serve his treasure at a swank dinner party and his demise in the back of a garbage track are both laughably ironic. But whether or not Lewis was clever enough to recognize such storytelling niceties is ultimately beside the point. Watching a film like *Blood Feast* is a unique experience in horror cinema, even if audiences may feel the need to flush out their brain afterwards.

Black Humor

From *Zombieland* to *Shaun of the Dead*, black humor has become one of the clichés of modern horror cinema. The bite of this once edgy approach to storytelling is now dull through overuse, but it was once a vital component in the filmmaker's toolbox. A wonderfully entertaining example of this is Roger Corman's 1959 mini-classic, *A Bucket of Blood*.

A Bucket of Blood tells the dark, comic tale of Walter Paisley, busboy for a local beatnik hangout, whose yearning for acceptance becomes the catalyst for an escalating spiral of murders. Dick Miller plays Paisley with convincing aplomb, and Miller became one of the stalwarts of Corman's informal repertory company. He enacts the role in convincing hangdog manner, following every word of his pretentious circle of friends and always putting his worst foot forward in an effort to be part of the crowd. When Walter echoes the existential musings of Maxwell (Julian Burton), the local poet laureate, the author steadfastly remains unimpressed. "I refuse to do anything twice," proclaims Maxwell in dismissive fashion, his enlightened demeanor a sharp contract to Walter's simple view of the world.

Satire also adds to the film's fun. Scriptwriter Charles Griffith throws sharp-edged barbs at the beatnik culture of the 1950s, as well as the modern phenomenon of sudden celebrity. Wannabe artists reciting free verse poetry share the stage with a jazz saxophonist, as the crowd expresses its ultra-hip approval. After the unveiling of Walter's first creation—a dead cat covered in clay—he unexpectedly becomes the focus of attention. Maxwell proclaims him a "master sculptor," while Carla (Barboura Morris), whom Walter worships from afar, is astounded by his craft. Walter's rise from nonentity to rising star becomes an ironic comment on the arbitrary nature of approval in today's celebrity-obsessed world.

Walter's series of murders illustrate both the humor and the satire of *A Bucket of*

Simon Pegg and Nick Frost stand ready in *Shaun of the Dead* (2004).

Walter Paisley (Dick Miller) stares at the dead cat covered in clay; Paisley will soon become an overnight celebrity in the beatnik world in *A Bucket of Blood*.

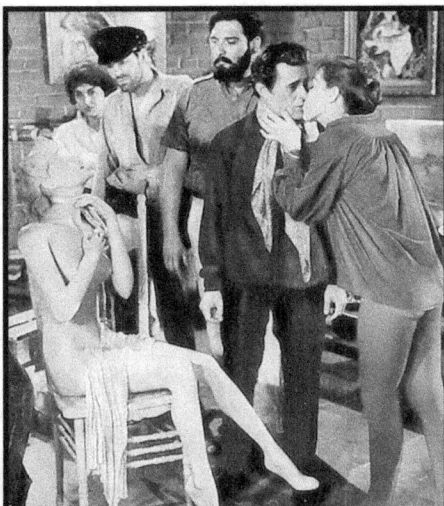

Walter Paisley (who begins as the bus boy) finds himself kissed in the local beatnik club, surounding himself with oddballs and pretentious friends in *A Bucket of Blood*.

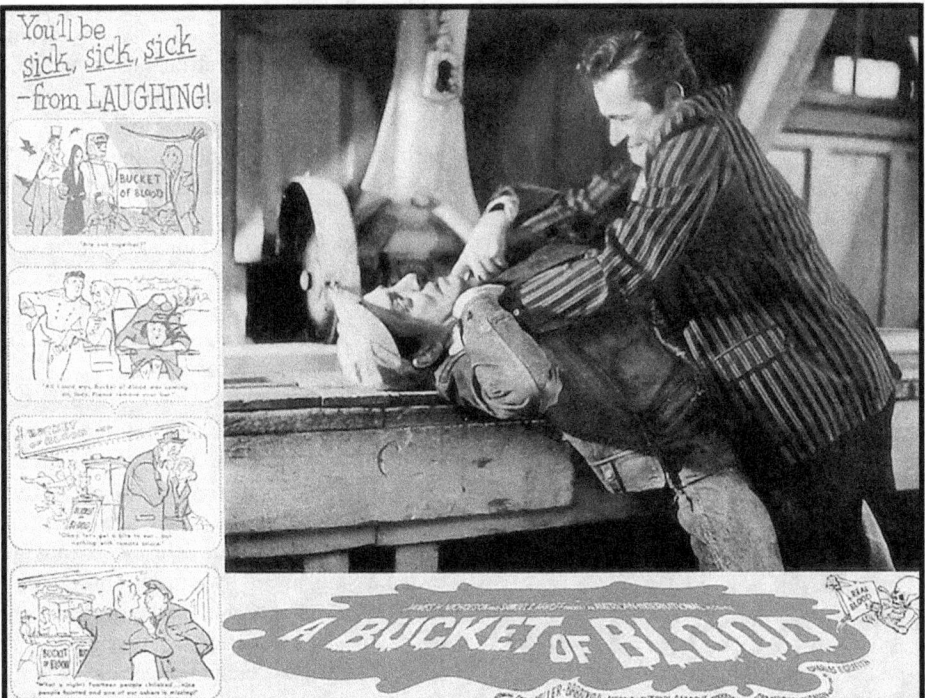

Water Paisley, in his journey from artist to murderer, dispatches his final vicitm in a lumberyard via the blades of an industrial band saw.

Blood. The cycle starts innocently enough when Walter advertently stabs a feline that has become entrapped within the walls of his apartment. The next death is likewise without malice—after Walter unknowingly receives a package of heroin from an admirer, an undercover cop approaches him. Panicky and fearing arrest, Walter brandishes a frying pan and beats the officer to death. With death number three, Walter begins to show criminal intent. After a local "model" ridicules Walter's newfound celebrity status, he invites the girl to pose for him and promptly claims her as his next victim. The last crime reveals full-blown premeditation; Walter, now engrossed in the identity of an "artiste," wanders the city in search of inspiration. By chance he wanders into a lumberyard and dispatches his final victim via the blades of an industrial band saw. Each crime advances Walter's career and further tightens the proverbial noose around his neck.

Roger Corman remains the most celebrated low-budget filmmaker of the 1950s for good reason. Working with the same wonky storylines, threadbare production values and competent but second-tier performers, Corman somehow packaged these leftover spare parts in a way that was more satisfying than the rest. *A Bucket of Blood* displays these qualities in abundance and its use of black humor helps the film zero in on its satiric targets. It's an approach that modern horror filmmakers, for all their edgy sensibilities, can't quite seem to master.

Zombies

Okay, it's a bit of a cheat to call *The Last Man on Earth* a zombie film. An adaptation of Richard Matheson's novella *I Am Legend* concerns a vampire infestation that impacts the entire civilized world. But in style, tone and assorted plot details, the nightwalkers that haunt the film's narrative would be right at home in *28 Days Later*, *ParaNorman* and any George Romero movie.

The Last Man on Earth (1964) features Vincent Price as Bob Morris, sole survivor of a fatal plague that devastated mankind. After death, victims of the infection become reanimated as dead/alive beings that roam at night looking for fresh blood on which to feed. Morris' existence becomes a fatalistic game of hide and seek. By day he hunts and destroys his monstrous adversaries, and

In the shadowy world of *28 Days Later* (2002), it is virtually impossible to tell the humans from the zombies, those former people infected with "the rage."

Having lost his wife and child to the plague, Morris fortifies his defenses with planks of wood and bottles of booze, from *The Last Man on Earth*.

by night he takes refuge in his boarded up home from the unholy undead storm that rages outside.

The film's mind-numbing sense of despair foreshadows today's zombie films in an uncanny way. A lengthy flashback shows us the world that Bob Morris once knew and how it quickly crumbled to pieces. Once a successful scientist, Bob was on ground zero when news of the devastating plague began to break. He works furiously and remains cautiously optimistic that a cure can be found, until tragedy touches his own world. First his young daughter succumbs, exhibiting signs of the telltale cough, progressive anemia and gradual blindness that inevitably leads to death. Morris' sense of denial persists even in a time of crisis; he struggles with authorities to retrieve his daughter's body prior to cremation, knowing full well the living hell that waits for the deceased. Bob's wife falls victim next and, despite his best efforts, she also perishes, leaving him alone to face a world gone mad. The golden memory of happy times hangs over Morris like a half-remembered dream, a constant reminder of life as it will never be again.

Many reviewers have noted the Romero-esque qualities of the walking dead in this film and with good reason. Slow moving and devoid of cognitive thought, these living dead are easy to thwart individually but gain the advantage by amassing into a swarming horde. The imagery is memorable and appropriately unsettling. Destruction of the undead is accomplished by cremation or by staking the bodies, a quest that gives Bob Morris a new, though ultimately futile, pursuit in life. The impressive effect is undercut only by a

Former scientist Bob Morris (Vincent Price) attempts to survive in a world gone mad, fighting off a predatory zombie in *The Last Man on Earth*.

Revivalist theater owner Ollie (Philip Coolidge) discusses personal problems with a gun pointed at Dr. Chapin (Vincent Price), from *The Tingler*.

menace is established with a complex and interesting, if somewhat unlikely, premise.

Even more fun is to be had as the film takes a turn into domestic disturbance territory. Vincent Price is cast as Dr. Warren Chapin, whose research on the human fear response results in a chance discovery of the Tingler. But the doctor has a problem in duplicitous wife Isobel (Patricia Cutts). The two endure a combative, anger-fueled relationship that threatens to turn murderous any minute. Although Warren's impulses are held in check by his financial dependence on his wife's inheritance, his contempt slips out via dialogue. "You're a scheming and evil woman," he tells Isobel after she returns from another late night rendezvous with one of her many male "friends." She retorts by telling Warren that he has "lost contact with living people," the remark made even more stinging by the insincere smile that beams across her angelic face. Verbal dollops of poison like these (a trademark of screenwriter Robb White) add an extra level of enjoyment to this already over-the-top monster fest.

The film's most celebrated moment, and surely one of the most bizarre in horror movie history, is saved for the final reel. Warren has removed a Tingler from the body of a woman who, he later discovers, was murdered. To confront the perpetrator, and to return the Tingler to its rightful resting place, Warren pays a call on her husband at the revival movie theater where he lives. And here is where the fun begins. The Tingler escapes and slithers to the occupied theater below. Realizing the potential danger, the pair enters the theater just in time to see the bizarre image of the Tingler crawling across a blank movie screen. The dulcet tones of Vincent Price warn us, "Please do not panic—but scream—scream for your lives! The Tingler is loose in this theater!!!" Imagine screaming your fool head off at the most audacious promotional stunt in movie history, while a buzzing motor vibrates your ass. Now *that's* entertainment!

These are but a few of the esoteric joys to behold in *The Tingler*. No one in his or her right mind would ever call William Castle a great filmmaker, but in terms of showmanship, the man had few equals. In the days when movie-going was an event, the promotional ballyhoo in which Castle specialized could turn an ordinary film into a "must see" experience and generate memories that could last a lifetime. Today's Internet-driven promotional campaigns may be slick and reach their target markets effortlessly, but the sense of fun generated by *The Tingler* is a quality that, sadly, is all but lost to today's movie audience.

Other recent horror film trends have their roots in the cinema of the past. Heart-throb vampires or monster rally matchups may be the flavor of the week, but a quick review of the films of decades past reveals that these too have antecedents on the horror movie family tree. Remakes of old favorites have become a reliable and oft-used corporate strategy. To be sure, these newer versions are dressed up with quick-cut editing, copious amounts of CGI and other effects to fulfill the expectations of contemporary audiences. But as for the basic premise, well, let's just say that this double feature has made the rounds before.

Pop culture is growing by leaps and bounds. In the decades to come, the movie-going experience is destined to change too. Trends may come and go as regularly as the changing of the seasons, exciting when they first come along but not all that different from what has come and gone before. Because, in many cases, it really has been done before.

Dr. Chapin and his young assistant David Morris (Darryl Hickman) work long hours in their home laboratory to solve the mystery of *The Tingler*.

Subterranean Chills
The Cave in Fantasy Cinema

by Barry Atkinson

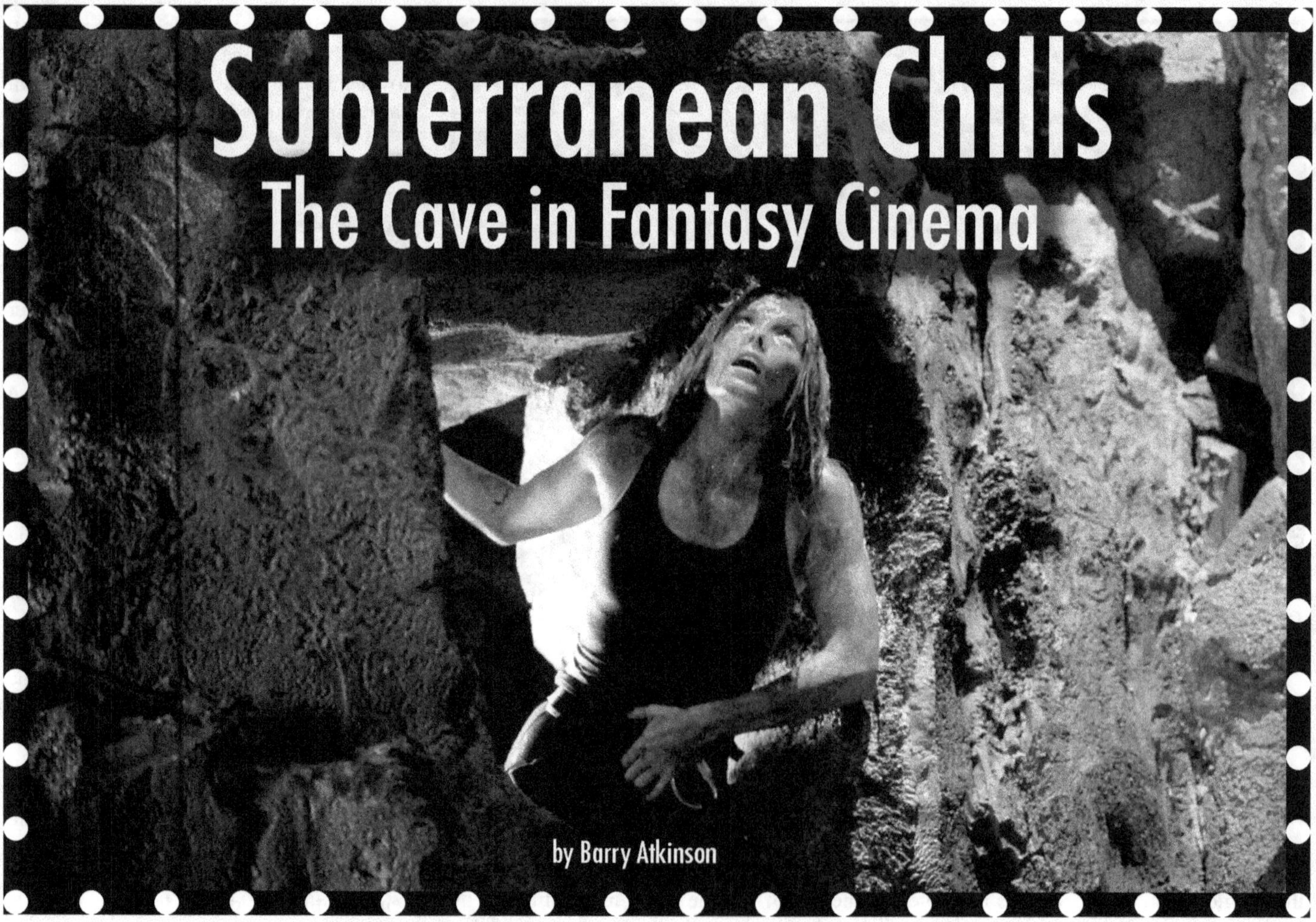

Female cavers face the fear of the dark and the horror contained within, from The Descent.

Saturday, December 5, 1953. Myself (aged six), Billy and Pete lined up on the edge of a ragged dark hole, in dense woods at the bottom of our respective gardens, leading to God knows where. To become a member of the local gang, I had to undergo an initiation ceremony, to prove my worth, and this was it. I chatted, stalling for time, when Billy gave me a gentle push in the back. "Off you go, Baz," he said, grinning, but I didn't find anything to grin about in my situation. Gingerly lowering myself into this pit, I realized, even at that tender age, that I had to face up to my own worst fears. What was crouching down there in the gloom? Would whatever it was reach out and tear me from limb to limb? What would "it" look like? Drawing breath, I dropped down about seven feet onto a damp earthy floor smelling of mildew. Now the hard part occurred. Heart racing, I doubled up in order to squeeze my skinny frame along a U-bend on hands and knees, emerging in daylight through another entrance, panting, dirty but victorious.

Billy and Pete's underground camp, dug out of Surrey's chalk soil, was my first introduction to what can loosely be described as a cave, and I was hooked. Sixty years later, I still am. Honeycombed with abandoned mine workings and sea

Doctor Blood's Coffin **was filmed around the abandoned mine workings that litter the cliffs in and around Cornwall in the United Kingdom.**

caves, a potholer's dream come true, is Cornwall, where I live, in the far southwest of the United Kingdom. But such caves are also a filmmaker's dream as well. Way back in 1960, United Artists filmed *Doctor Blood's Coffin* in and around the abandoned mine workings that litter the cliffs near St. Just, Botallack Head and Zennor; Kieron Moore used the underground levels of Wheal Owles to perform his experiments in illegal heart surgery and there bring the dead back to life. Six years later, Hammer's *The Plague of the Zombies* took place in a derelict Cornish tin mine (although actually filmed near Bray and Farnham). Then in 1971 Glendale's *Crucible of Terror* had satanic Mike Raven coating female corpses in bronze, shot amid the Tywarnhaile Mine ruins near Porthtowan and the Blue Hills Mine at St. Agnes. Horror moviemakers have never been afraid to venture underground for their thrills, as these three go to show. But Moore and Raven were carrying out their nefarious schemes in manmade caves. It's the cave made by the hand of Mother Nature where we will concentrate here, as opposed to mine workings, sewers, crypts, cellars, storm drains, catacombs, tombs, subways, bunkers, train tunnels, the bowels of a spaceship and any other cavity below our feet (plus, of course, the ultimate cave system of all—the inside of the human body [*Fantastic Voyage*, 1966]).

Since primitive Man first emerged from caves over a million years ago as a Pliocene ape, these geological formations in the Earth's crust have continued to hold a fascination, not gone unnoticed by the film studios, major and minor. The cave can be a key ingredient in any fantasy picture, either as the centerpiece or as part of a whole. In some ways, a cave can be likened to a physical extension of one's mind: Nightmares and visions of terror that suppress themselves within a person's thought processes can materialize inside the cranium-type confines of a black empty void surrounded by rocky walls, imagination running riot. What *is* it that's concealing itself in those pitch-black, unfathomable recesses beyond our torch beams? Freudian in concept, maybe, but very true, tapping into man's elemental phobia of dark, enclosed spaces and what lies waiting in the shadows. This psychological angle hasn't really been fully exploited in horror cinema, movies content to use a cave for all manner of nasty beasties to pounce on those foolhardy enough to wander into their domain. It *was* attempted in Universal's *Sanctum* (2011) where a team of cave divers carrying out a survey on an extensive system in Papua, New Guinea (actually shot in New Mexico's Cave of the Swallows) becomes cut off from the outside world when storm-water floods the exit

Filmed near Bray and Farnham but supposedly occurring around a Cornish tin mine, Hammer's *Plague of the Zombies* includes a shocking sequence where Alice (Jacqueline Pearce) is about to lose her head.

gallery, necessitating an urgent need to find another way out. The intriguing possibilities on offer, where the cave itself becomes the monster and forces everyone to confront his or her inner-most demons ("What could possibly go wrong, diving in caves?"), were ruined by over-dramatics from the cast and the grave error of making the surroundings too brightly lit, thus dissipating the fright factor. Cave regions are extremely dark verging on inky blackness, where one can see next to nothing beyond the sweep of a flashlight. Given a grittier approach and playing on the film's one great line, "Panic's the vulture that sits on your shoulder," this might have worked as a "man versus cave" thriller but failed to live up to expectations due to the glossy treatment given it, no doubt to make the movie appeal to a mass family audience.

George Melies' 65-foot short, *La Caverne Maudite* (*The Cave of Demons*), dating back to cinema's early years of 1898, can lay claim to being the very first fantasy motion picture where a cave played a major role; this one, encountered by a young woman, contained the spirits and skeletons of peo-

Richard Denning (right) is lowered into the monsters' lair in *The Black Scorpion*.

The Cyclops and the dragon exit the cave entrance, from *The 7th Voyage of Sinbad*

ple who had died there under mysterious circumstances. Since then, scores of fantasy movies have been released that feature a cave, or caves and caverns, as an integral element in their setup, stretching from the classic (*King Kong*, 1933) to the woeful (2008's 3-D *Journey to the Center of the Earth*). Caves can be many things to many people. They can be the portal to another realm (*Cesta do Praveku*, 1954); they can harbor monsters who regard caves as their home (*The Black Scorpion*, 1957); primitive cave-dwellers live in them (*Creatures the World Forgot*, 1971); something terrible can appear from a cave entrance (Ray Harryhausen's Cyclops in *The 7th Voyage of Sinbad*, 1958); experiments take place within their walls (*Mesa of Lost Women*, 1953); they can be the gateway to a lost civilization (*The Mole People*, 1956); they can be underwater (*The Incredible Petrified World*, 1959); vampires inhabit them (*Cave of the Living Dead*, 1964); they can be on the moon (*First Men in the Moon*, 1964); ferocious creatures hide from man in them (*The Monster of Piedras Blancas*, 1958); man hides from ferocious creatures in them (*The Cyclops*, 1957); the human race seeks refuge in them (*World Without End*, 1956); aliens plan world domination inside them (*It Conquered the World*, 1956); humans become trapped and lost in them (*The Descent*, 2005); classic monsters are found frozen in them (*House of Frankenstein*, 1944); and explorers can spend almost the entire length of a movie inside them (*Unknown World*, 1950). Cave fantasy flicks, to a lesser degree, persist right up to the present day. *The Cave* is a not-so-shining example dating from 2005 of the "monster is lurking in the darkness" category, while Magnet's tremendously different *Troll*

Hunter (2010) has a tribe of distinctly un-Grimm-like ugly giants inhabiting a murky Norwegian cavern.

I've listed the categories; let's examine in detail those movies that fall within their sphere, from scenes of sheer wonder (James Mason, Pat Boone, Arlene Dahl and Peter Ronson staring down into the dazzling crystal hollow in *Journey to the Center of the Earth*, 1959), through scenes of sheer alarm (the women cavers mercilessly assaulted by the subhuman flesh-eaters in *The Descent*), to scenes of sheer desperation (soapsuds cascading down cave walls masquerading as a hallucinogenic fungus in *The Unknown Terror*, 1957). Disregarding the *Batman*, *Star Wars* and *Star Trek* franchises, plus Peter Jackson's *Lord of the Rings* trilogy, modern-day fantasy movies (except those produced by independent film companies) tend to shun the good old cave unless one is encountered en route to another destination, as in the vast cavern (more like a colossal geode) of black crystals pierced by the burrowing machine in *The Core* (2003), and the similar crystal-encrusted chamber seen in UFO's 2000 *Deep Core* (Cinetel Films' *Descent* [2005] also presented us with a boring machine penetrating the Earth's crust and entering large caverns, but no crystals are on display in this lame offering). The

One of the moon cows that lives beneath the surface of the moon in *First Men in the Moon*

The Centaur from *The Golden Voyage of Sinbad*

genre's classic period, the 1950s, embraced caves wholeheartedly, adding a mixed sense of wonder and trepidation to many a worthy outing and boosting those less worthy, which is why so many of the movies mentioned in this article date from those heady days. We kick off with:

The Caves of Ray Harryhausen

The stop-motion maestro, who sadly passed away in May of this year, peppered his fantasy pictures with cave sequences, notably from *The 7th Voyage of Sinbad* onwards. Who, as a child, can ever forget the astounding sight of the roaring Cyclops striding out of a cave entrance and, at the end, the flamboyant dragon emerging from the same portal? Plus, of course, wily magician Torin Thatcher's devilish Arabian Nights' laboratory lies inside an ostentatious cavern, guarded by that fire-breathing dragon. *Mysterious Island* (1961) had three pivotal cave events: the cliff cave utilized as a hideout by Michael Craig and company, the humongous bee colony discovered by Michael Callan and Beth Rogan and the watery cavern in which Captain Nemo's Nautilus resided. Todd Armstrong went head-to-head with the Hydra in the creature's picturesque, shadowy lair (*Jason and the Argonauts*, 1963), and *First Men in the Moon* (1964) depicted a subterranean lunar world as entrancing as that envisaged in Fox's *Journey to the Center of the Earth*. From *One Million Years B.C.* (1966) to Harryhausen's final picture in 1981, *Clash of the Titans*, the cave was given prominence, mostly to accommodate mythical beings hidden away from the world of mortals: a tribe of cannibalistic ape men straight out of a Hammer horror movie terrifying John Richardson and Raquel Welch (*One Million Years B.C.*); Kali, the six-armed statue, the Gryphon and the Centaur (*The Golden Voyage of Sinbad*, 1974); the saber tooth tiger (*Sinbad and the Eye of the Tiger*, 1977); and the Kraken in *Clash of the Titans* all inhabited caves. And in 1957, the Ymir's egg was discovered in a sea cave in *20 Million Miles to Earth*, with the fully-grown space monster briefly retreating into a rocky cleft, away from a pesky helicopter. Yes, it has to be said that a Ray Harryhausen fantasy without a cave was like bread without butter, one complemented the other, heightening a sense of mystery in a production already steeped in it.

Keep Out, Earthlings!

If traveling millions of miles across space to our planet, where better to make plans for conquering Earth than a cave? *Invaders from Mars* (1953), *Killers from Space* (1954), *It Conquered the World* and *The Brain from Planet Arous* (1958) all told of aliens intent on taking over the Earth and using the seclusion of caves to plot their diabolical activities. Paul Blaisdell's cucumber-shaped alien with the beady eyes and big rubber claws from *It Conquered the World* represents classic '50s monster schlock, the alien trundled out of its cave hideout to face Lee Van Cleef and the army in one of sci-fi's most memorably corny finales. But at least it had an otherworldly look about it. The glowing brain in *The*

The watery cavern in which Captain Nemo's Nautilus resided, from *Mysterious Island*

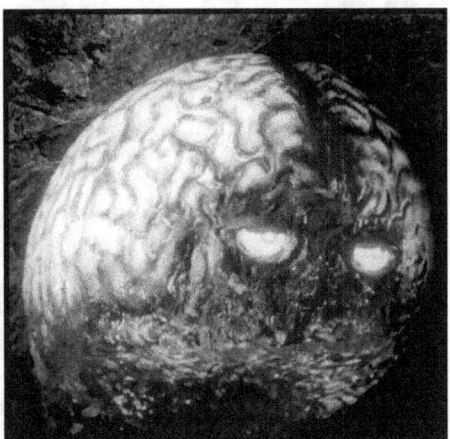

The evil brain Gor, residing within a cave, plots the conquest of Earth in *The Brain from Planet Arous*.

The military and young Jimmy Hunt use the alien death ray to burrow through stone caverns, from *Invaders from Mars*.

The invading aliens of *Killers from Space* operate from within a cave.

Space Children (1958) and the protoplasmic blob in *The Flame Barrier* (1958), both alien entities skulking secretively at the back of caves, made it hard for audiences to accept that such lowly forms of life could control man and do him harm. In this respect, the cave gave them an aura of dread they might not have otherwise deserved.

This is my Home—You're *Not* Welcome!

Spare a thought for old Kong as he ambles slowly through the Gothic arches of Byron L. Crabbe and Mario Larrinaga's fantastic Gustave Doré–inspired cathedral-sized cavern—he didn't ask for, or want, any interlopers trespassing on his territory. Neither did his white-furred youngster (*Son of Kong*, 1933), whose kingdom lay within Skull Island's network of lovingly rendered lofty rocky chambers. Also hacked off with being disturbed in their natural abode were the nest of giant scorpions in *The Black Scorpion*; the radiation-mutated crabs in *Attack of the Crab Monsters* (1957); the Gill-Man in *Creature from the Black Lagoon* (1954); the Yetis in *The Snow Creature* (1954), *Man Beast* (1955), *Half Human* (1955) and *The Abominable Snowman of the Himalayas* (1957); the mighty mollusks in *The Monster That Challenged the World* (1957); the overgrown leeches in *Demons of the Swamp* (1959); the huge spider in *World Without End* (1956), which also turned up in *Queen of Outer Space* (1958); and *Earth vs. the Spider*'s oversized tarantula (1958). All reacted violently to man butting in on their patch, in this instance a cave. In *Half Human*, the '50s finest Yeti movie, the enraged creature dragged Momoko Kochi into a wondrous cave system, intending to toss her into a volcanic vent in reprisal for its infant's death. Toho's atmospheric art direction in this prolonged finale can only be fully appreciated in the rare, uncut print of this film.

It was the after-effects of the H-bomb that awoke *Rodan* from its million-year-old slumber deep within Toho's fabulously concocted cavern; Kenji Sahara had the misfortune to stagger into this cave-of-caves seething with giant insects and witness the titanic flying reptile hatch from its egg. The radioactive blob known as *X: The Unknown* (1956) only got fed-up and started to create havoc when soldiers descended into its below-ground lair, as did the Munchkin-like mole people in *Superman and the Mole-Men* (1951), oil drillers disturbing their peaceful existence in caverns six miles under the Earth. Jim Davis and fellow scientists had to combat the big mutated wasps in *Monster from*

Dr. Anderson (Lee Van Cleef) goes on-on-one with the invader from Venus whose base of operation is a cave, from *It Conquered the World*.

Green Hell (1957) after walking into their volcanic cavity, and if one nosed around in that sea cave occupied by *The Monster of Piedras Blancas*, one stood a good chance of having his head ripped off. Meanwhile, the spidery horror in *Beast from Haunted Cave* (1959) cocooned its gangster victims for daring to enter its home unannounced.

More recent caving fare includes *Troll Hunter*. If one doesn't douse himself in Troll stench and renounce Christianity, so the old legends state, one stands no chance at all of escaping those killer elves the size of office blocks snoring merrily away in their cavern habitat; human scent makes them as angry as hell. Cinerenta's beautifully shot but only moderately successful *The Cave* has cave divers, led by Cole Hauser, battling for their lives against carnivorous flying flesh-eaters. And in *Outlander* (2008), a guilty pleasure from director Howard McCain, human-looking alien Jim Caviezel hunts down his stowaway nemesis, a fire-breathing Moorwen, in a network of caves in 8th-century Norway, where it and its offspring have retreated from the warring Vikings.

The lesson to be learnt here is to leave well enough alone unless we nurse a death wish and want to unleash something horrible on the populace. Approach any cave with caution—we never know what we may find!

Let's Experiment

Shut away from the interfering outside world, demented scientists carried on their work unmolested in secret caves. The heyday of the sci-fi serial, the '30s, '40s and start of the '50s, normally had villains up to no good in cave laboratories: *Flash Gordon's Trip to Mars* (1938), *The Crimson Ghost* (1946), *King of the Rocket Men* (1949) and *Flying Disc Man from Mars* (1950) all spotlighted caves in which mad scientists planned world domination. Jackie Coogan went bananas in *Mesa of Lost Women*, producing "tarantula" women, midgets and rather large spiders inside his cave lab, and Gerald Milton nurtured a slimy fungus in the legendary Cave of the Dead that changed natives into frothy-faced mutants in *The Unknown Terror*. *The Flying Saucer* (1951) turned out to be a UFO constructed by Roy Engel in an Alaskan cave, designed to swoop over American cities and force the authorities into blaming the Russians for spying on them. In Hammer's *The Damned* (1963), Alexander Knox and Viveca Lindfors experimented on the effects of radiation on humans in a remote coastal cave. However, by and large, underground laboratories in fantasy were built by man beneath their castles (*Frankenstein 1970*, 1958), under the house (*The Brain that Wouldn't Die*, 1959) and in deep-level installations (*Westworld*, 1973). Caves give sanctuary to all kinds of monsters that weren't necessarily created within them. Rock walls are nowhere near as intimidating as the cold sterility of a laboratory wall.

The intelligent Yeti appears inside a cave in *The Abominable Snowman of the Himalayas*.

The simian missing-link Yeti appears in Japan's *Half Human*.

Poor, pathetic humans (such as Russell Johnson and Mel Welles, standing) know better than to venture into the radiated crab monsters' lair, from *Attack of the Crab Monsters*.

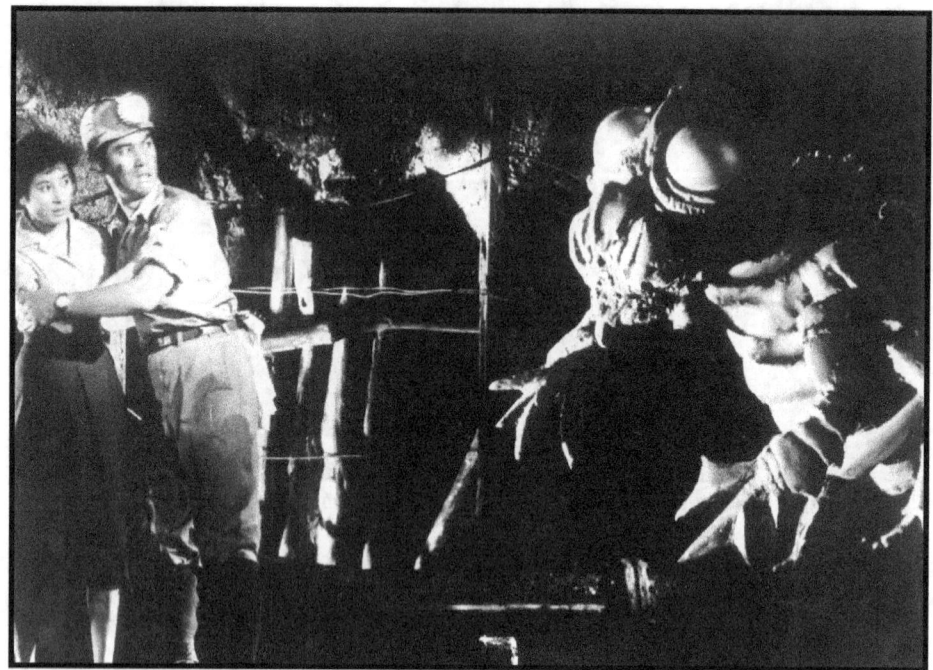

Deep beneath an inactive volcano, Japanese miners discover giant baby insects and other terrors, from *Rodan*.

In *Flying Disc Man from Mars*, criminals plan world domination from within caves, such as the one depicted here.

The Gateway to Other Worlds and Civilizations

When Josef Lukas, Petr Herrmann, Vladimir Bejval and Zdenek Hustak rowed their small boat through the portal of a dark cave, they emerged into the Ice Age in Karel Zeman's evocative *Cesta do Praveku* (aka, *Journey to the Beginning of Time*); that cave became the gateway to another universe (in this case, a prehistoric one), as far removed from the world we live in that anyone could possibly imagine. This writer isn't the only person fascinated with dark entrances and where they lead to—moviemakers have long since plunged their audiences into the depths of the Earth via cave systems, taking us on unforgettable journeys along the way. As far back as 1935, Mascot's 12-chapter serial *The Phantom Empire* saw, of all people, singing cowboy star Gene Autry and a gang of crooks stumbling across the underground civilization of Murania, ruled by despotic Wheeler Oakman and his force of tacky-looking slave robots. Moving forward to the 1950s, Lippert's enterprising *Unknown World* predated *The Core* and its ilk by 50 years: Scientist Victor Kilian invents the Cyclotram, a machine capable of tunneling through the Earth's mantle in search of a possible subterranean sanctuary (a geological shelter) should the planet be decimated by a nuclear holocaust. Partly filmed in New Mexico's Carlsbad Caverns, this low-budget venture, rarely seen these days, scores highly in the imagination stakes; the crew discovers a vast cave 1,640 miles down, encompassing the mother of all waterfalls, a boundless sea, and pinnacles of rock soaring into a hazy sky. Unfortunately, this underground paradise is unsuitable for human habitation because the atmosphere induces sterility. Jack Rabin and Irving Block were the men responsible for the cheap but impressive effects and visuals, as they were involved with many '50s fantasy films, proving conclusively that filmmakers didn't need an astronomical amount of money to present something creative to an audience.

The same can be said about *The Mole People* (1956). Anthropologists John Agar, Hugh Beaumont and Nestor Paiva descend

Carol (June Kenney) and Mike (Gene Persson) venture forth into the giant spider's cave lair to discover rotting former victims, from *Earth vs. the Spider*.

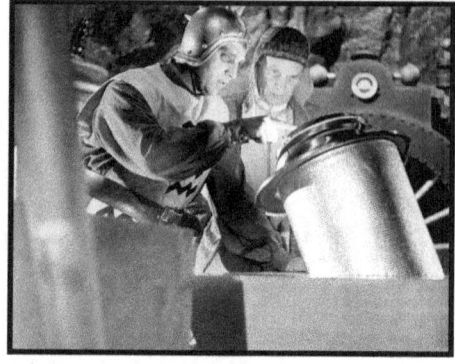

In *Commando Cody*, villains are up to no good in cave laboratories.

Baron Victor von Frankenstein (Boris Karloff) maintains his hidden lab within a cavern underground his castle, from *Frankenstein 1970*.

Doug McClure fights a prehistoric beast in *At the Earth's Core*.

King of the Rocketmen illustrates the typical underground lab used by the criminal element that planned to take over the world in serials of the 1940s and 1950s.

a narrow shaft on an Asian mountain and come upon the Sumerians, rulers of one of Universal's lesser, but nevertheless endearing, monsters, the warty Mole People of the title. Situated in immense caverns, the antiquated land of the Sumerians was well realized by Universal's set design department, despite the movie's medium-sized budget, as was the mole beasts' Hades-like habitation. Although sneered at by some critics, *The Mole People* is a worthy addition to the "cave movie" genre. Besides, John Agar is in it and that's reason enough for any fan to watch.

20th Century Fox released, in 1959, what many buffs consider to be the supreme fantasy spectacular taking place almost exclusively miles beneath the Earth's surface, *Journey to the Center of the Earth*. Expensively shot in color and CinemaScope, the design and effects work, supervised by L.B. Abbott, James B. Gordon and Joseph Kish, is nigh on faultless, presenting all budding speleologists with an array of underground delights: gleaming, multicolored crystalline grottos, a phosphorescent pool, fathomless gulfs, a cavern full of giant mushrooms, algae having the property of "cool chemical light," dinosaurs inhabiting dark passages, tortuous and twisting galleries, a salt labyrinth, and an ocean housed within a mammoth chamber. All this plus one of Bernard Herrmann's top scores—no wonder this subterranean extravaganza has stood the test of time. Subsequent modern, re-imagined versions have failed to match this peerless fantasy production, in particular the recent juvenile, CGI-loaded charade starring Brendan Fraser. Fox's unofficial follow-up to the 1959 original, *The Lost World* (1960), rounded off the action with a prolonged cave sequence, the cavity containing not only a tribe of natives but a dinosaur living in a lake of boiling water, a lively interlude in an otherwise flat picture. Also finding his way to the Earth's center was Reg Park in Mario Bava's eye-catching *Hercules at the Center of the Earth* (1961), released in the States as *Hercules in the Haunted World*, but no dinosaurs or lost cities appeared here, only Christopher Lee as a demonic priest lusting for eternal life.

The most bizarre version of Verne's tale comes in the form of *Where Time Began*, an English/German collaboration released in 1978 by Alemena Films. British actor Kenneth More played a German (?) professor who discovers a parchment giving cryptic clues of a route to the Earth's center via an extinct volcanic crater in Iceland. Fairly faithful to the book to begin with, the movie includes the obligatory forest of monster mushrooms, a big ape, giant tortoises, an underground ocean and plastic-looking dinosaurs. But what prompted

Peter Ronson, Pat Boone, Arlene Dahl and James Mason go underground to take a *Journey to the Center of the Earth*.

the makers to plonk a futuristic city in the Earth's depths, with guarded hints of time and space and "It's from 1914" clogging up the script, is anyone's guess. Added to this head-scratching puzzle, the photography inside the volcano's galleries showing the travelers traversing dangerous rock faces is so muddy that we can't see who's doing what and, further sabotaging the Victorian period feel, the title score is a pop song sung by Clean Wheat. One part success, two parts failure (Kenneth More is fine; his German co-stars less so), this oddity was never given a release date in Britain and America; looked at today, it's not too hard to understand why.

Much, much lower down the scale, Johnny Weissmuller's '40s/'50s *Jungle Jim* potboilers, all 16 produced by "Jungle Sam" Katzman, featured caves in abundance and one of these led to a lost civilization of sorts. In number 15 in the series, *Jungle Moon Men* (1955), our intrepid hero in the safari suit and slouch hat met up with legendary moon goddess Helene Stanton who, like She Who Must Be Obeyed, ruled her minuscule empire inside a huge art deco-designed cavern. Stanton wanted hunky Weissmuller as her next high priest, but the stony-faced one was having none of it, preferring the wide open spaces to the rocky confines of a cave, however attractive Stanton was. In the series' final entry *Devil Goddess* (1955), deluded scientist Billy Griffiths took on the mantle of Moses, conducting experiments inside a volcanic cave where he has set himself up as a sacred fire god to strike fear into the local natives. *Mark of the Gorilla* (1950) saw treasure-hunting Nazis hiding out in a cave

Professor Challenger (Claude Rains, third from right) leads his expedition party into a prolonged cave sequence in *The Lost World*.

and venturing forth in 1940s gorilla suits to scare off the inquisitive (look, we're talking *Jungle Jim* here, not high art!), while *Jungle Manhunt* (1951) had grade B stalwart Lyle Talbot concocting synthetic diamonds in a cave only accessible by negotiating mine tunnels. All this was good ramshackle fun for lovers of low-brow hokum everywhere.

Between 1975 and 1978, director Kevin Connor and producer John Dark made four fantasy/lost world movies that highlighted caves within their framework: *The Land that Time Forgot*, *At the Earth's Core*, *The People that Time Forgot* and *Warlords of Atlantis*. Remembered now for collectively hosting the largest assemblage of cardboard-looking prehistoric animals ever to hit the big screen, the movies dealt

From left, Hugh Beaumont and John Agar discover an ancient civilization that exists in the bowels of the Earth, from *The Mole People*.

Jungle Manhunt, starring Johnny Weissmuller as Jungle Jim (far right), features Lyle Talbot (left) as a criminal manufacturing synthetic diamonds in a secret cave.

with primitive tribes and communities inhabiting cave systems. Best of the bunch was *At the Earth's Core*, a cross between *Unknown World* and *Journey to the Center of the Earth*, based on an Edgar Rice Burroughs novel. Peter Cushing's Victorian burrowing machine transported himself and Doug McClure into the depths of the Earth to the mauve-tinted land of Pellucidar, populated by gigantic reptiles, savage, telepathic bird monsters and Caroline Munroe in a very skimpy bikini. Corny and amateurish looking, these films have grown in stature over the years because of a growing disillusionment among fans with computerized effects that tend to render everything a little too polished and bland. "Bland" is certainly one word audiences could never use to describe Connor and Dark's enchanting quartet of ancient world flicks with caves as their central focal point.

The Frankenstein Monster and the Wolf Man—on Ice!

Universal's *Frankenstein Meets the Wolf Man* (1943) had Lon Chaney, Jr. in werewolf mode crashing through the blackened foundations of Frankenstein's wrecked house and finding the Frankenstein monster preserved in an ice-filled cavern. This scene was expanded to better effect in *House of Frankenstein,* incorporating a splendid Gothic cave sequence amid all the horror shenanigans. Boris Karloff and J. Carrol Naish, while investigating the ruins of Frankenstein's castle, stumble into a frosty grotto crammed with glittering stalagmites and stalactites, an icy river

Boris Karloff (Niemann) and J. Carroll Naish (Daniel) are about to stumble into the frozen grotto from *House of Frankenstein.*

Lon Chaney, Jr. as Larry Talbot finds the frozen body of the Frankenstein Monster in an ice-filled cavern, from *Frankenstein Meets the Wolf Man.*

coursing through this fairy tale cavern. But not quite a fairy tale—frozen in ice are the Wolf Man and the Frankenstein Monster, both of whom Karloff thaws out to enable him to locate Frankenstein's records. A marvelous piece of set design, unusual in a horror film, this scene was more or less repeated frame-by-frame in Hammer's *The Evil of Frankenstein* (1964), featuring Peter Cushing as the Baron discovering monster Kiwi Kingston's body preserved in glacial ice inside a cave. Lon Chaney Jr.'s Wolf Man also turned up in a sea cave in *House of Dracula* (1945), pouncing on Onslow Stevens before changing back into human form. The classic horror movies of the '40s were virtually bereft of cave action; these are the only three sequences that really stand out.

In Hammer's *Evil of Frankenstein*, the Baron (Peter Cushing) discovers the Creature (Kiwi Kingston)—cheap plastic wrap substituting for ice—forzen in an ice cave, duplicating the similar sequence from *Frankenstein Meets the Wolf Man*.

Caves That Are Not of this Earth

Columbia's *First Men in the Moon* really set the standard for alien cave systems. Thanks to Ray Harryhausen's painstaking production details in bringing the subterranean realm of the Selenites to graphic life, Columbia's adaptation of H.G. Wells' vintage classic was a veritable feast for the eye: shafts, crystal prisms, caverns within caverns, hexagonal cubes, interconnecting tunnels and 100-foot moon-calves. This was a world of unearthly wonder that has never been surpassed. Certainly, the moon caves in *Cat-Women of the Moon* (1953) and its remake *Missile to the Moon* (1958) don't bear comparison; all they contain are the ropiest monster spiders ever to crawl across the silver screen and a bevy of ex-glamour girls masquerading as Moon Maidens, inhabiting cardboard cut-out cities viewed from a distance as poorly painted backdrops. Another contender for shabbiest alien cave appears in Sidney Pink's sub-*Solaris* clunker, *Journey to the Seventh Planet* (1961), where a brain living in a frozen cave on Uranus controls the minds of visiting astronauts; the cerebral monster is eventually destroyed by John Agar in what must count as one of the actor's weakest productions.

We have to look to Paramount's *Robinson Crusoe on Mars* (1964) to find an acceptable cave on another planet. Paul Mantee plays a castaway astronaut making his home in a series of caves where he finds water, oxygen and Vic Lundin, a Martian on the run from deadly fighting machines. Directed by Byron Haskin, who also directed *The War of the Worlds*, this movie remains oddly neglected among sci-fi films of the '60s, curious when we consider that it is one of the better examples from that period.

Running on similar lines to *Robinson Crusoe on Mars*, *Enemy Mine* (1985) saw astronaut Dennis Quaid and alien Lou Gossett, Jr. crash-landing on Fyrine IV and fighting against the planet's inhospitable elements inside a large cavern. Like Haskin's underrated space outing, this early effort from Wolfgang Petersen has gone strangely unnoticed over the years, becoming one of the best sci-fi films to emerge critically unscathed from the awful '80s. And of course that supposedly alien cave being excavated for disturbingly human-looking artifacts on the *Planet of*

In *Cat-Women of the Moon*, brave Earthlings explore moon caves and discover a gigantic spider that wants to devour them.

Alien Lou Gossett, Jr. fights Fyrine IV's inhospitable elements within a large cavern, from *Enemy Mine*.

the Apes (1968) wasn't alien in origin at all; it was (much to Charlton Heston's consternation) from planet Earth, thousands of years in the future. Also thousands of years in the future, 802,701 AD to be exact, Rod Taylor clambered down a shaft into the haunt of the savage Morlocks, a warren of caverns photographed in red/green hues, the floors littered with human bones, in George Pal's colorful *The Time Machine* (1960). Yes, once more, man had regressed back to an ape-like existence in caves, similar to his ancestors eons ago.

In *Pitch Black* (2000) Radha Mitchell, marooned with her crew on a distant planet, goes poking around in a cave system bathed in a blue light, unaware that Pteranodon-type carnivores scuttle in the semi-darkness, waiting for a total eclipse of the planet's two suns (one a double star). Then, when darkness falls, they fly out of their cave homes in the thousands, eating everything in sight, including stranded astronauts!

Indie Caves

Independent horror film outfits continue to perpetuate the cave as a means to scare or thrill a selective audience, however cheap the production usually is (well, most of them *are* straight-to-DVD/TV fodder). The major studios may have given up on the idea, but indie producers haven't. After all, what else (some might say) have they got to offer the punter? Copyists Asylum (anything the big boys can do, we can do as well, and for a lot less money) gives precedence to the cave in many of their questionable efforts. Most of the second half of *King of the Lost World* (2005) takes place in caves that house mega scorpions, an enormous spider and nubile lesbian natives, as well as providing shelter from the company's very own CGI-created King Kong. *The 7 Adventures of Sinbad* (2010) starred Patrick Muldoon as a modern-day descendant of the legendary sailor, encountering a Cyclops in an island cave that was *not* in the same class as the Columbia 1958 classic of near-enough the same title. Their updated version of *Journey to the Center of the Earth* (2008) was a stinker, and the underground cavern broken into by a posse of gun-toting bimbos in *Deep Digger I* seems more like the open prairie than the interior of the Earth, with the obligatory T-Rex stalking the team. Likewise their steal of *The Land that Time Forgot* (2009) couldn't equal Amicus' shoddy but entertaining values, the main cave home to a group of Germans stranded there since World War II who use it as protection from, yes, you've guessed it, a marauding T-Rex. Yet another T-Rex cropped up in present-day Los Angeles in *100 Million BC* (2008), but not before Michael Goss and his squad travel back to the Cretaceous period via a time portal to locate a missing scientist and his colleagues who were found inhabiting caves in Stone Age garb. With *Intermedio* (2006), Asylum struck the right balance in a plot involving a gang of teenagers, on the lookout for drugs, trapped in a series of creepy cave tunnels where the souls of the evil dead wait in limbo. No, despite being viewed as one of the bigger indie distributors, Asylum hasn't really done the cave justice—we have to look at other indie fare for half-decent cave excitement. It can be found—just.

Indie outfit Dead Crow Productions' *The Cavern* (2005) dispensed with a monster altogether and instead had a scarred, demented Russian rapist terrorizing eight

In *Missile to the Moon*, a moon maiden is attacked by a giant spider monster.

A huge brain living in a frozen cave on Uranus controls the minds of visiting astronauts in *Journey to the Seventh Planet*.

In the future, time traveler Rod Taylor descends into the cavern lair of the cannibalistic Morlocks, in George Pal's *The Time Machine*.

cavers in Kazakhstan's Kyle Desert locale, piling on the underground suspense with amateurish aplomb. Going back in time to the Iron Age, First Look International's *Minotaur* (2006) starred the snorting, slobbering mythical beast of the title, mightily upset because eight youths refuse to become sacrificial lambs after they are tossed into its cave labyrinth by gas-sniffing, incestuous High Priest Tony Todd, whose campy turn livened up a pretty good cheapo cave creature-feature. *Hydra* (Cinetel 2009) was also good, archaeologist Polly Shannon venturing into the Cave of Zeus and disturbing the multi-headed serpent of Greek legend, causing the writhing monster to bite off the heads of all those who get too close. Like so many other CGI beasties of myth, *Hydra*'s monster doesn't stand up to Harryhausen's animated Hydra from *Jason and the Argonauts*, and neither does the gargantuan five-headed snake in *SnakeMan* (Nu Image 2005), a reptilian monstrosity guarding a cave containing the secret of eternal life where the thing lives.

In American World Pictures' *Pterodactyl* (2005), Cameron Daddo and Coolio were up against a flock of prehistoric, head-plucking reptiles whose nest was situated in a cliff cave (and where Amy Sloan ends up as imminent food for the chicks). If one can manage to track it down, North American Pictures' wonderfully bizarre *Ariana's Quest* (2002) includes a lot of cave scenery of the papier maché kind in a nonsensical tale concerning Rena Mero's quest to regain her kingdom from wicked queen Katerina Brozova. And what about those colossal rhinoceros beetles in *Caved In* (Cinetel 2006) that Angela Featherstone and Christopher Akins come across while searching for emeralds in caves too well lit by far. Featherstone was also in one of independent cinema's finest moments, Full Moon's *Dark Angel: The Ascent* (1994). In this, the actress played a very attractive she-demon inhabiting a twilight cavern in Hell, yearning to visit human society above. Full Moon's depiction of the underworld—tortured souls slaving in a fiery cavern, especially Featherstone's fetching cave

The 7 Adventures of Sinbad features island caves housing a Cyclops.

dwelling, together with the blue-tinged grotto leading to the surface of our world—belied the film's humble leanings, producing a true indie masterpiece of some note. And in TNT's lively *The Librarian 2: Return to King Solomon's Mines* (2006), archaeologists Noah Wyle and Gabrielle Anwar finish their quest for the fabled King Solomon's treasure in caves underneath mountain peaks known as The Breasts of Sheba.

Post-apocalyptic mankind also has a habit of reverting back to the Stone Age and taking up their old haunts in caves: *Stryker* (HCI 1983) and *The Lost Future* (Tandem 2010) both had their heroes (Steve Sander and Sean Bean) tackling fur-clad tribes preferring caves to atomic-blasted buildings. For sheer weirdness, Kevin Sorbo's mission in *Fire From Below* (Black Chrome 2009) takes some beating. He has to blast to smithereens a renegade lithium lode with a mind of its own, running riot

Eight cavers confront a crazed Russian rapist in *The Cavern*.

Another T-Rex pops up in present-day Los Angeles, in *100 Million BC*.

deep underground in caverns and ejecting geysers of flame, fire tornadoes and ammonia gas.

Apart from Asylum's abysmal adaptation, there are two further versions of Jules Verne's *Journey to the Center of the Earth* on the market. The better of the two, released by Reunion Pictures in 2008, stuck more or less to Verne's Victorian vision but had the route to Earth's interior set in Alaska, not Iceland. Rick Shroder, Steven Grayhm and Victoria Pratt, after descending through miles of caves and galleries, emerge in a cavern where a lake harbors a Mosasaurus. But once Peter Fonda (Pratt's long-lost husband) appears on the scene with a band of Indians, the underground ambience evaporates, the movie petering out into standard adventure mode. At least it fared better than High Productions' 1993 effort that gave Oscar winner F. Murray Abraham a brief slot. Like Asylum's stab at the novel, the action was updated to the present time; the Avenger burrowing machine heads for the Earth's center where the crew find a Yeti, a tribe of missing links and manta ray creatures. Imitative sets are a poor substitute for the Carlsbad Caverns, and the script is full of gibberish relating to Atlantis and cosmic forces. The first of a proposed two-parter, the second installment was shelved, and it was just as well.

So independent horror/fantasy cinema continues with the tradition of incorporating a cave in its structure. The results may not always live up to expectations, but at least they're there, inviting us in to unseen worlds and horrors of the cheapskate variety.

The Best, and Worst, of the Rest

The Best: Witch Anna Orochko's baroque, cavernous place of residence on Procura in Suomi Filmi's *Sampo* (1959) impresses. Like the richly detailed backdrops in *King Kong*, inspired by the paintings of Gustave Doré, this nightmarish cave, bathed in vivid hues, is a place where ordinary souls would fear to tread. Mosfilm's *Sadko* (1952) featured another such marvel, a splendid cavern drenched in bold colors in which dwelt a mythical Phoenix known as the Bird of Happiness. *Turistas* (2006) may well have been standard slasher fodder for lovers of *Hostel* and its ilk, but it did include one outstanding moment in which the surviving teens evade their murderous pursuers by swimming through an underwater cave system; artful lighting produced a real feeling of claustrophobic terror in this one sequence. Bram Stoker's *The Lair of the White Worm* (1988) received the Ken Russell treatment, meaning going wildly over-the-top in all departments. The monstrous worm's cave dwelling was a corker, though, as was sexed-up priestess Amanda Donohue, charged with keeping the beast at bay.

The Worst: Jerry Warren's *The Incredible Petrified World* (1959) saw Robert Clarke and friends bumping into bearded hermit Maurice Bernard, marooned for 14 years in caves below the seabed. Thre were caves that consisted of a couple of sets shot at various angles to make them appear more extensive to a gullible audience. The tunnel walls in Richard Cunha's *She Demons* (1958) resembled gray papier maché and probably were, while in *The Night the World Exploded* (1957), Columbia's cheap rip-off of Universal's *The Monolith*

Deep within a studio mock-up of the Carlsbad Caverns, scientists attempt to neutralize black stones that can cause devastating earthquakes, in *The Night the World Exploded*.

Irish McCalla and Tod Griffin try to escape the terror of *She Demons*, an ex-Nazi experiment on native girls gone bad.

A group of female extreme sport enthusiasts explore an uncharted cave system, facing their own fears in *The Descent*.

Monsters, black stones expanding in the Earth's depths caused devastating earthquakes. Kathryn Grant spent a great deal of time in a studio mock-up of the Carlsbad Caverns attempting to neutralize the troublesome rocks to prevent worldwide catastrophe. And although *The Clan of the Cave Bear* (1986) had "cave" in the title, the hollows inhabited by Daryl Hannah and her Neanderthal buddies were far from captivating, becoming dull cavities in the rock to match the equally dull production values.

Cave Horror Par Excellence!

Horror, gore, sweat-inducing tension, suspense, claustrophobia, personal betrayal, loss, imploding relationships and repulsive, leprous creatures all wrapped up in utterly believable cave settings—Neil Marshall's brilliantly directed *The Descent* has all of these and more. No other horror movie set almost exclusively within the confines of a subterranean world can compare with Marshall's blood-curdling essay in underground nastiness. Filmed in Scotland (standing in for America's Appalachian Mountains) and shot almost entirely on sound stages, Marshall orchestrated his pet project for maximum impact, not afraid to plunge the entire screen into complete blackness (after all, caves *are* dark!) or simply position a red-lit image in center frame. There's little music to scupper the mood, just the slow drip-drip of water on rock, the echo of speech, heavy breathing through physical exertion and the noise of *something* prowling furtively in those dim corridors of stone, another world where *anything* might happen and does.

Six female extreme sport enthusiasts investigate a labyrinthine cave system, unaware that it's uncharted, all except egotistical Natalie Mendoza, that is. She's led them to this hellhole for kicks and, when the exit route becomes blocked, she not only has to face the wrath of her comrades but also find an alternative way out or perish in the attempt. For the picture's first half, the director builds on the claustrophobia and anxiety (felt by many) brought on by enclosed spaces, tight crawls, yawning drops and water-filled passages. The moment when Shauna Macdonald becomes stuck in a narrow, tortuous tunnel and gives in to panic is absolutely heart stopping and, for those of us who have spent time in caves, unnervingly true-to-life.

It's not until the 54th minute that Marshall ups the ante, introducing the loathsome, blind quasi-humans inhabiting this unknown region, his careful pacing switching to frenetic as the women, driven to hysteria, are picked off one by one in bloody fashion. Many of these savage scenes are so dim, or filmed through night vision optics, that the film needs more than one viewing to ascertain just who is being slaughtered and who isn't. But this adds to, rather than detracts from, the realism and hideousness and shows where efforts like the aforementioned *Sanctum* get it wrong: Caves are stygian environments. Okay, *The Descent* may be inscrutable at times, but if we were running for our lives underground, it wouldn't be down an illuminated gallery. This overall impenetrable darkness is what makes *The Descent* such a rewarding exercise in subterranean shock/horror. With its gruesome set pieces and a bleak ending tinged with poignancy (and let's not forgot that seat-jolting beginning), Neil Marshall presented fans with, as I write, the finest, most visceral cave-horror movie of them all—and I'm proud to say it's British!

2009's follow-up, *The Descent: Part 2*, was an unnecessary exercise, reun-iting a traumatized Macdonald with treacherous Mendoza as police and cavers go underground via a mineshaft to find out why Macdonald came out alive when five of her friends did not. Formulaic and spoiling the mood of Marshall's expertly crafted masterpiece, it offered contrived explanations for Macdonald's actions and bypassed the more ethereal elements that elevated its predecessor to modern-day classic status. However, it did manufacture a few shocks and scares along the way, and the "girls caught in the creatures' latrine" scene was enough to make audiences bring up their dinner!

Saturday, May 25, 2013. At age 66, I stand tentatively on the edge of a 300-foot-high cliff, waiting to scramble down a scree to barely accessible mine workings; then my mind returns to this article and ... I hesitate.

Shape of Fear to Come!

by Steven Thornton

When historians look back at the past 50 years, they are likely to echo the sentiments of the Grateful Dead and exclaim, "What a long, strange trip it's been!" Unprece-dented technological innova-tions, widespread social changes and economic upheavals have reshaped the cultural landscape in ways that are both profound and far reaching. The mind reels when thinking about such evolution.

Movies, of course, have been the mirror that reflects these cultural changes. Whether seen through the sober eyes of drama or the askew glance of comedy, the cinema is a blank canvas on which we view our changing world. Genre films, too, shed light on our evolving culture, especially those areas that inspire our greatest fears.

With the landmark passage of *MidMar*'s 50th anniversary, perhaps it is time to cast an analytical eye not just to the past but to the future as well and predict how the continued evolution of tomorrow's world might shape the look of genre films in the years to come. Our crystal ball may not always be accurate, but its vision may prompt us to contemplate the "long, strange trip" that we are on, collectively and individually. So join us as we look ahead to imagine the shape of fear to come.

The House Without Internet (2027)

The old dark house has been a reliable horror movie trope since the silent era. In its original inception, travelers become cut off from the outside world when they are trapped by circumstance to face the horrors of a temporary place of refuge. In this contemporary reimagining, a pair of young technicians unexpectedly finds itself separated from the only world they know in a real and very disturbing way.

The House Without Internet tells the gripping story of two techies, Bubb Fisher and Tyrell Jordon, sent to survey the high-speed Internet capabilities of private residences (part of President Britney Spears' initiative to stimulate the chronically depressed U.S. economy). To their surprise and shock, they encounter the Whitney clan, a family living in a remote dwelling that has absolutely no electronic ties to the world outside. What's more, any attempts to establish such connectivity appear destined

kid, has engineered a simulated electronic bubble around the house that restricts data transmission, thus keeping his clan safe from the "corrupting" influences of the outside world. When Bubb attempts to sabotage the mechanism, it begins to spin out of control and threatens to envelop the entire planet. The thought of permanently loosing all Internet/cable/smart phone connectivity proved to be too much for contemporary audiences in many urban locations, who reportedly fled the theaters in droves while screaming in terror.

Traditionally, the thrills in old dark house movies tended to eschew the supernatural, placing their emphasis instead on the instinctive vulnerability we feel in an unfamiliar environment. *The House Without Internet* builds on this pattern by commenting on our increasing dependence on electronic gadgetry for information, se-curity and a sense of community. Technology can be wonderful but it can also be a barrier that separates us from the human contact that previous generations took for granted. Perhaps the greatest fear that the film exploits is the realization that, for many people, the virtual world has become more appealing and more comfortable than the real one.

The Thing from the Recycling Center (2031)

Environmentally conscious consumers adopted recycling as a way of life in the early days of the 21st century. Public support for this practice grew so widespread that people who did not embrace the green-friendly lifestyle were looked upon as social pariahs. This change in social awareness is a driving force in the plot of the 2031 horror thriller, *The Thing from the Recycling Center*.

The city of Mudd Flats has just constructed a new, state-of-the-art recycling facility, which is the pride of the community. But budgetary restraints and the chance to make a fast buck motivate plant manager Myron Smalley to cut corners with the standard refuse handling procedures. When new employee Ernie Samson discovers that barges of raw recycling material are being trucked away and dumped in the local harbor, he begins to collect evidence that can be used to alert the local authorities. But Smalley gets wind of the plan and, with the help of corrupt union officials, devises a scheme to deal with the Samson situation. One night, Ernie is working the midnight shift when a sudden equipment malfunction occurs. As he climbs into the grinder hoppers to investigate, the machine "accidentally" roars to life, burying Ernie

to fail, as though the very Earth itself was cursed to forever belong to a distant, pre-modern past.

The situation is bemusing at first as Bubb and Tyrell observe the Whitneys' primitive lifestyle. The use of outdated devices like matches and doorknobs are exploited for unexpected comic potential. But things turn dark quickly and the tension builds to a level that is almost unbearable.

The tuning point comes when Bubb casually describes to the family the wonders of the Internet age. An inspired visual montage catalogs the endless entertainment and information options available in today's world, each image growing more vivid, compelling and frantic. The momentum of the scene culminates in a dramatic explosion as the Whitney children begin screaming in terror. The parents then take control, denouncing their uninvited guests as mad and declaring they must be prevented from leaving "for their own good."

Subsequent scenes reinforce the film's theme of social isolation and rejection of normalcy. Even the innocuous moments, such as when the Whitney children entertain themselves, turn unexpectedly dark when the imagery on their "card games" is revealed—sinister authority figures (kings, queens and jacks) with warlike regalia and arcane symbols (hearts, clubs and spades) that are assumed to be satanic in nature. The situation becomes too much for Tyrell, who becomes afflicted by a severe case of Internet withdrawal and is quickly reduced to a babbling, incoherent state of near idiocy.

In tried and true horror film fashion, the final denouement reveals a human agent at the source of the problem. Family patriarch Gus Whitney, a former electronics wiz under an avalanche of debris and seemingly silencing him forever.

But soon afterwards strange things begin to happen in Mudd Flats. Reports begin to circulate about a mysterious figure christened the "Garbage Man" who appears to be hell bent on enforcing the rules of recycling and proper refuse disposal. Dismissed by the local officials as an urban legend, the figure is alternatively benign—helping children dispose of empty bottles and gum wrappers—and vengeful—unleashing violent wrath on a junk dealer who disposes of used tires in a rural field. As the sightings of the Garbage Man increase in frequency, local residents begin to wonder if there might be more to the stories than mere childhood daydreams. And Myron Smalley begins to worry.

His fears soon prove to be justified. Myriad accidents begin to occur around the plant, always presaged by the appearance of an especially nasty pile of refuse in unusual places—the calling card of the Garbage Man. When Myron finds a steaming pile of fish heads, rotten eggs and animal dung in the front seat of his automobile, he is both outraged and terrified. Fearful over the potential discovery of his rampant mismanagement, he shuns the offer of police protection and decides to confront the mysterious vigilante on his own terms. In a scene that is celebrated as a classic of modern horror cinema, Smalley spends the late evening hours chasing down shadows in the darkened corners of the recycling plant in an attempt to vanquish his pursuer before it corners him. Just when it seems that Smalley's fears were all for naught, he turns and finds himself face to face with his ultimate nightmare—the Garbage Man, in the flesh. The unsuspected shock causes Myron Smalley to flee in terror until he meets his death, falling into a vat of untreated waste at the nearby sewage disposal facility.

The Thing From the Recycling Center had the strangest legacy of any 21st century horror film. Initially shunned as an exercise in poor taste, the character of the Garbage Man took on new life when it was embraced by school children the world over. Green advocacy groups also adopted the figure as a symbol for environmental awareness. Sequels, spinoffs, comic books and television appearances followed in short order, making the Garbage Man the most unconventional pop icon since the Batman craze of the 1960s. The popularity of its title character threatened to overshadow the impact and effectiveness of the film, which delivered more chills than any

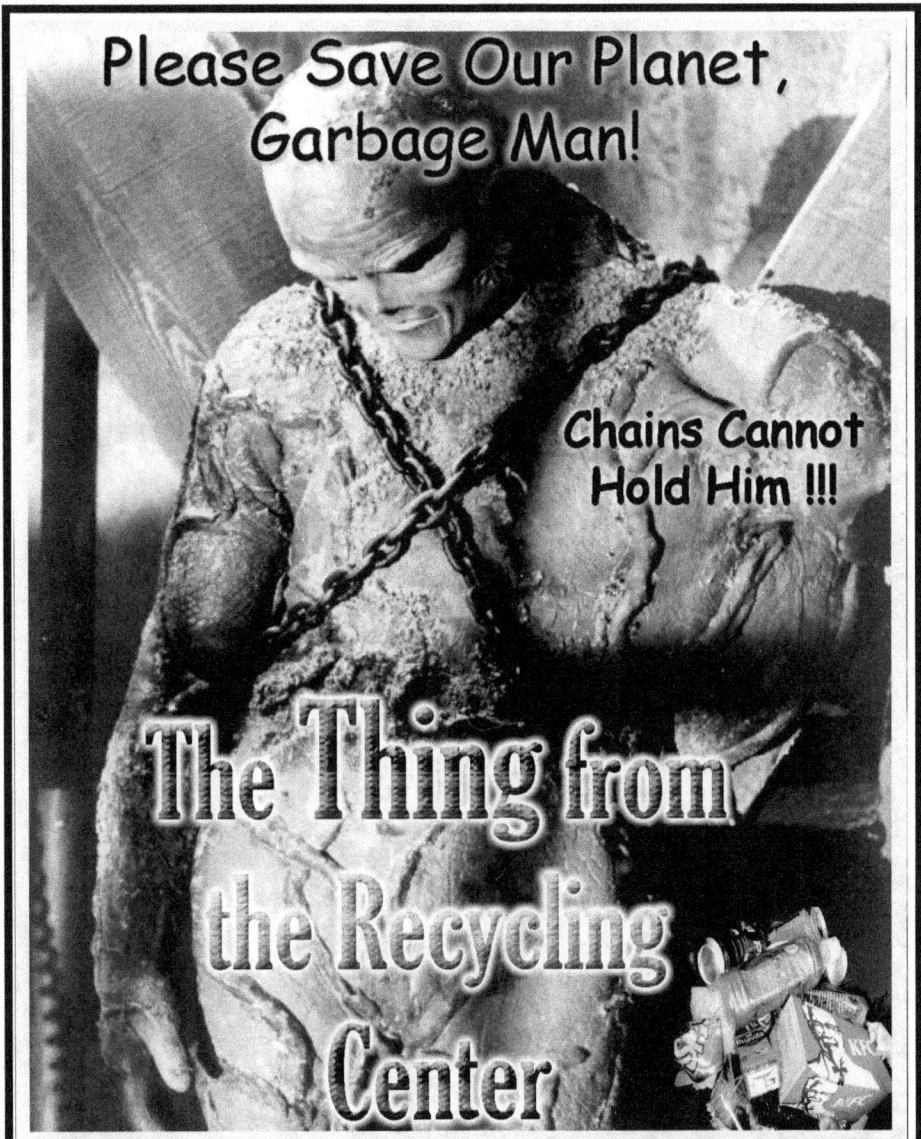

school teacher or advertising agency would willingly admit.

You Are What You Eat (2037)

The heightened awareness of dietary-related health issues became one of the noteworthy trends of the new millennium. Public recognition of the issue culminated with the passage of the National Junk Food Act of 2019, which banned 85% of food items from grocery and convenience stores around the country. Thumbing its nose at this social development was *You Are What You Eat,* a quirky black comedy rife with horror overtones, many of which referred to the carnivore-based lifestyles of the previous century.

In the remote regions of the South Pacific, anthropologists are amazed to discover E-tu-mup, the lone survivor of a people indigenous to the Pitcairn Islands. Researchers from the world over pounce upon the discovery, seeing it as a rare opportunity to observe man in his primitive state, unspoiled by the influence of the modern world. Politically motivated sociologists from America are especially zealous to study E-tu-mup, hopeful to demonstrate the positive influence of the newly revamped public education system as a vehicle to improve the lives of those on the lower end of the social spectrum.

E-tu-mup is indeed untouched by the ways of the world. Unfortunately, he is also unfamiliar with the many taboos of polite society. His treatment of the opposite sex, for example, is revealed in a series of comic vignettes in which our primitive protagonist tries to "hit" on various nurses in the medical facility where he is housed. Even more unsettling is his daily craving for the skeletal muscle tissue known as "meat," the consumption of which was largely abandoned in 2025. As various laboratory animals and other common pets disappear, it becomes clear that any meat will suffice for E-tu-mup's diet—hamster, dog, canary or goldfish.

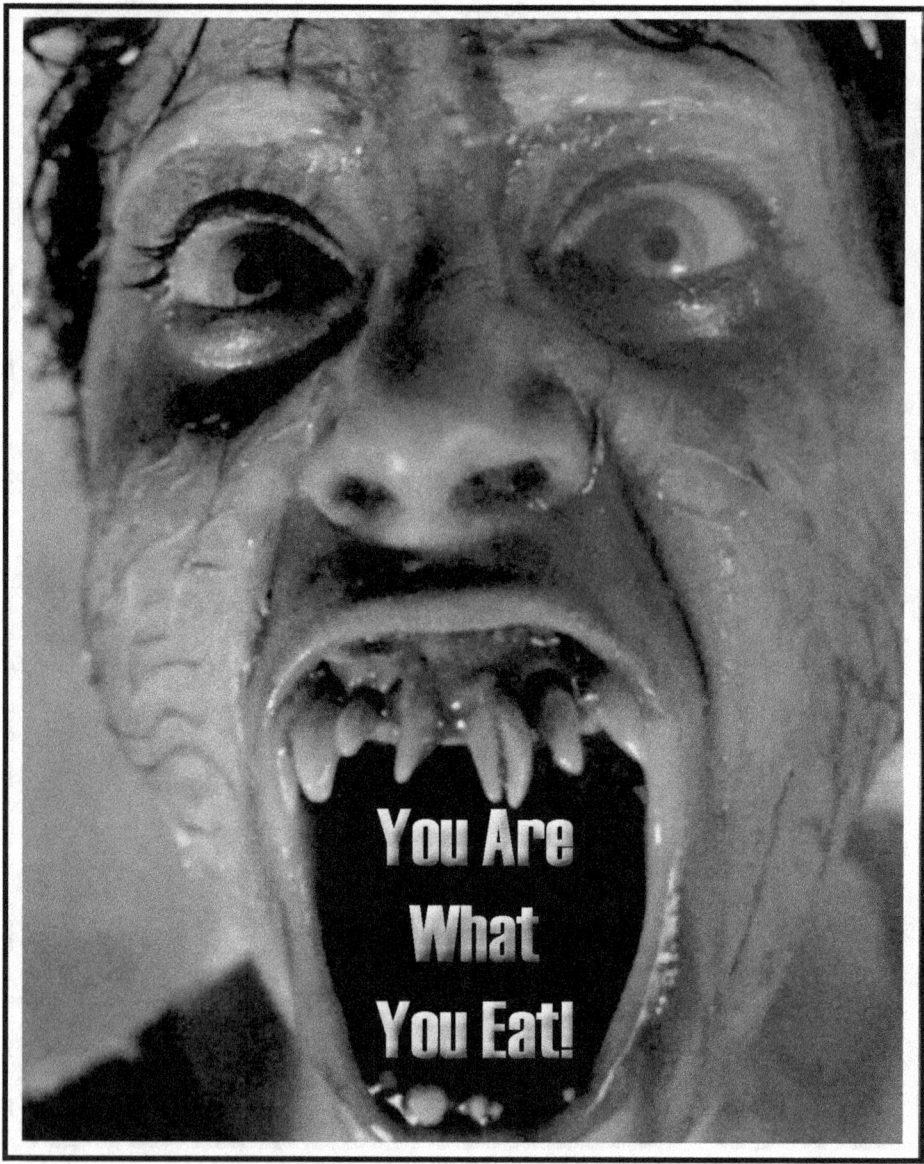

A firestorm of controversy erupts when word of E-tu-mup's lifestyle choices becomes common knowledge. The issue commands public attention to such an extent that it soon becomes a topic for high-level debate. In a scene that is remembered as the film's highlight, a far left news commentator asserts that E-tu-mup should be coached in the ways of the modern world, while a supporter of the far right contends that he is a menace to society and should be sent back "where he belongs." E-tu-mup brings the debate to an abrupt conclusion afterwards by attacking the taking heads backstage and making a meal out of them. The shot of E-tu-mup picking his teeth with the bones of the loquacious politicos was a hit with audiences of 2037.

With the help of sympathetic researchers, E-tu-mup avoids captivity and is relocated to one of the most desolate sections of the country, Federal Region A127 (the area formerly known as Detroit). Here, he can live on his own terms, unencumbered by the ways of the contemporary world. The crisis averted, society now feels safe knowing that its strict code of conduct will go unchallenged. But a final scene hints that there will be more to the story— E-tu-mup has started a family with a female liberal arts student and is shown instructing his progeny in the ways of hunting, fishing and living off the land. And that includes, of course, an appreciation for the taste of animal flesh in any form.

Its outlandish narrative aside, *You Are What You Eat* hints at some of the tensions beneath the surface of polite society. Our modern world, with its ever increasing complexity, shifting moral standards and overarching political correctness, leaves little room for the voices of dissent. E-tu-mup comes close to being a parody but at the core of his personality is a "be true to thine self" ethos that makes him seem more real than most of the other characters in the story. As a result, he retains our sympathy throughout the film's scant 98-minute running time. That itself is food for thought in an era when the average feature film is approaching five hours in length.

Vampires Over Iowa **(2041)**
The term "vampire" has changed meanings many times over the course of motion picture history. Its original inception dates from the silent era, when Theda Bara popularized the character as a sex-driven destroyer of men. Bela Lugosi and Christopher Lee became the faces of the vampire for the talkie generation and made Dracula one of cinema's enduring horror icons. In the early part of this century, teenage heartthrobs became synonymous with the character for a brief but intense period (a trend that reached a shocking apex with the unsolved murder of teen idol Justin Bieber, whose bloodless body was found in his Los Angeles apartment). In this most recent reinvention, the vampire becomes identified with the most loathsome creatures known to the modern world—bankers who specialize in home mortgages.

Newlyweds Shawn and DyeAnne Owens are overjoyed at the thought of purchasing their first home. A plethora of paperwork awaits them as they jump through hurdles to satisfy all of the bureaucratic obstacles involved in acquiring a home mortgage. One by one, the requirements are satisfied until there is but one item remaining. The young couple is nonplussed but accommodating when they are invited to their bank's corporate office for a midnight ceremony to finalize the signing of the mortgage.

The nocturnal gathering is a sinister harbinger of the events to come. A power outage necessitates the use of candlelight for illumination. A strange cadre of "witnesses" (including attorneys, legal aides and assorted financial advisors) takes a keen interest in observing the proceedings. As the clock chimes the witching hour, the writing on the contracts seems to change right before their very eyes. ("Don't worry about that," assures their legal council. "That's just legalese.") Lightning strikes as the pen is put to paper, leaving Shawn and DyeAnne shaken at the cumulative effective of so many weird coincidences.

As the couple settles into their new residence, a mood of uneasiness takes hold of them. Even Mouser, their pet cat, senses that something is wrong and stubbornly refuses to cross the threshold. Most disturbingly, they realize that their mortgage payments begin to escalate "like magic." They contact their mortgage representative, Mr. Bloodstone, who promises to look into the matter. But the problem quickly grows worse and the anguished pair soon finds themselves at wit's end.

Fortunately, the Owens have a friendly neighbor, Mr. Goodman, who is sympathetic to their plight. Though considered eccentric for his knowledge of obscure matters, Goodman recognizes the true nature of the threat facing the young family. "They intend to draw the lifeblood out of you," he warns them, "until you become their slaves forever." Goodman becomes Shawn and DyeAnne's friend, confidante and rock of support, helping them to cope with a labyrinth of legal obstacles that seem to have no end.

The film culminates with a climactic showdown initiated by Goodman that pits the Owens against Bloodstone and his management team. Evil is vanquished with the help of chance, providence and extensive knowledge of the intricacies of the modern legal system. The big reveal is that Goodman is a former corporate lawyer; being well versed in the forces of darkness, he is only too familiar with the strategies they employ. In a scene that found many viewers cheering out loud, Bloodstone and his associates are given termination notices and immediately consigned to the pits of Hell. The Owens are triumphant and order is restored, although the film's final image, a stack of foreclosure notices blown out the window by a sudden gust of wind, suggests that such evil will always be with us, ready to cast a dark shadow over all our lives.

Vampires Over Iowa struck a receptive chord with audiences who have come to distrust the predatory nature of modern corporate practices. Once business evolved into multi-trillion-dollar global leviathans, they gave up any pretense regarding the concept of social responsibility. Many a commentator has pointed out the dangers of capitalism unrestrained by the tempering influence of competition. To compare these corporate giants to supernatural entities is a bold but logical expression of this fear, hinting at the ambivalence that modern viewers feel toward organizations that, for all intents and purposes, have taken on lives of their own.

Zombies Are People Too (2048)

Zombies officially gained political recognition in 2045 after a lengthy and hard-fought struggle for full citizenship. This trend was not without controversy, as many

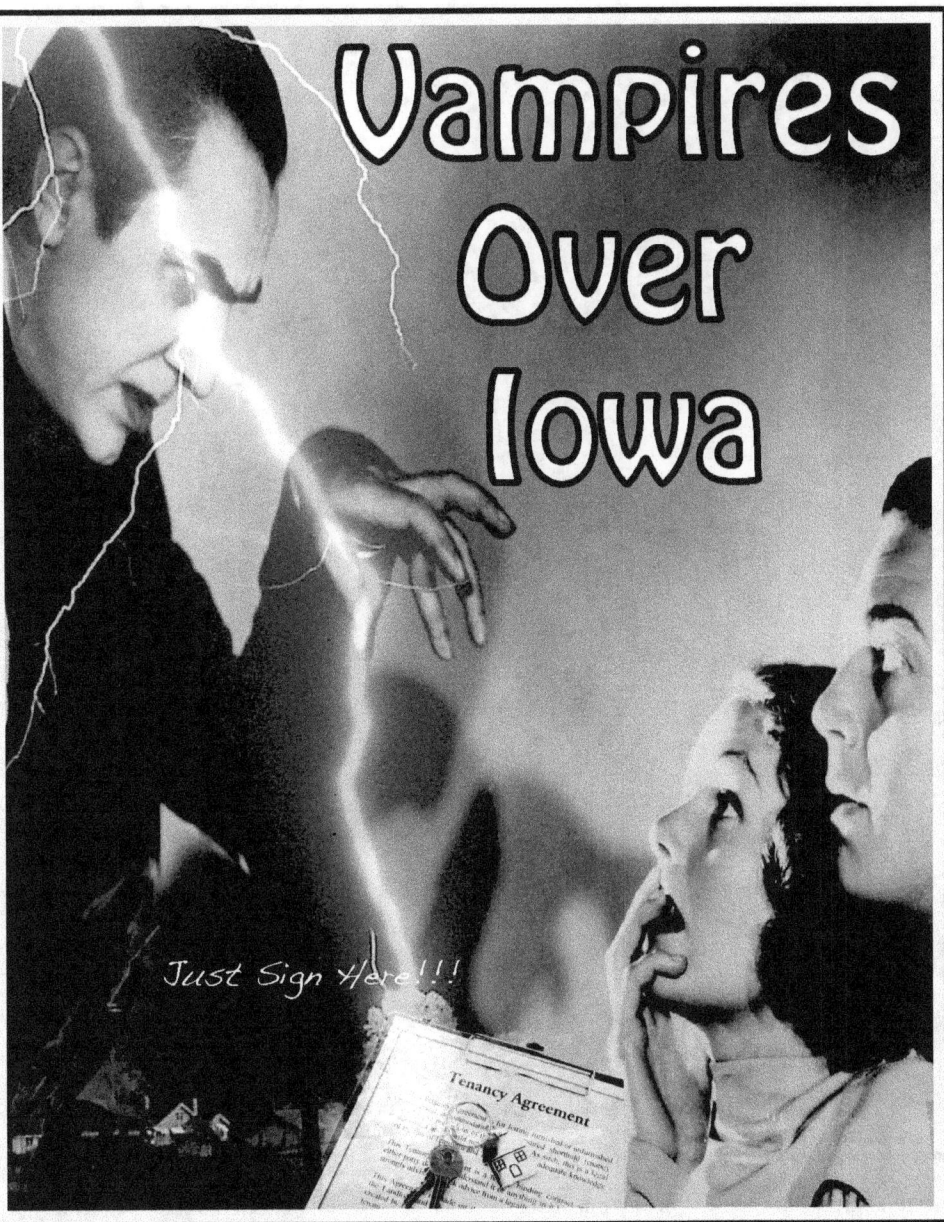

political commentators objected to granting recognition to a potential voting bloc that was incapable of coherent thought. But this firestorm eventually faded and the walls of discrimination finally came tumbling down.

Against this background, Leftover Cinema released *Zombies Are People Too*, a social satire that explores the complexities of this changing social dynamic. Like most movie monsters, the undead have endured stereotypes that are both unjust and unwarranted, a reality that has hindered their full integration into society at large. *Zombies Are People Too* explores the injustice of such a two-tiered society and reminds us that the differences between us are less important than one might believe.

Grad student Mickael Hather begins to question the direction of his life when his father passes away unexpectedly. After the funeral, he drives around aimlessly until he finds himself in the "bad" section of town where he observes firsthand the lives of the underprivileged. As his unplanned journey nears an end, his vehicle is attacked by the poorest of the poor—a marauding throng of zombies. The assault leaves him shaken due to its sudden severity and apparent lack of motivation. Mickael's discontent leads him to yearn for a greater understanding and his life suddenly acquires a new purpose—to help eliminate the prejudices and social inequalities that the undead and underprivileged endure in our culture.

But good intentions alone are not enough to bring about social change. Mickael soon learns how generations of economic hardship, lack of educational opportunities and long-standing social oppression create a vicious cycle of poverty from which zombies cannot escape. Even the name "zombie" proves problematic

Zombies Are People Too

as it conjures up stereotypical images of loathsome beings who crave human flesh. The "post living," as Mickael prefers to call them, are far more than that. But how can he convince the world at large?

Mickael's solution to this dilemma is novel and daring. He decides to immerse himself into this subculture so he can fully understand and inculcate himself with the zombie mindset and become their advocate to the outside world. Countless days and nights are spent living among the undead, learning and adapting his consciousness to match that of his dead/alive companions. Mickael's family and friends are understandably aghast at his newfound life's mission, especially girlfriend Rashell, who suspects that another woman is the real reason for his late-night sojourns. When Rashell follows Mickael on his nighttime journey to zombie land, she attracts their attention, a situation that triggers a panicked reaction in the girl and leads to her accidental death. Rashell's fate was widely interpreted by fans and critics alike as sad commentary on the dysfunctional state of human/zombie relations.

A line has been crossed in Mickael's life and he is no longer able to keep the two worlds apart. Zombies follow everywhere he goes—to work, to the market, to social outings. The beleaguered man has his hands full as he prevents the zombies from wreaking havoc while simultaneously dealing with the stigma of associating with such a lowly underclass. The situation becomes untenable when the walking dead surround him in the middle of a busy public square. Mickael issues a plea for tolerance and compassion in a desperate bid to bridge the chasm of social injustice. But the authorities, in their zeal to restore order, take charge and bring the film to a conclusion in a hailstorm of bullets.

Film commentators had a field day interpreting the climactic scenes of *Zombies Are People Too*. Was it an indictment of modern society's treatment of the underclass? Or did it imply that any attempt to elevate the status of those at the bottom of the socioeconomic ladder were inevitably doomed to failure? Political baggage hampers an honest assessment of the film, although these implications are surely a key reason why it still pushes the buttons of viewers on all sides of the cultural divide. Zombies have long been considered the "ne plus ultra" of movie monsters. But since the premiere of this film, their reputation has been somewhat restored, rebuilding the brand for a new, more culturally aware generation of moviegoers.

Agnostic Ghost Story (2055)

In a subtle but discernable way, the horror films of old were dependent on the prevailing belief systems of generations past. The mostly wild and wooly vampire and mad doctor yarns took on heightened significance when the mysteries of life and death were assumed to be sacred. All that changed, of course, in the 21st century when Western civilization abandoned the belief systems that were deemed to be at odds with progressive social and political movements. *Agnostic Ghost Story* explores this development and puts it in the context of the modern horror film, the genre in which the impact of this change is most keenly felt.

Science versus faith lies at the heart of the plot. Roothe Welling heads a research team that seeks the realization of a long-standing scientific goal—the artificial creation of self-sustaining life forms. Numerous failures have prompted the team to go back to the drawing board. During this reevaluation period, Roothe and her cohorts discover a unique energy aura as identifiable as a fingerprint that emits from each human brain. When one of their research subjects passes away suddenly, Roothe makes the curious discovery that the energy source is still active—weakened and variable but detectable nonetheless.

But Roothe's findings are met with resistance when she presents them to her peers. Citing everything from static electricity to faulty test procedures, the local scientific community rejects her evidence and deems it unworthy of further study. Stung by professional criticism on a level that she has never before experienced, Roothe decides to keep any further disclosures to herself. But her work continues.

Roothe's dedication and her doubt are driven by a long-denied curiosity concerning

SEE artificial life created in the laboratory

SEE Dawkins vs. Hitchens discuss existence!

spiritual matters. Like most denizens of the 21st century, she is the product of a culture that frowns upon traditional religious faith because of its refusal to adopt to contemporary political trends. This skepticism is given further weight by the highly rational nature of Roothe's scientific mindset, rendering her deaf to the quiet yearning for ultimate truth that stirs inside her heart. (The conflict is dramatized in a light-hearted way by a dream sequence in which the ghosts of Richard Dawkins and Christopher Hitchens appear and argue against their own existence.) Complicating matters further is the memory of Roothe's parents, who were recently euthanized due to their advanced age and chronic disabilities. "Those things happen," her coworkers advise in an obligatory display of comfort. "It's best not to dwell on it."

Fortunately, Roothe finds a kindred spirit in fellow researcher Rajesh Patel, whose non-Western background allows for a balance between the scientific and the spiritual. Together, they embark on an ambitious and clandestine project to confirm her team's earlier findings and, if possible, break through the barrier separating life and death. Ultra-sensitive energy recorders, digital imagery software, multi-dimensional sensors—all the resources of Roothe's department are stretched to the limit as the quest begins to consume her life. The sudden expenditures catch the attention of Roothe's supervisor, who has been searching for months to find grounds for her dismissal. As the film's climax approaches, Roothe's experiment kicks into high gear at the same moment that her termination notice is being prepared. A great conflagration ensues as the department head opens the laboratory door, just as Roothe breaks through and glimpses an image of the world beyond death. The end result: Roothe and Rajesh perish in the blaze, the research facility is closed due to financial improprieties and the records of the experiment are sealed from public view.

Agnostic Ghost Story generated no end of controversy on its initial release. Groups from both extremes of the social and political spectrum attacked the film, some saying that it recalled to the discredited beliefs of the past while others claimed that it insulted the legitimate spiritual impulse. The film unquestionably struck a nerve with contemporary audiences that, like Roothe Welling, are chaffed by the authoritarian restrictions of traditional religion but remain awestruck by the ultimate mystery of existence.

The Very Last Horror Film (2069)

Deep in the 21st century, evolving technologies have completely reshaped life in the developed world. Every avenue of industry, recreation and entertainment has been transformed by a revolution in the sharing of data and information. Left behind in this brave new world are the technologies of yesterday, many of which were embraced as cutting-edge marvels of their day. This conflict between the old and the new forms the backdrop for our final entry, *The Very Last Horror Film*.

Echoes of the past are made apparent in the film's opening scenes. Workmen are performing salvage operations in the earthquake-ridden region once known as California. The activity comes to a pause when an underground vault is unearthed—an inspection of the contents reveals hundreds of feet of damaged but still pliable nitrate film stock wound tightly on metal reels. "Movies," chuckles one worker with a knowing smile. "That's what people used to watch to kill time back in the old days."

One of the work crew, C.J. Johnson, volunteers to deliver the fragmented film to a local collector for identification. When Johnson arrives at the home of film buff Harvey Maxwell, Johnson is initially bemused at the sight of hundreds of film cans, empty metal reels and other artifacts of a time long gone. "Let's see what we have here," Maxwell mumbles as he fires up his antiquated 35mm film projector. Like magic, the flickering image comes to life.

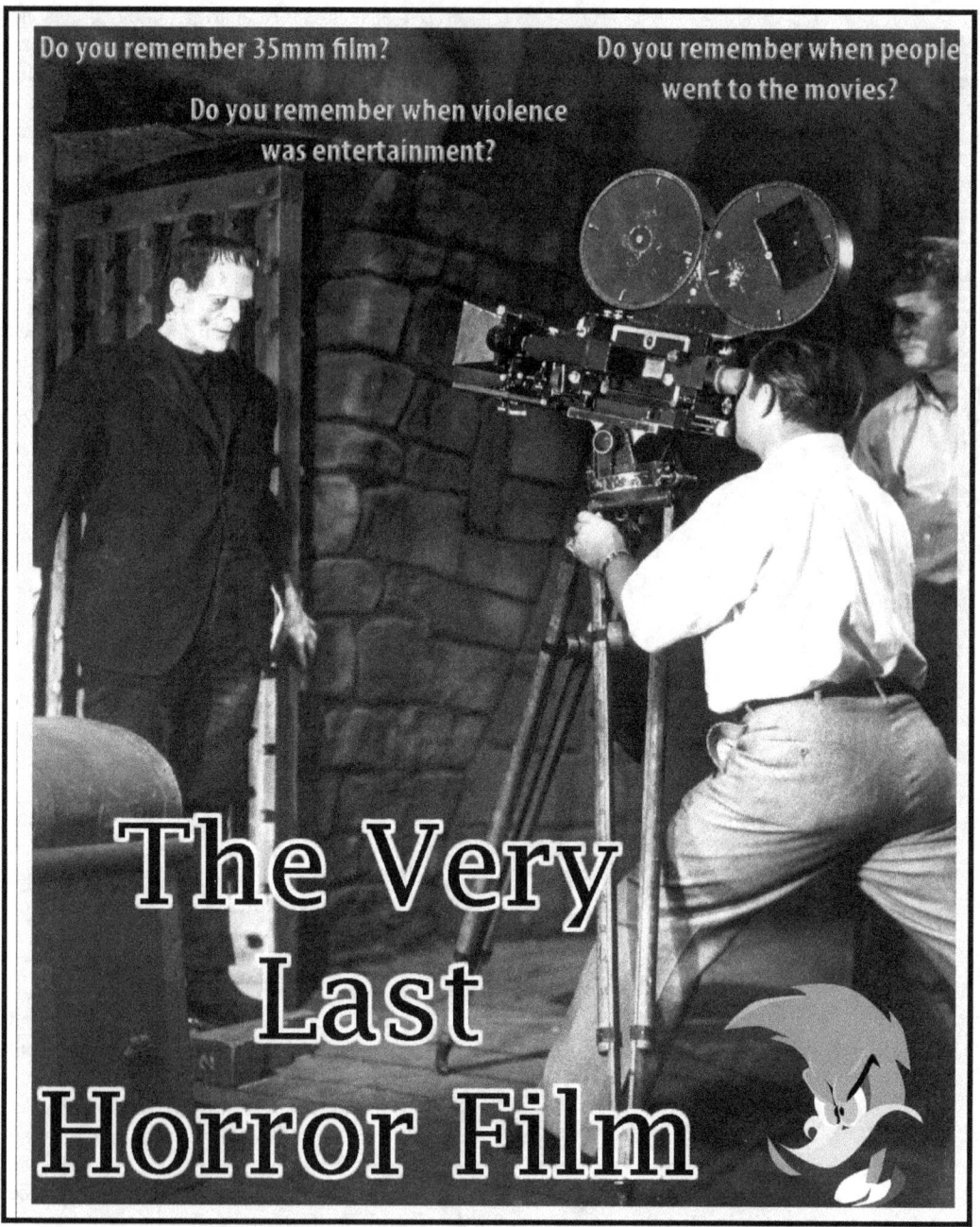

The Very Last Horror Film

Do you remember 35mm film?
Do you remember when violence was entertainment?
Do you remember when people went to the movies?

Although badly decomposed, the extant footage reveals the outline of a story. Two men—one young, one elderly—are engaged in a polite but heated discussion. "Have you never wanted to look beyond the clouds and the stars or to know what causes the trees to bud and what changes the darkness into light?" asks the junior member of the pair, his matinee idol looks contrasted by his stark intensity. From behind a doorway, footsteps approach. A man, entering backwards, slowly turns to reveal a ghastly but compelling face with a hideous forehead scar, lizard-like eyes, metallic neck bolts and a misshapen, flattened head. A few more images dance forth from the projector, then the film stock comes to a sputtering, abrupt finish.

The footage is quickly identified as belonging to the long-lost *Frankenstein*, a film that is rumored to have helped kick-start Hollywood's legendary Golden Age of Horror. Maxwell is dumbstruck at the rarity of the find and wonders if more might exist. For Johnson, the discovery sets off a cycle that proceeds from interest to deepest obsession. Following every lead and tracking every rumor, he sets out on a personal mission to restore the film to its original running length and, hopefully, score a financial bonanza in the process.

The big break comes when the pair learns of an avaricious collector who is rumored to be in possession of a full-length copy of the missing masterpiece. Despite repeated denials from the secretive film buff, Johnson and Maxwell remain convinced that they are on the right track. C.J. seizes the initiative one night, trespassing into the collector's private residence when the place appears to be deserted. Minutes pass slowly, seemingly like hours, as C.J. shines a flashlight on hundreds of carefully catalogued cans of motion picture film. As he locates his holy grail, footsteps approach from an adjoining hallway. C.J. grabs his purloined bounty and tries to escape, but the approaching figure reaches the exit first. There is a confrontation and a struggle. A handgun is produced—and a shot is fired. Unscathed, C.J. flees the scene with blood on his hands and the prized possession under his arms. He hurries to Maxwell's house and the pair excitedly loads the fragile film stock into the vintage projector. The lights are dimmed and the machine is brought to life. There, upon the screen, appears the image of Woody Woodpecker, greeting them with mocking laughter.

The production of horror films dropped off greatly in mid-2050s, the result of a social backlash against violent and otherwise provocative forms of entertainment. *The Very Last Horror Film* tapped into a feeling of nostalgia for the once thriving tradition of movie shockers that formed a profitable niche of the motion picture industry. A sad and well-documented reality was reflected in the plot too—most of the classic horror films of the 1930s were now considered lost after massive solar flares destroyed the surviving digital masters decades ago. The film, consequently, served as a symbolic stake in the heart for a school of filmmaking that is long gone but cannot be forgotten.

Times change but our need for entertainment does not. We may gaze at drawings on the walls of a cave or immerse ourselves in computer-generated 3-D imagery, but in the end, it all comes down to the fact that images give life to our innermost dreams. Sometimes those dreams are nightmares that find expression in flickering shadows that illuminate the dark. No matter how the cultural guardians of each era try to suppress it, the cinema of fear will endure, giving us those horrible yet comfortable thrills that call us back again and again.

Midnight Marquee Book Review
by Gary J. Svehla

Sixties Shockers: A Critical Filmography of Horror Cinema, 1960-1969 by Mark Clark and Bryan Senn; McFarland www.mcfarlandpub.com; Order 800-253-2187; 541 pages (7 by 10 inches); 345 photos; case bound $59.95

For me the decade of the 1960s concluded the Golden Age of horror cinema (which began with the decade of the 1930s). While much has been written about horror films produced from the 1930s through the 1950s, the decade of the 1960s awaits such astute critical investigation. The tag team tandem of Clark and Senn are perfectly suited to bring insightful analysis to this diverse decade (containing the beginnings of Euro-Horror; the importation of Mexican horror; the debut of widescreen and color period costume Gothic productions mounted by Roger Corman and AIP; the continuation of Hammer horror; the influx of low-budget independent productions; and mainstream Hollywood horror crafted by Hitchcock, Wise and Polanski). And while I enjoy the more thoughtful, analytical style of Mark Clark the most (although none of the individual films receive bylines, I am only second-guessing who wrote what, as I recognize each writer's style), Bryan Senn's contributions are equally important.

Clark focuses more on the literary criticism style analysis that I tend to favor. In his coverage of *The Birds*, Clark carefully examines why the production is the least compromising of Alfred Hitchcock's movies, allowing the director to have carte blanche and make radical artistic choices. His essay examines the reasons why the movie's resolution is so open ended, not cut-and-dried. Clark examines the reasoning of introducing a slow, character-building first half that quickly evolves into a carnage-filled second half. He links the subtle sequences of animal cruelty to nature's eruption against humanity. Likewise, during his dissection of Mario Bava's *Black Sabbath*, Clark does an outstanding job differentiating between the original European edit of the movie and AIP's shorter, re-arranged edit, explaining the superiority of the original cut and the damage done by AIP. Yet, Clark explains why *Black Sabbath* (in its director's cut) is the best anthology horror chiller of the decade, easily outdoing anything offered by Amicus Productions. And he faithfully spells out why Boris Karloff's performance as a vampire in the Wurdalak sequence is a late-period gem for the iconic actor. During the essay on *Brides of Dracula*, Clark lays out the reasoning why the original ending, later adapted for Hammer's *Kiss of the Vampire*, was rejected. In the original screenplay Van Helsing (Peter Cushing) uses black magic to evoke a swarm of devil bats to attack and kill the vampires, and director Terence Fisher rejected this premise. Fisher, a Christian advocate, envisioned Van Helsing as an evangelical adversary of black magic, so his pro-Christian faith was always on display, with good winning out over evil. The original scripted ending where Van Helsing evoked black magic did not further Fisher's philosophical vision. Finally, Clark's insight into *The Awful Dr. Orlof* demonstrates why this may be Jesse Franco's finest film, but the film also demonstrates the prolific director's major flaws as well (lapses in pacing, too much attention on mundane sequences that would be better served truncated or cut altogether, etc.). Clark draws parallels to Franco's film being one of the first films made as a direct influence of Georges Franju's *Eyes Without a Face*. And while many fans consider Franco to be an uninspired hack, Clark notes the director's artistic flourishes, describing specific sequences of inspired cinematography ("silhouetted shots of the two villains carrying a coffin towards a forbidding castle," etc.) and segments that take advantage of actual atmospheric settings. Mark Clark looks at these and other films closely and comes up with original insight that sparks the imagination. When it comes to the denser artistic productions of the decade, the intellectual Clark typically gets the nod because he can more easily convey the spiraling interconnections and tropes that make such productions classic.

But let's face it, the majority of the horror films produced during the 1960s were boilerplate productions, exploitation productions, movies made to round out required double features or fill drive-in theater screens. In other words, most of these movies were product and not cinematic classics. And Bryan Senn, who most likely researches production history and digs up published interviews with major cast members and the production crew, tends to assemble the "facts" of these and other productions the best. Senn appears to truly enjoy writing about the less-than-stellar productions.

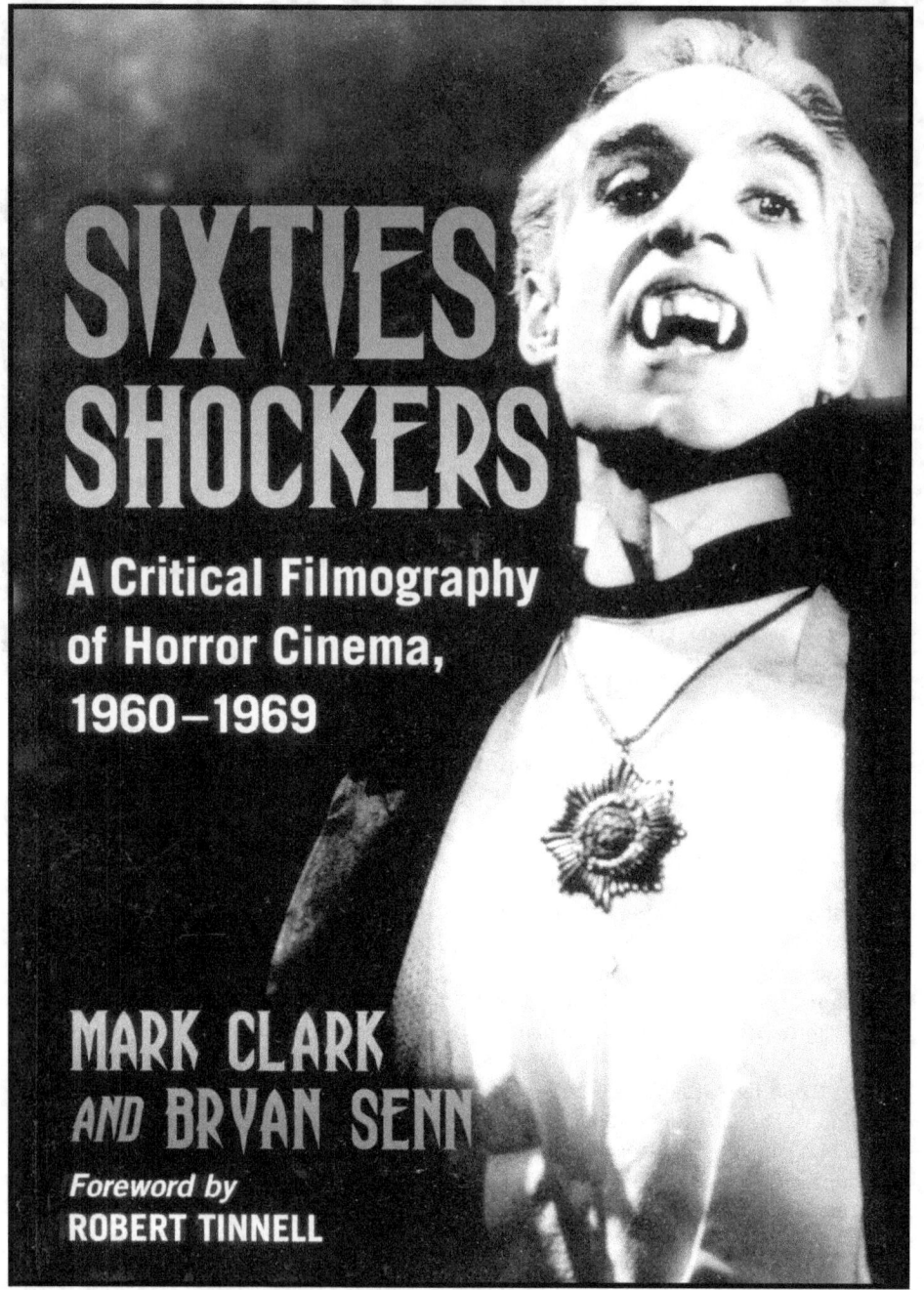

In his coverage of *The Astro-Zombies*, Senn reminds the reader "that any movie that opens with a skull-headed killer splattering the blood of an attractive woman on the side of a classic 1960s Mustang can't be all bad. Or can it?" Senn has a knack for finding interesting facts about grade Z productions (such as the screenplay being co-written by Wayne Rogers, who co-starred in the TV show *M*A*S*H*) and has a humorous flair for retelling synopses in interesting manners and emphasizing the one or two outstanding sequences that summarize the production. In his coverage of *The Brainiac* Senn succinctly tells the history of K. Gordon Murray and how he brought a package of redubbed Mexican horror movies to television. Noting that this movie is a classic of *le bad cinema*, Senn enjoys describing how the demon brain-eater has a huge head that inflates and deflates for horrific emphasis, noting its 12-inch forked tongue that sucks brains from its victims. But very interestingly, Senn explains how the production was photographed entirely indoors and notes how studio-bound sequences were made to appear as exteriors. The wonderful bad dialogue is noted, and the reasons why the movie becomes the South-of-the-Border *Plan 9 from Outer Space* are clearly laid out. So Senn can be just as insightful, but in his own way.

In other words, each writer's unique analytical style is well served in the context of detailing all the horror films released during the 1960s. Neither writer working alone would have been this successful. So the teaming of Clark and Senn works to the book's betterment, and by featuring different writers and different styles in separate essays, the book remains fresh and inviting.

Sixties Shockers is divided into three major sections. The first is an overview (quite detailed and insightful) of the entire decade, often dividing it into a two-year period of time, advancing from 1960 to 1969. Then the bulk of the book covers all the movies released during the decade, reviewed in alphabetical order. And finally the last section is "More Movies," which consists of shorter reviews of movies made during the 1960s but not released until the 1970s or beyond.

For me *Sixties Shockers* is one of the finest books on movies released during the past several years, an indispensable reference work and a simply irresistible read that is difficult to put down. The blending of writing styles contrasted with a decade of diverse horror product, from classics to schlock, makes the volume one that is always enjoyable, insightful and fresh.

Forry: The Life of Forrest J Ackerman by Deborah Painter; McFarland www.mcfarlandpub.com; Order 800-253-2187; 224 pages (7 by 10 inches); 88 photos; case bound $45

Deborah Painter creates the most comprehensive biography of Forrest J Ackerman to yet appear; it is a treat for all Forry fans. While the book is a noble effort and gets the specifics of his life correct, it is a biography that generally details the public persona of Mr. Science Fiction and never attempts to broach the true essence and inner workings of the more private Ackerman.

Don't misunderstand me, Painter did not discover *Famous Monsters of Filmland* until the mid-1970s, but did her homework. First she was a fan of the magazine, but soon became a contributor, essentially meeting and befriending Ackerman. She remains a fan of science fiction and horror film fandom and is an acolyte of Ackerman. So she mostly examines the life of Ackerman with star-struck eyes as a member of his close-knit cult. This might seem like criticism, but such loving and devoted fans not only spread the philosophy of Ackerman but also supported and cared for him during his declining years. We should all be so lucky to have non-family friends who would ask sympathetic bosses for time off to fly across the country to care for an elderly friend. But just as *Famous Monsters* presented a squeaky-clean "Uncle" Forry to a generation of Monster Kids, such devout readers, now adults, see themselves as caretakers of their aging prophet (and also see themselves responsible for maintaining his squeaky-clean legacy). For such people, writing objectively about Forry is impossible, as these people were part of the family of Ackerman, certainly not a bad thing to be. He was in many ways my mentor and person who influenced and encouraged my early efforts in the world of publishing. But I do not know if such emotionally attached individuals are the best choices to write a biography.

Deborah Painter is a fine writer but her style vacillates from the cool, detached chronicler of the facts to the obsessed fan writing with sentimentality over what this surrogate father meant to her. I won't say that this biography is minus warts, but it certainly attempts to avoid the scandalous and more salacious details of Ackerman's life. In very few sentences Painter recounts how vague tensions between Wendy's son, Wendy and Forry lead to divorce between Ackerman and his wife. This is quickly glossed over and we jump ahead to the couple's reconciliation and re-marriage. Forry's dalliance with nudist camps is mentioned but not so his attraction and friendship with much younger girls he met at conventions, nor his collection of science fiction-themed "adult" art. Somehow this biography comes off as detailed and fact-filled yet also sanitized and stripped of some of the darker aspects of Ackerman's personality. It was as though the biography were written by an adult who wanted it to be readable by younger fans who could grow up to admire mentor Ackerman just like they did. But writing such a party-line bio seems more propaganda rather than exposing the truth (the heart and soul?) of the flawed, shy man who established a milestone in pop culture.

Forry was fabulous in what he did for the science fiction and horror film genre, inspiring a younger generation of eager fans to remember and treasure the films made a generation before and keeping the past (in both film and literature) alive. However, Ackerman was never actually our uncle, and an objective biography needs to tell both the good and the bad and attempt to get inside the actual Ackerman psyche and reveal who and what he was. Painter treads lightly upon the fact that Ackerman remained a freelancer, hardly working in the traditional sense his entire life; in many ways his faithful wife Wendy held the traditional jobs, providing retirement security but also supporting Ackerman's boy-child lifestyle with her own financial investments and wealth.

What Painter does well is get the chronology and facts of Ackerman's professional and personal life correct. Perhaps the chapter on Ackerman's background, family and early years is the most insightful, as is the account of Ackerman's initiation into organized science fiction fandom and his friendships with other professionals in the field. All the major touchstones of his life are addressed: the rise and fall of *Famous Monsters of Filmland*, his souring relationships with James Warren and Ray Ferry, all the books and magazines that Forry wrote and/or edited over the years, all the Ackermansions in which he lived, his declining health during the final decade, etc. But the biography is told mostly as Forry Ackerman would most likely want his story told, and Painter tells that version well. The definitive biography of Ackerman is still waiting to be written, one that comes closest to revealing Forrest J Ackerman's private and inner workings, revealing the actual human being beyond the "Uncle" Forry persona.

Keep Watching the Skies! American Science Fiction Movies of the Fifties: The 21st Century Edition by Bill Warren; McFarland www.mcfarlandpub.com; Order 800-253-2187; 1,040 pages (8.5 by 11 inches); 273 photos (including full color poster reproductions); case bound with dust jacket (cover art by Kerry Gammill) $99

The current rage is for cinematic reference books, written a generation ago, to be revised, updated, re-designed, expanded and re-published. Such a philosophy works well for books such as Tom Weaver's *Universal Horrors* and Greg Mank's *Karloff and Lugosi* and a few others. However, Bill Warren's lovingly conceived double-volume *Keep Watching the Skies*, released in 1982 and 1986 (volume one and volume two), does not necessarily seem better served with an oversized, overweight, single-edition version (although the revision and expansion of the text is a boon for fans).

First of all, the bulky 6.5-pound book, the very definition of coffee table volume, works best if it were merely a visual art or photo book that could be leisurely gazed upon and flipped through. But Warren's book is essentially text based, a personal analysis of an important decade of the science fiction film genre, and is designed to be carefully read and reread. So simply maneuvering such a large and heavy text is, well, uncomfortable. Like McFarland's recent silent film analysis of the horror film written by John Soister et al., Warren's book would have been better served as a one price but two- or three-volume book, published concurrently, that would be much more lap-comfortable. But the use of heavy enamel stock and colorful poster reproduction (amid scores of black and white glossy photos) makes an impressive presentation. McFarland's rare use of a dust jacket with fabulous art is also a boon.

Reprinting the original Prefaces to the original editions, as well as adding a brand new Preface to the revised 21st Century edition, Bill Warren makes his book's purpose crystal clear: "In a sense, this is not really a book about the science fiction movies of the 1950s—actually, 1950-1962—it's a book about me, in that it's what I think of each movie that I define as science fiction." And Warren admits to loving all these films, even the ones that he most disparages, for all these films were his best friends as a child growing up. Warren states his analysis is very personal, often recalling the specific theaters where he saw a movie, the personal events leading up to the cinematic experience, the people he saw these movies with, etc. And this sense of personal passion is what made the original two-volume edition of the book exceptional and beloved. Bill Warren became the Everyman baby boomer Monster Kid who shared not only his thoughts on these movies but shared the experience of how it felt to first see these films as a kid. Warren made film criticism personal.

And Warren explains why he decided to re-visit *Keep Watching the Skies*. As Warren declares, tons of new information about the films became available since the 1980s, mostly collected interviews with actors, writers, directors, special effects people and others who worked on these science fiction movies of the 1950s, all easily accessible through a series of published interviews generated by Tom Weaver and others. Also, Warren revised his opinions and simply felt he had more to say about each movie reviewed. Warren admits that every single entry was rewritten, some only slightly but others extensively.

Admittedly when reviewing a 1,000-plus-page book, I did not have time to revisit the original editions of *Keep Watching the Skies*. So I was not able to compare Warren's original analysis of specific films to his revised analysis. But I got the impression in the revised edition that Warren tended to be less personal in his reviews and often more detached and *sometimes* negative. For a man who claimed to love all these movies, I see many reviews that fail to channel the love he felt. Even though Warren ultimately claims *The Amazing Colossal Man* to be "interesting and fun," he states "seen today" the movie would be observed as being "pretty bad." Warren admits the flaws outnumber the virtues but that the film "isn't a terrible film." Remember, the purpose of this book is to judge these films through the sensitive eyes of a boomer who grew up seeing them as his best friends. The review of *The Astounding She-Monster* begins with Warren stating, "This boring, dismal little picture … is astoundingly bad." When reflecting on Ed Wood and Alex Gordon's script for *Bride of the Monster*, Warren offers that it is "hopeless … it's worse than routine … it stinks." But then again, even the most faithful lover of 1950s s.f. cinema can't love it all.

Yet Warren proves to be quite astute at times, his critical eye adding nuances of meaning to movies that seemingly lack such levels. For his write-up of *Caltiki, The Immortal Monster*, Warren states: "Atmospheric and handsome most of the time, *Caltiki*'s beginning is slow-paced, but isn't the usual hackwork. It can't be called good, but is above average for monster thrillers of the period in the departments that really count for such films: design, photography and special effects." For his appraisal of *The Brain from Planet Arous*, Warren shares his displeasure with several critics who found the movie's plot "conventional": "Though the film is conventionally made, the premise is truly bizarre, anything but *conventional*. The idea is too grandiose for the budget level, and it's silly throughout, but at least it's imaginative and unusual."

Luckily, all of the reviews are insightful, detailed and demonstrate Warren's subtlety in differentiating between levels of incompetence vs. a film's struggling with lack of budget or limitations due to time. Not all B productions are treated equally, and Warren's ability to cut to the heart of the overall success or failure of any particular movie is the great strength of this book. True, some of Warren's biases disturb me, such as his blatant dislike of iconic hero John Agar, arguing that his clownish smile and round cheeks do not allow him to convey villainy in *The Brain from Planet Arous*, and when it comes to Agar's heroic roles, Warren can be equally harsh, especially in his appraisal of *The Mole People*. But at least the author is able to articulate his reasons cleverly and insightfully.

I disliked the decision to restructure this revised edition. In the original two-volume release, Warren listed the movies initially by year and then alphabetically within the framework of that specific year. However, in the revised edition, the movies are not listed chronologically; instead, we once again get the too common A-Z listing guide. Somehow the original edition was crafted as a journey through the 1950s, with readers right there with Bill Warren on his movie explorations, year-by-year; as we matured, the movies of the decade paraded by. But now, in the current edition, a review of a 1953 movie might be followed by another released in 1951, followed by one released in 1957. So a sense of a decade of like-minded movies evolving is somewhat

Bill Warren, in his review of *Caltiki, The Immortal Monster,* is quite astute, his critical eye adding nuances of meaning to movies that seemngly lack such levels.

lost in the new version. I would have preferred the chronological order structure that worked so well in the original volumes.

Warren does fill the final segment of the new edition with many clever appendices, including the total list of the films reviewed in their order of release; the "great pretenders" or movies that one would think should be included in the book but have not been; the science fiction movies of The Bowery Boys; 1950s movies that have been remade, and notable posters of the period (but why have them displayed here small, in black and white, when full color center section portfolios appear?).

For lovers of 1950s science fiction movies (and most of these could be labeled monster movies or s.f. *horror* movies, as Warren's definition is broad), this book is essential and remains an entertaining and informative read. I question the decision to include more outside research (quotes from Tom Weaver's books from actors, writers, producers and directors referencing the movie under discussion), as this produces a more generic critique approach in lieu of the personal approach found in the original edition. Sometimes I feel that Warren falls prey to what I half-jokingly refer to as the fan writer syndrome. Many excellent genre writers usually structure their analyses of movies in the same exact manner (no matter what the focus of the book necessitates), and this style is employed by Warren. Within the analysis of a specific movie, we get a snappy opening which leads to a brief synopsis, production details, short bios of all the major creative people and finally short snippets of reviews from outside sources, and all these elements always appear in the same order, film by film, so that by the 20th or 30th film the reader could draw up a template by which all reviews follow. Perhaps some might say this is a good thing, following a consistent formula that rarely varies. I feel that some films need a lot more of one element and perhaps none of another in their analysis, and that the spontaneity of need should dictate the format. But that's just me. It is a shame that many people will not be able to afford a $100 book or at least might be put off by the high cover price. Even though often second-guessed and diddled with, *Keep Watching the Skies* remains a superb read and a book that belongs on any film fan's library shelf.

Ingrid Pitt, Queen of Horror by Robert Michael "Bobb" Cotter; McFarland www.mcfarlandpub.com; Order 800-253-2187; 230 pages (7 by 10 inches); 98 photos; case bound $39.95

Ingrid Pitt's performance transformed vampire cinema when she made *The Vampire Lovers* (1970), generating a new level of sensuality and moral ambivalence for the movie's female Undead. Besides her blatant nudity, Pitt's performance was nuanced and subtle, as she was much more than just another "cutie nudie." Her cult

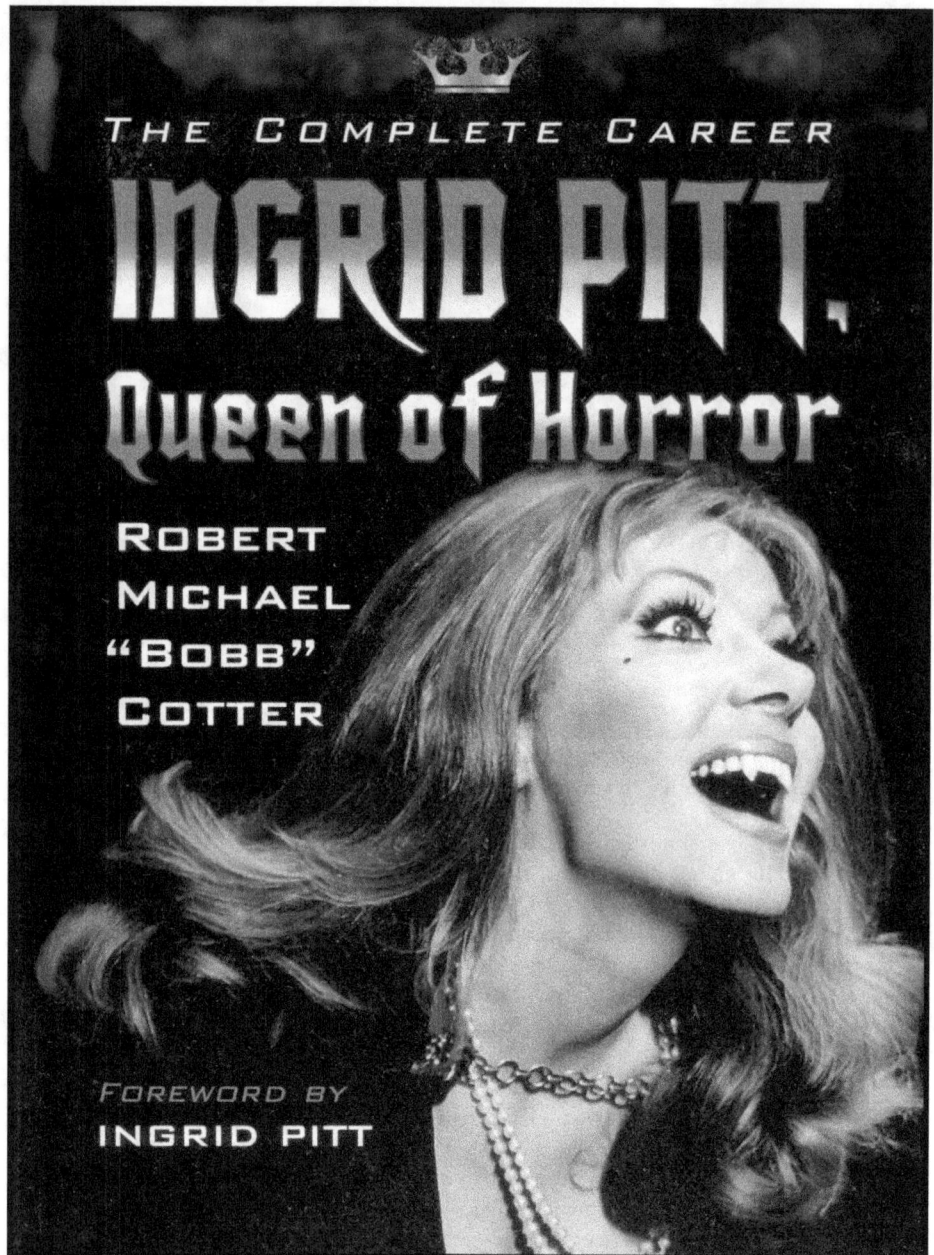

**The Complete Career
INGRID PITT, Queen of Horror
Robert Michael "Bobb" Cotter
Foreword by Ingrid Pitt**

stardom erupted from this point. However, looking to the past we are reminded that Ingrid appeared in very small parts in several mainstream movies. She also appeared on British television and on the European stage. As a major performer, hers was a limited career, although she remained a fan favorite. After so many convention appearances, she was a friend to Sue and me. We worked with husband Tony and her on publishing the Americanized version of her autobiography and we remained phone and convention buddies until the end (she always ended her conversations with her request for me to kiss my wife's belly-button). She was a gracious lady, humorous, kind and bursting with personality.

So how does one generate a book out of such a cult career, a rather limited one at that?

Bobb Cotter gives it a try, but his *Ingrid Pitt: Queen of Horror* is overly padded and appears slight compared to the coverage her career might have been accorded.

The late Ingrid Pitt delivers the Foreword, half humorously and humbly stating, "Aw shucks! Somehow Bobb Cotter has managed to turn my limited career into a thing of beauty and a joy forever." In his Introduction Cotter asks, "Is there anything else that can possibly be said about one of the most-loved icons of horror cinema?" By the end of the book the reader has to wonder how Cotter would have answered his own question.

After a marvelous initial chapter on Pitt's theatrical work, heavily illustrated with photos, ads and posters, we get to the heart of the book, the movie chapter that occupies its bulk. However, we must remember that Ingrid Pitt had virtual cameo parts in many of her earlier movies. So in the coverage of *Chimes at Midnight*, directed by Orson Welles, we get two pages of cast, production credits and a long synopsis, with one page of analysis briefly mentioning Pitt: "Ingrid Pitt is virtually indistinguishable in the crowd, although Mr. Welles' girth was such by this time that Mexico could have appeared in the film and not been spotted behind his massive frame." In the review of *Doctor Zhivago*, with over three pages of cast, credits and synopsis, we get less than one page of analysis, bare bones at best. At the end of Cotter's reviews he includes a generally brief "Tales from the Pitt" section where Ingrid reflects upon some aspect of the movie under discussion. However, while some quotes are credited to Cotter's book, most of the quotes are comments culled from Pitt's autobiography and a few other sources.

When the reader finally arrives at some of Ingrid Pitt's major movies, the ratio between synopsis, credits and analysis does not radically shift, as one might hope with Pitt becoming the central focus of the movie under discussion. For instance, the coverage of *Countess Dracula* contains roughly three pages of cast/credits and synopsis with less than one page of analysis (plus a long paragraph from Pitt herself). For *The House That Dripped Blood*, the same ratio of 3 pages (of cast/credits/synopsis) to one page (of analysis) continues. Perhaps most disturbing is Cotter's decision to give the Hammer Karnstein Trilogy (*The Vampire Lovers; Lust for a Vampire; Twins of Evil*) a detailed separate chapter, even though Ingrid Pitt appears only in the *first* movie.

Cotter must have realized that he did not have enough text for a book, written his way. However, I would have appreciated greater analysis of her performances. Why and how did she become the so-called "queen of horror"? Which performances stand out and why? I believe by focusing on the performance itself (and I am speaking about her major performances, not her barely noticeable walk-ons) that the book could have easily been expanded and become essential reading. The reader never gets the sense that Pitt has more to offer than her beautiful body (the article on her TV work is called "The Boob Tube") and that her performances contain plenty of merit. The problem appears to be that frequently Cotter simply reviews the movie in which Pitt appeared instead of focusing upon Pitt's artistic contribution. When Cotter focuses on Pitt's performance, as he does in his review of *The Vampire Lovers*, the results are far more insightful and informative. But such analysis is the exception.

The book closes out with several interesting chapters, the first about Ingrid Pitt's television work, with short and focused reviews never over-stating the case. Such an approach would have better served the reviews of some of Pitt's earlier movie productions, where she literally appears in brief walk-bys. It is in this television chapter where Cotter shines the brightest, because the reader is learning new information not readily available in other sources. Next we encounter a listing of documentary films or short features where Pitt appears as herself (perhaps being interviewed for a "making of" film as a supplement to one of her movies released on Blu-ray/DVD). Finally, a listing of books and articles about Ingrid Pitt appears, including her two autobiographies.

While Bobb Cotter has written a fan-friendly (light and breezy) book on the television, documentary and feature film work of cult actress Ingrid Pitt, the definitive reference book on Pitt has yet to be written. Cotter's research depends too heavily on other sources and he fails to properly investigate her performances and state what exactly is her legacy to the horror film genre. While this is an adequate book that will please fans of Pitt, Cotter's critical approach fails to go the extra mile to make his book truly worthy of its subject matter.

Women in the Horror Films of Vincent Price by Jonathan Malcolm Lampley; McFarland www.mcfarlandpub.com; Order 800-253-2187; 212 pages (7 by 10 inches); 49 photos; trade paperback $35

Originally conceived as a dissertation for his Ph.D., Jonathan Lampley's *Women in the Horror Films of Vincent Price* expands the concepts from that essay into book-length analysis. As a result the volume is academic in style and quotes extensively from a multitude of other published sources. After a wonderful (but brief) Foreword by actress Caroline Munro, who writes about working with Vincent Price (in the two Dr. Phibes films) and shares her reflections of him, Lampley writes a rather long and convoluted Introduction, "Welcome to My Nightmare: Vincent Price Considered," that meanders and is over-written, showcasing some of the worst aspects of scholarly writing. Lampley attempts to create an over-all context establishing the thematic issues of the horror film performances of Vincent Price. The writer suggests a "homo-horror approach" that addresses the "effete" performances sometimes created by Price

(always emphasizing his "camp" appeal). Lampley gravitates to the importance of supporting female performances in Price's horror films, thus establishing "gender ambivalence, anxiety about sexuality, romantic love and the ramifications of challenges to existing social and cultural paradigms." Women become "barometers of the 'dread of difference'" and are depicted as "villains, victims and objects of veneration or some combination thereof." Lampley continues to introduce various other thematic issues, while also giving an overview of the films under discussion. Of course a biography of Edgar Allan Poe and his literary theories enter the mix, and a definition of Gothic literature appears near the end. I am willing to bet that the heart of Lampley's dissertation appears here in the Introduction. Lampley jam-packs all his academic theories together in this Introduction.

Thank heavens the rest of the book demonstrates the finer aspects of academic writing and becomes far less verbose and pretentious, ultimately becoming a highly recommended and intelligent read that is just as entertaining as it is scholarly.

Two Vincent Price films released in 1946, not actually horror movies, establish two directions that would serve as templates for Vincent Price's future horror film roles. The film noir thriller *Shock* "foreshadows the mad doctors and scientists Price would frequently portray during his later career," with its reliance upon an evil doctor who

Vincent Price and Elizabeth Shepherd from *The Tomb of Ligeia*

runs a private sanitarium and murders his wife during a heated argument concerning his mistress, a nurse who works with him. Another innocent woman witnesses the crime and has to be locked away in Price's sanitarium where she might be driven insane by Price, murdered by Price or murdered by one of the unstable mental patients. Shades of *House on Haunted Hill* and *The Tingler* can be easily traced back to *Shock*. On the other hand, the historic costume drama *Dragonwyck* is "unquestionably a Gothic thriller and presents Price with an intriguing dress rehearsal for the Poe adaptations he would make in the 1960s." Here Price plays the last surviving male in an aristocratic family who is obsessed with a beautiful younger woman (driven by the urge to sire an heir and carry on the family name) and this theme is evident in many of the AIP Poe movies, especially *House of Usher*.

Calling *House of Wax* (1953) "the single most influential assignment in Vincent Price's cinematic career," Lampley makes the case that this film establishes the actor's connection to scary movies and defines his place in popular culture. Here Lampley makes a wonderful case for the importance of the female characters in the movie, addressing the theme of misogyny established by Professor Jarrod's (Vincent Price) "insane scheme" involving the "objectification of woman" when the mad doctor murders them to "preserve their beauty, to make them things, not human." The irony is that the now disfigured sculptor cannot use his hands to create beauty, so he can only create beauty through the act of murder. And Lampley points out that Jarrod's major wax creations—Joan of Arc and Marie Antoinette—are "famous women in history whose chief claims to fame are the circumstances surrounding their deaths … which result from the decisions of men," becoming examples of preserving female beauty "only by destroying female life." The author makes a fine point here.

In a dual chapter on *The Fly* (1958) and its sequel *Return of the Fly* (1959), Lampley focuses on Price's transitional roles to horror film stardom (claiming *House of Usher* in 1960 established his place alongside Boris Karloff and Bela Lugosi). And while Price's role in *The Fly* is a supporting one, it is a truly effective one. Lampley reminds us that second-billed star Patricia Owens is the "real star here" and that the film is "largely a female-centered project." Owens' character is the narrator of the story and her situation becomes the moral center of the film, exploring the motives she has for murdering her husband (will she be executed or spend the rest of her life in a mental institution?). Lampley demonstrates that Helene breaks the mold of helpless female heroines of the 1950s and becomes the active partner after the death of her husband.

The next dual chapter covers two of Price's most memorable movies, *House on Haunted Hill* (1958) and *The Tingler* (1959). Quite rightfully so, Lampley praises the sharp film noir-style dialogue created by screenwriter Robb White in the script for *House on Haunted Hill*, even though he calls the film "a mess" in terms of "its logical coherence." Stating the marriage between Loren (Price) and Annabelle (Carol Ohmart) has reached a "toxic point," Lampley points out they have not divorced, even though they now despise one another, because they share the aspects of "pride, greed, intelligence and determination" and are more similar than they would care to admit. But Lampley hits his target when he illuminates Loren's arrogance for the working stiffs he employs. The young Nora is first introduced by Price's own voice-over narration, describing her by saying, "Isn't she pretty?" Loren informs the audience that her income supports her entire family and that she could really benefit from the $10,000 prize money, if she stays overnight in the haunted house. "A sociopolitical conflict is thus established: the poor working girl already being exploited for her labor by the wealthy millionaire appears to be Loren's literal victim as well." Remember, Price orchestrates the chain of events to drive the sympathetic Nora to insanity so she will shoot and kill the man who is having an affair with his wife Annabelle. Nora is put through the wringer as far as scares go, confronting the witchy servant in the pitch dark room, being attacked by the dangling rope that supposedly kills Annabelle later in the picture, becoming the victim by finding a dismembered bloody head, etc. And after everything is resolved, "Loren makes no apology to Nora, nor does he appear to have any shame or guilt about involving this innocent person." In the companion film *The Tingler*, again written by Robb White, Lampley shows the parallels between three major female characters in both movies, demonstrating once again that two out of the three females in each "demonstrate characteristics of both villainy and victimization." But differences between the three parallel characters are also pointed out, as are their relationships with star Vincent Price. Remaining true to his title, Lampley constantly focuses on the females in each of the movies and spends quite some time establishing their relationship to the Vincent Price character in each movie.

The book continues following basically the same format, covering the pivotal classic *House of Usher* (1960) and all of Price's horror films that follow, concluding with *Madhouse* (1974). Lampley includes biography and background information where necessary, but his emphasis is upon analysis (there are almost no synopses) and tracing similar themes throughout the horror film genre work of Vincent Price. Lampley's text is intelligent and insightful. And most importantly, the book made me think and re-evaluate my impressions of the films and the performances. Skip the Introduction (or save it for last) and start with chapter one. Read in that way, the book comes recommended.

Midnight Marquee Movie Review

by Gary J. Svehla

Rating:
4 (excellent); 3 (good);
2 (fair); 1 (poor)

**Universal Classic Monsters
The Essential Collection (Blu-ray)**
Movies:
Dracula (3.5);
Spanish language *Dracula* (3.0);
Frankenstein (4.0);
The Invisible Man (3.0);
The Mummy (3.5)
Bride of Frankenstein (4.0);
The Wolf Man (3.0);
The Phantom of the Opera (2.5);
Creature From the Black Lagoon (3.0);
Disc: 4.0
Universal

And always remember, the analog picture was *never* perfect on Saturday late-night television back in the 1950s and 1960s.

Local TV stations usually screened well-circulated 16mm prints, often prints lacking enough silver to create the true blacks that a good contract print demanded. But even when viewed with jump cuts, scratches, ghost images and "snow," classic Universal features were always a treat to behold. Baby boomers initially encountered these horror movie classics under compromising conditions. And such initial crude broadcasts formed our critical reactions and appreciation. Later recordable VHS machines arrived and professionally released VHS releases appeared on shop shelves. Laserdics and DVDs followed. And in 2013 we have Blu-ray (and in years to come we will probably have 4k and 8k releases, if not on physical media, then as digital downloads).

At age 63 I feel I am *seeing* (and that is the operant word here) these Universal monster classics for the very *first* time. Never has any home video release done these movies justice—until *now*. Quite literally the cobwebs have been removed from Castle Dracula, the dank dust from the Watchtower in *Frankenstein*, the blinding snow removed from the inn where the Invisible Man traveled—you get the picture. And boy, do we get the picture in this magnificent box set! For any Universal horror film lover, these Blu-ray releases are life altering, for not even 35mm theatrical prints released since the 1960s have looked this good. And the presentation is so jaw dropping and brilliant that even my impressions of well-watched classics have changed because I am experiencing the films the way they most likely appeared 70-80 years ago. We can appreciate what an authentic restoration can offer. Universal has wisely preserved the look and sound of the original source material, maintaining the grain and film-like presentation. They haven't digitally added a 5.1 surround music mix (unless you count the secondary score offered for Dracula) or digitally erased or altered the original film (yes, one small segment of *Bride of Frankenstein* has been fiddled with). The restoration remains faithful and reverent to the original presentation during the film's year of release. In other words folks, Universal just about got it totally right! My only complaint is that Universal included the 1943 *Phantom of the Opera* when I would rather have seen *The Black Cat* (1934) or *Son of Frankenstein*, but hopefully another Blu-ray box set will be forthcoming.

Dracula (1931), directed by the long criticized Tod Browning, photographed by Karl Freund, with art direction by Charles D. Hall, looks absolutely majestic. Of course fans have criticized the production because, after its first third, the film becomes static and resembles a filmed stage play, losing the incredible cinematic look of

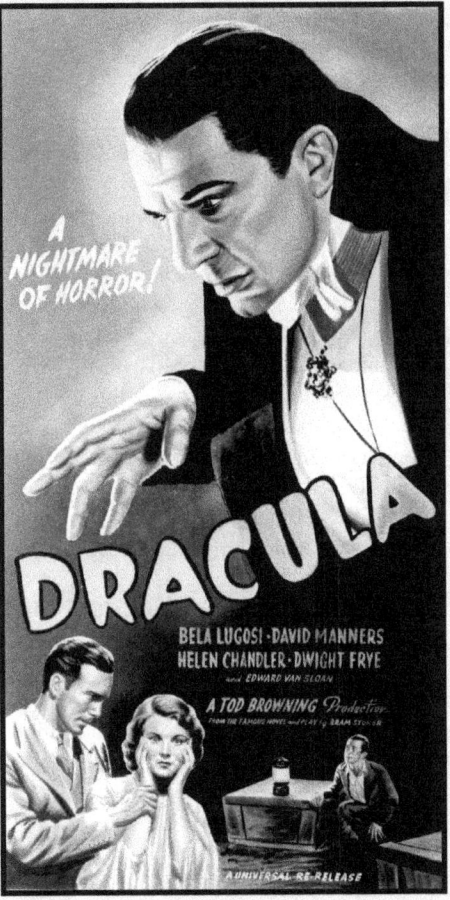

Helen Chandler, Bela Lugosi and Dwight Frye pose for a jumbo lobby card from *Dracula*.

the Transylvanian castle sequences. And I was one who also agreed that the final two-thirds of the film, while not exactly a bore, was disappointing when compared to the first third. But after watching the film once again in restored Blu-ray, I am shocked by how much I enjoy the so-called parlor sequences with bland Harker (David Manners) entertaining the kewpie doll Mina (Helen Chandler), while just simply weird Dr. Van Helsing (Edward Van Sloan) oversees. Sanitarium director Dr. Seward (Herbert Bunston) remains wallpaper but the dramatic intrusion of Renfield (Dwight Frye's iconic performance becomes even sharper) and his handler Martin (Charles Gerrard) spice things up.

Those initial castle sequences continue to be iconic, with the masterful set decoration framing Count Dracula (Bela Lugosi) as he delivers his oft-quoted dialogue, but now we can appreciate Lugosi's body language, piercing eyes, hand gestures and facial expressions even more because the photography and depth of field is now sharp as a tack, allowing subtlety to emerge that has long been diminished by years of wear and decay.

But what now impresses me the most is the effectiveness of the encounters between Van Sloan and Bela Lugosi, not only in the sequence where Van Helsing notices that Dracula does not cast a reflection in the mirrored cigarette box and triumphantly flashes the box his way, but also in the sequence where Dracula suddenly appears and reveals to his adversary Van Helsing that he realizes that the good doctor knows the truth about his legacy of evil—but since Dracula is so powerful and arrogant it does not matter. That is, until a smirk on his face (and my eyes keep going to Van Sloan's posture; he always stands half cocked leaning backwards, with one leg bent, almost as if he is trying to play his part a tad too elderly and weak, his stance always appearing odd) reveals he holds the trump card, in this case a small crucifix, which he uses to force Dracula to recoil in horror. These sequences are now framed by visual surroundings interesting enough to make us forget the stage-like presentation. Even the sequence out on the balcony is quite impressive, with Mina, formerly weak and fearful, perhaps morbid is the proper term. Now half vampire, energized but loving the nighttime and all its nocturnal attributes. When the big bat appears threateningly, and Harker fights it off, the minimal dialogue Mina delivers, speaking directly to Dracula in bat form, becomes quite unnerving. Another sequence, copied quite faithfully in *Horror of Dracula*, occurs when the housekeeper removes the wolf bane from Mina's room and Mina greets the immaculately attired Count Dracula, opening the French doors to allow him entrance. This sequence is spine tingling, something it never appeared to be before.

And of course, the sequences in the bowels of Carfax Abbey with Dracula's three earth boxes resting in an underground world of absolute death are more visually gripping than ever. Renfield's death, recoiling from the Count on the high stone staircase where Dracula stands with a mesmerized Mina, is one of the film's finest moments, the set and photography emphasizing the extreme heights and commanding Gothic nature of Dracula's undead world. And as Renfield falls silently tumbling down the stairs to his death, Dracula's world has never seemed more powerful.

In Tod Browning's *Dracula*, it is the little flourishes that matter most. The restored moans emanating from Dracula as Van Helsing stakes him in Carfax Abbey; those rats and armadillos traipsing around the bottom of the vampires' coffins; the sheer size of the interior of Dracula's castle; the simple but well-rehearsed gestures and carefully choreographed movements of Bela Lugosi; that smirk on Van Sloan's face whenever he feels he has one-upped Dracula; that powerful high-pitched whine that defines Dwight Frye's Renfield; that bright light that illuminates Lugosi's face when he rides the coach and first appears to Harker in his castle; Mina's lustful face as she stares at Harker after she has become seduced by the undead power of Dracula. And the list could just go on and on.

After too many years of disappointing and excuse-making reviews, I can finally appreciate Tod Browning's *Dracula* as a complete horror classic, a movie that shines from beginning to end (but that first third still remains the dramatic high point) and one that features a classic screen performance by Bela Lugosi, a quirky performance that never fails to elicit audience reaction. The presentation is flawless.

Included as an extra on the *Dracula* disc is the almost fully restored Blu-ray version of the Spanish-language version of *Dracula*, filmed on the same sets as the Lugosi version but at night, as the concurrently filmed American language version was filmed during the day. In place of Tod Browning and Karl Freund, George Melford directed and George Robinson photographed the Spanish-language version, and their contributions differ immensely. Although Charles D. Hall's fantastic sets were used by both productions, often the sets were slightly redressed (more cobwebs used for Dracula's entrance in the Spanish version) and some sequences were filmed differently. When Renfield confronts Dracula high on the arched staircase in the Browning version, Dracula throws Renfield's body down the stairs where his body crumbles and rolls slowly downward. However in the Melford version, Dracula simply throws Renfield off the side of the staircase where the fly-eater drops rapidly to his death. In the Browning version we see a hand slowly emerge from Dracula's earth-box, and then we cut to Lugosi hunched over as he slowly stands erect outside his box. In the Melford version, we have a similar spooky hand emerge from the box, but this time billowing fog is pumping from the earth-box. The casket lid opens and we have Carlos Villarias slowly stand up inside the box, giving the sequence more of a resurrection-from-the-dead effect. Lupita Tovar as Eva (Helen Chandler played her counterpart Mina in the Browning version) plays her role in sexier nightclothes and displays more cleavage, playing Eva for all the sensual appeal possible in 1931. While Chandler is the more prim and proper lady, in a sense her transformation to a seduced, undead parasite is more plausible since we see the wholesome being corrupted more clearly in the Browning version. Yet, the visceral and earthier performance submitted by Tovar is closer in spirit to Terence Fisher's Hammer vision. Both performances have their strengths.

However, where the Milford version falls completely flat is in the worthy yet inferior performance of Carlos Villarias as Count Dracula. In several sequences the actor's chubby cheeks and overplayed smile makes the performance almost laughable and appear overplayed. In repeated shots, Milford shows an extreme close-up of the top half of Villarias' face, focusing on his

Barry Norton (Juan Harker), Eduardo Arozamena (Professor Van Helsing), Carlos Villarias (Count Dracula) and Jose Soriana Viosca (Doctor Seward) from a lobby card of the Spanish language version of *Dracula*.

bulging eyes, and this effect is pretty intense. But when we see the actor perform, his Dracula is simply over-the-top and goofy. Lugosi's performance is eccentric and phonetically delivered, granted, but his body movements, his long-held glare and the use of his arms, hands and fingers are masterful. Lugosi—just in the way he smiles, stares, cocks his head and delivers his lines in a slowly delivered, halting manner—creates a masterful performance that Villarias cannot hope to capture. Bela Lugosi is truly Dracula, and even if the Spanish-language version has several strengths that the Browning-directed version lacks, the Universal English-language version stars Bela Lugosi, and quite simply stated, that makes all the difference.

Perhaps *Frankenstein* (1931) was not in need of the radical restoration that *Dracula* (1931) received, both aurally and visually, so the impression that *Frankenstein* leaves does not startle to the same degree that the restored *Dracula* does. I would have appreciated *Frankenstein* receiving the same pristine makeover, so I found myself slightly disappointed in *Frankenstein*'s restoration. Lacking the deep blacks and enhanced contrast that *Dracula* features, *Frankenstein* seems slightly softer in focus and lacks the clarity featured in *Dracula*. *Frankenstein* may very well be the innovator of the Universal horror cycle, becoming their first film actually marketed as a horror movie (since *Dracula* was billed more as the romantic Valentino from Hell or the mystery man who seduced young women with his eyes). *Frankenstein* is superior to *Dracula* and seems more cinematic, if ultimately creaky when compared to Universal classics released just a few years later (most noticeably *Bride of Frankenstein*). I still marvel at Boris Karloff's silent film acting style (with a few grunts and groans added) as the Monster re-animated from the dead, conceived as a patchwork quilt of stolen body parts. Karloff's Monster makes every motion nuanced and commands attention. The manner in which the Monster reaches its arms toward the skylight to experience sunlight for the first time, the manner in which Karloff stands erect but hunched stiffly forward, the manner in which the Monster attempts to plead for pity, totally fearful, at the cruel hands of bully Fritz (another too brief but masterful performance from Dwight Frye) and the manner in which the slowly revived Monster, lying on the examining table ripe for autopsy and dismemberment, slowly raises its powerful arm behind the head of Dr. Waldman (Edward Van Sloan) only attest to the artistry of the performance. Karloff's accomplishment as the re-born monster child, experiencing life for the first time, exiled to a dungeon of terror, is masterful.

And Colin Clive's haunted, obsessive performance as the overly curious scientist

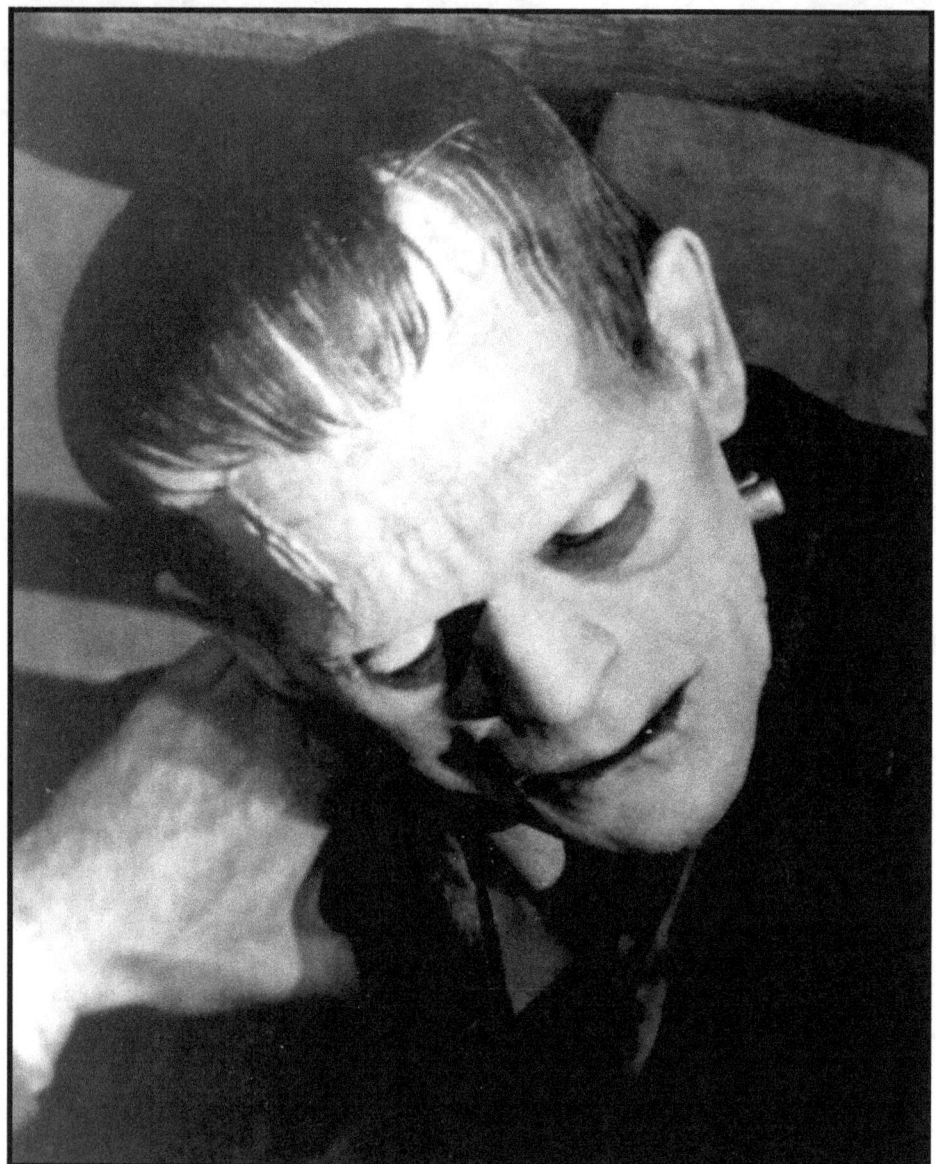
Boris Karloff creates the iconic Frankenstein Monster from Universal's *Frankenstein*.

who now knows what it means to be God becomes as manic as the Monster is scared. Seeing *Frankenstein* again and again only emphasizes just how similar Victor Frankenstein and his Monster are as characters. Each was literally made for the other. But that trio of terror, Frankenstein, Fritz and the Monster, become iconic screen characterizations that have stood the test of time.

Like *Dracula*, *Frankenstein* is burdened with slow sequences and chatty exchanges involving John Boles, Mae Clarke and Frederick Kerr, whose dusty performances have not aged well. When the film focuses on the world of the old Watchtower and its nearby environment—timeless, nation-less and existing in a fairy tale reality very distant from the actual world banging on the door outside—the film is masterful. In those stone-encrusted set designs with ceilings that almost touch the heavens, a haunted world of death attempts to bring light to the corpse that seems to exist in a scientific tomb. During the film's climax, a rotting corpse rises up to the sky to meet the fury of nature via a tremendous thunderstorm, and when the lightning touches the dead, a new type of half-living life is created. But this film's exploration of Boris Karloff's journey from death to life, and almost back to death again (ah, those sequels never allow that to occur), becomes aborted by narrative business far less exciting.

Despite the flaws, *Frankenstein* remains a true cinematic classic, but one fueled primarily by the physical conception and performance of Boris Karloff as the re-animated child (in mismatched adult body parts) from the grave who lives to experience life in an altered state that becomes both hellish and full of wonder. Just like regular human existence, the so-called Monster is shocked to a life he did not wish, experiences the wonder of existence, is treated to pain by his cruel handler Fritz, experiences the wonders of science such as hypodermic needles in the back and Waldman's attempt to dissect him as he lies semi-conscious on the examining table. Just like the life we all face, with unequal parts of misunderstanding, cruelty and pain, *Frankenstein* becomes a metaphor for life that touches upon the truth quite faithfully. While the film's restoration is good, it screams for the perfection of *Dracula*.

And speaking of exquisite restoration, James Whale's *The Invisible Man* (1933) rivals the marvelous dust-removal that occurred with *Dracula*. Once again it appears that *The Invisible Man* has been masterfully restored with over 90 years of dirt, scratches and wear removed, making the film appear very much as it must have appeared in 1933. All the hiss and scratches are gone from the soundtrack, and the digital print appears to be very sharp with flawless contrast and inky blacks. As stated before, *The Invisible Man* has never looked this good in my lifetime of watching this classic.

I certainly enjoy *The Invisible Man*, but consider it to be one of the least satisfying of all Universal horror classics. Just like *Dracula*, the film's first third is the most visually arresting and contains the power of Claude Rains' mostly aural performance (although the physical introduction of Rains wearing the bandages and shaded glasses as he attempts to rent a room produces a fine physical performance as well). Just the sight of the solitary, disfigured man approaching the inn emerging from the raging snowstorm speaks volumes. The Invisible Man's encounter with the innkeepers, Jenny (Una O'Connor) and Herbert Hall (Forrester Harvey), is both comical and sinister. And Una O'Connor's physical reactions and screams are classic. The introduction of the inn's patrons and the bloated bluster of Constable Jaffers (the wonderful E.E. Clive) maintains mounting tension laced with doses of humor. However, after the Invisible Man's disrobing sequence and his Keystone Cops-style chase around the rented room, resulting in slapstick bops on the heads of innocent interlopers as his mad laughter erupts, becomes a tad too much.

Remember, *The Invisible Man* is at heart a horror movie about an inquisitive scientist who dabbles in the unknown and gets in over his head. His only request is to be left alone to figure out an antidote, not just for the invisibility that plagues him, but for the insanity that is slowly overcoming his being. Claude Rains, an actor of short stature, becomes the perfect megalomaniacal madman whose inflated sense of self worth drives him insane as much as the chemical concoction he ingested. When we are focused at the snow-bound rural inn, the movie is at its best. When we transfer the action to the Cranley home and its scientific laboratory, focusing on Dr. Cranley (Henry Travers), daughter Flora (Gloria Stuart) and jealous assistant Dr. Kemp (William Harrigan), the movie falters and becomes visually and performance-wise far less exciting. Of course when the Invisible Man returns to renew his love affair with Flora at the house, things do brighten up considerably, and the Invisible Man's cruel stalking and murder of his rival in love Kemp is quite exciting, especially when the Invisible Man tells Kemp, in specific detail, how his short ride down the road and over the side of the ridge will result in a slow, painful death caused by a broken neck.

James Whale, always the eccentric and masterful director, merged black comedy with horror to far superior results with *Bride of Frankenstein* two years later. The problem with *The Invisible Man* is one of tone. Often the audience is not aware whether it is watching an out-right comedy (the Invisible One chasing the patrons of the inn around the small room as he partially disrobes and a floating shirt appears to be frightening grown adults), a black comedy (the verbal repartee between Kemp and the Invisible Man before Kemp's murder), a movie that is played seriously (Rains' pleading to be left alone to finish his scientific work) or far less seriously ("I've heard breathing in my barn!"). I just do not think *The Invisible Man* creates a consistent tone in which the audience can trust and knows how to feel. And I also think that *The Invisible Man* is masterfully directed in part, but that sequences of the movie meander and become far too talky, losing audience interest. However, from the vantage point of the restoration of the movie, *The Invisible Man* is spectacular and is worth another viewing for this aspect alone.

Karl Freund (who photographed *Dracula*) directed the similar narrative of *The Mummy* (1933), starring Boris Karloff in one of his finest performances ever. The wrapped Mummy make-up is only used in the film's opening sequence; the remainder of the film Imhotep is reborn as Ardeth Bey, the wrinkly Egyptian who appears to

Above: Claude Rains, as the invisible scientist who only wishes to be left alone to discover a cure for his invisibility, seems perplexed in *The Invisible Man*; Below: Boris Karloff as the reincarnated Imhotep from *The Mummy*

The blind hermit (O.P. Heggie) protects his friend the Frankenstein Monster (Boris Karloff) from the intruding woodsmen, from *Bride of Frankenstein*.

be very, very old and brittle. Because of the more subtle make-up execution, the thespian skills of Karloff are viewed, for the first time, in full frontal assault. We have the lumbering, slow-moving Ardeth Bey symbolize the 3,700 years of his existence, another subtle performance where his body movement alone provides a performance unto itself. But then we hear dialogue delivered by the self-obsessed high priest of Egypt, his monotone line readings, haltering and slow, again mirroring his age. Inspired lighting illuminates his eyes, or darkens them as though they were sinking into the abyss of time, and Karloff's facial movement and control adds another layer of complexity to the performance. For the first time Boris Karloff, although still playing a monster, executes a complex performance involving body language, body movement, facial performance and intense dialogue.

It is a shame that the movie's restoration resembles the adequate job provided *Frankenstein* and fails to approach the spectacular sprucing-up that *Dracula* and *The Invisible Man* both received. But even if the overall contrast is grayed out with inky blacks absent, the digital restoration is still very clean and speckle free, and the film's sharpness and clarity is evident from the Blu-ray resolution. The film has never looked better, but the film still does not look as wonderful as the aforementioned movies.

Fortunately, another inspired cast surrounds Karloff, making his performance even richer as he plays against the talents of Zita Johann (Helen), David Manners (Frank), Edward Van Sloan (Dr. Muller) and Noble Johnson (the Nubian). It is interesting to see the versatility of Edward Van Sloan, always underrated for his essential supporting performances as Van Helsing, Waldman and Muller, all very similar yet distinct personalities. My favorite is Dr. Van Helsing from *Dracula*, whose encounters with Bela Lugosi utilize words as swords to create sharp verbal duels, with Van Helsing always flashing a smirk or smile when he wins the upper hand. In *Frankenstein* he is the mentor/teacher to Dr. Frankenstein, but one who chastises his student for meddling in areas of science best left alone. Waldman becomes more the irate parent, and his performance is sparked with energy and anger. Finally as Muller he is the wise and calm voice of scientific reason, the wily adversary of evil, but a man who lacks the eccentric quirks that Van Helsing possesses.

The Mummy features so many iconic sequences, especially the sequence when Karloff gazes into his pool of time and views Sir Whemple (Arthur Byron) attempt to burn the scroll that gives him life. Using mainly his intense eye glare and a clenched fist, Ardeth Bey induces a fatal heart attack in Whemple, who dies a slow, painful death. Karloff also shines in the final sequence when he dresses Helen Grosvenor in her ancient clothing, returning Helen back to her original identity as an Egyptian Princess. Karloff plans to kill Helen so his Princess may be restored, as he has been, returning from the dead much like Count Dracula. With solemnity he tells the dazed beauty that only one moment of agony will deliver her to a life (as her previous self) of immortality. Raising the ceremonial knife above her half-exposed chest, Karloff's face slowly transforms first into decay and then the skin peels away revealing bone underneath as the scroll is finally burned. This is a solid performance where acting, make-up and special effects all meld into classic moviemaking that, like Ardeth Bey/ Imhotep, has stood the test of time.

Next up, *Bride of Frankenstein*, the crown jewel of all Universal horror classics, stands the test of time. Besides an inspired performance by Boris Karloff as the re-animated and horribly burned Monster, who comes to realize that "We belong dead," referring to Dr. Pretorius (Ernest Thesiger), the more evil of the two mad scientists. Henry Frankenstein (Colin Clive), the victimized monster-creator, is allowed to escape the exploding Watchtower to rejoin his formerly hostage-held wife Elizabeth (Valerie Hobson). With a tear in his eye, the Monster sadly, with integrity, pulls that darn lever, returning him to ashes and dust. It is an iconic moment in cinema history, not just horror film history. Karloff, who was the baby exiting the womb and facing the light of humanity for his first time in the original *Frankenstein*, progressed to tentative adolescence with emerging sexual desires (hidden beneath the excuse of being lonely and alone), hedonistic pleasures ("smoke ... good!") and aggression (he fights the woodsmen when they invade his rural solitude, ending the bliss he shares with the blind hermit). Though he speaks a few words here and there, Karloff's performance is hinged upon body movement (Karloff is still an outstanding mime) and facial expressions, accented with a flourish of an arm outstretched or flapping hands in front of his face. Boris Karloff's performance as the Monster is one of cinema's greatest works of art and he outdoes his 1931 performance by adding nuance, subtlety and greater doses of humanity to an otherwise splendid performance in the original.

When we add James Whale's inspired, idiosyncratic and quirky direction to what I consider his absolutely finest film, *Bride of Frankenstein* moves beyond a movie grounded on an iconic performance and becomes classic cinema by nature of its eccentricities. After fumbling around with black humor and abrupt shifts in tone in earlier movies such as *The Old Dark House* and *The Invisible Man*, Whale finally achieves that delicate balance between high drama and dark humor in *Bride of Frankenstein*. Dwight Frye re-imagines his earlier Fritz as Karl, the sinister stalker who gets fresh hearts by any means necessary (and his line delivery is spot on, milking the gallows humor for all it's worth). We also have a rave-up performance from odd Ernest Thesiger as Dr. Pretorius, the true transgressor of God's domain. Thesiger's performance is equally inspired when compared to Karloff's and his Pretorius is equal parts mad scientist, magician and playful transgressor. Colin Clive continues his inspired performance as Henry Frankenstein, the man haunted by his obsession to create life in the laboratory, but Thesiger's performance trumps him in this production. And when Whale places Pretorius in the burial vault, showing the demented scientist eating his elaborate lunch atop a casket, we know that Whale realizes that Pretorius has become the pivotal character in the movie besides the Monster. Elsa Lanchester's re-animated bride is fabulous and visually striking, but her performance, a hissing one, is simply too brief to rival these other two performances. Like Dwight Frye's Karl, O.P. Heggie's blind hermit and E.E. Clive's Burgomaster, Elsa Lanchester's supporting performance stands tall amid a production full of many exquisite supporting performances.

Bride of Frankenstein's art direction is immaculate and awe-inspiring, even when multiple viewings reveal that ornate archways aboveground are redressed with dust and cobwebs to become dank burial grounds belowground. Beginning with the revival of the Monster, who survived the windmill's burning and flooding afterwards, Whale opens his classic film with a very tall set that features cameras that swoop downward into the abyss and decaying hands that reach upward for help escaping from the watery grave below. When Karloff's face first emerges from the shadows, we can see that the Monster has been savagely burned, and he has suffered, his hateful face

People sometimes forget that Bela Lugosi played Bela the Gypsy in *The Wolf Man*, the original werewolf who bit Larry Talbot and turned him into a werewolf.

and pained grimaces registering the simple fact that he is not pleased with human existence. The Monster's life is one filled with pain, rejection and hatred from the human race that just does not understand him. True, he savagely tosses little Marie's mother downward to her watery death, but that brutal reaction and slaughter is most likely prompted by surprise, pain and fear. And later in the movie, it seems the Monster constantly wishes to remain isolated and alone (until he is taken in by the kindly hermit who cares for him), desperately trying to escape humanity. Karloff's interpretation makes the Monster inquisitive, playful, fearful, protective and, as we formerly said, hedonistic, but at heart he is humanity out of time, out of tune, a re-animated piecemeal corpse brought back to life in the most startling of ways, by having its sewed together body parts shocked by

a lightning storm and brought back to life. Talk about exiting the womb in the most violent of ways. Here is a living anomaly that never asked for life, yet at the same time he is forced to exist in a environment where everyone views him as a travesty of nature.

Greatly in need of restoration, *Bride of Frankenstein* has never looked better. While the restoration is not as startling as the restoration on a few of the other productions (*Dracula* is just awe-inspiring), the restoration is game-changing and for the first time allows audiences to see *Bride of Frankenstein* as it has not looked for generations. The blacks are approaching black (not grays as they formerly were) and the contrast and clarity are restored. Perhaps the most classic of all horror movie classics, *Bride of Frankenstein* once again demonstrates visual brilliance, eccentricity of tone and inspired performances wrapped around a fairy tale mythology of the blackest of black humor, resulting in one of filmdom's finest achievements.

Five years later Universal produced perhaps its finest horror movie of the 1940s with *The Wolf Man* (1941), an often misunderstood movie featuring a performance by the affable but awkward Lon Chaney, Jr. as the title creature. Juxtaposed within the character of Larry Talbot we find the snarky and arrogant ladies' man contrasted to the haunted and tragic "woe-is-me-and-I-want-to-die" victim. Chaney's performance is more than adequate, but I find myself just not believing his persona nor liking the character that Chaney creates. In many ways, besides the fact that he sacrifices himself trying to save his girlfriend's girlfriend, I tend to think that Larry Talbot deserves his cursed fate, and that might be the problem. In one sequence Talbot tries to be the ladies' man, a player, and in another sequence he seems arrogant. Then in another sequence he pleads with his father that he does not understand theory, that he needs a hands-on experience in order to prosper (thus we see the dichotomy between aristocratic birth and working class aesthetic, all wrapped together in the guise of a lunk who pictures himself as God's gift to women).

But once we get beyond Chaney's performance, we have an awful lot to like with *The Wolf Man*, especially the intriguing screenplay written by Curt Siodmak that single-handedly creates a monster mythos that stands to this day (full moon, silver bullets, the victim of a werewolf becoming a werewolf, the werewolf as tragic hero). True, *The Werewolf of London* attempted to create a similar werewolf mythos, but it never caught on to become iconic. Now in 1941 the incredible sets on the large soundstages, dank lighting and willowy trees, all spooked up in mountains of high rising fog, produce a mythic world in which the Wolf Man can prosper. While none of the performances rise above solid journeyman (even Claude Rains seems hamstrung by his lines and his awkward appearance playing the troll father to the lumbering son), each performance serves the material well. Perhaps Maria Ouspenskaya's supporting performance as Maleva, the Gypsy keeper of the doomed Talbot, rises above the rest. But even Ralph Bellamy, Warren William and Patric Knowles get lost in the proceedings. Leading lady and true beauty Evelyn Ankers seems to turn in a slightly better than adequate performance, but what we remember most about her is the way she falls backwards into the monster's arms. Bela Lugosi, haunted and also a victim of lycanthropy, submits an inspired performance, but he is killed off way too soon to really matter.

The werewolf sequences are few and far between, but when Chaney as the Wolf Man enters that large soundstage foggy forest set, the film threatens to become the classic that fans wish it to be. Chaney's physical performance is inspired—his mastery of facial gesturing, the way he walks on his tiptoes (perhaps more makeup design than artistic choice), the manner in which he holds his arms and claws, half hunched over, and the way his head darts quickly from side to side. To be honest, Chaney's performance shines as the beast; it's only the human counterpart that suffers. George Waggner's direction is serviceable yet never inspired, the film's rhythms only occasionally building. Instead the success of *The Wolf Man* is quite episodic, with specific sequences standing out rather than the film as a whole. Lon Chaney, Jr. is perhaps at his best as Talbot when he enters the church from the rear and meets the disapproving stares as others turn around in their pews to frown at him. Such rejection from the heart of his newly adopted community registers on Chaney's face as he flees, realizing only too well the extent of the curse inflicted upon him.

To be honest, after seeing the Blu-ray restoration of *The Wolf Man*, I never enjoyed the movie more or better appreciated its sparkling, well-lit cinematography. Since the film was released in 1941 and the camera lenses and film stock used were superior to that of the 1930s, the Blu-ray restoration impresses most noticeably. The movie looks pristine, with great contrast and a sharp, deep-focus image. The Wolf Man sequences, even when obscured beneath subdued lighting and fog, shimmer with their clarity. The subtlety of the make-up has never been better revealed. Simply put, *The Wolf Man* features a fantastic digital makeover, one that enhances the overall perception of the movie. Restoration cannot make a bad film suddenly appear good, but it can reveal aspects of a good movie that may have been hidden or over-looked in previous incarnations. *The Wolf Man* benefits greatly from such a facelift. While this movie may be the best Universal horror film of the 1940s, nonetheless, it still pales alongside the better classics of the 1930s.

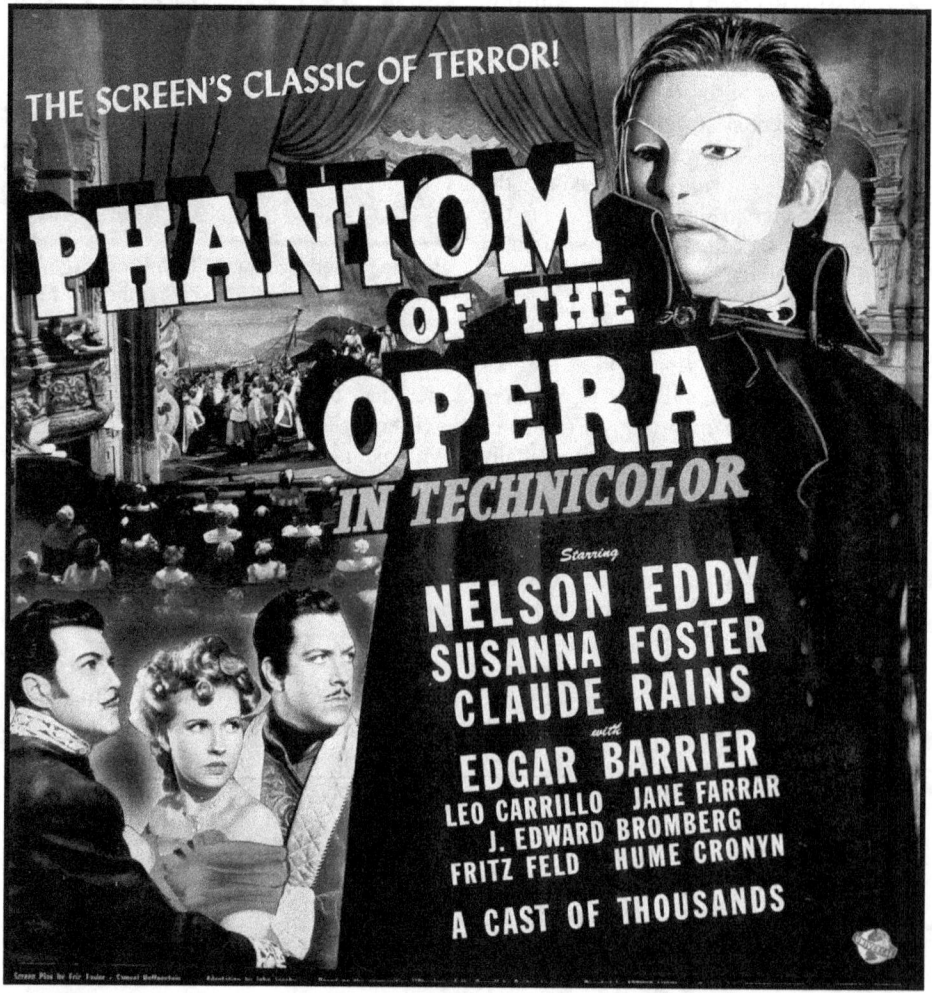

Universal's bookend movies of the 1940s, *The Wolf Man* and *Abbott and Costello Meet Frankenstein*, represent the artistic peaks during this decade of Universal's decline.

Phantom of the Opera (1943) might seem like a strange choice to be included among a package of Universal monster classics, but as first enacted by Lon Chaney in 1925, the monstrous Phantom is another of the iconic monsters that Universal created. However, the movie is actually here because of its stunning Blu-ray restoration and Technicolor photography, becoming a visual standout in the box set. The film has never looked or sounded better (the operatic orchestrations are impressive). When lovers of cinema speak of IB Technicolor and tout its virtue, *Phantom of the Opera* is one classic Blu-ray release that impressively exhibits what all the fuss is about. Dripping with perfect color saturation, boasting deep focus and a fine grain appearance, the cinematography by W. Howard Greene and Hal Mohr impresses.

The problem here is that *Phantom of the Opera* is not a very good film, and while it dazzles with its opulence during the 92-minute running time, the film is quite mediocre, appearing to have more substance than it actually does. As with many costume epics and melodramatic romances, the film is more a case of extreme style over substance. The film's opera segments are impressive with the full symphonic orchestra blazing, and this might be enough for many people to enjoy. But for me, character interaction is either played for tragedy or comedy, its changing tone grating, depending upon whether we are focused on the Erique Claudin (Claude Rains) tragic scenario or the lighter love triangle between the lovely rising opera star Christine (Susanna Foster) and her suitors Anatole Garron (Nelson Eddy) and Raoul D'Aubert.

Claude Rains as Claudin creates a sympathetic character. An important violinist in the orchestra of the Paris Opera, Claudin's arthritis cripples the fingers on his left hand so he can no longer play his instrument effectively. Given a free season pass to attend performances, Claudin is mercilessly fired without compensation or pension. He puts his passion into writing a concerto, but of course that music is stolen and another party takes credit for his creative sweat and blood. In the climactic moment, Claudin strangles the thief to death in front of his lover, and the lover throws a pan of acid in Claudin's face, thus relegating him to the sewers of the Paris opera house where he has free rein and access to his old world above. His goal is not actually to mentor the pretty young object of his obsession but to open doors, by any means possible, allowing the young talent to rise in the ranks. Star Biancarolli (Jane Farrar) drinks from a glass tampered with by the Phantom and she is unable to perform, so her understudy Christine gets her big break. However, Biancarolli will not allow the press to know of the switch because Christine brings the house down. Claudin, who lumbers around in the shadows and in masked disguise, murders people so his Christine advances in her career, and the audience sometimes wonders how the formerly kind and well-mannered violinist can suddenly becomes such a fiend.

It is only after Claudin cuts the heavy metal chain supporting the ornate chandelier, crashing it below and crushing a large segment of the audience, that the screenwriters attempt to demonstrate that Claudin is insane, most likely because of the acid bath. The Phantom forces Christine down below into his domain declaring that she will *only* sing for him and no one else. In these brief moments of dialogue among the dank underground settings, the viewing audience is supposedly convinced that the sympathetic Claudin is now a homicidal maniac, one not responsible for his actions.

Before their private concert can begin, the haunted underground chamber collapses and Claudin is crushed beneath the falling stone debris. Claudin's make-up is nicely handled, but it is simply an acid burn on half his face, not even approximating the more hideous make-up applied, say, to Vincent Price in *House of Wax*. Claudin is adorned with fluffy and poofy big hair, which slightly flattens near the end. Rains is impressive in his cape and light blue mask, but the diminutive actor, whose persona before the acid burning was so non-combative and unassertive, dazzles more than he terrifies. Claudin was a man without power, one facing debilitating crippling and loss of employment, and even in full costume with his protective mask, he still seems the nebbish man too willing to accept his manhandling by powers over which he has no control. Claudin begins the movie as a doormat who commands respect but he ends the movie as a doormat who is simply pathetic and twisted. A classic Universal monster he is not. But ah, that digital print is simply breathtaking.

The set concludes with both a 2-D and 3-D version of *Creature From the Black Lagoon* (1954), attempting to cash in on the current 3-D revival. The movie looks immaculate in Blu-ray. Somehow other

Universal's final classic monster, the Gill Man, threatens Julia Adams, from *Creature From the Black Lagoon*.

horror classics from the 1930s would have been better appreciated in this Blu-ray box set than *Creature From the Black Lagoon*, a movie best remembered for its classic monster rather than its status as a classic movie. Director Jack Arnold does himself proud in the creation of the Gill Man (played by Ben Chapman and Ricou Browning), a prehistoric, underwater missing link arriving in between the evolution of fish and man. Presenting the Gill Man in the so-called black lagoon (not very ominous) creates a sense of the claustrophobic, since the scientific exploration party uses the well-worn boat *Rita*, soon to be trapped by the Gill Man within the lagoon, as their base of operation. The mostly underwater Gill Man appears sporadically by jumping on and off the boat, able to appear and disappear at will. Tied to this conflict, we have the creature's attraction toward the lovely Kay (Julia Adams), who likes to take sensuous swims in her white bathing suit as the enamored Gill Man watches (sometimes his flaying claws inches away from Kay's wiggling toes) from below. Of course both hulking leading men, Mark (Richard Denning) and David (Richard Carlson), vie for Kay's romantic attention, as does the Gill Man. But Mark is the more insensitive scientist, the man who wants the publicity and financial rewards for his scientific discovery. David, on the other hand, is more the pure man of science who cares only about research and furthering the cause of scientific investigation. Of course in such a savage world, one of these men will die as the other claims Kay. That is, if the Gill Man does not get her first.

While *Creature From the Black Lagoon* lacks a sense of urgency and classic sequences needed to make the movie a horror film classic, Arnold does include marvelous moments, many of which are underwater, showing scuba divers pursue and attempt to capture the underwater beast. And when the Gill Man ventures aboard the *Rita* and grabs Kay and dives back into the water, the climax does generate thrills as David pursues Kay to bring her back alive. Venturing underwater and re-surfacing in the Gill Man's domain (a spooky grotto), David comes across the terrified and exhausted Kay as the Gill Man closes in for the final kill. After the Gill Man is shot by ordinary rifle bullets, David demands the gunfire cease as the mortally wounded creature, with dignity, returns to the dark waters and floats out of sight below. The implication is that the mighty monster adversary dies, but this is the studio known for its sequels and we realize the Gill Man will rise again.

Universal Classic Monsters is a marvelous box set of jaw-dropping restorations and Blu-ray presentations of horror movie classics produced as far back as over 80 years ago. Since the emphasis is upon classic monsters and not classic movies, we can understand the inclusion of *The Phantom of the Opera* and *Creature From the Black Lagoon*, but this initial box set only stresses the need for future sets to be released, so the entire array of Universal horror classics can be restored and released in Blu-ray and be viewed in the manner in which they deserve to be seen. The bonus features, usually comprising documentaries and features from earlier releases, are just fine, as these supplemental features were outstanding upon their original issues. A few new extras, most of which focus upon the latest restorations, are also appreciated. But when it comes to a loving presentation of these horror classics, Universal got it right and even included a wonderful collectors' booklet amid stunning graphic design. Hopefully this set's success will lead to the release of another box set next Halloween. Universal cannot allow just a handful of movies to be restored and released. They truly need to follow this ambitious endeavor through till the end.

Black Sunday [Mask of the Demon]
Movie: 4.0; Blu-ray Disc: 3.5
Kino Lorber

Some movies are destined to be classics, even when hindered by problematic editing, limited resources, artistic compromises and noticeable flaws that threaten to off-balance the other perfections. Mario Bava's *Black Sunday* is such a movie. Like recent DVD releases of the Bava classic, this first-time-

Arturo Dominici as Javutish/Javuto, the witch's servant, confronting John Richardson as Dr. Gorobec, from Mario Bava's *Black Sunday*.

ever Blu-ray release of *Black Sunday* is mastered from a British release print that contains the original musical score (by Roberto Nicolosi) and a slightly longer running time (American International used a Les Baxter score and re-edited the movie). Of course both versions are only available in a dubbed version where the voices and lips do not quite match up, but *Black Sunday* is simply so good that audiences can ignore these hindrances and appreciate a Gothic horror classic that still rings true more than 50 years after its release in 1961. While *Black Sunday* was not the first of the Euro-horrors (from Italy, Germany, France and Spain) to be produced, it rode in upon the first wave and in many estimations remains the crowning achievement of Euro-horror cinema (although Italian classics such as *Suspiria* and *Deep Red*, both directed by Bava's protégé Dario Argento, challenge Bava's crown, deservedly so).

Mario Bava, who served as both cinematographer and director, had total artistic control over the production and his vision created a horror film classic. We see bits and pieces of earlier horror milestones in *Black Sunday*, ascertaining that Bava was a student and fan of the genre. When the Innkeeper's daughter (Germana Dominici) takes that long walk to the barn to milk the cow, and Bava's camera becomes the roving, subjective eyes that look outside through the slotted hole in the wall of the old shack to observe Javutich (Arturo Dominici) resurrected from a shallow grave, ripping his spiked metal mask from his face, we are witnessing the latest incarnation of the infamous Val Lewton walk (done so effectively in *Cat People*, *I Walked With A Zombie* and *The Leopard Man*). In fact the little girl who is forced by her family to go out alone at night to purchase groceries during the gripping centerpiece sequence of *The Leopard Man*, her frightful walk accentuated by the natural sounds of the night, becomes a parallel sequence and inspiration for this walk in *Black Sunday*. In *The Leopard Man* the girl is confronted by a silent, monstrous leopard as she passes beneath a railroad bridge, and here the little girl is unaware of the satanic resurrection that the audience sees, but upon her return trip she encounters the ghostly slow-motion and gliding carriage housing the resurrected Javutich on his way to capture the doctor, who will be the first victim of vampire Princess Asa (Barbara Steele).

Black Sunday's spectacular set piece creation of the burial vault just beyond the decadent family chapel of the respected Prince Vajda (Ivo Garrani) is much more than a mere set. As our hero Dr. Gorobek (John Richardson) and doomed doctor Kruvajan (Andrea Checchi) enter the vault, Bava's camera creates a full panoramic pan of the entire chamber, circling back to focus on these human interlopers before they find the glass-topped vault of witch Asa, who is forced to remain in her eternal prison because a stone cross hovers in clear view just above her face. In one of the more predictable tropes of horror cinema, Kruvajan will cut his finger and bleed onto the soon broken glass top (a giant bat attacks and the doctor smashes both the bat and the glass lid with his cane), beginning the process of slow (this is no *Dracula, Prince of Darkness*) resurrection involving the witch's skull growing skin and sunken eyeballs bubbling upward to finish reconstructing her face). In Bava's cinematic world, audiences get little dialogue (thankfully meaning less re-dubbing) but gobs of moody art decoration and cinematography, all of which sinks slowly into our souls. Asa's resurrection occurs over the course of about 24 hours with cut-away shots showing more and more of her human features returning.

The film is carefully crafted using the doppelganger or doubling theme. Princess Asa, not quite burned at the stake two centuries ago with her servant Javutich, swore to destroy every living relative of the Vajda family, the people responsible for her destruction. And one of her intended victims is the current Princess Katia (also played by Barbara Steele as Asa's exact twin), the always-depressed young woman (who would not be depressed living in such a dank Gothic castle?) who seems to long for release from this world. That is until handsome Gorobek makes her acquaintance after seeing her standing alone at night with two spooky hounds by her side. But this leads to the second example of doubling, the heroic youthful doctor contrasted against the stoic older one, Kruvajan. After Kruvajan becomes the victim of Asa, he is last shown staring at her heaving breasts as she lies supine atop her burial vault and, powerless, he delivers a long and passionate kiss that leads to his blood being drained, off camera. When Kruvajan returns to Vajda's castle to claim Prince Vajda as Asa's next victim, the doctor's eyes are dead and cold. Instead of being the dedicated teacher to the young Gorobek, he is now a shifty-eyed demon shell working alongside Javutich as Asa's slave. So we have the contrast of two beautiful women, one haunted but innocent, the other vile and corrupted. These females will become interchangeable during the movie's climax, with the weakened witch able to drain Katia of her life force, making Asa youthful and beautiful once again and reducing Katia to a vile, withered shell. The same thing occurs with Gorobek and Kruvajan, where Bava contrasts the enthusiasm of youth, the healing power for good, with the corruption of satanic seduction and the transformation of the elder

Rachel Mayberry (Norma Eberhardt) is smitten with the worldly Cousin Bellac (Francis Lederer), actually Count Dracula looking for American blood, from *Return of Dracula*.

doctor to destroying life instead of saving it. Even the loving father Prince Vajda, weakened and confined to bed just because he observes the resurrected Javutich enter his bedroom, soon will find himself horribly disfigured (eaten from the inside as one character states) and drained dry of blood, fated to become a vampire himself. And instead of remaining the loving father, he soon will rise from his coffin and lust after his own daughter. Thankfully, his rotting shell will be destroyed in his own fireplace shortly after his satanic resurrection. Even the great room is riddled with this duality theme. Everyone sits around the grandeur that is the fireplace, trying to gain comfort from its warmth. But witches haunt the bowels of the castle behind the fireplace, their hidden passageways exposed once Javutich's portrait, hanging on the wall, is smashed and the hidden world behind is revealed. Once again we have that duality contrasting the world that comforts us and the other one, just as familiar, yet distant and corrupt. Bava's point here is simple. The faces of good and evil look virtually the same and even the most virtuous person can become seduced by the attractiveness of evil. All of us attempt to do the right thing, but any of us can be turned around by evil almost immediately, under the right circumstances. We are all vulnerable. We are all weak. And sooner than later, we will all die (or find ungodly immortality through the vile evil of vampirism).

Black Sunday shines because, in this black-and-white morbid and spiritually nihilistic world, Mario Bava creates a new mythology of vampires and evil. His is not the Technicolor world of vampires as created by Terence Fisher at Hammer. Instead we have vampires called witches, and vampire victims never act independently but always remain slaves to their master Asa. Such vampire witches are not destroyed by a stake through the heart but by a metal spike through the eye. They may also be destroyed by fire. These vampires may be beautiful, but as their evil reigns, the flesh on their skin decays (Javutich's decaying face and Asa's ghostly white and spiked face). At one point Gorobek grabs the cloak of Asa and sees the rotting skeletal corpse beneath. The vampires of *Black Sunday* are not the hedonistic cult that Hammer fabricated (most clearly illustrated by the dashing and youthful Baron Meinster in *Brides of Dracula*), but they become lonely, lethargic creatures fueled by their passion seeking unbridled power and dominance. Bava's world is one lacking light, energy and virtue.

No matter how many times I return to this movie, it never fails to transfix and weave a web of gripping horror. The Blu-ray digital print presents *Black Sunday* as it hasn't been seen since the early 1960s, even if the opening credits are a tad soft and other imperfections occur. Made from a fine-grade 35mm print, *Black Sunday* sparkles with its inky contrast and deep blacks. It remains one of the classics of horror cinema.

The Return of Dracula
The Vampire
Movies: *Return of Dracula* (3.5);
The Vampire (3.5); Disc: 3.5
[MGM]

Producers Arthur Gardner and Jules V. Levy released what I label the suburban Gothics, featuring mythic horror icons dressed up in all the accouterments of the 1950s. *The Vampire*, written by Pat Fielder and directed by Paul Landres, was released in 1957 by UA; *The Return of Dracula* followed one year later and was also written by Fielder and directed by Landres. To me, both of these productions are 1950s American classics, existing right up there with the best of Toho, AIP, Allied Artists, Film Group and any of the indies. Unfortunately Hammer's Technicolor *Horror of Dracula*, released only one month after *The Return of Dracula*, quickly overshadowed the less splashy production. And *The Vampire*, starring the mature, fatherly John Beal in a wonderful performance, lacked the youth appeal of other drive-in movie fare. These films were not drive-in programmers, they were released directly to the neighborhood (suburban) theaters and appealed both to the youth trade and to adults who fondly remembered the classic horror fare of a generation earlier. Both films were lower-budget film fare, but the ingenuity of vision and creativity made both stand out amid inferior but more widely heralded productions that made more money. I was lucky enough to have seen both of these movies theatrically, and my love for the genre was sparked by them when I was seven and eight years old. And let me stress, both of these productions delivered the goods and lingered long in my sense-of-wonder imagination.

First, *The Vampire* casts the mythic Euro-vampire in a bright new scientific sheen, filtered through shades of Jekyll and Hyde. Screenwriter Pat Fielder made sure she touched every one of the Gothic bases in this game of shudder déjà-vu. The film establishes its suburban roots in the very first sequence, where a drugstore delivery boy on his bike delivers a prescription to Dr. Campbell, who lives and works in a typical large (but run-down) suburban cottage. However, the boy finds the doctor near death and runs to fetch Dr. Beecher (John Beal), who hurries over to make a house call (something lost after the 1950s). With his dying breath Campbell delivers a speech, mumbling how his lifetime of experiments are contained within the pills that Beecher places in his lab coat pocket. Then Campbell dies. Returning to his suburban home/office (his daughter Betsy, played by Lydia Reed, dances ballet in a room directly outside the doctor's office), Beecher asks his daughter to get one of his migraine pills, and of course the adorable child reaches into the wrong pocket and produces Campbell's pills. Once Beecher takes the first pill, he becomes addicted and must have another pill around 11 p.m. every night. At first people on the street report a prowler lurking behind tree-lined streets, and Beecher wakes up with a worse headache and a grumpy disposition, even becoming surly with his daughter.

Three wonderful sequences occur. The first involves a bar/restaurant sequence where Beecher confesses his addiction to his pills and asks his lovely nurse Carol (Coleen Gray) to make sure she never gives him the pills, but when the doctor is called away, he finds a way to sneak the pills back into his possession. This sequence illustrates the tremendous acting performance that Beal creates in this quasi-Mr. Hyde/junkie performance. We feel sympathetic toward Dr. Beecher because he was the victim of an accident, yet we see the monster emerging. And for a B horror film production, John Beal creates one memorable performance.

Later, friend Dr. Beaumont (the wonderful Dabbs Greer) and Beecher are alone working in Dr. Campbell's lab late at night. Beaumont, hoping that their scientific work will occupy his mind and make him forget about the time, takes Beecher's pills and locks them in a drawer. As the clock speeds closer and closer to 11, Beecher becomes more unfocused and literally tries to claw inside the wooden desk drawer to get his pills. Beaumont's smile and reassuring voice only forces the good Beecher to bury his head in his hands, craving his medicine. However, in the best monster transformation tradition, Beecher turns into the vampire bat-fueled monster without any need of the chemical, and in a spooky, shadowy sequence, attacks and kills his friend, who was only trying to save him from himself.

The third memorable sequence involves misty sequences at night as the silent, stalking vampire attacks the nice old lady that everyone in town knows. Her dog tries to fight off the fiend, but the poor lady goes down as the creepily just out-of-

John Beal plays Dr. Beecher, in this frame grab looking more hung over than monstrous, but Beal's performance shines in *The Vampire*.

focus fiend goes for the jugular. In a similar sequence, the beautiful Coleen Gray is chased in a similar fashion, but she is able to make it home before the monster can get her. These scenes are effectively spooky and elicit screams and goose bumps. The cinematography of Jack Mackenzie (who also filmed *The Return of Dracula*) excelled in such sequences and audiences literally gasped out loud when the silhouetted monster appeared. The musical score of Gerald Fried also helped to maintain the chills and thrills.

Since our tragic hero is older and doomed to die, robust Kenneth Tobey plays the town sheriff, who ultimately saves Coleen Gray and destroys the vampire ... with ordinary bullets nonetheless! The climax and ending feel slightly rushed, but what comes before is suburban Gothic at its best.

One year later the same team upped the ante with the woefully forgotten *The Return of Dracula*, a modern day vampire film that works beautifully. This duo of movies is easily the best that Levy-Gardner produced.

First of all, Francis Lederer, an actor who had been working in Hollywood since the 1930s, submits what I consider his finest performance. And it just happens to be one of the best Count Dracula performances ever. Yes, Lederer dresses and speaks with a European accent, but he's not imitating Bela Lugosi. Lederer underplays every sequence as the vampire king, yet the intensity of his piercing eyes establishes his power and intelligence. During the 1950s most every horror performance tended to go over the top, but Lederer succeeds so admirably because he reins everything in and speaks at a conversational level that requires the audience to lean in toward the screen. In many ways screenwriter Pat Fielder is knocking off Alfred Hitchcock's *Shadow of a Doubt*, so the major relationship is between the reclusive Cousin Bellac (Lederer) and the young American teenager who wants an artistic life outside small-town America. Rachel Mayberry (Norma Eberhardt) is always wide-eyed and adoring in the presence of her fatherly (remember she lives in a single-parent household, ruled by her mother) cousin and she pines for a little attention from him. But Bellac is standoffish and needs time to adjust to the freedom that America offers, plus he appears more than a little weird as he rests quite rigidly in bed staring directly toward the ceiling as Rachel speaks to him. Again the cinematography of Jack Mackenzie shines in these sequences. Often he sets up his shots with Bellac standing in front of Rachel and the audience can see his facial expression while Rachel can only hear his voice. In several such sequences, the message of the voice (so supportive, nurturing and kindly) contrasts to the facial expressions where sometimes a sneaky smile slightly breaks through or Bellac's intensity is so severe that the audience knows that he is not the kindly man he tries to project to Rachel. The subtlety of Lederer's performance is only enhanced by such sequences.

Landres once again works overtime to embellish the suburban location with subtle Gothic trimmings. Even though Bellac appears to live in the Mayberry home (lined with dress-making equipment), his actual coffin is located in a mineshaft on the outskirts of town. While in 1958 suburbia Dracula would not be allowed to wear a cape, well, he does. Even though the actual Cousin Bellac is from peasant roots,

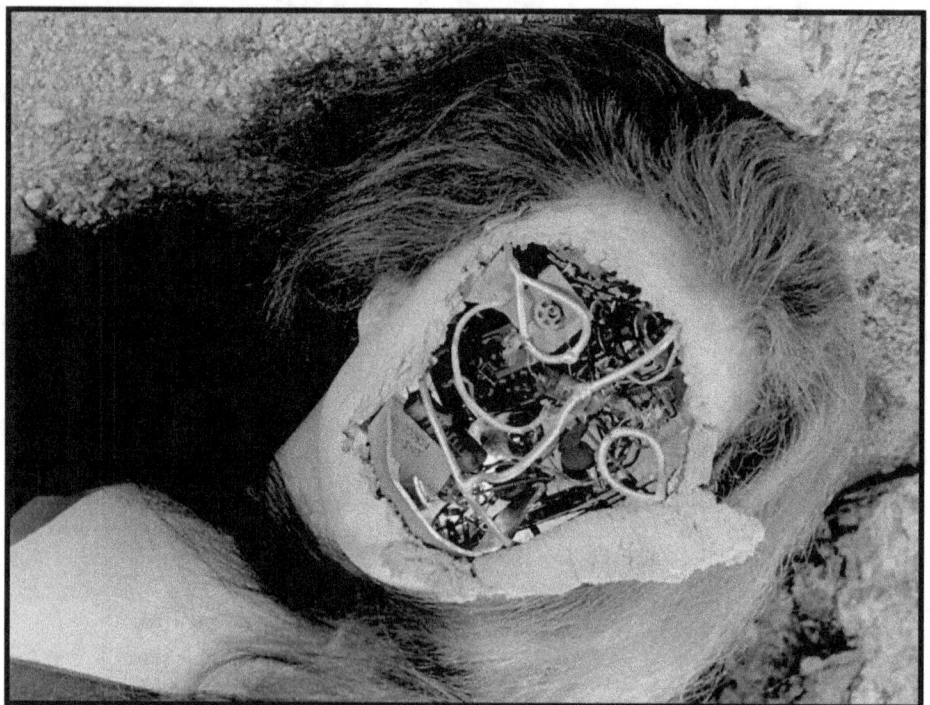
Corry (Jack Warden) is unable to return to Earth with his mechanical woman Alice (Jean Marsh), who is shot in the head at the end of *The Lonely*.

Dracula is aristocratic and wears body-sculpted suits that fit him to a tee. And he always wears a well-sculpted overcoat over his shoulders (in other words, he never puts his arms through the overcoat), allowing the coat to fall straight down. The draped overcoat's appearance mimics the look and majesty of an Old World cape, yet it is stylish for 1958. The small town has a dark and mysterious train depot and a church mission house which is actually the nursing home for the elderly and disabled. The heart of the community is the church and the annual Halloween dance is forthcoming, so everyone in town is creating his or her best costume for the affair. So the Gothic world of Europe has been masterfully transformed to Suburbia, USA.

Perhaps one of the key sequences from *The Return of Dracula* involves the young blind girl Jennie (Virginia Vincent) whom Rachel attends to at the Mission Home, where she reads to her. Rachel mentions that she will have her Cousin Bellac visit her here at the home. And visit her he does, appearing as mist outside her partially open window. Materializing as Dracula, he demands that Jennie open her eyes and look at him, and amazingly, she can see him after adjusting her vision. Dracula announces he will take her from the darkness into the light, and with these words he bends over her and bites her neck. The next morning Rachel is called to the Mission House when the reverend tells her that Jennie took a turn for the worse. When Rachel arrives, Jennie is fearful and talks about closing the window, and she gets up and goes over to the already closed window and pretends to shut it. Afterwards she drops to the floor dead. After she is buried in a vault, in a sequence very similar to one from *Horror of Dracula*, the vampire hunters find her casket empty and hide outside awaiting her return. When she returns they paralyze her with a crucifix and plunge a wooden stake through her heart, this scene appearing in vivid color.

The Vampire and *The Return of Dracula* are given widescreen 16:9 transfers that make both features appear flawless with wonderful contrast and intensity. The soundtracks are reproduced with strong phonics, making both Gerald Fried's scores powerful; he the master of the musical "stinger." The only negative is that both movies appear on one flipper disc, *The Vampire* on one side and *The Return of Dracula* on the other side. But when it comes to the best B pictures produced during the 1950s, these are outstanding movies to re-discover.

The Twilight Zone: Season One (Blu-ray)
Episodes: 3.5; Disc: 4.0
Image Entertainment

As a kid, everyone on the block, and even parents, watched the weird and wonderful half-hour TV series (well, one lesser season switched to the hour format) *The Twilight Zone*. Being an anthology series, it offered different types of stories and actors every week. When the series debuted episodes were, perhaps, too heavily dependent on teleplays written by the show's creator Rod Serling. Let's face it, even the greatest writers of the time would find it difficult to create classics week in and week out. As the series progressed, fine writers such as Richard Matheson, Charles Beaumont and others were added to the creative mix. Directors, musical scorers and cinematographers varied, but Rod Serling maintained a consistency of quality, tone and good storytelling as the series developed before our eyes as a television classic, still respected to this day. Classic episodes have been over-exposed to audiences since the series' introduction in 1959. But these episodes play differently to children (then) and adults (today). Few series capture the pulse of the emerging 1960s better than *The Twilight Zone*. Part of this was the heavy moral lesson spit in our face at the end of each story, but Serling was such a beloved icon that we as the child allowed the parent to preach to us. Remember, though, the preaching was secondary to well-written storytelling, and the series always presented classically composed short stories each week. Yes, not all were classics, but most were at least very good. From watching the series we observe all the dreams, the fears, the doubts, the flaws and, yes, the strengths that people during the 1960s held dear. Even when stories occurred in the past, say the Old American West, the concepts and morality expressed again mirrored the emerging consciousness of the 1960s. More so than any other series, *The Twilight Zone* was a mirror of its time.

To illustrate these and other points, allow me to review Season One of *The Twilight Zone* as a compilation discussing pieces of episodes together to demonstrate their symbiotic relationship. Certainly while the episodes varied and each story was unique, the overall series still managed to present common themes, concepts and feature various groups of people in similar patterns of thought and action. And as I touch upon a few stellar examples of Season One (1959-1960), I demonstrate that the series hit the ground running and never let up.

One common theme that exerts itself is the theme of loneliness. In fact one of the episodes is called *The Lonely* (script by Rod Serling; direction by Jack Smight) that concerns a good man, Corry (Jack Warden), convicted and sentenced to life imprisonment on a distant asteroid. Warden

Henpecked husband Walter Bemis (Burgess Meredith) has *Time Enough At Last* to read his beloved books after nuclear destruction wipes out the world. That is until he breaks his glasses.

is alone and only gets short visits from the rocket crew who drops him supplies every three months. Talk of a pardon always surfaces, but for four years only isolation and loneliness results. So the kindly captain Allenby (John Dehner), at risk for his job, drops off a mechanical woman, Alice (Jean Marsh), to keep him company. But when his pardon finally comes through, there isn't enough room or allowable weight to bring back his mechanical friend, a tool he now responds to as a human being. In a cruel ending, Allenby shoots Alice in the head, bursting out her face, and rendering the machine inoperative. Allenby tells Corry he is not leaving a friend or mate, but only leaving loneliness behind. Yet, the audience gets the feeling that Corry might opt to live the rest of his life on the barren asteroid with Alice, rather than return to a cruel yet familiar Earth where he would literally be starting all over again. Sadly, Corry was denied that final option in a rather cruel twist of fate.

The loneliness theme was first exercised in the pilot episode *Where Is Everybody?* (teleplay by Rod Serling, direction by Robert Stevens) where a man, Mike Ferris (Earl Holliman), clad in an Air Force uniform, wonders the deserted streets of a small town. No one is to be found. He thinks he spots a beautiful woman in a car, but it is a mannequin. He tries to make a phone call, but all he gets is a recorded message. Plenty of food exists and he has access everywhere, but the lack of companionship gradually pushes Ferris over the edge. At the heavy-handed surprise at the end we learn that Ferris is an astronaut and that he is being tested, at an aircraft hanger, to see how he (or anyone) will deal with isolation and loneliness for long space voyages. Even though the episode ends with Ferris being carted away on a stretcher looking up at the moon, the basic truth echoes that man can survive loneliness physically, but mentally, he will ultimately crack. As *The Lonely* demonstrates, once a man survives the long voyage to a desolated asteroid, it is the time alone there that will do him in. And in *Where is Everybody?* Mike Ferris does not step foot off our planet. The drama plays out in his head.

The theme of loneliness becomes a sidebar to another episode, *Escape Clause* (teleplay by Rod Serling; direction by Mitchell Leisen), a more humorous episode but one with a biting finale. In this tale Walter Bedeker (David Wayne), a hypochondriac, is offered immortality by the devil, the so-called Mr. Cadwallader (Thomas Gomez), in exchange for his soul. Cadwallader offers Bedeker an escape clause that any time he wishes, the devil will offer him a swift, painless death. At first boredom becomes his chief villain, as the devil has also made the selfish man indestructible. So he will not show his age, he will live for thousands of years and he cannot be killed. As a lark, when his wife accidentally falls to her death, Bedeker goes to the police and confesses to the crime, thinking perhaps going to the electric chair will be fun, especially since he cannot die. But when he receives a sentence of life in prison without parole, the immortal loneliness that he will face compels him to accept Cadwallader's escape clause.

This theme of immortality returns in *One For the Angels* (teleplay by Rod Serling; direction by Robert Parrish) where the superb Ed Wynn plays a "pitchman," Lew Bookman, who claims he can sell anybody anything. When a bland and overworked Mr. Death appears (Murray Hamilton), Bookman plans to trick the not-too-intelligent Mr. Death into granting him immortality if he can occupy Death's attention past midnight. But if that is the case, Death will claim the life of a neighborhood child hit by a car as his next victim instead. Creating the best pitch of his entire life, Bookman does make Death forget about the time and he occupies his attention until midnight. But Bookman willingly goes with Mr. Death, knowing he lived 69 years and that this innocent little girl now has a chance of living a longer life because of Bookman's sacrifice.

Time Enough At Last (teleplay by Rod Serling, based upon the story by Lynn Venable; directed by John Brahm) also plays upon these two themes of boredom and loneliness as a meek little man, Walter Bemis (Burgess Meredith), becomes henpecked by his overbearing wife and crushed under the thumb of his strict boss at the bank, where Bemis works as a teller. All that Walter, who wears thick Coke-bottle lenses, wants to do is read books and be left alone. He does become excited when his wife asks him to read some poetry aloud, but it is only a cruel trick of hers, since she defaced the book. While he is eating lunch and reading alone in the bank vault, an atomic holocaust occurs. Bemis is saved by the fact that he is underground and protected by the lead-lined and heavily reinforced vault. But once the smoke clears (of course the radiation would do him in, but all the science of nuclear annihilation was not readily known at the time) and Walter enters his brave new world, he observes total destruction of a world in ruins. No living creature is left alive. After first considering suicide, Bemis sees the upside of such new existence. Instead of being upset, Bemis finds a lifetime of books in the ruins of the city pubic library and creates little stacks, his present and future reading material year by year. But only when his glasses break and his vision is too blurred to read does the boredom and loneliness overtake him. Perhaps now he will put that gun he carries

Jacques Bergerac as the demented Desmond uses his hypnotic power to force beautiful women to disfigure themselves in *The Hypnotic Eye*.

in his coat pocket up to his head and pull the trigger. Finding books saved his life the first time he considered suicide; breaking his glasses and becoming virtually blind might now end his life. Irony has never seemed so cruel.

Of course lovers of the series can go on and on, reciting the virtues and surprises of almost every episode from Season One. But allow me to stop here. The less said about these cherished 30-minute morality plays the better. The Blu-ray restoration is fantastic, improving upon the restoration that first occurred on the standard definition release of the series. Until 4k comes along, this is the way to watch the entire series. The five-disc box set includes extras galore including new audio commentary tracks, related series pilot episodes, radio reenactments, and an interview with the late Rod Serling. And, of course, if Season One stimulates interest, all five seasons can be purchased either separately or collected into one huge box set. *The Twilight Zone* is one imaginative TV series that never seems old or dated. Even though technology and culture changes, the morality and humanistic view created by Serling will live forever.

The Hypnotic Eye
Movie: 3.0; Disc: 3.5
Warner Archive

Back in the early 1960s, horror movies first developed a gruesome streak, moving beyond family-oriented drive-in fare to a more sordid variety of suspense entertainment. One of the first examples out of the gate was a favorite of mine, *The Hypnotic Eye*, featuring enough gimmicks to make William Castle's head spin. Audiences were instructed to enjoy the audience participation "Hypno-Magic" during the climax of the movie. When we entered the theater, we received a balloon with the movie's title printed on it. During this special break, the movie's insidious hypnotist Desmond (Jacques Bergerac) pulls some tricks with the on-screen audience (who, of course, fall under his spell), demonstrating what they could do under the power of his suggestion. And then Desmond attempts this same "Hypno-Magic" on us! Continuing the trickery, Fred Demara appears in a cameo role, playing a doctor no less. He is the real-life criminal who gained notoriety as The Great Imposter, a man who assumed professional identities for which he had no training. He ultimately gravitated toward an acting career, but as seen by his performance, he had very little talent.

The movie involves criminal activities conducted by entertainment hypnotist Desmond, who invites beautiful women up on-stage every evening and plants a post-hypnotic suggestion that they will disfigure themselves at home. So far 10 cases of such mutilation have occurred, and the police, not very bright in these B productions, do not think to trace the victims back to having attended a Desmond performance. What is even more illogical is Desmond's motive for committing the crimes. He works with a female assistant, the always sleazy and beautiful Allison Hayes, who plays Justine. As the movie progresses it seems Justine is the one more in charge, and at the movie's end we observe that Justine too has been disfigured and that she somehow forces Desmond to commit the crimes of disfigurement as her vulgar attempt at revenge.

So as the movie opens, we observe a beautiful young woman wash her hair with shampoo over the kitchen range, and when her hair catches fire (via a not too convincing optical effect) and she screams, we cut to the title credits. Later we see a woman who sliced her face open with a knife, thinking it was a gentle massager. We then see a woman whose eyes have been burned out. And the list goes on and on. One exploitative and sensational death or mutilation occurs after another. Movies such as *Horrors of the Black Museum* (released one year earlier in 1959) and *Circus of Horrors* (1960) rode the same creative wave.

Of course the audience realizes from the get-go that Desmond is the fiend, but when police detective Kennedy (Joe Patridge) uses his lovely girlfriend Marcia (Marcia Henderson) as a decoy and she receives a mysterious post-hypnotic suggestion, Kennedy follows Marcia all over the city that night, leading to her late-night rendezvous with Desmond. Justine tells Desmond to take her home and Justine follows her there, pretending to be an old school friend. Justine instructs Marcia (under the post-hypnotic suggestion) to prepare to take a nice cool shower, but actually the water is hot and scolding. Kennedy arrives just in time to save her.

By the movie's end we go backstage at Desmond's show and watch as Justine continues to control Marcia. The two climb up the catwalk and walk onto a swinging platform, where Justine hopes to push her over the ledge. However, caught off guard by Kennedy, Justine rips off what turns out to be a mere mask that creates the illusion of a beautiful face, revealing the acid mutilation underneath. Distressed and off-balance, Justine tumbles to her death (landing near the dead body of Desmond).

Surprisingly sordid and exploitative for a juvenile audience, *The Hypnotic Eye* pointed toward a fresh decade of more explicit horror where beautiful women would becomes the victims of disfigurement and slow, painful death. However, as sold

What happened to ordinary names? Kodi Smit-McPhee and Chloe Grace Moretz play the troubled children in *Let Me In*.

by Allied Artists, the movie is still very youth oriented with its William Castle-styled gimmick of the audience participation "Hypno-Magic" segment. The script is often illogical and too simplistic for its own good. The motivation for Justine's actions becomes clear by the movie's end, but why Desmond went along with her is never adequately explained, although Jacques Bergerac is very effective with his suave French accent and showmanship. And Allison Hayes, as usual, is a hoot as the cruel assistant who is evil personified. The direction by George Blair is fine for the over-blown programmer on display here. But the movie needs a creative shot in the arm with a better-crafted script and make-up effects that would bring the movie to the realistic level of its thematically similar *Horrors of the Black Museum*. But, to be honest, this movie has always remained a personal guilty pleasure throughout the years and I still enjoy its better moments. The Warner Archive print looks and sounds just fine.

Let Me In
Movie: 4.0; Disc: 3.5
Anchor Bay

This is not your parents' Hammer Film Production!

One of many joys of watching this American remake of the Swedish film *Let The Right One In* is focusing on the new Hammer logo and seeing so many memorable images from Hammer classics drawn inside. Of course none of the original Hammer talent remains, but for the rebirth of the iconic name, Hammer could not have started with a finer movie than *Let Me In*. Unfortunately, while critics heaped praise upon the production, box-office revenue was pathetic, deeming the film a financial failure. But artistically, as the blurb from Stephen King on the Blu-ray states, this may very well be the best horror film of the past 20 years. Yes, it truly is that good. And of course, not many horror *classics* littered the past two decades.

I do not wish to spend too much time comparing the original 2008 Swedish version to this 2010 American remake. We must give credit where it is due. In the original, director Tomas Alfredson and screenwriter John Ajvide Lindqvist (working from his original novel) produced a critically well-received modern horror classic. Unfortunately, while wildly original, ambitious and containing classic sequences of true cinematic horror, the film, for some vague reason, left me cold. I felt the pacing, accented by the dreary snowy setting, was lethargic and my attention drifted. What is surprising is just how similar the remake is, often using the same dialogue and replicating sequences very closely. In fact, after seeing the remake I feel I need to see the original again, that perhaps I was sleepy or in a bad mood the evening I watched it.

But I am positive that upon multiple viewings that the Matt Reeves-directed Hammer remake, with a screenplay by Reeves based upon the original one by Lindqist, will be the superior production (and I hardly ever say this about remakes). And I think I know why.

First of all, Matt Reeves' direction is outstanding (his last film was the kinetic *Cloverfield*, featuring the jittery photography that left more than one audience member nauseated). Amazingly, Reeves brings an old school sensibility to *Let Me In* and emphasizes the stationary camera that relies on mood and traditional composition. Remember, I liked *Cloverfield* very much and found it very unnerving with style and get-under-your-skin creepiness. Here, Reeves wanted to demonstrate that he could go from the cutting edge and eccentric to the traditional. And *Let Me In* demonstrates his artistic growth.

First of all the movie does an outstanding job of creating three areas of focus. First we have the equally unnerving sequences of horror as a very old vampire occupies the body of a 12-year-old girl. A man who appears to be her father accompanies her, but in reality he is a childhood friend of hers who has aged while she remains perpetually in a pre-pubescent body. Abby's companion (receiving billing as "The Father") is veteran Richard Jenkins, who wears plastic trash bags over his face when he stalks and kills innocent victims to provide the needed blood for Abby. Of course in several sequences Abby proves she can find blood sources perfectly well all by herself. And perhaps preparing for the future after her companion dies, Abby (Chloe Grace Moretz) befriends a lonely and alienated boy her own age, Owen (Kodi Smit-McPhee). And this relationship forms the crux of the movie.

Second, perhaps the true horror of the movie evolves in its depiction of the bullying and torture of students at school. Owen lives alone with his mother in a run-down apartment complex. She is in the process of divorcing a father that Owen hardly ever sees. At school nasty Kenny (Dylan Minnette), the leader of the bullying school gang, calls the odd-looking Owen a girl. Sequences of the gang attacking Owen in the bathroom, the gym locker room, on the hockey field and at the school swimming pool are intense. In many ways the dominant vampire scenario does not contain the evil that we find in the bullying subplot.

Finally, *Let Me In* focuses on what it means to be on the threshold of adolescence, having to deal with raging hormones and uncontrolled emotional highs and lows. This is the period when Owen aches for a

Boris Karloff sported a distinctive shock of gray hair in his portrayal of a small-time criminal who rises from the dead, from *The Walking Dead*.

friend of the opposite sex and does not know how to handle such a friendship. When one's best friend happens to be a vampire who goes feral at the sight of a drop of blood. It only compounds the problems. But where the American feature excels is in its casting of and the sensitive performances by Smit-McPhee and Moretz (she was the star of *Kick Ass* and most recently *Hugo* and the remake of *Carrie*). Their performances are so real, perfectly capturing the awkwardness of first attraction and love (their relationship starts out as a close friendship but evolves into something higher). On the one hand we have Abby, shy and mysterious, announcing from the get-go to Owen that she cannot be his friend. She walks barefoot in the snowy New Mexico winter for most of the movie, accentuating her vulnerability and isolation. And then we have Smit-McPhee, with his feminine face, spending time alone looking through his telescope to spy on other tenants who live in the complex (at first trying to understand his over-active sex drive by watching a man and woman start to make love, but the woman notices his telescope far too early). Such imagery establishes Owen as not only a loner but as a shy individual who watches life from a distance, fearful of engaging in relationships that can end in pain or heartbreak. His inquisitive face and large, piercing eyes register the fact that Owen is an observer, but one from a safe distance. Where *Let Me In* excels is in the development of the relationship between Owen and Abby. After he witnesses Abby change into her feral vampire alter ego, with animalistic eyes, demonic face and non-human features, he still does not fear her. Even after he watches as she attacks a woman and her cat, Owen still understands that she is driven to drink blood just as the predatory human race slaughters animals on which to feed. Then after the sequence where a sympathetic policeman (Elias Koteas) accidentally discovers Abby hiding beneath a cover over the bathtub during the day, and she has to bleed him dry to protect herself, the cop's pleading eyes and outstretched hand only inches from Owen's hand does not diminish his opinion of Abby's character. A pivotal sequence occurs when Abby asks Owen to invite her into his house for the second time, and Owen momentarily hesitates. Yet Abby enters anyway, soon erupting into violent seizures with droplets of blood falling from her scalp onto her face. Owen hugs her immediately and invites her in (remember, a vampire may not cross any threshold unless invited). Abby knows that Owen would never let her suffer for long (and she tells him just that). For me these tender sequences of two quirky, isolated "people" trying to establish an intimate relationship (Abby uses terms like "let's hang out" in her notes to Owen) elevate the movie.

Sequences of horror are intense, well directed and crisply photographed (by Greig Fraser). We have several killings by Richard Jenkins, wearing his black trash bag, bleeding his victims and capturing their still sizzling blood in plastic containers. We have the far subtler than it sounds swimming pool massacre sequence with the decapitated head of one student tormentor drifting slowly beneath the water as Owen is being attacked. We have some marvelous sequences of Abby pretending to be lost and defenseless in underground tunnels, awaiting the arrival of her next victim. We have that ferocious attack on the woman and her cat and Abby's CGI escape climbing up poles or vaulting over fences. We have the disturbing murder of the policeman by Abby after he unwraps the cover shielding her from the sun as she lies in her bathtub. And we have the rapid disintegration of one of Abby's victims as she lies in her hospital bed, the nurse unknowingly letting sunshine touch her face, causing the vampire victim to catch fire, ignite the entire bed and also the nurse. And we even have one dandy sequence with a car rolling down the hill, out of control, as Richard Jenkins' attack on a new victim goes awry.

The film's ending is dazzling, with Abby hiding in a large carry-on trunk aboard a train, Owen occupying the nearby train seat showing his ticket to the conductor. With her adult companion dead, the implication is that Abby once again will start over with a new childhood friend who will grow, age and become a person very much like her former adult companion. And when Owen dies, she, always inhabiting a 12-year-old girl's body, will find another friend, making immortality seem as dreary and dull as it possibly can be. Bottom line, Abby is herself a pathetic victim and we pity her as much as we pity her victims. And Owen is perhaps the saddest victim of them all. Abby, even as a vampire, is the best thing that ever happened to Owen in his entire life. The wonderful original score by Michael Giacchino, whose symphonic and classical elements suit the regal and dreary mood of the film perfectly, is much appreciated. The music is never overpowering and its intensity and sadness seem just right.

Extras include a wonderful making-of documentary and two shorts detailing the creation of the film's special effects and car accident sequence. When it comes to classic horror, I think of *Let Me In* as synthesizing the best of Val Lewton with a more violent, modern edge. But just the relationship existing between the two children is very Lewton-esque in its loneliness and alienation (reminding me more than a little of both *Cat People* and *Curse of the Cat People*).

Karloff and Lugosi Horror Classics
Movie: *The Walking Dead* (3.0);
Frankenstein 1970 (3.0);
You'll Find Out (3.0);
Zombies on Broadway (2.5); Disc: 3.5
Warner Bros.

It's amazing to think that almost every horror film classic is now available on DVD/Blu-ray, the classics and B programmers alike. Surprisingly, Warner Bros.' Boris Karloff classic, *The Walking Dead*, has been often delayed because of so-called inferior source material, but it is finally available,

Peter Lorre, Bela Lugosi and Boris Karloff as they appeared in *You'll Find Out*

if perhaps still not in stellar condition. But alongside that classic is a hodge-podge of rare horror movie product starring either Karloff or Bela Lugosi and this box set is a gem of rare delights.

Let's start with what many may consider the bottom of the barrel, the comedy horror *You'll Find Out*, starring the trio of Boris Karloff, Bela Lugosi and Peter Lorre (at his most emaciated and smarmy). Many people consider this movie slow, not so funny and rather listless, but most likely those viewers are comparing this Karloff-Lugosi chiller to superior productions such as *The Black Cat* and *Son of Frankenstein*. I believe if we compare *You'll Find Out* to other old dark house mysteries of the 1930s and 1940s, the kind that Alpha Video, Warner Archive and others release, that this movie becomes more enjoyable. Compare the movie, say, to Universal's remake of *The Black Cat*, *Horror Island* or *Night Monster*, and we get the point. Remember, this is a starring vehicle for Southern big-band leader Kay Keyser, whose schlock is still mildly entertaining. This is a variation of say Bob Hope's *The Ghost Breakers*, a horror film based around Hope's comedic talents and personality. *You'll Find Out* even throws in a clever line of dialogue (a reference to an angered Bing Crosby fan) immediately after Keyser is almost sawed in half by a falling saber in an underground maze. While Keyser is not Crosby, this movie attempts to fuse humor, music and horror and does a pretty respectable job.

First of all, the production values are impressive, with Keyer and his Kollege of Musical Knowledge big band (augmented by comic Ish Kabibble, who sports a Moe Howard haircut) performing at a birthday party for a young heiress, Janis Bellacrest (Helen Parrish), at the family mansion (a typical creepy old dark house). Janis' Aunt

Funnymen Carney and Brown confront an intense Bela Lugosi in *Zombies on Broadway*.

Margo is enamored with phony spiritualist Prince Saliano (Lugosi) and pays him handsomely for his psychic services. So the main set piece of the production is the elaborate séance sequence where Margo attempts to contact her late husband (whose spiritual presence looks similar to Judge Mainwaring, played by Boris Karloff). Along for the ride is the professor, a seedy looking Peter Lorre. While Keyser and company realize from the get-go that Saliano is crooked, they are too trusting of the judge and professor, entrusting them into their scheme to expose the fake spiritualist and protect Aunt Margo from herself. In the meanwhile innocent Janis and Kay find their lives are in danger from parties unknown.

Besides the spiritualist séance featuring people wearing phosphorescent paint, objects flying around the room and huge globes shooting out fatal electrical sparks, we have the underground maze of hidden chambers with walls and doors mysteriously opening and closing. During these sequences, the production values really show, adding a creepy sense of whodunit to the proceedings. Of course by the movie's end it is apparent that Karloff, Lugosi, and Lorre are all working in cahoots, and while they attempt to dynamite the house and kill all the occupants, the cute little dog Prince saves the day by fetching the dynamite and instead blowing up the villains.

You'll Find Out is a minor diversion and a little variation of the old dark house murder mystery thriller, but the presence of the three horror icons, likeable Kay Keyser and a wonderful supporting cast creates enough thrills and chills to entertain for nearly an hour and a half. The digital restoration is superb and shimmers and sparkles, featuring deep blacks and great contrast. If viewers only remember the movie from the distant past, this revisiting might be quite a pleasant surprise.

Zombies on Broadway has got to be one of the greatest horror movie titles ever, and the fact that this RKO movie turns out to be somewhat of a sequel to Val Lewton's *I Walked With A Zombie* makes it all the more interesting. Director Gordon Douglas, most famous for directing the giant ant classic *Them!*, does a respectable job generating scares amid the comic antics. The movie occurs on the island of San Sebastian, the same locale as the Lewton movie, and chief zombie Darby Jones returns playing essentially the same role of Kolaga, the bug-eyed, half-dressed, lanky and muscular mute zombie.

As I get older, the comic shenanigans of Abbott and Costello seem a little less

Boris Karloff works alone in his cavern lab creating a giant humanoid in *Frankenstein 1970*.

funny and the talents of their imitators seem more inspired. *Zombies on Broadway*, a vehicle for the comedy team of Carney and Brown, works on a number of levels. True, Carney and Brown are never as original or as inventive as Abbott and Costello, the team they pattern themselves after, but they are enjoyable enough and create quite a few laughs along the way. Unfortunately, the chief villain, other than the mindless Kolaga, is Dr. Renault, played by Bela Lugosi. In every sequence in which the mad medico appears, Lugosi shines, playing both sinister and comedic in equal proportions. Besides strapping his victims to a gurney as he prepares to inject them with a zombie-inducing hypodermic, Lugosi shines in a sequence that requires him to open and close the drawers of a large chest to find a mischievous monkey. Lugosi's eyes perhaps bug out more than the make-up-enhanced zombies, but his comic timing is hilarious.

The movie gets off to a slow start, and Bela Lugosi is woefully underused and appears in only a few sequences, but once the spook show begins in Lugosi's island mansion, the pacing picks up and the movie flows into high gear. In one terrific sequence, we have Brown and Carney digging their own potential grave, with each idiot flinging a shovelful of dirt into the other's grave, but when Carney digs faster and deeper and falls through a trap door, pursued by both Lugosi and Kolaga, the movie becomes a lot of fun. Surprisingly the perky heroine Anne Jeffreys does an exceptional job of defeating both the dead-eyed zombie and Lugosi, as this woman can kick serious butt while the men fall by the wayside. Sheldon Leonard, as nightclub owner Ace Miller, is tons of fun as a former criminal going straight. He even promises to have a real zombie appear at his Zombie Hut nightclub for the premiere. Carney and Brown, as his press agents, have their jobs and lives on the line to make the zombie promise happen.

Ultimately, *Zombies on Broadway* has a listless middle section (meandering around San Sebastian, followed by seedy crooks and serenaded by Sir Lancelot, the guitar-strumming Calypso singer from the earlier Lewton classic) but fortunately features a funny opening and great final 20 minutes. The sequence with Alan Carney in bed talking to pal Wally Brown, screaming his head off when the zombie appears through the sliding bookcase, is very funny. Also the disturbing eye make-up that produces soulless, bugged-out dead eyes is quite effective. So effective that during the film's final moments, all the major players appear as zombies with the eye make-up applied. An effective B programmer, *Zombies on Broadway* looks good on the home theater screen.

Moving next to Boris Karloff, *Frankenstein 1970* has always been an underrated B programmer featuring Karloff's broad, over-the-top performance rivaling similar performances by Bela

Lugosi. When Lugosi plays these broad, ham-fisted roles he receives accolades and ovations, but when Karloff does them, he is accused of slumming, or worse yet, picking up a check and sleep-walking through the performance. In this well photographed (Carl E. Guthrie) black-and-white CinemaScope production, the camera lingers lovingly on Karloff's scarred, sad face. Often the photography is askew, with the angular photography bending the set to an odd, uneven composition. But whether shot from above, below or tight on the face, the camera loves that grizzled face with the spiked hair. Karloff delivers an emotional speech that rivals anything that Lugosi did in *Bride of the Monster*, asking his friend Wilhelm (Rudolph Anders), who would believe that we are the same age? As Baron Victor von Frankenstein, Karloff reflects upon the Nazi atrocities he was forced to commit, all for the cause of science. Now, old and in debt, he must rent out his family home to a movie production company to make a Frankenstein monster movie. Karloff's delivery, with quiet intensity, forces the audience to lean in to better understand such sad reflections. Even when servant Shuter (Norbert Schiller) wanders accidentally into Frankenstein's atomic-powered mad lab, Karloff almost whispers, "Why did it have to be you, Shuter???" Of course Frankenstein has found the brain for his gigantic creation (looking like 8 feet of gauze-wrapped inhumanity), but it is with regret that Karloff realizes that the servant he loves must be sacrificed for, once again, the cause of science. But Karloff's wistful line readings, so underplayed yet so dramatic, demonstrate that Karloff's talents had not faded over the decades. His body is sometimes hunched, his walk lumbering and unbalanced and his hands somewhat twisted by the arthritis he suffered from, but all the attention is on that face, those eyes and the words uttered from that mouth.

Most critics and fans criticize the movie, claiming that the best sequence occurs at the film's very beginning. True, in widescreen, we have a towering Frankenstein monster (but not the Karloff variety from the heyday of Universal as many claim), photographed at first only from the neck down. The monster, wearing a light gray burlap suit, drags one leg and foot, more akin to Lon Chaney's Kharis the mummy than Karloff's Frankenstein Monster. The actor's hands are the focus of attention, with his curling and sharp fingernails twitching and writhing, as his arms flail outwardly. This beastie is more Dr. Hyde than Frankenstein, and while the fiend is nothing similar to the

Boris Karloff, Edmund Gween and author H.G. Wells pose on the set of *The Walking Dead*.

Universal monster of the 1930s and 1940s, the sequence is a visual delight, culminating as the monster forces his pretty blonde female victim into the dark waters where he attempts to drown her. At this point the director yells cut and we are forced back to the future, to witness horror filmmaking in 1970, as seen from the eyes of moviemakers of 1958. How odd. Such a sequence is one of the movie's best, but it is a sequence of mood and monster, not one of any significant consequence; a sequence without the power and craftsmanship of Boris Karloff.

The movie benefits from the production design (Jack T. Collis), set design (Jerry Welch) and CinemaScope photography. Two of my favorite scenes involve a rehearsal sequence where a leading lady has to enter from the darkened edges of the unlighted set. As the woman focuses on her entrance, the audience sees the monstrous silhouette of the monster, its arms outstretched, advance upon the unaware victim. Demonstrating irony at its exploitative best, the audience screams out loud for the poor woman to look behind her, but all the focus on-screen is about getting the sequence framed properly. Another grand scene occurs when the cinematographer uses his hand-held lens to frame the shot, and as he pans to the left he sees the huge presence of the bandaged fiend a few feet away from him, advancing rapidly in a tight close-up.

Frankenstein 1970 has too much talent (in design, photography, acting and direction) to be dismissed so haphazardly by horror fans. Remember, when comparing this production to others released in 1957 and 1958, *Frankenstein 1970* has a veneer that makes the overall production stand above and beyond many of its peers. Never a great movie by any estimation, the film is a classy B horror thriller, one that shows Boris Karloff to fine advantage.

Finally, Warner Bros.' so-called definitive horror production, *The Walking Dead*, starring Boris Karloff, comes to DVD. While the 1936 production has not been restored to the extent of some other 1930s horror classics, it sure looks good enough. Unfortunately, I always felt the production to be over-rated, even though Karloff's performance is among his absolute best.

The merger of the gangster and horror genres (playing to the strength of Warner Bros. by emphasizing the gangster genre) is a novel idea, but somehow the gangster aspects of the production are boilerplate and never rise above pedestrian. Perhaps we needed a James Cagney or a Humphrey

The ungodly underground lair of Count Mitterhaus (Robert Taylor) finds the vampire king staked and the fair maiden rescued, from *Vampire Circus*.

Bogart to appear in the production as one of the chief villains, because the gangster aspects never sizzle. The idea of the mob taking out a judge and framing a lower-echelon criminal to take the rap seems a little too pat. Even the mad doctor aspects never achieve Universal greatness. Not in the creation of the mad lab itself or in the creation of the dedicated mad scientist (Edmund Gwenn is always delightful but his performance here is fairly bland—he is too nice and never eccentric or obsessed enough). When Karloff is on-screen, the movie creates energy, and the idea to revive Karloff with that white puff of hair was inspired.

But Karloff's almost robotic re-animation leads to members of the mob dying one by one, mostly from being frightened to death or doing something stupid to cause their demise. Yes, the hand of the creator guides Karloff's John Elman, but that is precisely what is sometimes wrong. We want to see Karloff acting on his own volition and become responsible for his own acts of revenge. Instead, under Michael Curtiz' direction, Elman becomes a pawn in the hand of an angry god. While this creates a quietly intense, almost ghost-like performance, it is a performance that fails to explore the emotional depths of Karloff's conflicted character. The key question becomes what is death like, and Karloff never has the opportunity to answer. The film's religious overtones become, at least near the end, mechanical and heavy-handed, and the attempt to merge the gangster genre and horror genre, with a heavy dose of Old Testament vengeful God thrown in for good measure, simply does not work.

The Walking Dead becomes a fantastic vehicle for Boris Karloff, but as a movie, the 66-minute-long production lacks a sense of dramatic power and the cross-genre plotline meanders and sometimes becomes dull for a production barely over an hour long. Don't get me wrong, *The Walking Dead* Karloff has the look and delivers an incredible performance, but the other aspects of the production disappoint. Once again it should become clear that Universal knew how to put these productions together, and even Warner Bros. pales in comparison to Universal when it comes to horror films.

Vampire Circus (Blu-ray/DVD combo)
Movie: 3.0; Disc: 3.5
Synapse

With the birth of *The Vampire Lovers*, Hammer, for commercial consideration, reinvented itself as an erotically charged Gothic horror movie company, one that emphasized violence, blood, nudity and sexuality. Hammer now lacked essential creative components such as Anthony Hinds, Michael Carreras and Terence Fisher. I can understand that a new generation, fueled by new creative talent, tried desperately to keep the company relevant in the 1970s when mainstream horror hit back hard against the independents, fueled by the success of Warner Bros.' *The Exorcist*. For me, these final chapters in the Hammer legacy never came close to thrilling me to the extent that their finest productions did from the 1950s and 1960s. But I confess my fondness for *The Vampire Circus*, a flawed yet energetic Hammer offering. Director Robert Young, working from a screenplay written by Judson Kinberg, creates an atypical vampire movie and Hammer production that until now never had been released in the United States uncut. With the restored footage and magnificent digital presentation, oversaturated with intense colors and clarity akin to 35mm, *Vampire Circus* becomes one of the truly delightful Hammer debuts on Blu-ray.

What I love most about Terence Fisher's classic Hammer vampire movies is the otherworldly presence that his undead characters create, be it the doe-eyed David Peel as Baron Meinster, Martita Hunt as the gaunt and goose-like Baroness Meinster, the on-fire sensual aggressiveness of Andree Melly, the blood-smeared feral-faced Christopher Lee as Count Dracula or the sinister sexuality of predatory Valerie Gaunt as Dracula's vampire mate. In *Vampire Circus* we have the curly-haired, almost purring, Anthony Corlan (Higgins) as Emil, the panther vampire shape-shifter whose performance consists mainly of intense facial expressions, all of them mesmeric and haunting. Merely the way he commands our attention with his effortless off-putting stance makes him a marvelous vampire. Again, perhaps the man cannot act his way out of a body bag, but the manner in which director Robert Young uses Higgins to create an ungodly creature of the night is inspired. Count Mitterhaus (Robert Tayman), on the other hand, seems little more than stereotypical and his performance seems too kitschy. Luckily, he lies in suspended animation throughout most of the movie, and when he returns to life near the end, his performance is so brief that audiences can tolerate his overly dramatic put-on poses.

The movie blends a circus backdrop with the community curse inflicted upon the descendants of the people who destroyed Mitterhaus. Throw in the plague that isolates the vampire-infested village and add the magical manner in which vampires become shape shifters that occupy a parallel universe. All this attests to the imagination that conceived this theater of death. Many standout sequences populate the movie and the stark photography imbues this darkly magical universe with a veneer of evil. This is not Terence Fisher's vampire world.

We have the weirdly fascinating walk down the hall of mirrors with characters joking and laughing as they see their images distorted, only to arrive at the final mirror, one that seems uneventful. Suddenly writhing vampires with extended fangs appear in the mirror's reflection but not in the actual world. The fact that the vampires actually exist in an underground cave that can be entered only by one narrow entrance makes this colony of vampires a very claustrophobic one (the cave is very small and not very deep—a result of budget restrictions probably, but the result is still unnerving). We have arrogant brother and sister vampires, defined by their vanity and physical beauty, confront a victim-to-be who uses a giant cross on the ledge above-ground as the means to destroy the undead below. The mostly adolescent audience must be thrilled that a few vampires even attack while in the nude. The movie is outrageous in that the antics of the vampires are way over the top and their cult of the undead seems far removed from reality. These vampires are monsters and the actors who portray them make their performances otherworldly.

Vampire Circus has never looked this spectacular. Synapse's attention to detail should be applauded. The two-disc set includes additional extras such as the making-of documentaries, interactive comics and related short features. These added features are extensive, highly information and entertaining. *Vampire Circus* becomes an essential Hammer to own because of the diligent care taken in making the presentation so spectacular.

The Awful Dr. Orlof
Movie: 2.5; Disc: 3.5
Redemption

Spanish director Jess (Jesus) Franco became one of the most prolific directors in horror cinema history, directing about 200 films before his death in April 2013 at age 82. His final credit was *Revenge of the Alligator Ladies* (2013), a title that sums up the type of movies he made for decades. When thinking of Franco the phrase *quantity over quality* immediately comes to mind, as Franco made movies that are gripping (or sometimes simply odd or visually compelling) in short spurts, but overall his movies contain more passion than craft. When it comes to surreal, dream-like cinema with a heavily erotic bent, Franco does have his admirers, and when it comes to Euro-horror, Franco is an iconic name. But his career is mainly one for admirers of *le bad cinema* and a small, dedicated niche who appreciate his creative longevity.

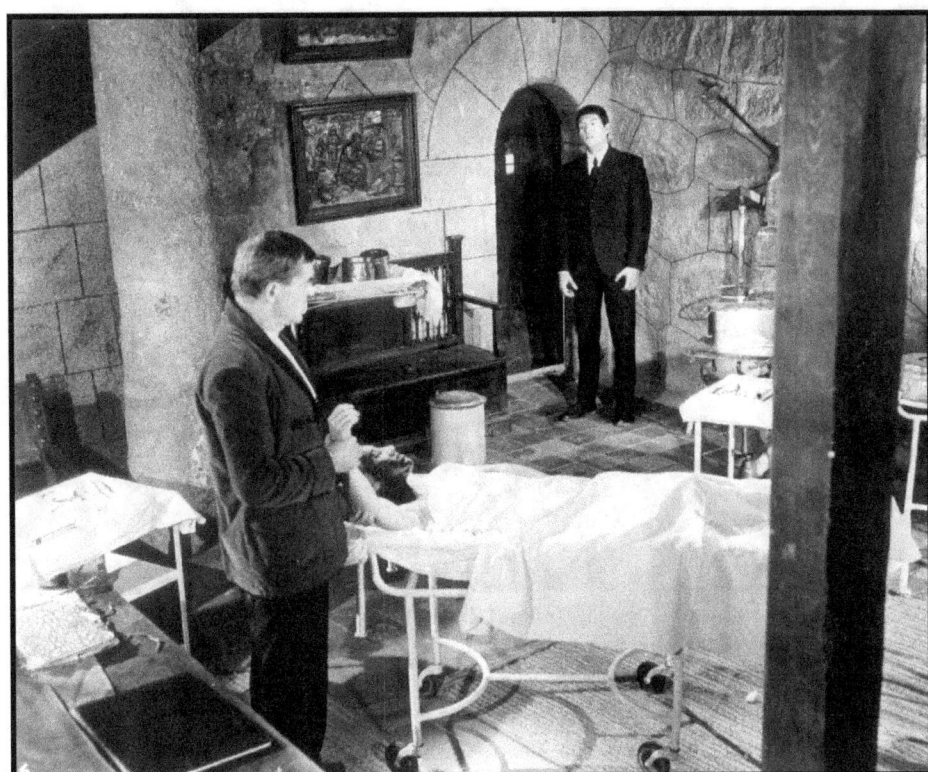

Evil surgeon Dr. Orlof (Howard Vernon) stands over his latest victim, as the well dressed but disfigured Morpho (Ricardo Valle) hovers in the background, in *The Awful Dr. Orlof*.

The Awful Dr. Orlof, a Spanish-French co-production released in 1962, was Jess Franco's first horror feature, and many consider it to contain his best work. Photographed in gloomy black-and-white, the movie borrows heavily from *Eyes Without a Face*, the French classic released a few years earlier in 1960. Both films deal with a doctor/surgeon who kidnaps and mutilates beautiful women, cutting up their faces to perform skin grafts on his disfigured daughter, desperately attempting to restore her beauty. In both films the cold-hearted doctor employs an assistant to help him procure and restrain the female victims. In the superior *Eyes Without a Face,* the doctor uses an attractive woman to do his dirty work, but in the Franco movie the doctor uses a disfigured criminal to overpower his victims. In spite of the copycat nature of the Franco film, *The Awful Dr. Orlof* is actually quite mesmerizing, containing eerie photography that generates unsettling mood. Simply watching Orlof (Howard Vernon) and Morpho (Ricardo Valle) in a small boat float slowly across a fog-shrouded river at night, travelling to a castle on the other side, is memorable simply for the dream-like cinematography. Such moody river sequences, repeated several times during the movie, leisurely allows the audience to become hypnotized by the rhythmic cadence of the small craft crossing the haunted body of water, approaching the shadowy castle looming in the background. And even when Orlof and Morpho (sometimes with one of their victims) exit the boat and march up toward the castle, the haunted landscape and camerawork only increases the creepiness of this dank journey. The river crossing is almost like experiencing a dream, in that the action occurs in slow motion and the haunting visuals are repeated multiple times. Actually it becomes a recurring nightmare that the sleeper just cannot get out of his or her head.

Morpho, Orlof's mute, zombie-like assistant, is simply creepy to behold. Well dressed in a fashionable suit, Morpho has acid-burned eyes that bulge outward, never close or blink. But a round scar on his face reveals that the center portion of his face had been cut out and sewn back on, giving his character an off-putting eeriness that makes the victimizer also appear to be a victim. And when the tall and lanky henchman approaches Orlof's victim, the female cowers in fear as the blind predator manages to use all his senses to ultimately find and over-power the object of his pursuit. In a horrifying climax, Morpho

Grandfatherly and seemingly kind Dr. Paul Carruthers (Bela Lugosi) transports one of his bats from one secret chamber to another, from *The Devil Bat*.

always lurches toward and appears to caress and bite his victims, rendering them unconscious, a beautiful limp doll carried in his strong arms. But simply watching Morpho hover, slowly approach and finally render helpless his victims is again another visual treat. Morpho's disfigured facial make-up execution is not perfectly crafted, but Valle's rhythmic and lumbering stalking of his victims is expertly acted and well photographed. Even with limited finances Jess Franco manages to do much with little and his creation of haunting atmosphere overcomes many of the other obvious flaws.

And luckily for genre fans, Redemption has released a Blu-ray version of this pivotal Franco debut. Made from a fine grain 35mm print, Kino's digital presentation is far from a frame-by-frame restoration. Some splices and white speckling are apparent in sections, mostly appearing at the beginning of reels and especially at the beginning of the film. But the Blu-ray presentation creates sharpness and an enhancement of the grays and blacks that help restore rich contrast. Enough grain is apparent to maintain the true 35mm movie look, and the depth of field helps to maintain the unease and dream-like quality the film so effectively conveys. For a foreign movie, a rather non-important one at the time of release, Redemption has done wonders making *The Awful Dr. Orlof* look the best it could over 50 years after its original release. Extras include an insightful audio commentary by Tim Lucas, one of the final on-screen interviews with Jess Franco, and moving tributes to the late director by film historians and Franco's peers. Even with all its shortcomings, *The Awful Dr. Orlof* manages, in relatively modern 1962, to create visual Gothic horror that harkens back to the decade of the 1940s, reminding us of the classic horror style that was fast becoming a relic of the past.

The Devil Bat
Movie: 2.5; Disc: 3.5
Kino Lorber

Never in a million years would anyone expect one of Poverty Row's most infamous B movies to be released on Blu-ray disc. PRC's *The Devil Bat* (1940), starring Bela Lugosi, is often compared favorably to the slew of Monogram shockers that Lugosi made during the 1940s. Perhaps *The Invisible Ghost*, *Voodoo Man*, *The Return of the Ape Man* and *The Corpse Vanishes* may compete with *The Devil Bat* for being Lugosi's finest schlock B thriller of the decade (but we won't dare compare these to the Ed Wood classics of the 1950s).

Director Jean Yarbrough's first horror movie project, *The Devil Bat* (screenplay by John T. Neville) employs a staple of the mystery/suspense genre by having the villain use a special chemical fragrance to lure the monster to the hapless victim. Lugosi plays the kindly small-town doctor, Dr. Paul Carruthers, who enacts revenge on the corporate suits he feels cheated him out of a fortune when they got wealthy and he accepted a buyout and only received pennies. So of course he uses an electronic apparatus to transform ordinary bats into giant killer bats that are attracted to a fragrance, telling intended victims that he invented a new aftershave. Lugosi is at his absolute best when he slyly advises potential victims to be sure to put a dab on their necks and throats, erupting into a subtle smile knowing that the little dab will seal their fate.

The entire production is ridiculous, with the Carruthers character lurking in his seedy out-of-the-way home, slithering from one hidden chamber to the text, grabbing one specimen from the room of ordinary bats and transforming, one at a time, the harmless creature into a giant swooping fiend that roams the night skies (mostly on a fairly visible wire). Surprisingly, the sets are varied and well dressed, and the cinematography is respectably creepy. The music score, chiefly comprised of dramatic "stingers," works effectively, and the supporting cast, including exploitation star Dave O'Brien and a cast of recognizable B players, does a fine job creating enough energy and tension when it is required. But none of this hokum would be remembered without Bela Lugosi, who approached this film as if it were *Dracula* (or at least *Return of the Vampire*). The non-stop, dry and insightful commentary by *Video Watchdog* contributor Richard Harland Smith makes the point that Lugosi is having the time of his life as Carruthers, and Smith feels Lugosi approaches the performance as black comedy, always showing that little "wink" in his performance. In a sense I think Smith attributes too much subtlety to Lugosi's performance. Lugosi never succumbed to black comedy, for he always played his characters in the Bs as seriously as he performed in major studio productions. I do not think Lugosi was capable of winking or playing a role for its comic nuance. I believe that Lugosi enjoyed commanding the screen and dominating productions in which he appeared. Realizing that he would be playing supporting roles like Ygor in mainstream productions such as *Son of Frankenstein* (1939), eating up the scenery (delightfully and wholly inspired) with only limited screen time, I believe his ego enjoyed starring in Poverty Row productions that gave him the opportunity to totally overpower the production by having a top-starring role. Lugosi was never a subtle performer, he was always an actor, theatrically trained, who perhaps thought he was playing the stage when he was delivering lines in a camera close-up in a movie. He jerked his head a little too dramatically, arched an eyebrow a little too noticeably, smiled a little too villainously and used hand gesturing a little too theatrically. But even with this acting overkill, Bela Lugosi was perhaps the screen's greatest horror film personality, whose performances, while over the top, still dazzled and thrilled. Unlike Vincent Price, Lugosi was never aware of chewing the scenery. For him these were the qualities that the production demanded and *The Devil Bat* shows Lugosi at his over-dramatic best.

Once again, this HD digital print was made from an archival 35mm print with about 9 minutes of replacement 16mm footage. So do not mistake this for a Criterion Collection restoration. Merely finding such an excellent 35mm print and digitizing it as a Blu-ray is enough to make this the finest home video release ever of *The Devil Bat*. Original negatives no longer exist and no one would spend the fortune it would cost to restore this little programmer frame by frame. *The Devil Bat* will never look better (until its 4k Ultra HD release). Bela Lugosi, known for his A list work in *Dracula, The Black Cat, The Raven, Son of Frankenstein* and *Murders in the Rue Morgue*, is just as remembered for his work in Poverty Row Hollywood, where he was allowed to run wild (to every horror movie fan's delight). And when it comes to remarkable Poverty Row performances, Lugosi's Paul Carruthers is among his finest.

White Zombie
Movie:3.0; Disc: 3.5
Kino Lorber

The Halperin brothers' independent production *White Zombie*, featuring Bela Lugosi's as Murder Legendre, demonstrates Lugosi's artistic powers at the peak of his professional career, one year after *Dracula*. Young and wealthy Charles Beaumont (Robert Frazer) desires to marry the fiancée of new acquaintance Neil Parker, whom Beaumont invites to be married at his Haitian plantation. Beaumont uses everything in his power to steal beautiful Madeline (Madge Bellamy) from Neil, including the powers of black magic and voodoo. Enter Murder Legendre. Legendre is the lanky man who runs the mill for Beaumont, using zombie slaves as an unlimited source of free labor. Legendre begins the movie as Beaumont's employee and underling, but as Beaumont needs Murder's power to win over the body (if not the heart and intellect) of Madeline, the zombie master gains more and more control over Beaumont, ultimately turning his employer into a weak-willed emotional cripple, unable to lift a finger against him. Lugosi is at his best as Legendre, his slick hair, floppy hat and brushy eyebrows, often seen in close-up with intense, twitching eyes and an insidious all-knowing smile.

Bela Lugosi, in *White Zombie*, looks like his character would be named Murder Legendre.

The character appears so different from vampire king Dracula, yet his performance as Legendre is mesmerizing. Working with a cast of second-raters, Lugosi's supporting role actually dominates the production by nature of his charisma and talent. Even though the production is creaky, its on-location sets and masterful dressing of soundstages produce a movie that seems different from Universal productions, yet it oozes with atmosphere and malevolence.

A major controversy erupted when this Blu-ray release included both the "raw" 35mm source print unaltered (and it is a dense contrast print in really good condition) and a digitally enhanced "restored" version. Many people understand how PhotoShop, the software program, can take scratches out of photos, sharpen the image, lighten, darken or increase the contrast. Imagine a PhotoShop program that can perform the same enhancements for digitized movies. This is exactly what Kino has done with the 35mm print of *White Zombie*.

And in a sense they created a bruha-ha by releasing both the raw and restored version on one disc (a wonderful move and one I applaud, in that it gives fans the option of viewing one or both versions). Like many older black-and-white movies, the 35mm print of *White Zombie* is sharp to the point that film grain is too noticeable, becoming a distraction in some sequences. If we stand close to the screen, it appears as though a black net is covering the movie image with small black dots dancing about. But film grain gives projected film its movie-like look. The print runs to the dark side with night sequences a tad too dark and detail is sometimes lost in black shadows. Of course the well-worn print has its share of minor scratches and white speckling. But the

Bela Lugosi and one of his zombie labor force from *White Zombie*

35mm print looks rather nice, considering its age.

Now on to the restored digitized version. First of all almost all scratches, speckling and surface flaws have been removed. The contrast has been boosted to the print's betterment, and lightness and darkness of specific sequences has been improved. No longer are images lost in inky shadows. For close-up sequences, faces have been cleaned up and sharpened, but in medium or long shots, faces appear to have been waxed too clean and often the pupils seem to blend in with the whites of eyes. In other words, the restoration has gone a tad too far with all the grain eliminated, producing human faces that appear digitized and too perfect. Some sequences look spectacular, while others seem odd, almost as though something indescribable has gone wrong, but viewers may find it difficult to explain what bothers them. Film restoration is fraught with simply too many choices.

Generally the best digital restorations tend to meet somewhere in the middle, by reducing film grain but not eliminating it. Contrast boosts and light-dark corrections only improve the presentation, but digital over-correction produces a cinematic image that is sometimes off-putting.

In other words, neither version of *White Zombie* is perfect and both contain advantages that the other version lacks. When I watch the movie next time, I will most likely watch the restored digital version, even knowing that it contains flaws. But with the clean-up of the 35mm print, I simply marvel at the intensity of scenes that now are minus decades of age and wear.

With 35mm being phrased out by the end of this year, and with digital photography replacing 35mm film, we now have younger generations who do not understand how film grain enhances the movie watching experience and makes movies, well, movies. Today's younger audiences will watch movies that are digitally smooth and will most likely view film grain as an inherent flaw, one that necessitates correction. And while baby boomers will argue that movies must have that specific projected look, younger movie fans will argue that the look of movies that boomers grew up with is ancient and outmoded technology, something to be admired for what it was, back in its day. As our movie theaters convert from 35mm projection to pure digital projection, the look of movies is changing and technology continues to march onward.

And isn't it amazing that this fabulous release of *White Zombie*, a film released over 80 years ago, stands symbolically at the heart of such controversy. Whatever version of the film we watch, the fact remains that Bela Lugosi's performance is spectacular and that *White Zombie*, an ancient classic, still entertains, with waxy faces or fine grain either present or absent.

www.ingramcontent.com/pod-product-compliance
Lightning Source LLC
Chambersburg PA
CBHW081718100526
44591CB00016B/2421